NOLO® Products & Services

Books & Software

Get in-depth information. Nolo publishes hundreds of great books and software programs for consumers and business owners. They're all available in print or as downloads at Nolo.com.

Legal Encyclopedia

Free at Nolo.com. Here are more than 1,400 free articles and answers to common questions about everyday legal issues including wills, bankruptcy, small business formation, divorce, patents, employment and much more.

Plain-English Legal Dictionary

Free at Nolo.com. Stumped by jargon? Look it up in America's most up-to-date source for definitions of legal terms.

Online Legal Documents

Create documents at your computer. Go online to make a will or living trust, form an LLC or corporation or obtain a trademark or provisional patent at Nolo.com. For simpler matters, download one of our hundreds of high-quality legal forms, including bills of sale, promissory notes, nondisclosure agreements and many more.

Lawyer Directory

Find an attorney at Nolo.com. Nolo's unique lawyer directory provides in-depth profiles of lawyers all over America. From fees and experience to legal philosophy, education and special expertise, you'll find all the information you need to pick a lawyer who's a good fit.

Free Legal Updates

Keep up to date. Check for free updates at Nolo.com. Under "Products," find this book and click "Legal Updates." You can also sign up for our free e-newsletters at Nolo.com/newsletters/index.html.

1st edition

Bankruptcy for Small Business Owners: How to File for Chapter 7

by Attorney Stephen Elias &
Bethany K. Laurence, J.D.

First Edition	MARCH 2010
Editor	LISA GUERIN
Book Design	TERRI HEARSH
Cover Design	JALEH DOANE
Proofreading	ROBERT WELLS
Index	THÉRÈSE SHERE
Printing	DELTA PRINTING SOLUTIONS, INC.

Elias, Stephen.
Bankruptcy for small business owners : how to file for chapter 7 / by attorney Stephen R. Elias and Bethany K. Laurence, J.D. -- 1st ed.
p. cm.
ISBN-13: 978-1-4133-1080-1 (pbk.)
ISBN-10: 1-4133-1080-X (pbk.)
1. Small business--United States. 2. Bankruptcy--United States--Popular works. I. Laurence, Bethany K., 1968- II. Title.
HD2346.U6E45 2010
346.7307'8--dc22
2009041933

Please note

We believe accurate, plain-English legal information should help you solve many of your own legal problems. But this text is not a substitute for personalized advice from a knowledgeable lawyer. If you want the help of a trained professional—and we'll always point out situations in which we think that's a good idea—consult an attorney licensed to practice in your state.

Acknowledgments

The authors gratefully acknowledge Lisa Guerin's superb editorial assistance and Jake Warner's helpful tips. And much thanks to Terri Hearsh and the great staff in Nolo's production department for getting out the book.

Table of Contents

Appendixes

Your Small Business Chapter 7 Personal Bankruptcy Companion

If you're considering filing for bankruptcy because your small business is drowning in debt, you're not alone. The economic downturn that began in 2008 took many small business owners (not to mention politicians, bankers, and economists) by surprise. For a variety of reasons—from reduced consumer spending to cutthroat competition, cutbacks by business customers, and shrinking (or disappearing) lines of credit—the number of bankruptcies filed by small business owners has skyrocketed.

You might be considering bankruptcy because:

- Your business debts have grown so large that you'll never be able to pay them back.
- You want to get out of an expensive commercial lease, sales contract, or vehicle or equipment lease that's preventing you from operating profitably.
- You want creditors and bill collectors to stop harassing you and your employees.
- Your business lost a lawsuit and was ordered to pay a judgment that's well beyond your means.
- You racked up a lot of business debt and need to lighten the load so you can pay your mortgage, car loan, or current accounts payable.
- You want to stop (at least temporarily) a vehicle repossession, a garnishment on your spouse's wages, or a foreclosure.
- You want to remove a lien from your home or get out of your mortgage without owing a deficiency.

This book explains how to file for Chapter 7 personal bankruptcy, which could be the right solution to many of these problems. However, it won't be the answer for every small business owner, for two reasons:

- **Chapter 7 personal bankruptcy covers only debts for which you are personally liable.** If your business is a sole proprietorship or general partnership, you are personally liable for all of your business's debts, and you can get them wiped out in Chapter 7 personal bankruptcy. If your business is a separate legal entity—for example, a corporation or limited liability company (LLC)—you are personally liable for its business debts only if you personally signed for them or guaranteed them, as explained in Ch. 1. Otherwise, the corporation or LLC is responsible for its own debts and must file its own business bankruptcy case to discharge them. This book doesn't cover the special process that corporations and LLCs must follow for Chapter 7 business bankruptcy (which requires an attorney).
- **You may have to close your business if you file for Chapter 7 personal bankruptcy.** If you've already decided that you want out of your business, this won't be an important consideration. Some business owners—especially those who own service businesses with few assets—may be able to stay open during Chapter 7. And, plenty of business owners have closed down, used Chapter 7 to get out from under their debts, and then started a similar business later. However, if you want to continue operating your business, and particularly if you have any valuable business assets (which you are likely to lose in a Chapter 7 personal bankruptcy), Chapter

7 bankruptcy may not be the best option. Instead, you may want to reorganize your business in Chapter 13 bankruptcy, negotiate a workout with your creditors, or consider other options (as explained in Ch. 3).

Part I of this book will help you decide whether Chapter 7 personal bankruptcy is the best option for handling your small business debt. First, we explain how to determine whether you or your spouse are personally liable for your business debt. Second, we describe what effect filing for Chapter 7 personal bankruptcy will have on your debts, your creditors, your property (both business and personal), and your business. We also cover the other options available to those who want to close their business down, as well as to those who want to stay in business, and explain how those options compare to Chapter 7 bankruptcy.

If you decide that it makes sense to file for Chapter 7 personal bankruptcy, Part II of this book provides step-by-step instructions and detailed information that will help you figure out what property you'll get to keep (and what property you may lose), decide how to handle your various debts, fill out all the necessary paperwork, and handle routine issues that may come up as your case progresses.

If your small business finances have reached the point where bankruptcy is a serious consideration, you may feel anxious, isolated, or even like a failure. But you're not alone: The current recession is taking down thousands of businesses, large and small, including many that were well-established stalwarts of our economy. Our bankruptcy system recognizes that financial missteps, overextension, and simple bad luck happen—and it provides relief to those who are willing to let the court help them get out from under.

Filing for bankruptcy can even be an important step toward future business success. Chapter 7 personal bankruptcy gives small business debtors the opportunity to wipe out some or all of their debt while protecting their personal assets to the extent possible. In fact, many bankruptcy filers go on to start another business and become successful the second or third time around. So if you're ready for a fresh financial start, let this book help you navigate the bankruptcy process and get back on your feet.

Part 1:

Making the Decision—Is Chapter 7 Personal Bankruptcy Right for You?

CHAPTER

1

Evaluate Your Debts and Your Business

This book is for business owners who are considering filing for personal Chapter 7 bankruptcy—not for those who want to file a bankruptcy case for the business itself. Why this distinction? Because there is a big difference between debts that only your business owes and debts that you are personally responsible to repay. Chapter 7 personal bankruptcy wipes out your personal liability for debts; it doesn't wipe out debts that a corporation or limited liability company (LLC) owes separately.

If your business is a separate legal entity that offers limited liability—such as a corporation or LLC—and you have not personally guaranteed or otherwise taken legal responsibility for its debts, the business is responsible for paying its own debts. If the assets of the corporation or LLC aren't sufficient to satisfy those debts, business creditors are out of luck. They usually cannot come after your personal assets, such as your personal bank account and your equity in your house, other real estate, or vehicles, for repayment (unless a court rules that you have failed to treat your business as a separate entity and, therefore, are not entitled to the limited liability protection you'd otherwise enjoy; see "Fraud, Misrepresentation, or Sloppy Record Keeping," below, for more information on this exception).

But if your business is a sole proprietorship or general partnership, your business is not a separate entity, and you are legally responsible for paying its debts. If the business can't pay its own way, your personal assets are at risk.

To decide whether filing for Chapter 7 personal bankruptcy makes sense, you must first understand which debts (if any) you are personally liable for. This chapter will help you evaluate your (and your spouse's) liability for your business's debts. It will also help you assess the condition of your company and decide whether you want to close the business down and or try to stay in business. Answering these preliminary questions will give you the information you need to weigh your options for dealing with your business debt.

Assess Your Personal Liability for Business Debts

Many small business owners see their businesses as an extension of themselves. It can be tough (not to mention stressful and costly) to start a business, and the daring entrepreneurs who make a go of it often pour their energy, time, and money into their ventures. Perhaps you started your business with your personal savings or money from an inheritance, use your spouse's paycheck (or your paycheck from a day job) to fund its operations, use your own car for deliveries or sales calls, or have pledged your own property and used your own credit to get the money you need to keep the business running. Practices like these can make it hard to figure out where your business's finances end and yours begin.

Because their business and personal finances are so often intertwined, small business owners often face collection efforts against their business assets and their personal property. In looking at your options, one of your first tasks will be to figure out which business debts you are personally liable for and which are owed only by your business.

If you are personally liable for some or all of your business's debts, they can be wiped out by filing for Chapter 7 personal bankruptcy. On the other hand, if you are not personally liable for any business debts—for example, because your business is organized as a corporation or LLC and you have not voluntarily pledged your personal credit—you won't need to file a Chapter 7 personal bankruptcy action for your business debts. Although your business might need to file its own business bankruptcy, that's a different process (one that we don't cover in detail in this book).

To figure out whether you are personally liable for your business's debts, you'll need to start by looking at how your business is structured (as a sole proprietorship, partnership, corporation, or LLC). Even if you've formed a separate business structure that offers limited liability, you may still be responsible for its debts if you've personally guaranteed them or taken other actions that might put you on the hook, such as signing a lease or contract in your personal name rather than your capacity as a corporate officer, or pledging personal property as collateral for a business debt.

CAUTION

Whether your business is organized as a corporation, LLC, partnership, or sole proprietorship, you are legally responsible to pay taxes your business withheld from employee paychecks. The IRS isn't interested in any of the details: If you withheld those taxes, you are personally liable if you don't pay that money to the government.

Sole Proprietorships and Partnerships

If you are the sole owner of your business, and you haven't filed paperwork with your state to incorporate or form an LLC, you are a sole proprietor. The same is true for some businesses owned by a husband and a wife: If you live in a community property state (discussed below), you and your spouse can run the business and still call it a sole proprietorship.

Legally, a sole proprietorship is inseparable from its owner; the business isn't a separate entity that can take on its own debt. You are personally liable for every penny that your business can't pay. If your business doesn't have enough cash or assets to pay its debts, creditors can, and often will, go after your personal assets.

If you are a sole proprietor considering bankruptcy to get rid of your business debts, you need to file a personal bankruptcy, not a business bankruptcy. A personal bankruptcy will help you wipe out most types of debts, whether or not they are related to your business.

The same is true of general partnerships. In a general partnership, each partner is personally liable for 100% of the partnership's debts. If there aren't enough business assets to pay those debts, and your partners are broke, creditors can take your personal assets to pay *all* of the business's debts, not just your pro rata share. But fortunately, filing a personal bankruptcy will get rid of all of your liability for the partnership's debts, as well as any money you owe to your partners.

Corporation or LLC

If your business is organized as a corporation or LLC, you and your business are separate legal entities. You have limited liability for the business's debts. In theory at least, this means you aren't personally liable for the debts of your business, so creditors can't take your house or other personal assets to pay business debts, even if your business can't pay them.

> EXAMPLE: Cook's Nook, Inc., orders kitchen supplies from 20 wholesalers before the business tanks. Unable to pay its expenses, the corporation closes its doors. Talia, the corporation's sole owner, auctions off the store's inventory and uses the proceeds to pay Cook's Nook's creditors, who receive a few cents on the dollar. She then dissolves the corporation by filing dissolution papers with the state. Because the business is a corporation, Talia is not personally responsible for paying any of Cook's Nook Inc.'s remaining debt. Its creditors are simply out of luck.

Unfortunately for small business owners, legal theory is not necessarily legal reality. There are many ways corporate shareholders or LLC members can make themselves personally liable for business debts. In fact, most owners of small corporations and LLCs voluntarily take on personal liability for at least some business debts.

Below are some common ways an owner of a corporation or an LLC might become personally liable for the business's debts. If you *are* personally liable for some or all of your business debts, you will have to file a personal bankruptcy, rather than a business bankruptcy, to rid yourself of these debts.

Signing a Personal Guarantee

Because most suppliers, banks, and landlords know that corporate shareholders and LLC members aren't personally liable for business debts, they often won't extend credit or lend money to a small corporation or LLC without an owner's personal guarantee: a legally binding agreement that the owner will repay the debt if the business can't. And many small business owners are willing to sign a personal guarantee, even though they incorporated or formed an LLC precisely to limit their liability for obligations relating to the business, because they can't get the money otherwise.

Check to see whether you signed a personal guarantee on any of your business contracts, such as a loan for a business vehicle or business equipment, trade terms with a supplier, a bank line of credit, or a commercial lease. If so, the creditor can go after your personal assets for repayment.

Offering Your Property as Collateral

Banks often require the owners of small corporations or LLCs to put up their home or other real estate as security for a loan. If you secured a business loan or debt by pledging personal property, such as your house, boat, or car, you are personally liable for the debt. If your business defaults on the loan, the lender or creditor can sue you to foreclose on the property (collateral) and use the proceeds to repay the debt. Filing for Chapter 7 personal bankruptcy will wipe out your personal liability for this type of loan, but the lender's lien on the collateral will survive. This means you'll eventually have to pay off the debt if you sell the property; what happens to liens in bankruptcy is covered in Ch. 8.

Signing a Contract in Your Own Name

You may also have given up your limited liability if you were careless about signing purchase agreements and service contracts for your business. Sometimes these agreements display the personal name of the business owner without the name of the corporation or LLC. If you signed an agreement in your personal name and not on behalf of the corporation or LLC, you're personally liable for the underlying debt, even if it was a simple mistake. If you're not sure whether you signed an agreement or loan personally, check the language of the agreement and the signature block to see whether you signed it in your name or in your capacity as an owner or officer.

> **EXAMPLE:** Talia signs a loan contract as Talia Smith, CEO of Cook's Nook, Inc., which means only her incorporated business is liable to repay the loan. But Talia then signs her commercial lease as just Talia Smith (without any mention of Cook's Nook, Inc.). Talia will be personally liable to the landlord if her business can't pay the rent.

Using Credit Cards or Personal Loans to Fund the Business

If you used credit cards or home equity loans to obtain funds for your business, you are personally liable for those debts. (Under the terms of most credit card applications, even those used in the name of a corporation or LLC, you agree to be personally liable for making all payments.)

> **EXAMPLE:** Amy and Adam open a coffee roastery and café offering weekly poetry readings. To get their business started, they file LLC formation papers with the state and spend $35,000 on a brand new roaster that can crank out a thousand pounds of coffee per day. Unable to get a small business loan, they charge the coffee roaster on their personal credit cards, figuring they will pay it off quickly with income from the business. They also sign a two-year lease on a corner building in an artsy neighborhood, for which the landlord requires their personal signatures. They arrange for weekly deliveries of beans from a nearby wholesaler, with invoices in the name of Cozy Roast LLC.
>
> Unfortunately, when they open their doors, crowds fail to appear, and Amy and Adam

realize that their original sales forecast was too optimistic by half. Five months later, still operating in the red, they decide to close down. They are personally liable for their $35,000 credit card debt for the coffee roaster as well as the remaining months on their two-year lease (unless the landlord can find a replacement tenant). Because Amy and Adam didn't personally sign or guarantee a contract for the coffee bean deliveries, only the business is liable to pay the bean invoices (assuming Amy and Adam have properly followed LLC formalities). Amy and Adam consider filing for Chapter 7 personal bankruptcy to get rid of their credit card debt and obligation to the landlord.

Tortious Conduct

Generally, owners of corporations and LLCs are not personally liable for mistakes in management, but they can be held personally liable for injuring others. An owner who commits a tort (the legal term for an act that harms another person and causes monetary loss) can be held personally liable.

EXAMPLE: Brian, the owner of an LLC, speeds through a residential neighborhood and runs a red light, causing an accident. Damages to the other vehicles, which were totaled, exceed his $50,000 liability insurance policy by $40,000 (he hit a Lexus and a Mercedes). Even though Brian was driving on work-related business, the LLC's limited liability does not protect Brian from being sued personally for the automobile damages.

Fraud, Misrepresentation, or Sloppy Record Keeping

If you misrepresented or lied about any facts when you applied for a loan or credit on behalf of your corporation or LLC, you could be held personally liable for the debt. Likewise, if you failed to maintain a formal legal separation between your business and your personal financial affairs, creditors could try to hold you personally responsible for the business's debts under a theory known as "piercing the corporate veil." This happens when a court finds that your corporation or LLC is really just a sham and you are personally operating the business as if the corporation or LLC didn't exist. In this situation, a court may decide that you aren't entitled to the limited liability that your business structure would ordinarily provide.

One way creditors try to pierce the corporate veil is by showing that you didn't observe the legal formalities imposed on corporations and LLCs. For instance, you may have made important corporate or LLC decisions without recording them in minutes of a meeting. Or, you may have paid business bills from a personal checking or credit card account or paid personal bills from your business bank account. Even corporations or LLCs owned by a single individual or a married couple have to obey the rules and formalities imposed on these business structures; otherwise, they risk losing their limited liability protection.

TIP

List all business debts in your personal bankruptcy filing, just in case your "veil" is pieced. Even if you don't think you are personally liable for a corporate or LLC debt, you should list *all* business debts when you file for Chapter 7 personal bankruptcy. Business creditors might try to pierce your corporate veil and sue you personally for those debts. But if you list your business creditors in your personal Chapter 7 paperwork, any potential personal liability for the business debt will be extinguished in the Chapter 7 personal bankruptcy—even though the business debt will remain on the corporation or LLC's books. If you're concerned about personal liability for your corporation's or LLC's debts, you should also talk to a lawyer to make sure you're doing all you can to protect yourself. At a minimum, when you list these business debts in your bankruptcy forms, check the "disputed" column (see Ch. 9), so you won't be admitting liability down the road if any of these debts survive your bankruptcy.

Assess Your Spouse's Liability for Business Debts

After reading the section above, you should be able to figure out which debts you are personally liable for and which you are not. But that isn't the end of the story: Your spouse's personal liability for your business debts could also affect your decision about filing for Chapter 7 personal bankruptcy. For instance, if your spouse *is* liable for your business debts and has assets or income to lose, it might make sense for both of you to file for personal bankruptcy.

Whether your spouse is liable for your business debts turns mostly on where you live. So, it's time for a little geography lesson.

CAUTION

If you live in a state that allows same-sex marriage, same-sex spouses are subject to the same rules about joint and separate debt that apply to other married couples. Some states that don't recognize same-sex marriage allow same-sex couples to register their union in some form (for example, as domestic partners) and thereby gain some of the benefits and obligations of marriage—which may include joint obligations for debt. If you are concerned about your same-sex partner's liability for business debts, consult with an attorney. As explained in Ch. 5, however, same-sex couples may not file jointly for bankruptcy, even if they are married.

Community Property States

In the community property states (listed below), all income either spouse earns during marriage, as well as all property bought with that income, is community property, owned equally by husband and wife. For the most part, any debt incurred by one spouse during marriage is owed by both of them, too; it's a community debt, and the spouse's creditor can go after community property as a source of repayment (although they rarely do when the debt is in one spouse's name). So, if you live in a community property state, you may want to file for bankruptcy to wipe out your business debts and protect your community income and property; even if you currently have little or no income, your spouse may have a good job.

In Ch. 9, we discuss the pros and cons of filing jointly or separately in a community property state.

Community and Common Law Property States

Community Property	Common Law
Alaska*	Everywhere else
Arizona	
California**	
Idaho	
Louisiana	
Nevada	
New Mexico	
Texas	
Washington	
Wisconsin	

*In Alaska, couples can elect to treat their property as community property.

**In California, community property laws also apply to registered domestic partners.

EXAMPLE: Shelley runs a sporting goods store in Tacoma, Washington, as a sole proprietor; her husband is a local bank executive. Even though Shelley's husband isn't involved in the business, he and Shelley own the business jointly, because Shelley started the business with income earned after they married. Over the last few years, Shelley's store has been suffering from poor sales. She finally decides to close her doors, owing $40,000 to suppliers, $25,000 to her landlord, and $15,000 in other debt.

Because Shelley and her husband live in a community property state, her business creditors can sue both Shelley and her husband personally to collect the money owed. Shelley no longer has any income to take, but her husband's earnings are significant. To prevent her creditors from garnishing her husband's income or suing the couple to take their personal assets, Shelley files for personal bankruptcy, which discharges her business debts, Shelley's personal debts, and any personal debts owed jointly by Shelley and her husband. (If Shelley's husband has separate personal debts, such as a lawsuit judgment against him that predates their marriage, those debts will not be affected by Shelley's bankruptcy filing.)

Common Law States

The law works differently in what we refer to as "common law" marital property states (that is, the states that don't appear on the list of community property states, above). In these states, debts incurred by one spouse—even during the marriage—are generally that spouse's debts alone, and only that spouse's income and property are liable for the debt. Debts are jointly owed by both spouses only if they were jointly undertaken. A debt might be jointly owed if any of the following are true, for example:

- Both spouses signed a contract requiring them to make payments.
- Both spouses' names appear on an account or title to property.
- A creditor was given both spouses' credit information as part of an application for a loan.
- The debt benefited the marriage. In other words, it was for food, clothing, child care, necessary household items, or similar items of direct benefit to the family.

All other debts, such as a business debt from one spouse's business, a loan for a car whose title is in only one spouse's name, or credit card debt in one spouse's name only, are considered that spouse's separate debts.

One spouse's creditors cannot legally reach the other spouse's separate money, property, or wages to repay a separate debt. However, if income earned by one spouse is put into a joint bank account or investment account, that income becomes a joint asset, which a creditor can go after. Fortunately, in most common law states, a creditor can take only half of the money in a joint account to pay a spouse's separate business debts.

In many common law states, spouses can jointly own property in a form known as tenancy by the entirety. The rules for when creditors can proceed against property held in tenancy by the entirety are complex (see Ch. 5 for more information). However, the basic idea is that property held in tenancy by the entirety is protected from the separate creditors of a spouse.

SEE AN EXPERT

If you're concerned about your spouse's liability, see a lawyer. If you have run up a pile of business debts and your spouse owns lots of separate property (whether or not it's kept in a joint account), we recommend that you see a lawyer to find out how to best protect your spouse's assets.

EXAMPLE: Robert Horton, the sole owner of Horton Rental, rents construction equipment and party furniture and supplies in Albany, New York. His wife Amanda is an independent jewelry appraiser who makes a good living. Robert hasn't been able to pay Horton Rental's bills for several months, and a creditor is threatening to sue the couple.

Because the Hortons live in a common law property state, the creditor can't sue Amanda and garnish her income. And, because the Hortons hold title to their house in tenancy by the entirety, New York law prevents creditors from forcing its sale, as long as Amanda is alive. If Amanda and Robert were to sell the house, however, the creditor would be entitled to payment from Robert's half of the proceeds.

If you and your spouse have not kept your income and property separate, and your spouse brings significant income and/or assets to the table, filing together for bankruptcy can be advantageous. We discuss the pros and cons of filing separately in Ch. 9.

Assess Whether Your Business Is Viable

Now you know how much of your business debt you (and perhaps your spouse) are personally liable to repay. If you are personally liable for a significant amount of debt, Chapter 7 personal bankruptcy might be a good choice for you. Before making the decision, however, you also need to take a hard look at your business. Undoubtedly, you're considering bankruptcy because the business hasn't done well. But could it do better in the future, or is it time to close the doors for good? And if you think prospects could improve for the business, do you want to continue at the helm?

Is Your Business Economically Viable?

Let's focus first on whether your business can be saved. The answer affects whether you decide to keep your business open and which strategy for handling your business debt makes the most sense.

You wouldn't be reading this book if your business was going gangbusters. So we'll start with the assumption that your business is performing poorly and deep in debt. But does this mean that your business could never turn a profit?

If your past-due debts to your suppliers, landlord, utility providers, and other creditors were erased, either through negotiating settlements or through a bankruptcy process that allowed your business to stay open, could your business begin to break even? Could it stay in the black for the foreseeable future and produce enough income to cover your living expenses? To answer these questions, use your recent expense and income figures to come up with a profit-and-loss forecast and cash-flow analysis—using real numbers, not guesses or rosy estimates.

RESOURCE

Help with financial spreadsheets and business viability. For help assessing whether your business can return to profitability, read *Save Your Small Business: 10 Crucial Strategies to Rescue Your Business or Close Down and Move On*, by Ralph Warner, J.D, and Bethany Laurence, J.D. (Nolo). This book explains in detail how to make a profit (including, for those who need it, how to complete a profit-and-loss forecast and cash-flow analysis) and offers an entire toolkit of marketing ideas that will help you turn your business around.

If you've looked at the financials and you think your business can turn a profit in the long run, it may make sense to stay open while trying to reduce your debt, either through negotiating settlements with your creditors (called a debt workout) or filing a type of bankruptcy that will allow you to keep running your business. If you run a service business with few assets, you might even be able to keep your doors open while you file for Chapter 7 personal bankruptcy. Ordinarily, however, the owner of a business with significant assets or inventory would have to file for Chapter 13 bankruptcy to stay open. (As explained in Ch. 3, Chapter 13 bankruptcy requires you to come up with a plan to pay off some or all of your debts over three to five years.)

Before you spend a lot of time and money trying to save your business by arranging a debt workout or filing for bankruptcy, make sure your business plan will allow your business to become profitable in the next 12 to 18 months, not just to break even. It doesn't make sense to invest the time, trouble, and sleepless nights required to turn your business around unless you see a pot of gold at the end of the rainbow. If you can't become profitable within that time, it may make more sense to cut your losses now by closing the business, filing for Chapter 7 personal bankruptcy to wipe out your debt, and deciding whether to start over with a new business.

While it can be agonizing to decide to close your business down, the sooner you make this decision, the better off you will be if you decide to file for Chapter 7 personal bankruptcy. Bankruptcy law prohibits certain transactions close to the time of a bankruptcy filing, including actions you might want to take to preserve your assets or pay off favored creditors. The more time you have, the more flexibility you will have in arranging your affairs before filing for bankruptcy.

Do You Want to Continue Owning the Business?

If you think your business has a financial future, you'll need to decide whether you want to be part of it. This decision might depend on lots of factors beyond the prospects of your business, including your health, age, family situation, and career alternatives.

If you've come to realize that running a business (or running this particular business) isn't your cup of tea, this may be your opportunity to move on to more fulfilling opportunities. In this situation, you'll want to look at how much money you can squeeze out of the business, in or out of bankruptcy, before you close the doors. On the other hand, if you love running your business, your financial assessment may be focused more on how to keep it running at all costs.

Once you decide either that you want to keep running the business or that you want to move on to other things, you'll have an easier time assessing the financial condition of your business. This is especially true if you are willing to let the business go, because you will no longer be tempted to exaggerate the chances of a turnaround.

Some Personal History

For many years, Steve's father worked in—and owned part of—the family department store (Lee's Department Store in the Los Angeles area). His specialty was men's clothing. He hated going to work, and his family knew it. After several years, he sold out his interest in the family business and purchased a small men's clothing store in partnership with a brother-in-law, where he worked for many years.

After the first flush of enjoyment at being his own boss, he realized he was still unhappy working in retail and often wished out loud for a more creative line of work. Finally, Steve's father said, "Enough!" and made the jump to commercial development. He was a transformed human being for most of the rest of his life. The moral of this little story is simple: Facing up to the need to make a career change—even one forced upon you—can be a positive life event.

At this point, you should have a good sense of whether you want to continue operating your business—and whether that's a good idea financially. You also know the extent of your (and your spouse's) personal liability for the business's debts. Armed with this information, it's time to consider whether Chapter 7 personal bankruptcy is the best strategy for dealing with your business debt.

CHAPTER

2

How Chapter 7 Personal Bankruptcy Works

If you determined, after reading Ch. 1, that you (and perhaps your spouse) are personally liable for all or a good portion of your business debt, filing for Chapter 7 personal bankruptcy might be a wise choice. Chapter 7 personal bankruptcy wipes out your personal liability for most debts, including most business debts. But in exchange, you may have to give up any valuable business assets you own, and perhaps some of your personal property, so they can be sold and the proceeds used to pay down your unsecured debt. You may also have to close down your business. Bankruptcy has other downsides as well, including bankruptcy court fees, attorney fees if you use a lawyer, and a damaged credit rating.

For these reasons, Chapter 7 bankruptcy may not be the best strategy for those who want to stay in business, have valuable property that they could lose in bankruptcy, or wouldn't benefit much from the process because too many of their debts would survive a bankruptcy filing. And, some debtors aren't eligible to file for Chapter 7 personal bankruptcy because their income is too high, they have already received a bankruptcy discharge in the recent past, or they are otherwise disqualified.

This chapter explains the basics of Chapter 7 personal bankruptcy, so you'll have a general sense of how it works, what effect it will have on your property and debts, and whether it's available to you in the first place. Once you understand the Chapter 7 process, you can compare it to other options, covered in Ch. 3, to make a final decision about whether to file for Chapter 7 personal bankruptcy.

The Chapter 7 Process

Chapter 7 bankruptcy is sometimes called "liquidation," or "straight" bankruptcy. It wipes out most types of debt, but you have to let the bankruptcy trustee liquidate (sell) your nonexempt property to repay your creditors.

Property is exempt—which means it can't be taken by creditors or the bankruptcy trustee—if your state law (or federal law, in some cases) has declared it off-limits for collection efforts. Exempt property typically includes basic living essentials, such as clothing, furniture, health aids, the tools of your trade, most retirement accounts, and some amount of equity in a vehicle and a home. Nonexempt property, which you stand to lose in bankruptcy, often includes things like luxury items, a second car, antiques, artwork, and real estate other than your home. Most business assets, such as inventory, machinery, equipment, and supplies, are typically nonexempt, which means they can be taken and sold in Chapter 7 bankruptcy. (You'll find more information on exemptions in "What Happens to Your Property in Chapter 7 Bankruptcy?" below, and in Ch. 6.)

The typical Chapter 7 personal bankruptcy is a routine process that lasts three to six months, costs $299 in filing fees, and requires no special courtroom or analytical skills. Most filers will have to follow only these steps:

- Get credit counseling from an approved agency before filing for bankruptcy.
- File a packet of official forms and documents.
- Attend a short meeting outside of court (called the meeting of creditors) with a bankruptcy official called the trustee.
- Take a two-hour course in budget management.

This section summarizes how a typical Chapter 7 personal bankruptcy case proceeds. If you decide to file for Chapter 7 personal bankruptcy, you'll find much more detail on every step of the process in later chapters.

Starting Your Chapter 7 Personal Bankruptcy Case

To begin your Chapter 7 bankruptcy case, you must complete a packet of forms and file them with the bankruptcy court in your area. The forms require you to provide a lot of information, including basic information about yourself; lists of your creditors, assets, debts, income, expenses, and financial transactions prior to filing; a list of property you are claiming as exempt; information on what you plan to do with property that serves as collateral for a loan (such as a car or home); and more. You also have to file documents, such as your most recent tax return and wage stubs.

In addition, you'll also have to file a form certifying that you have completed a mandatory credit counseling course with an agency approved by the U.S. Trustee's office. (You can find more on this requirement in Ch. 9.)

Along with your paperwork, you must pay the $299 bankruptcy filing fee. If you can't afford the whole fee, you can apply to pay the fee in installments or apply for a fee waiver. (Ch. 9 explains how.) Plus, if you use a lawyer, you can expect to pay several thousand dollars in legal fees. Of course, you can save most of this money by representing yourself with the help of this book (and, perhaps, by using typing services from a bankruptcy petition preparer or legal advice from a limited practice lawyer). Many small business owners can handle their Chapter 7 bankruptcy cases on their own. For more information on situations when it might make sense to hire a lawyer or petition preparer, and help finding one, see Ch. 12.

The Role of the Trustee and the Court

When you file for bankruptcy, you are technically placing the property you own and the debts you owe—called your "bankruptcy estate"—in the hands of the bankruptcy court. The court exercises control over your bankruptcy estate through an official called a "trustee," who is appointed to manage your case. The trustee's primary duty is to see that your creditors are paid as much as possible, so trustees are mostly interested in what you own and what property you claim as exempt. The trustee will examine your papers to make sure they're complete and to look for property that can be taken and sold for the benefit of your creditors. Trustees are paid on a sort of commission system: The more assets the trustee recovers for your creditors, the more the trustee is paid.

While your case is open, you must get the trustee's consent before you sell or give away any of the property in your bankruptcy estate. With a few exceptions, however, you can do what you wish with property you acquire and income you earn after you file for bankruptcy. You are also allowed to borrow money during your bankruptcy case (if you can find someone who will lend it to you).

You aren't the only one prevented from selling or disposing of your property during bankruptcy: Creditors also generally have to keep their hands off. As soon as you file your papers, a federal court order called the "automatic stay" goes into effect, which requires your creditors to immediately stop all collection efforts. Although the automatic stay is not absolute (as explained in Ch. 4), it typically puts a swift end to collection calls and letters, and efforts to garnish wages, take property, or cut off your utilities.

The Meeting of Creditors

At some point during your bankruptcy case, you must show up at a meeting of creditors and answer questions about your paperwork. Usually, the meeting is held somewhere in the courthouse or federal building. The trustee will swear you in, and then ask you questions like whether the information in your papers is complete and accurate, whether you've given anything away in the last year, or how you arrived at the value you gave for a particular item of property listed on your forms. All told, the process rarely takes more than a few minutes.

Despite the name, creditors rarely attend this meeting. If they do, they will also have a chance to question you under oath, usually about the location of collateral for a debt or the accuracy of information you provided to obtain a loan or credit. In most bankruptcy cases, this will be the only personal appearance you have to make. You'll find more information on the creditors' meeting, as well as other situations when you might have to appear in court, in Ch. 10.

How a Bankruptcy Case Ends

Before your bankruptcy case can be closed and your debts wiped out, you must attend a two-hour course on managing your finances. (This is in addition to the credit counseling course you must complete before filing your papers.) You must take this course from an agency approved by the U.S. Trustee, as explained in Ch. 9. Once you complete your counseling, you must file a form certifying that you have met this requirement.

A couple of months after your meeting of creditors, you will receive a Notice of Discharge from the court. This notice doesn't list which of your particular debts are discharged, but it provides some general information about the types of debts that are and are not affected by the discharge order. For information on what happens to your debts in Chapter 7 personal bankruptcy, see "Which Debts Are Discharged in Chapter 7?" below, and Ch. 11.

Once you receive your bankruptcy discharge, you are free to resume your economic life without reporting your activities to the bankruptcy court unless you receive (or become eligible to receive) an inheritance, insurance proceeds, or proceeds from a divorce settlement within 180 days after you initially filed your bankruptcy case. (Ch. 5 explains these exceptional circumstances in more detail.)

After bankruptcy, you cannot be discriminated against by public or private employers solely because of the bankruptcy, although there are some exceptions (discussed in Ch. 11). You can start rebuilding your credit almost immediately, but it will take several years to get decent interest rates on a credit card, mortgage, or car note. You can't file another Chapter 7 bankruptcy case until eight years have passed since your last filing date. In addition, you can't get a discharge in a Chapter 13 bankruptcy case unless you filed it at least four years after you filed your earlier Chapter 7 case.

Who Can File for Chapter 7

Chapter 7 personal bankruptcy isn't available to everyone. If you have a higher income, you may not be eligible for Chapter 7. In addition, previous bankruptcies or fraud may disqualify some filers.

The Means Test

In 2005, Congress changed the bankruptcy law to require some higher-income filers to repay some of their debts over time in Chapter 13 bankruptcy rather than have their debts discharged outright in Chapter 7. The calculations you must perform to figure out whether you can use Chapter 7 bankruptcy or will be forced into Chapter 13 are called the means test.

Here's how the means test works: If your average monthly income over the six months before you file is no more than the median income in your state, you are eligible to use Chapter 7. If your average monthly income is more than the median, however, you have to calculate how much disposable income you will have left after making your required debt payments and paying your allowed expenses. If you would have enough left over (in theory, at least) to pay down part of your debt in Chapter 13, you may be prohibited from using Chapter 7.

In our experience, very few entrepreneurs whose businesses are so troubled that they are contemplating bankruptcy will fail the means test, so hopefully this won't be a concern for you. But if you have had fairly high income over the past six months (after you deduct ordinary and necessary business expenses) and most of your debt is personal (rather than business related), you may have a problem.

Do You Have to Take the Means Test?

Congress carved out a potentially big exception to the means test for business debtors. If your debts stem primarily from business operations, you don't have to take the means test. If most of your total debt is business related, you are exempt from the means test requirement

All of your debt counts toward the total, even if your business caused your financial difficulties. If you have a lot of personal debt (such as a substantial mortgage on your home or student loans), you may have to take the means test—even if you are current on those debts and they aren't the source of your problems.

> **EXAMPLE:** Petra, a small business owner, uses her personal credit cards and home equity line of credit to fund her high school tutoring business. She uses the same sources of credit for personal expenses unrelated to her business, such as taking a trip to visit her grandfather, vacationing in Vermont, and buying a new bedroom set. She has run up a total of $50,000 in debt.
>
> When Petra tallies up her debt, she finds that she spent just under $30,000 on her business and the rest on personal expenses. Because most of her debt was incurred for business reasons, Petra doesn't have to take the means test.
>
> If Petra also had a sizable home mortgage, the balance would tip. For example, say Petra owes $150,000 on her home mortgage (not including the home equity line discussed above). Because most courts consider a home mortgage to be a personal debt, Petra would have to add $150,000 to the "personal" side of the debt scale, and would have to take the means test to see whether she can use Chapter 7.

Certain disabled veterans who will use Chapter 7 to discharge debts incurred while on active duty or engaged in homeland defense activities can also skip the means test.

Is Your Income Higher Than the State Median?

If you have to take the means test, your first step is to compare your "current monthly income" to your state's median income. If your income is equal to or less than the state median, you can file for Chapter 7 without doing any further calculations.

The bankruptcy law defines your "current monthly income" as your average monthly income over the six months before you filed for bankruptcy. All gross income, whether taxable or not, must be included in the total, except for Social Security and Temporary Assistance to Needy Families (TANF). Include your business income, rents, pension, disability insurance, wages, and so on. (You can find a list of income you must include in Ch. 9, along with the instructions to complete the means test form; you can also do this calculation—and find your state's median income—online free, at www.legalconsumer.com.) Importantly, your business income is not your gross business income—it's your gross receipts minus your ordinary and necessary business expenses (the same expenses you list on Schedule C of your tax return).

Once you have a monthly average, multiply it by 12 to come up with an annual figure. Then compare that number to your state's median for a household of the same size (you can find the state median figures online at www.legalconsumer.com or www.usdoj.gov/ust; select "Means Testing Information"). If your income is at or below the median, you have passed the means test and can use Chapter 7. If your income is more than the median, however, you have to do some more calculations.

TIP

Take the means test free, online. This section explains how the means test works, so you can make a rough determination of whether you qualify for Chapter 7. If you want more precise calculations, or you'd simply rather not look up the required figures and do all of the math, go to www.legalconsumer.com. Once you type in your zip code, this information-rich site will give you all of the state and regional information you need and run the figures for you. You'll need to gather your personal and business financial information (on income, expenses, and so on) in order to use the online calculator. If you decide to file for Chapter 7, you'll find line-by-line instructions in Ch. 9 on how to complete the official means test form (Form 22A—*Chapter 7 Statement of Current Monthly Income and Means Test Calculation*), which you must submit with the rest of your bankruptcy paperwork.

Secured vs. Unsecured Debt

Secured debts and unsecured debts are handled differently in bankruptcy. A secured debt gives the creditor the right to take particular property (called collateral) if you fail to pay. For example, a car note is often secured by the car, which the creditor can repossess if you miss your payments. Similarly, a mortgage is secured by your house, on which the creditor can foreclose. Filing for bankruptcy does not wipe out a secured creditor's lien on the collateral, which means the creditor still has the right to take it back if you don't keep up with your payments.

An unsecured debt is not tied to any particular piece of property. Typical unsecured debts include credit card bills, legal fees, medical bills, and bills from suppliers or service providers. If you fail to pay an unsecured debt, the creditor isn't entitled to simply take your money or property. Instead, the creditor usually has to go to court, win a judgment against you or your business, and then institute collection proceedings. In a bankruptcy case, unsecured creditors receive a share of the proceeds from the trustee's sale of your nonexempt property (if you have any). Most unsecured debts are wiped out in bankruptcy.

Do You Have Enough Disposable Income to Pay Your Debts?

If your "current monthly income" exceeds the state median, you don't necessarily fail the means test. However, you have to do a lot more math to see whether you pass: You need to subtract your allowed personal expenses from your income and see whether you'd have enough left over to pay certain debts that will survive your bankruptcy (such as child support and some tax debts), make required payments on your secured debts (like your mortgage or car note), and pay a certain minimum amount (currently, about $110 per month) toward your unsecured debts. If your income will cover all of these costs, you might be forced out of Chapter 7 bankruptcy.

As you can see, these calculations can get complicated. What's more, you might have to use expense amounts as determined by the IRS for your area, not the actual amount you spend on particular items. In Ch. 9, we explain how to fill in each line of the required form to find out whether you pass the test. Or, you can complete the means test using the free online calculator at www.legalconsumer.com (it supplies the IRS amounts for you).

CAUTION

The bankruptcy court can second-guess the results of the means test. Even if you pass the means test, the bankruptcy court could dismiss your Chapter 7 bankruptcy case or order it converted to a Chapter 13 case if the court believes you have enough income to repay your debts. For example, if the current monthly income you used in the means test was very low, but you've recently been rehired at the high-paying job you left to start your business, the judge might decide that you shouldn't be allowed to use Chapter 7.

Other Disqualifying Circumstances

Even if you pass the means test, you might still be ineligible for Chapter 7 bankruptcy. Here are the most common situations in which debtors aren't allowed to use Chapter 7.

Previous Bankruptcy Discharge

If you obtained a discharge of your debts in a Chapter 7 case filed within the last eight years, or a Chapter 13 case filed within the last six years, you cannot file for Chapter 7. This rule bars only the same person or entity from filing. So, for example, if you already received a discharge in a Chapter 7 personal bankruptcy you filed to deal with debts from your sole proprietorship business, you may not file another Chapter 7 personal bankruptcy until eight years have passed—even if your current debts were incurred for a different business or for entirely personal reasons.

> **EXAMPLE:** Seven years ago, Fred filed for Chapter 7 personal bankruptcy to discharge debts arising from his computer repair service, which he owned as a sole proprietor. As part of that bankruptcy proceeding, Fred closed down his business. Once he received his discharge, Fred got a job with a large computer company as a network troubleshooting specialist.
>
> After a few years, Fred decided to go back into business for himself. He left his job and opened a new sole proprietorship called "Doctor Network." His business is doing fairly well, but Fred has run up huge medical bills as a result of a car accident. He's considering filing for bankruptcy again.
>
> If Fred wants to use Chapter 7 personal bankruptcy, he'll have to wait another year. Even though he's now running a different business, and his debts are personal this time around, he is subject to the eight-year bar. Regardless of the source of his debts, he is filing personally in both cases—and he's still the same Fred.

If your current business is a separate entity (a corporation or an LLC), it can file for Chapter 7 business bankruptcy even if you filed a Chapter 7 personal bankruptcy case within the past eight years. Because you and your business are legally separate, you are different filers, and the bar wouldn't apply (unless the corporate veil is pierced and you and the corporation or LLC are deemed to be the same entity; see Ch. 1 for more on this). Similarly, you can file for Chapter 7 personal bankruptcy even if your corporation or LLC has filed a business bankruptcy case in the last eight years.

> **EXAMPLE:** Laura is the sole owner of an incorporated beauty salon business. The corporation owns the salon's fixtures and beauty supplies and is obligated on the salon's ten-year lease. Laura is also personally liable on the lease, because the landlord insisted that she cosign in her own name. Due to recent business downturns, Laura decides to close the business.
>
> The business's assets are worth about $15,000, and it owes vendors a total of $20,000. Laura and the corporation are both liable for the rent due for the remainder of the lease period, a potential liability of $75,000 (depending on whether, and when, the landlord can find a replacement tenant).
>
> Laura received a discharge in a Chapter 7 personal bankruptcy case she filed six years ago. The corporation has never filed for bankruptcy. The corporation may file a business bankruptcy case now, in which its assets will be sold off and used to pay its creditors. Laura will still be personally liable for the lease, however, and she must wait another two years to file for Chapter 7 personal bankruptcy to discharge that debt. If she is personally liable for any of the other corporate debts (which would happen if her corporate veil is pierced), that liability could also be wiped out in a personal Chapter 7 bankruptcy.

The eight-year bar applies only if you received a discharge in your earlier bankruptcy case. If your case was dismissed or otherwise ended without a discharge, it doesn't count.

Previous Bankruptcy Dismissal

You cannot file for Chapter 7 bankruptcy if your previous Chapter 7 or Chapter 13 case was dismissed in the last 180 days because you violated a court order, the court found that your case was fraudulent or abusive (as explained below), or you requested the dismissal after a creditor asked for relief from the automatic stay. (See Ch. 4.)

Abuse of the System

Even if you pass the means test, the court can dismiss your Chapter 7 case if it finds, considering all of the circumstances, that your case is an "abuse" of the remedy that Chapter 7 provides. For example, courts have dismissed cases in which debtors failed to explain how they got so deeply in debt; couldn't (or wouldn't) say how they spent cash advances, personal injury settlements, or money received from a mortgage refinance; or were voluntarily unemployed.

Fraud

If you lie or attempt to hide assets, your current debt crisis may no longer be your biggest legal problem. You must swear, under oath, that everything in your bankruptcy papers is true. If you are caught deliberately failing to disclose property, omitting important information about your financial transactions, or using a false Social Security number, your bankruptcy case will be dismissed—and you may even be prosecuted for perjury or fraud on the court.

As explained in "Property You Transferred or Payments You Made," below, the trustee has the right to undo certain transfers you made before filing for bankruptcy, if it appears that the transfers were made for inadequate consideration (in other words, you gave the property away or sold it for substantially less than its market value). If the trustee believes a particular transfer that occurred within the previous year was made to cheat or defraud a creditor, or to temporarily unload your property to keep it out of bankruptcy, your right to receive a discharge of your debts may be challenged.

What Happens to Your Property in Chapter 7 Bankruptcy?

When you file for Chapter 7 bankruptcy, you may have to give up some of your property in exchange for having some or all of your debt wiped out. If, despite your business's money problems, you still own a significant amount of property free and clear (such as investments, real estate, vehicles, business equipment, or inventory), the bankruptcy trustee may be able to take it, sell it, and distribute the proceeds to your unsecured creditors. As it turns out, however, most Chapter 7 filers have few assets or owe a lot of money on their property, so they aren't likely to lose much. State exemption laws allow you to keep the basic necessities of life, including clothing, furniture, possibly a vehicle, and some or all of your equity in your house.

The trustee will look for assets in your bankruptcy estate that can be sold for the benefit of your creditors. However, the amount of money a trustee can recover from taking and selling your property is limited by any debts secured by the property and by applicable exemption laws:

- **Secured debt.** If a trustee wants to seize and sell property, he or she must first pay any claims that are secured by the property (collateral) first. For example, if you own a $15,000 car, and you still owe $10,000 on the car note, the trustee would have to pay the lender its $10,000 first, which would leave only $5,000 (less the costs of taking and selling the car) to be distributed among your unsecured creditors.
- **Exemption laws.** State laws entitle you to keep certain property. Some exemption laws allow you to keep all of a particular type of property (for example, your clothing); some allow you to exempt certain types of property up to a dollar limit. For example, many states allow you to exempt up to a certain amount of your equity in a vehicle. If your vehicle is worth more, you may not get to keep it, but you are entitled to be paid your exempt amount. Often, an exemption makes the difference between keeping and losing your property. Using the example above, if you still owe $10,000 on your $15,000 car, and your state allows you to exempt $5,000 of equity in a vehicle, the trustee isn't going to take your car and sell it. After paying off the car

note ($10,000) and giving you your exempt amount ($5,000), there wouldn't be anything left for your other creditors.

Let's take a look at what could happen to various types of property.

Your Business

If you file for Chapter 7 personal bankruptcy, the trustee will examine your business for cash to take and assets to sell. What will happen to your business—and any assets it has—in bankruptcy depends largely on how you have structured it and whether you own it alone or with others.

Legally, the trustee "stands in your shoes" and can do anything with your assets that you could have done, had you not filed for bankruptcy. This means that the trustee not only can sell your property, but also can hold a meeting and vote your corporate or LLC membership shares. In essence, this enables the trustee to dissolve and sell the assets of corporation or LLC if you are the sole (or even the majority) owner.

Will You Have to Close Your Business?

You may have to shut your business down if you file for Chapter 7 personal bankruptcy. However, if you own an LLC or corporation with others, you may be able to keep your doors open, even if you are personally liable for a significant portion of its debt. Let's take a closer look.

TIP

An owner's personal bankruptcy can save a corporation or LLC. When most of a corporation or LLC's debt is owed by its owners rather than by the business itself, the corporation or LLC's debt problems can be often be solved if the owners file for Chapter 7 personal bankruptcy. For example, let's say a corporation's sole owner has racked up debt for the business on personal credit cards. The credit card debt can be wiped out in the owner's personal Chapter 7 bankruptcy case, allowing the business to move forward, debt-free.

Sole Proprietorships

If your business is a sole proprietorship, the trustee may insist that you close it, at least until the trustee can assess the value, exempt status, and likely sales price of any business assets in your bankruptcy estate. This assessment usually lasts a couple of months or more. Closing the business also prevents you from incurring any additional liabilities during your bankruptcy case, whether for regular business debts you might take on during the bankruptcy or for potential legal claims against your business (for example, if someone gets hurt on your premises).

Businesses that operate without assets, such as service providers, consultants, or freelancers, might be allowed to remain open during bankruptcy, especially if your chances of running up debt or incurring legal liabilities are small. But even a small service business might be shut down if it has significant accounts receivable that the trustee could collect. For example, if you own a real estate business and have commissions in the pipeline that haven't been paid yet, the commissions will become part of your bankruptcy estate when they are paid. Any proceeds generated by the business while you're in bankruptcy are also part of your bankruptcy estate.

Partnerships and Multimember LLCs

If your business is a partnership or multimember LLC (it has more than one owner), your share of the business will be part of your bankruptcy estate. Unless you are a majority owner, however, most states prohibit the trustee from interfering with the partnership or LLC or taking its assets.

Here's how it works. A creditor or bankruptcy trustee can obtain a "charging order" against the debtor-owner's interest in the business. Essentially, a charging order acts as a lien against the business interest, allowing the creditor or trustee to receive the profits that would otherwise be paid to the owner of the interest. However, a charging order won't do a creditor or trustee much good if a partnership or LLC doesn't regularly distribute profits to its members. The trustee takes over only the economic right to receive income from the partnership or LLC; typically, a person assigned economic rights is not allowed to manage or vote in the partnership or LLC nor to assume other membership rights granted to full owners under the partnership or LLC operating agreement. The trustee can assign or sell the economic rights in your ownership interest to someone else, but generally cannot transfer or sell your share of the partnership or LLC.

CAUTION

You may need to get out of a partnership or LLC before filing for bankruptcy. If you are a partner in a partnership or a member of an LLC, you may have signed a buy-sell agreement that requires you to terminate your ownership interest before filing for bankruptcy. If you violate a provision like this, you could be facing a lawsuit from your co-owners. A small business attorney can help you assess your obligations and options here.

Corporations and Single-Member LLCs

Your bankruptcy estate includes your corporate shares or LLC membership. If you are the sole or majority owner of the corporation or LLC, the bankruptcy trustee can take over your shares or membership interest and vote to sell or liquidate the business, then distribute the proceeds to the business's creditors.

In deciding whether to dissolve a single-owner corporation or LLC, the trustee will take a cost/benefit approach. The trustee will look at the cost of dissolving and liquidating the business, how much the assets can be sold for, and whether any of the assets are exempt. In many cases, the business owes almost as much as (or more than) it owns, so liquidating the business wouldn't make financial sense. But if the business has a moderate amount of debt and valuable, nonexempt assets, the trustee is likely to dissolve the corporation or LLC and sell the assets.

EXAMPLE: Ned, a truck driver, is the sole owner of a corporation that has few debts and holds title to an 18-wheeler. Ned wants to file for personal bankruptcy to get rid of a huge amount of credit card debt. Because Ned's corporate stock becomes part of his bankruptcy estate, the trustee can exercise all powers conferred by the stock, including dissolving the corporation, selling the corporation's sole asset (the truck), and distributing the proceeds to Ned's unsecured creditors (unless Ned can claim the truck as exempt under his state's laws).

If you own a viable corporation with other members, then your personal bankruptcy may or may not affect your business. For example, if you own a corporation equally with two or three other shareholders, you may be able to file for personal bankruptcy without any consequences to the corporation. Although the trustee has the right to vote shares in a corporation, he or she generally won't be able to call a meeting and force a dissolution of the corporation to get at its assets unless you are the majority shareholder. Your stock is still part of your bankruptcy estate, but it won't have much value to the bankruptcy trustee unless one of the other owners wants to buy it.

CAUTION

Trustees may be able to dissolve even a multiowner corporation or LLC. When one person, or a small group of related or closely associated people, have complete control over a corporation or LLC, and the corporation or LLC has been used in questionable ways (perhaps it has recklessly borrowed and lost money or perpetrated financial fraud), a trustee can try to "reverse pierce" the corporation or LLC's veil of liability protection. This is similar to piercing the corporate veil, discussed in Ch. 1, but instead of holding the owner liable for the business's debts, reverse piercing allows the trustee to hold the business liable for the owner's debts. If there was commingling of personal and business funds, the corporation or LLC was inadequately capitalized, or corporate or LLC formalities were neglected, the trustee might be able to dissolve the business and sell the assets attributable to the bankruptcy filer for the benefit of the bankruptcy filer's creditors.

Your Business Assets

The bankruptcy trustee has the power to take valuable business equipment and supplies in your bankruptcy estate and sell them for the benefit of your unsecured creditors. The trustee, however, can't take and sell:

- property that secures a loan (collateral)
- exempt property, or
- property that belongs to your corporation or LLC.

Property Acting as Collateral

Here's a brief overview of what happens to property acting as collateral for a loan (secured property); for more detailed information, see Ch. 8. If your property serves as collateral for a loan, the trustee can petition the bankruptcy court for permission to sell the property. The trustee will do this only if he or she believes that there will be money left over after selling the property, paying off the lender, and paying you any exempt amount you are entitled to. The money left over would be paid to your unsecured creditors.

Unless the collateral is worth much more than the loan securing the property, the bankruptcy trustee will often allow the secured creditor to take the property (the trustee will "abandon" the property to the secured creditor), because there wouldn't be any money left over from a sale to distribute to the unsecured creditors.

> **EXAMPLE:** Kevin opens Kitchen Playpen, a sole proprietorship that carries a select inventory of upscale home kitchen products. To stock his shelves, Kevin borrows $60,000 from a local community bank at a low interest rate. The loan is secured by the store's entire inventory. As business falters, Kevin substantially cuts down on inventory. As a result, the value of the bank's security for the loan decreases as well. Under the terms of the loan, the bank calls for immediate payment of the loan in full.
>
> Realizing that he can't pay off the loan (and that his business is no longer economically viable), Kevin closes his doors and files for Chapter 7 personal bankruptcy. In addition to Kevin's personal assets, the bankruptcy estate includes the store's remaining inventory, valued at roughly $40,000. Because Kevin owes the bank more than the inventory is worth, all of the proceeds from auctioning off the inventory would go to the bank. There would be nothing left for Kevin's other creditors, and the trustee couldn't claim a commission for the sale. The trustee decides instead to leave the inventory alone (in bankruptcy terms, to "abandon" the property) and let the bank take it back.

Exempt Property

If any of your business property is entirely exempt, the trustee can't take it and sell it. There are two types of exemptions that may apply to business assets:

- "wildcard" exemptions, which give you a lump sum exemption amount you can apply to any type of property, including business property (wildcard exemptions range from several hundred dollars to $20,000 or $30,000, depending on your state's law), and
- "tools of the trade" exemptions, which let you keep tools or equipment up to a certain dollar amount in value (typically, several thousand dollars). However, most states allow you to exempt property as tools of the trade only if you will continue to use them to make a living.

> **EXAMPLE:** Chuck, a sole proprietor, has a car repair and restoration shop in a trendy area of Venice, California. Four years ago, he signed a ten-year lease for $48,000 per year, payable in $4,000 monthly installments. After suffering

some health problems and seeing a sharp decline in his business, Chuck decides to close his doors. Because he can't pay off what he owes on the lease, his landlord is unwilling to negotiate, and he has a growing pile of medical and personal bills, Chuck files for Chapter 7 personal bankruptcy.

Chuck's bankruptcy estate consists primarily of used shop equipment and tools, the possible value of the six years remaining on his lease, and Chuck's house. Chuck values the shop equipment at $20,000 in his bankruptcy papers and claims a full wildcard exemption under California law. If the trustee takes the equipment and sells it, Chuck is entitled to his exempt amount before one penny can be distributed to his unsecured creditors. Figuring that Chuck's valuation is pretty accurate and taking into account the costs of an asset sale, the trustee lets him keep the equipment instead of selling it.

As for the lease, the trustee is legally entitled to "assume" it and then sell it off to a willing buyer, or "reject" it and let it die with the bankruptcy. If Chuck's space was worth much more than $4,000 a month, the trustee could probably make some money for Chuck's creditors by selling the right to take over the lease to an interested customer. Because times are so bad, however, the lease is now greatly overpriced, so the trustee chooses to reject it. Finally, Chuck's house is "underwater" (he owes more than it is worth), so the trustee has no interest in selling it; all of the proceeds from a sale would go to the mortgage lender.

These examples illustrate the typical facts on the ground: People who declare bankruptcy don't tend to own much valuable property, especially not free and clear. Often, the trustee won't be able to sell property belonging to the bankruptcy estate, either because the property (or the owner's equity in it) is exempt or because the property is collateral for a secured debt, and the creditor would get all the proceeds if it were sold.

Property That Belongs to Your Corporation or LLC

If your business is a corporation or LLC, the trustee can take and sell its assets only if you are the sole or majority owner and the trustee votes to dissolve the business, as explained above. If you are a minority owner, the corporation's or LLC's property is off limits to the trustee.

EXAMPLE: Heather starts a gelato shop on a busy corner in San Francisco and organizes it as a corporation. After Heather spends a fortune on expensive equipment (purchased with a small business loan), the business does poorly and Heather has to shut down. She arranges to keep her equipment in a storage facility, hoping that she can use it to restart the business in a different location when the economy improves. Mired in credit card debt and burdened by a mortgage that's higher than the current value of her house, Heather files for personal Chapter 7 personal bankruptcy.

She doesn't list her shop equipment as an asset because the equipment belongs to the corporation, which isn't filing for bankruptcy. Heather does, however, list her stock in the corporation as one of her assets. Heather hopes the trustee will "abandon" the stock, because there's really no market for it, and leave Heather with her equipment. This is wishful thinking, however. Because the corporation owns valuable assets, the trustee becomes owner of the corporation and "votes" to dissolve it and liquidate its assets, including the shop equipment, for the benefit of Heather's unsecured creditors.

Had Heather formed the corporation equally with a couple of friends, the situation would have been different. The trustee would have had the right to vote Heather's shares, but wouldn't have had the power to force a dissolution of the corporation over the objections of the other shareholders. Because the shop equipment belongs to the corporation, it's not part of Heather's bankruptcy estate, and the trustee wouldn't have been able to take it and sell it.

TIP

Records of asset ownership are essential. It's important to know which business assets belong to you and which belong to the business entity (if any), so you know what will be part of your bankruptcy estate. This is especially important if you are one of several co-owners of your corporation or LLC; the trustee has no right to take any assets belonging to the corporation or LLC if you are a minority owner.

Your House

Ch. 7 explains in detail what happens to your house in a Chapter 7 bankruptcy, but here's a brief overview. Small business owners often pledge their homes as collateral for business loans or lines of credit. If you default on this type of loan (or you stop making your mortgage payments for any reason), the lender can foreclose. Filing for Chapter 7 bankruptcy can delay the foreclosure, but ultimately, if you don't make the payments, you'll lose your house. (Note: Chapter 13 bankruptcy can provide a more long-term solution to keeping your home—see Ch. 3.)

What about debts that aren't secured by your home? To determine whether your house might be sold to pay debts you owe your commercial landlord, suppliers, or other business creditors, you need to understand your state's homestead exemption law. Most states let you keep your principal residence if your equity in it doesn't exceed the state's homestead exemption amount (assuming, of course, that you keep making the mortgage payments). In most states, $10,000 to $70,000 of your home equity is exempt from creditors. A few states, including Tennessee, Ohio, Maryland, Kentucky, and Alabama, exempt $5,000 or less, and New Jersey and Pennsylvania don't have a homestead exemption at all. At the other end of the spectrum, Texas, Florida and a few other states exempt your residence no matter how much it's worth (though some have large acreage limits). Note that the homestead exemption applies only to main residences, not second houses, vacation houses, or rental property.

If your equity in your home is less than your state's exemption amount, the trustee wouldn't get anything from a sale; what you owe to the mortgage lender and your exempt amount would together eat up all of the sale proceeds. You'll be able to keep your house—again, if you keep up on your mortgage payments during and after the bankruptcy. But if your equity significantly exceeds the exempt amount, the trustee will want to sell the house, pay off your mortgage and any other loans secured by the house, give you the exempt amount, and distribute the rest of your equity among your unsecured creditors.

EXAMPLE: Andy's New York travel company, a sole proprietorship, goes under. Andy owes $40,000 on a small business loan, $10,000 in rent for his commercial space, and $25,000 in credit card bills for both personal and business expenses. He decides to file for Chapter 7 personal bankruptcy.

Andy's house is worth $300,000, and he owes $245,000 on his mortgage, leaving him with $55,000 in equity. New York's homestead exemption protects up to $50,000 in equity. In theory, the bankruptcy trustee could sell the house, give Andy his $50,000 exemption amount, and pay the remaining $5,000 toward Andy's creditors. However, the trustee knows that it will cost more than $5,000 to take the house and sell it. This makes the sale a losing proposition for the trustee, so Andy gets to keep it.

TIP

Chapter 7 bankruptcy can buy you some breathing room. When you file for bankruptcy, the court issues an "automatic stay," an order that requires all creditors to immediately stop their collection activities (including foreclosure) and prevents them from filing lawsuits, taking assets, or shutting off utilities. This delay might give you at least a few months to bring in the income you need to get current on your mortgage or other secured debt, so you can keep the house or other collateral. After a month or two, however, secured lenders can usually get the court's permission to proceed with a foreclosure, repossession, or collection. The automatic stay is discussed in detail in Ch. 4.

Your Vehicle

If your car secures your car loan, and you default on the loan, the lender can repossess your car. Bankruptcy can delay the repossession for a while and give you a chance to get current on the loan. Ultimately, however, you'll lose your car if you can't make your payments.

If your car doesn't serve as collateral for a debt, the trustee can still take it and sell it to pay your unsecured creditors if your equity exceeds your state's vehicle exemption amount. Most states allow you to keep one vehicle with equity up to a certain amount—usually between $1,000 and $5,000. Your state may also have a wildcard exemption you can apply to your car, either instead of or in addition to the vehicle exemption.

> **EXAMPLE:** Carlos and Melyssa have two vehicles. One is a newish Dodge Sprinter on which they are making payments; its value went down quite a bit in the last year, so they don't have any equity in it. The other is a ten-year-old car they own free and clear, worth about $3,000.
>
> When Carlos and Melyssa file for bankruptcy, the Sprinter goes back to the lender because they can't afford the payments. The amount the lender is able to sell it for doesn't cover what they still owe on the loan, but the remaining debt (called a "deficiency") will be wiped out in bankruptcy. Their state exempts up to $5,000 worth of equity in a vehicle, so they get to keep their older car.

You may get to keep your car even if your equity significantly exceeds your state's vehicle exemption. The costs of taking and selling a car can be substantial, and a bankruptcy sale typically yields less than the car is worth. Recognizing this, the trustee is likely to give you an opportunity to "buy back" the car for substantially less than the nonexempt amount. For example, if your vehicle exemption is $5,000, your car is worth $10,000, and you own the car free and clear, the trustee might let you keep the car for $2,000 cash, since the trustee would likely not receive any much more than that after deducting the costs of sale. If you decline this "generous" offer, the trustee will sell it, give you the exempt amount, and use the rest to pay your creditors.

You'll find more information on what happens to your car and other personal property in bankruptcy in Ch. 6.

CAUTION

Don't pay off your car before you file for bankruptcy. Many people are under the erroneous impression that they get to keep one vehicle when they file for bankruptcy, no matter how much it's worth. They do whatever they can to pay off their best car or truck before they file. This is exactly the wrong strategy, however. Because exemption laws protect only a limited dollar amount, it's usually better to owe money on your car when you go into bankruptcy. The less equity you have in the car, the more likely it is to be protected by an exemption, which means you get to keep it (assuming you can keep up the payments on it).

Your Other Personal Property

Every state's exemption laws allow you to keep a certain amount of essential personal property, such as clothing, appliances, and furniture. As is true of vehicles, even if your personal property is worth somewhat more than the exemption in your state, the trustee is not likely to take it; the costs of a legal sale are considerable, and used personal property doesn't typically bring a high price. Pensions and retirement accounts are also exempt, although some types of "retirement" annuities may not be.

If you own valuable nonexempt property, such as expensive art, collectibles, boats, antiques, stocks, bonds, and highly valuable jewelry, you should expect them to be taken and sold by the bankruptcy trustee. See Ch. 6 for more information on how your personal property is handled in bankruptcy.

TIP

You might be able to buy back nonexempt assets. You might be able to negotiate with the bankruptcy trustee to keep some nonexempt property. If you have exempt property that you don't want, you may be able to substitute it for nonexempt property of the same value. Or, you could make a lump-sum payment to "buy back" your exempt property. For example, if you wanted to keep your car, which is worth $10,000 more than the exempt amount, the trustee might allow you to keep it if you could come up with $7,500 in cash (the discount represents the costs that would be saved and the lower value the car would fetch at auction) or the trustee might be willing to take and sell several valuable pieces of exempt household furniture instead.

Property You Transferred or Payments You Made

In some cases, the trustee can take back payments you made and property you transferred or sold before you filed for bankruptcy. The trustee will look at your prior transactions to see whether you sold property for less than it was worth, transferred property to someone else with the intent of preventing your creditors from getting it, or made "preference" payments to insider creditors, such as relatives and close business associates.

A bankruptcy court can reverse certain previous transfers or payments and use the proceeds to repay all of your creditors equally. If any money you paid to family or friends has been spent, the trustee can sue them to get it back. To make things worse, if the bankruptcy judge decides you made the payment or transfer for fraudulent purposes, your bankruptcy case could be dismissed.

How far back the trustee can look depends on the type of transaction and your relationship to the other party to the transaction. The time limits can be anywhere from a few months to four years. Ch. 5 covers fraudulent transfers and preference payments in detail.

EXAMPLE: Tommy grows walnuts on a ten-acre farm he owns with his brother. Tommy decides to leave the walnut business. Although the farm is worth $250,000, Tommy sells his half to his brother for $75,000; $50,000 goes to pay off Tommy's half of the farm's $100,000 mortgage, and Tommy pockets the remaining $25,000.

Tommy files for Chapter 7 bankruptcy a year later and, as is required, lists the sale of the farm in his bankruptcy paperwork (all transfers made within the previous two years must be listed). The bankruptcy trustee challenges the transfer as a fraudulent attempt by Tommy to keep the farm out of his bankruptcy estate. The trustee demands that Tommy's brother deed Tommy's share of the property back to the trustee so that it can be included in Tommy's bankruptcy estate and possibly sold for the benefit of Tommy's creditors. Tommy must also account for what he did with the $25,000 from the sale. Had Tommy sold his half of the farm for its full $125,000 fair value, the transfer would not be considered fraudulent and Tommy's brother could keep the farm. However, Tommy would be held to account for how he spent the $125,000.

Which Debts Are Discharged in Chapter 7?

Although many types of debts are wiped out in Chapter 7 personal bankruptcy, certain debts may survive your bankruptcy, depending on the circumstances. What happens to debts in Chapter 7 bankruptcy is discussed in detail in Ch. 11. Here is a brief overview.

Debts That Are Discharged

Many of the debts that drive business owners to bankruptcy are dischargeable. This means that you are no longer responsible for paying them once your Chapter 7 personal bankruptcy case is complete. Once the trustee sells your nonexempt assets (if you have any) and distributes the proceeds among your unsecured creditors, then the court discharges any amount that remains unpaid on the debts when your case ends.

Here are some common types of debts that are discharged in Chapter 7 personal bankruptcy:

- credit card bills
- lawsuit judgments
- medical bills
- unsecured business debts owed by a sole proprietor, such as debts to suppliers, consultants, and professionals (accountants or architects, for example)
- obligations under leases and contracts entered into by a sole proprietor, including commercial and residential property leases and leases to rent equipment, and
- personal loans and promissory notes.

Secured debts are handled differently. As explained above (and in detail in Ch. 8), the lender can take back the collateral securing the loan if you don't make your payments, even if you file for bankruptcy. If you owe more on a secured debt than the collateral is worth, the difference (called a "deficiency") is discharged in bankruptcy. But the lender still has the right to take back the collateral if you default.

Debts That Survive Chapter 7 Bankruptcy

Several types of debt are not dischargeable in Chapter 7, which means you will still owe them when your case is over, just as if you hadn't filed for bankruptcy. Which debts are and are not discharged is covered in detail in Ch. 11; here are some of the most common types of debts that cannot be discharged in Chapter 7 bankruptcy:

- back child support, alimony, and other domestic support obligations
- court-imposed fines, penalties, and restitution
- certain tax debts, including recent back taxes; any back taxes for which you didn't file a tax return; trust fund taxes (the employee portion of Social Security and Medicare taxes); and debts you incurred to pay nondischargeable taxes (for example, if you took a cash advance on your credit card to pay your most recent tax bill)
- debts of more than $550 to any one creditor for luxuries in the 90 days before you file (charges for reasonably necessary items don't count)
- cash advances of more than $825 taken within 70 days before you file
- loans you owe to your pension plan (such as money you borrowed from your 401(k))
- student loans, unless repaying them would constitute an extreme hardship (this is very hard to prove)
- debts arising from your fraudulent activity (for example, lying on a loan application), if the creditor proves the fraud to the bankruptcy court's satisfaction, and
- debts resulting from an incident in which you kill or injure someone while you are driving under the influence.

Debts Owed By Others (Your Company, Partners, and Cosigners)

Chapter 7 personal bankruptcy wipes out only your debts (and possibly those of your spouse, as explained in Ch. 1). It does not get rid of:

- **Debts owed by your corporation or LLC.** Chapter 7 personal bankruptcy discharges your personal liability for debts, but does not affect your corporation's or LLC's liability. To

What Not to Do If You Might File for Bankruptcy

If you've concluded that Chapter 7 bankruptcy may be in the cards, there are certain actions you should avoid taking. While it's natural to try to come up with "creative" methods to pay down your debt or protect your assets, you can harm your bankruptcy case—or lose your right to file for bankruptcy altogether—if you do any of the following:

- **Hide assets.** You may be tempted to give assets to your friends and relatives, change the title to property so it looks like you don't own it, or "sell" property to loved ones for far less than it's worth. Creditors' attorneys and trustees are experienced in ferreting out these tactics, which can lead the trustee to take the property back or even charge you with fraud and prevent you from receiving a discharge of your debt.
- **Lie on loan applications.** We know you need money to stay afloat. But overstating the value of your assets, inflating your income, or failing to disclose other debts on a loan application can lead to fraud charges. The bankruptcy court may refuse to discharge any debt that you took on through fraud.
- **Make preference payments.** As explained above, the trustee will take a close look at all payments you made to creditors during the year before you file—and may take those payments back to distribute among all of your creditors. Any payments above a certain threshold made within 90 days before you file might be considered a preference; if the payment was to an insider creditor (a relative or close business associate), the court can take payments made over the past year.
- **Engage in shopping sprees and cash advances.** If you buy luxury goods or services within three months before filing, the trustee will assume that you intended to defraud the court and your creditors. If you really splurge and buy a new car, vacation time-share, or similarly opulent purchase on credit, the creditor can argue that the debt is fraudulent, no matter when you took it on. And, cash advances for more than $825 taken within 70 days before you file may also be deemed fraudulent (if the creditor can prove fraud, even smaller advances will be suspect). In any of these situations, the debt won't be discharged.
- **Pay off your unsecured debt or car loan.** If you're planning to file for bankruptcy, don't bother paying debts that will be fully discharged. And, as discussed above, you're better off owing money on your car when you go into bankruptcy; the more equity you have in the car, the more likely you are to lose it.
- **Take property from your LLC or corporation.** If your corporation or LLC is insolvent, its assets belong to its creditors. If you take that property, you're committing theft—which could result in the dismissal of your bankruptcy case or even criminal charges.
- **Pay yourself a bonus or back pay.** The bankruptcy system treats you as an insider creditor. If you pay yourself a bonus, repay a loan you made to the business, or pay yourself back wages in the year before you file, these will be considered preference payments that the court can take back. It could also be considered fraud, which might result in dismissal of your case or worse.
- **Let your insurance lapse.** If you may stay in business, or you simply need to keep your liability insurance while you wind down, file for bankruptcy just after you renew your policy. After you file, you may have a tough time finding a carrier willing to renew your coverage or issue a new policy. As long as you continue your payments, your insurance can't be canceled just because of your bankruptcy.

take care of debts owed by the corporation or LLC, the business will have to file its own business bankruptcy (or settle them).

- **Debts owed by your partners in a partnership.** Your Chapter 7 personal bankruptcy wipes out your personal liability for partnership debts, but your partner(s) will still be on the hook for the full amount.
- **Debts someone else cosigned.** If someone else cosigned a loan or otherwise took on a joint obligation with you, that person can be held wholly responsible for the debt if you don't pay it. Your Chapter 7 personal bankruptcy discharges only your personal liability for the debt, not the debt itself. Your cosigner will still be stuck with it.

Is Chapter 7 the Right Choice?

Chapter 7 personal bankruptcy can be a powerful solution to overwhelming business debts, but it isn't the right choice for everyone. As you now know, Chapter 7 personal bankruptcy may be the best option for business owners who:

- have personal liability—either alone or with a spouse—for many of their business debts
- are willing to shut down their business if the trustee requires it
- don't have much valuable, nonexempt property
- aren't concerned about leaving a partner or cosigner on the hook for debt
- have mostly debts of the type that are discharged in Chapter 7, and
- are willing to put up with a damaged credit rating, at least for a few years.

After reading this far, you should have a pretty good idea of whether Chapter 7 will work for you. Before making a final decision, however, you should evaluate other options for handling your business debt. Ch. 3 covers some alternative strategies and explains how they compare to Chapter 7 personal bankruptcy.

CHAPTER 3

Other Options for Handling Business Debt

Chapter 7 personal bankruptcy is a powerful tool—but it isn't the only strategy available for dealing with business debt. Depending on your situation, it might make more sense to try to settle your debts outside of bankruptcy, use another form of bankruptcy, or even just sit tight for a while and see what happens. This chapter explains how each of these alternatives compares to Chapter 7, so you can make sure that filing for Chapter 7 personal bankruptcy is the right way to go.

In some circumstances, you'll need to consider other options for handling business debt in addition to—rather than instead of—Chapter 7 personal bankruptcy. Chapter 7 personal bankruptcy takes care of your personal liability for business debts, but a separately structured business might have its own debt problems. For example, perhaps you've decided to file for Chapter 7 personal bankruptcy to wipe out your personal liability for certain corporate debts, but your corporation also needs to take care of its liability for its own debts. Options for handling corporate and LLC debt are covered briefly at the end of this chapter.

RESOURCE

Want detailed information on other strategies for handling debt? Pick up a copy of *Save Your Small Business: 10 Crucial Strategies to Rescue Your Business or Close Down and Move On*, by Ralph Warner, J.D, and Bethany Laurence, J.D. (Nolo). This valuable resource is filled with great ideas for dealing with a struggling business, whether you decide to keep operating or shut your doors. You'll also find more information on each of the options in this chapter.

If You Want to Close Your Business

As explained in Ch. 1 and Ch. 2, Chapter 7 personal bankruptcy can be a good choice if you've decided your business is not going to survive, or you aren't interested in spending the effort or capital necessary to save it. In this situation, you are probably looking at closing your business with a good-sized pile of debts—to landlords, suppliers, utilities, service providers, and possibly a bank or private lender.

You have several options for handling your personal liability for business debt in addition to filing for Chapter 7 personal bankruptcy:

- **Do nothing and see what happens.** Some creditors may conclude that trying to collect from someone with a pile of debt and few assets isn't worth the trouble.
- **Sell your business** and use the proceeds to pay off your business debts to the extent possible.
- **Close your business**, sell its assets, and pay off your business debts to the extent possible.

Do Nothing

One option that some business owners take, often as a result of sheer exhaustion rather than careful planning, is to just wait and see what happens. Some creditors, perhaps realizing that the debtor has nothing valuable to take, will give up their collection efforts after sending a threatening letter or two. On the other hand, some creditors will sue, get a judgment, and try to take your personal assets to satisfy your debt. If you have nothing worth taking now, these creditors may simply wait and hope you get a job or acquire some valuable property in the future, when they'll come back to collect.

If you really are "judgment proof" (that is, you don't have anything a creditor can take), you may not need to file for bankruptcy. To figure out if just doing nothing is a viable option, however, you should understand what your creditors can do, and what will happen to your property, if you go this route.

You can't be thrown in jail for not paying your debts (unless you refuse to pay child support that you are able to pay). And unless you owe back taxes or you've defaulted on a student loan, creditors can't just take money out of your bank account or intercept your tax refund. A creditor with a secured debt can generally take back the collateral if you default on the loan (although in some states, a lender has to go to court before foreclosing on a home mortgage). But most other creditors have to sue you and win a money judgment against you before they can actually go after your property and wages. And even after they get a judgment, creditors can't take property that's exempt. Let's look at how secured and unsecured creditors can collect their debts.

Secured Debts

Lenders with secured debts generally have the right to take back the property that secures the collateral if you default. Here are the rules for particular types of property.

Vehicle repossessions. If you default on a car loan secured by your car, the lender has the legal right to repossess it: to physically take the car and sell it to recover the money you owe, plus the costs of the sale and attorney's fees. The lender doesn't have to get permission or a court judgment. You will still owe the difference between what the lender can get for the car (typically only a fraction of what it's worth) and what you owed on the loan, called a "deficiency."

To collect a deficiency, the lender will have to sue you and obtain a money judgment. As with other unsecured debts, this debt can be wiped out in a Chapter 7 personal bankruptcy. Absent bankruptcy, the repossession will appear on your credit report for seven years.

Vehicle leases usually also give the dealer the right to take the car without a court order, but the dealer will have to take you to court for any damages owed as a result of your breach of the lease if it wants to collect them.

Other repossessions. Vehicles are the most commonly repossessed type of property, but the same procedures apply to other property. For example, if you borrowed money to buy business equipment or machinery and pledged the equipment as security for the loan, the creditor will have the same repossession rights discussed above. Also, some department store credit card contracts give the creditor a security interest in the property you buy; if you don't pay the bill, the creditor might try to repossess the property. However, because creditors must get a court order to enter your home or business, repossession of personal property other than vehicles is rare, except for business property that's valuable enough to justify the creditor's time and trouble.

Foreclosures. If you have a home equity line of credit or you refinanced your mortgage to take cash out for your business, you must make your payments on time to keep the house. If you don't, the lender can foreclose on the collateral for your debt: your house. But foreclosures are not as quick as vehicle repossessions. In about half of the states, a lender has to go to court for what's called a judicial foreclosure proceeding before foreclosing when you default on a mortgage. In the other states, the lender has to at least give you some advance notice before foreclosing. Either way, it can take several months to a year or more to lose your house, which gives you time to save some money and, if necessary, find a new place to live.

If you pledged your house as collateral for a business loan or line of credit and you default on that loan, the lender can also foreclose on your house. In this situation, however, the lender must always file a foreclosure action in court, no matter what state you live in. To avoid having the lender foreclose, you must either repay the debt or, if the debt exceeds your equity in the house, at least pay the lender the amount of your equity so that it no longer has a reason to foreclose.

RESOURCE

Foreclosure information. For up-to-date information about your options if you are facing foreclosure, see *The Foreclosure Survival Guide*, by attorney Stephen Elias (Nolo).

If You Are Underwater on Your Line of Credit or Second Mortgage

It's not uncommon for homes to be worth far less than the total of all the liens against them. Assume, for example, that Juliet's home is worth $200,000 but she owes $250,000 on a first mortgage. She has no equity in her house. In addition, to keep her freelance engineering business in operation, she took out $50,000 on a line of credit back when her home was worth $400,000. If Juliet defaults on her line of credit, the lender of the credit line has no foreclosure remedy; if the house were taken and sold, all the proceeds would go to the first mortgage holder. If defaulting on a line of credit or second mortgage would help you stay current on your first mortgage, the default would be a relatively safe strategy to stay in your house. Of course, the secondary lender will still have a lien on the home that it can enforce if you attempt to sell it or if the home appreciates in value. Also, the secondary lender could sue you for breach of contract, but that may be the least of your worries.

Right to offset. If you owe money to a bank on a loan or credit line, and you have other accounts at the same bank (such as a checking or saving account), the bank can take cash from your account to pay off the debt without getting a court order. This is called a "setoff" or an "offset." So, if you're about to default on a loan, it makes sense to move your other accounts to another institution first.

Unsecured Debts

As we've mentioned, most unsecured creditors—including credit card companies, doctors, lawyers, contractors, and suppliers—must sue you and win a money judgment before they can collect. To sue you, a creditor has to hire and pay a lawyer, pay court fees, and wait around for up to a year to win the lawsuit (unless you fail to respond, in which case the creditor can obtain a default judgment very quickly). In either case, the creditor then may have to wait a while if you don't have any assets to pay the judgment. Unless there's a lot of money at stake, and you have or anticipate getting significant cash or valuable assets the creditor could go after, the creditor might not bother to sue you at all.

Before seriously considering a lawsuit, a creditor usually tries to collect the debt for several months, and then turns it over to a collection agency or attorney, who will restart the process with a series of demand letters and phone calls. If you don't pay, the creditor may decide that it isn't worth the trouble to sue. Let's say, for example, that your consulting business has few assets and is doing poorly, your house is worth less than you owe on your mortgage, and your income now comes mostly from Social Security (which can't be taken to pay debts). A creditor, or any collection attorney or agency your debt is turned over to, might look at these circumstances, decide there's no point trying to collect from you, and write off your debt as a deductible business loss. Typically, in four to six years (depending on your state's statute of limitations), the debt will become legally uncollectible.

You can, however, expect to be sued if there is significant money at stake and you have valuable personal or business assets (or the creditor expects you to get some in the future). For instance, if your dress shop is failing but you have an MBA, your creditor might assume you'll eventually make a good salary. If so, chances are the creditor will sue you, get a judgment, and wait for you to start earning again. In many states, a court judgment can be collected for at least ten years.

How Creditors Can Collect on a Judgment

It can be even harder for a creditor to collect a judgment than to win it in the first place. Theoretically, if a creditor has gone to court and won a judgment to collect an unsecured debt, the creditor will be able to take your business assets, business income, and any cash in your business bank account to pay off the debt. The creditor can also get a court to order customers and clients to pay any money they owe to your business directly to the court (although this collection device is rarely used).

If you're a sole proprietor or partner, or you signed a personal guarantee for a debt, the judgment creditor can also garnish your wages (and in community property states, your spouse's wages) and take money from your personal bank account, as well as your nonexempt personal property, to pay off the debt.

Of course, all of this is possible only if you have nonexempt property or income to take, the creditor finds it, and the creditor then gets a court order and pays the sheriff, marshal, or constable to take it. Many creditors won't go to these lengths to get your property. Instead, if your business owns real estate, valuable equipment, or other tangible assets, the creditor will simply file a judgment lien against that property (or any valuable personal property or real estate that you own, if you are personally liable for the debt). The lien allows the creditor to collect when you or the business sells or refinances the property.

A creditor cannot take exempt property. As explained in Ch. 2, certain types of property are exempt and cannot be taken and sold in Chapter 7 personal bankruptcy. Depending on your state's exemption laws, the types of property you get to keep include your clothing, furniture, appliances, and other necessities; your retirement or pension plan; some equity in a car; and some equity in a home (you can find lists of each state's exemptions in Appendix A). For the most part, these exemptions apply whether or not you file for bankruptcy. In other words, just as the bankruptcy trustee can't take this property and sell it for the benefit of your creditors, your creditors can't take it directly, either.

Special Rules for Leases

Back rent is treated like any other unsecured debt, but if you don't pay your rent, you can be evicted in fairly short order. And a commercial eviction happens even faster than a residential eviction, often in just a few weeks.

If you have time remaining on a residential or commercial lease when you move out, your landlord can sue you for the remaining months' rent. However, in most states the landlord is obligated to try to find a new tenant to minimize the loss. This is called "mitigating the damages." If the landlord can rent the place for at least what you were paying, you are off the hook for the remaining rent. However, the landlord can charge you rent for the time the space was vacant, plus the costs of finding a new tenant. If the landlord is not able to find a replacement tenant with reasonable effort, you will be on the hook for the rent for the remainder of the lease. (This debt can be discharged in Chapter 7 personal bankruptcy.)

You may be able to negotiate a lease termination with your landlord in exchange for paying an extra month or two of rent. Your landlord will probably be happy to arrive at a negotiated solution rather than risk getting nothing if you file for bankruptcy.

If you have a month-to-month rental rather than a lease, you can simply give your landlord written notice that you're terminating your agreement. If you are current in your rent payments, you won't owe anything. You'll probably have to give 30 days' notice, but some commercial agreements require more. Check your lease or rental agreement.

TIP

Negotiate your way out of an equipment lease before you return the equipment. If you return equipment before your lease term ends, the same rule usually applies: You will be liable for the remainder of the payments in the lease term (or at least for an early return penalty). Try to negotiate a better deal while you've still got the equipment. For example, you might offer to return two forklifts to the leasing company along with two months' additional payments, in exchange for a complete release of further obligations. If lots of money is at stake and the leasing company won't cooperate, having a lawyer call, possibly with the suggestion that you may file for bankruptcy, can be a huge help. The leasing company will want its property back as soon as possible, without having to wait for months and deal with the bankruptcy court.

Doing Nothing Compared to Chapter 7

Ignoring your creditors and hoping they will ignore you in return might be tempting, but think hard before you go this route. If your debts are significant—and especially if you have valuable nonexempt property such as equity in real estate or the prospect of earning a decent wage—creditors are likely to sue you and try to collect their judgment. Doing nothing probably also means that you'll spend the next couple of years hounded by collection agencies, repossessors, lawyers, lawsuits, and wage garnishments.

If you file for Chapter 7 personal bankruptcy, you can wipe out many types of business debt. If you truly are "judgment proof," most of the property you own is probably exempt, which means you won't lose it if you file for bankruptcy. Plus, filing for bankruptcy allows you to resolve all of your outstanding debt issues *now*; you won't have to worry about collection actions in the future. If you later acquire valuable property or get a high-paying job, you won't have to feel anxious that you'll lose your assets to creditors.

In short, it almost always makes more sense to file for Chapter 7 personal bankruptcy than to take a "wait and see" approach. Only those who have few assets, little prospect of employment, and a high tolerance for uncertainty should even consider ignoring their debts.

Sell Your Business

Some debtors get out of business not by closing down, but by selling their business as a going concern.

Is Selling an Option?

In the best of times, it can be tough to sell a profitable small business. When times are tough and a business is losing money, it can be nearly impossible to arrange even a bargain-basement sale. But there are exceptions. A business with a great reputation, market position, or location might find a buyer even when profits have disappeared. Businesses that have been historically profitable usually retain at least some value, even when they stop making money.

Your competitors are the most likely buyers. They know that buying up your customers, and perhaps your equipment and employees, will allow them to corner the local market, gaining significant pricing power. Talk to a local business broker to see if you might be able to sell your business.

RESOURCE

Information on selling. *The Complete Guide to Selling Your Business*, by Fred Steingold (Nolo), is a helpful companion for those planning to sell. It will help you decide whether it makes more sense to approach likely purchasers yourself or hire a business broker to do it for you, and it takes you through a typical sales contract clause by clause, identifying the key issues you'll need to negotiate.

Selling Your Business Compared to Chapter 7 Bankruptcy

Most business owners won't have the option to sell their business, simply because they won't be able to find a buyer. If you're one of the lucky few who is able to sell, it can be a better option than filing for bankruptcy—as long as you are able to wipe out your personal liability for your business debts by paying off or settling all the business's debts with the sales proceeds.

CAUTION

Disclose all debts, liabilities, and problems with your business. If you are contemplating selling your business, be careful that you don't misrepresent its financial condition or cash flow. If the buyer is unable to turn a profit, he or she may turn around and sue you for fraud. If the buyer wins this type of lawsuit, you will have to return the sales proceeds and you probably won't be able to discharge that debt if you later file for bankruptcy. Because the outcome of fraud lawsuits is always uncertain, be absolutely clear about the business's financial problems—or file for Chapter 7 bankruptcy instead of selling.

Liquidate Your Business and Settle Your Debts

Rather than trying to sell their business as a going concern, some business owners close the business down, sell its assets, and then use the proceeds (perhaps along with some personal assets) to negotiate settlements with their creditors, often for a fraction of what they owe. By liquidating your business on your own rather than allowing the bankruptcy trustee to do it, you will likely get more money for your assets (and therefore, have more money to pay your creditors) than a bankruptcy trustee could get, and you won't have a bankruptcy on your credit report for the next ten years.

How Liquidation and Settlement Works

To liquidate your business, you shut down, sell the assets, then contact your creditors and try to settle your debts. When you negotiate with your creditors, you will be asking them to accept partial payment of the debt as payment in full—and to give you a full written release of your liability for the debt. Why would a creditor agree to this? Because it often makes more sense than suing you and trying to chase down your remaining assets while hoping you don't file for bankruptcy (which would probably leave your creditors with nothing).

How little will your creditors settle for? It depends on the type of creditor, the legal details of the debt, and the creditor's attitude. For example, if your business is an LLC or corporation and you haven't personally guaranteed its debts, a creditor will know that it can't collect from you personally, so it may be more willing to accept a small fraction of what your business owes as full settlement of the debt. But if you owe a debt personally and have valuable personal assets, or worse, a wealthy friend or relative cosigned for it, the creditor has much more leverage and will likely demand a larger portion of the amount owed. In our experience, if you can pay 30% to 70% cash on the barrelhead, you may be able to interest your creditors in a deal.

EXAMPLE: Quinn runs Read More Books LLC, which sells new books upstairs and used books downstairs. It has a loyal following, but when the economic downturn hits the book industry especially hard, Quinn can't earn enough to pay her expenses. When she decides to close the business, she owes three publishers a total of $80,000, owes $4,000 to her landlord on the month-to-month lease that she personally guaranteed, and has $1,000 in utility bills. She gives her landlord the required 30 days' notice. She returns as much book inventory as possible to the publishers, reducing the amount she owes them to $40,000, and notifies them in writing that she's going out of business. Of course, they call her immediately to press for payment on their invoices, but Quinn says she'll get back to them.

She then sells off her used book inventory as well as her bookshelves, cash registers, and computers (mostly to a competitor, the rest on craigslist), leaving her with $25,000 in cash. She pays her landlord the $4,000 past due—this is a high priority debt for her because she personally guaranteed the lease—and writes checks to the utility companies. She has $20,000 left. Quinn then writes to each of the publishers offering a final payment of 50 cents on the dollar ($20,000 to satisfy her debts of $40,000). She makes the offer contingent upon all of the publishers' signing a written release that releases Read More Books LLC, Quinn, and her spouse from any liability for the debts. The publishers know that Read More Books is an LLC, which means that Quinn can walk away from the business or the LLC can file a Chapter 7 business bankruptcy; either way Quinn won't be personally liable for these debts. They decide that half a loaf is better than none, so they take the deal.

TIP

Don't settle any debts if you can't settle them all. It won't help you much to settle a few small debts for a reasonable amount if you can't settle larger ones: You might end up having to file for bankruptcy to get rid of your remaining debts anyway. In this case, the money you paid to settle with your other creditors could be taken back ("recaptured") by the bankruptcy trustee as preference payments. Even if your other settlements aren't treated as preference payments, you might have been able to save that money by just filing for bankruptcy in the first place and having those debts discharged as well. To avoid these problems, don't pay any creditor before you settle with all of them. When you negotiate, tell your creditors that your offers are contingent upon all of your creditors agreeing to settle their debts with your business.

It can be difficult to haggle and come to terms with creditors, especially if you have a fairly complicated debt and asset situation. Many business owners wisely choose to get some help from a lawyer with debt and bankruptcy experience. Although this may cost a few thousand dollars, the lawyer's negotiating skills—and ability to convincingly threaten creditors that you'll file for bankruptcy if the negotiations fail—may save you more than the lawyer's fee in the form of frugal settlements. Creditors know that once you file for bankruptcy, they are unlikely to see any money for months (if there's anything left once costs are paid and other creditors line up for their share). And, if your creditors agree to settle, your lawyer can also help you prepare the necessary releases to be sure that, in exchange for your partial payment, you, your spouse, and any cosigners will be fully absolved from future liability.

CAUTION

Debt forgiveness can be taxed as income. If creditors agree to settle your debts for less than you owe, the IRS and state tax agencies may view the forgiven amount as taxable income to you. This could result in you having to report positive taxable income, rather than an operating loss, in the year you close. Owners of corporations won't be personally liable to pay these taxes, but other business owners should talk to a tax adviser to see whether this income can be applied to previous years' net operating losses or otherwise wiped out.

Liquidation and Settlement Compared to Chapter 7

Whether liquidating your business on your own is a better option than Chapter 7 depends entirely on whether you could raise enough cash from selling your business assets (and maybe some personal property as well) to settle all of the debts for which you are personally liable.

If you can wind down your business and resolve your debts on your own, that's often a better approach. It gives you the flexibility to decide how much to offer creditors and who to pay first, without worrying about preference payments. As explained in Ch. 2 and Ch. 5, the bankruptcy trustee can take back money you pay to certain creditors before your bankruptcy filing, in order to divide that money equally among all of your creditors. For instance, if you made payments on a loan to a relative or close business associate in the past year or two, a bankruptcy court could take back these payments and distribute them among all of your creditors. If you liquidate and settle your debts outside of bankruptcy, you determine who gets paid how much, and in what order. As long as you can convince your creditors to go along with it and sign a release, you won't have to worry about preference payments.

Settling your debts yourself, however, can be quite time-consuming and stressful—and, if you decide to save yourself some anxiety by hiring a lawyer, it can costs thousands of dollars in attorney fees as well.

In addition, you may not be able to convince all of your creditors to settle their debts, or you may not have sufficient assets to make it worth their while. In this situation, you're probably better off filing for bankruptcy in the first place and having all of your debt wiped out, rather than paying out money to some creditors that you could have saved by filing for bankruptcy or that the trustee could treat as a preference.

RESOURCE

Information on settling your debts. For help negotiating with your creditors, making settlement offers, and getting signed agreements that release you from liability, read *Save Your Small Business: 10 Crucial Strategies to Rescue Your Business or Close Down and Move On*, by Ralph Warner, J.D, and Bethany Laurence, J.D. (Nolo).

If You Want to Continue Your Business

Most readers of this book will be planning to shut down. Their businesses are in such poor shape, with so much debt, that the best strategy is close their doors, settle their debts or discharge them in bankruptcy, and move on to new opportunities. But some business owners will want to continue operations after getting some relief from their debts. This is most common when the owner believes the business could succeed once one or two missteps are corrected. For example, perhaps the underlying business could be profitable if not for debts resulting from an ill-timed expansion.

As explained in Ch. 1 and Ch. 2, most business owners who file for Chapter 7 personal bankruptcy will have to shut down: If your business sells or manufactures products and/or owns significant assets, you probably won't be able to continue the same business after Chapter 7 personal bankruptcy, unless the business can recover after being shut down while your bankruptcy is pending, perhaps three to six months.

If you can raise enough money after filing for bankruptcy, or you are willing to give the trustee some exempt property, you might be able to buy back some of your business assets from the bankruptcy trustee to start a new business. But the business you once ran will most likely be liquidated and long gone.

If you run a sole proprietor service business that has few assets and no essential location, and you aren't likely to incur new debt during bankruptcy, the trustee might let you to stay in business. A trustee might allow a small service business, such as a bookkeeping, graphic design, or massage therapy business, to continue during the owner's Chapter 7 personal bankruptcy if the business can be operated without using up or damaging assets that should be taken and sold to repay creditors. In that case, Chapter 7 bankruptcy may be a fine solution for you.

But if you own a larger business and want to keep operating without interruption (or having to try to buy back your business assets from the bankruptcy trustee), you'll have to file for another type of bankruptcy or try to negotiate and settle your debts through a "workout": a plan you reach with all of your creditors to settle your business's debts outside of court.

Other Types of Bankruptcy

Chapter 7 bankruptcy is sometimes called "liquidation" bankruptcy because the trustee has the right to take and sell (liquidate) the debtor's nonexempt property, in exchange for wiping out most debt. Chapter 7 provides a true clean slate: In just a few months, the debt is gone and the debtor has a fresh start.

In contrast, other types of bankruptcy—including Chapter 11, Chapter 12, and Chapter 13—are referred to as "reorganization" bankruptcies. These procedures allow a person or a business (or in the case of Chapter 12, a farm) to put creditors on hold while the bankruptcy filer comes up with a plan to repay debts over the next few years. In a reorganization bankruptcy, the debtor doesn't have to give up any property. Instead, the debtor uses income to repay debts. If the debtor makes all of the payments required by the repayment plan, most debts that remain after the plan ends are wiped out.

SEE AN EXPERT

If your debt comes primarily from the operation of a family farm, Chapter 12 might be the answer. Because it won't be available to most businesses, we don't cover Chapter 12 here. For more information on Chapter 12 bankruptcy, speak to a lawyer with experience in this area.

Chapter 13 Bankruptcy

Chapter 13 bankruptcy is the only type of reorganization bankruptcy that's appropriate for most small business owners. In Chapter 13, you use your income to fund a repayment plan that lasts from three to five years. If you make all of the payments required by the plan, most remaining debts are discharged when the plan ends.

Only individuals can file for Chapter 13. You can use Chapter 13 to rid yourself of business debts for which you have personal liability (for example, if you are a sole proprietor or you have taken on personal liability for some corporate or LLC debts), but a corporation, an LLC, or a partnership cannot file for Chapter 13 as an entity. Also, Chapter 13 bankruptcy is available only to those who have unsecured debt of up to $336,900 and secured debts of up to $1,010,650; those with higher debt totals can't use Chapter 13.

How Chapter 13 Works

In a Chapter 13 bankruptcy, you don't necessarily lose any property. Instead, you use a portion of your future income to pay some or all of what you owe your creditors over time. The length of your repayment plan will depend on your income. If your average monthly income in the six months before you file for bankruptcy is less than or equal to the median income for your state, your repayment plan need not last more than three years. But if your income is more than the state median, your plan must last long enough to repay all of your debt, or five years, whichever is shorter. (See "The Means Test," in Ch. 2, for information on calculating your income and comparing it to the state median.)

Your repayment plan must devote all of your anticipated disposable income to repaying your debts over the repayment plan period. In Chapter 13 bankruptcy, you must pay some debts in full (back taxes, child support, and short-term secured loans are the most common examples). For your other debts, the rule is that your unsecured creditors must receive at least as much as they would have gotten if you had filed for Chapter 7 bankruptcy. That is, you will have to pay out an amount equal to the value of your nonexempt property (the property that the trustee could have taken and sold in a Chapter 7 bankruptcy). If you have a lot of nonexempt assets, you'll have to pay more toward your debts during your Chapter 13 repayment plan, unless you voluntarily sell the assets and make the proceeds available to the trustee.

If you successfully complete the repayment plan, most categories of remaining debt are wiped out. The same categories of debt that are discharged in Chapter 7 are also discharged in Chapter 13. And, some debts that aren't dischargeable in Chapter 7 bankruptcy can be discharged in Chapter 13, including:

- cash advances for more than $825 taken within 70 days before filing for bankruptcy
- recent debts for luxuries
- loans owed to a pension plan or 401(k)
- marital debts (other than for spousal support) created in a divorce or settlement agreement

- debts taken out to pay a nondischargeable tax debt, and
- court fees.

Chapter 13 Bankruptcy Compared to Chapter 7

Unfortunately, Chapter 13 bankruptcy doesn't work for most small business owners. Overall, only about 35% of all Chapter 13 filers complete their repayment plans. And for entrepreneurs, it's even harder. If you decide to continue your business during your Chapter 13 plan, you'll be operating under the scrutiny of the bankruptcy trustee and devoting all of your money to paying off the business's debts—often an impossible task for an enterprise struggling to stay afloat.

It's difficult to run a business while in bankruptcy. All of your personal and business property is under the bankruptcy court's control. You must get court permission to borrow money or to buy or sell business assets (other than typical, day-to-day operating decisions). You can't use credit cards, and you have to submit monthly reports to the bankruptcy trustee. If business picks up or you take on a side job, the extra money will have to go toward your debts.

It might be even harder for a business owner to keep up with plan payments for three to five years. You need to make every plan payment on time, even if your income is seasonal or fluctuates with the economy. If you can't keep up with your payments, the bankruptcy judge can modify the plan to some extent. However, if it appears that you won't be able to make at least the payments required by the bankruptcy code, the judge will likely convert your case to a Chapter 7 bankruptcy or dismiss it. If your case is dismissed, you'll owe your creditors the balance of your debts: what you owed at the start of your bankruptcy case, plus the interest that stopped accruing while you were in bankruptcy, less whatever you paid through your repayment plan.

Chapter 13 typically costs more—and always takes longer—than Chapter 7. Although the filing fees are comparable (currently, $274 for Chapter 13 versus $299 for Chapter 7), you will almost certainly need a lawyer to file for Chapter 13, which can cost thousands of dollars. In addition, you'll usually be required to repay at least some of your unsecured debt (although some courts approve what are known as 0% plans, in which unsecured creditors receive nothing), something you wouldn't have to do in Chapter 7. What's more, a Chapter 7 bankruptcy case is over in a matter of months, compared to the three to five years you'll spend in Chapter 13.

For all of these reasons, Chapter 7 personal bankruptcy is almost always the better choice for business owners. Rather than trying to continue your debt-ridden existing business under the close supervision of the bankruptcy court, it usually makes more sense to close down, file a Chapter 7 personal bankruptcy to deal with your debts, and then start a new—but similar—business free of debt.

This isn't always the case, however. For some business owners, Chapter 13 might make more sense than Chapter 7:

- Those who can't pass the means test or are otherwise ineligible to use Chapter 7 will have to use Chapter 13 to get bankruptcy relief. (The means test is covered in Ch. 2 and Ch. 9.)
- Those who want to keep an asset-rich business open during bankruptcy shouldn't use Chapter 7, because the trustee will likely shut the business down and sell its assets. (However, these business owners might be best served by avoiding bankruptcy altogether and trying to settle their debts, as discussed below.)
- Debtors might choose Chapter 13 if they don't want to lose particular, perhaps unique, nonexempt assets that they would lose in a Chapter 7 bankruptcy. (This is a tricky area and you should probably go over the details with a lawyer).
- Debtors might want to use Chapter 13 if they have significant debts that wouldn't be discharged in Chapter 7, but would be discharged in Chapter 13.

- Those who will need the long-term protection of the bankruptcy court while they get current on their personal mortgage or car payments might choose Chapter 13 rather than Chapter 7.

Cramdowns

One additional advantage of a Chapter 13 over a Chapter 7 bankruptcy is that it lets you reduce what you owe if you are significantly upside down on certain secured debts—that is, you owe more than the collateral for the debt is worth. You can reduce what you owe on a secured debt down to the value of the collateral in what's called a "cramdown." Once you cram down your debt to the value of the property securing it, you usually get to keep the collateral.

For example, let's say you owe $20,000 on a car loan and the car is worth only $11,000. Assuming you took the loan out at least 30 months ago, the court will probably approve a provision in your repayment plan that calls for the loan to be modified so you owe only the value of the car ($11,000) at a very low interest rate, to be paid in full while your bankruptcy is pending. The additional amount that you would otherwise owe will be discharged at the end of your repayment plan along with your other unsecured debts.

Although the cramdown remedy is powerful, its usefulness is limited because you can use it only for certain types of secured debt. First and foremost, you can't cram down the mortgage on your primary residence. Although Congress has considered allowing cramdowns on residential mortgages, it hasn't yet been willing to make this amendment to the bankruptcy law. You also can't cram down debts for cars incurred within the previous 30 months (unless the vehicle was purchased for your business, in which case the 30-month restriction doesn't apply). And, you can't cram down debts for other property you bought within a year before filing.

RESOURCE

More on Chapter 13 bankruptcy. If you are interested in filing for Chapter 13 bankruptcy, see *Chapter 13 Bankruptcy: Keep Your Property & Repay Debts Over Time,* by Stephen Elias and Robin Leonard (Nolo).

Chapter 11 Bankruptcy

Chapter 11 bankruptcy has been in the news a lot lately. Plenty of businesses, from banks to car manufacturers, department stores, and airlines have been using Chapter 11 to try to reorganize their operations and get out from under their debts. However, because Chapter 11 is expensive—think $50,000 to $100,000 or more in legal fees—and extraordinarily complex, it's rarely appropriate for any but the largest small businesses.

How Chapter 11 Works

In Chapter 11, a company uses a set of procedural rules in the bankruptcy code to come up with a plan under which it will be able to continue its operations. Any business entering Chapter 11 must be represented by an attorney, who prepares a complicated set of disclosures and meets and negotiates with various creditor groups (secured, unsecured, equity holders, licensees, lessees, bond holders, and so on). All of the major creditor groups (which are organized into "committees") must agree to the Chapter 11 plan proposed by the debtor business through its attorney, or the judge can approve the plan in spite of any creditor objections if the plan generally meets the best interests of the creditors overall. Once the plan is approved, it governs the business's future relationships with its creditors, including any decisions the business might make that could adversely affect those relationships.

Many Chapter 11 bankruptcies fail—and attorney fees are often responsible. The business filing for bankruptcy is responsible for paying both its own attorney *and* the attorneys who represent the various creditor groups. Attorneys seldom charge less than a $10,000 retainer just to get things started, and the expenses for creditor attorneys can be astronomical; lengthy meetings and negotiations are necessary in a Chapter 11 bankruptcy, and the attorney fee meter is always ticking. As a result, a business that limps into Chapter 11 bankruptcy often feeds its meager remaining operating capital to attorneys, accountants, appraisers, and other professionals to come up with a plan the court will confirm. Unless the business can obtain a loan to finance its bankruptcy (called "debtor-in-possession" financing), once the business's money is gone, the case is typically converted to Chapter 7 business bankruptcy where the business is liquidated and the proceeds distributed under various bankruptcy priority rules.

Chapter 11 Compared to Chapter 7

Chapter 11 is rarely the right choice for a small business. You should consider it only if your business has enough income—and the ability to swing debtor-in-possession financing—to both stay in business and pay tens or even hundreds of thousands of dollars in legal fees to successfully emerge from the bankruptcy intact. If you are interested in Chapter 11 bankruptcy, speak to an attorney who is experienced in Chapter 11 filings. If you receive advice that a Chapter 11 is your best option, either for your business or for you personally, make sure you understand exactly where the money will come from to pay the various players—including the one trying to talk you into Chapter 11.

Workouts

A workout is sort of like a Chapter 13 repayment plan, without the bankruptcy court. In a workout, you negotiate with all of your business's creditors to settle the business's debts out of court.

How a Workout Works

In a workout, you make an offer to each of your creditors, asking them to take less than the full amount you owe to help you stay in business. But making a workout work isn't easy, primarily because you'll have to come up with some money for your creditors.

Because your business probably doesn't have the cash available to pay off your creditors in a lump sum, you would need to get a loan, attract new equity investment, or pay your creditors regular installments from your business's income. All of these options are fairly difficult for a struggling business to pull off. Finding a lender or an investor who's willing to invest money in a small company on the verge of bankruptcy may be next to impossible, unless you can find a sympathetic friend or family member with cash to spare.

If your business plans to pay your creditors from future cash flow, you have to find a way to turn the business around, stop losing money, and eventually become profitable. And, your plan will have to be convincing to creditors. They won't accept more of the same: They'll want to see that something big is going to change in a way that's likely to turn your fortunes around (for example, that you are picking up a major new customer or a new revenue stream from a new service). You'll have to show that you can earn enough to pay your current expenses and make your installment payments on your debt, too.

If you're interested in attempting a workout that goes beyond asking for an installment plan, you will no doubt need a business lawyer to help you negotiate; otherwise, your creditors probably won't take you seriously. A lawyer can explain the situation to your creditors and the consequences of not cooperating. A lawyer can also help you offer creditors more creative options. For instance, if you need to keep doing business with a particular creditor, you can offer a lien on your inventory, equipment, or accounts receivable. Even offering a small ownership stake in your corporation or LLC can work. A lawyer can explain these options and will probably offer more ideas as well.

Workout Compared to Chapter 7

If you file for Chapter 7 personal bankruptcy, you will likely have to close down your business, at least temporarily. So, if you are determined to stay in business and you can come up with the money, either up front or in installments, to bring your creditors on board, a workout may be your best option. However, a couple of cautions are in order if you're considering this route:

- **You won't have the protection of the bankruptcy court.** Remember that, if you file for either Chapter 7 or Chapter 13 bankruptcy, creditors won't be able to take your property or demand that you pay them back during your bankruptcy case. Because a workout is an out-of-court solution, your creditors can pull the plug on your settlement or repayment plan if you're late with a payment or you can't come up with your installment for the month. So be very certain that you can meet your obligations under the workout plan before you start.
- **Make sure you can afford it.** Before you agree to obligate yourself to pay back all of your business debt, take a long, hard look at your business's chances of success. Are you really going to earn enough to pay off all of your debt, pay your operating expenses, and make a living? Is keeping this business open worth obligating yourself to years of debt repayment? Keep in mind that if you file for bankruptcy, you could wipe out much of your debt rather than paying it back. And if you spend months or even years faithfully following your workout plan and then can't keep up the payments, you may end up in bankruptcy anyway—and all of the debt you repaid could have simply been erased instead.

Options for Dealing With Corporate and LLC Debt

Because corporations and LLCs are legal entities separate from their owners, they will owe the debts of the business after they close down unless those debts are paid, settled, or discharged in a business bankruptcy. Even if the owners of a corporation or an LLC file for personal bankruptcy to wipe out their personal liability (if any) for the business's debts, the corporation or LLC itself will still owe the debts that the business incurred. Corporations and LLCs have a few options here:

- **Allow the corporation or LLC to simply lapse.** Creditors to whom you have also obligated yourself personally will likely go after your personal assets. If you don't have much they can take, however, these creditors may conclude that it's more sensible to just write off their debts.
- **Assign the corporate or LLC assets to a liquidation company or law firm**, which will pay off your creditors (called an assignment for the benefit of creditors).
- **File for Chapter 7 *business* bankruptcy.**

Allow Your Corporation or LLC to Lapse

If you file for personal bankruptcy to wipe out your own liability for your corporation or LLC's debts—or you aren't personally liable for any of those debts in the first place—there's probably no reason to file a business bankruptcy case. Instead, you can use the business's remaining assets to pay off its debts to the extent possible, and then just dissolve your corporation or LLC. You do this by filing dissolution documents with your state's corporate or LLC office; that office will have the proper form, usually called a certificate of dissolution, certificate of cancellation, articles of dissolution, or something similar. By dissolving your entity, you ensure that you are no longer liable for paying annual fees, filing annual reports, and paying business taxes.

If a corporation or an LLC owes debts when it's dissolved, and it owns cash or assets, the owners (and the directors and officers) have a statutory duty to pay off the business's debts to the extent possible. Only after you have paid all creditor claims and repaid all loans can you legally distribute any remaining cash and assets to the owners. If your corporation or LLC distributes its assets to its owners without following the proper procedures to notify and pay back creditors, creditors can sue the business owners personally after the corporation or LLC dissolves. In addition, some states won't *allow* the corporation or LLC to dissolve until it has repaid its debts. The state corporate and LLC registration lists are full of business that have been suspended: They have debts that can't be paid, which prevents them from being dissolved.

You could simply sell the remaining assets of the business, use the proceeds to pay business creditors on a pro rata basis, and then officially dissolve the entity. But it's a better idea to insist on signed releases from all creditors, releasing the business and its owners from liability for the debt. As explained in "Liquidate Your Business and Settle Your Debts," above, creditors are often willing to sign releases so they can recover at least part of what you owe them, especially if the request comes from a lawyer. Assigning your assets to a law firm or liquidation company can also avoid personal lawsuits, as can putting the corporation or LLC through a business bankruptcy, both of which are discussed below.

CAUTION

Don't cheat your creditors. The directors and officers of an insolvent corporation or LLC (one whose assets are worth less than its liabilities) have a legal duty to minimize losses to the company's creditors. This obligation includes the duty to try to get fair market value for business assets. You commit fraud if you give away or sell business assets at below market rates, or put your interests ahead of those of creditors. In other words, forget about selling assets cheaply and pocketing the cash or giving assets to friends or family.

RESOURCE

Information on dissolving your corporation or LLC. For help in giving proper notice (which will reduce the chance of personal liability for the corporation or LLC's debt), winding down a corporation or LLC, and filing dissolution papers, read *Save Your Small Business: 10 Crucial Strategies to Rescue Your Business or Close Down and Move On*, by Ralph Warner, J.D, and Bethany Laurence, J.D. (Nolo). It has a comprehensive chapter on how to avoid personal liability while closing down a business.

Assignment for Benefit of Creditors

You (and your co-owners, if you have them) may feel you don't have the knowledge or time necessary to liquidate the corporation or LLC's assets and pay off the business's debts. If your corporation or LLC has a significant amount of debt, it can take many months to wind things down—and you may need to spend your time earning some money. For many business owners, it makes more sense to hire someone else for the job.

You could hire a local lawyer to negotiate for you. Or, you could make an "assignment for the benefit of creditors" (ABC). In this process, you hire one of the many ABC companies or law firms that specialize in liquidating insolvent businesses. The company or law firm (called the assignee) sells the company's assets and pays off its creditors while you and your co-owners move on with your lives. The assignee collects a percentage of the funds it is able to distribute to your creditors after selling your assets, much like a bankruptcy trustee. ABC companies or firms are regulated by state law, so the details vary depending on the location of your business.

Here's how it works in general terms: In an ABC, your business assigns (transfers) all of its assets and debts to the assignee. The assignee then owns the business assets and is liable for its debts, just as your business was. The assignment makes it easier for the ABC firm to sell assets and negotiate with creditors, because the firm doesn't have to consult with you every time it wants to do something. Instead, the firm can sell the assets and settle the debts as it sees fit, motivated to get top dollar by its commission payment structure.

EXAMPLE: Emile's French Laundry, Inc., has been suffering from poor sales for the past year as restaurants have cut back on their linen requirements. French Laundry's accounts payable list is growing, creditors are demanding payment, and the company will be out of cash within a few months. Emile decides to close down and wants help paying off the many debts French Laundry owes.

Emile consults with a few ABC firms and finds one with experience liquidating companies that have made big investments in commercial equipment. Because this ABC firm may be more likely to get top dollar for French Laundry's equipment, Emile signs a contract with the firm (now called the assignee) and provides a list of the company's creditors and business assets.

First, the assignee investigates whether Emile's company can be sold as a going concern. If not, it will send a letter to all creditors, telling them that the assignment has been made and providing a form each creditor can use to submit a claim to the assignee. At the same time, the assignee advertises the assets for sale in industry publications and, using its contacts, searches for another company that might be willing to pay a fee to take over Emile's lease. It also publishes a press release stating that it has acquired the assets of French Laundry, Inc. After all of the assets have been liquidated, the assignee takes a percentage of the proceeds as its fee, and then distributes the rest to the creditors, based on their claims. In six months, it's all done—and Emile has been free to spend that time on other pursuits.

This option may work better than doing it yourself or working with a local lawyer, but only if your business has a lot of debts *and* assets. An assignee can often get more for your assets than you could on your own (and certainly more than a bankruptcy trustee could get). An assignee can also often monetize hard-to-sell assets such as the intellectual property your business owns—your business name, customer lists, and trademarked product names or patents—which a bankruptcy trustee usually won't even try to do. If you haven't also filed for Chapter 7 personal bankruptcy, you will still be personally liable for debts you have personally guaranteed, so you will want to make sure the assignee understands the importance of settling these debts and getting rid of your personal liability to repay them.

Assigning your debts to an assignee is quicker than liquidating your business yourself, and it can also be faster than a business bankruptcy. To learn more about ABCs, speak to a local business lawyer or search online.

Chapter 7 Business Bankruptcy

Like hiring a lawyer to help you negotiate debt settlements or making an assignment for the benefit of creditors, filing for business bankruptcy means someone else steps in to liquidate your business's assets and settle its debts (in this case, the bankruptcy trustee).

TIP

One-owner LLCs or corporations may not need business bankruptcy. If you are the sole owner of a corporation or LLC, filing for Chapter 7 personal bankruptcy may be the solution to both your and your business's debt problems. In this case, the bankruptcy trustee might decide to take over your corporation or LLC and liquidate and dissolve the business for you. Your Chapter 7 personal bankruptcy would free you of any personal liability for the business's debts.

A corporation or an LLC files a Chapter 7 *business* bankruptcy, a different animal than a Chapter 7 personal bankruptcy. Filing a business bankruptcy lets the owners turn their business over to the trustee for an orderly liquidation. The business stops operating, and the court liquidates its assets and pays what it can to business creditors.

Exemptions don't apply in a business bankruptcy, so the trustee can take anything the business owns: The entire company is liquidated.

When the liquidation is complete and the proceeds have been paid out to creditors, the business won't owe any remaining debts. Lease obligations, contracts, utility bills, credit cards, loans, overdue accounts, and all other business debts will have been paid to the extent possible by the bankruptcy trustee. If creditors aren't fully paid, that's their tough luck. The business owners are off the hook unless they are personally liable for the debts.

In theory, the business owners receive anything left over after the creditors are paid. Typically, however, a business that files for Chapter 7 business bankruptcy has liabilities that exceed its assets, and there is nothing left for the owners.

CAUTION

Business bankruptcy does not erase personal liability. If you are personally liable for corporate or LLC debts, you'll still be on the hook even after your business's liability is discharged in business bankruptcy. You will need to discharge your personal liability for the debts by filing for Chapter 7 personal bankruptcy or by negotiating a settlement with the creditor(s). Otherwise, the creditor(s) can still come after you for full repayment of the debt, even after the business is closed and its liability for the debts is discharged in business bankruptcy.

The court fees in a Chapter 7 business bankruptcy are the same as for Chapter 7 personal bankruptcy. The trustee is likely to get a bigger fee, because the trustee is paid on commission: The more of your business property and assets the trustee can liquidate and distribute to your creditors, the more the trustee is paid. This money comes out of what the creditors would otherwise get, however; you don't have to pay it directly.

The real added expense in a business bankruptcy is attorney fees. You must hire a lawyer to file for business bankruptcy; you can't do it yourself.

In a business bankruptcy, the trustee will undoubtedly sell your assets for less than you (or an ABC firm) could get for them, and the process won't be private. In contrast, if you sell your business's assets and settle the business's debts yourself (or with the help of a lawyer or ABC firm), there may be little reason to file for business bankruptcy. As long as you aren't personally liable for any remaining debts—or you file a personal Chapter 7 bankruptcy to wipe out that liability—you are off the legal hook, your business is closed, and the debts can't be collected.

CAUTION

Business bankruptcy is not suitable for partnerships. Partnerships rarely file for Chapter 7 business bankruptcy because it doesn't rid the partners of their personal liability for the business's debts. In fact, it actually makes it easier for creditors to reach the partners' personal assets, because the trustee in a Chapter 7 bankruptcy case may sue the partners personally to recover some cash to pay the partnership's debts. Speak to a business lawyer if you're interested in filing a business bankruptcy for your partnership.

Part 2:

Filing for Chapter 7 Personal Bankruptcy

CHAPTER

4

The Automatic Stay

One of the most powerful features of bankruptcy is the automatic stay: a court order that protects you from collection actions by your creditors. The automatic stay goes into effect as soon as you file for bankruptcy. It stops most debt collectors dead in their tracks and keeps them at bay for the rest of your case. Once you file for bankruptcy, all collection activity (with a few exceptions, explained below) must go through the bankruptcy court. Most creditors cannot take any action against you directly while your case is pending.

The purpose of the automatic stay is, in the words of Congress, to give debtors a "breathing spell" from their creditors, and a break from the financial pressures that drove them to file for bankruptcy. In a Chapter 7 bankruptcy, it serves another purpose as well: to preserve the status quo at the time you file. The automatic stay ensures that the bankruptcy trustee—not your creditors—will be responsible for ultimately deciding which property you will be able to keep, which property you will have to give up, and how the proceeds will be divided among your creditors if the trustee takes and sells any of your belongings.

This chapter explains how the automatic stay applies to typical debt collection efforts, including a couple of situations in which you might not get the protection of the automatic stay. It also covers how the automatic stay works in eviction proceedings, vital information for any renter who files for bankruptcy.

TIP

You don't need bankruptcy to stop your creditors from harassing you. Many people begin thinking about bankruptcy when their creditors start phoning them at home and at work. Federal law (and the law of many states) prohibits consumer debt collectors from contacting you once you tell the creditor, in writing, that you don't want to be called. If you tell a consumer debt collector orally that you refuse to pay, the collector is legally barred from contacting you again except to send a final letter demanding payment before filing a lawsuit. While just telling the creditor to stop contacting you usually works, you may have to send a follow-up letter. Unfortunately, there are no federal protections from collectors of business debts, but the automatic stay will put a stop to the collection of business debts.

Who the Stay Protects

When you file for Chapter 7 personal bankruptcy, the automatic stay applies only to you personally. If your business is a separate entity, such as a corporation or limited liability company, the stay will not prevent your business creditors from trying to collect debts your business owes them. If you are personally liable for the debts, the automatic stay will protect you personally. But collection activities may still proceed against the business if it is also liable for the debts.

EXAMPLE: Harry has operated Sweet Treats Plus, Inc., a bakery, for two years. He is the sole owner, shareholder, and officer of the corporation. When business takes a nose dive, he is unable to pay the main supplier of his ingredients (such as assorted flours, butter, yeast, and nuts). The supplier extends Harry some short-term credit, but requires him to personally cosign for the order.

When Harry finally files for Chapter 7 personal bankruptcy, he (and his business) owe the supplier $10,000. One reason Harry decided to file for bankruptcy was that the supplier not only stopped delivering ingredients, but also turned the bill over to an aggressive collector, who calls Harry several times a day demanding payment. These calls will be prohibited by the automatic stay, but only to Harry personally as cosigner for the credit. The automatic stay doesn't protect Harry's corporation, so he should expect more calls—this time to him in his capacity as owner of the corporation—to collect the corporation's debt. Only if the corporation files its own bankruptcy action or settles the debt will all of the calls finally stop.

If your business is a sole proprietorship, you and your business are considered a single debtor. If you file for Chapter 7 personal bankruptcy, the automatic stay will apply to both your personal and your business creditors, and the stay should stop all collection efforts against you, at least temporarily.

Actions Prohibited by the Automatic Stay

The automatic stay goes into effect as soon as you file for bankruptcy. It's "automatic" because you don't have to ask the court to issue the stay, and the court doesn't have to take any special action to make it effective. Once you file, the stay is in place, automatically. The stay prohibits creditors and collection agencies from taking any action to collect most kinds of debts you owe them, unless the law or the bankruptcy court says they can.

In some circumstances, the creditor can file an action in court (called a motion) asking the judge to lift the stay and allow the creditor to proceed with its collection efforts. In others, the creditor can simply begin collection proceedings without advance permission from the court.

The good news is that the most common type of creditor collection actions are stopped by the stay, including harassing calls from debt collectors, threatening letters from attorneys, and lawsuits to collect payment for credit card bills. This section explains which collection actions are stopped by the automatic stay.

Credit Card Debts, Medical Debts, and Attorney Fees

Anyone trying to collect credit card debts, medical debts, attorney fees, debts arising from breach of contract, or legal judgments against you (other than for child support and alimony) must stop all collection activities after you file your bankruptcy case. They cannot:

- call you or send letters to you
- file a lawsuit or proceed with a pending lawsuit against you
- record liens against your property
- report the debt to a credit reporting bureau, or
- seize your property or income (such as money in a bank account or your paycheck) to repay the debt.

EXAMPLE: For years, Michelle and Brad ran a business making and selling wooden handcrafted canoes, but in 2009 their sales plummeted. They close up shop owing various suppliers $35,000. They file for Chapter 7 personal bankruptcy. Under the automatic stay, suppliers can't call them, send them letters, sue them, report their bad debt to a credit bureau, or seize any remaining supplies or inventory.

Public Benefits

If you were overpaid public benefits such as SSI, Medicaid, or Temporary Assistance to Needy Families (welfare) benefits, the government agency cannot reduce or terminate your benefit payments to get that money back while your bankruptcy is pending. If, however, you become ineligible for benefits, including Medicare, the agency may deny or terminate your benefits because of your ineligibility, even if you are in the midst of a bankruptcy proceeding. In other words, bankruptcy doesn't allow you to keep collecting benefits to which you are no longer entitled.

Debt Associated With Criminal Proceedings

If a criminal case against you can be broken down into criminal and debt components, only the criminal component will be allowed to continue. The debt component will be put on hold while your bankruptcy is pending. For example, if you were convicted of writing a bad check and have been sentenced to community service and ordered to pay a fine, your obligation to pay the fine will be stopped by the automatic stay, but you will still have to perform your community service.

IRS Liens and Levies

Certain tax proceedings are not affected by the automatic stay (see "When the Automatic Stay Doesn't Apply," below, for more information). The automatic stay does, however, stop the IRS from issuing a lien or seizing (levying against) your property or income.

Foreclosures

Foreclosure is the procedure a mortgage holder must use to regain title to the property securing the mortgage. It is the main (and sometimes only) remedy available to a mortgage holder when a homeowner defaults.

Foreclosure procedures differ from state to state. In about half the states, foreclosures are carried out in court just like any other civil proceeding; these are called "judicial" foreclosures. In other states, the mortgage holder doesn't have to go to court, but must follow complex state rules regarding notices, reinstatement periods, and redemption periods. These are called "nonjudicial" foreclosures.

When you file for bankruptcy, the automatic stay stops all foreclosure proceedings. They can't resume until you receive your final discharge or the bankruptcy judge lifts the stay, upon request by the mortgage holder.

Filing for bankruptcy doesn't stop the clock on foreclosure notice requirements, however. For instance, in California, a foreclosing bank or mortgage company must provide the homeowner with a notice of default at least 90 days before setting a date for the actual foreclosure sale. If the mortgage holder issued a notice of default before you filed for bankruptcy, the 90-day notice period would continue to run right through the bankruptcy proceedings. However, if the mortgage holder did not issue a notice of default before you filed for bankruptcy, the mortgage holder is prevented from issuing the notice of default until the bankruptcy is over. In other words, filing for bankruptcy before the 90-day notice would substantially delay the foreclosure process, but filing after the 90-day notice would have little or no effect on the foreclosure. (See *The Foreclosure Survival Guide,* by Stephen Elias (Nolo), for a more detailed look at how bankruptcy can work to delay or prevent foreclosure.)

CAUTION

You can't delay a foreclosure by filing serial bankruptcies. Although foreclosure activities are stayed initially by your bankruptcy filing, the automatic stay won't apply if you filed another bankruptcy case within the past two years and the court, in that proceeding, lifted the stay and allowed the lender to proceed with the foreclosure.

If a court has ordered you to leave your home following foreclosure and the sheriff is trying to evict you, filing for bankruptcy will legally postpone the eviction until you receive a bankruptcy discharge or until the judge lifts the automatic stay, whichever happens first. Although changes to the bankruptcy law in 2005 make it somewhat easier for property owners to evict tenants who have filed for bankruptcy (see "Residential Evictions," below), these rules don't apply in actions to evict property owners rather than tenants.

Utilities

Companies providing you with utilities (such as gas, heating oil, electricity, telephone service, and water) may not cut off your services because you file for bankruptcy. However, they can stop providing services 20 days after you file for bankruptcy if you don't provide them with a deposit or other means to assure future payment. They can also terminate services if you fail to pay for them after you file. (See *In re Jones*, No. 06-10105-RS (D. Mass. 2006).)

If your utilities were shut off, either at your house or at your place of business (if it's a sole proprietorship), before you filed for bankruptcy, you are entitled to have them turned back on immediately after you file for bankruptcy.

One court has found that cable television isn't a utility, and service can therefore be stopped if you fail to pay the bill before filing for bankruptcy. (*In re Darby*, 470 F.3d 573 (5th Cir. 2006).)

When the Automatic Stay Doesn't Apply

The stay doesn't put a stop to every type of collection action, nor does it apply in every situation. Congress has determined that certain debts or proceedings are sufficiently important to "trump" the automatic stay. In these situations (described in "Actions Not Stopped by the Automatic Stay," below), collection actions can continue just as if you had never filed for bankruptcy.

In addition to the specific types of collection actions that can continue despite the stay, there are circumstances in which you can lose the protection of the automatic stay through your own actions. These are described below as well.

Actions Not Stopped by the Automatic Stay

The automatic stay does not prohibit the following types of actions from proceeding.

Divorce and Child Support

Almost all proceedings related to divorce or parenting continue unaffected by the automatic stay. These include actions to:

- set and collect current child support and alimony
- modify child support and alimony
- report overdue child support to credit bureaus
- collect back child support and alimony from property that is not in the bankruptcy estate (Ch. 5 explains what property is part of the bankruptcy estate, such as income you earn after filing for bankruptcy)
- withhold income to collect child support
- intercept tax refunds to pay back child support
- withhold, suspend, or restrict drivers' and professional licenses as leverage to collect child support
- determine child custody and visitation
- establish paternity in a lawsuit, and
- protect a spouse or child from domestic violence.

Tax Proceedings

The IRS can continue certain actions against someone who files bankruptcy. These actions include:

- conducting a tax audit
- issuing a tax deficiency notice (including for unpaid payroll taxes)
- demanding a tax return
- issuing a tax assessment, or
- demanding payment of an assessment.

Pension Loans

The automatic stay doesn't prevent withholding from a debtor's income to repay a loan from an ERISA-qualified pension (this includes most job-related pensions and individual retirement plans). See Ch. 5 for more on how pensions are treated in bankruptcy.

How You Can Lose the Protection of the Automatic Stay

Even if the stay would otherwise apply, you can lose its protection through your own actions. The stay may not protect you from collection efforts if:

- you had a bankruptcy case pending within the year before you filed your current case, and the court refuses your request to allow the stay to kick in, or
- you don't meet the deadlines set out in the bankruptcy code for dealing with property that serves as collateral for a secured debt.

Let's look at these exceptions in a bit more detail.

Prior Bankruptcy Case Pending in the Past Year

Under the 2005 amendments to the bankruptcy law, the automatic stay will last only 30 days if a prior case you filed was pending but dismissed within the year before you file, unless you can get the court to extend the stay. And if you have had more than one case pending in the last year, the automatic stay will never kick in at all, unless the court orders otherwise.

If the automatic stay terminates because of one or more prior pending cases, the property of the bankruptcy estate—in your current bankruptcy filing—is still protected. (As explained in more detail in Ch. 5, your bankruptcy estate includes most types of property that you own or are entitled to receive when you file your bankruptcy papers, but does not include money earned or most property received after filing.) For example, a creditor would not be entitled to seize money that was in your bank account on the date you filed, but it could levy on income you earned after filing, which is not part of the bankruptcy estate.

Bankruptcy Case Dismissed in the Past Year

With a couple of exceptions, if you had a bankruptcy case pending and dismissed during the previous year for any reason, voluntarily or involuntarily, the court will presume that your new filing is in bad faith, and the automatic stay will terminate after 30 days in your new case. You, the trustee, the U.S. Trustee, or the creditor can file a motion asking the court to continue the stay

When Is a Case Pending?

For this exception to the automatic stay to kick in, the previous pending case must have been dismissed. If the case was fully administered and a discharge was granted, then the exception does not apply. For instance, if you file a Chapter 7 bankruptcy case and receive a discharge, you can file a Chapter 13 case within the next year and get the full benefit of the stay (even though you can't receive a discharge in the Chapter 13 case). See *In re Chaudhry*, 411 B.R. 282 (Bkrtcy E.D. Va., 2009).

If you've had a bankruptcy case dismissed within the last couple of years, you may be wondering exactly when that case is no longer "pending" and, therefore, when the one-year time period for losing the automatic stay begin to run. This can be tough to figure out, partly because some cases remain open long after they are dismissed. But the general rule is that a dismissed case is no longer pending, even if it continues to be open after that date. In other words, the one-year period starts on the date a case is dismissed.

EXAMPLE: Clayton's Chapter 7 bankruptcy case is dismissed by the court on January 20, 2010, because Clayton missed a deadline for filing required documents. Before the case is closed, Clayton files a motion to set aside the dismissal and be allowed to proceed with his case; the court denies his motion. The case is ultimately closed on March 20, 2010. Clayton files for bankruptcy again on January 21, 2011. Because at least one year has passed since Clayton's previous case was dismissed, he is entitled to the full protection of the automatic stay.

beyond the 30-day period, but the court will grant the motion only if you (or whoever else makes the request) can show that your current case was not filed in bad faith.

The motion to continue the stay must be scheduled for hearing within 30 days after you file for bankruptcy and must give creditors adequate notice of why the stay should be extended. This means the motion must:

- be filed within several days after you file for bankruptcy (unless you obtain an "Order Shortening Time" from the judge, a simple procedure)
- be served on all creditors to whom you want the stay to apply, and
- provide specific reasons why your current filing is not in bad faith and the stay should be extended.

When deciding whether to extend the automatic stay beyond 30 days, the court will look at a number of factors to decide whether your current filing is in good faith. Here are some of the factors that will work against you:

- More than one prior bankruptcy case was filed by (or against) you in the past year.
- Your prior case was dismissed because you failed to file required documents on time (for instance, you didn't file your credit counseling certificate within 15 days or didn't amend the petition on a timely basis when required to do so). If your failure was inadvertent or due to a careless error, that won't help you with the judge unless you used an attorney in the prior case. Judges are more willing to give debtors the benefit of the doubt if an attorney was responsible for the mistake.
- The prior case was dismissed while a creditor's request for relief from the automatic stay was pending.
- Your circumstances haven't changed since your previous case was dismissed.

More Than One Bankruptcy Case Dismissed in the Past Year

If you had two or more cases pending and dismissed during the previous year, no automatic stay will apply in your current case. You won't even get the initial 30-day stay that would apply if you had only one bankruptcy case pending within the past year. The only way to get the benefit of the automatic stay in this case is to convince the court, within 30 days of your filing, that your current case was not filed in bad faith and that a stay should therefore be granted. The court will look at the factors outlined above to decide whether you have overcome the presumption of bad faith.

Missing Deadlines for Handling Secured Debts

If you have property that secures a debt—that is, property that the creditor has a right to take if you don't pay the debt—you will have to file a form called a "Statement of Intention" with the court and serve it on your creditors. The Statement of Intention explains what you want to do with the collateral. If you don't meet the deadlines for handling your secured debts, the automatic stay will no longer apply to that property (although it will continue to protect you otherwise).

For example, assume you want to keep your car and continue making payments on your car note, but you don't serve your Statement of Intention on time. The automatic stay will no longer protect your car or prevent the creditor from repossessing it, but your other property will still be protected. Secured debts and the Statement of Intention are covered in detail in Ch. 8 and Ch. 9.

Rules for Commercial Leases

In 2005, Congress made significant changes regarding the application of the automatic stay to residential tenants. These are discussed in "Residential Evictions," below. Importantly, however, none of those changes apply to commercial tenancies. If you file for bankruptcy while your commercial lease is in effect, you are entitled to remain for the duration of your bankruptcy case unless the court lifts the automatic stay and permits an eviction or the bankruptcy trustee decides to assume the lease (see Ch. 9 for more on how leases and contracts are treated in bankruptcy). But the stay won't protect you from eviction proceedings if your lease expired by its own terms before or as a result of your bankruptcy filing.

Residential Evictions

In the past, many renters filed for Chapter 7 bankruptcy to stop the sheriff from enforcing a judgment for possession (an eviction order). While landlords could come into court and ask the judge to lift the automatic stay so the eviction could proceed, many landlords didn't know they had this right—and many others didn't have the wherewithal to hire attorneys (or the confidence to handle their own cases). In other words, filing for Chapter 7 bankruptcy often stopped eviction proceedings for the duration of the bankruptcy.

Today, things are a bit different. The 2005 bankruptcy law gives landlords the right to evict a residential tenant, despite the automatic stay, if:

- the landlord got a judgment for possession —that is, took the tenant to court for eviction and won—before the tenant filed for bankruptcy (however, if the judgment was for failing to pay rent, there is a possible exception to this rule, discussed below), or
- the landlord is evicting the tenant for endangering the property or illegal use of controlled substances on the property (more on this below).

If the landlord does not already have a judgment for possession when you file for bankruptcy, and he or she wants to evict you for reasons other than endangering the property or using controlled substances (for example, the eviction is based on your failure to pay rent or violation of another lease provision), the automatic stay will prevent the landlord from beginning or continuing with eviction proceedings. However, the landlord can always ask the judge to lift the automatic stay.

CAUTION

Landlords can always ask the court to lift the automatic stay. Although the automatic stay will kick in unless one of the above exceptions applies, the judge can lift the stay upon the landlord's request. And many courts are willing to do so, because most evictions will have no effect on the bankruptcy estate—that is, your tenancy isn't something that the trustee can turn into money to pay your creditors. As a general rule, bankruptcy courts are inclined to let landlords exercise their property rights regardless of the tenant's debt problems.

If the Landlord Already Has a Judgment

If your landlord has already obtained a judgment of possession against you when you file for bankruptcy, the automatic stay probably won't help you. The landlord may proceed with the eviction just as if you had never filed for bankruptcy. But if the eviction order is based on your failure to pay rent, you may be able to get the automatic stay reinstated. This exception applies only if your state's law allows you to stay in your rental unit and "cure" (pay back) the rent delinquency after the landlord has a judgment for possession. Here's what you'll have to do to take advantage of this exception:

Step 1: As part of your bankruptcy petition, you must file a certification (a statement under oath) stating that your state's laws allow you to cure the rent delinquency after the judgment is obtained and to continue living in your rental unit. Very few states allow this. To find out whether yours is one of them, ask the sheriff, someone at your local legal aid office (if you have legal aid in your area), or a tenants' rights group. In addition, when you file your bankruptcy petition, you must deposit with the court clerk the amount of rent that will become due during the 30-day period after you file.

Once you have filed your petition containing the certification and deposited the rent, you are protected from eviction for 30 days unless the landlord successfully objects to your initial certification before the 30-day period ends. If the landlord objects to your certification, the court must hold a hearing on the objection within ten days, so theoretically you could have less than 30 days of protection if the landlord files and serves the objection immediately.

Step 2: To keep the stay in effect longer, you must, before the 30-day period runs out, file and serve a second certification showing that you have fully cured the default in the manner provided by your state's law. However, if the landlord successfully objects to this second certification, the stay will no longer be in effect and the landlord may proceed with the eviction. As in Step 1, the court must hold a hearing within ten days if the landlord objects.

SEE AN EXPERT

If you really want to keep your rental, talk to a lawyer. As you can see, these rules are somewhat complicated. If you don't interpret your state's law properly, file the necessary paperwork on time, and successfully argue your side if the landlord objects, you could find yourself put out of your home. A good lawyer can tell you whether it's worth fighting an eviction—and, if so, how to go about it.

Endangering the Property or Illegal Use of Controlled Substances

Under the 2005 bankruptcy law, an eviction action will not be stayed by your bankruptcy filing if your landlord wants you out because you endangered the property or engaged in the "illegal use of controlled substances" on the property. And your landlord doesn't have to have a judgment for possession in hand when you file for bankruptcy: The landlord may start an eviction action against you or continue with a pending eviction action even after your filing date if the eviction is based on property endangerment or drug use.

To evict you on these grounds after you have filed for bankruptcy, your landlord must file and serve on you a certification showing that:

- the landlord has filed an eviction action against you based on property endangerment or illegal drug use on the property, or
- you have endangered the property or engaged in illegal drug use on the property during the 30-day period prior to the landlord's certification.

If your landlord files this certification, he or she can proceed with the eviction 15 days later unless, within that time, you file and serve on the landlord an objection to the truth of the statements in the landlord's certification. If you do that, the court must hold a hearing on your objection within ten days. If you prove that the statements in the certification aren't true or have been remedied, you will be protected from the eviction while your bankruptcy is pending. If the court denies your objection, the eviction may proceed immediately.

As a practical matter, you will have a very difficult time proving that you weren't endangering the property or using drugs. Similarly, once allegations of property endangerment or drug use are made, it's hard to see how they would be "remedied." In short, this is another area where you'll need a lawyer if you have to fight it out.

RESOURCE

Need help with your residential landlord? For more information on dealing with landlords—including landlords that are trying to evict you—see *Every Tenant's Legal Guide*, by Janet Portman and Marcia Stewart (Nolo).

CHAPTER

5

Your Bankruptcy Estate

When you file for Chapter 7 personal bankruptcy, most of the property you own—and even some property that you used to own or that you haven't received yet—is subject to the jurisdiction of the bankruptcy court. This property, referred to as your "bankruptcy estate," is under the bankruptcy trustee's authority.

The trustee will be very interested in the contents of your bankruptcy estate. The trustee earns a commission on property that can be taken from your estate and sold to come up with some money to distribute to your creditors. However, the trustee will take property only if it could be sold for a profit. You won't lose property in which you have no equity, property that is protected by an exemption (see Ch. 6), or property that won't fetch enough to cover the costs of sale. Many Chapter 7 filers are pleased to discover that they can keep most or all of their personal property through the bankruptcy process.

This chapter explains which types of property are part of your bankruptcy estate and come under the bankruptcy court's jurisdiction. It also covers situations in which the trustee can take back property or money you transferred to others and make it part of your bankruptcy estate.

Property in Your Bankruptcy Estate

When you file for Chapter 7 personal bankruptcy, almost everything you own when you file becomes part of your bankruptcy estate, which is subject to the bankruptcy court's authority. This includes:

- property you own and possess on the date you file
- property you are entitled to receive as of the date you file (tax refunds, for example)
- your share of marital property (including all community property, in community property states)
- property you used to own but improperly transferred to someone else
- "preference" payments (money you paid to favored creditors shortly before filing), and
- certain types of property that you acquire within six months after you file.

Property You Own and Possess When You File

With a few exceptions, the contents of your bankruptcy estate are determined as of the date you file for bankruptcy. As a small business owner, your estate may include:

- the tangible assets of a sole proprietorship business (such as equipment, machinery, or supplies)
- the intangible assets of a sole proprietorship business (customer lists, patents, copyrights, business name, and so on)
- the value of your ownership interest in a business entity such as an LLC or a corporation (even though it may not be worth much by the time you get around to thinking about bankruptcy)
- your home and other real estate
- your personal property, including your furniture, vehicle, and various electronics (TVs, computers, cell phones, and personal digital assistants)
- personal investments (such as stocks, bonds, and CDs) and deposit and money-market accounts
- personal retirement plans such as 401(k)s and IRAs, and
- miscellaneous items, such as guns, collectibles, art, recreational vehicles, farm and show animals, or musical instruments.

TIP

If you convert from Chapter 13. If you originally filed for Chapter 13 bankruptcy and convert your case to a Chapter 7 bankruptcy, your bankruptcy estate in your Chapter 7 case includes everything you owned when you filed your Chapter 13 case (as long as you still own it when you convert). In one case, a trustee required debtors who converted from Chapter 13 to Chapter 7 to hand over their clothes, $3,660 worth of personal property, and their family dog, because the debtors hadn't claimed an exemption for any of this property. (*In re John*, 352 B.R. 895 (N.D. Fla. 2006).) Although you get to keep all of your property in Chapter 13 bankruptcy, you still have to claim exemptions to calculate your minimum plan payment.

Property in a Revocable Living Trust

A revocable living trust is a popular estate planning tool in which the grantor puts property in trust to be managed by the trustee, for the benefit of one or more beneficiaries. The trust is revocable because the grantor can change his or her mind and revoke it at any time. If the grantor owns a sole proprietorship business, it's typically included in the trust.

If you are both the grantor and the trustee of your revocable living trust (the most common arrangement), property in the trust is considered property of your bankruptcy estate, even though the trust technically "owns" the property. Courts haven't yet determined what happens if you name someone else to be the trustee, but it's likely that the same result would occur: The trust would be considered part of your (the grantor's) bankruptcy estate because you could still change you mind and revoke the trust.

If, however, the trust is irrevocable (that is, you can't change your mind and dissolve or amend it), property in the trust won't be considered part of your bankruptcy estate unless:

- the trust was created within the previous two years (or even earlier if you were trying to avoid your creditors) and qualifies as a fraudulent transfer, or
- the trust was created within the previous ten years and is self-settled (that is, you created the trust and are also its beneficiary).

Both of these situations are described in "Property You Transferred Improperly," below.

Property You Are Entitled to Receive

As a small business owner, you may be entitled to receive money or property that hasn't yet found its way into your hands (a bird that's still in the bush, so to speak). Property that might fall into this category includes the following (some are explained in more detail below):

- accounts receivable
- stock options
- commissions
- tax refunds that are due and payable
- causes of action (legal grounds for bringing a lawsuit)
- vacation or severance pay you earned before filing
- proceeds from property in your bankruptcy estate (such as royalties you have earned on copyrighted material)
- proceeds of an insurance policy, if the injury or other event that triggers payment has already occurred when you file, and
- an inheritance that you are entitled to but haven't yet received.

These types of assets are part of your bankruptcy estate because you are already entitled to them when you file. Although a typical Chapter 7 bankruptcy case is over in just a few months, your case can be held open, for years if necessary, until these assets materialize. For example, if you are a named heir of someone who has already died, but the will is held up in probate for months, the bankruptcy judge will keep your case open until the will is finally settled and you receive the inheritance, so that if can be taken to pay your creditors.

If, however, the asset will be protected by an exemption when it finally arrives, your bankruptcy case will probably be closed on schedule. For example, if you are still owed $5,000 in accounts receivable, but the exemption system you plan to use include a "wildcard" exemption for up to $5,000, the trustee won't keep your case open (see Ch. 6 for more on exemptions). Because you'll get to keep the money when it comes, there's no reason to delay the end of your bankruptcy.

Let's look in more detail at a few types of property you may receive in the future.

Accounts Receivable

Even if you don't think you'll be paid by a particular creditor, any debt owed to you is part of your bankruptcy estate. It's the trustee's job to go after the money, if possible, so it can be distributed to your creditors (unless you are able to protect it with an exemption). Leaving current or overdue accounts receivable off the bankruptcy forms can get you into trouble.

Stock Options

If you own stock options, you have the right to purchase company stock at the price that was assigned when the stock options were granted. When you actually buy the stock, you are "exercising" your stock options.

As a general rule, stock options that you own when you file for bankruptcy are part of your bankruptcy estate. In addition, any stock you purchase by exercising your stock options is also part of the estate, even if you exercise those options after you file for bankruptcy. Courts treat these postfiling stock purchases as proceeds of the bankruptcy estate.

Most of the time, you have to wait for a while after you are awarded options before you are entitled to buy the stock. When the waiting period ends, the stock options "vest" and you may exercise them. Whether stock options are part of your bankruptcy estate depends on when you received them and when they vest. If your stock options do not vest until you have been with your company for a certain period of time, your bankruptcy estate will include only those stock options that have already vested on the date you file for bankruptcy.

To calculate the value of your stock options, multiply the number of vested stock options you own by the difference between your option price and the fair market value of the stock. (Value of options = [number of vested stock options] x [fair market value – option price].) Even if the value of your options is uncertain, they are still part of your bankruptcy estate and the trustee will take them if they are marketable.

Causes of Action

If you have a potential legal claim for money damages against another person or business, it is part of your bankruptcy estate even if the value of the claim hasn't yet been determined. For example, if you entered into a purchase agreement with a vendor, and the vendor failed to deliver supplies as promised, you have a legal claim for breach of contract. Even if you haven't yet filed a lawsuit—and may never do so—you must include this potential source of money in your bankruptcy papers.

If you don't list your potential causes of action in your bankruptcy petition, you may lose the right to bring a lawsuit on the claims after your bankruptcy. Under a legal principal known as judicial estoppel, failing to raise a legal claim in one judicial proceeding could prohibit you from raising it in a later proceeding. For example, if you file for bankruptcy to prevent a foreclosure sale of your home, but fail to list a cause of action you may have against the lender under the Truth in Lending Act, you may be prevented from suing the lender after your bankruptcy is completed. (See *In re Lopez*, 283 B.R. 22 (9th Cir. BAP 2002).)

Proceeds From Property in Your Bankruptcy Estate

This category of property includes, for example, rent from commercial or residential real estate, royalties from copyrights or patents, and dividends earned on stock. If property in your bankruptcy estate earns income or otherwise produces money after you file for bankruptcy, this money is also part of your bankruptcy estate. For example, suppose you have a contract to receive royalties for a book you wrote before filing bankruptcy. That contract is part of your bankruptcy estate, as are any royalties you earn after you file for bankruptcy. The one exception to this rule is money you earn from providing personal services *after* filing for bankruptcy; this money isn't part of your bankruptcy estate. Continuing our example, work you do to create a new edition of the book after you file for bankruptcy would be considered personal services. The royalties you earn for that new work would not be part of your bankruptcy estate.

Proceeds from a "contingent future interest" are also part of the bankruptcy estate. This bit of legalese refers to money that you will receive if certain things happen in the future. The mere possibility that you will receive property after filing for bankruptcy is enough to put that property in your bankruptcy estate once you do file. In one case, for example, an employee had the right to participate in a profit-sharing plan, but only if he was still employed by the company at the end of the year. He filed for bankruptcy before the end of the year, but remained employed and at the end of the year received a hefty check, which the trustee claimed belonged to the bankruptcy estate, at least in part. The court ruled that the check the employee received belonged in the bankruptcy estate even though the employee didn't receive it until after the filing date, because the employee's interest in the profit-sharing plan was a contingent future interest. (*In re Edwards*, 273 B.R. 527 (E.D. Mich. 2000).)

Inheritances

If you are entitled to receive an inheritance, that money or property is part of your bankruptcy estate, even if you have not yet received it. Generally, you are "entitled" to receive an inheritance only after the person leaving the inheritance has died. After all, that person could always spend the money, sell the property you hope to one day inherit, or change his or her estate plan to cut you out.

There are a few exceptions to this rule. If you are the beneficiary of an irrevocable trust, the person who created the trust is not legally entitled to change it. Technically, this type of arrangement qualifies as a gift to the beneficiary rather than an inheritance, and it's part of your bankruptcy estate.

Property you inherit within six months after filing is also part of your bankruptcy estate. Even if the person leaving the inheritance is still alive when you file your bankruptcy, property left to you by will or by intestate succession (the way property passes when no will or other estate planning device dictates who will receive it) will be part of your bankruptcy estate if the person dies within 180 days after you file for bankruptcy (see "Certain Property Acquired Within 180 Days After You File," below).

Some inheritances are set up so that you receive periodic payments from a trust, although you are not entitled to the full amount of the trust yet. For example, you may be the beneficiary of a spendthrift trust, which pays you a certain amount each year until you reach a particular age, when you are entitled to whatever's left in the trust. Because spendthrift trusts restrict the trustee's ability to use the funds to pay creditors, the funds in the trust are not technically part of your bankruptcy estate.

Nonetheless, when you complete your paperwork in Ch. 9, you should identify any such trust on your Schedule B (where you list all your personal property) and describe it as a spendthrift trust that isn't part of your bankruptcy estate. You don't want to be accused of trying to hide it. The trustee may want a copy of the trust paperwork to find out whether it's a true spendthrift trust or whether there is a way for creditors (and thus the trustee) to get at the funds.

Your Share of Marital Property

How much of your marital property—the property you and your spouse own together—is included in your bankruptcy estate depends on two factors: (1) whether you file jointly or alone, and (2) the laws of your state regarding marital property.

If you file jointly, all marital property that fits into any of the categories discussed in this section belongs to your bankruptcy estate.

However, if you are married and you file for bankruptcy alone, some marital property may not be part of your bankruptcy estate. Whether property is part of the estate depends on whether you live in a community property, tenancy by the entirety, or "common law" property state.

Community Property States

These are the community property states: Alaska (only if the spouses sign a written agreement to treat the property as community property), Arizona, California, Idaho, Louisiana, Nevada, New Mexico, Texas, Washington, and Wisconsin.

As explained in Ch. 1, the general rule in community property states is that all property either spouse earns or receives during the marriage is community property and is owned jointly by both spouses. Exceptions are gifts and inheritances received by only one spouse, and property owned by one spouse before the marriage or acquired after the spouses permanently separate: These types of property are the separate property of the spouse who acquired or received them.

If you are married, live in a community property state, and file for bankruptcy, all the community property you, and your spouse, own is considered part of your bankruptcy estate, even if your spouse doesn't file. This is true even if the community property might not be split evenly if you were to divorce.

> EXAMPLE: Paul and Sonya live in California, a community property state. Sonya contributed $20,000 of her separate property toward the down payment on their home. The rest of the money for the house came from community funds, and the house is considered community property. If Paul and Sonya were to divorce and divide the house proceeds, Sonya would be entitled to $20,000 more than Paul as reimbursement for her down payment.
>
> But they aren't divorced, and Paul files for bankruptcy separately after his consulting business fails. Their house is worth $250,000. Paul must list that entire value as part of his bankruptcy estate on his bankruptcy papers—that is, he can't list only half of that amount because he owns the house jointly with Sonya, nor can he subtract the $20,000 Sonya would be entitled to if they divorced.

When Are Family Sole Proprietorships Considered Community Property?

Family businesses purchased with community funds are also community property, even if only one spouse is involved in the business. For example, Pablo and Maya got married in 2009. At the time, Pablo was unemployed and Maya was a schoolteacher. Shortly after the marriage, Pablo used some of their savings to open a sole proprietor business called Pablo's Landscaping. Pablo took out all of the necessary licenses and permits in his own name, and only his name appeared on the business checking account. Despite the fact that the business appears to belong only to Pablo, it is actually a community property business because it was formed during the marriage with community property. The business would also be community property if Pablo had formed a corporation and was the sole stockholder.

If, however, Pablo already owned the landscaping equipment prior to the marriage, used his own savings from before the marriage to get the business off the ground, and kept a separate account for business income and expenses, the business would likely be considered Pablo's separate property. But, if Maya quit her teaching job and started working in the preexisting business, it might still qualify as community property, despite all of Pablo's separate contributions.

The separate property of the spouse filing for bankruptcy is also part of the bankruptcy estate. But the separate property of the spouse *not* filing for bankruptcy is not part of the bankruptcy estate.

EXAMPLE: Paul owns a twin-engine Cessna as his separate property (he owned it before he married Sonya). Sonya came to the marriage owning a grand piano. Because Paul is filing for bankruptcy alone, Paul's aircraft will be part of his bankruptcy estate, but Sonya's piano won't be.

You may need to do some research into your state's property laws to make sure you understand which of your property is separate and which is community. (See Ch. 12 for tips on legal research.)

Tenancy by the Entirety States

States that recognize some form of tenancy by the entirety for married couples are Delaware, Florida, Hawaii, Illinois, Indiana, Maryland, Massachusetts, Michigan, Missouri, North Carolina, Ohio, Pennsylvania, Rhode Island, Tennessee, Vermont, Virginia, and Wyoming, along with the District of Columbia.

Real estate (and personal property, in some states) that a couple owns as tenants by the entirety belongs to the marriage, rather than to one spouse or the other. If both spouses file for bankruptcy, property held in tenancy by the entirety is property of the bankruptcy estate. If only one spouse files for bankruptcy, however, this property is not part of the bankruptcy estate and is generally exempt from claims for which only one spouse is liable. Because the property belongs to the marriage, one spouse cannot give it away or encumber it with debts on his or her own. The property is not exempt from debts the couple takes on jointly, however. We discuss this further in Ch. 7.

Common Law Property States

If your state is not listed above as a community property or tenancy by the entirety state, it is a "common law" property state. When only one spouse files for bankruptcy in a common law property state, all of that spouse's separate property plus half of the couple's jointly owned property goes into the filing spouse's bankruptcy estate.

The general rules of property ownership in common law states are:

- Property that has only one spouse's name on a title certificate (such as a car, a house, or stocks) is that spouse's separate property, even if it was bought with joint funds.
- Property that was purchased or received as a gift or inheritance by both spouses is jointly owned, unless title is held in only one spouse's name (which means it belongs to that spouse separately, even if both spouses use it).
- Property that one spouse buys with separate funds or receives as a gift or inheritance for that spouse's separate use is that spouse's separate property (unless, again, a title certificate shows differently).
- If one spouse owns and operates a business under his or her name, and the other spouse is not engaged in operating the business, the business will be the separate property of the first spouse.

Same-Sex Couples and Domestic Partners

If you are married to, or in a domestic partnership with, someone of the same sex, you may be wondering whether you can file for bankruptcy together with your partner—and what effect bankruptcy will have on property you own together. Many issues involving these relationships are still up in the air, and, because same-sex marriage has only recently become possible, it isn't clear how things will shake out.

If you and your partner have married (currently allowed in Massachusetts, Iowa, Vermont, Connecticut, and New Hampshire) or registered as domestic partners in a state that offers registered partners some of the benefits of marriage, you might be considering a joint bankruptcy filing. Thus far, however, such efforts have not been successful, primarily because federal law does not recognize same-sex marriage and allows states to disregard such marriages performed in other states. This law, known as the Defense of Marriage Act

(DOMA), also defines marriage, for purposes of federal law, as a union between a man and a woman. The DOMA has led at least one court to deny a lesbian couple who had married in Canada the right to file jointly for bankruptcy.

Separate but Equal Can Be Helpful in Bankruptcy

Believe it or not, the federal bankruptcy system's discrimination against same-sex couples can also be an advantage. An example of this is the exemption system. In many states, married couples are not allowed to double exemptions, whether they file together or separately. And in community property states, all of the couple's community property is part of the bankruptcy estate, even if only one spouse files. These problems disappear for unmarried couples. Because unmarried partners must file separately, each can claim the full amount of every exemption, and one partner can file for bankruptcy without worrying that his or her partner's property will be considered part of the bankruptcy estate. The downside—beyond being prohibited from classifying your relationship as you wish—is having to pay a separate filing fee (and some extra attorney fees if you are using an attorney).

There is even less certainty as to how state exemptions and property ownership laws will be applied to same-sex couples who are married or registered as civil or domestic partners. For example, a New Jersey Tax Court allowed a disabled veteran's claim that the home he owned with his male partner was exempt from taxes, because the men had registered as domestic partners in New Jersey and owned the home in tenancy by the entirety—a form of property ownership previously reserved to married couples.

This uncertainty extends only to couples that have married or registered, however. If you and your partner are neither married nor registered in a state that gives partners marriage-like benefits, any property you own together will be treated like property owned with any other person: The share that you own will be part of the bankruptcy estate and subject to the court's jurisdiction. Your partner will be treated as a codebtor on any debts you owe jointly. But your partner will not be part of your bankruptcy case.

If you and your partner or spouse are considering filing jointly or have concerns about the treatment of your debts and property in bankruptcy, you should consult with a bankruptcy attorney who is familiar with legal issues facing same-sex couples.

Property You Transferred Improperly

Even property you no longer possess or own can be pulled back into your bankruptcy estate if you transferred it improperly. For example, if you sold or gave away property during the two-year period immediately before you file for bankruptcy (or even longer in some cases), you will have to disclose those transfers on your bankruptcy forms. And if you gave away or sold the property for less than it was worth within the past year, the trustee can get it back and sell it for the benefit of your creditors.

Fraudulent transfers take place when debtors try to unload their assets so that their creditors (or the bankruptcy trustee) won't be able to take and sell them. These transactions often take the form of selling property to a friend or relative for a nominal amount (such as a dollar), with the understanding that the friend will give back the property once the bankruptcy case is closed. Another common example of a fraudulent transfer is taking one's name off a joint account, deed, or vehicle title (which is really a gift of half of the property to the other joint owner). Or, a debtor might try to reduce his or her equity in property by using it as collateral for a new loan shortly before filing for bankruptcy.

Even if you didn't intend to improperly shield your assets, a transfer can be set aside—and the property returned to the bankruptcy estate—if you received less than reasonably equivalent value in exchange for the property, and:

- you were insolvent when you made the transfer (or as a result of it)
- you were engaged in business or about to engage in a business transaction with an unreasonably small amount of capital
- you intended to incur debts that you couldn't repay, or
- you made the transfer to or for the benefit of an insider under an employment contract, and not in the ordinary course of business.

TIP

Some charitable donations don't count. Charitable contributions to qualified religious or charitable organizations are not fraudulent transfers as long as they comprise less than 15% of your gross annual income or are consistent with your past charitable giving practices (even if more than 15%).

Depending on the type of transfer and the state where the improperly transferred property was located, the trustee can look back for up to ten years before you filed for bankruptcy, searching for improperly transferred property that can be pulled back into your bankruptcy estate and sold for the benefit of your creditors. The trustee will be looking for signs that you intended to cheat your creditors, called "badges of fraud."

Badges of Fraud

Under state and federal law, converting property (selling it or giving it away) before you file for bankruptcy may constitute fraud if you did it to "cheat, defraud, delay, or hinder your creditors." To figure out whether a particular conversion meets this standard, judges look at a list of factors, called "badges of fraud." The more of these facts are present in your transaction, the more likely a judge is to find a fraudulent conversion of assets.

The badges of fraud list typically includes:

1. The transfer was made to an insider (a business associate, friend, or relative).

Selling Your Business

It's not uncommon for people to file for Chapter 7 bankruptcy shortly after selling a business (or its assets). The sale of a business or business assets is treated just like any other transfer in the two years before filing: If you sell for considerably less than fair market value, the trustee can undo the sale and get the property back. If you make a sale like this within the year before filing for bankruptcy, your whole bankruptcy case might be at risk.

Of course, it can be tough to put a fair price on a business, especially one that's relatively new. As long as the sale was made at arms length (that is, not to an insider, such as a friend or family member) and you tried to get a fair price, the sale probably won't be challenged by the trustee. If, however, you sold to a business associate or relative, you should expect serious scrutiny from the trustee, especially if you sold for a low price.

Even if you sell the business for fair value, you'll have to disclose the sale and answer any questions the trustee has about it. For example, assume Cindy sells her skin care business for $25,000 (a fair price) and files for bankruptcy a few months later. When Cindy completes her paperwork, she'll have to explain what she did with the money. If Cindy gave the money to her Aunt Rose to help Rose start a business, the bankruptcy trustee would demand that Rose fork over the money to the bankruptcy estate, because it would constitute a transfer within the previous two years. On the other hand, if Cindy used the money to pay her own living necessities or to buy exempt items, then the trustee would probably allow the transfer to stand, and there would be no adverse consequences.

If Cindy's business were a separate entity (such as a corporation or an LLC), any proceeds Cindy received from the sale would be part of the bankruptcy estate and subject to any exemption Cindy could claim, just like any other asset. If the business entity had debts, the sale proceeds would have be used to pay them first. If there were money left over after the creditors were paid, it would be part of Cindy's personal bankruptcy estate.

2. The debtor retained possession or control of the transferred property after the transfer (for example, the property was transferred to a trust in which the debtor continued to possess the property as trustee).
3. The transfer or obligation was not disclosed (for example, the debtor tried to conceal the transfer from the court by failing to list it on the bankruptcy paperwork).
4. Before the transfer was made, the debtor had been sued or threatened with a lawsuit.
5. The transfer included substantially all of the debtor's assets (if the debtor transferred only a small part of his or her assets, the court is less likely to find fraud).
6. The debtor changed his or her address or moved out of state for no apparent reason other than to avoid the creditor.
7. The debtor removed or concealed assets (for example, the debtor changed bank accounts, moved his or her money to a foreign jurisdiction or off-shore account—often called "situs trusts"—or changed the name on the property's title).
8. What the debtor received for the property was not reasonably equivalent to its value (that is, the property was either given away or sold for an amount far lower than could be obtained on the open market).
9. The debtor became insolvent shortly after the transfer was made.
10. The transfer occurred shortly before or shortly after a substantial debt was incurred.
11. The debtor transferred the essential assets of a business to a lienholder, who then transferred the assets to an insider (a business associate, friend, or relative) of the debtor.

It can be tough to predict how a particular judge will weigh the presence or absence of particular factors to decide whether a transfer was fraudulent. The badges of fraud are nothing more than a laundry list of suspicious acts for judges to consider, but judges are free to disregard certain badges—or give certain badges more weight—depending on the circumstances. A judge could decide that a transfer is fraudulent even if only one or two badges are present; similarly, a judge might decide that a transfer is not fraudulent even if a number of badges are present.

While fuzzy logic may work in certain types of math, it tends to undercut the certainty that people look for in the law. If you've made a transfer that you're concerned about, you'll need to examine the circumstances surrounding the conversion, consider which "badges of fraud" might apply, and be prepared to argue with the trustee.

Time Limits

The bankruptcy court can undo transfers like these only if you make them within a certain time before filing for bankruptcy. Generally, the trustee can look back two years before you filed for bankruptcy to find fraudulent transfers; that's why the bankruptcy paperwork requires you to list all transactions in the two years before you filed. If, however, you made a fraudulent transfer within the year before filing, the trustee may decide to go a step further and ask the court to deny you a bankruptcy discharge of your debts.

> EXAMPLE 1: You want to file for Chapter 7 bankruptcy, but you are listed on a deed as the co-owner of property where a friend is living (which was necessary to allow the friend to buy the property because he has bad credit). After learning that the trustee could take and sell that property for the benefit of your unsecured creditors, you take yourself off the deed before you file for bankruptcy. Because you're unwilling to commit perjury, however, you have to list the transaction on your bankruptcy papers, and your entire bankruptcy case could go down the tubes.

> EXAMPLE 2: You own a used book store as a sole proprietor, and business isn't good. If you file for Chapter 7 bankruptcy, you'll

have to close down your business (at least temporarily), and you'll lose most of your inventory and fixtures to the bankruptcy trustee, who will try to sell them to raise money for your creditors. To avoid this result, you "sell" the business to a friend. Although the business has a fair market value of $50,000, your friend pays only $1,000.

When you file for bankruptcy a month later, you leave the business—and the sale to your friend—off of your paperwork because you don't see any way the bankruptcy trustee could find out about it. However, you are required to file your most recent tax return with the bankruptcy court, from which the trustee learns that you own a store. At the creditors' meeting, the trustee questions you closely about the store. At this point, you fess up and show the trustee your bill of sale. Because this was a recent transfer for far less than fair market price, the trustee can oppose your entire bankruptcy discharge. And, because you deliberately left the transfer off your paperwork despite clear instructions on the form to list it, you risk being prosecuted for perjury (a felony).

These one- and two-year look-back periods come from federal bankruptcy law. However, all states also have laws that forbid unlawful transfers and allow creditors to sue to get back property that was improperly transferred. These fraudulent transfer laws often have a statute of limitations of four years, which means the trustee can look back that far into the past for property to pull back into the bankruptcy estate.

If one of these laws gives a creditor the right to sue, the trustee can step in and exercise that same right in the creditor's place. Trustees don't often use these laws because they require a lot of time and effort. The trustee must file a lawsuit in the bankruptcy court, win it, and then enforce the judgment before actually laying hands on the property. Also, the person to whom you transferred the property might win the lawsuit if he or she wasn't aware of the fraud. Still, if you transferred valuable property within the last four years, you might want to consult with a lawyer.

EXAMPLE: The fraudulent transfer act in Pete's state has a statute of limitations of four years. Three years ago, Pete transferred ownership of a real estate parcel to his Uncle Paul to hide it from a vendor that was threatening to sue for breach of contract. No money changed hands; Pete just changed the name on the title, and Uncle Paul agreed to transfer the property back to Pete after the dust had settled. The vendor sued Pete, but settled for pennies on the dollar; the vendor didn't know about the property.

After settling the lawsuit, Pete files for Chapter 7 bankruptcy (in part, to get out of making the payments required by the settlement agreement). Pete leaves the transfer to Uncle Paul off his records because it happened more than two years ago. As part of a routine search of public records, the bankruptcy trustee discovers the transfer and learns of the fraud by questioning Pete at his creditors' meeting. After the trustee threatens to sue him to get the property back, Uncle Paul willingly transfers the parcel to the trustee, who sells it and distributes the proceeds to Pete's unsecured creditors. Had Pete known this would happen, he may have decided not to file for bankruptcy until another year had passed. If more than four years had passed between the transfer and Pete's bankruptcy filing, the transfer would have been beyond the trustee's reach.

If You've Made a Fraudulent Transfer

Whatever form they take, gifts and sales of property for substantially less than the property is worth are frequently judged to be improper or fraudulent transfers. This means the property can be taken—from its new owner—and sold for the benefit of the creditors, and the bankruptcy case could be dismissed. Even if you're able to convince the trustee that your intentions were good, the trustee can still require the person to whom you gave or sold the property to give it back. In these situations, you may not have the opportunity to claim that the property is exempt, so you won't even get any of the sale proceeds.

If you made a mistake like this, you may be tempted to try to undo it by, for example, getting the property back, putting your name back on the deed or title certificate, and so on. This looks even worse to the trustee, however: It indicates that you are trying to deceive the court. The best way to handle these transfers is simply to wait out the two-year (or four-year) period, if possible. For example, if you sold your car to a relative on the cheap, you should wait two years before filing.

Unfortunately, it's not always possible to wait. You may have a wage garnishment in the works, or you may be trying to buy some time in a foreclosure or eviction situation. What then? Probably the next best strategy is to disclose the transfer and attempt to use your exemptions to keep the property. Some lawyers advocate undoing recent transactions, even if the trustee may see this as further evidence of deception. You can list the property on your schedules as part of your bankruptcy estate, explaining that you earlier transferred it but now have it back. Then, you should be able to claim any exemptions that apply to the property.

In some cases, the property you transferred may not exist or be available for the trustee to seize. For example, say you took your name off the title to a car you owned jointly with your brother, and he pays you nothing in return. Several months later, your brother sells the car to raise money to pay off his child support arrearages. If you filed for bankruptcy, there is little the trustee can do to get this money back. The car is gone, your brother is broke, and the trustee can't go after his ex for the child support money. In a situation like this, a fraudulent transfer won't have any effect on your bankruptcy.

Often, property that people try to transfer before filing for bankruptcy would have been exempt anyway. In other words, these transfers often occur simply because the debtor doesn't understand the bankruptcy laws. Had the person just kept the property and claimed it as exempt, he or she could have held on to it and avoided a whole lot of trouble.

How Do Trustees Find Out?

People often wonder how the trustee would find out about a particular transfer. If the transferred property has a title document (as with cars, boats, and real estate), the transfer might show up in the trustee's routine search of state and local databases (for example, at the state DMV). And the tax return you are required to provide will give the trustee useful information about your previous possessions and transactions. Also, when you attend the creditors' meeting, you must affirm, under oath, that you truthfully answered the questions in your bankruptcy papers, including questions about property you transferred in the past two years. Because trustees profit directly from finding property they can take and sell, they are very skilled at picking up on any hesitancy or anxiety you may show at the creditors' meeting. A trustee who senses trouble can question you under oath in a deposition-like proceeding. Most importantly, it's a bad idea to commit perjury. Period.

Self-Settled Trusts

If you created an irrevocable "self-settled" trust within the last ten years, intending to defraud your creditors, this might also count as a fraudulent transfer. A self-settled trust is one that you created and funded with your own property, and for which you are the beneficiary. A trust is irrevocable if you can't take it back; once you create an irrevocable trust, it's final. If the trustee finds that you created a self-settled trust in the past ten years with fraudulent intent (based on the badges of fraud discussed above), the trustee can undo it and distribute all of the assets of the trust to your creditors, without letting you claim any exemption.

Unequal Divorce Settlements

People frequently file for bankruptcy within a year or two of ending a marriage. Is it a fraudulent transfer if one spouse gives all or most of the marital property to the other spouse and then files bankruptcy? While some trustees have attempted to recover property transferred to an ex-spouse under these circumstances, most courts have ruled that property given up in a divorce is deemed to be transferred for fair consideration, even if the spouse filing for bankruptcy got little or nothing in return. There are many reasons why one spouse might come out with the short end of the stick in a divorce, and these judges have found that it's not appropriate for a federal bankruptcy court to second-guess the outcome of a state court divorce settlement or decree.

Preference Payments

A basic principle of bankruptcy law is that all creditors deserve to be treated fairly in comparison to each other. In many cases, fair treatment means that no one gets anything. In some cases, it means that your unsecured creditors share equally in the proceeds if the trustee takes your nonexempt property and sells it.

This principle is undermined if you make a payment to some creditors and not others before you file for bankruptcy. Payments like these may be considered "preferences" because you are favoring some creditors over others. When payments qualify as preferences, the trustee can demand that the creditor return the money to your bankruptcy estate, where it will be divided equally among all of your creditors (subject to any exemptions you can claim).

For consumer debtors (those whose debts are primarily for personal debt rather than business debt), any payment of more than $600 might be considered a preference if it was made within a year to insider creditors (business associates, friends, or relatives), or within three months to others (see below). If, however, you are a business debtor—that is, a majority of your debt arises from your business activities—the court will look only at transactions that exceed $5,475. (Ch. 2 explains how to determine whether you are a business debtor for purposes of this rule.)

Payments to Insiders

The time period during which payments will be considered a preference depends on whether the creditor is an insider (a business associate, friend, or relative). If you pay more than $600 (or $5,475 if you are primarily a business debtor) to any creditor who's an insider during the year before you file for bankruptcy, that payment is a preference. For example, if you use your tax refund to pay back an emergency loan from your sister, brother, or mother, you have preferred that creditor over your other unsecured creditors. Bluntly put, when in bankruptcy, you are required to treat your mother and Visa equally.

> **EXAMPLE:** In October, Robin borrows $2,000 from her mother to pay off a supplier. In March of the following year, Robin receives a tax refund of $3,000. She pays her mother back and uses the remaining $1,000 to catch up on other bills. Even though no one could blame Robin for paying back her mom, this would likely be considered a preference payment if she files for bankruptcy within the year. She'll have to disclose it in her bankruptcy paperwork, and her mom may have to cough up the money.

There is one important exception to this rule: A payment to an insider won't be considered a preference if you made the payment more than 90 days prior to filing for bankruptcy and you weren't insolvent at the time. For example, if you repaid a $3,000 loan from your mother more than three months before you file, and you can show that the value of your assets was greater than your liabilities at the time you repaid her, the payment won't be considered a preference. This insolvency rule also applies to preferences to noninsiders.

Insolvency is presumed during the 90-day period before you file for bankruptcy, so if you made a preference payment within the past 90 days, you should expect it to be undone if you file for bankruptcy.

Payments to Others

If the creditor is not an insider, but instead is a regular "arms-length" creditor like most of your business creditors, such as a vendor or credit card company, the rules are different. The court will look at your transactions with that creditor for only three months before you file for bankruptcy. During this time period, any payment of more than $600, or $5,475 if you are primarily a business debtor, will be considered a preference

Antecedent Debt Rule

To qualify as a preference, the payments must be made on an "antecedent" debt. In other words, the debt must already be past due and owing. Even if you are current on an account, it might still qualify as an antecedent debt. For example, you may be current on a large credit card debt because you have been making the minimum monthly payments. As long as interest is being charged on the underlying debt, however, it will be considered an antecedent debt, and paying off the debt would be considered a preference.

Payments Made in the Ordinary Course of Business or Financial Affairs

A payment is not a preference if it is made in the ordinary course of business or the debtor's financial affairs.

> EXAMPLE: Tim, a masonry contractor, owes Tom's Tile $3,500 from a past job. Although it's always been Tim's practice to immediately pay for his supplies as soon as he's paid for the job, he hasn't paid Tom's Tile because of a dispute over the quality of materials provided. Tim lands another job, for which he secures $10,000 worth of tile on credit from ABC Masonry Supplies. Two months later, when he is paid for the job, he pays ABC $10,000, which brings his ABC account current. This transaction would most likely qualify as one made in the ordinary course of Tim's business, because it meets his normal practice of immediately paying his suppliers.

Regular payments for personal expenses—such as utilities or services—typically also qualify as payments made in the ordinary course of business or financial affairs, rather than preferences. And regular monthly payments on long-term debt (for example, making a usual monthly payment on a mortgage, credit card bill, or student loan) also fall within this exception.

Even if a payment to a creditor was not made in the ordinary course of business or financial affairs, it still may escape the trustee's clutches if the debtor receives "new value" as a result of making the payment. This means the debtor is receiving some current benefit for making the payment, not just paying off an old debt. For instance, let's say Tim, from the example above, paid off Tom's Tile so he could order more materials on credit from that company. This extension of credit might be considered new value received for paying off the old debt, which means the payment wouldn't be a preference.

TIP

Transferring balances may be a preference. At least one court has found that transferring your balance from one credit card to another might be considered a preference. In that case, the debtor used her credit on one credit card to pay off her debt on another credit card. Because she made the transfer within three months of filing for bankruptcy, and she could have used the money for any purpose (in other words, she didn't have to use it to pay off her other card), the court ruled that the transfer was a preference. (*In re Dilworth*, 560 F.3d 562 (8th Cir. 2009).)

If You've Made Preference Payments

The consequences of violating the preference rules can be harsh. The bankruptcy trustee is authorized to take back the money and distribute it among your creditors. If you paid back a family member, this may cause some tension. Even if you paid back a creditor that isn't an insider, it could cause problems. For example, if you paid back a credit card issuer so you could keep your card, the issuer will probably revoke your credit card if it has to cough up the money to the trustee. The same problem could come up if you paid a debt to a core vendor or a commercial landlord or equipment leasing company.

The trustee may not go after every preference payment. For example, the trustee might decide not to go after a preference if the cost of suing to collect it would outweigh the amount to be gained. If you can claim an exemption that covers the preference, the trustee has even less incentive to pursue it. For example, assume your state has a wildcard exemption (discussed in Ch. 6) for up to $5,000 of any property. If the trustee discovers a preference payment of up to $5,000, and you haven't used any of the wildcard exemption, the trustee has no reason to undo the preference. Even if the trustee went to the trouble to get the preference back, you would get to keep the money when it is returned to the bankruptcy estate; forcing your creditor to pay the money back wouldn't raise any money for your other creditors.

Even though you can't pay a favorite creditor before you file, nothing prevents you from doing so after you file, as long as you do it with income earned after you file for bankruptcy or with property that isn't in your bankruptcy estate.

Certain Property Acquired Within 180 Days After You File

Most property you acquire—or become entitled to acquire—after you file for bankruptcy isn't included in your bankruptcy estate. But there are exceptions. If you acquire (or become entitled to acquire) certain items within 180 days after you file, you must report them to the bankruptcy court—and the trustee may take them if you can't protect them with an exemption.

The 180-day rule applies to:

- property you inherit during the 180-day period (some courts have held that property that passes to you as a beneficiary of a revocable living trust is not part of your bankruptcy estate; see, for example, *In re Mattern*, 55 Collier Bankr. Cas. 2d 1677 (D. Kan. 2006) and *In re Roth*, 289 B.R. 161 (D. Kan. 2003))
- property from a property settlement agreement or divorce decree that goes into effect during the 180-day period (excluding child support and alimony payments), and
- death benefits or life insurance policy proceeds that become owed to you during the 180-day period.

You must report these items on a supplemental form, even if your bankruptcy case is over before the 180-day time period is up. (You can find instructions for filing the supplemental form in Ch. 10.)

If you convert from a Chapter 7 bankruptcy to a Chapter 13 bankruptcy, the 180-day period runs from the date you originally filed for Chapter 7, not from the date you converted to Chapter 13. (*In re Carter*, 260 B.R. 130 (W.D. Tenn. 2001).)

Property That Is Not in Your Bankruptcy Estate

Property that is not in your bankruptcy estate is not subject to the bankruptcy court's jurisdiction, which means that the bankruptcy trustee can't take it to pay your creditors under any circumstances.

Property that belongs to someone else is not part of your bankruptcy estate—even if you control the property—because you don't have the right to sell it or give it away.

EXAMPLE 1: A parent establishes a trust for her child and names you as the trustee to manage the money in the trust until the child's 18th birthday. You possess and control the money, but it's solely for the child's benefit under the terms of the trust; you cannot use it for your own purposes. It isn't part of your bankruptcy estate.

EXAMPLE 2: Your sister has gone to Zimbabwe for an indefinite period and has loaned you her computer system while she's gone. Although you might have use of the equipment for years to come, you don't own it. It isn't part of your bankruptcy estate.

EXAMPLE 3: You are making monthly payments on a leased car. You are entitled to possess the car as long as you make the monthly payments, but you don't own it. It is not part of your bankruptcy estate (but the lease itself is).

EXAMPLE 4: Your name appears on the title (and note) to your son's car because he was too young to get a loan when he bought it. Your son makes all the payments. While the two of you probably consider the car to "belong" to your son, the bankruptcy laws initially consider it to be yours, and you have to disclose it in your bankruptcy paperwork. You can explain that you have "bare legal title" and your son is the equitable owner, which means it shouldn't be considered part of your bankruptcy estate. However, the court may disagree, which means your son could lose the car unless it fits within an available exemption. Courts have gone both ways on this issue; you should definitely talk to a lawyer if valuable property held this way is at stake.

Other types of property that don't fall within your bankruptcy estate are:

- property you buy or receive after your filing date (with the few exceptions described in "Certain Property Acquired Within 180 Days After You File," above)
- pensions and retirement plans
- property in a spendthrift trust that cannot be reached by the debtor's creditors
- tax-deferred education funds, with certain conditions and restrictions
- property pledged as collateral for a loan, if a licensed lender (pawnbroker) retains possession of the collateral
- property in your possession that belongs to someone else (for instance, property you are storing for someone)
- wages that are withheld, and employer contributions that are made, for employee benefit and health insurance plans, and
- child support arrearages owed to the debtor, because the parent is entitled to the funds only in his or her capacity as trustee for the child. (*In re Perry*, No. 06-50237 (Bkrtcy D. So. Dak. 2009).)

TIP

Retirement accounts are exempt. When Congress passed the new bankruptcy law in 2005, it created a broad exemption for all types of tax-exempt retirement accounts, including 401(k)s, 403(b)s, profit sharing and money purchase plans, IRAs (including Roth, SEP, and SIMPLE IRAs), and defined-benefit plans. These exemptions are unlimited—that is, the entire account is exempt, regardless of how much money is in it—except in the case of traditional and Roth IRAs. For these types of IRAs only, the exemption is limited to a total value of $1,095,000 per person (this figure is adjusted every three years for inflation).

Under the 2005 bankruptcy law, funds placed in a qualified tuition program or Coverdell education savings account are also not part of your bankruptcy estate, as long as:

- the beneficiary of the account is your child, stepchild, grandchild, step-grandchild, or in some cases, foster child, and

If You Are Named on Someone Else's Bank Account

It's common for older parents to put an adult child's name on the parent's bank account. This allows the child to write checks and otherwise manage the account if the parent becomes unable to do so; it also means the account goes straight to the child when the parent dies, outside of probate or other inheritance procedures.

If you are named on someone else's account and file for bankruptcy, however, that account could be considered property of your bankruptcy estate, subject to being taken by the trustee for the benefit of your unsecured creditors. Of course, it's not really your money while your parent is living, but if the trustee thinks you are free to withdraw the money and use it for your own purposes (as lowdown as that would be), the trustee may consider at least some of it to be part of your bankruptcy estate.

In this situation, it's important to tell the trustee, up front, that it really isn't your money to use as you wish. It would be a breach of your fiduciary duty (duty of trust) toward the account holder—and possibly elder abuse—for you to use the money for any purpose other than his or her welfare. To make sure that the trustee understands why you are named on the account, you should declare the account on your property schedule (Schedule B) but explain that it really isn't yours. You should identify the account and explain why you are named on it in Question 14 on the Statement of Financial Affairs. Finally, you would be well advised to gather documents showing that the sources of the money in the account clearly belong to the main account owner. (See Ch. 9 for more on these paperwork requirements.)

If you are able to exempt the account, you can just list it on Schedule B as your own property and avoid any argument over who owns it. For example, suppose your mother has put your name on her savings account, which has a balance of $4,000. If the exemption system you are using in your bankruptcy protects that amount of money (and you don't have an account of your own to protect), you could list the account on your personal property schedule (Schedule B) and claim the full amount as exempt on your Schedule C. That way you won't have to argue over who owns the money; either way, the trustee can't take it.

To avoid all this trouble, you may be tempted to remove your name from the account before you file bankruptcy. Don't do it. Removing your name makes it look like you are trying to hide the whole issue from the bankruptcy court. The trustee might well convince the court to dismiss your bankruptcy altogether, on the ground that you committed fraud on the court. You're better off leaving your name on the account and explaining the situation to the trustee. If there is significant money in the account, consider consulting with a lawyer about the best way to handle the situation in your paperwork. Incidentally, if you are thinking that the trustee won't find out about the account if you don't list it, don't go there. They have their ways.

Custodian Note: If you are listed as a custodian or a trustee of the account funds for a minor under the Uniform Transfers to Minors Act, you don't have to worry about the bankruptcy trustee taking the funds. The law is clear that those funds belong to the minor, not to you in your fiduciary capacity as a custodian or trustee.

- you deposit the funds into the account at least one year before filing for bankruptcy.

In other words, contributions made within the year before filing for bankruptcy are not excluded from your bankruptcy estate. As to contributions you make between one and two years before filing, you can exclude only $5,475 of them. As to contributions made more than two years before you file, they are excluded from the bankruptcy estate without limit.

CAUTION

Experts disagree over how to interpret this provision. Some bankruptcy lawyers believe that, although the statute appears to exclude from the bankruptcy estate all contributions made more than two years before filing, the total exclusion for educational accounts and tuition programs will be capped at $5,475, regardless of when the funds were deposited. Talk to a bankruptcy lawyer if you need more information on this issue.

CHAPTER

6

Understanding Property Exemptions

After reading Ch. 5, you should have a good idea of what property is part of your bankruptcy estate. But how much of that property will you get to keep, and how much is at risk of being taken and sold by the trustee? The answer to this question depends on whether you can protect the property—or your equity in it—with exemptions.

For example, if you own a used car outright, you will be able to keep it if the car's value is within the vehicle exemption in your state. If your car is worth $5,000 and the exemptions you are using protect equity in a car up to $5,000, you can keep the car.

On the other hand, you may lose property that isn't protected by an exemption. For instance, let's say you run a trucking business and own a tractor and trailer in which you have $30,000 equity. If the exemption system you are using protects a maximum of $10,000 for a commercial vehicle, you'll most likely have to give up the rig. The trustee would sell the tractor and trailer and pay you your $10,000 exemption amount, but your remaining equity (less the costs of sale) would be used to repay your creditors.

Whether you can protect property with an exemption frequently depends on the value of the property and how much equity you have in it. Often, you are entitled to keep a certain amount of equity—for example, up to $5,000 in a vehicle or $30,000 in a house. Knowing what you own and how much you could get for it will help you decide whether or not to file for Chapter 7 personal bankruptcy. If your property is worth enough, it may be easier to sell some of it (especially property that you would have to give up if you filed for bankruptcy) and pay your creditors directly rather than go through bankruptcy.

For those who have equity in valuable property, a Chapter 7 personal bankruptcy case often comes down to a fight between the trustee, who will try mightily to take your property and distribute it to your creditors, and you—and your lawyer, if you have one—who will try to keep every penny by carefully applying the available exemptions and valuing your property in the most advantageous way. It's your responsibility—and to your benefit—to claim all exemptions to which you're entitled. If you don't claim property as exempt, you could lose it unnecessarily to your creditors.

Equity vs. Value

Your equity in a piece of property may be less than the value of the property. In that case, as long as your equity in the item is no more than the amount you can exempt, you'll get to keep it. For example, if your car is worth $10,000 and you still owe $5,000 on your car loan, you have $5,000 equity in your car. If the exemptions you are using protect equity in a car at least up to $5,000, you can keep the car: The trustee wouldn't bother to sell it because once the car loan was paid off and you got your $5,000 exempt amount, there wouldn't be anything left for your other creditors.

Alternatively, you might have a very valuable vehicle in which you have no equity. For example, if your car is worth $19,000 but you still owe $20,000 on your car loan, you have zero (or negative) equity in your car. The trustee wouldn't bother to sell the car because there wouldn't be anything left for your other creditors after the car loan was paid off. (In both of these scenarios, you would need to keep making your monthly payments to keep the car.)

This chapter describes how exemptions work and how to figure out which exemptions you can use. Once you know which exemptions are available to you, you can start applying those exemptions to your personal property to figure out which items you'll be able to keep. To help you keep track, we've included a Personal Property Checklist, which you can use to take an inventory of your property. Then, using the Property Exemption Worksheet, you'll be able to figure out, item by item, whether you'll be able to hang on to your property. If you decide to file for bankruptcy, you'll need to fill out forms listing what property you own, how much it's worth, and what you claim as exempt. The work you do in this chapter can be transferred to those forms.

RELATED TOPIC

For home and real estate exemptions, see Ch. 7. This chapter explains how exemptions work generally, and provides detailed information on exemptions for personal and business property. For many bankruptcy filers, however, the main concern is whether they'll be able to keep their home. Because this is such an important issue, we've devoted a separate chapter (Ch. 7) to exemptions that apply to your home and other real estate.

How Exemptions Work

Each state's legislature has created a set of exemptions primarily for use by people who are residents of that state. These state exemptions apply both to bankruptcy cases and to all other collection efforts. In addition, 16 states (and the District of Columbia) allow debtors to choose between their state's exemptions or another set of exemptions created by Congress, called federal bankruptcy exemptions.

States That Allow Debtors to Choose the Federal Exemptions	
Arkansas	New Jersey
Connecticut	New Mexico
District of Columbia	Pennsylvania
Hawaii	Rhode Island
Kentucky	Texas
Massachusetts	Vermont
Michigan	Washington
Minnesota	Wisconsin
New Hampshire	

If you are entitled to choose between state or federal exemptions, you must select one system or the other: You can't mix and match, using some exemptions from one list and some from the other. However, if you use one system when you first file your petition and later decide that the other system would work better for you, you can usually amend your bankruptcy paperwork to change systems.

California has adopted its own unique exemption system. Although California law doesn't allow debtors to use the federal exemptions, California offers two sets of state exemptions. With a few important exceptions, the second set of California exemptions are the same as the federal exemptions. As in the states that have the federal bankruptcy exemptions, people filing for bankruptcy in California must choose one or the other set of state exemptions.

TIP

You might be able to keep your nonexempt property. If you have property that does not fall within an exemption, the trustee won't necessarily take it. You may not have to surrender nonexempt property if you have the cash to buy it back from the trustee, who will often accept less than its replacement value to avoid having to collect, store, and sell it at auction (probably for far less than its full value). Instead of cash, the trustee may be willing to accept exempt property of roughly equal value instead. Also, the trustee might choose to reject or abandon the item (in other words, to let you keep it), if it would be too costly or cumbersome to sell and you aren't willing or able to buy it back. So when we say that you have to give up property, remember that you still might be able to keep it, depending on the circumstances.

Types of Exemptions

Both state and federal exemptions come in several basic flavors.

Exemptions to a Limited Amount

Some exemptions protect the value of your ownership in a particular item only up to a set dollar limit. For instance, the New Mexico state exemptions allow you to keep $4,000 of equity in a motor vehicle. If you filed for Chapter 7 bankruptcy in that state and used the state exemption list, you could keep your car if it was worth $4,000 or less. You could also keep the car if selling it would not raise enough money to pay what you still owe on it and give you the full value of your $4,000 exemption. For example, if you own a car worth $20,000 but still owe $16,000 on it, selling it would raise $16,000 for the lender and $4,000 for you (thanks to the exemption). The trustee wouldn't take the car because there would be nothing left over to pay your other creditors. Instead, you would be allowed to keep it as long as you remain current on your payments.

However, if your equity in the car significantly exceeded the exemption, the trustee might sell the car to raise money for your other creditors. To continue our example, let's say you owe only $10,000 on that $20,000 car. Selling the car would pay off the lender in full, pay your $4,000 exemption, and leave some of the remaining $6,000 (after the costs of sale are deducted) to be distributed to your other creditors. In this scenario, you are entitled to your exemption—$4,000—but not to the car itself.

Exemptions Without Regard to Value

Another type of exemption allows you to keep specified property items regardless of their value. For instance, the Utah state exemptions allow you to keep a refrigerator, freezer, microwave, stove, sewing machine, washer, and dryer with no limit on their value. For comparison purposes, another Utah state exemption places a $500 limit on "sofas, chairs, and related furnishings." Go figure.

Wildcard Exemptions

Some states (and the federal exemption list) also provide a wildcard exemption. This exemption gives you a dollar amount that you can apply to any type of property. If you play poker, you undoubtedly have played a game where a particular card is designated a wildcard, which means you can use it as a queen of diamonds, a two of spades, or any other card you want to make the most of the other cards in your hand. The same principle applies here. For example, suppose you own a computer system and software worth $2,000 in a state that doesn't exempt these items but does have a wildcard exemption of $5,000. You can take $2,000 of the wildcard exemption and apply it to the computer and software, which means they will now be considered exempt. And if you have other nonexempt property, you can apply the remaining $3,000 of the wildcard exemption to that property.

You can also use a wildcard exemption to increase an existing exemption. For example, if you have $5,000 worth of equity in your car but your state has a motor vehicle exemption of only $1,500, you will likely lose the car. However, if your state has a $5,000 wildcard exemption, you could use the $1,500 motor vehicle exemption and $3,500 of the wildcard exemption to exempt your car entirely. And you'd still have $1,500 of the wildcard exemption to use on other nonexempt property.

Tools of the Trade

Many states provide a "tools of the trade" exemption, which lets you keep tools or equipment up to a certain dollar amount in value (typically, several thousand dollars). In some states, these exemptions allow you to exempt property as tools of the trade only if you will continue to use them to make a living. If you are closing down your business and getting out of that field altogether, your business assets may not be exempt tools of the trade. In other states, you may be able to use the tools of the trade exemption even if you have no plans to use that property to make a living in the future.

Tools of the trade used to include only hand tools, but now it refers more broadly to the things you need in order to do the job you rely on for support. Here are some examples:

- art camera, scanner (artist)
- car or van that is used for more than just commuting (sales manager, insurance adjuster, physician, traveling salesperson, real estate salesperson)
- truck (logger, tire retreader, truck driver, farmer, electrician, mechanic)
- cream separator, dairy cows, animal feed (farmer)
- drills, saws (carpenter)
- electric motor, lathe (mechanic)
- guitar, acoustic amplifier, coronet, violin and bow, organ, speaker cabinet (musician)
- hair dye, shampoo, cash register, furniture, dryer, fan, curler, magazine rack (barber, beauty parlor operator)
- oven, mixer (baker)
- personal computer, printer (insurance salesperson, lawyer, accountant)
- photographic lenses and darkroom equipment (photographer)
- power chain saw (firewood salesperson)
- sewing machine (tailor).

Why State Exemptions Vary So Much

Each state's exemptions are unique. The property you can keep, therefore, varies considerably from state to state. Why the differences? As mentioned, state exemptions are used not only for bankruptcy purposes but also to shelter property that otherwise could be taken by creditors who have obtained court judgments. The exemptions reflect the attitudes of state legislators about how much property, and which types of property, a debtor should be forced to give up when a creditor collects on a judgment. These attitudes are rooted in local values and concerns. But in many cases there is another reason why state exemptions differ. Some state legislatures have raised exemption levels in recent times, while other states haven't looked at their exemptions for decades. In states that don't reconsider their exemptions very often, you can expect to find lower dollar amounts.

Exemptions and Business Assets

Other than the "tools of the trade" exemption, there are almost no state exemptions explicitly for business assets or the value of the business as reflected in its goodwill. Historically, business owners have used Chapter 7 bankruptcy to liquidate the business (sell the business or, more frequently, its assets in an auction). Those who wanted to keep the business operating used Chapter 11 bankruptcy. In keeping with this practice, legislatures have seen no reason to extend exemptions to business assets or goodwill in Chapter 7 bankruptcies. (See Ch. 3 for more on Chapter 11 bankruptcy.)

If your business is a sole proprietorship, however, you may be able to protect your business assets using personal exemptions. For example, if you have a truck that you use in your handyman sole proprietorship business, you can apply a state vehicle exemption. And, if your state offers a wildcard exemption, you can use that for any property you wish, including your business assets and inventory. (As explained in Ch. 1, if your business has assets or inventory that could easily be sold while you are in bankruptcy, you may have to close your business, at least temporarily, so the trustee has an opportunity to appraise the assets and analyze whether they fit within your claimed exemptions.)

Domicile/Residency Requirements for Using State Exemptions

Prior to the 2005 bankruptcy law revisions, filers used the exemptions of the state where they resided when they filed for bankruptcy. Under the revised rules, however, some filers have to use the exemptions of the state where they *used* to reside. Congress was concerned about people gaming the system by moving to states with generous exemptions, just to file for bankruptcy. As a result, it created domicile requirements that filers have to meet before they can use a state's exemption system.

To apply these rules, you must first understand where your domicile is. Domicile has been defined as the place where someone has his or her "true fixed and permanent home and principal establishment" and to which the person intends to return after any period of absence. This means something more than your residence, which generally means wherever you are living at any given time.

Your domicile is the place where you are living and intend to live for the indefinite future, the place where you work, vote, receive your mail, pay taxes, do your banking, own property, participate in public affairs, register your car, apply for your driver's license, and send your children to school. Your domicile might not be the state where you are actually living when you file for bankruptcy. For example, members of the military, professional athletes, and corporate officers all might spend significant amounts of time working in another state or country, but their domicile is the state where they make their permanent home.

Here are the rules that govern which state's exemptions you must use:

- If you have made your domicile in your current state for at least two years, you can use that state's exemptions.
- If you have had your domicile in your current state for more than 91 days but less than two years, you can file in that state. However, you must use the exemptions of the state where you were domiciled for the better part of the 180-day period immediately prior to the two-year period preceding your filing.
- If you have had your domicile in your current state for less than 91 days, you can either file for bankruptcy in the state where you lived immediately before (as long as you lived there for at least 91 days) or wait until you have logged 91 days in your new home and file in your current state. Once you figure out where you can file for bankruptcy, you'll need to use whatever exemptions are available to you according to the rules set out above.
- If the state you are filing in offers a choice between the state and federal bankruptcy exemptions, you can use the federal exemption list regardless of how long you've been living in the state. In other words, the rules of the state where a person files for bankruptcy determine whether the filer can use the federal exemptions, even if the filer has not lived in the state long enough to use its *state* exemptions.
- If these rules deprive you of the right to use *any* state's exemptions, you can use the federal exemptions, even if they aren't otherwise available in the state where you file. For example, some states allow their exemptions to be used only by current state residents, which might leave former residents who haven't lived in their new home state for at least two years without any available state exemptions. (See, for example, *In re Underwood*, 342 B.R. 358 (N.D. Fla. 2006); *In re Crandall*, 346 B.R. 220 (M.D. Fla. 2006); and *In re West*, 352 B.R. 905 (M.D. Fla. 2006).) If you have recently returned to the U.S. after being domiciled in another country, and no state

exemption system is available to you under these rules, you are also entitled to use the federal exemptions.

CAUTION

A longer domicile requirement applies to homestead exemptions. If you acquired a home in your current state within the 40 months before you file for bankruptcy (and you didn't purchase it with the proceeds from selling another home in that state), your homestead exemption will be subject to a cap of $136,875, even if the state homestead exemption available to you is larger. For detailed information on homestead exemptions, see Ch. 7.

EXAMPLE 1: Sammie Jo lives in South Carolina from July 2008 until January 2010, when she gets lucky at a casino, moves to Texas, and starts a dog walking business with her winnings. She buys a Dodge Sprinter for $20,000 and has her new business name, VanDog, painted on the side. Her business really never takes off, and in March 2011, Sammie Jo files for Chapter 7 personal bankruptcy in Texas. Her van is now worth $14,000. Because Sammie Jo has been living in Texas for only 14 months—not two years—she can't use the Texas exemption for vehicles, which can be up to $30,000, depending on the value of other personal property that a filer claims as exempt. Because Sammie Jo filed for bankruptcy in March 2011, she must use the exemptions of the state where she lived for most of the six-month period ending two years before she filed for bankruptcy, or March 2009. Sammie Jo lived in South Carolina for the six months prior to March 2009, so she must use the South Carolina exemptions. As it turns out, the South Carolina exemption for vehicles is only $5,000, which means that Sammie Jo will probably lose her van if she uses the South Carolina exemptions.

As it turns out, however, Texas gives filers the option of using either its state exemptions or the federal bankruptcy exemptions. Because the rules of the state where a person files for bankruptcy determine whether the federal exemptions are available, Sammie Jo can use the federal exemptions instead of the South Carolina state exemptions. Under the federal exemptions, Sammie Jo is entitled to exempt a motor vehicle worth up to $3,225—still not enough to cover her van. But wait: The federal exemptions also provide a wildcard of $1,075, plus $10,125 of homestead exemption (together $11,200). Sammie Jo doesn't own her home, so she can add the entire wildcard exemption of $11,200 to her $3,225 vehicle exemption, for a total exemption of $14,425, which she can apply to her van to keep it.

EXAMPLE 2: Julia ran a day care center in North Dakota for many years. As part of her health care and retirement plan, she had set up a high-deductible health care plan with a health care savings account (HSA). In January 2010, when she has $20,000 in her HSA, she closes down her business and moves to Florida. She files for bankruptcy in Florida on November 30, 2011, 23 months later. Because she has lived in Florida for slightly less than two years when she files, she must use the exemptions from the state where she lived for the better part of the 180-day period that ended two years before she filed—which is North Dakota. As it turns out, Julia's most valuable possession is her $20,000 HSA. While the account would be exempt under Florida law, North Dakota has no exemption for this type of property. Nor are the federal exemptions available in Florida. So the trustee will probably seize the HSA and use the money in it to pay Julia's creditors. Had Julia waited another month to file, she would have been able to use Florida's exemptions and keep her HSA to use in retirement.

If You Are Married and Filing Jointly

If you and your spouse file jointly for bankruptcy, you may be able to double your exemptions. If the federal bankruptcy exemptions are available in the state where you file and you decide to use them, spouses filing jointly may double all of the exemptions. This means that you and your spouse can each claim the full amount of each federal exemption. You must both use the same exemption system; for example, you can't use the federal system while your spouse uses the state system.

If you decide to use your state's exemptions, you may be able to double some exemptions but not others. For instance, in the California System 1 exemption list, the $2,550 limit for motor vehicles may not be doubled, but the $6,750 limit on tools of the trade may be doubled in some circumstances. In order for you to double an exemption for a single piece of property, title to the property must be in both of your names. In Appendix A, we've noted whether a court or state legislature has expressly allowed or prohibited the doubling of exemptions. If the chart doesn't say one way or the other, it is probably safe to double the exemption. However, keep in mind that this area of the law is subject to change—and legislation or court decisions issued after the publication date of this book will not be reflected in the chart. (See Ch. 12 for information on doing your own legal research. The Nolo website helps you do this at www.nolo.com/legal-research/state-law.html; you can also find the latest exemption laws at www.legalconsumer.com.)

Applying Exemptions to Your Property

The Personal Property Checklist and Property Exemption Worksheet will help you inventory all of the personal property you own and figure out whether you will get to keep it if you file for bankruptcy. You also can use this information to complete the official forms that accompany your bankruptcy petition, if you do decide to file for bankruptcy.

Inventory Your Property

If you file for bankruptcy, you will have to list all property that belongs in your bankruptcy estate. Whether or not you can hold on to that property, or at least some of the property's value in dollar terms, depends on what the property is worth and which exemptions are available to you. The best way to start figuring out what you'll be able to keep—and get a jump on your filing paperwork—is to create an inventory (list) of your property.

Use the Personal Property Checklist shown below—you can find a blank, tear-out copy in Appendix B—to create an inventory of your possessions. Place a checkmark in the box next to each item you own. If you are married and filing jointly, list all property owned by you and your spouse.

As you'll see, there are a number of boxes to check for business property, such as customer lists, fixtures, accounts receivable, and so on. You should check these boxes only if you own this property as a sole proprietor or an individual. If your corporation or LLC actually owns the business property, leave these boxes blank, and instead check the box "Stocks and interests in incorporated and unincorporated companies."

Personal Property Checklist

Cash on hand (include sources)

- ☐ In your home
- ☐ In your wallet
- ☐ Under your mattress

Deposits of money (include sources)

- ☐ Bank account
- ☐ Brokerage account (with stockbroker)
- ☐ Certificates of deposit (CDs)
- ☐ Credit union deposit
- ☐ Escrow account
- ☐ Money market account
- ☐ Money in a safe deposit box
- ☐ Savings and loan deposit

Security deposits

- ☐ Electric
- ☐ Gas
- ☐ Heating oil
- ☐ Security deposit on a rental unit
- ☐ Prepaid rent
- ☐ Rented furniture or equipment
- ☐ Telephone
- ☐ Water

Household goods, supplies, and furnishings

- ☐ Antiques
- ☐ Appliances
- ☐ Carpentry tools
- ☐ China and crystal
- ☐ Clocks
- ☐ Dishes
- ☐ Food (total value)
- ☐ Furniture (list every item; go from room to room so you don't miss anything)
- ☐ Gardening tools
- ☐ Home computer (for personal use)
- ☐ Iron and ironing board
- ☐ Lamps
- ☐ Lawn mower or tractor
- ☐ Microwave oven
- ☐ Patio or outdoor furniture
- ☐ Radios
- ☐ Rugs
- ☐ Sewing machine
- ☐ Silverware and utensils
- ☐ Small appliances
- ☐ Snow blower
- ☐ Stereo system
- ☐ Telephone and answering machines
- ☐ Televisions
- ☐ Vacuum cleaner
- ☐ Video equipment (VCR, camcorder)

Books, pictures, and other art objects; stamp, coin, and other collections

- ☐ Art prints
- ☐ Bibles
- ☐ Books
- ☐ Coins
- ☐ Collectibles (such as political buttons, baseball cards)
- ☐ Family portraits
- ☐ Figurines
- ☐ Original artworks
- ☐ Photographs
- ☐ Records, CDs, audiotapes
- ☐ Stamps
- ☐ Videotapes

Apparel

- ☐ Clothing
- ☐ Furs

Jewelry

- ☐ Engagement and wedding rings
- ☐ Gems
- ☐ Precious metals
- ☐ Watches

Firearms, sports equipment, and other hobby equipment

- ☐ Board games
- ☐ Bicycle
- ☐ Camera equipment
- ☐ Electronic musical equipment
- ☐ Exercise machine
- ☐ Fishing gear
- ☐ Guns (rifles, pistols, shotguns, muskets)
- ☐ Model or remote-controlled cars or planes
- ☐ Musical instruments
- ☐ Scuba diving equipment
- ☐ Ski equipment
- ☐ Other sports equipment
- ☐ Other weapons (swords and knives)

Interests in insurance policies

- ☐ Credit insurance
- ☐ Disability insurance
- ☐ Health insurance
- ☐ Homeowners' or renters' insurance
- ☐ Term life insurance
- ☐ Whole life insurance

Annuities

Pension or profit-sharing plans

- ☐ IRA
- ☐ Keogh
- ☐ Pension or retirement plan
- ☐ 401(k) plan

Stock and interests in incorporated and unincorporated companies

- ☐ Corporate shares
- ☐ Stock options
- ☐ LLC membership
- ☐ Sole proprietorship business

Interests in partnerships

- ☐ Limited partnership interest
- ☐ General partnership interest

Government and corporate bonds and other investment instruments

- ☐ Corporate bonds
- ☐ Municipal bonds
- ☐ Promissory notes
- ☐ U.S. savings bonds

Accounts receivable

- ☐ Accounts receivable from business
- ☐ Commissions already earned

Family support

- ☐ Alimony (spousal support, maintenance) due under court order
- ☐ Child support payments due under court order
- ☐ Payments due under divorce property settlement

Other debts for which the amount owed you is known and definite

- ☐ Disability benefits due
- ☐ Disability insurance due
- ☐ Judgments obtained against third parties you haven't yet collected
- ☐ Sick pay earned
- ☐ Social Security benefits due
- ☐ Tax refund due under returns already filed
- ☐ Vacation pay earned
- ☐ Wages due
- ☐ Workers' compensation due

Any special powers that you or another person can exercise for your benefit, other than those listed under "real estate"

- ☐ A right to receive, at some future time, cash, stock, or other personal property placed in an irrevocable trust
- ☐ Current payments of interest or principal from a trust
- ☐ General power of appointment over personal property

An interest in property due to another person's death

- ☐ Any interest as the beneficiary of a living trust, if the trustor has died
- ☐ Expected proceeds from a life insurance policy where the insured has died
- ☐ Inheritance from an existing estate in probate (the owner has died and the court is overseeing the distribution of the property), even if the final amount is not yet known

- ☐ Inheritance under a will that is contingent on one or more events occurring, but only if the owner has died

All other contingent claims and claims where the amount owed you is not known, including tax refunds, counterclaims, and rights to setoff claims (claims you think you have against a person, government, or corporation, but you haven't yet sued on)

- ☐ Claims against a corporation, government entity, or individual
- ☐ Potential tax refund on a return that is not yet filed

Patents, copyrights, and other intellectual property

- ☐ Copyrights
- ☐ Patents
- ☐ Trade secrets
- ☐ Trademarks
- ☐ Trade names

Licenses, franchises, and other general intangibles

- ☐ Building permits
- ☐ Business goodwill
- ☐ Cooperative association holdings
- ☐ Exclusive licenses
- ☐ Liquor licenses
- ☐ Nonexclusive licenses
- ☐ Patent licenses
- ☐ Professional licenses
- ☐ Customer lists

Automobiles and other vehicles

- ☐ Car
- ☐ Minibike or motor scooter
- ☐ Mobile or motor home if on wheels
- ☐ Motorcycle
- ☐ Recreational vehicle (RV)
- ☐ Trailer
- ☐ Truck
- ☐ Van

Boats, motors, and accessories

- ☐ Boat (canoe, kayak, rowboat, shell, sailboat, pontoon, yacht)
- ☐ Boat radar, radio, or telephone
- ☐ Outboard motor

Aircraft and accessories

- ☐ Aircraft
- ☐ Aircraft radar, radio, and other accessories

Office equipment, furnishings, and supplies

- ☐ Artwork in your office
- ☐ Computers, software, modems, printers
- ☐ Copier
- ☐ Fax machine
- ☐ Furniture
- ☐ Rugs
- ☐ Supplies
- ☐ Telephones
- ☐ Typewriters

Machinery, fixtures, equipment, and supplies used in business

- ☐ Equipment
- ☐ Fixtures
- ☐ Machinery
- ☐ Supplies
- ☐ Tools of your trade

Business inventory

Livestock, poultry, and other animals

- ☐ Birds
- ☐ Cats
- ☐ Dogs
- ☐ Fish and aquarium equipment
- ☐ Horses
- ☐ Other pets
- ☐ Livestock and poultry

Crops—growing or harvested

Farming equipment and implements

Farm supplies, chemicals, and feed

Other personal property of any kind not already listed

- ☐ Church pew
- ☐ Health aids (such as a wheelchair or crutches)
- ☐ Hot tub or portable spa
- ☐ Season tickets

Using the Property Exemption Worksheet

Now that you have a comprehensive list of your property, you can decide how to use the exemptions available to you to your best advantage. This will require you to come up with a value for each item, decide which exemption system to use (if you have a choice), then figure out how to apply those exemptions to your property.

To do this, use the Property Exemption Worksheet in Appendix B. A portion of the worksheet is set out below. As you can see, it includes four columns:

1. a description of the property
2. the property's replacement value
3. the exemption (if any) that applies to the property, and
4. the number of the statute where that exemption appears (you'll need this information when you complete your bankruptcy forms).

Complete each of these columns following the instructions below.

Column 1: Property Description

Using your completed checklist as a guide, describe each item of property and its location. For personal property, identify the item (for example, 1994 Ford Mustang) and its location (for example, residence). For cash on hand and deposits of money, indicate the source of each, such as wages or salary, insurance policy proceeds, or the proceeds from selling an item of property. Although cash on hand is usually not exempt, you may be able to exempt all or some of it if you can show that it came from an exempt source, such as unemployment insurance.

Column 2: Replacement Value

Enter the replacement value of each item of property in Column 1. (Under the former rules, filers used the market value—what they could get for the property if they sold it at their own garage sale. The 2005 bankruptcy law requires filers to use the replacement value, which is typically a higher figure.)

TIP

Trustees are often more interested in what the property would fetch at auction. You are supposed to use the replacement value of property in your bankruptcy papers. However, the trustee will be more interested in how much money could be made from selling the property, often at auction at an extreme discount. For example, a car with a replacement value of $10,000 might sell for $6,000 at auction, and the trustee might let you keep it if you can come up with about $3,000 in cash. Why? Because the trustee would have to take the car, store it, get permission from the judge to

Property Exemption Worksheet

1 Property	2 Replacement Value	3 Exemption	4 Statute No.
1. Cash on hand			
______	______	______	______
______	______	______	______
______	______	______	______
______	______	______	______
2. Checking/savings account, certificate of deposit, other bank accounts			

sell it, and then sell it, typically for less than it's worth. To save these costs, most trustees will be willing to take significantly less than the replacement value—and even less than the property would sell for at auction—and let you keep the property. Be aware, however, that some trustees are more inclined to squeeze every last dollar out of a debtor's property; if your case is assigned to one of them, you shouldn't count on keeping property that isn't fully exempt (or close to it).

It's easy to enter a dollar amount for cash, bank deposits, bonds, and most investment instruments. For items that are tougher to value, such as business equipment, machinery, inventory, an ownership interest in an LLC or a corporation, insurance, annuities, and pensions, you may need to get an appraisal from someone who has some financial expertise.

For your other property, estimate its replacement value—that is, what you could buy it for from a retail vendor, considering its age and condition. As long as you have a reasonable basis for your estimates, the lower the value you place on property, the more of it you will be allowed to keep. But be honest when assigning values. Trustees have years of experience and a pretty good sense of what property is worth. It's okay to be wrong as long as you have an arguable basis for the value you list and briefly explain any uncertainties. If you can't come up with a replacement value, leave this column blank. If you file for bankruptcy, you can simply indicate that the value is unknown. If the trustee is concerned about the value, you will be asked at your creditors' meeting to provide more detail.

Putting a value on personal property can be a difficult task. Here are some tips for valuing specific items.

Tangible property. If the property you are trying to value can be readily purchased from a vendor on the open market, you can use what you'd have to pay for it. You can visit local stores to get a price; for instance, many areas have used appliance stores, and used furniture can readily be purchased from the Salvation Army or Goodwill. But where do you go for a used laptop computer, lathe, or mechanics tools? These days, your best bet for valuing property may be Google, Craigslist or eBay on the Internet. If you can't find it there, you'll have to value your property by estimating what it would sell for in a local flea market or classified section of a newspaper, online or off.

Small businesses typically have property that can readily be valued. For retail or manufacturing businesses, for example, you may have inventory that could easily be liquidated on the open market. Here are some examples of other business assets you might need to list:

- business equipment, such as computers, phones, cash registers, credit card machines
- inventory, components, and materials
- office furniture, art, and supplies
- vehicles and tools
- real estate
- security deposits with landlords, utilities, or taxing agencies, and
- prepaid insurance premiums you can get refunded to you.

As a general rule, tangible business assets are fairly easy to value. You can use eBay, craigslist, or bid4assets.com to find prices for comparable items. There also may be specialized auction sites for your industry that you could consult.

Intangible business property. In addition to tangible property, your business may own intangible property you should record on your Property Exemption Worksheet, such as:

- accounts receivable (see below)
- works in progress that could have some value
- your customer list and your company name (essentially, the goodwill your company has built up—see below)
- intellectual property such as copyrights, patents, and trademarks (see below)
- a commercial lease at below-market rent and/or at a good location
- contracts with suppliers at below-market rates, and
- contracts with customers at profitable rates.

Accounts receivable. The value of accounts receivable depends on whether they are current or past due, so you shouldn't just list their face value. A current account receivable (one that fell due within the last 30 days) is worth much more than a 90-day past due account that you've already tried to collect with no results. The most common method to estimate the collectability of receivables is to use an aging schedule. In a typical aging schedule, accounts receivable are divided into categories of current, 31-60 days, 61-90 days, and over 90 days past due. But it will be up to you to estimate how collectible your accounts receivable are based on your past collection experiences. For instance, you might estimate that 90% of your current accounts receivable will be paid, 70% of those between 31 and 60 days, 50% of those between 61 and 90 days, and 40% of those over 90 days. You would then multiply the amount of accounts receivable in each category by these percentages to come up with a value for the accounts receivable in each category, and then total them up for the total value of your accounts receivable.

Sample Aging Schedule

Category	Amount	Percentage Collectible	Discounted Amount
<30 days	$50,000	90%	$45,000
31-60 days	$40,000	70%	$28,000
60-90 days	$30,000	50%	$15,000
over 90 days	$40,000	40%	$16,000
Total	$160,000		$104,000

Goodwill. Goodwill represents how customers feel about your business, as evidenced by the business's history of customer recognition and patronage. For example, if Joe's Liquor has been doing business on the corner of 5th and Main in Whoseville for 25 years, the store's "goodwill" may be worth many thousands of dollars because of the number of customers who have patronized it over the years. However, most small businesses that are newer or don't have a widely recognized name do not have goodwill worth a significant amount. The value of goodwill is what's left when you subtract all property, accounts receivable, and intangible assets such as intellectual property, from the value of the business. If you think your business has enough goodwill that someone would want to buy your business name or your customer list, you may need to contact an expert in business valuations—a business appraiser—who can determine how much this intangible aspect of your business might be worth. (See "Finding a Business Appraiser," below.) Appraisers are expensive, however, so it might be best to wait and let the trustee decide on what the value of the company's goodwill might be.

Finding a Business Appraiser

Anyone can value a business—generally, there are no licensing requirements for business appraisers. However, we suggest hiring an independent appraiser with professional credentials. While many appraisers are also certified public accountants, the American Society of Appraisers (a widely respected private accreditation group) uses these designations:

- AM (Accredited Member): requires two years of full-time appraisal experience
- ASA (Accredited Senior Appraiser): requires five years of full-time appraisal experience
- FASA (Fellow Appraiser): an Accredited Senior Appraiser who has been recognized by ASA's International Board of Governors for outstanding services to the appraisal profession and/or the Society of Appraisers.

Another group, which accredits appraisers of closely held businesses according to education and experience qualifications, is the Institute of Business Appraisers—see its website at www.go-iba.org.

Intellectual property. Your business may have valuable intellectual property, such as trademarks, patents, trade secrets, and copyrights. For example, assume Valerie is half-owner of a start-up LLC that manufactures solar-powered eyeglasses with mini windshield wipers, for use in snowy climates. Valerie's company might own a patent in its eyeglass wiper design, a valuable and unique trademark under which to market the eyeglasses (Vision Wipes), a trade secret involving its innovative manufacturing techniques, and maybe even a copyright in pamphlets explaining the care and use of the product.

Valuing intellectual property is often difficult in bankruptcy because its value lies in its potential to yield future profits, not as a present source of cash that the trustee can use to pay off your creditors. However, the trustee may shop your company's intellectual property around to appropriate businesses (perhaps your competitors) to see whether there are any takers. Copyrights owned by small businesses, by themselves, are often essentially worthless.

RESOURCE

Need more information on intellectual property? Pick up a copy of *Patent, Copyright and Trademark,* by Richard Stim (Nolo), a desk reference that includes all you need to know about these important business assets.

Ownership of business entities. If you are sole or part owner of a limited liability company (LLC), corporation, or partnership, you'll need to know the value of your ownership interest to figure out whether you can protect it with the exemptions available to you.

Ownership shares in small business entities are notoriously hard to value. Of course, if a corporation's stock is trading on an exchange, you can use that value. But small, private corporations and LLCs pose a much tougher valuation problem. Unless the board or management is in the practice of deciding on a value for the company on a routine basis, some guesswork will have to take place. For one thing, unlike publicly traded corporations, there is no public market for small business interests, so it's hard to establish comparative prices for similar businesses, particularly when a business is floundering. For example, assume Valerie's LLC is roughly $50,000 in the red and isn't expected to make much money over the next several years. What is the LLC worth? Possibly not much, but if the LLC showed promise of making a decent profit in the future, the ownership interest might be worth a considerable sum, and the trustee could market the ownership interest to interested members of the public, competitors, or co-owners.

One way to put a value on a business (which you can use to come up with a value for a partial ownership interest) is to find out how much similar businesses are selling for. But, depending on the competitive pressures in your industry, the economy, the financial wellbeing of your business, plus other factors, the value of your company could be more or less than what a similar business sold for.

Another way to value a business is by using a formula such as assets minus liabilities (that is, the current fair market value of the company's assets minus the company's liabilities) or a capitalization of earnings method (the company's average annual earnings multiplied by a certain number of years). If the ownership interest is likely to be worth a significant amount of money, you may want to consult with an appraiser to put a value on the company; see "Finding a Business Appraiser," above."

If you own a minority share of the business, however, there may be no market for your ownership interest—that is, no one may want to buy it, assuming the other owners aren't in the market to sell the business. It's often impossible to find an interested buyer for a minority interest in a company. After all, a minority share gives an owner little or no control over how the business is run and no guarantee of profits. Because of this, the IRS allows a valuation discount of 20–40% to be applied to the value of minority interests because of their lack of marketability. And if there are restrictions on whether you can sell your minority interest, the ownership interest might even be worth 30–60% less than an unrestricted, majority interest in the company. (A restriction on freely selling your ownership interest to an outsider is called a buy-sell restriction or transfer restriction—look at your corporate bylaws or LLC operating agreement to see if you are subject to one.)

As a general rule, you'll be better off with a low value for your shares of a business entity (and your other property). A lower value makes it more likely that you'll be able to protect your shares with an exemption. Even if your shares aren't exempt, a lower value means the trustee will be less likely to try to sell your shares: The time and expense of selling will probably outweigh whatever the trustee will be able to get for them.

Cars. Unfortunately, the replacement value requirement doesn't exactly square with the way car values are determined by the *Kelley Blue Book*, the most common source for car prices. To be absolutely safe in your estimate, use the average retail price for your car (based on its mileage), listed at the website of the National Automobile Dealers Association, www.nada.com. If your car is inoperable or in poor condition (with obvious and significant body damage or serious mechanical problems), you can reasonably list whatever you could sell it for on the open market. Because such cars are not sold by car dealers, there's no way to figure out what a retail merchant would charge for such a car.

Life insurance. If you have a whole life insurance policy, list the current cash surrender value of the policy (call your insurance agent to find out what it is). Term life insurance has a cash surrender value of zero. Don't list how much the policy will pay, unless you're the beneficiary of an insurance policy and the insured person has died.

Jewelry, antiques, and other collectibles. Any valuable jewelry or collections should be appraised prior to filing for bankruptcy. You don't want to learn—only after filing for bankruptcy—that your jewelry or other treasured property is worth much more than you thought, and will therefore be taken and sold by the trustee.

TIP

Ignore liens against your personal property when computing the property's value. If you owe money to a major consumer lender (such as Beneficial Finance), the lender may have a lien on some or all of your personal property. You can ignore this lien when calculating the item's replacement value because you can often remove this lien in the course of your bankruptcy. Similarly, there may be a lien against your personal property if a creditor has obtained a court judgment against you. These liens, too, can frequently be removed. See Ch. 8 to find out more about personal property liens and your options for dealing with them.

Columns 3 and 4: Exemptions

You can find every state's exemptions in Appendix A. If the state exemption system you're using allows you to choose the federal exemptions instead of your state's exemptions, you can find these listed directly after Wyoming.

TIP

Focus on the property you really want to keep. If you have a lot of property and are afraid of getting bogged down in exemption jargon and dollar signs, start with the property you would feel really bad about losing. After that, if you are so inclined, you can search for exemptions that would let you keep property that is less important to you.

If Only One Set of Exemptions Is Available to You

Many filers won't have a choice of exemptions: Only one set of exemptions will be available. For example, you must use your state's exemptions (subject to the domicile rules discussed above) unless you are subject to the exemption rules for a state that allows you to choose the federal exemptions (Arkansas, Connecticut, D.C., Hawaii, Kentucky, Massachusetts, Michigan, Minnesota, New Hampshire, New Jersey, New Mexico, Pennsylvania, Rhode Island, Texas, Vermont, Washington, or Wisconsin). Similarly, if the domicile requirements leave you with no available state exemptions, you must use the federal exemption list; you don't have a choice of exemptions.

If you have only one set of exemptions to consider, follow these steps:

Step 1: In Column 3, list the amount of the exemption or write "no limit" if the exemption is unlimited. In Column 4, list the number of the statute identified in Appendix A for the exemption that may reasonably be applied to that item. If you need more information or an explanation of terms, check the notes at the beginning of Appendix A and the glossary. In evaluating whether your cash and deposits are exempt, look to the source of the money, such as welfare benefits, insurance proceeds, or wages.

TIP

Err on the side of exemption. If you can think of a reason why a particular item might be exempt, list it even if you aren't sure that the exemption applies. If you file for Chapter 7 bankruptcy, you will only be expected to do your best to fit the exemptions to your property. Of course, if you do misapply an exemption and the bankruptcy trustee or a creditor files a formal objection within the required time, you may have to scramble to keep the property that you mistakenly thought was exempt. If you have property that you would hate to lose but you aren't sure whether it fits within an exemption, pay for a consultation with a bankruptcy attorney on the issue. (See Ch. 12 for more on bankruptcy attorneys.)

Step 2: If a particular exemption has no dollar limit, then apply that exemption to all property items that seem to fall into that category. For example, if you can exempt all household furnishings without limit, list all furniture, appliances, home theater and stereo equipment, tableware, linens, rugs, and so on in this category. If there is a limit (for instance, an exemption allows you to keep up to $1,000 worth of electronic products), total the value of all property items you wish to claim under that exemption. Then compare the total with the exemption limit. If the total is less than the limit, then there is no problem. However, if the total is more than the limit, you may have to either give the trustee enough property to bring your total back under the limit or apply a wildcard exemption to the extra property, if the system you are using has one. The trustee may not be interested in used furniture or other items that will fetch little or nothing at an auction, even if the replacement value is officially higher than the exemption limit. In these instances, the trustee will simply "abandon" the property, which means you can keep it even if it doesn't fit entirely within the exemption.

If You Have a Choice of Exemption Systems

If the state system you're using allows you to use the federal exemptions or you qualify to use the California exemptions (which give you a choice between two state systems), you'll need to decide which exemption system to use. You can't use some exemptions from one system and some from the other. If you own a home in which you have equity, your choice will often be dictated by which system gives you the most protection for that equity. In California, for example, the homestead exemption in System 1 protects from $75,000 to $175,000 in equity (depending on factors such as age, income, and disability), while the System 2 list protects only $21,825 (including the $1,100 wildcard). While System 1 used to be the system of choice for California homeowners, that's not necessarily the case since home values have declined so sharply.

Unless your choice of exemption lists is dictated by your home equity, you'll be best served by going through the Property Exemption Worksheet twice. The first time through, use the state exemptions (or System 1 in California). The second time, use the federal exemptions (or System 2 in California).

After you apply both exemption lists to your property, compare the results and decide which exemption list will do you the most good. You may find that one set of exemptions is more generous or better protects the property you really want to keep. You may be sorely tempted to pluck some exemptions out of one list and add them to the other list. Again, this can't be done. You'll either have to use your state's exemption list or the federal exemptions—you can't mix and match.

EXAMPLE: Paula Willmore lives in Detroit, Michigan, and runs a storefront computer repair shop. Business has been dwindling over the last two years. Paula decides she can't continue to lose money and float the business with her personal credit cards, so she closes her doors. Deep in personal debt, Paula files for Chapter 7 personal bankruptcy. Other than clothing, household furniture, and personal effects, Paula owns several computers, accessories (such as scanners and zip drives), and some inventory (computer parts, spare hard drives, and so on). Paula often reads computer magazines and knows that her computers and parts are worth about $12,000, total. Paula wants to know if she will lose her property.

Because Paula has lived in Michigan for more than two years, she will use that state's exemption rules. Her first step is to locate the exemptions for Michigan in Appendix A. Near the bottom of the Michigan exemption listings for personal property, Paula finds an entry for computers and accessories and sees that the exemption is $575. Paula begins to worry that she may lose her computers, which she'd like to keep in the hopes that she can continue to work with computers on a freelance basis from home.

Paula's next step is to search the Michigan state exemptions for a tools of trade exemption. Paula discovers that she has a $2,300 tools of trade exemption that she can apply to tools, materials, and other property. Paula next looks for a wildcard exemption, but Michigan doesn't offer one. Add the tools of trade exemption to the $575 computer exemption, and Paula can now exempt $2,875. This doesn't begin to cover the value of her computer equipment, which means that if Paula uses the Michigan state exemptions the trustee would probably sell the equipment, give Paula her $2,875 exemption, and distribute the rest of the sales proceeds to Paula's unsecured creditors.

Paula next checks to see whether Michigan allows debtors to use the federal bankruptcy exemptions. She looks at the top of the exemption page and sees a note that the federal bankruptcy exemptions are available to Michigan filers. Hoping that the federal exemptions will give her a higher exemption limit for her computer equipment, she turns to the end of Appendix A (right after Wyoming) and finds the federal bankruptcy exemption list. Under personal property she sees household goods to $525 per item. Even if computers fall into this category (they usually don't if they're used for business purposes), it's still not enough to do her much good. She next notes a tools of trade exemption for $2,025, which won't cover much of her equipment. Paula then examines the federal bankruptcy exemptions to see whether they provide a wildcard exemption. She discovers that the federal bankruptcy exemptions let you use up to $10,125 of the homestead exemption as a wildcard. Because Paula has no home equity to protect, she can apply the wildcard to the computer equipment, in addition to the tools of trade exemption for $2,025. Further, Paula sees that she can get an additional wildcard exemption of $1,075 under the federal exemption list. Putting these exemptions together, Paula sees she can exempt up to $13,225 of property—more than the value of her computer equipment.

Because the federal bankruptcy exemptions let Paula keep all of her computer equipment while the state exemptions don't, Paula decides to use the federal bankruptcy exemption list.

Five Steps to Applying Exemptions to Property

1. Check the exemptions you are using for specific items you want to keep.
2. If the exemptions don't cover the property you want to keep (either because they don't exempt that property at all or because they exempt less than your property is worth), look for a wildcard exemption in the list.
3. If you have a choice of exemption systems, check the other list for an exemption that covers your property.
4. If the federal bankruptcy exemptions are available to you but don't seem to cover your property specifically, see whether the federal bankruptcy wildcard exemption will work.
5. If you have the choice of two exemption systems, decide which exemption list you want to use. Don't mix and match. (In California, if you own your home and have more than $20,000 in equity, you'll likely want to use System 1. If you don't own a home, System 2 will often be a better choice.)

TIP 1

Double your exemptions if you're married and filing for bankruptcy jointly, unless the state exemption list in Appendix A says that doubling isn't allowed. If you're using the federal bankruptcy exemptions, you may double all exemptions.

TIP 2

While you're figuring out which of your property is exempt, write down in Column 4 the numbers of the statutes that authorize each exemption. (You can find these in Appendix A.) You will need this information when you fill out Schedule C of your bankruptcy papers.

Using Federal Nonbankruptcy Exemptions

If you are using state exemptions, you are also entitled to use a handful of exemptions called "federal nonbankruptcy exemptions." As the name suggests, these exemptions are generally used in cases other than bankruptcies, but you can also use them in a bankruptcy case. (In California, they are available only if you're using System 1.)

Skim the list at the end of Appendix A to see whether any of these exemptions would help you. If they would, you can use them in addition to the state exemptions. If they duplicate each other, though, you cannot add them together for any one category. For example, if both your state and the federal nonbankruptcy exemptions let you exempt 75% of disposable weekly earnings, you cannot combine the exemptions to keep all of your wages—75% is all you get.

Selling Nonexempt Property Before You File

If you want to reduce the amount of nonexempt property you own before you file for bankruptcy, you might consider selling it and using the proceeds to buy exempt property. Or you might want to use the proceeds to pay certain types of debts.

But be careful: If the trustee learns that you sold the nonexempt property and bought exempt property with the proceeds, and he or she believes that you did so in order to defraud a creditor, your efforts to shelter that value may fail. The court may find that you made a fraudulent transfer (as explained in Ch. 5), and decide to treat any exempt property you purchase as nonexempt property, which may be taken and sold. And, if the court believes you made a fraudulent transfer within the past year, your entire bankruptcy discharge may be at risk.

CAUTION

Talk to a lawyer first. Before you sell nonexempt property, consult a bankruptcy attorney. Your local bankruptcy court may automatically assume that these kinds of transfers are attempts to defraud a creditor. The only sure way to find out what is and isn't permissible in your area is to ask an attorney familiar with local bankruptcy court practices. A consultation on this sort of issue should not run more than $100 and is well worth the cost if it will help you hold on to more property.

Replacing Nonexempt Property With Exempt Property

Depending on the practices in your local bankruptcy court, there may be several ways to turn your nonexempt property into exempt property. Keep in mind, however, that selling property for substantially less than it's worth will look like a fraudulent transaction to the trustee. If you sell nonexempt property, make sure you get as close to full value for it as possible.

You might be able to:

- Sell a nonexempt asset and use the proceeds to buy an asset that is completely exempt. For example, you can sell business equipment that isn't exempt in your state (such as a printer, lathe, drill, or press), and purchase clothing, which in most states is exempt, with no dollar limit.
- Sell a nonexempt asset and use the proceeds to buy an asset that is exempt up to the amount received in the sale. For example, you can sell a nonexempt table saw worth $1,200 and purchase a computer that is exempt up to $1,200 in value.
- Sell an asset that is only partially exempt and use the proceeds to replace it with a similar asset of lesser value. For example, if a television is exempt up to a value of $200, you could sell your $500 television and buy a workable secondhand one for $200, putting the remaining cash into other exempt assets such as clothing or appliances.
- Use cash (which isn't exempt in many states) to buy an exempt item, such as furniture, work tools, or a commercial vehicle.

Paying Debts With Proceeds From Nonexempt Property

You might choose to reduce your nonexempt property by selling it and using the proceeds to pay debts. For example, you could use the money to pay off debts that wouldn't be discharged in bankruptcy, such as back child support, recent tax debts, or student loans. If you are considering this strategy, however, keep the following points in mind:

- **It's usually unwise to pay off a debt that could be discharged in bankruptcy.** Many debts (such as credit card bills) can be completely discharged in bankruptcy. The only reason you should consider paying a dischargeable debt is when a relative or friend is a cosigner, so that the friend or relative is not stuck paying the whole debt after your liability for the debt is discharged in bankruptcy. Also, you might want to pay off a small credit card balance in order to keep the card out of your bankruptcy (you don't have to list it if you don't owe anything on it), so that you can continue to use it.
- **If you pay a creditor more than $600, you may want to wait to file for bankruptcy.** You should wait at least 90 days before you file for bankruptcy if the total payments to any one regular creditor (not a relative, associate, or friend) during that period exceed $600. The $600 limit applies only if you owe primarily consumer debts; if you owe primarily business debts or taxes, you can pay a creditor up to $5,475 during the 90-day prefiling period without it being considered a preference. (See Ch. 2 for more on making this business versus consumer

decision.) Payments over these limits may be considered a preference, and the trustee may be able to get the money back and add it to your bankruptcy estate. (See Ch. 5 for more on preference payments.) If the creditor you pay is a relative, close friend, or company in which you are an officer, you should wait at least one year before filing, rather than just 90 days.

- **You can pay regular bills.** You can pay regular monthly bills right up until you file for bankruptcy. So you can keep paying your utilities and mortgage or rent with the proceeds you make from selling nonexempt property.
- **Think twice before paying secured debts.** If you want to use the proceeds from nonexempt property to pay off a debt secured by collateral, read Ch. 8 first. If the collateral for the debt isn't exempt, paying off the debt won't do you much good because the trustee will take the collateral when you file for bankruptcy. If you have equity in the collateral that you can exempt, you will be able to keep it even if you don't pay off the debt before filing for bankruptcy.

  EXAMPLE: John owes $5,000 on the 2004 Toyota utility truck he used in his plumbing business. The truck is worth $4,000. John sells some nonexempt musical equipment for $5,000, pays off the $5,000 truck loan, and files for bankruptcy. It turns out that John can exempt only $1,000 in the motor vehicle. The trustee orders John to turn over the truck, which John does. The trustee sells the truck and gives John his $1,000 exemption amount. Not only did John lose his truck, but he also no longer has his musical equipment or $4,000 of the money he earned by selling it.

  A better alternative: Because John owes more on the truck than it's worth, he could hold on to it through bankruptcy, making regular payments on the loan. The trustee would not take the truck to sell it, because there would be no money left for unsecured creditors if the truck were sold with $5,000 in debt still hanging over it. And John might be able to hold on to the musical equipment by paying a small price to the trustee.

You Can Pay Favored Creditors After You File

You may be tempted to leave certain creditors off your bankruptcy papers, perhaps because the creditor is a relative or a provider of services that are important to you personally (a veterinarian or doctor, for example) or in your business (such as a major supplier or vendor), and you want to pay that person or business off rather than having the debt discharged in bankruptcy. Unfortunately, bankruptcy requires that all creditors be identified on the appropriate schedules. However, you can still pay a debt that has been (or will be) wiped out in bankruptcy, as long as you wait until after you file and don't use property of the estate. For instance, if you file for bankruptcy on March 12, 2011, you can use income you earn on March 13 and afterwards to pay the creditor, because that income is not part of your bankruptcy estate. One last point: While you are free to pay off a discharged debt, the creditor is not permitted to hound you for it.

CAUTION

If you own your home. If you own your home and plan to claim a homestead exemption to protect your home equity (see Ch. 7), your exemption can be reduced, dollar for dollar, by the value of nonexempt property you converted if (1) the conversion took place in the ten years before you filed for bankruptcy, and (2) you converted the property to defraud your creditors. (Homestead exemptions, including these conversion rules, are covered in detail in Ch. 7.) Because the amount of your homestead exemption often determines whether or not you can keep your home, you should definitely not try to convert nonexempt property without first talking to a lawyer who knows how your local bankruptcy court handles this issue.

Six Guidelines for Prebankruptcy Planning

Here are six important guidelines for staying out of trouble when you're making these kinds of prebankruptcy transactions.

1. **Don't convert nonexempt property if you have equity in your home.** As noted above, you risk losing some or all of your homestead exemption if you engage in this type of planning. Our advice is not to do it until you talk to a lawyer.
2. **Accurately report all your transactions** on Form 7, the Statement of Financial Affairs. (See Ch. 9 for more on completing the official bankruptcy forms.) If the subject comes up with the trustee, creditors, or the court, freely admit that you tried to arrange your property holdings before filing for bankruptcy so that you could better get a fresh start. Courts see frankness like this as a sign of honorable intentions. If you lie or attempt to conceal what you did or why you did it, the bankruptcy trustee or court may conclude that you had fraudulent intentions and either not allow the transaction or—even worse—deny you a bankruptcy discharge.
3. **Sell and buy for equivalent value.** If you sell a $2,000 nonexempt item and purchase an exempt item obviously worth $2,000, you shouldn't have a problem. If, however, you sell a $2,000 nonexempt item and purchase a $400 exempt item, be prepared to account for the $1,600 difference. Otherwise, the court will probably assume that you're trying to cheat your creditors and either force you to cough up the $1,600 (if you still have it) or, possibly, dismiss your bankruptcy case.
4. **Sell and buy property at reasonable prices.** When you sell nonexempt property in order to purchase exempt property, charge an amount as close to the item's market value as possible. This is especially true if you sell to a friend or relative. If you sell your brother a $900 stereo system for $100, a creditor or the trustee may cry foul, and the judge may agree. At the other end of the transaction, if you pay a friend or relative significantly more for exempt property than it is apparently worth, the court may suspect that you're just trying to transfer your assets to relatives to avoid creditors.
5. **Don't make last-minute transfers or purchases.** The longer you can wait to file for bankruptcy after making these kinds of property transfers, the less likely the judge is to disapprove. For example, judges frequently rule that a hasty transaction on the eve of filing shows an intent to cheat creditors. The open, deliberate, and advance planning of property sales and purchases, however, is usually considered evidence that you didn't intend to defraud. But even this isn't foolproof. One court ruled that the debtor's deliberate planning more than a year before filing was evidence of intent to cheat creditors. This conflict reinforces our earlier warning: You must find out your bankruptcy court's approach before you sell nonexempt property.
6. **Don't just change the form of property ownership.** Simply changing the way property is held from a nonexempt form to an exempt form is usually considered fraudulent.

    EXAMPLE: Although he's married, Jeff owns a house as his separate property. Also, Jeff incurred virtually all of his debts alone, so he plans to file for bankruptcy alone. In Jeff's state, the homestead exemption is only $7,500, but Jeff's equity in his home is nearly $30,000. Jeff finds out that his state also exempts property held as tenancy by the entirety, so Jeff transfers ownership of the house to himself and his wife as tenants by the entirety.

That would normally exempt the house from all debts Jeff incurred separately. But because Jeff merely changed the form of property ownership, rather than buying exempt property or paying off debts to give himself a fresh start, the bankruptcy court would probably find the transfer fraudulent and take Jeff's house. (Jeff might get $7,500 from the sale for his homestead exemption amount, but not necessarily.)

CAUTION

Community property warning. As mentioned earlier, if you're married and live in a community property state (Alaska, Arizona, California, Idaho, Louisiana, Nevada, New Mexico, Texas, Washington, or Wisconsin), the trustee can usually take both your share of community property and your spouse's, even if your spouse doesn't file for bankruptcy. But if you're tempted to change all or a portion of the community property into your spouse's separate property, beware: Creditors or the trustee are apt to cry fraud, and the trustee is likely to take the property anyway.

To give you an idea of what judges consider improper behavior shortly before filing for bankruptcy, here are some transactions that courts have found to be fraudulent:

A debtor bought goods on credit but never paid for them. He then sold those goods and bought property that he tried to exempt.

A debtor with nonexempt property was forced into involuntary bankruptcy by a creditor. The debtor convinced the creditor to drop the forced bankruptcy. Then the debtor sold the nonexempt property, purchased exempt property, and filed for Chapter 7 bankruptcy.

- A debtor sold nonexempt property that was worth enough to pay off all her debts (but didn't pay them off).
- A debtor sold nonexempt items for considerably less than they were worth.
- A debtor sold valuable property to a nonfiling spouse for one dollar.
- A debtor transferred nonexempt property the day after a creditor won a lawsuit against him, then filed for bankruptcy.
- A debtor in a state with an "unlimited" homestead exemption sold all of her nonexempt property and used the proceeds to pay off a large portion of her mortgage.
- A debtor bought a piano and harpsichord and a whole life insurance policy, all exempt in his state. He didn't play either instrument, and he had no dependents who needed insurance protection.

Taking Out Loans to Pay Nondischargeable Debts

Some people are tempted to borrow money to pay off debts that aren't dischargeable—for instance, a student loan—and then list the new loan as a dischargeable unsecured debt. Be careful if you do this. A court could consider your actions fraudulent and dismiss your bankruptcy. If the court doesn't dismiss your case, the creditor may ask the court to declare the debt nondischargeable. In short, if you take out the loan while you're broke and file for bankruptcy soon after, you probably will be penalized. And, if you borrow money or use your credit card to pay off a nondischargeable tax debt, you will not be able to discharge the loan or credit card charge in a Chapter 7 bankruptcy (although you could in a Chapter 13 bankruptcy).

CHAPTER

7

What Happens to Your Home

As a small business owner, you may have had to pledge your home as security (collateral) for a business debt or line of credit. Or, you may have had to put up other real estate you own, such as rental property or a vacation home. If you default on the business debt secured by the house—or if you stop making mortgage payments on the house—the lender can foreclose on the house. Chapter 7 bankruptcy can delay the foreclosure for a while, but ultimately, if you don't make the payments, you'll lose your house.

Even if you don't have a lender knocking at your door, you need to know how much equity you have in your house. If the equity is not protected by an exemption, the trustee can sell your house to pay debts to your unsecured creditors—your commercial landlord, suppliers, or vendors, for example. Fortunately, almost all states have a homestead exemption, which should protect at least some amount of equity in your house. This chapter explains how filing for Chapter 7 personal bankruptcy will affect your home or other real property, including how the homestead exemption works.

TIP

If your business "owns" your home. It's not uncommon for business owners to purchase or lease homes in the name of their business. This makes it harder for creditors to uncover home ownership (and put a lien on the home) if they win a money judgment. Also, people with damaged credit might get a better interest rate if their business is the purchaser. If your business owns your home, you are still considered the homeowner if your business is a sole proprietorship. Even if your business is an LLC or a corporation, the material in this chapter will apply if you have personally cosigned the mortgage. In this situation, you are on the hook personally to pay the mortgage, and you are entitled to use available homestead exemptions to keep your equity in the home.

If you have little or no equity in your home—that is, you owe about as much or more on your home than it is worth—you won't lose it to the bankruptcy trustee if you file for Chapter 7 personal bankruptcy. Once the mortgage and any other debts secured by your home were paid off, there wouldn't be anything left to give to your unsecured creditors (and no commission for the trustee). Because selling your home wouldn't generate any cash, your home won't be at risk because of your bankruptcy filing.

If you have substantial equity in your home that you can't protect with a homestead exemption, however, the trustee may take your home, sell it, pay off the mortgage and other debts secured by the home, give you your exempt amount, and distribute the rest of the sales proceeds to your unsecured creditors.

When You Need a Lawyer

If you have any concerns about keeping your home or other real estate, you should at least consult with a bankruptcy lawyer before filing for bankruptcy. The laws, procedures, and strategies discussed in this chapter can be complex and are subject to change as foreclosures escalate and real estate values fluctuate. A mistake in estimating your equity or applying a homestead exemption could cost you your home. And, your state's law may offer you rights and options that aren't covered here.

You should also consult with a bankruptcy lawyer if:

- you own two homes or you want to protect equity in a home that isn't your residence, or
- you are married, own a home with your spouse, and plan on filing for bankruptcy separately. Because the rules for how community property and "tenancy by the entirety" property are treated in bankruptcy can get complicated, it's a good idea to get some legal advice geared to your situation.

Whether you have some equity in your home or you are completely underwater (that is, you owe more than your home is worth), filing for Chapter 7 bankruptcy won't ultimately prevent a foreclosure on your property if you are behind on your payments. The automatic stay will put foreclosure proceedings on hold while your bankruptcy case is pending, but they will start up again once your bankruptcy is over—or sooner, if the mortgage holder convinces the court to lift the stay. The bottom line is, no matter how you decide to deal with your debts, you must keep making your payments if you want to keep your home for the long run.

Real Estate Other Than Your Home

As explained in this chapter, most exemption systems (including the federal exemption list) include a homestead exemption, which protects some or all of your equity in the home where you live. However, most exemption systems don't have a specific exemption that covers real estate you aren't using as a residence, such as a vacation home, commercial real estate, or rental property. You may be able to protect your equity in other real estate using a wildcard exemption (see Ch. 6). In some states, you may use any portion of your homestead exemption that you don't use for your home as a wildcard, which you could use to protect other real estate. For example, if you used the West Virginia $25,000 homestead exemption, and you had only $10,000 equity in your home, you could apply the remaining $15,000 of the homestead exemption to any other property, including other real estate.

How Bankruptcy Affects a Typical Homeowner

Most homeowners don't really "own" much of their home—a bank or other lender that has a mortgage or deed of trust on the home probably owns most of it. (Throughout this chapter, we use the term "mortgage" to include deeds of trust.) In addition, some homeowners have taken out a second mortgage or home equity loan. And some homes are encumbered by mechanics' liens, tax liens, or judgment liens.

What Happens to Your Mortgage(s)

Mortgages have two parts: a promissory note, which is your agreement to repay the debt, and a lien on the property, which gives the lender the right to foreclose on the property to get its money back. The promissory note will be wiped out when your bankruptcy case is over, unless you reaffirm it—that is, you tell the lender you want to keep the house and you enter into a new loan agreement with the lender, which will survive your bankruptcy. (See Ch. 8.) On the other hand, the lien on your home is not wiped out in bankruptcy. This means that you must keep making your payments or face foreclosure. Once the lien is paid off, you will own the home just as if you had been paying off the promissory note.

Sometimes, mortgage holders refuse to accept payments from a debtor who is in bankruptcy. If you tender your payments but the lender rejects them, create a separate bank account in which to deposit the payments each month—and be prepared to pay these funds to the lender whenever it agrees to start taking your money again. Why create a separate bank account? To make sure it's there when you need it. If you leave that money in your regular bank account, you may end up spending it on other things. For example, if your mortgage payment is $1,500 a month, and your bankruptcy lasts four months, you may be in hock for $6,000 by the time your bankruptcy ends and you have to bring your account current. That's a lot of money that you might be tempted to spend unless you lock it away in its own dedicated account.

Mortgage Modification and Reaffirmation

If you are interested in modifying your mortgage following bankruptcy (you usually may not modify during your bankruptcy case), you may need to reaffirm the promissory note. Unless you reaffirm, there will be no promissory note to modify. But reaffirming a mortgage can leave you with a huge debt that you'll still be responsible for after your bankruptcy, which often makes it a bad idea. Check with your bank or HUD-approved housing counselor (call 888-995-HOPE to find one) to see how bankruptcy may affect your mortgage modification efforts. The best approach is often to hold off filing for bankruptcy until your modification efforts are completed—whether successfully or not.

If you don't reaffirm your mortgage, your lender may allow you to keep making payments on the house under the old terms. The lender won't report your payments to the credit reporting agencies, which means your payments won't help you rebuild your credit. But it's a bad idea to reaffirm a mortgage solely to rehabilitate your credit: For the relatively small benefit of some positive credit history, you'll be obligating yourself to repay an enormous debt for years to come.

What Happens to Your Equity in Your Home

Even if you keep up with your mortgage payments, you may still lose your home unless a homestead exemption protects your equity. How do you measure your equity? If you were to sell your home today, without filing for bankruptcy, the proceeds from the sale would go first to the mortgage lender(s) to pay off the mortgage(s), then to any lien holders to pay off the liens, and finally to real estate agents to pay the costs of sale and to city or county governments to pay off any property taxes due. You would get to keep anything left over: your equity.

Second or Third Mortgages

These days, many people have second or third mortgages on their homes that are no longer secured by home equity, due to the recession.

EXAMPLE: A few years ago, Toni took out a mortgage and bought a house. As the property rose in value, Toni took out two additional mortgages (a second deed of trust and a home equity line of credit). Now, the house's value has declined from $300,000 to $150,000. Toni owes $175,000 on her first mortgage and $50,000 each on the second and third mortgages. When the house was worth $300,000, all of the mortgages ($275,000) were covered by the home's value. Any of the mortgage holders could have foreclosed on their lien if Toni defaulted. If the second or third mortgage holder tried to foreclose now, however, all the money from the sale would go to the first mortgage holder; the second and third mortgage holders would get nothing.

If your home's value has declined so much that a second or third mortgage holder no longer has any equity upon which to foreclose, and you discharge the underlying debt (the promissory note) in your bankruptcy, there will be no immediate consequence if you stop making payments on those mortgages. The mortgage holders can't hold you personally liable on the promissory note because it will have been discharged in your bankruptcy. And there's no reason for the holder to foreclose on the lien, because it wouldn't get any money from the foreclosure. If, however, your home later regains enough equity to cover the additional liens, those liens could become valuable again; they might once more be secured by your home, and could be enforced through foreclosure.

The moral of this story is pretty simple. If you have more than one mortgage and are having trouble keeping up with your house payments, default on the second and third mortgages first. The consequences are likely to be far less severe than if you default on your first mortgage.

If you file for bankruptcy and the trustee has your house sold to get at your equity, the creditors will get paid in pretty much the same order—mortgage holders, lien holders, real estate agents, and city and county governments—with one big difference. In a bankruptcy sale, whatever is left after the mortgages, liens, costs of sale, and taxes have been paid goes not to you, but to your unsecured creditors, unless a homestead exemption available to you entitles you to some or all of it.

The amount and availability of the homestead exemption varies widely by state. For example, in Texas, Florida, and a few other states (plus the District of Columbia), the dollar amount of the homestead exemption is unlimited: It protects your entire residence no matter how much it's worth (subject to acreage limits in some states). However, in many states, only $10,000 to $50,000 of your equity is exempt from creditors. In a few states, the homestead exemption is $5,000 or less, and in New Jersey and Pennsylvania, it's zero. Your state's homestead exemption amount is listed in Appendix A; in "Will You Lose Your Home In a Chapter 7 Bankruptcy?" below, we explain how to determine whether a homestead exemption will prevent the trustee from selling your home.

The amount of your equity in your home, and your ability to protect the equity with a homestead exemption, will determine whether or not you'll lose your home in bankruptcy. As a practical matter, the trustee won't bother to sell your home if there will be nothing left over for your unsecured creditors. On the other hand, if the bankruptcy trustee calculates that, after selling your home and applying the homestead exemption, there would be enough money left to give to your unsecured creditors, the trustee will probably take your home and sell it to get that money, unless you can somehow buy it back—that is, pay the trustee the amount that your unsecured creditors would get from the sale.

If Your Home Is Appreciating in Value

In most areas of the country, home values have declined significantly in the last few years. However, if you happen to live in an area where the prices are not declining but appreciating, even modestly, this question may arise: Who owns appreciation in the property's value after you file for bankruptcy, you or the trustee? Some courts have found that the value of that appreciation technically belongs to the trustee. (See *In re Farthing*, 340 B.R. 346 (D. Ariz. 2006); *In re Reed*, 940 F.2d 1317 (9th Cir. 1991).) If your bankruptcy court follows these cases, your equity may be protected by your state's homestead law when you file, but not be fully protected six months or a year after you file (if the trustee keeps your case open to see what happens). For example, assume the equity in your home is $100,000 and your state's homestead exemption is $100,000. In that case your entire equity is protected. But if, while your bankruptcy is still open, the home's value appreciates to $125,000, the trustee may be able to sell the home, give you your exemption, and pay the appreciated value to your unsecured creditors.

At the height of the housing bubble, trustees were known to keep bankruptcies open in the hope that the debtor's home would appreciate sufficiently in value to warrant a sale. To counter this, debtor's attorneys were asking courts to order their clients' cases closed as soon as possible. If you find yourself in a similar situation—that is, your home is appreciating in value—ask the court to close your case sooner than later, and hire an attorney if you run into problems. It will be worth it.

How a Homestead Exemption Works

This chart applies only to those states that use dollar-amount homestead exemptions. If your state bases the homestead exemption on acreage, your lot size will determine whether or not you keep your home. (See "Will You Lose Your Home?" below.)

This example is based on a home worth $100,000, with a $35,000 homestead exemption.

If you have nonexempt equity in your home, the trustee will sell it. Here, the homeowner's total equity is $60,000 ($100,000 [value of home] – $40,000 [mortgages and liens against home]). The homeowner's nonexempt equity is $25,000 ($60,000 [total equity] – $35,000 [homestead exemption]). Because the homeowner has $25,000 in nonexempt equity, the trustee will sell the house and use the nonexempt equity to pay unsecured creditors.

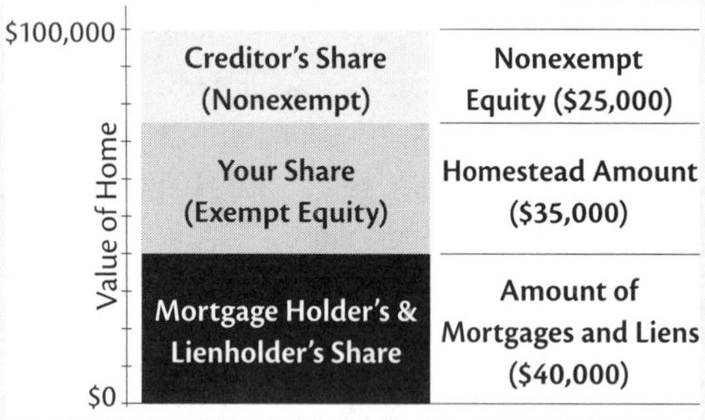

If you don't have any nonexempt equity, the trustee won't sell your home. Here, the homeowner's total equity is $30,000 ($100,000 [value of home] – $70,000 [mortgages and liens against home]). The homeowner doesn't have any nonexempt equity ($30,000 [total equity] – $35,000 [homestead exemption] = less than zero).

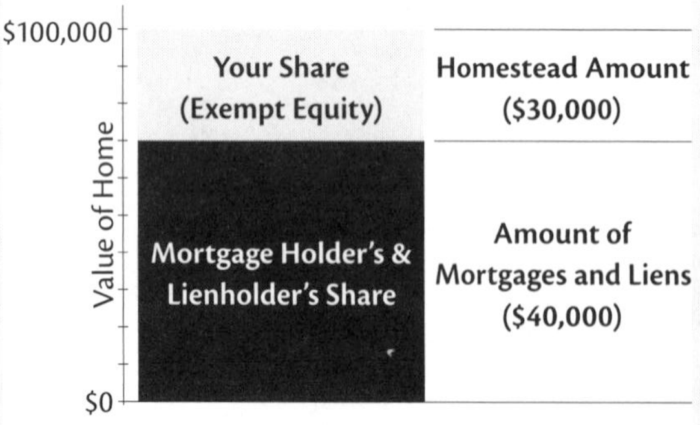

What Happens to Liens on Your Home

Chapter 7 bankruptcy won't eliminate liens on your home that were created with your consent, nor will it eliminate certain nonconsensual liens (such as tax liens or mechanics' liens). If you've pledged your home as security for loans other than a mortgage—for example, you used your home as security for a bank loan to pay ongoing business expenses—those creditors, too, have claims against your home.

If there is a judgment lien on your home—that is, a creditor sued you, won a court judgment, and recorded a judgment lien against your home at the land records office—you may be able to get rid of the lien entirely without paying a cent to the lien holder. This will depend on whether you would have exempt equity in the home if not for the presence of the judgment lien. The basic rule is that you can get rid of a judgment lien if it impairs your ability to claim an exemption. But if you have no equity in your home, then the judgment lien isn't impairing an exemption and you can't get rid of it.

> EXAMPLE: Canada and Robin run a struggling construction company and own a house worth $400,000. They owe $350,000 on their mortgage. Prior to filing for bankruptcy, they are sued over a construction defect and lose in court. A judgment lien of $60,000 is recorded against their house. When their construction company is losing more money than it brings in, they close down and file for bankruptcy because they can't pay all of their debts. Their state gives them a homestead exemption of $50,000, so after paying the mortgage holder its $350,000, there is no nonexempt equity left for the judgment creditor (the holder of the judgment lien) to take ($400,000 – $350,000 – $50,000 = 0). Canada and Robin file a motion in bankruptcy court to get rid of the judgment lien. The judge grants their motion and the lien is wiped out.

If the lien would impair your ability to claim an exemption, you can get rid of the lien by filing a motion to avoid the lien. You may also be able to get rid of some liens by filing a separate lawsuit in bankruptcy court. You can find more information on lien avoidance in Ch. 8.

What Happens to Foreclosure Proceedings

Chapter 7 bankruptcy's automatic stay (covered in Ch. 4) won't prevent an eventual foreclosure if you fall behind on your mortgage payments. At most, it will delay foreclosure for a few months. In many cases, the lender will just wait out your bankruptcy case and then proceed with the foreclosure. And if your lender gets impatient and files a motion to lift the automatic stay, the judge might allow the lender to process the foreclosure during your bankruptcy case.

Fighting a Motion to Lift the Stay and Foreclose

Until the housing bubble burst, bankruptcy judges routinely granted lenders' motions to lift the stay and proceed with a foreclosure. However, in some recent cases, bankruptcy courts have taken a closer look at these motions and discovered that the institutions filing them aren't necessarily entitled to ask the court to lift the stay. Only the holder of a promissory note is a "party in interest" with the right to request that the stay be lifted. Because of the way mortgages have been divided, bought, and sold lately, the institution asking to lift the stay often cannot produce a valid copy of the promissory note or otherwise prove that it is the legal holder of the note. (See *In re Kang Jin Hwang*, 396 B.R. 757 (Bkrtcy C.D. Cal. 2008) for more on this argument.)

Judges are increasingly likely to deny motions to lift the stay. Instead, they might make the party wait until the bankruptcy case is over to pursue the foreclosure. (Even if you defeat a motion to lift the stay by questioning the institution's right to do so, your bankruptcy will provide only temporary relief from the foreclosure.)

About the only way Chapter 7 bankruptcy can help you hang on to your home for the long haul is by discharging your other debts, which will allow you to devote more money to getting current on your mortgage to prevent foreclosure. Also, if your property has sufficiently decreased in value, Chapter 7 bankruptcy can effectively eliminate the need to pay your second and third mortgages, as explained above.

If foreclosure is inevitable, you should know that losing your home in a bankruptcy sale might be better for you than losing it in a foreclosure sale, for two reasons: First, a forced sale of real estate in bankruptcy is supervised by the bankruptcy court, which wants to sell the house for as much as possible. In a foreclosure sale, the foreclosing creditor cares only about getting enough to cover its own debt. So, a bankruptcy sale often yields a higher price—and if you have a homestead exemption on the house, the amount you get increases as the amount your home sells for goes up.

Second, debtors are rarely entitled to the homestead exemption if the house is sold through foreclosure. In a bankruptcy sale, however, you are entitled to your homestead amount in cash, if there are proceeds left over after the secured creditors have been paid.

Will You Lose Your Home in a Chapter 7 Bankruptcy?

If you file for Chapter 7 bankruptcy, the fact that you've kept up on your house payments may not protect you from losing it. As explained above, if selling your house will produce some cash for your unsecured creditors (and you aren't able to pay the trustee an equivalent amount), the trustee may well decide to sell it. But if the sale won't produce cash, the trustee will not take the house.

Whether the sale will produce cash depends on two factors:

- whether you have any equity in your home, and

- if so, whether you can protect that equity with an exemption.

Use the Homeowners' Worksheet below to figure out the answers to these questions. (You'll find a tear-out copy of the worksheet in Appendix B.) Here are the instructions for filling out the form.

Part I: Do You Have Any Equity in Your Home?

Line 1: Estimated market value of your home

Estimate how much money your home could produce in a quick, as-is sale. The trustee will often use this value in deciding whether to sell the home. However, some trustees will instead use the full market value of your property, so if there is a significant difference between the quick sale value and the full value of the home, use the latter to be on the safe side. To get a rough idea of what your home is worth in either type of sale, ask a realtor what comparable homes in your neighborhood have sold for. Or, look in newspaper or online real estate sections. You can also generate rough home valuation estimates from websites such as www.zillow.com, www.domania.com, www.homegain.com, or www.realtor.com.

Line 2: Costs of sale

Costs of sale vary, but they tend to be about 6%–8% of the sales price. The trustee is not required to subtract the costs of sale in determining whether to take your home, but most do. (If you want to err on the side of caution, put "0" in this blank.) When you complete your bankruptcy paperwork, you can note that you are deducting the costs of sale from the property's fair market value.

Line 3: Amount owed on mortgages and other loans

Enter the amount needed to pay off your mortgage and any other loans that are secured by the home as collateral. If you can't come up with a reasonably reliable estimate, contact each lender and ask how much is necessary to cancel the debt.

Line 4: Amount of liens

Enter the amount of all liens recorded against your home (other than liens created by mortgages and home equity loans). Liens are claims against your home that have been recorded with the land records office. The three most common types of liens are tax liens, mechanics' liens, and judgment liens. Tax liens can be recorded against your home by the county, state, or federal government for failure to pay property taxes, income taxes, payroll taxes, collected sales taxes, or other taxes. People who do work on your home and claim that you didn't pay them what you owe can record mechanics', or materialmen's, liens against your home. And judgment liens can be recorded by anyone who has sued you in court and won.

If you think there might be liens on your home, visit the county land records office. Tell the clerk you'd like to check your title for liens. The clerk should direct you to an index (often computerized) that lists all property in the county by the owner's last name. Next to your home should be a list of any liens recorded against it. In come counties you can also use an online database to check for liens against your home.

Line 5: Total costs = Line 2 + Line 3 + Line 4

Add up the total costs that would have to be paid if you were to sell your home.

Line 6: Your equity = Line 1 – Line 5

If Line 1 is more than Line 5, subtract Line 5 from Line 1, and put the result on Line 6. For bankruptcy purposes, this is your equity in the property: the amount that would be left over after all mortgages, loans, liens, and costs of sale are paid.

If the amount on Line 5 is more than the amount on Line 1, you have no equity; you can stop here. There will be no reason for the trustee to take your home in bankruptcy—once all of the liens and mortgage(s) are paid off, there would be nothing left to distribute to your unsecured creditors.

Homeowners' Worksheet

Part I. Do you have any equity in your home?

1. Market value of your home .... $__________
2. Costs of sale (if unsure, put 5% of market value) .... $__________
3. Amount owed on all mortgages .... $__________
4. Amount of all liens on the property .... $__________
5. Total of Lines 2, 3, and 4 .... $__________
6. Your equity (Line 1 minus Line 5) .... $__________

   If Line 6 is less than zero, skip the rest of the worksheet. The trustee will have no interest in selling your home.

Part II. Is your property protected by an exemption?

7. Does the available homestead exemption protect your kind of dwelling?

   ☐ Yes. *Go on to Line 8.*

   ☐ No. *Enter $0 on Line 11, then continue on to Line 12.*

8. Do you have to file a "declaration of homestead" to claim the homestead exemption?

   ☐ Yes, but I have not filed it yet. *(You should. See instructions.)*

   ☐ Yes, and I have already filed it.

   ☐ No.

9. Is the homestead exemption based on lot size?

   ☐ No, it is based on equity alone. *Go to Line 10.*

   ☐ No, it is unlimited (true only of the exemptions for Washington, DC).

   If you are using the D.C. exemptions, you can stop here. Your home is protected.

   ☐ Yes. The exemption is limited to property of __________ acres.

   If your property is smaller than this limit, you can stop here. Your home is protected. If your property exceeds this limit, see the instructions.

   ☐ Yes, but there is an equity limit as well. The exemption is limited to property of __________ acres.

   If your property is smaller than this limit, go on to Line 10. If your property exceeds this limit, see the instructions.

10. Do you own the property with your spouse in "tenancy by the entirety"?

    ☐ Yes. *See the instructions and talk to a bankruptcy attorney to find out whether your house is fully protected.*

    ☐ No. *Go on to Line 11.*

11. Is the dollar amount of the homestead exemption limited?

    ☐ Yes. *Enter the dollar limit here:* $ ______________

    ☐ No dollar limit. *You can stop here. Your home is protected.*

12. Can you protect more equity with a wildcard exemption?

    ☐ Yes. *Enter the dollar amount here:* $ ______________

    ☐ No.

13. How much of your equity is protected?

    Total of Lines 11 and 12: $ ______________

    If the total exceeds $136,875 and you are subject to the cap on homestead exemptions, write "$136,875" on this line. See the instructions for more information.

14. Is your home fully protected?

    Subtract Line 13 from Line 6: $ ______________

    If this total is a negative number, your home is protected. If this total is a positive number, you have unprotected equity in your home, and the trustee might choose to sell it (or allow you to keep it in exchange for cash or exempt property roughly equal in value to your unprotected equity).

If you do have equity, go on to Part II to determine how much of it is protected by an applicable exemption.

TIP

Legal research note. If you do legal research about equity and homestead exemptions, note that the word "equity" has multiple meanings. Unencumbered equity is the value of your home, minus the mortgage and the liens you can't get rid of. (That's what we mean when we say equity.) Then there's "encumbered" equity, which is the value of your home minus only the mortgage. Sometimes courts refer to encumbered equity simply as "equity."

Part II: If You Have Equity, Is It Protected by an Exemption?

We're assuming that, in Part I, you found that you have some amount of home equity. Here in Part II, we'll determine how much of that equity you can claim as exempt—that is, how much of it you're entitled to keep.

Before you can figure out how much of your equity is protected by an exemption, you must determine which set of exemptions to use. The 2005 bankruptcy law imposes strict domicile requirements on filers seeking to use a homestead exemption. Filers who don't meet these requirements may have to use the exemptions of

The Trustee's Power to Eliminate Liens—And How It May Cost You Your Home

When property has liens on it for more than the property is worth, it is "oversecured." If a trustee were to sell oversecured property, there wouldn't be enough money to pay off all of the liens, which means that one or more lienholders would be left with nothing. And there certainly wouldn't be any money to pay unsecured creditors, who get paid only after all lienholders have been paid off.

The trustee's job is to find money to pay unsecured creditors, so the trustee usually won't bother trying to sell an oversecured home. The picture changes, however, if the trustee can successfully petition the bankruptcy court to knock out enough lienholders to free up some equity. Once that happens, it might make sense to sell the home.

If a lien hasn't been perfected, the trustee may try to knock it out, turning an oversecured property into one that, when sold, will yield some cash after the remaining lienholders get their share. All states have laws specifying the procedures that must be followed to make a mortgage or other secured agreement or lien valid (called "perfecting" the lien). These typically include a proper acknowledgement signed in front of a notary public and recorded in the local land records office. While real estate practitioners usually have a firm grasp of these rules, mistakes can happen. If the trustee finds that a lien wasn't perfected properly, it could be knocked out, meaning there is more equity in the house than you thought, maybe enough for the trustee to justify a sale.

The trustee can also knock out liens that have been created to enforce a money judgment. If getting rid of such a lien would free up some equity over and above any exemption you could claim, you may lose the house for that reason. This means that you shouldn't rely on judgment liens to keep your home unless you are able to claim a homestead exemption in the equity that would be produced by getting rid of the lien.

Before you file for bankruptcy, check on the legal status of any liens you are relying on to save your home or other property. In particular, make sure the document creating the lien is recorded and contains a proper acknowledgement. If not, you may have more equity than you think—and the trustee may have a greater incentive to sell your home.

the state where they used to live—and they may be subject to a $136,875 limit on the amount of equity they can exempt. (Because many states protect less than $136,875 in home equity anyway, this cap won't affect the majority of filers.) The purpose of these rules is to prevent filers from moving to another state to take advantage of its better homestead protection.

Here are the rules:

- If you bought your home at least 40 months ago, you can use the homestead exemption of the state where your home is.
- If you bought your home at least two years ago, you can use the homestead exemption of the state where your home is. However, if you bought your home within the last 40 months, your homestead exemption is capped at $136,875, unless you bought the home with the proceeds from the sale of another home in the same state.
- If you bought your home within the last two years, then you must use the homestead exemption of the state where you were living for the better part of the 180-day period that ended two years before your filing date. And you are still subject to the $136,875 limit.
- If the state you are filing in offers a choice between the state and federal bankruptcy exemptions, you can use the federal exemption list regardless of how long you've been living in the state. In other words, the rules of the state where a person files for bankruptcy determine whether the filer can use the federal exemptions, even if the filer has not lived in the state long enough to use its *state* exemptions.

EXAMPLE 1: Four years ago, John and Susie retired and moved from Massachusetts to Maine, where they bought a home. If they file for bankruptcy in Maine, they can use Maine's exemptions, because they have lived there for more than 40 months. If they had moved to Maine three years ago, they would still be able to use Maine's exemptions, but their homestead exemption would be capped at $136,875. Maine's homestead allowance for joint filers who are at least 61 years old is $180,000, so John and Susie would have lost just over $43,000 worth of homestead exemption ($180,000 exemption minus the $136,875 cap).

EXAMPLE 2: After moving from Vermont to Boston in 2009, Julius and his family buy a fine old Boston home for $700,000. After borrowing heavily against the home because of financial reversals, Julius files for bankruptcy in early 2011, when he owns $250,000 in equity. Although the Massachusetts homestead exemption of $500,000 would cover Julius's equity, he can claim only $136,875 of that exemption because he moved to Massachusetts from another state within the last 40 months.

EXAMPLE 3: Eighteen months ago, Fred moved from Florida to Nevada, where he purchased his current home with $400,000 he received from an inheritance. Fred files for bankruptcy in his current home state of Nevada. Because Fred lived in Florida for two years prior to moving to Nevada, he must use Florida's homestead exemption—and because Fred hasn't lived in Nevada for 40 months, his exemption is subject to the $136,875 cap. The cap imposes an extreme penalty on Fred, because Florida offers an unlimited homestead exemption and Nevada's homestead exemption is $550,000, but because of the cap, Fred can protect only $136,875 of his equity, which means that the trustee will undoubtedly sell his home, give Fred his $136,875, and use the rest to pay off his unsecured creditors.

EXAMPLE 4: Joan moves from Maryland to Vermont, where she buys a home for $250,000, with a $225,000 mortgage. Less than two years after moving, Joan files for bankruptcy. Because Joan was living in Maryland for years before moving to Vermont, she must use either Maryland's state homestead allowance or the federal homestead allowance (Maryland gives filers a choice of exemptions). Maryland provides no homestead exemption at all, but the federal homestead exemption is approximately $21,000. It isn't hard for Joan to figure out that she should use the federal exemption system if protecting the equity in her home is her top priority. However, if Joan's other property is more important to her, and she would be able to keep more of it using the Maryland state exemptions, she might choose the state exemptions and let the trustee sell her home.

If you are filing in a state that allows you to choose between the state and federal exemption lists, you are always entitled to use the federal exemptions, regardless of how long you have lived in the state. The federal homestead exemption allows you to protect about $21,000 in equity (this amount is scheduled to change in April, 2010), and married couples can double that amount.

CAUTION

The homestead cap also applies to filers who commit certain types of misconduct. No matter how long you have lived in the state where you are filing, your homestead exemption will be capped at $136,875 if you have been convicted of a felony demonstrating that your bankruptcy filing is abusive, you owe a debt arising from a securities act violation, or you have committed a crime or an intentional, willful, or reckless act that killed or caused serious personal injury to someone in the last five years. However, the court may lift the cap if it finds that the homestead exemption is reasonably necessary for you to support yourself and your dependents.

How Bankruptcy Affects Homes in Revocable Living Trusts

Revocable living trusts have become a popular way to pass valuable property on when you die. The property owner creates a trust document naming him- or herself as the trustee, another person as successor trustee to take over when the owner dies, and typically one or more beneficiaries to receive the property upon the owner's death. When the original property owner dies, the successor trustee steps in and distributes the property to the beneficiaries. All of this happens without going through court. (It's called a living trust because it takes effect during the property owner's life, not when he or she dies; it's revocable because the property owner can undo it any time.)

Legally, the trustee owns the property in the trust, although it's common to refer to the trust itself as the legal owner of the property. So, if John Henry creates a revocable living trust and puts his house in it, he will be the initial trustee and he will own his house as "trustee of the John Henry Revocable Living Trust." If John Henry files for bankruptcy, can he claim a homestead exemption for the house he owns as trustee?

Almost every court to consider this issue has allowed homestead exemptions to be claimed on homes held in the typical revocable living trust. When you create a revocable living trust, you retain actual ownership of the property even though it's titled as a trust rather than outright ownership, so it's only fair to allow you to claim an exemption. Despite this trend, however, it's probably safest to remove the property from a living trust by executing a new deed (giving the property from yourself as trustee(s) to yourself as a person or married couple). After your bankruptcy, you can execute a new deed placing the property back in the trust.

If you have commercial or rental property in a living trust, the property will be considered part of your bankruptcy estate, like your home. However, you can't use a homestead exemption to protect commercial property unless your state's homestead exemption can also be used as a "wildcard." (You can find all exemptions in Appendix A.)

Line 7: Does the available homestead exemption protect your kind of dwelling?

Only three states do not have a homestead exemption. If you are using the exemptions in one of these three states, enter $0 on Line 11.

States With No Homestead Exemption		
Maryland	New Jersey	Pennsylvania

For all other states, check Appendix A to see whether your type of dwelling is protected. Some types of dwellings may not be covered, including:

- **Mobile homes.** Most states specifically include mobile homes in their homestead exemptions. Other states state that any "real or personal property used as a residence" can use the homestead exemption. This covers a trailer, mobile home, or houseboat, as long as you live in it. Some states don't detail the types of property that qualify as a homestead. If your mobile home does not qualify for a homestead exemption, it would be protected only by the exemption for a motor vehicle.
- **Co-ops or condominiums.** Some homestead exemption laws specifically cover co-ops or use language that says the exemption protects "any property used as a dwelling."
- **Apartments.** Most homestead exemption statutes do not protect rental apartments, because tenants don't have equity in an apartment. If you have a long-term lease in an apartment, the exemption statutes of a few states may provide protection if the trustee were inclined to sell the lease.

If your type of dwelling is not covered, enter $0 on Line 11.

If it is unclear whether your type of dwelling is covered by the available homestead exemption, you may need to do some legal research. (See Ch. 12 for help getting started.)

Line 8: Do you have to file a "declaration of homestead" to claim the exemption?

States That May Require a Declaration of Homestead		
Alabama	Montana	Utah
Idaho	Nevada	Virginia
Massachusetts	Texas	Washington

To claim a homestead exemption in Virginia, you must have a declaration of homestead on file with the land records office for the county where the property is located when you file for bankruptcy. The other states on this list vary in what they require and when. If you are using the homestead exemption for one of these states, the safest approach is to file a declaration of homestead.

Requiring you to record a declaration before you can get the benefit of a homestead exemption may violate the bankruptcy laws. (*In re Leicht*, 222 B.R. 670 (1st Cir. BAP 1998).) Regardless of the legalities, however, you will be best served by filing your declaration of homestead before you file for bankruptcy.

Other states allow (but do not require) you to file a homestead declaration in certain circumstances. In Texas, for example, you may file a homestead declaration to claim protection for property you own but are not currently living in.

> **EXAMPLE:** John and Doris live in Texas. They have retired and have decided to rent out their spacious country home and move to an apartment closer to town. They can still claim their country home as their homestead by recording a declaration of homestead with the land records office in the county where their country home is.

In some states, a "declared" homestead offers additional protection in situations other than bankruptcy. Also, if you own more than one piece of real estate, some states allow a creditor to require you to file a declaration of homestead to clarify which property you are claiming as your homestead.

Line 9: Is the homestead exemption based on lot size?

Most states place a limit on the value of property you can claim as your homestead exemption, but a few states have no such limits. Find out what kind of homestead exemption system your state uses by looking at the lists below.

Unlimited Homestead Exemption
District of Columbia

If you are lucky enough to be using the District of Columbia exemptions, congratulations: You can skip the rest of this chapter. Your home is not at risk in a Chapter 7 bankruptcy.

Homestead Exemption Based on Lot Size Only		
Arkansas	Kansas	South Dakota
Florida	Oklahoma	Texas
Iowa		

In these states, you can easily determine whether your home is exempt. The homestead exemption is based simply on acreage. Look in Appendix A for the acreage limitation for the state. (In Oklahoma, if you use more than 25% of the property as a business, the one-acre urban homestead exemption cannot exceed $5,000.)

If your property is smaller than the maximum allowable acreage, your home is fully protected. You can skip the rest of this chapter.

If your property exceeds the maximum allowable acreage, the trustee will sell the excess acreage if you have any equity in it (unless you are able to buy it back from the trustee for a negotiated amount). Enter $0 in Line 11 of the worksheet.

Homestead Exemption Based on Lot Size and Equity		
Alabama	Michigan	Nebraska
Hawaii	Minnesota	Oregon
Louisiana	Mississippi	

These states use the size of your lot and the amount of your equity to determine whether your home is exempt. First look in Appendix A for the state acreage limitation and enter it on Line 9.

If your property exceeds the maximum allowable acreage, the trustee will want to sell the excess acreage (or get the equivalent in value from you) if you have enough equity in it.

If your lot size is within the allowed acreage, your exemption is determined by the equity amount limit. Proceed to Line 10.

Homestead Exemption Based on Equity Alone		
Federal exemptions	Maine	Rhode Island
Alaska	Massachusetts	South Carolina
Arizona	Missouri	Tennessee
California	Montana	Utah
Colorado	Nevada	Vermont
Connecticut	New Hampshire	Virginia
Georgia	New Mexico	Washington
Idaho	New York	West Virginia
Illinois	North Carolina	Wisconsin
Indiana	North Dakota	Wyoming
Kentucky	Ohio	

If the state homestead exemption is based on equity alone, or you are using the federal exemptions, go to Line 10.

Line 10: Do you own the property with your spouse in "tenancy by the entirety"?

If you are married and live in the right state, you may be able to exclude your home from your bankruptcy estate—which means you can keep it, no matter how much equity you own or how large your state's homestead exemption is—if you own it with your spouse in tenancy by the entirety.

Tenancy by the entirety (TBE) is a form of property ownership available to married couples in about half of the states, some of which have laws that prohibit TBE property from being sold to pay debts that are owed by only one spouse. If this type of law applies, you can keep TBE property, regardless of its value, if your debts are separate. Some states also protect personal property owned in tenancy by the entirety, such as checking accounts.

To qualify for this type of property protection, all of the following must be true:

- You are married.
- You, or your spouse, are filing for bankruptcy alone, without the other spouse. If you file jointly, your TBE property will not be protected unless a homestead exemption applies.
- You and your spouse own property in one of the states that recognize TBE (see below).
- You and your spouse own the home as tenants by the entirety. In some of these states, the law presumes that married people own their property as tenants by the entirety, unless they specify that they wish to own it in some other way (as joint tenants, for example); in a few states, the deed must explicitly state that the property is owned as tenants by the entirety.
- The debts that are causing you to file for bankruptcy are solely owned by the spouse who will be filing; debts that are jointly owed will not be discharged if only one spouse files.

If you meet these five criteria, this protection could be extremely valuable to you. You may want to see a bankruptcy attorney to figure out the best way to take full advantage of it.

States That Recognize TBE

These states recognize TBE home ownership (as does the District of Columbia): Delaware, Florida, Hawaii, Illinois, Indiana, Maryland, Massachusetts, Michigan, Missouri, North Carolina, Ohio, Pennsylvania, Rhode Island, Tennessee, Vermont, Virginia, and Wyoming.

Unlike exemptions, tenancy by the entirety protection generally depends on the law of the state where your property is, not where you live. For example, if you and your spouse live in Minnesota but own a condo in Florida as tenants by the entirety, Florida law protects your condo from being seized to pay debts owed by only one spouse, even though Minnesota law offers no such protection. Recently, however, an Illinois case reached the opposite conclusion: The court found that debtors filing in Illinois could claim tenancy by the entirety protection only for property in Illinois, not for property located in Michigan—even though Michigan is a state that recognizes tenancy by the entirety. (*In re Giffone, Jr.*, 343 B.R. 893 (N.D. Ill. 2006).) If you own property in another state, you should talk to a lawyer to find out whether you can protect it.

Line 11: Is the dollar amount of the homestead exemption limited?

Most states place a dollar limit on the homestead exemption—for example, New York allows you to exempt up to $50,000 in equity, while Massachusetts allows you to exempt up to $500,000. If the state homestead exemption you're using works this way, write down the amount of equity the exemption protects on Line 11. If your state allows you to use the federal exemptions and you plan to do so, write down the federal exemption instead. (See Appendix A for these figures.)

In some states, if you own your home with your spouse and you file jointly for bankruptcy, you can each claim the full homestead exemption amount (called "doubling"). Other states don't allow doubling. When you look at Appendix A, check to see whether doubling is prohibited. If the chart doesn't mention doubling, assume that you and your spouse can double the exemption amount.

Line 12: Can you protect more equity with a wildcard exemption?

Some states allow you to add a wildcard exemption to the amount of your homestead exemption. Although these wildcard amounts are usually small, they might be enough to tip the balance in favor of keeping your home.

Check Appendix A to see whether the state where you're filing has a wildcard exemption you can use for real estate; if so, write the amount on Line 12. If your state doesn't have a wildcard exemption that you can use for real estate, leave this line blank.

Line 13: How much of your equity is protected?

Add Lines 11 (the state homestead exemption available to you) and 12 (any wildcard exemption

If You Converted Nonexempt Property in the Last Ten Years

The 2005 bankruptcy law allows the court to look back ten years before you filed for bankruptcy to find out whether you have "defrauded" your creditors by selling nonexempt property and using the proceeds to buy exempt property (often real estate). If the court finds that you converted property with the intent to cheat your creditors out of their lawful right to take it, the value of your homestead exemption will be reduced by the value of the property your converted. (11 U.S.C. § 522(o); *In re Maronde*, 332 B.R. 593 (D. Minn. 2005); *In re Lacounte*, 342 B.R. 809 (D. Mont. 2005).)

Your homestead exemption may be at risk only if all of the following are true:

- Within the last ten years, you converted any type of nonexempt property into any type of exempt property.
- You used the converted property as a means of acquiring or improving residential property you or a dependent currently inhabits (or a real estate co-op or a burial plot). (For example, you sold valuable antiques to raise the down payment for your house.)
- You have some equity in the property that could be protected by an exemption.
- You are using a state exemption system rather than the federal exemptions.
- When you converted the property in question, you intended to cheat, defraud, delay, or hinder your creditors.

If all of these statements are true, the homestead exemption available to you for that property will be reduced by the value of the property you improperly converted.

> EXAMPLE: You have $50,000 of equity in your home, and your state offers a $50,000 homestead exemption. Nine years ago, you were sued by a creditor over a real estate deal that went bad. To protect a $50,000 investment portfolio you owned at the time, you cashed it out and bought an exempt life insurance policy. Five years ago, you cashed out the life insurance policy and used the proceeds as a down payment for your home. Because you meet all of the factors listed above, you could lose your homestead exemption entirely, and your house could be sold so your equity can be distributed to your creditors.

Few real-life situations are this clear-cut, of course. It's usually easy to tell whether or not you converted nonexempt property to exempt property. However, the question of whether you converted the property to cheat, defraud, delay, or hinder your creditors is not so simple. Generally, bankruptcy courts use the badges of fraud list (covered in Ch. 5) to determine whether you intended to cheat your creditors.

you can add to your homestead exemption). This is the amount of home equity you can protect in bankruptcy. If you aren't subject to the $136,875 cap (explained above), a reduction of your homestead protection because you converted nonexempt property to defraud a creditor, or the creation of a self-settled trust (see Ch. 5), write this amount on Line 13.

If you are subject to the $136,875 cap, it might limit the amount of equity you can protect. If the total of Lines 11 and 12 doesn't exceed $136,875, it doesn't matter—the cap won't affect you, and you can write the total amount on Line 13. However, if the total is more than $136,875 and the cap applies, you can protect only $136,875 in equity. Even if your state law would otherwise allow you to take a larger exemption, you'll be limited to $136,875, and this is what you should write on Line 13.

Line 14: Is your home fully protected?

Subtract Line 13 from Line 6, and enter the total on Line 14. If you generate a negative number, all of your home equity should be protected by the applicable exemptions, if your estimates are correct. The trustee probably won't have your home sold, because there would be no proceeds left over (after your mortgage holder was paid off and you received your exempt amount of equity) to pay your unsecured creditors.

If, however, you generate a positive number, your equity exceeds the applicable exemption—in other words, you have unprotected (nonexempt) equity in your home. If your estimates are right, and a sale would produce a profit to be paid to your unsecured creditors after the costs of sale are deducted (5% to 10% of the sale price), the trustee can force the sale unless you can pay the trustee the value of your unprotected equity. From the proceeds of the sale, your secured creditors will be paid their mortgages, liens, and so forth; you will receive your exempt amount; and your unsecured creditors will get the rest.

If you have significant unprotected equity in your home (over and above the costs of sale), you shouldn't file for Chapter 7 bankruptcy if you want to keep it. The trustee will almost certainly sell it, unless you can come up with the cash to keep it. You'll probably fare better—and hold on to your home longer—by using your equity to help pay off your debts, either directly or through a reverse mortgage, or to fund a Chapter 13 reorganization plan. Some of these strategies are discussed in "Ways to Keep Your House" below.

CAUTION

This worksheet is for estimate purposes only. If this worksheet shows that your equity is equal to or near the maximum amount of your state's homestead exemption, take note: The trustee can challenge the value you claim for your home and may determine that it's worth more than you think. If this happens, and the trustee concludes that your equity exceeds the amount you can claim as exempt, the trustee may seek to have your home sold. If your estimates show that you might be close to the exemption limit, arrange for a formal appraisal or get some advice from an experienced bankruptcy lawyer.

Ways to Keep Your House

If you have nonexempt equity in your home, there are a few strategies that might be available that will allow you to keep your house even if you file for bankruptcy. We outline them briefly here, but you should ask an experienced bankruptcy lawyer for help. (For a quick overview of strategies to keep your house if you decide not to file for bankruptcy, as well as a list of resources, see "Alternatives to Chapter 7 Bankruptcy If You Might Lose Your Home," below.)

Reduce Your Equity Before Filing for Bankruptcy

If you can reduce your nonexempt equity before you file for bankruptcy, you may be able to save your home. (You may even be able to avoid bankruptcy altogether if you use the money to pay off your other debts.)

There are two ways to reduce your equity:

- borrow against the equity, or
- sell part ownership of your house.

You can use the proceeds to buy exempt property or to pay off other debts.

CAUTION

Consult a local bankruptcy lawyer before reducing your equity. If you file for bankruptcy after reducing your equity, the bankruptcy court in your area might view your actions as an abuse of the bankruptcy process and dismiss your bankruptcy petition. This is more likely if you reduced your equity within two years of filing. How to stay out of trouble when converting property from nonexempt to exempt status is covered in Ch. 6.

Borrow Against Your Equity

If you borrow against your equity, you won't reduce your overall debt burden. You may be able to lower your overall monthly bills, however, if you can get a lower interest rate mortgage or a longer-term equity loan to pay off short-term, high-interest debts. You can also fully deduct the interest you pay on mortgages and home equity loans from your income taxes.

Be careful when you shop for a loan. Many lenders offer loans with very high rates to people in

Alternatives to Chapter 7 Bankruptcy If You Might Lose Your Home

If you want to keep your home but you have unprotected (nonexempt) equity and/or you are behind on your mortgage and facing foreclosure, Chapter 7 personal bankruptcy may not be the best way to deal with your debt. Some alternative strategies you might consider include:

- Negotiate a plan with your lender to make up the missed payments.
- Agree to a mortgage workout, in which you renegotiate the payment terms of your mortgage to avoid foreclosure.
- Refinance your loan with another lender.
- Negotiate a "short sale," in which the lender agrees to accept whatever you can sell the house for as payment in full on your mortgage.
- If you are at least 62 years old, look into the possibility of a reverse mortgage.
- Consider whether you have any defenses to a foreclosure action, such as an interest rate that's too high, violations of the Truth in Lending Act, or the lender's failure to prove that it owns the loan and has the right to foreclose.
- File for Chapter 13 bankruptcy, in which you can propose to make up your missed payments over the life of your repayment plan. (You can also use Chapter 13 to get rid of second or third mortgages that are no longer secured by your home due to depreciation.)

For debtors who have a lot of home equity, filing for Chapter 13 bankruptcy may be the better bankruptcy choice, because Chapter 13 filers aren't required to give up any property. While business owners typically find it very difficult to complete a Chapter 13 repayment plan (as explained in Ch. 3), Chapter 13 might be a viable option if you can propose a plan that will pay your creditors at least the value of your nonexempt equity in your home.

For more information on these and other strategies for dealing with home debt outside of bankruptcy, talk to a HUD-approved housing counselor (you can find one by calling 800-569-4287 or visiting HUD's website at www.hud.gov/foreclosure/index.cfm). You can learn more about government-sponsored mortgage modification programs at www.makinghomeaffordable.gov. You may also want to pick up a copy of *The Foreclosure Survival Guide*, by Stephen R. Elias (Nolo), which includes lots of tips and strategies for saving your home.

financial trouble. Although you may be desperate to save your home, taking out another loan with high interest rates or high costs and fees will only get you into deeper financial trouble. Also, be extra cautious about taking out a loan with a balloon payment (a large lump sum of money due at the end of the loan term). If you can't make the balloon payment when it comes due, you will lose your home. Most people can't come up with $25,000, $50,000, or $100,000 all at once. You might be able to refinance your home to pay off the balloon, but don't count on it.

CAUTION

Beware of foreclosure and mortgage modification scams. When people are close to foreclosure, they become targets for an army of con artists who have descended into their communities to give them one last kick. Unless you know the person who is offering to help you save your home—for instance, a neighborhood real estate or mortgage broker, or a community bank, or credit union—we recommend that you decline all offers of foreclosure and mortgage modification assistance unless you first consult with a HUD-approved nonprofit housing counselor (see "How to Find a HUD-Approved Housing Counselor," above). Nolo's *The Foreclosure Survival Guide* has a large section on the various scams and some dos and don'ts that will help you avoid being a victim.

Sell Some of Your Equity

Another way to protect your equity is to sell some of your house. By owning your home jointly with someone else, your equity is reduced.

Selling a portion of your equity may appeal to you—after all, what you need now is more cash, not another monthly bill. Perhaps a friend or relative would be willing to buy a half share in your home. If you pursue this strategy, you may need to wait two years after the sale before filing for bankruptcy. Otherwise, the bankruptcy trustee might void the sale, especially if it appears that you gave your friend or relative a bargain on the price.

Even two years may not be sufficient in some courts if the trustee views your actions as defrauding your creditors under your state's fraudulent transfer laws (see Ch. 5.) Be sure to consult a bankruptcy attorney who is aware of local practice before you try this.

Also, think long and hard about whether you want to share ownership of your home. A co-owner can sell his or her interest, force a sale of the property, die and leave it to someone else, and so on. Again, consult a bankruptcy lawyer before you sell. This strategy can be fraught with complications and traps for the uninformed.

After You File for Bankruptcy

Once you file for Chapter 7 bankruptcy, you may be able to keep the trustee from selling your house through one of the following methods:

- **Offer to substitute cash for the amount of nonexempt equity.** You may be able to convince the trustee not to sell your house if you can come up with enough cash to cover your nonexempt equity. In other words, you would give the trustee the amount that would be available from selling the house to pay unsecured creditors. You may be able to raise the cash by selling exempt property or using income you earn after you file.

  EXAMPLE: The Robertsons have approximately $5,000 of nonexempt equity in their home. All of their home furnishings are exempt. After discussing the matter with the trustee, they sell three pieces of furniture and a camera for a total of $1,800 and scrape together $2,700 extra cash from income earned since they filed for bankruptcy. They offer the cash to the trustee as a substitute for the nonexempt equity. The trustee accepts the money, because the creditors will end up with almost as much as they would have gotten if the home were sold—and the trustee will be spared the hassle and expense of selling the Robertsons' home.

- **Convert to Chapter 13 bankruptcy (or file for Chapter 13 in the first place).** Chapter 13 bankruptcy lets you pay your debts out of your income rather than by selling your property. If you file for Chapter 13 bankruptcy, you won't have to give up your home, even if you have nonexempt equity. (However, you will have to pay your unsecured creditors at least the value of your nonexempt property over the life of your plan.) Chapter 13 bankruptcy also permits you to spread out repayments of missed installment payments, taxes, and late charges on a mortgage. And, if your lender has begun foreclosure proceedings, Chapter 13 bankruptcy can halt them as long as your house hasn't yet been sold. (For more information on Chapter 13, see *Chapter 13 Bankruptcy: Keep Your Property & Repay Debts Over Time*, by Stephen Elias and Robin Leonard (Nolo).)

You can convert to Chapter 13 bankruptcy any time during a Chapter 7 bankruptcy proceeding. If you miss mortgage payments after you file for Chapter 7 bankruptcy, however, some courts won't let you include them in your Chapter 13 repayment plan. So try to make all payments due after you file for Chapter 7.

CHAPTER

8

Secured Debts

This chapter explains how Chapter 7 bankruptcy affects secured debts: debts that give the creditor the right to take back a particular piece of property (the collateral) if you don't pay. We tell you how to recognize a secured debt when you see one and explain your options for dealing with secured debts (and the collateral that secures them) in bankruptcy. A couple of these options involve considerable paperwork beyond what you'll have to complete for your bankruptcy case; we provide some sample forms and instructions for these procedures in Appendix D.

TIP

Chapter 13 may provide better protection for secured property you want to keep. As explained in Ch. 3, debtors who use Chapter 13 may "cram down" many types of secured debts. In a cramdown, the court reduces the principal owed on the debt to the property's replacement value (and often reduces the interest rate, too). Although you can't cram down mortgages on your home or newer car loans, many other types of debts are eligible. If you are significantly upside down on a secured debt and you want to keep the collateral, review the material in Ch. 3 to make sure Chapter 7 is the right bankruptcy choice.

What Are Secured Debts?

A debt is secured if it is linked to a specific item of property, called collateral, that guarantees payment of the debt. Mortgages and car loans are the most common examples of secured debts, but small business owners might also take on secured debts to purchase machinery, equipment, and inventory. If you don't make your payments when they come due, the creditor can repossess the collateral. Often, the collateral is the property you purchased with the debt. For example, a mortgage typically gives the lender the right to foreclose on your home if you don't pay. However, you can also pledge property you already own as collateral for a debt. For example, if you take out a $50,000 business line of credit, you could pledge $50,000 worth of inventory as collateral to secure the line of credit.

An unsecured debt, on the other hand, is not secured by any type of collateral. Credit card and medical debts are common examples of unsecured debt. Debts owed to lawyers and other professionals are also typically unsecured, as are "deficiency judgments" arising from foreclosures and car repossessions (if the lender sells the property for less than you owe, the remainder of the debt that you owe is called a deficiency judgment).

For bankruptcy purposes, there are two types of secured debts:

- those you agree to (called security interests), such as a mortgage or car note, and
- those created without your consent, such as a lien the IRS records against your property because you haven't paid your taxes.

Security Interests

Security interests are secured debts you have taken on voluntarily. If you pledge property as collateral for a loan or line of credit—that is, as a guarantee you will repay the debt—the lien on your property is a security interest. A security interest created to buy the collateral is called a purchase-money security interest. If you use property you already own as collateral (for instance, you refinance a car or pledge business assets as collateral for a loan), the debt is a non-purchase-money security interest. These two types of security interests may be treated somewhat differently in bankruptcy, as discussed later in this chapter.

Usually, you must repay a security interest by making installment payments. If you fail to make your payments on time or to comply with other terms of the agreement (for example, a mortgage lender's requirement that you carry homeowner's insurance), the lender or seller has the right to take back the property.

Lenders Must Perfect Their Security Interests

For bankruptcy purposes, security interest agreements qualify as secured debts only if they have been perfected: recorded with the appropriate local or state records office. For instance, to create a lien on real estate, the mortgage holder (the bank or other lender) must typically record it with the recorder's office for the county where the real estate is located. To perfect security interests in cars or business assets, the holder of the security interest must typically record it with whatever statewide or local agency handles recordings under the Uniform Commercial Code (these are called "UCC recordings," and they are usually filed with the secretary of state, or department of state).

It's not uncommon for informal business documents to provide that one party will receive a "security interest" in some collateral in exchange for granting a loan or business credit to the other party. Informal agreements like these, called security agreements, can be enforced generally, but the seller will have a lien on the collateral only if the agreement is properly recorded.

> EXAMPLE: Clear Water, a swimming pool maintenance firm, buys a high-power vacuum from Acme Vacuum for $25,000. Clear Water signs a boilerplate promissory note and security agreement, agreeing to pay the debt in monthly installments over one year and giving Acme a security interest in the vacuum. Acme doesn't record the agreement with the appropriate government agency. Soon afterwards, Clear Water files bankruptcy. Acme believes it has a security interest in the vacuum that will be protected in the bankruptcy proceedings. However, the bankruptcy trustee takes the vacuum and sells it without paying Acme the amount due on its loan. Because Acme didn't perfect the agreement by recording it, it has no security interest that would require the trustee to pay off its debt before distributing any remaining proceeds to Clear Water's unsecured creditors.

Common Examples of Security Interests

Many everyday loans qualify as security interests, including:

- **Mortgages.** Called deeds of trust in some states, mortgages are loans to buy or refinance a house or other real estate. The real estate is collateral for the loan. If you fail to pay, the lender can foreclose.
- **Home equity loans or HELOCs.** You can borrow against the equity in your home to provide your business with cash flow, remodel your home, or pay for other things, such as college tuition or a car. No matter how you spend the money, the house is collateral for the loan. If you fail to pay, the lender can foreclose.
- **Loans for cars, boats, tractors, motorcycles, or RVs.** Here, the vehicle is the collateral. If you fail to pay, the lender can repossess it.
- **Loans for business equipment, machines, or inventory.** The lender can repossess the property you pledged as collateral if you don't repay the loan.
- **Store charges with a security agreement.** Almost all purchases on store credit cards are unsecured, as are major credit cards. Some stores, however, print on the credit card slip or other receipt that the store "retains a security interest in all hard goods (durable goods) purchased," meaning that if you don't pay the credit card bill, the store will have the right to take back the purchased items. If you didn't specifically sign a security agreement setting out repayment terms, debts like these are generally considered unsecured debts in bankruptcy. However, if the store makes you sign an actual security agreement setting out the amount financed, the interest rate, and the number of required payments (the basics required by the Truth in Lending Act for installment payments) when you use the store's credit card, the

debt may be secured. For example, if you buy building supplies on credit, the store may require you to sign a security agreement in which you agree that the items purchased are collateral for your repayment. If you don't pay back the loan, the seller can repossess the property, as long as it perfects its security interest.

- **Title loans, or personal loans from banks, credit unions, or finance companies.** Often, you must pledge valuable personal property you already own, such as a paid-off motor vehicle, as collateral for this type of loan. This is a non-purchase-money secured debt, which will be treated as a secured debt in your bankruptcy as long as it has been perfected by the lender.

Nonconsensual Liens

In some circumstances, a creditor can get a lien on your property without your agreement. These are called nonconsensual liens. In theory, a nonconsensual lien gives the creditor the right to force a sale of the property in order to get paid. In practice, however, few creditors exercise this right because forcing a sale is expensive and time-consuming. Instead, they typically wait until you sell or refinance the property, at which point the lien has to be paid off with the proceeds, to give the new owner or lender clear title to the property.

For bankruptcy purposes, there are three major types of nonconsensual liens:

- judgment liens
- statutory liens, and
- tax liens.

Judgment Liens

A judgment lien can be imposed on your property only after somebody sues you and wins a money judgment against you. In most states, the judgment creditor (the person or company who won) must then record the judgment by filing it with the county or state. In a few states, a judgment entered against you by a court automatically creates a lien on the real estate you own in that county—that is, the judgment creditor doesn't have to record the judgment to get the lien.

A judgment lien affects real estate you own in the county where the lien is recorded or the judgment is entered. In many states, a judgment lien also applies to your personal property (property other than real estate) for a period of time after the judgment, if certain judgment collection techniques are employed. However, judgment liens on personal property are generally ineffective, because most personal property has no title, and the liens are not recorded. This means that the personal property could easily be sold to a third party who has no idea that the lien existed. However, if the personal property is business equipment and inventory, and the lien has been recorded under the Uniform Commercial Code because the equipment or inventory is collateral for a loan, the lien will prevent you from selling the property with clear title if the buyer conducts a UCC search.

TIP

How to find liens recorded against you. The secretary of state's office in every state maintains a registry of liens, listing judgment liens, tax liens, and security interests that creditors claim in your property. You can do your own lien search online by searching the Uniform Commercial Code (UCC) records database at your secretary of state or department of state's website, to see whether any liens have been recorded against you and your business. (Search for your personal name and your business names.) If you find any incorrect information—for example, you have paid off a debt but there's still a lien against you—ask the lender in question for a UCC release, which it is legally required to provide.

A judgment creditor can also file a judgment with your state motor vehicles department to get a judgment lien on any car, truck, motorcycle, or other motor vehicle you own. You may not know about this type of lien unless you check with the motor vehicles department or the creditor files a proof of claim in your bankruptcy case, describing its interest as "secured."

Typically, judgment liens that have been recorded in your county will attach to property that you acquire later. For example, a judgment may be recorded in your county land records office even if you don't own any real estate. If you buy some real estate a few years later, you'll discover that it is now burdened by that pesky old lien that was just sitting there, waiting for you to make a move. Most real estate liens expire after a certain number of years (seven to ten in most states), though they can typically be renewed.

Statutory Liens

Some liens are created by law. For example, in most states, when you hire someone to work on your house, the worker or supplier of materials is entitled to obtain a mechanic's lien (also called a materialman's lien) on the house if you don't pay. In some states, a homeowners' association has the same right if you don't pay your dues or special assessments.

Statutory liens affect only your real estate. They don't attach to your personal property, such as a car or equipment.

Tax Liens

Federal, state, and local governments have the authority to impose liens on your property if you owe delinquent taxes. If you owe money to the IRS or another taxing authority, the debt is secured only if the taxing authority has recorded a lien against your property (and you still own the property) or has issued a notice of tax lien, and the equity in your home or retirement plan is sufficient to cover the debt. For example, in these times of upside down or underwater mortgages, a debt to the IRS may be unsecured even if a lien has been imposed on your home, if you don't have enough equity to secure the debt.

If you don't pay an IRS bill, the IRS can record a Notice of Federal Tax Lien at your county land records office or your secretary of state's office. While the federal tax lien attaches to all of your property, for practical purposes a lien will be effective only if your real estate equity, your retirement account, or your bank account is sufficient to cover the debt. Similarly, your local government can attach a lien to your real estate for unpaid property taxes. And, if your state taxing authority sends you a bill and you don't contest or pay it, the state can record a tax lien against your real estate in that state.

What Happens to Secured Debts When You File for Bankruptcy

Unsecured debts and secured debts are treated differently in Chapter 7 bankruptcy. Creditors with unsecured debts may receive some money in the bankruptcy process, if the trustee is able to take and sell any of your nonexempt property. (The proceeds from a sale of your nonexempt property are divided among all of your unsecured creditors according to priorities established in the bankruptcy code.) Once your case is over, however, unsecured creditors have no rights. Most types of unsecured debts are wiped out in bankruptcy, whether or not the creditor was paid off, and the creditor has to simply take the loss and move on.

Secured debts are different in two ways: First, if the trustee takes and sells property that secures a debt, the secured creditor is entitled to be paid in full before unsecured creditors get anything. This may effectively allow you to keep the property securing the debt, because the trustee has no incentive to take the property and sell it if the secured creditor would be entitled to all of the nonexempt proceeds.

Second, even though bankruptcy wipes out your personal obligation to repay a secured debt, the creditor's lien on your property survives your bankruptcy case (unless the property is returned to the creditor). A secured debt consists of two parts:

- **Your personal liability for the debt, which obligates you to pay back the creditor.** Bankruptcy wipes out your personal liability for the debt, assuming the debt qualifies for the bankruptcy discharge (See Ch. 11.) This means the creditor cannot later sue you to collect the debt.

- **The creditor's legal claim (lien or security interest) on the collateral for the debt.** A lien gives the creditor the right to repossess the property or force its sale if you do not pay the debt. If the collateral is unavailable, the lender can sue you for the value of the collateral. A lien sticks with the property even if you give the property to someone else. Bankruptcy, by itself, does not eliminate liens. However, during bankruptcy, you may be able to take additional steps to eliminate, or at least reduce, liens on collateral for security interests.

EXAMPLE: Mary buys a multipurpose copier/fax machine on credit from an office supply store. She signs a contract agreeing to pay for the machine over the next year. The contract also states that the creditor (the store) has a security interest in the copier and can repossess it if any payment is more than 15 days late. The creditor records a UCC statement for the property, which perfects the lien. In this type of secured debt, Mary's obligation to pay the debt is her personal liability, and the store's right to repossess the copier is part of the lien. Bankruptcy eliminates Mary's obligation to pay for the copier (unless she reaffirms the debt in bankruptcy—see below), but the creditor retains its lien and can repossess the copier if Mary doesn't keep up her payments as specified in the security agreement.

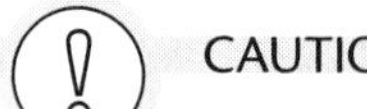
CAUTION

If you "lose" the collateral. Some bankruptcy debtors lose, sell, or give away property serving as collateral for a secured debt. This can get you into big trouble with the bankruptcy court. For example, Fred used a heavy-duty metal lathe in his machine shop to manufacture metal puzzles. The lathe is collateral for the loan he used to purchase the lathe. Six months ago, Fred shipped the lathe to a friend in a different state (to pay a gambling debt) and stopped making payments to the lender, then filed for Chapter 7 bankruptcy. The lender sought and obtained permission from the bankruptcy court to continue its repossession efforts. The lender contacted Fred to arrange to pick up the lathe; Fred told the lender he no longer had it. After the bankruptcy, the lender sued Fred and recovered an award for the value of the lathe. Most bankruptcy courts would consider what Fred did to be a "willful and malicious" act, which means the debt cannot be discharged in bankruptcy. Fred will never be able to discharge the judgment, even if he files a second bankruptcy case down the road.

Options for Handling Secured Debts in Chapter 7 Bankruptcy

As part of your Chapter 7 bankruptcy paperwork, you must list all creditors who hold secured debts. You must also tell the bankruptcy trustee and the secured creditors what you plan to do with the collateral that secures those debts: whether you plan to surrender the property or keep it. You do this in an official form called the "Statement of Intention," which you must file with the court along with your other bankruptcy papers and mail to your creditors. Then, you must carry out your stated intention within the applicable time limits. (You'll find step-by-step instructions for completing all of the necessary bankruptcy forms in Ch. 9; Ch. 10 explains how to follow through on your intentions.)

This section explains the basic options for handling secured debts in bankruptcy, including the advantages and disadvantages of each option, any restrictions that may apply, when each option makes sense, and what steps you have to take to use each option. You should review this material carefully and decide how you want to treat the collateral for each secured debt before you file for bankruptcy. If you plan on keeping the collateral, call the lender before filing to see whether you will have to reaffirm the debt (agree to be liable for it under a new contract after your bankruptcy, as explained further below) or whether you can keep the collateral by simply remaining current on your payments.

Once you've filed for bankruptcy, the automatic stay prevents secured creditors from repossessing property that serves as collateral for a secured debt, unless the court gives permission or you miss the deadline for carrying out your stated intention. It's much easier to hold on to property in the first place than to get it back after the creditor repossesses it. So, if you have some secured property that a creditor is about to take and you haven't filed for bankruptcy yet, you may want to file right away to prevent the seizure.

CAUTION

You may lose your property if you fail to choose. If you don't make a choice about how you intend to treat collateral, the secured creditor might have the right to repossess the collateral 30 days after you file for bankruptcy, whether or not you have kept up with your payments. Most security agreements contain what's known as an "ipso facto" clause, which says that filing for bankruptcy qualifies as a default allowing the creditor to repossess the property, even if you are current on your payments. If you don't use one of the choices provided by the bankruptcy code, the creditor may use the ipso facto clause to grab your property. However, some states don't honor these ipso facto clauses as long as you remain current on your payments.

Option 1: Surrender the Collateral

If you don't want or need to keep the property, you can surrender it. Surrendering the collateral simply means allowing the creditor to take it back or foreclose on the lien. This is the simplest option for dealing with secured property. It completely frees you from the debt: Giving back the property satisfies the terms of the lien, and the bankruptcy discharges your personal liability for the original debt (and prevents the creditor from seeking a deficiency judgment).

Advantages. A quick and easy way to completely rid yourself of a secured debt.

Disadvantages. You lose the property.

Restrictions. None. You can surrender any kind of collateral for a secured debt.

When to use it. For property that you don't need or want or that would cost too much to keep.

How it works. On the Statement of Intention form, check the box indicating that you will surrender the property. You must file the form and send a copy to the secured creditor. It's then up to the creditor to contact you and arrange a time to pick up the property. You must make the property available to the creditor within 30 days after the creditors' meeting. If the creditor doesn't take the property, and the trustee doesn't claim it, it's yours to keep. This might happen if the property isn't worth much. For example, it probably isn't worth the creditor's time to pick up, store, and auction off used household furniture or old computer equipment, no matter how much you still owe on it.

Option 2: Redeem the Collateral

If you want to keep certain types of property, you may "redeem" it by paying the secured creditor the property's current replacement value (what you would have to pay a retail vendor for that type of property, considering its age and condition), usually in a lump sum. Essentially, you are buying the property back from the creditor. In return, the creditor delivers title to you in the same manner as if you had followed through on your original agreement. You then own the property free and clear.

Advantages. Redemption is a great option if you owe significantly more than the property is worth. The creditor must accept the current replacement value of the item as payment in full. If you and the creditor don't agree on the replacement value of the property, the court will decide the issue in a proceeding called a "valuation" hearing. (Ch. 6 explains how to figure out the replacement value of various types of property.)

Disadvantages. Most debtors will have to pay the full replacement value of the item in a lump sum in order to redeem it. It may be difficult for you to come up with that much cash on short notice. You may be able to get a loan; some companies specialize in lending to people seeking to redeem their collateral in bankruptcy. Or, you can try to get the creditor to agree to accept installment payments, but courts cannot require creditors to make this type of deal. Importantly, redemption is not available for business property.

Restrictions. You have the right to redeem property only if all of the following are true:

- The debt is a consumer debt: one incurred "primarily for a personal, family, or household purpose." This includes just about everything except collateral for loans and credit obtained for business purposes.
- The property is tangible personal property. Tangible property is anything you can touch. A car, furniture, a boat, a computer, and jewelry are all examples of tangible property. Stocks are intangible. The property must also be "personal property," which simply means it can't be real estate. You aren't allowed to redeem property you use in your business, even in a sole proprietorship.
- The property is either:
  - claimed as exempt (exempt property is explained in Ch. 6), or
  - abandoned by the trustee. A trustee will abandon property that has little or no nonexempt value beyond the amount of the liens. The trustee may notify you of the abandonment or may simply wait for your discharge to be granted, at which time the property will automatically be considered abandoned. Either way, once the property is abandoned, you can redeem it by paying the secured creditor its replacement value. If you know you'll want to redeem property if the trustee abandons it, check the "redeem" box on the Statement of Intention. If you haven't done this and the trustee abandons the property, you may have to amend your Statement of Intention (instructions for amending a form are in Ch. 10). Call the trustee to find out.

When to use it. Redemption may be a good idea if you really want to keep personal property, but you don't want the debt to survive your bankruptcy (this is a consequence of reaffirmation, discussed below). Use redemption only if you owe more than it would cost to purchase the property and you would not be able to get rid of the lien (lien avoidance is covered below in Option 5). It often makes sense to redeem small items of household property that you want to keep, because raising money for the lump sum payment probably will not be that difficult.

How it works. You and the creditor must agree on the value of the property, then draft and sign a redemption agreement. Agreeing on the replacement value may take a little negotiation. Sometimes, you can get the creditor to accept installment payments if you agree to pay a higher total amount. Whatever you agree to, put it in the redemption agreement. (See Appendix D for sample agreements and instructions.)

Option 3: Retain and Pay (the "Ride-Through" Option)

Before the bankruptcy law changed in 2005, a majority of bankruptcy courts recognized the "ride-through" or "retain and pay" option for dealing with secured debts. Where this option was available, debtors could keep the collateral for a secured debt without reaffirming the debt or redeeming the property, as long as they stayed current on their payments. Debtors who took advantage of this option wouldn't owe a deficiency balance if they had to give the property back after receiving their bankruptcy discharge.

The ride-through option is no longer an explicit part of the bankruptcy code, and it isn't recognized in the bankruptcy courts of every state. However, some lenders (and some courts) still allow debtors to keep the collateral without reaffirming a secured debt, as long as they remain current on the payments. These lenders would rather continue to receive payments from a reliable borrower than have to repossess and auction off the property only to receive a fraction of what they're owed.

Advantages. The ride-through option allows you to keep property without obligating yourself to a debt that will survive your bankruptcy or having to come up with lump-sum payment. You can keep the property as long as you can keep up with your payments. If you reach a point where you can't afford the payments, you can essentially surrender the property: give it back without owing a deficiency balance.

Disadvantages. Because the ride-through option is no longer part of the bankruptcy code, your lender usually gets to decide whether to allow it or not. And, the ride-through option isn't allowed in every judicial district. Even if you are allowed to use this option, you'll have to keep making your payments if you want to keep the property. In contrast, surrendering or redeeming the property both allow you to exit your bankruptcy case without ongoing payment obligations (unless your lender allows you to redeem on an installment plan).

Restrictions. Generally, your lender gets to decide whether to allow you to use the ride-through option or to require you to redeem or reaffirm the debt. Whether or not your creditor will be so accommodating depends on how close you are to paying off the debt, your history with the creditor, and the creditor's experience with the reaffirmation process.

If your lender doesn't want you to use this option, it might still be available to you if one of the following is true:

- Your state's law forbids lenders from repossessing property as long as you stay current on your payments. In this situation, if you don't redeem or surrender the property, or reaffirm the debt, the debtor can't do anything to enforce its security interest as long as you keep making those payments. (For information on researching your state's law, see Ch. 12.)
- The court rejects your reaffirmation agreement. In this situation, most courts have allowed debtors to keep their property as long as they continue making their payments. These courts have held that, as long as you sign and file a valid reaffirmation agreement and attend the hearing, you will be protected from repossession, even if the court ultimately rejects the agreement (typically, because it looks like you won't be able to make the payments required by the contract). (See *In re Chim*, 381 B.R. 191 (Md. 2008); *In re Moustafi*, 371 B.R. 434 (Ariz. 2007).)

In at least one federal judicial circuit—the 11th Circuit, which covers Alabama, Florida, and Georgia—debtors may not use the ride-through option. If debtors in these states want to keep property, they must either redeem it or sign a reaffirmation agreement for the debt. (See *In re Linderman*, Case No. 6:09-BK-02087-KSJ (M.D. Fla. 2009).

When to use it. If your lender will allow it and you think you'll be able to make your payments, the ride-through option is often the best choice for property you really want to keep. It allows you to retain the property and avoid any penalty (in the form of a deficiency judgment) if you later have to give it back.

How it works. First, you'll have to contact your lender to see whether it will allow you to "retain and pay for" the collateral rather than reaffirm. If the lender agrees, check the box on the Statement of Intention indicating that you will retain the property. Then, check the "Other" box, and write this in the space provided: "Debtor will retain collateral and continue to make regular payments."

If you default to the ride-through option because the court rejects your reaffirmation agreement, you should complete your Statement of Intention as explained in the instructions for reaffirming a debt, below.

Option 4: Reaffirm the Debt

When you reaffirm a debt, you agree that you will still owe the debt after your bankruptcy case is over. Both the creditor's lien on the collateral and your personal liability for the debt under the original promissory note survive bankruptcy intact—often, just as if you never filed for bankruptcy. For example, if you owe $25,000 on your car before you file for Chapter 7 bankruptcy, you most likely will continue to owe $25,000 on your car after you file for bankruptcy (unless you negotiate a lower amount in your reaffirmation agreement). If you can't keep up your payments and the car is repossessed, you'll owe the difference between the amount you reaffirm for and the amount the lender is able to sell the car for at auction (considerably less than you owe, in most cases). This is called a "deficiency balance." Nearly all states permit a creditor to sue for a deficiency balance for most types of property. About half of the states, however, don't allow deficiency balances on repossessed personal property if the original purchase price was less than a few thousand dollars.

Whether or not you reaffirm the debt, if you default on your payments once your bankruptcy case is over, the creditor can repossess the collateral. But if you don't reaffirm the debt, and instead use the ride-through option of keeping the property and continuing your payments, you won't owe a deficiency balance if you have to give back the property.

Advantages. Reaffirmation provides a sure way to keep collateral as long as you abide by the terms of the reaffirmation agreement and keep up your payments. Reaffirmation also provides a setting in which you may be able to negotiate new terms to reduce your payments, your interest rate, and/or the total amount you will have to pay over time.

Disadvantages. Because reaffirmation leaves you personally liable for the debt, you can't walk away from the debt after bankruptcy. You'll still be legally bound to pay the deficiency balance even if the property is damaged or destroyed. And because you have to wait eight years before filing another Chapter 7 bankruptcy case, you'll be stuck with that debt for a long time.

> EXAMPLE: Tasha owes $35,000 on a pickup truck she uses in her masonry contracting business. Because she needs the truck for her business, she enters into a reaffirmation agreement with the dealership financing company that is subsequently approved by the bankruptcy judge. Two months after her bankruptcy case is over, Tasha's income plummets when her main general contractor goes out of business. Tasha is forced to give back the truck. Shortly afterwards, the lender auctions off the truck for $15,000, then sends Tasha a deficiency notice for the $20,000 remaining on the loan. When Tasha doesn't pay up, the lender sues Tasha, obtains a judgment, and begins aggressive collection efforts that won't let up until Tasha can file another bankruptcy case, eight years later.

Restrictions. Reaffirmation can be used with any kind of property and any kind of lien, but the creditor must agree to the terms of the reaffirmation if they are different from the current agreement. You or the lender must file the agreement in court as part of your bankruptcy case. Unless an attorney is representing you in the bankruptcy or in the reaffirmation process, the bankruptcy court must review the agreement in a reaffirmation or discharge hearing. At that hearing, the judge will review your bankruptcy paperwork to see how the reaffirmation might affect your post-bankruptcy budget and whether you can afford the payments. The judge can disapprove the agreement if it is not in your best interest or would create an undue hardship for you. The judge is likely to reject the agreement if it looks like you won't be able to make the payments after paying your basic living expenses or if you owe much more on the debt than the property is worth.

When to use it. Because reaffirmation comes with the very serious disadvantage of leaving you in debt after your bankruptcy case is over, you should consider it only if:

- it's the only way to hang on to collateral that you really need to keep, or
- you are able to negotiate new payments terms that are attractive enough to warrant the reaffirmation.

Even if your creditor doesn't require you to reaffirm the debt, it may make sense to do so anyway if you can use the process to negotiate a significantly lower payment. Your leverage will often be considerable. After all, you have the option of surrendering the collateral and walking away without owing a dime, while the lender will be stuck having to sell the collateral at auction for a small fraction of the property's value.

You generally shouldn't reaffirm a debt for more than the property is worth unless your credit score and other circumstances would make replacing the property too difficult. As you undoubtedly know, it's hard to buy a new car, business equipment, or inventory without a good credit score—and filing for bankruptcy will certainly lower your score. Even if reaffirmation doesn't make the best economic sense, you may be inclined to do it anyway, if it's the only way to hold on to assets you really need. Only you can decide whether the property you want to keep is worth saddling yourself with a large debt for years to come.

> EXAMPLE: Joanie borrowed $25,000 three years ago to purchase three computer servers she uses in her Web-based bookkeeping service. Joanie still owes the lender about $20,000 because of the 12% interest she pays on the loan. However, because computer hardware depreciates so fast, the servers are now worth only $8,000. Joanie tells the lender that she's willing to reaffirm only if it reduces the balance on the note to $8,000 and cuts the interest rate to 5%, which would lower her monthly payments by more than half. When the lender refuses, Joanie says that she will have to simply surrender the servers and buy new ones for much less. Caught between the proverbial rock and hard place, the lender makes a counteroffer of $10,000, at an interest rate of 6.5%. Joanie agrees to reaffirm the debt under these new terms. Even though she might be able to replace the servers for less, that would take more time and effort than she has to spare.

If you need to reaffirm a debt in order to keep the collateral, make sure you keep up your payments prior to filing for bankruptcy so you can stay on the creditor's good side. If you fall behind, the creditor has the right to demand that you make your account current before agreeing to a reaffirmation contract, but you will probably have some room to negotiate. If the creditor rejects your payments during bankruptcy (which often happens), deposit that money into a separate account so it's available once the creditor decides to accept it. If you can't make these rejected payments when the creditor wants them, you might lose your property.

How it works. There are several official forms you must use to reaffirm a debt: a form cover sheet

(Form 27), and the reaffirmation forms themselves (Form 240A, Form 240B, and Form 240C). You'll find blank copies of these forms in Appendix C. Most large creditors will complete the paperwork, ask you to sign it, and file it with the court. If you're dealing with a smaller creditor, you may have to file it yourself.

The reaffirmation agreement includes a number of legally required disclosures and warnings. These provisions are intended to put you on notice of how much you'll be paying overall, the interest rate, and your liability to pay the debt in full, even if something happens to the collateral. In Part D of the agreement, you must explain why you are reaffirming the debt and provide information on your income and expenses, so the court can determine whether the agreement creates an undue hardship for you. Your income and expense information should be in the same ballpark as the information you include in Schedules I and J (see Ch. 9). If these figures indicate that you can't afford the required payments, the court may reject your reaffirmation agreement. (See *In re Laynas*, 345 B.R. 505 (E.D. Penn. 2006).) If this happens, you will probably be able to keep the property as long as you stay current on your payments under the old loan; see Option 3, above, for more information.

You can cancel a reaffirmation agreement by notifying the creditor before the later of:

- the date of your discharge, or
- 60 days after you filed the reaffirmation agreement with the bankruptcy court

If your case is already closed, however, you will not be able to switch to the other options listed in this chapter.

Option 5: Eliminate (Avoid) Liens

Lien avoidance is a procedure by which you ask the bankruptcy court to eliminate or reduce liens on some types of exempt property. Lien avoidance is neither automatic nor required: You have to request it in a separate legal proceeding in your bankruptcy case.

One common lien avoidance procedure lets you eliminate or reduce liens on certain types of exempt personal property, depending on the value of the property and the amount of the exemption available to you. This procedure is available only for what are called "nonpossessory, non-purchase-money liens": liens on property that you already owned when you pledged it as security for a loan. It can't be used for real estate.

A different lien avoidance procedure allows you to eliminate judgment liens on personal property or real estate that falls within an exemption. By eliminating the judgment lien, you get to keep the property free and clear without paying anything more to the creditor, assuming the underlying debt can be discharged in bankruptcy (which it usually can).

Nonpossessory, Non-Purchase-Money Liens

If you have pledged some item of personal property (not real estate) that you already owned as security for a loan, and the property is completely or partially exempt, you may be able to eliminate a lien on the property. (You'll find sample forms for this remedy in Appendix D; you will need to modify them to fit your situation.)

How much of the lien can be eliminated depends on the value and type of property and the amount of the exemption. If the property (or your equity in it) is entirely exempt, the court will eliminate the entire lien, and you'll get to keep the property without paying anything. If the property (or your equity in it) is worth more than the exemption limit, the lien will be reduced to the difference between the exemption limit and either the property's value or the amount of the debt, whichever is less.

EXAMPLE: A creditor has a $5,000 lien on Dena's professional embroidery and monogramming machine, which is worth

$3,000. In Dena's state, the embroidery machine is exempt as a tool of trade only to $2,000. Dena could get the lien reduced to $1,000. The other $4,000 of the lien is eliminated (avoided); $3,000 (value of item) – $2,000 (exemption amount) = $1,000 (amount of lien remaining after lien avoidance).

Advantages. This type of lien avoidance costs nothing (if you are representing yourself), involves only a moderate amount of paperwork, and often allows you to keep property without paying anything.

Disadvantages. Some paperwork is involved. Also, by trying to avoid a lien on exempt property, you may reopen the issue of whether the property really is exempt in the first place. This may happen if the property was deemed exempt by default (that is, the property is exempt because the trustee and creditors didn't challenge your claim of exemption within the applicable time limit). Some courts have allowed creditors to argue that the property is not exempt at a hearing on a motion to avoid a lien.

As a practical matter, however, motions to avoid a lien are usually not contested.

Restrictions. There are several important limits on this type of lien avoidance. First, as noted above, you may avoid only nonpossessory, non-purchase-money security interests. That sounds complicated, but it makes sense when you break it down:

- Nonpossessory means the creditor does not physically keep the property you've pledged as collateral. It stays in your possession; the creditor only has a lien on it. (In contrast, if you leave your property at a pawnshop to get a loan, that is a possessory security interest—for which this lien avoidance procedure is not available.)
- Non-purchase-money means that you didn't use the money you borrowed to purchase the collateral. Instead, you used property you already owned as collateral for the loan.
- Security interest means the lien was created by voluntary agreement between you and the creditor. In other words, the lien wasn't involuntary, like a tax or judgment lien.

Second, the property you pledged as collateral must be exempt under the exemption system you are using. (Remember that domicile requirements may limit the exemptions available to you—see Ch. 6 for more information.) If the property isn't exempt, then the lien doesn't impair your exemption rights, and it can't be eliminated.

Third, only certain types of property are covered. Unfortunately, the property most commonly pledged as collateral for nonpossessory, non-purchase-money security interests don't qualify—homes and cars (unless the vehicle qualifies as a tool of trade, discussed below). You may eliminate a nonpossessory, non-purchase-money security interest lien only if the collateral falls into one of these categories:

- household furnishings, household goods, clothing, appliances, books, and musical instruments or jewelry that are primarily for your personal, family, or household use
- health aids professionally prescribed for you or a dependent
- animals or crops held primarily for your personal, family, or household use (but only the first $5,575 of the lien can be avoided), or
- implements, machines, professional books, or tools used in a trade (yours or a dependent's), but only the first $5,575 of the lien can be avoided.

You can remove up to $5,575 of a lien from a vehicle that qualifies as a tool of your trade. Generally, a motor vehicle is considered a tool of trade only if you use it as an integral part of your business—for example, if you do door-to-door sales or delivery work. It is not considered a tool of trade if you simply use it to commute, even if you have no other means of getting to work.

What Are Household Goods?

Household goods are limited to:

- clothing
- furniture
- appliances
- one radio
- one television
- one VCR
- linens
- china
- crockery
- kitchenware
- educational equipment and materials primarily for the use of your minor dependent children
- medical equipment and supplies
- furniture exclusively for the use of your minor children, or your elderly or disabled dependents
- your personal effects (including your wedding rings and the toys and hobby equipment of your minor dependent children) and those of your dependents, and
- one personal computer and related equipment.

Items in the following categories are not considered to be household goods, and you cannot avoid liens on them:

- works of art (unless they were created by you or a relative)
- electronic entertainment equipment with a fair market value of more than $550 total (not including the one television, one radio, and one VCR listed above)
- items acquired as antiques that have a fair market value of more than $550 total
- jewelry (other than wedding rings) that has a fair market value of more than $550 total, and
- a computer (excluding the personal computer and related equipment listed above), motor vehicle (including a tractor or lawn tractor), boat, motorized recreational device, conveyance vehicle, watercraft, or aircraft.

Judgment Liens

A nonconsensual judgment lien on property can be avoided if all of the following are true:

- The lien resulted from a money judgment issued by a court.
- You are entitled to claim an exemption in at least some of your equity in the property.
- The lien would result in a loss of some or all of this exempt equity if the property were sold.

If these three conditions are met, you can remove judgment liens from any exempt property, including real estate and cars.

When to use it. Use lien avoidance if it's available, especially if a lien can be completely wiped out. Even if you don't need or want the property, you can avoid the lien, sell the property, and use the money for other things.

To keep things simple, you may want to avoid liens only on property that is completely exempt. The lien will be eliminated entirely and you'll own the property free and clear, without paying anything to the creditor.

Even partial lien avoidance can be beneficial, but sooner or later you'll have to pay the amount remaining on the lien if the property has a title document or is subject to repossession or foreclosure on what's left of the lien. Most often, you'll have to pay off the lien in a lump sum, but some creditors may be willing to accept installments, especially if you compromise on the value of the lien.

How it works. You request lien avoidance by checking the column "Property is claimed as exempt" on the Statement of Intention, and by typing and filing a motion. (Forms and instructions for preparing and filing a motion to avoid a judgment lien on real estate are contained in Appendix D; the form must be modified if the lien is on personal property, such as a car or boat.) Although it may sound complicated, lien avoidance is often a routine procedure that can be accomplished without a lawyer.

Some bankruptcy filers don't realize they have liens on their property, or don't realize that they could eliminate those liens. Others may not be able to eliminate liens when they file for bankruptcy (typically, because they have no exempt equity in the property), but later they become eligible to do so. Fortunately, bankruptcy courts are very liberal about allowing debtors to reopen a case so they can file a motion to avoid the lien. Reopening a bankruptcy case is a routine procedure, described in Ch. 10.

CAUTION

The economic downturn has made lien avoidance on real estate less common. Until 2007, many debtors were able to avoid judgment liens on real estate. The value of the property almost always exceeded the voluntary liens, leaving at least some exempt equity. These days, however, it is increasingly rare for homeowners to have any equity. In fact, one-third of all *first* home mortgages exceed the value of the home, and the figure is much higher if you add second mortgages. If you have no equity in your home, a judgment lien can't "impair"

Eliminating Judgment Liens on Oversecured Property

To determine whether you can eliminate a judicial lien, apply this simple formula. Add the following items:

- all consensual liens on the property (for example, a mortgage and home equity loan)
- all tax liens, and
- your exemption amount.

If the total of all these items is greater than the value of the property, then you can completely eliminate judicial liens on the property. The Judicial Lien Worksheet, below, will help you do the math. Here are a few sample calculations:

Example A

Value of property	$ 200,000
Mortgage	$ 100,000
Second mortgage	20,000
Exemption	10,000
Total	$ 130,000
Amount available for judicial liens	$ 70,000
Amount of judicial lien	$ 30,000

RESULT: Lien cannot be eliminated.

Example B

Value of property	$ 200,000
Mortgage	$ 150,000
Second mortgage	20,000
Exemption	10,000
Total	$ 180,000
Amount available for judicial liens	$ 20,000
Amount of judicial lien	$ 30,000

RESULT: $10,000 of lien can be eliminated, $20,000 of lien cannot be eliminated.

Example C

Value of property	$ 200,000
Mortgage	$ 160,000
Second mortgage	40,000
Exemption	10,000
Total	$ 210,000
Amount available for judicial liens	$ 0
Amount of judicial lien	$ 30,000

RESULT: Judicial lien can be completely eliminated.

One more point to remember: For the purposes of bankruptcy lien avoidance provisions, judicial liens get the lowest priority, behind consensual liens and tax liens, regardless of when the liens were placed on the property and regardless of what state law says. So, in Example C above, it would not matter if the $30,000 judgment lien was created before or after the $40,000 second mortgage: The judicial lien can be eliminated either way.

Judicial Lien Worksheet

1. Value of your home .... $ ______
2. Amount of first mortgage .... $ ______
3. Amount of other mortgages and home equity loans .... $ ______
4. Amount of tax liens .... $ ______
5. Amount of mechanics' liens .... $ ______
6. Total of Lines 2 through 5 .... $ ______
   (Total of all liens that are not judicial liens)

   If Line 6 is greater than Line 1, you can stop here—you can eliminate all judicial liens. Otherwise, go on to Line 7.
7. Line 1 minus Line 6 .... $ ______
   This is the amount of equity you can protect with an exemption.
8. Exemption amount .... $ ______

   If Line 8 is greater than Line 7 you can stop here—you can eliminate all judicial liens. Otherwise, go on to Line 9.
9. Line 7 minus Line 8 .... $ ______
   This is the amount of the judicial liens that you can't eliminate.
10. Amount of judicial liens .... $ ______

   If Line 9 is greater than Line 10, you can stop here—you cannot eliminate judicial liens from this property. Otherwise, go on to Line 11.
11. Line 10 minus Line 9 .... $ ______
   This is the portion of the judicial lien that you can eliminate.
   (Line 9 is the portion of judicial lien you cannot eliminate.)

an exemption and can't be avoided. If your home's value later increases enough to give you some equity, you might consider reopening the bankruptcy and bringing a lien avoidance action.

Lien Elimination Techniques Beyond the Scope of This Book

Deep in the recesses of the bankruptcy code are other procedures for eliminating certain kinds of nonconsensual liens. Section 11 U.S.C. § 522(h) gives a debtor the power to use a wide range of lien avoidance techniques that have been made available to the bankruptcy trustee. The techniques are found in Sections 545, 547, 548, 549, 553, and 724(a) of the bankruptcy code. These liens include:

- nonjudgment liens securing the payment of penalties, fines, or punitive damages, and
- nonconsensual liens that were recorded or perfected while you were already insolvent or within the 90 days before you filed for bankruptcy.

To use these procedures, you'll need the help of a bankruptcy attorney.

TIP

You can pay off a lien in a follow-up Chapter 13 bankruptcy. Another way to handle liens is through what some bankruptcy practitioners call a "Chapter 20" bankruptcy: filing for Chapter 13 bankruptcy after completing a Chapter 7 bankruptcy. You use the Chapter 13 bankruptcy to deal with or eliminate any liens remaining after your Chapter 7 case has wiped out your personal liability. And, if a lien exceeds the value of the property, you can often get the lien fully discharged by simply paying the current replacement value of the item, rather than the full amount of the lien. However, you can do this only if you file the Chapter 13 case at least four years after the date when you filed for Chapter 7 bankruptcy. (The revised bankruptcy law prohibits you from receiving a Chapter 13 discharge within four years of filing a Chapter 7 case in which a discharge was granted.) Because this book covers Chapter 7 bankruptcies only, space does not permit us to give a full explanation of how to do a successful follow-up Chapter 13 case. For more information, see *Chapter 13 Bankruptcy: Keep Your Property & Repay Debts Over Time,* by Stephen Elias and Robin Leonard (Nolo).

Reclaiming Exempt Property Repossessed Just Before Bankruptcy

If, during the 90 days before you filed for bankruptcy, a secured creditor took exempt property that would qualify for either lien avoidance or redemption, you may be able to get the property back. But you must act quickly, before the creditor resells the property. If the creditor has already resold the property, you are probably out of luck. Repossessed cars are usually resold very quickly, but used furniture may sit in a warehouse for months.

Legally, the creditor must give back the property because the repossession was an illegal preference, which means that the property is still part of the bankruptcy estate (as explained in Ch. 5) and can be "recaptured." In practice, however, most creditors won't give the property back unless the court orders it (which usually means you'll need the help of a lawyer) or you make a reasonable cash offer for the item.

Assuming you don't want to hire a lawyer, you probably won't be able to get an item back unless you talk the creditor into allowing you to redeem it or reaffirm the debt. The creditor might prefer to have cash in hand rather than used property sitting in a warehouse. If you plan to avoid the lien on the exempt item and not pay anything, however, the creditor probably won't turn over the property unless forced to by court order.

Whether hiring a lawyer is worth the expense to get back an exempt item so you can avoid the lien depends on how badly you need the property and what you'll save through lien avoidance. Compare what it would cost to redeem the property and what it would cost to buy replacement property. If those options are cheaper, or you decide you can get along without the property, don't bother with the court order.

CHAPTER

Complete and File Your Bankruptcy Paperwork

This chapter shows you how to take all of the necessary steps to prepare your bankruptcy case for filing under Chapter 7. For the most part, the process is simple, as long as you follow all of the instructions we provide.

Gather the Necessary Documents

Along with your official and local bankruptcy forms, you will also have to provide these documents:

- a certificate showing that you completed a credit counseling workshop within the last 180 days
- your most recent federal tax return or a transcript of the return (this goes to the trustee, not the court), and
- your wage stubs for the last 60 days, if you received any.

Before you can get your bankruptcy discharge, you must also file a certification showing that you completed counseling on personal financial management (Form 23—Debtor's Certification of Completion of Postpetition Instructional Course Concerning Personal Financial Management, covered in Ch. 10).

The Credit Counseling Certificate

Every person who files a consumer bankruptcy—including small business owners filing a personal Chapter 7 bankruptcy—must first attend credit counseling. This counseling must be provided by an agency approved by the United States Trustee's Office and must take place within 180 days before you file for bankruptcy. (At least one court has held that you must get counseling at least one day before you file—not earlier the same day. To be safe, don't get same-day counseling.) The counseling can be done by phone, on the Internet, or in person.

You can find a list of approved counselors at the U.S Trustee's Office website at www.justice.gov/ust (click "Credit Counseling & Debtor Education"). The agencies are listed by state, but you can use any agency in any state or region.

Once you complete your counseling, the agency should give you a certificate of completion. You must either attach this certificate to Exhibit D of your bankruptcy petition (see the instructions for completing the petition below) or file the certificate within 14 days after you file. Although you don't have to file your certificate of completion when you file your petition, you must have completed your counseling by that time unless you fit within one of the exceptions discussed below.

Repayment Plans

The purpose of credit counseling is to get you to sign up for a debt repayment plan instead of filing for bankruptcy. Indeed, if the plan makes sense and you believe you can make the payments required to complete it, you might reasonably consider signing up for it. However, keep in mind that even if you make the payments faithfully month after month, the creditors can pull out of the plan if you later fall behind—and they can go after you for the remaining debt. If you then decide to file for Chapter 7 bankruptcy, you will have paid back all that money for no good reason. This is why most bankruptcy professionals discourage their clients from signing up for a debt repayment plan.

Even if you have no intention of signing up for a plan, you are still required to cooperate with the debt counseling agency in fashioning a plan if they think one is possible. You then have to file this plan along with your certificate of completion and your other bankruptcy papers. If the U.S. Trustee suspects that you might be able to complete a Chapter 13 bankruptcy repayment plan, it will review the agency's plan as part of its decision-making process.

Counseling Fees

Most agencies charge a modest sum ($25–$50 is common) for the credit counseling, coming up with a repayment plan, and the certificate of completion that you'll need to file with your

Follow These Rules to Stay Out of Trouble

Chapter 7 bankruptcy can be a very straightforward process, but only if you follow the rules. If you don't—even by accident—your bankruptcy case might be dismissed. Not only will you continue to owe your debts and face creditor collection actions, but you might also lose the protection of the automatic stay in any future bankruptcy case you file (see Ch. 4 for more information on the automatic stay).

If you keep these golden rules in mind, you'll save yourself a lot of time and trouble:

- Don't file for Chapter 7 bankruptcy unless you are sure it is the right choice (Part I explains how to make this decision).
- Don't file until you have completed all of your documents as directed in this chapter.
- Don't file until you have a certificate showing that you have completed your credit counseling.
- If you can, pay your filing fee in full rather than in installments, so you don't have to worry about your case being dismissed if you miss a payment.
- Be absolutely complete and honest in filling out your paperwork. Except for Form 23, file all of your documents at the same time (unless you have to file an emergency petition to stop an impending foreclosure, wage garnishment, or repossession).
- Don't file your case until you have your most recent federal tax return (or a transcript) in your hands.
- Serve your tax return (or transcript) on the trustee and any creditors who request it as soon after you file as possible. If you don't serve it at least seven days before the creditors' meeting, your case could be dismissed.
- Immediately amend your paperwork if the trustee asks you to.
- Don't forget your personal financial management counseling. You won't receive a discharge unless, within 45 days after your creditors' meeting, you file Form 23 certifying that you have completed this course. (Ch. 10 explains how.)

other bankruptcy papers. Some credit counseling agencies don't charge anything for the counseling, but require a fee of $50 or more for the certificate.

Agencies are legally required to offer their services without regard to your ability to pay. (11 U.S.C. § 111(c)(2)(B).) If an agency wants to charge more than you can afford, inform the agency of this legal requirement. If the agency doesn't back down, make notes of your conversations (including who you talked to, what was said, and the date of the conversation), and then inform the agency that you are going to report it to the U.S. Trustee's Office for failing to take your poverty into account. If that doesn't bring down the price, go ahead and report the agency. You'll be doing others in the same situation a great favor. (You can find contact information at www.justice.gov/ust.)

Exceptions to the Counseling Requirement

You don't have to get counseling if the U.S. Trustee certifies that there is no appropriate agency available to you in the district where you will be filing. However, counseling can be provided by telephone or online if the U.S. Trustee approves, so it is unlikely that approved debt counseling will ever be unavailable.

In one case, however, a bankruptcy court found that counseling was not "available" to a debtor who spoke Creole because none of the credit counseling agencies in his area could accommodate his language needs. (*In re Petit-Louis,* 344 B.R. 696 (S.D. Fla. 2006).) Presumably, this same rule would apply to any debtor who doesn't speak standard English and can't obtain counseling in his or her native language (or through a translator). Since this case was decided, the U.S. Trustee has begun to approve multilingual credit counseling agencies.

You can also avoid the requirement if you file a motion asking the court to grant an exception because "exigent circumstances" prevented you from getting counseling. You'll have to show that:

- you had to file for bankruptcy immediately (perhaps to stop a creditor from levying on your paycheck or bank account), and
- you were unable to obtain counseling within seven days after requesting it.

CAUTION

A pending foreclosure may not be "exigent" enough. One court has found that a debtor who waits until the last minute to seek credit counseling might not qualify for an exception to the counseling requirement. In *Dixon v. La Barge, Jr.*, 338 B.R. 383 (BAP 8th Cir., 2006), the court found that no exigent circumstances existed when a debtor filed for bankruptcy on the day of a scheduled foreclosure sale. In that case, the debtor claimed to have learned that he could file for Chapter 7 bankruptcy—and that he would have to complete credit counseling—on the night before he filed.

If the court grants an exception based on exigent circumstances, you must complete the counseling within 30 days after you file (and you can ask the court to extend this deadline by 15 days if necessary).

You may also escape the credit counseling requirement if, after notice and hearing, the bankruptcy court determines that you couldn't participate because of:

- a physical disability that prevents you from attending counseling (this exception probably won't apply if the counseling is available on the Internet or over the phone)
- mental incapacity (you are unable to understand and benefit from the counseling, as in cases involving dementia or developmental disabilities), or
- you're on active duty in a military combat zone.

Consequences of Failing to Get Counseling

Courts have handled a debtor's failure to get counseling in two different ways. Some courts dismiss the debtor's bankruptcy case. (See *In re Mills*, 341 B.R. 106 (D.C. 2006).) Other courts have "stricken" the debtor's case instead. (See *In re Carey*, 341 B.R. 798 (M.D. Fla. 2006); *In re Thompson*, 344 B.R. 899 (S.D. Ind. 2006).) This seemingly technical difference can be very important: If your case is stricken, you may refile for bankruptcy without any of the negative consequences of dismissal (including losing the protection of the automatic stay) explained in Ch. 4.

Your Tax Return or Transcript

You will have to give the trustee and the U.S. Trustee your most recent federal tax return no later than seven days before your creditors' meeting. You also have to provide the return to any creditor who asks for it. To protect your privacy, you can redact (black out) your birthdate and Social Security number. If you don't provide your tax return on time, your case could be dismissed.

If you can't find your most recent tax return, you can ask the IRS to give you a transcript of the basic information in your return, then provide the transcript to the trustee. Because it can take some time to receive the transcript, you should make your request as soon as you can.

CAUTION

If you haven't filed tax returns. Although some commentators believe otherwise, you don't have to be current on your tax returns when you file for Chapter 7 bankruptcy. The law requires only that you provide a copy of your "most recently filed" tax return. Of course, most small business owners are current on their tax returns, but for many senior citizens and people who have been living on disability benefits, federal tax returns may be a thing of the past. The trustee probably won't be interested in seeing ancient tax returns, and the IRS may not be able to issue a transcript for a return filed ten or more years ago. So don't lose any sleep if you don't have a relatively recent tax return to show the trustee.

Wage Stubs

As a small business owner, you may not receive a regular "paycheck" or have any wage stubs, because you aren't employed as that term is generally understood. That's fine: If you don't receive wage stubs, you don't have to produce them.

However, if you or your spouse have been employed recently, you are required to produce the stubs you received during the 60-day period prior to filing. If you have already tossed your stubs, you have two options: Wait 60 days (and keep your stubs) before filing, or go ahead and file, hand over the stubs you have, and explain why you don't have 60 days' worth. This second option might not work, however: The law states that failing to provide all wage stubs for the prior 60 days can result in dismissal of the bankruptcy case. (*In re Wilkinson*, 346 B.R. 539 (D. Utah 2006).)

Many bankruptcy courts require you to use a local form as a cover sheet for wage stubs. (See "Get Some Information From the Court," below, for more on local rules and forms.) You should be able to get a copy of this form from the court or its website. Some of these local forms require you to provide information about income that comes from other sources too, not just wages, or at least to certify that you haven't received wages within the past 60 days. However, one court has found that failing to provide this extra information (in that case, proof of disability payments) was not grounds for dismissing the case. (*In re LaPlante*, No. 06-00174B, (W.D. N.Y. 2006).) Our advice on this uncertain issue is to get your court's local form and provide all of the information it requests.

Finding the Right Bankruptcy Court

Because bankruptcy is a creature of federal, not state, law, you must file for bankruptcy in a special federal court. There are federal bankruptcy courts all over the country.

The federal court system divides the country into judicial districts. Every state has at least one judicial district; most have more. Debtors filing personal bankruptcies can file in any of the following districts:

- the district where you have been living for the greater part of the 180-day period before you file, or
- the district where you are domiciled—that is, where you maintain your home, even if you have been living elsewhere (such as on a military base) temporarily.

To find a bankruptcy court nearest to one of these locations, check the government listings in your white pages (under "United States, Courts"), call directory assistance, ask your local librarian, or visit the court directory link at www.bankruptcydata.com. If you live in a state with more than one district, call the court in the closest city and ask whether that district includes your county or zip code.

> **EXAMPLE:** For the past two months, Tom has lived and operated his sole proprietor business in San Luis Obispo, which is in California's Central Judicial District. Before that, he was based in Santa Rosa, in California's Northern Judicial District. Because Tom spent more of the past six months in the Northern District than in the Central, he should file in the bankruptcy court in the Northern District. If it's too inconvenient to file there, he could wait another month, when he would qualify to file in the Central District.

Get Some Information From the Court

Every bankruptcy court has its own requirements for filing bankruptcy papers. If your papers don't meet these local requirements, the court clerk may reject them. So, before you begin preparing your papers, you should find out your court rules.

In urban areas especially, you may get no response to a letter or phone call to the court clerk. You may need to visit the court and get the information in person. Or, the information may be available on the Internet. Almost all bankruptcy courts have websites with this sort of information. To find your court's website, visit www.uscourts.gov/courtlinks.

Fees

The current fee charged by the court to file for Chapter 7 bankruptcy is $299. Fees change, however, so make sure you verify the amount with the court. This fee is due upon filing, unless the court waives the fee or gives you permission to pay in installments. (To make these requests, you must complete Form 3A or 3B, as explained below.)

Local Forms

In addition to the official forms that every bankruptcy court uses (they are listed below), your local bankruptcy court may require you to file one or two additional forms that it has developed. For example, different courts have different forms that you must file along with your wage stubs (as explained above). You can get any required local forms from your local bankruptcy court or you can download them from your court's website. (Go to www.uscourts.gov/courtlinks for a list of links to local courts.) There are far too many local forms for us to explain them here. Most, however, are easy to complete. If you need help obtaining or understanding a local form, ask a bankruptcy lawyer or visit a bankruptcy petition preparer. (See Ch. 12 for information on bankruptcy petition preparers.)

Local Court Rules

Most bankruptcy courts publish local rules that govern that court's procedures. These rules mainly govern hearings conducted by the bankruptcy judge; they aren't relevant in routine bankruptcy cases, which usually involve only filing papers and appearing before a trustee at a creditors' meeting. Still, some rules may affect routine Chapter 7 bankruptcy cases. You can get your local rules from the bankruptcy court—in person or on its website—but be prepared to comb through reams of material to find the one or two rules that might apply in your case.

Number of Copies

Before filing your papers, find out how many copies your court requires. Most ask for an original and one copy. The original will be scanned into the court's database, and your copy will be "conformed" for your records. (A conformed copy is either stamped or receives a computer-generated label, with information showing that you filed, the date of your filing, your case number, and the tentative date of your creditors' meeting.) A few courts still require you to provide an original and four copies.

Order of Papers and Other Details

Every court has a preferred order in which it wants to receive the forms in the package you submit for filing. Most courts also have rules indicating whether the forms should be hole-punched or stapled, and other details. If you mess up, most clerks will put your forms in the correct order or punch and staple your papers in the right way. Some, however, will make you do it yourself. This can be a major pain if you are filing by mail. Every court has an exhibit of the standard Chapter 7 bankruptcy filing with the forms arranged correctly. If you want to get it right the first time, visit the court and carefully examine the court's sample filing, taking notes on which forms fall in which order.

Below is a sample letter you can adapt to your situation and send to the court, requesting the information discussed above. Include a large, self-addressed envelope. Call and ask the court if you need to affix return postage. Again, if you live in an urban area, you'll probably have to visit the court to get this information.

Sample Letter to Bankruptcy Court

Sandra Smith
432 Oak Street
Cincinnati, OH 45219
513-555-7890

July 2, 20xx

United States Bankruptcy Court
Atrium Two, Room 800
221 East Fourth Street
Cincinnati, OH 45202

Attn: COURT CLERK

TO THE COURT CLERK:

Please send me the following information:

1. Copies of all local forms required by this court for an individual (not corporation) filing a Chapter 7 bankruptcy and for making amendments.
2. The number of copies or sets required for filing.
3. The order in which forms should be submitted.
4. Complete instructions on this court's emergency filing procedures and deadlines.

I would also appreciate answers to four other questions:

1. Do you require a separate creditor mailing list (matrix)? If so, do you have specific requirements for its format?
2. Is the filing fee still $299? If not, please advise.
3. Should I two-hole punch my papers or is that done by the court?
4. Should I staple the papers or use paper clips?

I've enclosed a self-addressed envelope for your reply. Thank you.

Sincerely,

Sandra Smith
Sandra Smith

For Married Filers

If you are married, you and your spouse will have to decide whether one of you should file alone or whether you should file jointly. To make this decision, you'll first have to make sure that you're married in the eyes of the federal law (a trickier issue than you might think), then consider how filing together or separately will affect your debts and property.

Are You Married?

If you are married to a person of the opposite sex, with a valid state license, you are married for purposes of filing a joint petition and you can skip down to "Should You File Jointly?" below. However, if you were not married with a license and ceremony, or if you are married to a same-sex partner, read on.

Common Law Marriage

Some states allow heterosexual couples to establish "common law" marriages, which the states will recognize as valid marriages even though the couples do not have a state marriage license or certificate. Contrary to popular belief, a common law marriage is not created by two people simply living together for a certain number of years. In order to have a valid common law marriage, the couple must do all of the following:

- live together for a significant period of time (not defined in any state)
- hold themselves out as a married couple—typically this means using the same last name, referring to the other as "my husband" or "my wife," and filing a joint tax return, and
- intend to be married.

Alabama, Colorado, the District of Columbia, Georgia, Idaho, Iowa, Kansas, Montana, New Hampshire (only for inheritance), Ohio, Oklahoma, Pennsylvania, Rhode Island, South Carolina, Texas, and Utah recognize some form of common law marriage, but the rules for what constitutes a marriage differ from state to state. And, several of these states will only recognize common law marriages that were created before a certain date.

If you live in one of these states and you meet your state's requirements for a common law marriage, you may file jointly if you wish.

Same-Sex Marriage

If you married your same-sex partner in a state, country, or province that recognizes same-sex marriage, the prevailing opinion among bankruptcy lawyers and judges is that the federal Defense of Marriage Act (1 U.S.C. § 7 and 28 U.S.C. § 1738C) prohibits federal courts from recognizing your marriage for bankruptcy purposes. In other words, you have to file for bankruptcy separately.

At least one court has refused to allow a lesbian couple that had married in Canada to file a joint bankruptcy petition. If you choose to file jointly with your same-sex spouse, you may well face opposition on these grounds from the trustee or the U.S. Trustee. Consider consulting with a bankruptcy attorney who has some experience with issues facing same-sex couples before you decide how to proceed. While filing separately will require you to pay an extra $299 filing fee, it also effectively doubles the amount of exemptions you can claim in states where spouses are not allowed to double.

Should You File Jointly?

Unfortunately, there is no simple formula that will tell you whether it's better to file alone or with your spouse. In the end, it will depend on which option allows you to discharge more of your debts and keep more of your property, and whether at least one of you still has good credit that can be maintained by a separate filing. Here are some of the factors you should consider:

- **If you have recently married**, you haven't acquired any valuable assets as a married couple, and one of you has all the debts, it may make sense for that spouse to file for bankruptcy alone (especially if the nonfiling spouse has good credit to protect).
- **If you are living in a community property state**, most of your debts were incurred during marriage, and most of your money and property was acquired during marriage, you should probably file jointly. Even if only one spouse files, all community property is considered part of that spouse's bankruptcy estate. The same is generally true for debts—that is, all community debts are listed and discharged even though only one spouse files (although some creditors may attempt to collect community debts that are listed in the names of both spouses). See Ch. 1 and Ch. 5 for more on community property.
- **If you and your spouse own property as tenants by the entirety** (see Ch. 7), you owe most of your debts in your own name, and you live in a state that excludes property held in a tenancy by the entirety from the bankruptcy estate when only one spouse files, you may want to file alone. This is a particularly important consideration if you own your home as tenants by the entirety—filing jointly could cause you to lose your home unnecessarily.
- **If the exemption system you are using allows spouses to double their exemptions**, filing for bankruptcy jointly may help you hang on to more of your property. (See Ch. 6 for more information on exemptions, and Appendix A for state-by-state information on whether doubling exemptions is allowed.)
- **If you are married and share finances,** you should consider a joint filing. The court will look at your total household income to determine whether you pass the bankruptcy means test (and are therefore eligible to use Chapter 7). If your spouse's income is significantly larger than your own, filing alone could lead the court to dismiss your

case for abuse, particularly if the court believes that you filed alone to prevent the court from considering your spouse's income. If the debts you are trying to discharge benefited both of you, and your finances are combined, a court may consider your nonfiling spouse's income in determining whether you could afford a Chapter 13 repayment plan. (See *In re Haney*, No. 06-40350 (W.D. Ky. 2006), in which the court considered the nonfiling spouse's income of $6,000 or $7,000 a month in dismissing the bankruptcy case of the filing spouse, who brought in less than $400 a month.)

- **If you are still married but separated**, you may have to file alone if your spouse won't cooperate (for example, by providing financial information, signing the papers as a codebtor, attending the mandatory counseling sessions, and appearing at the creditors' meeting).

When deciding whether to file jointly or alone in a community property state, you'll need to know whether you both own the "family business" or whether only one of you owns it. This isn't as easy as you may think. As a general rule, if the filing spouse owned the business going into the marriage, and the nonfiling spouse has not been added as an owner on any of the business-related documents—such as fictitious business name registration—then the nonfiling spouse isn't an owner and won't be held liable for any of its debts. On the other hand, if the nonfiling spouse owned the business prior to the marriage and the filing spouse hasn't been added as an owner, the business assets needn't be included in the bankruptcy. If the business was started during the marriage, it will generally be considered community property and included in the bankruptcy even if only one of you files.

In "common law" marital property states, the business belongs to the spouse whose name appears on the title documents (such as a fictitious business name statement, bank account, or other formal business documents).

SEE AN EXPERT

The decision to file jointly or alone can have significant consequences. Because the best choice will depend on your situation and the laws of your state, we advise you to talk to a bankruptcy lawyer if you have any questions about which option makes more sense. We've provided some general guidelines, but you should definitely consult with a local lawyer regarding what will happen to your business assets and debts if only one of you files.

Required Forms and Documents

Bankruptcy uses official forms prescribed by the Federal Office of the Courts. In addition, you must file certain documents, as described above in "Gather the Necessary Documents." Here we provide complete lists of (1) the official forms you will be completing in this chapter, and (2) the documents that you will have to file along with the official forms. We also explain how to get these forms and documents.

Checklist of Required Bankruptcy Forms

These are the standard forms that must be filed in every Chapter 7 bankruptcy:

- ☐ Form 1—Voluntary Petition
- ☐ Form 3A (if you want to pay your filing fee in installments)
- ☐ Form 3B (if you apply for a fee waiver)
- ☐ Form 6, which consists of:
  - ☐ Schedule A—Real Property
  - ☐ Schedule B—Personal Property
  - ☐ Schedule C—Property Claimed as Exempt
  - ☐ Schedule D—Creditors Holding Secured Claims

- ☐ Schedule E—Creditors Holding Unsecured Priority Claims
- ☐ Schedule F—Creditors Holding Unsecured Nonpriority Claims
- ☐ Schedule G—Executory Contracts and Unexpired Leases
- ☐ Schedule H—Codebtors
- ☐ Schedule I—Current Income
- ☐ Schedule J—Current Expenditures
- ☐ Summary of Schedules A through J
- ☐ Statistical Summary of Certain Liabilities
- ☐ Declaration Concerning Debtor's Schedules

- ☐ Form 7—Statement of Financial Affairs
- ☐ Form 8—Chapter 7 Individual Debtor's Statement of Intention
- ☐ Form 21—Full Social Security Number Disclosure
- ☐ Form 22A—Statement of Current Monthly Income and Means-Test Calculation
- ☐ Form 23—Certification of Instructional Course on Financial Management
- ☐ Form 201—Notice to Consumer Debtors Under § 342 of the Bankruptcy Code
- ☐ Mailing Matrix
- ☐ Required local forms, if any.

With the exception of Form 22A, which might require you to do a fair bit of math, the forms are straightforward and easy to complete, as long as you take them one at a time. Also, you probably won't have to spend time on each of them, even though they will be part of your filing package. For instance, if you don't own real estate, you can simply check the "None" box on Schedule A and proceed to Schedule B.

All together, these forms usually are referred to as your "bankruptcy petition," although technically your petition is only Form 1. (In case you're wondering, Forms 2, 4, and 5 aren't used in voluntary Chapter 7 bankruptcy filings.)

Fee Waivers

You may ask the court to waive the bankruptcy fees by filing Form 3B. To qualify, you must be unable to pay the fee in installments and your income must be below 150% of the federal poverty level (you can find up-to-date poverty guidelines at the Department of Health and Human Services' website at http://aspe.hhs.gov/poverty.) You will have to appear in court so the judge can ask you questions. You can find a blank copy of the form in Appendix C; as you'll see, it asks you to repeat much of the information from your other papers.

If the court won't grant your request to waive the fee entirely, it may allow you to pay in four installments. In this situation, you must be very careful. If you miss even one installment, the court will dismiss your case without giving you a chance to explain yourself. It's best to deliver your payments directly to the court and get a receipt from the clerk. A second, not-as-good alternative is to send the payments by registered mail, return receipt requested. Whether you use first class or registered mail, if the court fails to apply the payments to your account, it will be the court's word against yours. And guess who wins?

Checklist of Required Documents

As explained above, the bankruptcy law passed in 2005 requires filers to submit some documents along with their forms. The documents you must file are:

- your most recent federal tax return (or a transcript of the return obtained from the IRS)
- a certificate showing that you have completed the required credit counseling
- any repayment plan that was developed during your credit counseling
- your pay stubs for the previous 60 days (along with an accompanying form, if your local court requires one), and

- proof that you have completed a course in personal financial management (you must attach this to Form 23).

Where to Get the Official Forms

Appendix C of this book includes tear-out copies of all of the required bankruptcy forms. You can type the necessary information in the blanks or complete the forms by hand. Some of these forms may be out of date by the time you use this book, so you should always check the dates on the forms against the dates on the most current versions available online. The website of the United States Courts offers a complete and current set of official forms at www.uscourts.gov/bkforms/index.html, which you can fill in electronically and print (but not save on your computer).

Tips for Completing the Forms

Here are some tips that will make filling in your forms easier and the whole bankruptcy process smoother. A completed sample form accompanies each form's instructions. Refer to it while you fill in your bankruptcy papers.

Use your worksheets and credit counseling plan (if you have one). If you've completed the worksheets in previous chapters, you've already done a lot of the work. These worksheets will save you lots of time when you prepare your bankruptcy forms, so keep them handy. If you skipped any of those chapters, refer to the worksheets and accompanying instructions for help in figuring out what to put in your bankruptcy forms.

Make several copies of each form. Having several copies allows you to make a draft, changing things as you go until the form is complete and correct. Prepare final forms to file with the court only after you've double-checked your drafts. If you use the PDF fill-in-the-blanks forms available on the official U.S. courts' website (see above), remember that you can't save the information in the forms. It's easiest to do a draft by hand, then complete the form and print it all at once.

Type your final forms. If you are using the Nolo forms or the PDF forms available from the U.S. courts' website (see above), you may enter your information by hand. Unless your handwriting is very neat, however, your case will likely go a lot more smoothly if your forms are typewritten. If you don't have access to a typewriter, many libraries have typewriters available to the public (for a small rental fee), or you can hire a bankruptcy form preparation service to prepare your forms using the information you provide. (See Ch. 12 for more on these services.)

Be ridiculously thorough. Always err on the side of giving too much information rather than too little. If you leave information out, the bankruptcy trustee may become suspicious of your motives or delay your case until you provide more information. Bankruptcy law requires you to disclose all of your creditors. Your bankruptcy may be jeopardized if you intentionally omit anyone. The debts you owe creditors who are left off your forms might even survive your bankruptcy—hardly the result you want. If you intentionally or carelessly fail to list all your property and debts, or fail to accurately describe your recent property transactions, the court may find that you acted with fraudulent intent. It may deny your bankruptcy discharge altogether, and you may lose some property that you could otherwise have kept. The three basic rules of bankruptcy form preparation are disclose, disclose, and, you guessed it, disclose.

Respond to every question. Most of the forms have a box to check when your answer is "none." If a question doesn't have a "none" box and the question doesn't apply to you, type in "N/A" for "not applicable." This will let the trustee know that you didn't overlook the question. Occasionally, a question that doesn't apply to you will have a number of blanks. Put "N/A" in only the first blank if it is obvious that this applies to the other blanks as well. If it's not clear, put "N/A" in every blank.

Explain uncertainties. If you can't figure out which category on a form to use for a debt or an item of property, list the debt or item in what you think is the appropriate place and briefly note next to your entry that you're uncertain. The important thing is to disclose the information somewhere. The bankruptcy trustee will sort it out, if necessary.

Be scrupulously honest. As part of your official bankruptcy paperwork, you must complete declarations, under penalty of perjury, swearing that you've been truthful. It's important to realize that you could be prosecuted for perjury if it becomes evident that you deliberately lied.

Use continuation pages if you run out of room. The space for entering information is sometimes skimpy, especially if you're filing jointly. Most of the forms come with preformatted continuation pages that you can use if you need more room. But if there is no continuation form in Appendix C, prepare one yourself, using a piece of regular, white 8½" × 11" paper. Write "see continuation page" next to the question you're working on and enter the additional information on the continuation page. Label the continuation pages with your name and the form name, and indicate "Continuation page 1," "Continuation page 2," and so on. Be sure to attach all continuation pages to their appropriate forms when you file your bankruptcy papers.

Get help if necessary. If your situation is complicated, you're unsure about how to complete a form, or you run into trouble when you go to file your papers, consult a bankruptcy attorney or do some legal research before proceeding. (See Ch. 12.)

Refer to—but don't copy—the sample forms. Throughout this chapter, we have included the completed sample forms of Annie Justine Kaye, a small business owner who lives and does business in her hometown of Freshstart, in the fictional state of Anonymous (AA). These forms are intended to be used as examples, so you can see what a completed form should look like. However, everyone's bankruptcy situation is different—and obviously, you will owe different debts, own different property, have different bank accounts and Social Security numbers, live in an actual state, and otherwise be utterly dissimilar from this fictional gal. DO NOT COPY THESE EXAMPLES VERBATIM.

About Our Fictional Debtor

Annie is a recently divorced mother of one who owns a boutique women's accessories store. Her business has been steadily going downhill since 2007, along with the economy. Her commercial landlord likes Annie and would like to keep her in her retail space, but he isn't willing to reduce her rent to an amount she can afford or forgive the back rent she owes him. This means that Annie will have to close her business whether or not she files for bankruptcy. She is looking for a job to tide her over, but hopes to open a new boutique when the economy improves.

Because Annie's business is a sole proprietorship, she can use her state's personal exemptions to keep some of her business assets. She has decided to try to protect her customer list and inventory but give up her store's hard assets (fixtures, office equipment, and so on). She can't really place a value on her store's good will, so she's decided not to claim an exemption for that. As is true of many small business owners, Annie can only provide a best guess as to the value of some of her business assets. If some assets turn out to be worth more than she thought, she can amend her paperwork to try to exempt the items that are most important to her. (Coincidentally, Annie's fictional state of Anonymous follows California's exemption system, and Annie has chosen to use the System 2 exemptions.)

Annie's debts are primarily from her business, so she doesn't have to take the means test (although she still has to file Form 22A).

Form 1—Voluntary Petition

A completed sample Voluntary Petition and line-by-line instructions follow.

Emergency Filing

Although people usually file all of their bankruptcy forms at once, you don't absolutely have to. If you really need to stop creditors quickly—because of an eviction, a foreclosure, or a threatened repossession, you can simply file the Voluntary Petition (including Exhibit D, concerning credit counseling), the statement of your Social Security number (Form 21), and a form called a matrix, which lists the name, address, and zip code of each of your creditors. The automatic stay, which stops most collection efforts against you, will then go into effect. You have 14 days to file the rest of the forms. (Bankruptcy Rule 1007(c).)

Although it's an option if you're really in a jam, we urge you to not do an emergency filing unless it's absolutely necessary. That 14-day extension goes by fast; many people blow the deadline, then have their cases dismissed. So, if possible, file all your paperwork at the same time.

First Page

Court Name. At the top of the first page, fill in the name of the judicial district you're filing in, such as the "Central District of California." If your state has only one district, fill in your state's name. If your state divides its districts into divisions, enter the division after the state name, such as "Northern District of California, Santa Rosa Division." (See "Finding the Right Bankruptcy Court," above, for information on where to file.)

Name of Debtor. Enter your full name (last name first), as used on your checks, driver's license, and other formal documents. If you are married and filing jointly, put one of your names as the debtor (on the left) and the other as the "joint debtor (spouse)," on the right. If you are married but filing separately, enter "N/A" in the second blank.

All Other Names. The purpose of this box is to make sure that your creditors know who you are when they receive notice of your bankruptcy filing. If you have been known by any other name in the last eight years, list it here. If you've operated a business as a sole proprietorship during the previous eight years, include your trade name (fictitious or assumed business name) preceded by "dba" for "doing business as." But don't include minor variations in spelling or form. For instance, if your name is John Lewis Odegard, you don't have to put down that you're sometimes known as J.L. But if you've used the pseudonym J.L. Smith, you should list it. If you're uncertain, list any name that you think you may have used with a creditor. Do the same for your spouse (in the box to the right) if you are filing jointly. If you're married and filing alone, type "N/A" in the box to the right (and the remaining joint debtor boxes on the form). If your business is an LLC, corporation, or partnership, do not list its name here.

Last four digits of Soc. Sec. or Individual-Taxpayer I.D. Enter only the last four digits of your Social Security number or taxpayer's ID number. Do the same for your spouse (in the box to the right) if you are filing jointly.

Street Address of Debtor. Enter your current street address. Even if you get all of your mail at a post office box, list the address of your personal residence.

Street Address of Joint Debtor. If filing jointly, enter your spouse's current street address (even if it's the same as yours)—again, no post office boxes.

County of Residence. Enter the county in which you live. Do the same for your spouse if you're filing jointly. Otherwise, type "N/A" in the box.

Mailing Address of Debtor. Enter your mailing address if it is different from your street address. If it isn't, put "N/A." Do the same for your spouse (in the box to the right) if you are filing jointly.

Location of Principal Assets of Business Debtor. This question is only for business entity (LLC or corporation) filings, not for personal Chapter 7 bankruptcy cases (including sole proprietor filings). You can leave this blank.

Sample Voluntary Petition

B1 (Official Form 1) (1/08)

United States Bankruptcy Court State of Anonymous	Voluntary Petition

Name of Debtor (if individual, enter Last, First, Middle): **Kaye, Annie Justine**	Name of Joint Debtor (Spouse) (Last, First, Middle):
All Other Names used by the Debtor in the last 8 years (include married, maiden, and trade names): **DBA Annie's Beauty Accessories**	All Other Names used by the Joint Debtor in the last 8 years (include married, maiden, and trade names):
Last four digits of Social Security or Individual-Taxpayer I.D. (ITIN) No./Complete EIN (if more than one, state all): **xxx-xx-9999**	Last four digits of Social Security or Individual-Taxpayer I.D. (ITIN) No./Complete EIN (if more than one, state all):
Street Address of Debtor (No. & Street, City, and State): **XXXX First St.** **Freshstart, AA 99999-9999** ZIP CODE **99999-9999**	Street Address of Joint Debtor (No. & Street, City, and State): ZIP CODE
County of Residence or of the Principal Place of Business: **Independence**	County of Residence or of the Principal Place of Business:
Mailing Address of Debtor (if different from street address): **PO Box XXXX** **Freshstart, AA 99999-9999** ZIP CODE **99999-9999**	Mailing Address of Joint Debtor (if different from street address): ZIP CODE

Location of Principal Assets of Business Debtor (if different from street address above):

Type of Debtor
(Form of Organization)
(Check one box.)

- [X] Individual (includes Joint Debtors) *See Exhibit D on page 2 of this form.*
- [ ] Corporation (includes LLC and LLP)
- [ ] Partnership
- [ ] Other (If debtor is not one of the above entities, check this box and state type of entity below.)

Nature of Business
(Check **one** box.)

- [ ] Health Care Business
- [ ] Single Asset Real Estate as defined in 11 U.S.C. § 101(51B)
- [ ] Railroad
- [ ] Stockbroker
- [ ] Commodity Broker
- [ ] Clearing Bank
- [X] Other

Tax-Exempt Entity
(Check box, if applicable.)

- [ ] Debtor is a tax-exempt organization under Title 26 of the United States Code (the Internal Revenue Code).

Chapter of Bankruptcy Code Under Which the Petition is Filed (Check one box)

- [X] Chapter 7
- [ ] Chapter 9
- [ ] Chapter 11
- [ ] Chapter 12
- [ ] Chapter 13
- [ ] Chapter 15 Petition for Recognition of a Foreign Main Proceeding
- [ ] Chapter 15 Petition for Recognition of a Foreign Nonmain Proceeding

Nature of Debts
(Check one box)

- [ ] Debts are primarily consumer debts, defined in 11 U.S.C. § 101(8) as "incurred by an individual primarily for a personal, family, or household purpose."
- [X] Debts are primarily business debts.

Filing Fee (Check one box.)

- [X] Full Filing Fee attached
- [ ] Filing Fee to be paid in installments (Applicable to individuals only) Must attach signed application for the court's consideration certifying that the debtor is unable to pay fee except in installments. Rule 1006(b). See Official Form 3A.
- [ ] Filing Fee waiver requested (Applicable to chapter 7 individuals only). Must attach signed application for the court's consideration. See Official Form 3B.

Check one box: **Chapter 11 Debtors**

- [ ] Debtor is a small business debtor as defined in 11 U.S.C. § 101(51D).
- [ ] Debtor is not a small business debtor as defined in 11 U.S.C. § 101(51D).

Check if:

- [ ] Debtor's aggregate noncontingent liquidated debts (excluding debts owed to insiders or affiliates) are less than $2,190,000

Check all applicable boxes:

- [ ] A plan is being filed with this petition.
- [ ] Acceptances of the plan were solicited prepetition from one or more classes of creditors, in accordance with 11 U.S.C. § 1126(b).

Statistical/Administrative Information

THIS SPACE IS FOR COURT USE ONLY

- [X] Debtor estimates that funds will be available for distribution to unsecured creditors.
- [ ] Debtor estimates that, after any exempt property is excluded and administrative expenses paid, there will be no funds available for distribution to unsecured creditors.

Estimated Number of Creditors

[X] 1-49	[ ] 50-99	[ ] 100-199	[ ] 200-999	[ ] 1,000-5,000	[ ] 5001-10,000	[ ] 10,001-25,000	[ ] 25,001-50,000	[ ] 50,001-100,000	[ ] OVER 100,000

Estimated Assets

[ ] $0 to $50,000	[X] $50,001 to $100,000	[ ] $100,001 to $500,000	[ ] $500,001 to $1 million	[ ] $1,000,001 to $10 million	[ ] $10,000,001 to $50 million	[ ] $50,000,001 to $100 million	[ ] $100,000,001 to $500 million	[ ] $500,000,001 to $1 billion	[ ] More than $1 billion

Estimated Debts

[ ] $0 to $50,000	[ ] $50,001 to $100,000	[X] $100,001 to $500,000	[ ] $500,001 to $1 million	[ ] $1,000,001 to $10 million	[ ] $10,000,001 to $50 million	[ ] $50,000,001 to $100 million	[ ] $100,000,001 to $500 million	[ ] $500,000,001 to $1 billion	[ ] More than $1 billion

Type of Debtor. Check the first box—"Individual(s)"—even if you are self-employed or operate a sole proprietorship.

Nature of Business. See a bankruptcy lawyer if any of these descriptions apply to you or your spouse. For instance, if you or your spouse owns an assisted living facility (11 U.S.C. § 101 (27A)), you would need a lawyer's services, because the law has gotten quite complicated regarding how health care businesses are treated in bankruptcy.

Tax-Exempt Entity. Leave this blank. This box is for nonprofits only.

Chapter of Bankruptcy Code Under Which the Petition is Filed. Check "Chapter 7."

Nature of Debts. Check the box for consumer debts if most of your debts are personal debts rather than business debts. If, however, the bulk of your debts are due to the operation of a business, check the business debts box. If you are in doubt, check the business debts box. If the bulk of your debts are business debts, you don't have to take the means test (see Ch. 2 for more information).

Filing Fee. If you will attach the entire fee, check the first box. If you plan to ask the court for permission to pay in installments, check the second box. (Instructions for applying to the court are in "How to File Your Papers," below.) If you wish to apply for a full waiver of the filing fee, check the third box and see "How to File Your Papers," below.

Chapter 11 Debtors. Leave this section blank.

Statistical/Administrative Information. There are a number of boxes here. The first set of boxes tells the trustee whether you think there will be assets available to be sold for the benefit of your unsecured creditors. If you did your homework in Ch. 5 and Ch. 6, you will have a good idea of whether all of your assets are exempt, or whether some will have to be surrendered to the trustee. Check the top or bottom box accordingly. If you check the bottom box, your creditors will be told that there is no point in filing a Proof of Claim unless they hear differently from the trustee. If you check the top box, your creditors will be told to file Proof of Claim forms. If you haven't a clue yet about your property and exemptions, come back to this question after you've completed Schedules A, B, and C.

Similarly, if you can provide pretty good estimates of the other information requested (estimated number of creditors, assets, and liabilities), fill in the appropriate box on the form. If not, come back to these questions when you've completed more of your paperwork.

Second Page

Name of Debtor(s). Enter your name, and your spouse's if you are filing jointly.

All Prior Bankruptcy Cases Filed Within Last 8 Years. If you haven't filed a bankruptcy case within the previous eight years, type "None" or "N/A" in the first box. If you—or your spouse, if you're filing jointly—have, enter the requested information. A previous Chapter 7 bankruptcy discharge bars you from filing until eight years have passed since you filed the previous case. And, if you filed a Chapter 7 bankruptcy case that was dismissed for cause within the previous 180 days, you may have to wait to file again, or you may not be able to discharge all your debts. (See Ch. 2 for more information.) If either situation applies to you, see a bankruptcy lawyer before filing.

Pending Bankruptcy Case Filed by any Spouse, Partner, or Affiliate of this Debtor. "Affiliate" refers to a related business under a corporate structure. "Partner" refers to a business partnership. Again, you shouldn't use this book if you're filing as a corporation, partnership, or other type of business entity. If your spouse has a bankruptcy case pending anywhere in the country, enter the requested information. Otherwise, type "None" or "N/A" in the first box.

Exhibit A. This is solely for people who are filing for Chapter 11 bankruptcy. Leave it blank.

Exhibit B. This is solely for people who are represented by an attorney. If you are representing yourself or using a bankruptcy petition preparer, leave this section blank.

Sample Voluntary Petition—page 2

B1 (Official Form 1) (1/08) Page 2

Voluntary Petition *(This page must be completed and filed in every case)*	Name of Debtor(s): **Annie Justine Kaye**	
All Prior Bankruptcy Cases Filed Within Last 8 Years (If more than two, attach additional sheet.)		
Location Where Filed: **- None -**	Case Number:	Date Filed:
Location Where Filed:	Case Number:	Date Filed:
Pending Bankruptcy Case Filed by any Spouse, Partner, or Affiliate of this Debtor (If more than one, attach additional sheet.)		
Name of Debtor: **- None -**	Case Number:	Date Filed:
District:	Relationship:	Judge:

Exhibit A

(To be completed if debtor is required to file periodic reports (e.g., forms 10K and 10Q) with the Securities and Exchange Commission pursuant to Section 13 or 15(d) of the Securities Exchange Act of 1934 and is requesting relief under chapter 11.)

☐ Exhibit A is attached and made a part of this petition.

Exhibit B

(To be completed if debtor is an individual whose debts are primarily consumer debts.)

I, the attorney for the petitioner named in the foregoing petition, declare that I have informed the petitioner that [he or she] may proceed under chapter 7, 11, 12, or 13 of title 11, United States Code, and have explained the relief available under each such chapter. I further certify that I delivered to the debtor the notice required by 11 U.S.C. § 342(b).

X ______________________________

Signature of Attorney for Debtor(s) Date

Exhibit C

Does the debtor own or have possession of any property that poses or is alleged to pose a threat of imminent and identifiable harm to public health or safety?

☐ Yes, and Exhibit C is attached and made a part of this petition.

☒ No

Exhibit D

(To be completed by every individual debtor. If a joint petition is filed, each spouse must complete and attach a separate Exhibit D.)

☒ Exhibit D completed and signed by the debtor is attached and made a part of this petition.

If this is a joint petition:

☐ Exhibit D also completed and signed by the joint debtor is attached and made a part of this petition.

Information Regarding the Debtor - Venue

(Check any applicable box)

☒ Debtor has been domiciled or has had a residence, principal place of business, or principal assets in this District for 180 days immediately preceding the date of this petition or for a longer part of such 180 days than in any other District.

☐ There is a bankruptcy case concerning debtor's affiliate, general partner, or partnership pending in this District.

☐ Debtor is a debtor in a foreign proceeding and has its principal place of business or principal assets in the United States in this District, or has no principal place of business or assets in the United States but is a defendant in an action or proceeding [in a federal or state court] in this District, or the interests of the parties will be served in regard to the relief sought in this District.

Certification by a Debtor Who Resides as a Tenant of Residential Property

Check all applicable boxes.

☐ Landlord has a judgment against the debtor for possession of debtor's residence. (If box checked, complete the following.)

____
(Name of landlord that obtained judgment)

____
(Address of landlord)

☐ Debtor claims that under applicable nonbankruptcy law, there are circumstances under which the debtor would be permitted to cure the entire monetary default that gave rise to the judgment for possession, after the judgment for possession was entered, and

☐ Debtor has included in this petition the deposit with the court of any rent that would become due during the 30-day period after the filing of the petition.

☐ Debtor certifies that he/she has served the Landlord with this certification. (11 U.S.C. § 362(l))..

Sample Voluntary Petition—page 3

B1 (Official Form 1) (1/08) Page 3

Voluntary Petition *(This page must be completed and filed in every case)*	Name of Debtor(s): **Annie Justine Kaye**

Signatures

Signature(s) of Debtor(s) (Individual/Joint)

I declare under penalty of perjury that the information provided in this petition is true and correct.

[If petitioner is an individual whose debts are primarily consumer debts and has chosen to file under chapter 7] I am aware that I may proceed under chapter 7, 11, 12 or 13 of title 11, United States Code, understand the relief available under each such chapter, and choose to proceed under chapter 7.

[If no attorney represents me and no bankruptcy petition preparer signs the petition] I have obtained and read the notice required by 11 U.S.C. § 342(b).

I request relief in accordance with the chapter of title 11, United States Code, specified in this petition.

X ______________________________

Signature of Debtor **Annie Justine Kaye**

X ______________________________

Signature of Joint Debtor

XXX-XXX-XXXX

Telephone Number (If not represented by attorney)

____

Date

Signature of a Foreign Representative

I declare under penalty of perjury that the information provided in this petition is true and correct, that I am the foreign representative of a debtor in a foreign proceeding, and that I am authorized to file this petition.

(Check only one box.)

☐ I request relief in accordance with chapter 15 of title 11, United States Code. Certified copies of the documents required by 11 U.S.C. § 1515 are attached.

☐ Pursuant to 11 U.S.C. § 1511, I request relief in accordance with the chapter of title 11 specified in this petition. A certified copy of the order granting recognition of the foreign main proceeding is attached.

X ______________________________

Signature of Foreign Representative

____

Printed Name of Foreign Representative

____

Date

Signature of Attorney*

X ______________________________

Signature of Attorney for Debtor(s)

____

Printed Name of Attorney for Debtor(s)

____

Firm Name

____

Address

____

Telephone Number

____

Date

*In a case in which § 707(b)(4)(D) applies, this signature also constitutes a certification that the attorney has no knowledge after an inquiry that the information in the schedules is incorrect.

Signature of Non-Attorney Bankruptcy Petition Preparer

I declare under penalty of perjury that: 1) I am a bankruptcy petition preparer as defined in 11 U.S.C. § 110; 2) I prepared this document for compensation and have provided the debtor with a copy of this document and the notices and information required under 11 U.S.C. §§ 110(b), 110(h), and 342(b); and, 3) if rules or guidelines have been promulgated pursuant to 11 U.S.C. § 110(h) setting a maximum fee for services chargeable by bankruptcy petition preparers, I have given the debtor notice of the maximum amount before preparing any document for filing for a debtor or accepting any fee from the debtor, as required in that section. Official form 19 is attached.

____

Printed Name and title, if any, of Bankruptcy Petition Preparer

____

Social-Security number (If the bankruptcy petition preparer is not an individual, state the Social Security number of the officer, principal, responsible person or partner of the bankruptcy petition preparer.)(Required by 11 U.S.C. § 110.)

____

Address

X ______________________________

____

Date

Signature of Bankruptcy Petition Preparer or officer, principal, responsible person, or partner whose social security number is provided above.

Names and Social-Security numbers of all other individuals who prepared or assisted in preparing this document unless the bankruptcy petition preparer is not an individual

If more than one person prepared this document, attach additional sheets conforming to the appropriate official form for each person.

A bankruptcy petition preparer's failure to comply with the provisions of title 11 and the Federal Rules of Bankruptcy Procedure may result in fines or imprisonment or both 11 U.S.C. § 110; 18 U.S.C. § 156.

Signature of Debtor (Corporation/Partnership)

I declare under penalty of perjury that the information provided in this petition is true and correct, and that I have been authorized to file this petition on behalf of the debtor.

The debtor requests relief in accordance with the chapter of title 11, United States Code, specified in this petition.

X ______________________________

Signature of Authorized Individual

____

Printed Name of Authorized Individual

____

Title of Authorized Individual

____

Date

Exhibit C. If you own or have in your possession any property that might cause "imminent and identifiable" harm to public health or safety (for example, real estate that is polluted with toxic substances, or explosive devices such as hand grenades or dynamite), check the "yes" box, fill in Exhibit C (see Appendix C), and attach Exhibit C to this Petition. If you are unsure about whether a particular piece of property fits the bill, err on the side of inclusion.

Exhibit D. As explained above, debtors filing for Chapter 7 bankruptcy are required to participate in debt counseling sessions within 180 days of their bankruptcy filing. Exhibit D tells the court whether you've complied with this requirement. Instructions for completing Exhibit D are set out below. Check the top box in this part of the petition if you are filing individually and have completed Exhibit D; if you are filing jointly and your spouse has completed Exhibit D, check the bottom box.

Information Regarding the Debtor—Venue. Check the top box.

Certification by a Debtor Who Resides as a Tenant of Residential Property. Certain evictions are allowed to proceed after you file for bankruptcy, despite the automatic stay. The questions in this section are intended to show whether your landlord has already gotten a judgment for possession (eviction order), and whether you still may be able to postpone the eviction. See Ch. 4 for the information you need to complete these boxes, if they apply.

Third Page

Signature(s) of Debtor(s) (Individual/Joint). You—and your spouse, if you are filing jointly—must sign, date, and provide your telephone number where indicated. By signing, you—and your spouse, if you are filing jointly—declare that you are aware that you may file under other sections of the bankruptcy code, and that you still choose to file for Chapter 7 bankruptcy.

Signature of Attorney. Assuming you are representing yourself, type "debtor not represented by attorney" in the space for the attorney's signature.

Signature of Non-Attorney Bankruptcy Petition Preparer. If a bankruptcy petition preparer typed your forms, have that person complete this section.

Exhibit D

At the top of the page, fill in the court name, your name(s) as debtor(s), and the case number (if you have it).

The warning in bold letters explains that you have to check one of the five statements regarding credit counseling listed in Exhibit D.

Most people will check box 1, which means you obtained the certificate of completion from the credit counseling agency and can attach the certificate (and any debt repayment plan developed through the agency) to your petition.

If you have received counseling but haven't got your certificate yet, check box 2. To remain in bankruptcy, you'll need to obtain and file your certificate (and debt repayment plan if any) within 14 days after your bankruptcy filing date.

Checking box 3 indicates that you have requested credit counseling but were unable to obtain the services within seven days after your request, and have not yet received counseling. If you check this box, you'll have to explain why you couldn't complete the credit counseling before your filing date. Read the bold type for additional information regarding your obligations if you wish to remain in bankruptcy.

Box 4 summarizes the exceptions to the credit-counseling requirement and asks you to check the appropriate reason.

Box 5 only applies if the credit-counseling requirement doesn't apply in your district. This exception is very rare.

Sign and date this document under penalty of perjury and file it with your petition.

Sample Exhibit D—page 1

B 1D (Official Form 1, Exhibit D) (12/09)

United States Bankruptcy Court
State of Anonymous

In re **Annie Justine Kaye** Debtor(s) Case No. ______ Chapter **7**

EXHIBIT D - INDIVIDUAL DEBTOR'S STATEMENT OF COMPLIANCE WITH CREDIT COUNSELING REQUIREMENT

Warning: You must be able to check truthfully one of the five statements regarding credit counseling listed below. If you cannot do so, you are not eligible to file a bankruptcy case, and the court can dismiss any case you do file. If that happens, you will lose whatever filing fee you paid, and your creditors will be able to resume collection activities against you. If your case is dismissed and you file another bankruptcy case later, you may be required to pay a second filing fee and you may have to take extra steps to stop creditors' collection activities.

Every individual debtor must file this Exhibit D. If a joint petition is filed, each spouse must complete and file a separate Exhibit D. Check one of the five statements below and attach any documents as directed.

☒ 1. Within the 180 days **before the filing of my bankruptcy case**, I received a briefing from a credit counseling agency approved by the United States trustee or bankruptcy administrator that outlined the opportunities for available credit counseling and assisted me in performing a related budget analysis, and I have a certificate from the agency describing the services provided to me. *Attach a copy of the certificate and a copy of any debt repayment plan developed through the agency.*

☐ 2. Within the 180 days **before the filing of my bankruptcy case**, I received a briefing from a credit counseling agency approved by the United States trustee or bankruptcy administrator that outlined the opportunities for available credit counseling and assisted me in performing a related budget analysis, but I do not have a certificate from the agency describing the services provided to me. *You must file a copy of a certificate from the agency describing the services provided to you and a copy of any debt repayment plan developed through the agency no later than 14 days after your bankruptcy case is filed.*

☐ 3. I certify that I requested credit counseling services from an approved agency but was unable to obtain the services during the seven days from the time I made my request, and the following exigent circumstances merit a temporary waiver of the credit counseling requirement so I can file my bankruptcy case now. *[Summarize exigent circumstances here.]* ____

If your certification is satisfactory to the court, you must still obtain the credit counseling briefing within the first 30 days after you file your bankruptcy petition and promptly file a certificate from the agency that provided the counseling, together with a copy of any debt management plan developed through the agency. Failure to fulfill these requirements may result in dismissal of your case. Any extension of the 30-day deadline can be granted only for cause and is limited to a maximum of 15 days. Your case may also be dismissed if the court is not satisfied with your reasons for filing your bankruptcy case without first receiving a credit counseling briefing.

☐ 4. I am not required to receive a credit counseling briefing because of: *[Check the applicable statement.] [Must be accompanied by a motion for determination by the court.]*

Sample Exhibit D—page 2

B 1D (Official Form 1, Exhibit D) (12/09) - Cont. Page 2

☐ Incapacity. (Defined in 11 U.S.C. § 109(h)(4) as impaired by reason of mental illness or mental deficiency so as to be incapable of realizing and making rational decisions with respect to financial responsibilities.);

☐ Disability. (Defined in 11 U.S.C. § 109(h)(4) as physically impaired to the extent of being unable, after reasonable effort, to participate in a credit counseling briefing in person, by telephone, or through the Internet.);

☐ Active military duty in a military combat zone.

☐ 5. The United States trustee or bankruptcy administrator has determined that the credit counseling requirement of 11 U.S.C. § 109(h) does not apply in this district.

I certify under penalty of perjury that the information provided above is true and correct.

Signature of Debtor: ______________________________
Annie Justine Kaye

Date: ______________________

Form 6—Schedules

Form 6 refers to a series of schedules that provides the trustee and court with a picture of your current financial situation. Most of the information needed for these schedules is included in the Personal Property Checklist, Property Exemption Worksheet, and Homeowners' Worksheet that you (hopefully) completed already.

CAUTION

Use the correct address for your creditors. Many of these schedules ask you to provide addresses for your creditors you list. For creditors who have sent you written requests or demands for payment, provide the address that the creditor listed as a contact address on at least two written communications you received from the creditor within the 90-day period prior to your anticipated filing date. If the creditor has not contacted you within that 90-day period, provide the contact address that the creditor gave in the last two communications it sent to you. If you no longer have the address of your original creditor, use the contact address of the entities that have most recently attempted to collect the debt (such as a collection agency or attorney's office). If a creditor is a minor child, simply put "minor child" and the appropriate address. Don't list the child's name.

Schedule A—Real Property

Here you list all the real property you own as of the date you'll file the petition. If you completed the Homeowners' Worksheet in Ch. 7, much of that information goes on Schedule A.

A completed sample of Schedule A and line-by-line instructions follow. If you don't own any real estate, you still must complete the top of this form.

TIP

Tab this page. You might want to put a sticky note alongside the instructions for Schedule A, because we'll keep referring back to these instructions as you complete the rest of your schedules.

Real Property Defined

Real property—land and things permanently attached to land—includes more than just a house. It can also include unimproved land, vacation cabins, condominiums, duplexes, rental property, business property, mobile home park spaces, agricultural land, airplane hangars, and any other buildings permanently attached to land.

You may own real estate even if your name isn't on the deed or you can't walk on it, live on it, or get income from it. This might be true, for example, if:

- your spouse purchased real estate in his or her name after you were married and you live in a community property state (which means you own half), or
- someone else lives on property that you are entitled to receive in the future under a trust agreement.

There's a separate schedule (Schedule G) for leases and time-shares. If you hold a long-term commercial lease for your sole proprietory business, a time-share lease in a vacation cabin or property, lease a boat dock, lease underground portions of real estate for mineral or oil exploration, or otherwise lease or rent real estate of any description for any purpose, don't list it on Schedule A. Again, all leases and time-shares should be listed on Schedule G. (See the instructions for that schedule below.)

In re. (This means "In the matter of.") Type your name, and the name of your spouse if you're filing jointly. "In re [your name(s)]" will be the name of your bankruptcy case.

Case No. If you made an emergency filing, fill in the case number assigned by the court. Otherwise, leave this blank.

SKIP AHEAD

If you don't own real estate, type "N/A" anywhere in the first column, type "0" in the total box at the bottom of the page, and move on to Schedule B.

Description and Location of Property. For each piece of real property you own, list the type of property—for example, house, office building, farm, or undeveloped lot—and street address. You don't need to include the legal description of the property (the description on the deed).

Nature of Debtor's Interest in Property. In this column, you need to provide the legal definition for the interest you (or you and your spouse) have in the real estate. The most common type of interest—outright ownership—is called "fee simple." Even if you still owe money on your mortgage, as long as you have the right to sell the house, leave it to your heirs, and make alterations, your ownership is fee simple. A fee simple interest may be owned by one person or by several people jointly. Normally, when people are listed on a deed as the owners—even if they own the property as joint tenants, tenants in common, or tenants by the entirety—the ownership interest is in fee simple.

Other types of real property interests include:

- **Life estate.** Fairly uncommon, this is the right to possess and use property only during your lifetime. You can't sell the property, give it away, or leave it to someone when you die. Instead, when you die, the property passes to whomever was named in the instrument (trust, deed, or will) that created your life estate. This type of ownership is usually created when the sole owner of a piece of real estate wants his surviving spouse to live on the property for the rest of her life, but then have the property pass to his children. In this situation, the surviving spouse has a life estate. Surviving spouses who are beneficiaries of AB, spousal, or marital bypass trusts have life estates.
- **Future interest.** This is your right to own property sometime in the future. A common future interest is owned by a person who—under the terms of a deed or irrevocable trust—will definitely inherit the property when its current owner dies. Simply being named in a will, revocable living trust or beneficiary designation instrument doesn't create a future interest, because the person who signed any of these documents could change it to cut you out.
- **Contingent interest.** This ownership interest doesn't come into existence unless one or more conditions are fulfilled. Wills sometimes leave property to people under certain conditions. If the conditions aren't met, the property passes to someone else. For instance, Emma's will leaves her house to John provided that he takes care of her until her death. If John doesn't care for Emma, the house passes to Emma's daughter Jane. Both John and Jane have contingent interests in Emma's home.
- **Lienholder.** If you are the holder of a mortgage, deed of trust, judgment lien, or mechanics' lien on real estate, you have an ownership interest in the real estate
- **Easement holder.** If you are the holder of a right to travel on or otherwise use property owned by someone else, you have an easement.
- **Power of appointment.** If you have a legal right, given to you in a will or transfer of property, to sell a specified piece of someone's property, that's called a power of appointment and should be listed. You may have authority to sell someone's property under a power of attorney, but that's not the same as a power of appointment and shouldn't be listed as a real estate interest on Schedule A.
- **Beneficial ownership under a real estate contract.** This is the right to own property by virtue of having signed a binding real estate contract. Even though the buyer doesn't yet own the property, the buyer does have a "beneficial interest"—that is, the right to own the property once the formalities are completed. For example, property buyers have a beneficial ownership

Sample Schedule A

B6A (Official Form 6A) (12/07)

In re **Annie Justine Kaye**, Debtor — Case No. ____________

SCHEDULE A - REAL PROPERTY

Except as directed below, list all real property in which the debtor has any legal, equitable, or future interest, including all property owned as a cotenant, community property, or in which the debtor has a life estate. Include any property in which the debtor holds rights and powers exercisable for the debtor's own benefit. If the debtor is married, state whether husband, wife, both, or the marital community own the property by placing an "H," "W," "J," or "C" in the column labeled "Husband, Wife, Joint, or Community." If the debtor holds no interest in real property, write "None" under "Description and Location of Property."

Do not include interests in executory contracts and unexpired leases on this schedule. List them in Schedule G - Executory Contracts and Unexpired Leases.

If an entity claims to have a lien or hold a secured interest in any property, state the amount of the secured claim. See Schedule D. If no entity claims to hold a secured interest in the property, write "None" in the column labeled "Amount of Secured Claim." If the debtor is an individual or if a joint petition is filed, state the amount of any exemption claimed in the property only in Schedule C - Property Claimed as Exempt.

Description and Location of Property	Nature of Debtor's Interest in Property	Husband, Wife, Joint, or Community	Current Value of Debtor's Interest in Property, without Deducting any Secured Claim or Exemption	Amount of Secured Claim
None				

Sub-Total > **0.00** (Total of this page)

Total > **0.00**

(Report also on Summary of Schedules)

0 continuation sheets attached to the Schedule of Real Property

interest in property while the escrow is pending.

If you have trouble figuring out which of these definitions best fits your type of ownership interest, leave the column blank and let the trustee help you sort it out.

Husband, Wife, Joint, or Community. If you're not married, put "N/A." If you are married, indicate whether the real estate is owned:

- by the husband (H)
- by the wife (W)
- jointly by husband and wife as joint tenants, tenants in common, or tenants by the entirety (J), or
- jointly by husband and wife as community property (C).

If the real property is held in the name of a sole proprietorship business, check the column indicating the business owner. If you are married and live in a community property state, the business is most likely the community property of both spouses (C). If the business was owned by one spouse prior to marriage, it would belong to that spouse alone, at least for purposes of filling out this form. If you live in a common law property state, ownership will depend on who signed the deed, registered the business, or otherwise indicated ownership on formal documents.

Current Value of Debtor's Interest in Property, without Deducting any Secured Claim or Exemption. Enter the current fair market value of your real estate ownership interest. If you filled in the Homeowners' Worksheet in Ch. 7, use the value you came up with there (assuming the real property is your home).

Don't figure in homestead exemptions or any mortgages or other liens on the property. Just put the actual current market value as best you can calculate it. However, you can deduct the costs of sale from the market value and enter the difference, as long as you explain what you did on the schedule. (See Ch. 7 for information on valuing real estate.)

If you own the property with someone else who is not joining you in your bankruptcy, list only your ownership share in this column. For example, if you and your brother own a home as joint tenants (each owns 50%), split the property's current market value in half and list that amount here.

If your interest is intangible—for example, you are a beneficiary of real estate held in trust that won't be distributed for many years—enter an estimate provided by a real estate appraiser or put "don't know" and explain why you can't be more precise.

Mobile Home Owners

If you own a mobile home in a park, use the value of the home in its current location, even though the mobile home itself might qualify as personal property. Many parks are located in desirable areas, and the park itself adds value to the motor home even though you may not have any ownership interest in the park itself. A mobile home that might not be worth much on its own could be worth quite a bit if it's sitting in a fancy park.

Total. Add the amounts in the fourth column and enter the total in the box at the bottom of the page. The form reminds you that you should also enter this total on the Summary of Schedules (see the instructions for completing the Summary, below).

Amount of Secured Claim. List mortgages and other debts secured by the property. If there is no secured claim of any type on the real estate, enter "None." If there is, enter separately the amount of each outstanding mortgage, deed of trust, home equity loan, or lien (judgment lien, mechanic's lien, materialmen's lien, tax lien, or the like) that is claimed against the property. If you don't know the balance on your mortgage, deed of trust, or home equity loan, call the lender. To find out whether there are liens on the property—and if so, for how much—visit the land records office in your county (or check online) and look up the parcel in the records; the clerk can show you how. Or, you can order a title search through a real estate attorney or title insurance company. If you own several pieces of real estate and there is one lien on file against all of it, list the full amount of the lien for each separate parcel. Don't worry if, taken together, the value of the liens is higher than the value of the property; it's quite common.

How you itemize liens in this schedule won't affect how your property or the liens will be treated in bankruptcy. The idea here is to notify the trustee of all possible liens that may affect your equity in your real estate.

If you are simply unable to obtain this information, and you can't afford the help of a lawyer or title insurance company, put "unknown." This will be okay for the purpose of filing your papers, but you may need to get the information later. For example, a question might come up as to whether the equity in your home is protected by your exemption. Suppose your state's homestead exemption is $10,000 and your equity is $30,000. You would probably lose the house and receive $10,000 for your exemption, and your creditors would get $20,000, less the cost of sale and the trustee's commission. But if there were an unknown lien on the property for $20,000, then you wouldn't lose the house because the trustee wouldn't sell the property because there would be nothing left over for the unsecured creditors after the lienholder was paid. So it's to your benefit to get this information any way you can.

How to List Property That Is Subject to Foreclosure Proceedings

Even if your property is subject to foreclosure proceedings, you still own the property until the foreclosure sale is held and a new deed is recorded either in the lender's name (if the property fails to sell) or in the purchaser's name (if the foreclosure auction ends in a successful bid). You should list the property in Schedule A and include all of the required information. You should also explain that the house is in foreclosure and provide the date set for the foreclosure sale (if it has gotten that far) or, if not, when you expect the property to be sold.

Schedule B—Personal Property

Here you must list and evaluate *all* of your personal property, including intangible property (such as accounts receivable and possible legal claims), property that is security for a debt, and property that is exempt. If you didn't fill in the Personal Property Checklist and Property Exemption Worksheet in Ch. 6, turn to that chapter for explanations and suggestions about what property you should list in each of the schedule's categories. Remember that the assets of your sole proprietorship business are your personal property and must be listed on Schedule B.

When listing all of your stuff on a public document like Schedule B, you might feel tempted to cheat a little. Don't give in to the temptation to "forget" any of your assets. Bankruptcy law doesn't give you the right to decide that an asset isn't worth mentioning. Even if, for example, you've decided that your CD collection is worthless given the advent of the iPod, you still have to list it. You can explain on the form why you think it's worthless. If you omit something and get caught, your case can be dismissed—or your discharge revoked—which means you'll get no bankruptcy relief for your current debts. Remember, you can use exemptions to keep much of your property; if no exemption is available, you may be able to buy the property back from the trustee.

A completed sample of Schedule B and line-by-line instructions follow. If you need more room, use an attached continuation page, or create a continuation page yourself.

In re and Case No. Follow the instructions for Schedule A.

Type of Property. The form lists general categories of personal property. Leave this column as is.

None. If you own no property that fits in a category listed in the first column, enter an "X" in the "None" column. But make sure that you really don't own anything in this category.

Description and Location of Property. List specific items that fall in each general category. If you filled out the Personal Property Checklist and Property Exemption Worksheet in Ch. 6, you already have this information. If not, be sure to go over the Personal Property Checklist, which lists types of property to include in each category. Although the categories in the checklist correspond to the categories in Schedule B, the checklist describes some of them differently (where we felt the Schedule B descriptions weren't clear).

CAUTION

Start with the property's replacement value. Although some bankruptcy commentators believe that you must use the property's replacement value—what it would cost to purchase the property from a retail vendor, given the property's age and condition—for your estimates on Schedule B, we are not convinced that this is legally required. The only value that matters in this context is its "fire sale" value (what the trustee would get for the property in a trustee's sale), which would likely be less than the property's replacement value. Despite our view of this matter, we recommend that you at least start with the property's replacement value. If that value renders the property nonexempt to a significant degree, then consider listing the lower "fire sale" value and disclosing that fact along with the description of the property. Chances are that the trustee will choose not to take the property because there would be little or nothing left to pay the creditors with after you receive your exemption amount. (See Ch. 6 for more on how exemptions work.)

Separately list all items worth $50 to $100 or more (there is no hard and fast rule about this). Combine small items into larger categories whenever reasonable. For example, you don't need to list every spatula, colander, garlic press, and ice cream scoop; instead, put "kitchen cookware" (unless one of these items is worth a lot). If you list numerous items in one category (as is likely for household goods and furnishings), you may need to attach a continuation sheet.

For each category of property listed, you must indicate where the property is. If your personal property is at your residence, just enter "Residence" or your home address beneath the property description. If the property is at your business, enter the business address beneath the property description. If someone else holds property for you (for example, you loaned your woodworking tools to a friend), put that person's name and address in this column.

Here are further instructions for some of the categories:

Items 1 and 2. List the amount and source of any cash on hand or money in financial accounts—for example, from business receipts, wages (if you have a day job to supplement your business income), Social Security payments, or child support. Listing everything will help you (and the trustee) decide later whether any of this money qualifies as exempt property. You must list the amount in your account on the day you file for bankruptcy, even if you have written checks on the account that haven't yet cleared. All money in your accounts on the day you file is property of your bankruptcy estate, and the trustee can take that money unless it's exempt (even if that means you bounce a check or two). (*In re Schoonover*, No. 05-43662-7 (D. Kan. 2006).) The amount you list should be about what will be in the account when you file your bankruptcy paperwork (and shortly afterwards). If you list a small amount on your forms but your account balance grows significantly just after you file, the trustee may freeze the account pending further investigation.

Sample Schedule B—page 1

B6B (Official Form 6B) (12/07)

In re **Annie Justine Kaye** , Debtor   Case No. ____________

SCHEDULE B - PERSONAL PROPERTY

Except as directed below, list all personal property of the debtor of whatever kind. If the debtor has no property in one or more of the categories, place an "x" in the appropriate position in the column labeled "None." If additional space is needed in any category, attach a separate sheet properly identified with the case name, case number, and the number of the category. If the debtor is married, state whether husband, wife, both, or the marital community own the property by placing an "H," "W," "J," or "C" in the column labeled "Husband, Wife, Joint, or Community." If the debtor is an individual or a joint petition is filed, state the amount of any exemptions claimed only in Schedule C - Property Claimed as Exempt.

Do not list interests in executory contracts and unexpired leases on this schedule. List them in Schedule G - Executory Contracts and Unexpired Leases.

If the property is being held for the debtor by someone else, state that person's name and address under "Description and Location of Property." If the property is being held for a minor child, simply state the child's initials and the name and address of the child's parent or guardian, such as "A.B., a minor child, by John Doe, guardian." Do not disclose the child's name. See, 11 U.S.C. §112 and Fed. R. Bankr. P. 1007(m).

Type of Property	N O N E	Description and Location of Property	Husband, Wife, Joint, or Community	Current Value of Debtor's Interest in Property, without Deducting any Secured Claim or Exemption
1. Cash on hand		**Location: XXXX First St., Freshstart AA** **Cash at home.**	-	**500.00**
2. Checking, savings or other financial accounts, certificates of deposit, or shares in banks, savings and loan, thrift, building and loan, and homestead associations, or credit unions, brokerage houses, or cooperatives.		**Bank of America Checking Account #12345** **Location: XXXX Third St., Freshstart AA**	-	**2,000.00**
		Freshstart Credit Union **XXXX Fourth St.** **Freshstart, AA 99999** **Personal savings account**	-	**1,000.00**
		Freshstart Community Bank **XXXX Sixth St.** **Freshstart, AA, 99999** **Personal checking account**	-	**200.00**
3. Security deposits with public utilities, telephone companies, landlords, and others.		**$1000 Security Deposit for lease on store** **XXX Seventh St. Freshstart AA 99999**	-	**1,000.00**
4. Household goods and furnishings, including audio, video, and computer equipment.		**All items at replacement value** **Stereo system ($300), washer dryer set ($200), refrigerator ($400), electric stove ($250), misc furniture (couch, 2 chairs) $450, minor appliances (blender, toaster, mixer) $125, vacuum ($50), 42" HDTV (purchased two years ago for $800, currently $500),** **Location: XXXX First St., Freshstart AA**	-	**2,275.00**
		2 end tables ($500), bed and bedding ($800), oriental rug ($1500) **Location: XXXX First St., Freshstart AA**	-	**2,800.00**
5. Books, pictures and other art objects, antiques, stamp, coin, record, tape, compact disc, and other collections or collectibles.		**250 books at used bookstore prices** **Location: XXXX First St., Freshstart AA**	-	**100.00**
6. Wearing apparel.		**Normal clothing at used clothing store prices** **Location: XXXX First St., Freshstart AA**	-	**800.00**

Sub-Total > **10,675.00**
(Total of this page)

3 continuation sheets attached to the Schedule of Personal Property

If You Are Listed on Someone Else's Account

As explained in Ch. 5, if you are named on a parent's bank account (typically, to manage the parent's finances if he or she becomes incapacitated or otherwise needs help), the trustee might believe that account should be part of your bankruptcy estate. To prevent the trustee from getting a false idea about the nature of the account, the best approach is to list it under Item 2 and then explain the true facts, which usually are that the money in the account came from and belongs to the parent, that the bankruptcy filer was only added to the account as a fiduciary (a trusted assistant), and that it would be a breach of the fiduciary duty for the filer to use any of the parent's money for the filer's own purposes.

If the exemptions you are using allow you to exempt bank accounts or cash up to a certain amount, and you have enough of that exemption left over to apply to the money in your parent's account, it makes sense to claim the money in your parent's account as exempt on Schedule C (explained below). The claim of exemption is legally unnecessary, but it will prevent the trustee from trying to prove that the money should be considered part of your bankruptcy estate; even if it is, you'll be able to keep it all anyway.

Item 11. Although an education IRA and a qualified state tuition plan may technically not be part of the bankruptcy estate, list them here anyway. Also, you are required to file any records you have of these interests as an attachment to Schedule B.

Item 12. Although ERISA-qualified pension plans, 401(k)s, IRAs, and Keoghs may not be part of your bankruptcy estate, list them here anyway and describe each plan in detail. In the Current Value column, enter the value of the pension, if known. Otherwise, list the value as "undetermined."

Item 13. Here is where you describe your ownership interest in your business, unless it is a partnership or joint venture (see Item 14). Sole proprietors should list their business here, whether or not it's conducted under a different name. If you are a sole or partial owner of a corporation or LLC, describe the exact nature of your interest in the company or entity (for instance, "sole owner with wife of a C corporation," or "owner of 50% stocks in ABC Inc." or "owner of a 40% interest in an LLC"). If you have stock options, describe them here.

If your business is a sole proprietorship, its value will most readily be measured by the value of its assets (equipment, machines, inventory, accounts receivable, goodwill, and so on). You should itemize your assets as best you can, attaching as many continuation sheets as you need. For instance, if you have a retail business, you can attach a recent inventory (if you have one), or bring your inventory current if you haven't done one in a while. If you have a service or professional business, or otherwise don't have inventory, list your larger assets and summarize the small stuff (for instance, desk $200, chair, $300, labeling machine $500, stationary and supplies $400).

If you own shares in a publicly traded corporation, use the listed value of the shares. If your corporation is a close corporation or LLC, it will be difficult to value your interest. (See Ch. 6 for more in how to value ownership interests in business entities.) If the corporation or LLC has been capitalized, then the value of your interest can be measured by its capital (assets minus liabilities). Or, for a corporation, the corporate accountant may be able to give you an estimate based on the number of shares issued and the book value of the corporation used for taxation and bank loan purposes. An alternative is to list the value as "unknown" and let the trustee help you sort it out.

Item 14. If you own a partnership or joint venture, list it here. You'll almost certainly need help from the business CFO or accountant to place a value on your ownership interest.

Sample Schedule B—page 2

B6B (Official Form 6B) (12/07) - Cont.

In re **Annie Justine Kaye**, Debtor   Case No. ____________

SCHEDULE B - PERSONAL PROPERTY

(Continuation Sheet)

Type of Property	NONE	Description and Location of Property	Husband, Wife, Joint, or Community	Current Value of Debtor's Interest in Property, without Deducting any Secured Claim or Exemption
7. Furs and jewelry.		**Diamond earrings at used jewelry store price ($800), watch at flea market price ($300) Location: XXXX First St., Freshstart AA**	-	**1,100.00**
8. Firearms and sports, photographic, and other hobby equipment.		**Mountain bike at used bicycle store price ($250), digital camera priced at ebay ($200), 16 ga over and under shotgun ($300) Location: XXXX First St., Freshstart AA**	-	**750.00**
9. Interests in insurance policies. Name insurance company of each policy and itemize surrender or refund value of each.	**X**			
10. Annuities. Itemize and name each issuer.	**X**			
11. Interests in an education IRA as defined in 26 U.S.C. § 530(b)(1) or under a qualified State tuition plan as defined in 26 U.S.C. § 529(b)(1). Give particulars. (File separately the record(s) of any such interest(s). 11 U.S.C. § 521(c).)	**X**			
12. Interests in IRA, ERISA, Keogh, or other pension or profit sharing plans. Give particulars.		**Roth IRA, $10,000, located at Freshstart Credit Union (See Item 2)**	-	**10,000.00**
13. Stock and interests in incorporated and unincorporated businesses. Itemize.		**Sole proprietor owner of Annie's Beauty Accessories, business consists of inventory for sale, fixtures and furniture, and possible good will. Most inventory is consignment items from local artisans. Items owned by Debtor are itemized in other parts of Schedule B. Location: XXX Seventh St. Freshstart, AA**	-	**Undetermined**
		250 shares in my brother's private C Corporation. Brother is majority stockholder and corporation has five total shareholders, including me. Corporation currently is engaged in producing iPhone apps. Corporation has not produced a profit for over three years. My brother is willing to purchase my shares at $4 a share, or a total of $1000. XXX 9th St. Freshstart, AA	-	**1,000.00**
14. Interests in partnerships or joint ventures. Itemize.	**X**			

Sub-Total > **12,850.00**
(Total of this page)

Sheet **1** of **3** continuation sheets attached to the Schedule of Personal Property

Item 15. As a small business owner, you may not own government or corporate bonds. However, you may own other instruments that carry some value, such as promissory notes. If so, describe them here and provide their face value in your description (for example, "promissory note in the amount of $4,500 signed by Bob Pascarelli, dated 2/10/2010").

Item 16. If you are a sole proprietor or independent contractor, one or more of your customers probably owe you some money that isn't formally documented in a promissory note or other written instrument. If so, list each debt by customer name, the reason for the debt, and the date the debt was incurred. These debts belong to your bankruptcy estate and may be collected by the trustee unless you are able to claim them as exempt.

Item 17. List all child support or alimony arrears—that is, money that should have been paid to you but hasn't been. Specify the dates the payments were due and missed, such as "$250 monthly child support payments for June, July, August, and September 20xx." Also list any debts owed you from a property settlement incurred in a divorce or dissolution.

Item 18. List all other money owed to you and not yet paid, other than accounts receivable (those go in Item 16) and child support, alimony, and property settlements (which should be listed in Item 17). If you've obtained a judgment against someone but haven't been paid, list it here. State the defendant's name, the date of the judgment, the court that issued the judgment, the amount of the judgment, and the kind of case (such as "car accident"). If you are filing for bankruptcy early in the year and know how much your tax refund will be, you should list the amount here even though you haven't received it yet. If your state's exemption system allows you to exempt cash, you can exempt the tax refund on Schedule C (explained below).

Item 19. An "equitable or future interest" means that sooner or later you will get property that is currently owned by someone else. Your expectation is legally recognized and valuable. For instance, if your parents' trust gives them the right to live in the family home, that's a "life estate." If the trust gives you the home when they die, you have an "equitable interest" in the home while they're alive. "Powers exercisable for the benefit of the debtor" means that a person has been given the power to route property to you, but it hasn't happened by the time you file your bankruptcy petition. In sum, if it looks like property is coming your way eventually, and that property hasn't been listed in Schedule A, list it here. These kinds of interests are hard to value. You'll need to get some help from an appraiser or list the value as "unknown" and let the trustee sort it out.

Item 20. You have a contingent interest in property if, for example, you are named the remainder beneficiary of an irrevocable trust (a trust that can't be undone by the person who created it). It's contingent because you may or may not get something from the trust—it all depends on whether there's anything left by the time it gets to you. A noncontingent interest means you will definitely get the property sooner or later, for example, under the terms of an insurance policy. Also list here any wills or revocable living trusts on which you are named as a beneficiary. Even though you don't have any right to inherit under these documents (because they can be changed at any time prior to the person's death), the trustee wants to know this information because the inheritance becomes part of your bankruptcy estate if the person dies within six months after you file for bankruptcy.

Item 21. List all claims that you have against others that might end up in a lawsuit. For instance, if you were recently rear-ended in an automobile accident and are struggling with whiplash, you may have a cause of action against the other driver (and that driver's insurer). Or, you might have contractual claims against a vendor or customer of your business. Make sure you list and do your best to value all possible "causes of action." If you don't list this type of claim here, you may be prohibited from pursuing it later.

Sample Schedule B—page 3

B6B (Official Form 6B) (12/07) - Cont.

In re **Annie Justine Kaye**, Case No. ______
Debtor

SCHEDULE B - PERSONAL PROPERTY
(Continuation Sheet)

Type of Property	NONE	Description and Location of Property	Husband, Wife, Joint, or Community	Current Value of Debtor's Interest in Property, without Deducting any Secured Claim or Exemption
15. Government and corporate bonds and other negotiable and nonnegotiable instruments.		**Negotiable promissory note from Jonathan Kaye, Annie's brother, dated XX/XX/XXXX Location: XXXX First St., Freshstart AA ($500)**	-	**500.00**
16. Accounts receivable.		**25 customers owe money for goods purchased on credit Location: XXX Seventh St., Freshstart AA**	-	**1,100.00**
17. Alimony, maintenance, support, and property settlements to which the debtor is or may be entitled. Give particulars.	X			
18. Other liquidated debts owed to debtor including tax refunds. Give particulars.		**Refund for 20XX Taxes (expected but not yet received) Location: XXXX First St., Freshstart AA**	-	**1,000.00**
19. Equitable or future interests, life estates, and rights or powers exercisable for the benefit of the debtor other than those listed in Schedule A - Real Property.	X			
20. Contingent and noncontingent interests in estate of a decedent, death benefit plan, life insurance policy, or trust.		**Named by recently-deceased brother in his will to inherit one half of $10,000 Bond due to mature on January 1, 2016 on the contingency that my younger sister has not married by that date. Location: XXXX First St., Freshstart AA**	-	**Undetermined**
21. Other contingent and unliquidated claims of every nature, including tax refunds, counterclaims of the debtor, and rights to setoff claims. Give estimated value of each.		**Potential cause of action against parents of teenager who vandalized my store. Total damages were $3000. Case is awaiting resolution in criminal court and no lawsuit has yet been filed Location: XXXX First St., Freshstart AA**	-	**3,000.00**
22. Patents, copyrights, and other intellectual property. Give particulars.		**See Item 24 for trade secret maintained in customer list**	-	**Undetermined**
23. Licenses, franchises, and other general intangibles. Give particulars.		**Business good will**	-	**Undetermined**

Sub-Total > **5,600.00**
(Total of this page)

Sheet 2 of 3 continuation sheets attached to the Schedule of Personal Property

Item 22. This question asks about intellectual property assets. State the type of intellectual property you own (patent, copyright, trademark, or similar right) and its subject matter. Give the number assigned by the issuing agency and the length of time the patent, copyright, trademark, or other right will last. Keep in mind that both copyright and trademark rights may exist even if you haven't registered them with a government agency. If you claim trademark rights through usage, or copyright through the fact that you created the item and reduced it to tangible form, describe those rights here.

Your business may also have trade secrets. A trade secret is confidential information that gives you a competitive advantage precisely because it's a secret. Examples include recipes, manufacturing techniques, marketing strategies, product designs, and computer algorithms. (Although customer lists are often categorized as trade secrets, they go in Item 24, below.) Trade secrets are very difficult to value: You may want to list the value as "unknown" for now. The important thing is to tell the trustee that a trade secret exists, which gives the trustee a chance to sell it if it's marketable and you can't use an exemption to keep it.

Item 23. List all licenses and franchises, what they cover, the length of time remaining, who they are with, and whether you can transfer them to someone else. Franchises and licenses are contracts in which an owner of tangible or intellectual property gives another party permission to use it under the conditions set out in the contract. Examples include a license to drill or mine for oil or minerals on real estate, a fast food or carpet cleaning franchise, or the right (license) to use a software program for a certain customer base. As a bankruptcy debtor, you may be on either side of this type of contract (that is, you may own the property or have the owner's permission to use the property). Either way, you should list the license or franchise here.

Item 24. Describe customer lists or other compilations of personally identifiable information that you obtained from people as part of providing them with consumer goods or services. For example, if you have a database of customers' email addresses and contact information for your graphic design business, state "database with customer contact information," or simply "customer list" (no need to list any names). If you have promised your customers not to share the information or sell the information to third parties, or otherwise safeguard the information, note that here. The trustee may or may not be able to sell your customer list, and the value of your customer list will depend on whether the list can be sold.

Items 25–27. Include the make, model, and year of each vehicle or accessory.

Item 28. Most small businesses have offices, or at least home offices. Here, you should list and value your office fixtures, desks, chairs, computers, telephones, and other equipment and supplies. In Item 13, you had to value your interest in your business. That value might be the same as the value you list here, if your office holds all of your business assets. You can use the same number here or simply refer back to Item 13.

Item 29. This is where you list everything else—other than your office furniture and supplies—that you use in your business. If you already listed everything in Item 13, you can refer to that answer. Make sure your responses match: If you remember an additional an additional piece of equipment here, for example, you should also go back and add it to Item 13.

Item 30. List all inventory here, in broad strokes. For instance, a restaurant might list "wine, liquor, and food"; a retail store might list "clothing, shoes, and accessories"; and a manufacturing company might list various categories of parts and materials to be used in making its products. In Item 20 of the Statement of Financial Affairs (see below), you are asked to detail inventories you have taken. You can use the most recent inventory to guide your description here.

Items 32-34. For crops, list whether they've been harvested, whether they've been sold (and, if so, to

Sample Schedule B—page 4

B6B (Official Form 6B) (12/07) - Cont.

In re **Annie Justine Kaye**, Debtor Case No. ______

SCHEDULE B - PERSONAL PROPERTY

(Continuation Sheet)

Type of Property	NONE	Description and Location of Property	Husband, Wife, Joint, or Community	Current Value of Debtor's Interest in Property, without Deducting any Secured Claim or Exemption
24. Customer lists or other compilations containing personally identifiable information (as defined in 11 U.S.C. § 101(41A)) provided to the debtor by individuals in connection with obtaining a product or service from the debtor primarily for personal, family, or household purposes.		**Trade secret consisting of mailing list compiled by various owners over 22 years of operating the store and acquired by debtor when store was purchased. Location: XXX Seventh St., Freshstart AA**	-	**4,500.00**
25. Automobiles, trucks, trailers, and other vehicles and accessories.		**2009 Honda Accord Location: XXXX First St., Freshstart AA**	-	**21,000.00**
		01 23 Foot Travel Trailer Location: XXXX First St., Freshstart AA	-	**5,000.00**
26. Boats, motors, and accessories.	X			
27. Aircraft and accessories.	X			
28. Office equipment, furnishings, and supplies.	X			
29. Machinery, fixtures, equipment, and supplies used in business.		**Fixtures in store ($1500), equipment (accounting, cleaning, etc) ($500) Location: XXX Seventh St. Freshstart, AA**	-	**2,000.00**
30. Inventory.		**Inventory in store is 75% artisan products (necklaces, earrings, scarves, pendents, theme T-shirts, etc.) Consignment contracts are available for inspection. These items are not part of bankruptcy estate (See SFA #14]** **Items in bankruptcy estate are bath and massage oils, perfumes, shawls, costume jewelry, shampoos. Retail value is $2200.** **Location: XXX Seventh St. Freshstart, AA**	-	**2,200.00**
31. Animals.	X			
32. Crops - growing or harvested. Give particulars.	X			
33. Farming equipment and implements.	X			
34. Farm supplies, chemicals, and feed.	X			
35. Other personal property of any kind not already listed. Itemize.	X			

Sub-Total > **34,700.00**
(Total of this page)
Total > **63,825.00**

Sheet **3** of **3** continuation sheets attached to the Schedule of Personal Property

(Report also on Summary of Schedules)

whom and for how much), whether you've taken out any loans against them, and whether they are insured. In Items 33 and 34, list your farming equipment and supplies.

Item 35. This is the catchall question. If you have any type of personal property that you haven't been able to squeeze into the other categories, list it here and do your best to give it a value.

Husband, Wife, Joint, or Community. If you're not married, put "N/A" at the top of this column.

If you are married and live in a community property state, then property acquired during the marriage is community property and you should put "C" in this column. Gifts and inheritances received by one spouse are separate property, as is property a spouse owned prior to marriage or after separation. Identify this property with an "H" (for husband) or "W" (for wife), as appropriate.

If you live in any state that is not a community property state, write "J" if you own the property jointly with a spouse, and "H" or "W" if a spouse owns that property as an individual.

Current Value of Debtor's Interest in Property, without Deducting any Secured Claim or Exemption. You can take the information requested here from the Property Exemption Worksheet in Ch. 6. List the replacement value of the property, without regard to any secured interests or exemptions. For example, if you own a car with a replacement value of $6,000, you still owe $4,000 on the car note, and your state's motor vehicle exemption is $1,200, put down $6,000 for the market value of the car.

Providing values for intangible personal property can be tricky. For instance, the actual value of a promissory note may not be the same as its face value, because the note is only worth what it can be sold for. For example, a $500 promissory note may be worth less if you would have to pay someone to collect it, and if you went to sell it, you likely would get pennies on the dollar. (Ch. 6 provides some tips on valuing commercial paper.) If you can't come up with a value for intangible assets, list it as "unknown" and let the trustee sort it out.

Total. Add the amounts in this column and put the total in the box at the bottom of the last page. If you used any continuation pages in addition to the preprinted form, remember to attach those pages and include the amounts from those pages in this total.

Schedule C—Property Claimed as Exempt

On this form, you claim all property you think is legally exempt from being sold to pay your unsecured creditors. In the overwhelming majority of personal Chapter 7 bankruptcies, all—or virtually all—of the debtor's personal property is exempt.

The same is not necessarily true for business assets, however. Most state exemption systems do not specifically address business assets other than as "tools of the trade," an exemption that usually covers a very limited dollar amount. To the extent that any of your business assets cannot reasonably be listed in this category, the only way you can exempt them is through a wildcard exemption. For example, if your state allows you to use the federal exemptions, you can use any portion of the homestead allowance that you don't use to protect home equity for any type of property, including business assets. (See Ch. 6 for more on exempting business-related assets.)

When you work on this form, you'll need to refer frequently to several other documents. Have in front of you:

- the worksheets from Ch. 6 and Ch. 7
- your drafts of Schedules A and B
- the list of state or federal bankruptcy exemptions you'll be using, provided in Appendix A, and
- if you're using a state's exemptions, the additional nonbankruptcy federal exemptions, also provided in Appendix A.

Set out below is a sample completed Schedule C and line-by-line instructions. Looking at the sample Schedule C exemptions, you might notice that a particular exemption could apply to more than one category of personal property from Schedule B. That's because the exemption categories are set up by each state, but the property categories are determined by the feds, who also wrote Schedule B. As a result, the property and exemption categories don't necessarily match up neatly. For example, the California "tools of the trade" exemption (see Appendix A) could apply to a number of the property categories, including Item 28 (office equipment, furnishings, and supplies), Item 33 (farming equipment and implements), Item 25 (automobiles, trucks, trailers and other vehicles, and accessories), and Item 5 (books, etc.). On Schedule C, you'll group the property you want to claim as exempt by the categories printed on Schedule B. For example, you'd list "Office Equipment, Furnishings and Supplies," and "Machinery, fixtures, equipment, and supplies used in business," rather than creating one big category of your own making for "tools of the trade."

Give Yourself the Benefit of the Doubt

When you claim exemptions, err in your own favor. If an exemption seems to cover an item of property, claim it. You may find that you're legally entitled to keep much of the property you're deeply attached to, such as your home, car, and family heirlooms, though not all of your business assets if they are valuable and easily liquidated.

Your exemption claims will be examined by the trustee and possibly a creditor or two, although historically few creditors monitor bankruptcy proceedings. In close cases, bankruptcy laws require the trustee to honor your exemption claims. In other words, you're entitled to the benefit of the doubt. If the trustee or a creditor successfully objects to an exemption claim, you've lost nothing by trying. See Ch. 10 for more on objections to claimed exemptions.

In re and **Case No.** Follow the instructions for Schedule A.

Debtor claims the exemptions to which the debtor is entitled under. If you're using the federal exemptions, check the top box. Everybody else, check the second box. See Ch. 6 for information on residency requirements for using a state's exemptions and tips on how to choose between the federal and state exemption systems. If you are living in a state that offers the federal exemption system, but you haven't been there long enough to meet the two-year residency requirement to use the state exemptions, you can still choose the federal system (and check the top box on Schedule C).

SEE AN EXPERT

If you own property out of state. You'll generally choose the exemptions of the state where you live when you file as long as you've lived there for at least two years. Most exemptions for home equity require that you be living in the home when you file for bankruptcy, but this isn't always the case. If you want to protect your equity in a home in a state other than the one where you plan to file, see a lawyer.

Check if debtor claims a homestead exemption that exceeds $136,875. Check this box if:

- the exemptions of the state you are using allow a homestead of more than $136,875
- you have more than $136,875 equity in your home, and
- you acquired your home at least 40 months prior to your bankruptcy filing date.

If you acquired your home within 40 months of filing, and you didn't purchase it using the proceeds from selling another home in the same state, your homestead exemption may be capped at $136,875, regardless of the exemption available in the state where your home is located. (See Ch. 7 for detailed information on the homestead exemption cap.)

The following instructions cover one column at a time. But rather than listing all your exempt property in the first column before moving on to the second column, you might find it easier to list one exempt item and complete all of the columns for that item before moving on to the next exempt item.

Description of Property. To describe the property you claim as exempt, take these steps:

Step 1: Turn to Ch. 6 to find out which exemptions are available to you and which property to claim as exempt (if you have already used the Property Exemption Worksheet to identify your exempt property, skip this step).

Step 2: Decide which of the real estate you listed on Schedule A, if any, you want to claim as exempt. Remember that state homestead allowances usually apply only to property you are living in when you file, but that you can use a wildcard exemption for any type of property. Use the same description you used in the Description and Location of Property column of Schedule A.

Step 3: Decide which of the personal property you listed on Schedule B you want to claim as exempt. For each item identified, list both the category of property (preprinted in the Types of Property column) and the specific item, from the Description and Location of Property column. If the exemptions you are using apply to an entire category, such as clothing, simply list "clothing" as the item you are exempting.

Specify Law Providing Each Exemption. You'll find citations to the specific laws that create exemptions in the state and federal exemption lists in Appendix A. Remember to use the rules for choosing your exemptions explained in detail in Ch. 6.

You can simplify this process by entering the name of the statutes you are using at the top of the form. For example, you might type "All law references are to the Florida Statutes Annotated unless otherwise noted." The name of the statute is noted at the top of each exemption list in Appendix A.

For each item of property you are claiming as exempt, enter the citation (number) of the specific law that creates the exemption, as set out on the exemption list. If you are combining part or all of a wildcard exemption (an exemption that can be used for any type of property) with a regular exemption, list both citations. If the wildcard and the regular exemption have the same citation, list the citation twice and put "wildcard" next to one of the citations. If you use any reference other than one found in the state statutes you are using, such as a federal nonbankruptcy exemption or a court case, list the entire reference for the exempt item.

Value of Claimed Exemption. Claim the full exemption amount allowed, up to the value of the item. The amount allowed is listed in Appendix A.

Bankruptcy law allows married couples to double all exemptions unless the state expressly prohibits it. Doubling exemptions means that each of you can claim the entire amount of each exemption, if you are filing jointly. If your state's chart in Appendix A doesn't say your state forbids doubling, go ahead and double. You are entitled to double all federal exemptions, if you use them.

If you are using part or all of a wildcard exemption in addition to a regular exemption, list both amounts. For example, if the regular exemption for an item of furniture is $200, and you plan to exempt $500 worth of furniture by adding $300 from your state's wildcard exemption, list $200 across from the citation you listed for the regular exemption and $300 across from the citation you listed for the wildcard exemption (or across from the term "wildcard").

CAUTION

Don't claim more than you need. For instance, if you're allowed household furniture up to a total amount of $2,000, don't inflate the value of each item of furniture simply to get to $2,000. Use the actual property values from Schedule B.

Current Value of Property Without Deducting Exemption. Enter the current (replacement) value of the item you are claiming as exempt. For most items, this information is listed on Schedules A and B. However, if you listed the item as part of a group in Schedule B, list it separately here and assign it a separate replacement value.

Sample Schedule C—page 1

B6C (Official Form 6C) (12/07)

In re **Annie Justine Kaye**, Debtor   Case No. ________

SCHEDULE C - PROPERTY CLAIMED AS EXEMPT

Debtor claims the exemptions to which debtor is entitled under:
(Check one box)
☐ 11 U.S.C. §522(b)(2)
■ 11 U.S.C. §522(b)(3)

☐ Check if debtor claims a homestead exemption that exceeds $136,875.

Description of Property	Specify Law Providing Each Exemption	Value of Claimed Exemption	Current Value of Property Without Deducting Exemption
Cash on Hand **Location: XXXX First St., Freshstart AA** **Cash at home.**	**C.C.P. § 703.140(b)(5)**	**500.00**	**500.00**
Checking, Savings, or Other Financial Accounts, Certificates of Deposit **Bank of America Checking Account #12345** **Location: XXXX Third St., Freshstart AA**	**C.C.P. § 703.140(b)(5)**	**2,000.00**	**2,000.00**
Freshstart Credit Union **XXXX Fourth St.** **Freshstart, AA 99999** **Personal savings account**	**C.C.P. § 703.140(b)(5)**	**1,000.00**	**1,000.00**
Freshstart Community Bank **XXXX Sixth St.** **Freshstart, AA, 99999** **Personal checking account**	**C.C.P. § 703.140(b)(5)**	**200.00**	**200.00**
Security Deposits with Utilities, Landlords, and Others **$1000 Security Deposit for lease on store** **XXX Seventh St. Freshstart AA 99999**	**C.C.P. § 703.140(b)(5)**	**1,000.00**	**1,000.00**
Household Goods and Furnishings **All items at replacement value** **Stereo system ($300), washer dryer set ($200), refrigerator ($400), electric stove ($250), misc furniture (couch, 2 chairs) $450, minor appliances (blender, toaster, mixer) $125, vacuum ($50), 42" HDTV (purchased two years ago for $800, currently $500),** **Location: XXXX First St., Freshstart AA**	**C.C.P. § 703.140(b)(3)**	**2,275.00**	**2,275.00**
2 end tables ($500), bed and bedding ($800), oriental rug ($1500) **Location: XXXX First St., Freshstart AA**	**C.C.P. § 703.140(b)(5)**	**2,800.00**	**2,800.00**
Books, Pictures and Other Art Objects; Collectibles **250 books at used bookstore prices** **Location: XXXX First St., Freshstart AA**	**C.C.P. § 703.140(b)(5)**	**100.00**	**100.00**
Wearing Apparel **Normal clothing at used clothing store prices** **Location: XXXX First St., Freshstart AA**	**C.C.P. § 703.140(b)(3)**	**800.00**	**800.00**
Furs and Jewelry **Diamond earrings at used jewelry store price ($800), watch at flea market price ($300)** **Location: XXXX First St., Freshstart AA**	**C.C.P. § 703.140(b)(4)**	**1,100.00**	**1,100.00**

__2__ continuation sheets attached to Schedule of Property Claimed as Exempt

Sample Schedule C—page 2

B6C (Official Form 6C) (12/07) -- Cont.

In re **Annie Justine Kaye**, Debtor — Case No. ____________

SCHEDULE C - PROPERTY CLAIMED AS EXEMPT
(Continuation Sheet)

Description of Property	Specify Law Providing Each Exemption	Value of Claimed Exemption	Current Value of Property Without Deducting Exemption
Firearms and Sports, Photographic and Other Hobby Equipment			
Mountain bike at used bicycle store price ($250), digital camera priced at ebay ($200), 16 ga over and under shotgun ($300) Location: XXXX First St., Freshstart AA	**C.C.P. § 703.140(b)(5)**	**750.00**	**750.00**
Interests in IRA, ERISA, Keogh, or Other Pension or Profit Sharing Plans			
Roth IRA, $10,000, located at Freshstart Credit Union (See Item 2)	**11 U.S.C. § 522(b)(3)(C)**	**10,000.00**	**10,000.00**
Stock and Interests in Businesses			
Sole proprietor owner of Annie's Beauty Accessories, business consists of inventory for sale, fixtures and furniture, and possible good will. Most inventory is consignment items from local artisans. Items owned by Debtor are itemized in other parts of Schedule B. Location: XXX Seventh St. Freshstart, AA	**C.C.P. § 703.140(b)(5)**	**0.00**	**Undetermined**
250 shares in my brother's private C Corporation. Brother is majority stockholder and corporation has five total shareholders, including me. Corporation currently is engaged in producing iPhone apps. Corporation has not produced a profit for over three years. My brother is willing to purchase my shares at $4 a share, or a total of $1000. XXX 9th St. Freshstart, AA	**C.C.P. § 703.140(b)(5)**	**1,000.00**	**1,000.00**
Government & Corporate Bonds, Other Negotiable & Non-negotiable Inst.			
Negotiable promissory note from Jonathan Kaye, Annie's brother, dated XX/XX/XXXX Location: XXXX First St., Freshstart AA ($500)	**C.C.P. § 703.140(b)(5)**	**500.00**	**500.00**
Accounts Receivable			
25 customers owe money for goods purchased on credit Location: XXX Seventh St., Freshstart AA	**C.C.P. § 703.140(b)(5)**	**1,100.00**	**1,100.00**
Other Liquidated Debts Owing Debtor Including Tax Refund			
Refund for 20XX Taxes (expected but not yet received) Location: XXXX First St., Freshstart AA	**C.C.P. § 703.140(b)(5)**	**1,000.00**	**1,000.00**
Other Contingent and Unliquidated Claims of Every Nature			
Potential cause of action against parents of teenager who vandalized my store. Total damages were $3000. Case is awaiting resolution in criminal court and no lawsuit has yet been filed Location: XXXX First St., Freshstart AA	**C.C.P. § 703.140(b)(5)**	**3,000.00**	**3,000.00**

Sheet **1** of **2** continuation sheets attached to the Schedule of Property Claimed as Exempt

Sample Schedule C—page 3

B6C (Official Form 6C) (12/07) -- Cont.

In re **Annie Justine Kaye**, Debtor

Case No. ____________

SCHEDULE C - PROPERTY CLAIMED AS EXEMPT

(Continuation Sheet)

Description of Property	Specify Law Providing Each Exemption	Value of Claimed Exemption	Current Value of Property Without Deducting Exemption
<u>Customer lists or other compilations containing personally identifiable info</u>			
Trade secret consisting of mailing list compiled by various owners over 22 years of operating the store and acquired by debtor when store was purchased. Location: XXX Seventh St., Freshstart AA	**C.C.P. § 703.140(b)(5)**	**4,500.00**	**4,500.00**
<u>Machinery, Fixtures, Equipment and Supplies Used in Business</u>			
Fixtures in store ($1500), equipment (accounting, cleaning, etc) ($500) Location: XXX Seventh St. Freshstart, AA	**C.C.P. § 703.140(b)(5)**	**0.00**	**2,000.00**
<u>Inventory</u>			
Inventory in store is 75% artisan products (necklaces, earrings, scarves, pendents, theme T-shirts, etc.) Consignment contracts are available for inspection. These items are not part of bankruptcy estate (See SFA #14] Items in bankruptcy estate are bath and massage oils, perfumes, shawls, costume jewelry, shampoos. Retail value is $2200. Location: XXX Seventh St. Freshstart, AA	**C.C.P. § 703.140(b)(5)**	**2,200.00**	**2,200.00**
Total:		**35,825.00**	**37,825.00**

Sheet 2 of 2 continuation sheets attached to the Schedule of Property Claimed as Exempt

Schedule D—Creditors Holding Secured Claims

In this schedule, you list all creditors who hold claims secured by your property. This includes:

- holders of a mortgage or deed of trust on your real estate
- creditors who have won lawsuits against you and recorded judgment liens against your property
- contractors who have filed mechanics' or materialmen's liens on your real estate
- taxing authorities, such as the IRS, that have obtained tax liens against your property
- creditors with either a purchase-money or non-purchase-money security agreement (see "Nature of Lien" below)
- doctors or lawyers to whom you have granted a security interest in the outcome of a lawsuit, so that the collection of their fees would be postponed (the expected court judgment is the collateral), and
- all parties who are trying to collect a secured debt, such as collection agencies and attorneys.

For more information about secured debts, see Ch. 8.

Line-by-line instructions and a completed sample of Schedule D follow.

In re and **Case No.** Follow instructions for Schedule A.

Check this box if debtor has no creditors holding secured claims to report on this Schedule D. Check the box at the bottom of the Schedule's instructions if you have no secured creditors, then skip ahead to Schedule E. Everyone else, keep reading.

Creditor's Name and Mailing Address Including Zip Code, and Account Number. List all secured creditors, preferably in alphabetical order. For each, fill in the last four digits of the account number, if you know it; the creditor's name; and the complete mailing address, including zip code. As mentioned earlier, the mailing address should be the contact address shown on at least two written communications you received from the creditor during the previous 90 days. Call the creditor to get this information if you don't have it.

If you have more than one secured creditor for a given debt, list the original creditor first, followed by the other creditors. For example, if you've been sued or hounded by a collection agency, list the information for the collection agency after the original creditor.

If, after typing up your final papers, you discover that you've missed a few creditors, don't retype your papers to preserve perfect alphabetical order. Simply add the creditors at the end. If your creditors don't all fit on the first page of Schedule D, make as many copies of the preprinted continuation page as you need to list them all.

If the creditor is a child, list the child's initials and the name and address of the child's parent or guardian. For example, "A.B., a minor child, by John Doe, Guardian, 111 Alabama Avenue, San Francisco, CA 94732." Don't state the child's name.

Codebtor. Someone who owes a creditor money with you probably isn't the first person you think of as your creditor. But if someone else agreed to cosign your loan, lease, or purchase, then creditors can go after your codebtor, who will then look to you to cough up the money. So, if someone else (other than a spouse with whom you are filing jointly) can be legally forced to pay your debt to a listed secured creditor, list that person in the creditor column of this Schedule and put an "X" in this column. You'll also need to list the codebtor as a creditor in Schedules E, F, and H (explained below).

The most common codebtors are:

- cosigners
- guarantors (people who guarantee payment of a loan)
- ex-spouses with whom you jointly incurred debts before divorcing
- joint owners of real estate or other property
- coparties in a lawsuit
- nonfiling spouses in a community property state (as explained earlier, most debts

Sample Schedule D

B6D (Official Form 6D) (12/07)

In re **Annie Justine Kaye**, Debtor Case No. ______

SCHEDULE D - CREDITORS HOLDING SECURED CLAIMS

State the name, mailing address, including zip code, and last four digits of any account number of all entities holding claims secured by property of the debtor as of the date of filing of the petition. The complete account number of any account the debtor has with the creditor is useful to the trustee and the creditor and may be provided if the debtor chooses to do so. List creditors holding all types of secured interests such as judgment liens, garnishments, statutory liens, mortgages, deeds of trust, and other security interests.

List creditors in alphabetical order to the extent practicable. If a minor child is a creditor, the child's initials and the name and address of the child's parent or guardian, such as "A.B., a minor child, by John Doe, guardian." Do not disclose the child's name. See, 11 U.S.C. §112 and Fed. R. Bankr. P. 1007(m). If all secured creditors will not fit on this page, use the continuation sheet provided.

If any entity other than a spouse in a joint case may be jointly liable on a claim, place an "X" in the column labeled "Codebtor" ,include the entity on the appropriate schedule of creditors, and complete Schedule H - Codebtors. If a joint petition is filed, state whether the husband, wife, both of them, or the marital community may be liable on each claim by placing an "H", "W", "J", or "C" in the column labeled "Husband, Wife, Joint, or Community".

If the claim is contingent, place an "X" in the column labeled "Contingent". If the claim is unliquidated, place an "X" in the column labeled "Unliquidated". If the claim is disputed, place an "X" in the column labeled "Disputed". (You may need to place an "X" in more than one of these three columns.)

Total the columns labeled "Amount of Claim Without Deducting Value of Collateral" and "Unsecured Portion, if Any" in the boxes labeled "Total(s)" on the last sheet of the completed schedule. Report the total from the column labeled "Amount of Claim" also on the Summary of Schedules and, if the debtor is an individual with primarily consumer debts, report the total from the column labeled "Unsecured Portion" on the Statistical Summary of Certain Liabilities and Related Data.

☐ Check this box if debtor has no creditors holding secured claims to report on this Schedule D.

CREDITOR'S NAME AND MAILING ADDRESS INCLUDING ZIP CODE, AND ACCOUNT NUMBER (See instructions above.)	CODEBTOR	Husband, Wife, Joint, or Community H W J C	DATE CLAIM WAS INCURRED, NATURE OF LIEN, AND DESCRIPTION AND VALUE OF PROPERTY SUBJECT TO LIEN	CONTINGENT	UNLIQUIDATED	DISPUTED	AMOUNT OF CLAIM WITHOUT DEDUCTING VALUE OF COLLATERAL	UNSECURED PORTION, IF ANY
Account No. **#XXXX** **Freshstart Credit Union** **XXX Third St.** **Freshstart, AA 99999**		-	**February, 2009** **Purchase Money Security** **2009 Honda Accord** **Location: XXXX First St., Freshstart AA** Value $ **21,000.00**				**23,000.00**	**2,000.00**
Account No. **Freshstart Credit Union** **XXX Third St.** **Freshstart, AA 99999**		-	**01 23 Foot Travel Trailer** **Location: XXXX First St., Freshstart AA** Value $ **5,000.00**				**10,000.00**	**5,000.00**
Account No.			Value $					
Account No.			Value $					
						Subtotal (Total of this page)	**33,000.00**	**7,000.00**
						Total (Report on Summary of Schedules)	**33,000.00**	**7,000.00**

0 continuation sheets attached

incurred by a nonfiling spouse during marriage are considered community debts, making that spouse equally liable with the filing spouse for the debts), and

- nonfiling spouses in states other than community property states, for debts incurred by the filing spouse for basic living necessities such as food, shelter, clothing, and utilities.

Husband, Wife, Joint, or Community. Follow the instructions for Schedule A.

Date Claim Was Incurred, Nature of Lien, and Description and Value of Property Subject to Lien. This column calls for a lot of information for each secured debt. If you list two or more creditors on the same secured claim (such as the lender and a collection agency), simply put ditto marks (") in this column for the second creditor. Let's take these one at a time.

Date Claim Was Incurred. For most claims, the date the claim was incurred is the date you signed the security agreement. If you didn't sign a security agreement with the creditor, the date is most likely the date a contractor or judgment creditor recorded a lien against your property (perfected the lien) or the date a taxing authority notified you of a tax liability or assessment of taxes due.

Nature of Lien. What kind of property interest does your secured creditor have? Here are the possible answers (see Ch. 8 for more information):

- **First mortgage.** You took out a loan to buy your house. (This is s specific kind of purchase-money security interest.)
- **Purchase-money security interest.** You took out the loan to purchase the property that secures the loan—for example, a promissory note for an industrial coffee roasting machine.
- **Nonpossessory, non-purchase-money security interest.** You borrowed money for a purpose other than buying the collateral. This includes business loans or lines of credit, refinanced home loans, home equity loans, or loans from finance companies.
- **Possessory, non-purchase-money security interest.** This is what a pawnshop owner has when you pawn your property.
- **Judgment lien.** This means someone has sued you, won a court judgment, and recorded a lien against your property.
- **Tax lien.** This means a federal, state, or local government agency recorded a lien against your property for unpaid taxes.
- **Child support lien.** This means that your child's other parent or a government agency has recorded a lien against your property for unpaid child support.
- **Mechanics' or materialmen's lien.** This means someone performed work on your property but didn't get paid, and recorded a lien on that property. Such liens can be an unpleasant surprise if you paid for the work, but your contractor didn't pay a subcontractor who took out the lien.
- **Unknown.** If you don't know what kind of lien you are dealing with, put "Don't know nature of lien" after the date. The bankruptcy trustee can help you figure it out later.

Description of Property. Describe each item of real estate and personal property that is collateral for the secured debt listed in the first column. Use the same description you used on Schedule A for real property or Schedule B for personal property. If a creditor's lien covers several items of property, list all items affected by the lien.

Value of Property. The amount you put here must jibe with what you listed on Schedule A or B for the collateral. If you put only the total value of a group of items on Schedule B, you must now get more specific. For instance, if a department store has a secured claim against your washing machine, and you listed your "washer/dryer set" on Schedule B, now you must provide the washer's specific replacement value. You may have already done this on the Property Exemption Worksheet. If not, see the instructions for "Current Value" on Schedule B.

Contingent, Unliquidated, Disputed. Indicate whether the creditor's secured claim is contingent, unliquidated, or disputed. Here's what the terms mean:

- **Contingent.** The claim depends on some event that hasn't yet occurred and may never occur. For example, if you cosigned a secured loan, you won't be liable unless the principal debtor defaults. Your liability as cosigner is contingent upon the default.
- **Unliquidated.** This means that a debt may exist, but the exact amount hasn't been determined. For example, say you've sued someone for injuries you suffered in an auto accident, but the case isn't over. Your lawyer has taken the case under a contingency fee agreement—he'll get a third of the recovery if you win, and nothing if you lose—and has a security interest in the final recovery amount. The debt to the lawyer is unliquidated because you don't know how much, if anything, you'll win.
- **Disputed.** A claim is disputed if you and the creditor do not agree about the existence or amount of the debt. For instance, suppose the IRS says you owe $10,000 and has put a lien on your property, and you say you owe $500. List the full amount of the lien, not the amount you think you owe.

Check all categories that apply. If you're uncertain of which to choose, check the one that seems closest. If none apply, leave them blank. Although these categories aren't really important in a Chapter 7 personal bankruptcy (because your debts are discharged regardless of the category you choose), you must check the boxes.

TIP

You're not admitting you owe the debt. You may think you don't really owe a contingent, unliquidated, or disputed debt, or you may not want to "admit" that you owe the debt. By listing a debt here, however, you aren't admitting anything. Instead, you are making sure that, if you owe the debt after all, it will be discharged in your bankruptcy, if possible.

Amount of Claim Without Deducting Value of Collateral. For each secured creditor, list the amount it would take to pay off the secured claim, regardless of what the property is worth. The lender can give you this figure. In some cases, the amount of the secured claim may be more than the property's value.

> EXAMPLE: Your original business loan was for $13,000, plus $7,000 in interest (for $20,000 total). You've made enough payments so that $15,000 will cancel the debt, which is what you should list in this column.

If you have more than one creditor for a given secured claim (for example, the lender and a collection agency), list the debt only for the lender and put ditto marks (") for each subsequent creditor.

Subtotal/Total. Total the amounts in the "Amount of Claim" column for each page. Do not include the amounts represented by the ditto marks if you listed multiple creditors for a single debt. On the final page of Schedule D (which may be the first page or a preprinted continuation page), enter the total of all secured claims.

Unsecured Portion, If Any. If the replacement value of the collateral is equal to or greater than the amount of the claim, enter "0," meaning that the creditor's claim is fully secured. If the replacement value of the collateral is less than the amount of the claim(s) listed, enter the difference here.

> EXAMPLE: If the current value of your truck is $5,000 but you still owe $6,000 on your truck loan, enter $1,000 in this column ($6,000 – $5,000). This is the amount of the loan that is unsecured by the collateral (your truck).

If you list an amount in this column for a creditor, do not list this amount again on Schedule F (where you will list all other creditors with unsecured claims). Otherwise, this unsecured amount will be counted twice.

How to List Creditors Associated With Foreclosed Property

Until your property is sold in a foreclosure sale and a deed has been recorded showing a transfer of ownership to the lender or new purchaser, you still own the property and any mortgages on the property are secured debts. You must list all lenders, mortgage servicers, foreclosing trustees, and attorneys listed on foreclosure papers as secured creditors on Schedule D. You should list the amounts of the mortgages only once, however. After a deed has been recorded showing that you no longer own the property, your mortgage debt is no longer secured debt, and you should list all these parties on Schedule F as unsecured creditors.

Schedule E—Creditors Holding Unsecured Priority Claims

Schedule E identifies creditors who hold priority claims. These creditors may be entitled to be paid first (by the trustee) out of your nonexempt assets. Even if you don't have any nonexempt assets to be distributed, you still need to fill out this form if you have any unsecured priority debts. Most debtors won't care too much about who gets paid first, but you should still identify your priority debts carefully to avoid having to amend your papers later.

Set out below are a sample completed Schedule E and line-by-line instructions.

In re and **Case No.** Follow the instructions for Schedule A.

Check this box if debtor has no creditors holding unsecured priority claims to report on this Schedule E. Priority claims are claims that must be paid first in your bankruptcy case. The most common examples for personal bankruptcy debtors are unsecured, nondischargeable income tax debts and past due alimony or child support. There are several other categories of priority debts that may also apply to small business owners, including payroll taxes and money owed to employee benefit plans. Read further before deciding whether to check this box.

Types of priority claims. These are the categories of priority debts, as listed on Schedule E. Check the appropriate box on the form if you owe a debt in that category.

☐ **Domestic support obligations.** Check this box for claims for domestic support that you owe to, or that are recoverable by, a spouse, former spouse, or child; the parent, legal guardian, or responsible relative of such a child; or a governmental unit to whom such a domestic support claim has been assigned.

☐ **Extensions of credit in an involuntary case.** Don't check this box. You are filing a voluntary, not an involuntary, bankruptcy case.

☐ **Wages, salaries, and commissions.** If your business owes a current or former employee wages, vacation pay, or sick leave that was earned within 180 days before you filed for bankruptcy or ceased doing business, check this box. If you owe money to an independent contractor who did work for you, and the money was earned within 180 days before you filed your petition or ceased doing business, check this box only if, in the 12 months before you filed for bankruptcy, this independent contractor earned at least 75% of his or her total independent contractor receipts from you.

☐ **Contributions to employee benefit plans.** Check this box if your business owes contributions to an employee benefit fund for services rendered by an employee within 180 days before you filed your petition or ceased doing business.

☐ **Certain farmers and fishermen.** Check this box only if you operate or operated a grain storage facility and owe a grain producer, or you operate or operated a fish produce or storage facility and owe a U.S. fisherman for fish or fish products.

☐ **Deposits by individuals.** If you took money from someone who planned to purchase, lease, or rent goods or services from you that you never delivered, you may owe a priority debt. For the debt to qualify as a priority, the goods or services must have been planned for personal, family, or household use.

Sample Schedule D—page 1

B6E (Official Form 6E) (12/07)

In re **Annie Justine Kaye**, Debtor — Case No. ____________

SCHEDULE E - CREDITORS HOLDING UNSECURED PRIORITY CLAIMS

A complete list of claims entitled to priority, listed separately by type of priority, is to be set forth on the sheets provided. Only holders of unsecured claims entitled to priority should be listed in this schedule. In the boxes provided on the attached sheets, state the name, mailing address, including zip code, and last four digits of the account number, if any, of all entities holding priority claims against the debtor or the property of the debtor, as of the date of the filing of the petition. Use a separate continuation sheet for each type of priority and label each with the type of priority.

The complete account number of any account the debtor has with the creditor is useful to the trustee and the creditor and may be provided if the debtor chooses to do so. If a minor child is a creditor, state the child's initials and the name and address of the child's parent or guardian, such as "A.B., a minor child, by John Doe, guardian." Do not disclose the child's name. See, 11 U.S.C. §112 and Fed. R. Bankr. P. 1007(m).

If any entity other than a spouse in a joint case may be jointly liable on a claim, place an "X" in the column labeled "Codebtor," include the entity on the appropriate schedule of creditors, and complete Schedule H-Codebtors. If a joint petition is filed, state whether the husband, wife, both of them, or the marital community may be liable on each claim by placing an "H," "W," "J," or "C" in the column labeled "Husband, Wife, Joint, or Community." If the claim is contingent, place an "X" in the column labeled "Contingent." If the claim is unliquidated, place an "X" in the column labeled "Unliquidated." If the claim is disputed, place an "X" in the column labeled "Disputed." (You may need to place an "X" in more than one of these three columns.)

Report the total of claims listed on each sheet in the box labeled "Subtotals" on each sheet. Report the total of all claims listed on this Schedule E in the box labeled "Total" on the last sheet of the completed schedule. Report this total also on the Summary of Schedules.

Report the total of amounts entitled to priority listed on each sheet in the box labeled "Subtotals" on each sheet. Report the total of all amounts entitled to priority listed on this Schedule E in the box labeled "Totals" on the last sheet of the completed schedule. Individual debtors with primarily consumer debts report this total also on the Statistical Summary of Certain Liabilities and Related Data.

Report the total of amounts not entitled to priority listed on each sheet in the box labeled "Subtotals" on each sheet. Report the total of all amounts not entitled to priority listed on this Schedule E in the box labeled "Totals" on the last sheet of the completed schedule. Individual debtors with primarily consumer debts report this total also on the Statistical Summary of Certain Liabilities and Related Data.

☐ Check this box if debtor has no creditors holding unsecured priority claims to report on this Schedule E.

TYPES OF PRIORITY CLAIMS (Check the appropriate box(es) below if claims in that category are listed on the attached sheets)

☐ **Domestic support obligations**

Claims for domestic support that are owed to or recoverable by a spouse, former spouse, or child of the debtor, or the parent, legal guardian, or responsible relative of such a child, or a governmental unit to whom such a domestic support claim has been assigned to the extent provided in 11 U.S.C. § 507(a)(1).

☐ **Extensions of credit in an involuntary case**

Claims arising in the ordinary course of the debtor's business or financial affairs after the commencement of the case but before the earlier of the appointment of a trustee or the order for relief. 11 U.S.C. § 507(a)(3).

☐ **Wages, salaries, and commissions**

Wages, salaries, and commissions, including vacation, severance, and sick leave pay owing to employees and commissions owing to qualifying independent sales representatives up to $10,950* per person earned within 180 days immediately preceding the filing of the original petition, or the cessation of business, whichever occurred first, to the extent provided in 11 U.S.C. § 507(a)(4).

☐ **Contributions to employee benefit plans**

Money owed to employee benefit plans for services rendered within 180 days immediately preceding the filing of the original petition, or the cessation of business, whichever occurred first, to the extent provided in 11 U.S.C. § 507(a)(5).

☐ **Certain farmers and fishermen**

Claims of certain farmers and fishermen, up to $5,400* per farmer or fisherman, against the debtor, as provided in 11 U.S.C. § 507(a)(6).

☐ **Deposits by individuals**

Claims of individuals up to $2,425* for deposits for the purchase, lease, or rental of property or services for personal, family, or household use, that were not delivered or provided. 11 U.S.C. § 507(a)(7).

■ **Taxes and certain other debts owed to governmental units**

Taxes, customs duties, and penalties owing to federal, state, and local governmental units as set forth in 11 U.S.C. § 507(a)(8).

☐ **Commitments to maintain the capital of an insured depository institution**

Claims based on commitments to the FDIC, RTC, Director of the Office of Thrift Supervision, Comptroller of the Currency, or Board of Governors of the Federal Reserve System, or their predecessors or successors, to maintain the capital of an insured depository institution. 11 U.S.C. § 507 (a)(9).

☐ **Claims for death or personal injury while debtor was intoxicated**

Claims for death or personal injury resulting from the operation of a motor vehicle or vessel while the debtor was intoxicated from using alcohol, a drug, or another substance. 11 U.S.C. § 507(a)(10).

* Amounts are subject to adjustment on April 1, 2010, and every three years thereafter with respect to cases commenced on or after the date of adjustment.

1 continuation sheets attached

☐ **Taxes and certain other debts owed to governmental units.** Check this box if you owe unsecured back taxes or any other debts to the government, such as payroll or other trust fund taxes, or fines imposed for driving under the influence of drugs or alcohol. Not all tax debts are unsecured priority claims. For example, if the IRS has recorded a lien against your real property, and the equity in your property fully covers the amount of your tax debt, your debt is a secured debt. It should be listed on Schedule D, not on this schedule. Also, if your tax debts are dischargeable (see Ch. 11), they should be listed on Schedule F as nonpriority unsecured debts.

☐ **Commitments to maintain the capital of an insured depository institution.** Don't check this box. It is for bankruptcies brought by corporations or other business entities.

☐ **Claims for death or personal injury while debtor was intoxicated.** Check this box if there are claims against you for another's death or personal injury resulting from your operation of a motor vehicle or vessel while intoxicated from using alcohol, a drug, or another substance. This priority applies only to personal injury or death, not property damage.

If you didn't check any of the priority debt boxes, go back and check the first box, showing you have no unsecured priority claims to report. Then go on to Schedule F.

If you checked any of the priority debt boxes, make as many photocopies of the continuation page as the number of priority debt boxes you checked. You will need to complete a separate sheet for each type of priority debt, as follows:

In re and **Case No.** Follow the instructions for Schedule A.

Type of Priority. Insert the category for one of the boxes you checked (for example, "Domestic support obligations").

Creditor's Name, Mailing Address Including Zip Code, and Account Number. List the name and complete mailing address (including zip code) of each priority creditor, as well as the account number, if you know it. The address should be the one provided by the creditor in two written communications you have received from the creditor within the past 90 days, if possible. You may have more than one priority creditor for a given debt. For example, if you've been sued or hounded by a collection agency, list the collection agency in addition to the original creditor.

If the creditor is a child, list the child's initials and the name and address of the child's parent or guardian. For example, "A.B., a minor child, by John Doe, Guardian, 111 Alabama Avenue, San Francisco, CA 94732." Don't state the child's name.

Codebtor. If someone else can be legally forced to pay your debt to a priority creditor, enter an "X" in this column and list the codebtor in the creditor column of this schedule. You'll also need to list the codebtor as a creditor in Schedule F and Schedule H. Common codebtors are listed in the instructions for Schedule D.

Husband, Wife, Joint, or Community. Follow the instructions for Schedule A.

Date Claim Was Incurred and Consideration for Claim. State the date you incurred the debt—this may be a specific date or a period of time. Also briefly state what the debt is for. For example, "goods purchased," "hours worked for me," or "deposit for my services."

Contingent, Unliquidated, Disputed. Follow the instructions for Schedule D.

Amount of Claim. For each priority debt other than taxes, list the amount it would take to pay off the debt in full, even if it's more than the priority limit. For taxes, list only the amount that is unsecured (and therefore a priority). You should list the secured amount on Schedule D. If the amount isn't determined, write "not yet determined" in this column.

Amount Entitled to Priority. If the priority claim is larger than the maximum indicated on the first page of Schedule E (for example, $10,950 of wages owed to each employee; this amount will increase in April 2010), put the maximum here. If the claim is less than the maximum, put the amount you entered in the Total Amount of Claim column here.

Sample Schedule D—page 2

B6E (Official Form 6E) (12/07) - Cont.

In re **Annie Justine Kaye**, Case No. ______
Debtor

SCHEDULE E - CREDITORS HOLDING UNSECURED PRIORITY CLAIMS

(Continuation Sheet)

Taxes and Certain Other Debts Owed to Governmental Units

TYPE OF PRIORITY

CREDITOR'S NAME, AND MAILING ADDRESS INCLUDING ZIP CODE, AND ACCOUNT NUMBER (See instructions.)	CODEBTOR	Husband, Wife, Joint, or Community (H W J C)	DATE CLAIM WAS INCURRED AND CONSIDERATION FOR CLAIM	CONTINGENT	UNLIQUIDATED	DISPUTED	AMOUNT OF CLAIM	AMOUNT NOT ENTITLED TO PRIORITY, IF ANY / AMOUNT ENTITLED TO PRIORITY
Account No. **XXXX** **Business Tax Board** **12345 XX St.** **Freshstart, AA 99999**		-	**State income taxes withheld from employee (payroll taxes)**				**4,000.00**	**0.00** **4,000.00**
Account No.								
Account No.								
Account No.								
Account No.								

Sheet **1** of **1** continuation sheets attached to Schedule of Creditors Holding Unsecured Priority Claims

Subtotal (Total of this page)	**4,000.00**	**0.00** **4,000.00**
Total (Report on Summary of Schedules)	**4,000.00**	**0.00** **4,000.00**

Amount Not Entitled to Priority, If Any. List any portion of the debt that is not entitled to priority here. For example, if you owe an employee $15,000 in wages, only the first $10,950 is entitled to priority (this amount will increase in April 2010). That amount should be listed in the "Amount Entitled to Priority" column; here, you would list the remaining $4,050.

Subtotal/Total. At the bottom of each continuation page, list the subtotals of the "Amount of Claim," "Amount Entitled to Priority," and "Amount Not Entitled to Priority, If Any" columns. Enter the total amounts for each of these categories on the final page of Schedule E.

Schedule F—Creditors Holding Unsecured Nonpriority Claims

In this schedule, list all creditors you haven't listed in Schedules D or E. You should include creditors on debts that are or may be nondischargeable, such as student loans. Even if you believe that you don't owe the debt or you owe only a small amount and intend to pay it off, you must include it here. It's essential that you list every creditor to whom you owe, or possibly owe, money. The only way you can legitimately leave off a creditor is if your balance owed is $0.

You may be tempted to leave some creditors (like your doctor, a favorite electrician, an indispensable vendor, or a relative who loaned you money) off of your bankruptcy schedules, in order to stay in their good graces. Don't do it. You must list all of your creditors. However, there is nothing to prevent you from paying a dischargeable debt after your bankruptcy is complete. The only effect bankruptcy has on the debt is that the creditor can't pursue it through collections or place it on your credit report. If you plan to pay certain creditors after your bankruptcy, let them know. This will lessen the sting of your bankruptcy filing. Although your promise is unenforceable, creditors will gladly accept your money.

EXAMPLE: Peter Kinson, owner of a sole proprietorship called PK Plumbing, owes his local hardware store $2,000 for various materials he ordered prior to filing bankruptcy. Peter plans to continue his business and would prefer not to list the debt, so he can keep doing business at the store. However, he understands that must list all debts on Schedule F, which he does. The hardware store debt is discharged along with Peter's other debts. After his bankruptcy, Peter approaches the store owner and voluntarily settles up on his bill. The store restores his credit rating. Peter can once again obtain materials on credit so he can continue his business. But repaying the debt was completely voluntary on Peter's part. The store can't sue him to collect the debt.

Inadvertent errors or omissions on this schedule can come back to haunt you. If you don't list a debt you owe to a creditor, it might not be discharged in bankruptcy if your creditor has been harmed by not learning of your bankruptcy. For example, an omitted creditor would be harmed if you had assets that were liquidated for the benefit of your creditors, and the creditor missed out on its share of the distribution. (Fortunately, it is sometimes possible in these circumstances to reopen the bankruptcy and include the creditor retroactively.) Also, leaving a creditor off the schedule might raise suspicions that you deliberately concealed information, perhaps to give that creditor preferential treatment in violation of bankruptcy rules.

TIP

Use your credit reports. You aren't required to use a credit report to find creditors when filing for bankruptcy, but it will help you make sure you don't miss anyone. You will likely find entries on your credit report for debts you didn't know you owed. But it never hurts to list a creditor in your bankruptcy, even if you don't think you owe the debt (you can always check the "disputed" box). If you can get credit reports for free, it's a good idea to get a copy of your report from all three major credit reporting agencies; the information in them does vary. Don't rely exclusively on credit reports, however; you must disclose every debt on your bankruptcy forms, whether or not it appears in a credit report.

Below are a sample completed Schedule F and line-by-line instructions. Use as many preprinted continuation pages as you need.

In re and **Case No.** Follow the instructions for Schedule A.

Check this box if debtor has no creditors holding unsecured claims to report on this Schedule F. Check this box if you have no unsecured nonpriority debts. This would be very rare.

Creditor's Name, Mailing Address Including Zip Code, and Account Number. List, preferably in alphabetical order, the name and complete mailing address of each unsecured creditor, as well as the account number (if you know it). If you have more than one unsecured creditor for a given debt, list the original creditor first, followed by the other creditors. For example, for a particular debt, you might have the name, address, and account number for the original creditor, a collection agency run by the original creditor, an independent collection agency, an attorney debt collector, and an attorney who has sued you.

It's best to list every creditor. But you could omit the intermediate collectors and just list the original creditor and the latest collector or attorney. Or, if you no longer have contact information for the original creditor, listing the latest collector will do.

When you are typing your final papers, if you get to the end and discover that you left a creditor off, don't start all over again in search of perfect alphabetical order. Just add the creditor to the end of the list.

Creditors That Are Often Overlooked

One debt may involve several different creditors. Remember to include:

- your ex-spouse, if you are still obligated under a divorce decree or settlement agreement to pay joint debts, turn any property over to your ex, or make payments as part of your property division
- anyone who has cosigned or guaranteed a promissory note or loan application you signed
- any holder of a loan or promissory note that you cosigned for someone else
- the original creditor, anybody to whom the debt has been assigned or sold, and any other person (such as a bill collector or attorney) trying to collect the debt, and
- anyone who may sue you because of a car accident, business dispute, or the like.

Codebtor. If someone else can be legally forced to pay your debt to a listed unsecured creditor, enter an "X" in this column and list the codebtor as a creditor in this schedule. Also, list the codebtor in Schedule H. The instructions for Schedule D list common codebtors.

Husband, Wife, Joint, or Community. Follow the instructions for Schedule A.

Date Claim Was Incurred and Consideration for Claim. If Claim Is Subject to Setoff, So State. State when the debt was incurred. It may be one date or a period of time. With credit card debts, put the approximate time over which you ran up the charges, unless the unpaid charges were all made on one or two specific dates. Then state what the debt was for. You can be general ("office supplies" or "furnishings") or specific ("refrigerator" or "Dell laptop computer").

If you are entitled to a setoff against the debt—that is, the creditor owes you some money, too—list the amount and why you think you are entitled to the setoff. If there is more than one creditor for a

Sample Schedule F—page 1

B6F (Official Form 6F) (12/07)

In re **Annie Justine Kaye**, Debtor   Case No. ________

SCHEDULE F - CREDITORS HOLDING UNSECURED NONPRIORITY CLAIMS

State the name, mailing address, including zip code, and last four digits of any account number, of all entities holding unsecured claims without priority against the debtor or the property of the debtor, as of the date of filing of the petition. The complete account number of any account the debtor has with the creditor is useful to the trustee and the creditor and may be provided if the debtor chooses to do so. If a minor child is a creditor, state the child's initials and the name and address of the child's parent or guardian, such as "A.B., a minor child, by John Doe, guardian." Do not disclose the child's name. See, 11 U.S.C. §112 and Fed. R. Bankr. P. 1007(m). Do not include claims listed in Schedules D and E. If all creditors will not fit on this page, use the continuation sheet provided.

If any entity other than a spouse in a joint case may be jointly liable on a claim, place an "X" in the column labeled "Codebtor," include the entity on the appropriate schedule of creditors, and complete Schedule H - Codebtors. If a joint petition is filed, state whether the husband, wife, both of them, or the marital community may be liable on each claim by placing an "H," "W," "J," or "C" in the column labeled "Husband, Wife, Joint, or Community."

If the claim is contingent, place an "X" in the column labeled "Contingent." If the claim is unliquidated, place an "X" in the column labeled "Unliquidated." If the claim is disputed, place an "X" in the column labeled "Disputed." (You may need to place an "X" in more than one of these three columns.)

Report the total of all claims listed on this schedule in the box labeled "Total" on the last sheet of the completed schedule. Report this total also on the Summary of Schedules and, if the debtor is an individual with primarily consumer debts, report this total also on the Statistical Summary of Certain Liabilities and Related Data.

☐ Check this box if debtor has no creditors holding unsecured claims to report on this Schedule F.

CREDITOR'S NAME, MAILING ADDRESS INCLUDING ZIP CODE, AND ACCOUNT NUMBER (See instructions above.)	CODEBTOR	Husband, Wife, Joint, or Community H W J C	DATE CLAIM WAS INCURRED AND CONSIDERATION FOR CLAIM. IF CLAIM IS SUBJECT TO SETOFF, SO STATE.	CONTINGENT	UNLIQUIDATED	DISPUTED	AMOUNT OF CLAIM
Account No. **86-3** **ABC Bank** **XXXXX Second St.** **Freshstart, AA 99999-9999**		-	**8/XX** **Student loan**				**3,000.00**
Account No. **5656** **ABCDE Beauty Supplies** **XXX P St.** **Freshstart, AA 99999**		-	**5/XX** **Inventory (misc new products for store inventory)**				**9,000.00**
Account No. **Alan Accountant** **5 Green St.** **Freshstart, AA 99999**		-	**4/XX** **Tax preparation and bookkeeping services for the business**				**2,500.00**
Account No. **#5556** **American Allowance** **Po Box 1** **Freshstart, AA 99999**		-	**1/xx-4/XX** **credit card charges for business operations**				**5,600.00**
2 continuation sheets attached			Subtotal (Total of this page)				**20,100.00**

Sample Schedule F—page 2

B6F (Official Form 6F) (12/07) - Cont.

In re **Annie Justine Kaye**, Debtor   Case No. ______

SCHEDULE F - CREDITORS HOLDING UNSECURED NONPRIORITY CLAIMS
(Continuation Sheet)

CREDITOR'S NAME, MAILING ADDRESS INCLUDING ZIP CODE, AND ACCOUNT NUMBER (See instructions above.)	CODEBTOR	Husband, Wife, Joint, or Community H W J C	DATE CLAIM WAS INCURRED AND CONSIDERATION FOR CLAIM. IF CLAIM IS SUBJECT TO SETOFF, SO STATE.	CONTINGENT	UNLIQUIDATED	DISPUTED	AMOUNT OF CLAIM
Account No. **XXX** **Angel of Mercy Hospital** **XXXX A St.** **Freshstart, AA 99999**		-	**3/XX** **Uninsured emergency room visit for gall bladder attack**				**2,000.00**
Account No. **Cecilia Kaye Brunner** **XXX C St.** **Freshstart, AA 99999**		-	**4/XX** **Personal loan from sister to get business started**				**5,000.00**
Account No. **Freddie Fencer Esq** **XXX H St.** **Freshstart, AA 99999**		-	**6/XX** **Legal fees incurred for representation in two cases involving implied warranties for products sold in store. Both cases were dismissed over two years ago.**				**22,250.00**
Account No. **Margaret Jones III** **XXX B St.** **Freshstart, AA 99999**		-	**9/XX** **Claim for alleged injuries to skin caused by bath oil product sold at the store. Claimant has recently filed a personal injury action in court against debtor and her business.**			**X**	**25,000.00**
Account No. **Rural Industries Leasing Service** **XXX M St.** **Freshstart, AA 99999**		-	**7/XX** **Store lease delinquent payments**				**4,000.00**

Sheet no. **1** of **2** sheets attached to Schedule of Creditors Holding Unsecured Nonpriority Claims

Subtotal (Total of this page) **58,250.00**

single debt, put ditto marks (") in this column for the subsequent creditors.

Contingent, Unliquidated, Disputed. Follow the instructions for Schedule D.

Amount of Claim. List the amount of the debt claimed by the creditor, even if you dispute the amount. If there's more than one creditor for a single debt, put the debt amount across from the original creditor and put ditto marks (") across from each subsequent creditor you have listed. Be as precise as possible when stating the amount. If you must approximate, write "approx." after the amount.

Subtotal/Total. Total the amounts in the last column for this page. Do not include the amounts represented by the ditto marks if you listed multiple creditors for a single debt. On the final page (which may be the first page or a preprinted continuation page), enter the total of all unsecured, nonpriority claims. On the first page in the bottom left-hand corner, note the number of continuation pages you are attaching.

Listing Debts on Foreclosed and Repossessed Property

Debts that were secured prior to a foreclosure or repossession become unsecured debts after title reverts to the secured lender when the foreclosure or repossession is complete, and you should list them on Schedule F as unsecured debts. If you know what the alleged deficiency was (the difference between what you owed and what the lender ultimately got in the foreclosure or repossession sale), list that amount. If you don't yet know—because the foreclosure or repossession was so recent—list the entire debt.

Schedule G—Executory Contracts and Unexpired Leases

In this form, you list every executory contract or unexpired lease to which you're a party. "Executory" means the contract is still in force—that is, both parties are still obligated to perform important acts under it. Similarly, "unexpired" means that the contract or lease period hasn't run out—that is, it is still in effect. Common examples of executory contracts and unexpired leases are:

- car leases
- residential leases or rental agreements
- business leases or rental agreements
- service contracts
- business contracts
- vendor contracts
- time-share contracts or leases
- contracts of sale for real estate
- personal property leases, such as equipment used in a beauty salon
- copyright and patent license agreements
- leases of real estate (surface and underground) for the purpose of harvesting timber, minerals, or oil
- future homeowners' association fee requirements
- agreements for boat docking privileges, and
- insurance contracts.

CAUTION

If you're behind in your payments. If you are not current on payments that were due under a lease or executory contract, the delinquency should also be listed as a debt on Schedule D, E, or F. The sole purpose of this schedule is to identify existing contractual obligations that you still owe or that someone owes you. Later, when completing the Statement of Intention, you will be given the opportunity to state whether you want the lease or contract to continue in effect.

Below are a sample completed Schedule G and line-by-line instructions.

In re and **Case No.** Follow the instructions for Schedule A.

Check this box if debtor has no executory contracts or unexpired leases. Check this box if it applies; otherwise, complete the form.

Sample Schedule G

B6G (Official Form 6G) (12/07)

In re **Annie Justine Kaye**, Debtor   Case No. ______

SCHEDULE G - EXECUTORY CONTRACTS AND UNEXPIRED LEASES

Describe all executory contracts of any nature and all unexpired leases of real or personal property. Include any timeshare interests. State nature of debtor's interest in contract, i.e., "Purchaser", "Agent", etc. State whether debtor is the lessor or lessee of a lease. Provide the names and complete mailing addresses of all other parties to each lease or contract described. If a minor child is a party to one of the leases or contracts, state the child's initials and the name and address of the child's parent or guardian, such as "A.B., a minor child, by John Doe, guardian." Do not disclose the child's name. See, 11 U.S.C. §112 and Fed. R. Bankr. P. 1007(m).

☐ Check this box if debtor has no executory contracts or unexpired leases.

Name and Mailing Address, Including Zip Code, of Other Parties to Lease or Contract	Description of Contract or Lease and Nature of Debtor's Interest. State whether lease is for nonresidential real property. State contract number of any government contract.
Beauty Products Leasing Co. XXX R St. Freshstart, AA 99999	**Laser skin treatment machine. Lease for five year period that expries on 2013**
Rural Industries Leasing Service XXX M St. Freshstart, AA 99999	**Five year lease on business property. Four months behind and three years to go**

0 continuation sheets attached to Schedule of Executory Contracts and Unexpired Leases

Name and Mailing Address, Including Zip Code, of Other Parties to Lease or Contract. Provide the name and full address (including zip code) of each party—other than yourself—to each lease or contract. These parties are either people who signed agreements or the companies for whom these people work. If you're unsure about whom to list, include the person who signed an agreement, any company whose name appears on the agreement, and anybody who might have an interest in having the contract or lease enforced. If you still aren't sure, put "don't know."

Description of Contract or Lease and Nature of Debtor's Interest. For each lease or contract, give:

- a basic description (for instance, residential lease, commercial lease, car lease, business obligation or contract, or copyright license)
- the date the contract or lease was signed
- the date the contract is to expire (if any)
- a summary of each party's rights and obligations under the lease or contract, and
- the contract number, if the contract is with any government body.

Schedule H—Codebtors

In Schedules D, E, and F, you identified those debts for which you have codebtors—usually, a

What Happens to Executory Contracts and Unexpired Leases in Bankruptcy

The trustee has 60 days after you file for bankruptcy to decide whether an executory contract or unexpired lease should be assumed as property of the estate (continued in force) or terminated (rejected). If the lease or contract could be sold to raise funds for your unsecured creditors, then the trustee will assume it; otherwise, it will be rejected. As a general matter, most leases and contracts are liabilities rather than assets, and are rejected by the trustee. However, even if the trustee rejects the lease or contract, you have the right to assume it if it is for personal property (for instance, a car lease or vendor contract), provided you give the creditor written notice and the creditor agrees. (11 U.S.C. § 365(p).) You provide this written notice in the Statement of Intention, discussed below.

Generally, people filing Chapter 7 bankruptcies are not parties to leases or contracts that would likely add value to their bankruptcy estates. This isn't an absolute rule, however. If the trustee could sell a lease to someone else for a profit (because you're paying less than market rent for prime commercial space, for example), the trustee might assume the lease and assign it for a lump sum that could be distributed to your creditors.

It's also possible that you'll want to get out of a contract or lease, such as a commercial lease when your business is closing down, or a residential lease, auto lease, or time-share you can't afford. Be sure to state at the bankruptcy meeting or even on your papers that you would like the trustee to terminate the agreement. But remember this is up to the trustee to decide.

If the lease is assigned or terminated or the contract is terminated, you and the other parties to the agreement are cut loose from any obligations, and any money you owe the creditor will be discharged in your bankruptcy, even if the debt arose after your filing date. For example, say you are leasing a car when you file for bankruptcy. You want out of the lease. The car dealer cannot repossess the car until the trustee terminates the lease, which normally must occur within 60 days of when you file. During that 60-day period, you can use the car without paying for it. The payments you don't make during this period will be discharged as if they were incurred prior to your bankruptcy.

Bankruptcy law has special rules for executory contracts related to intellectual property (copyright, patent, trademark, or trade secret), real estate, and time-share leases. If you are involved in one of these situations, talk to a bankruptcy lawyer.

Sample Schedule H

B6H (Official Form 6H) (12/07)

In re **Annie Justine Kaye**, Debtor   Case No.________________

SCHEDULE H - CODEBTORS

Provide the information requested concerning any person or entity, other than a spouse in a joint case, that is also liable on any debts listed by debtor in the schedules of creditors. Include all guarantors and co-signers. If the debtor resides or resided in a community property state, commonwealth, or territory (including Alaska, Arizona, California, Idaho, Louisiana, Nevada, New Mexico, Puerto Rico, Texas, Washington, or Wisconsin) within the eight year period immediately preceding the commencement of the case, identify the name of the debtor's spouse and of any former spouse who resides or resided with the debtor in the community property state, commonwealth, or territory. Include all names used by the nondebtor spouse during the eight years immediately preceding the commencement of this case. If a minor child is a codebtor or a creditor, state the child's initials and the name and address of the child's parent or guardian, such as "A.B., a minor child, by John Doe, guardian." Do not disclose the child's name. See, 11 U.S.C. §112 and Fed. R. Bankr. P. 1007(m).

☐ Check this box if debtor has no codebtors.

NAME AND ADDRESS OF CODEBTOR	NAME AND ADDRESS OF CREDITOR
Frida Sanford **XXX 18th St.** **Freshstart, AA 99999** **Co-signed on commercial loan from XYZ Bank**	**XYZ Bank** **XXX D St.** **Freshstart, AA 99999**

0 continuation sheets attached to Schedule of Codebtors

cosigner, guarantor, ex-spouse, nonfiling spouse in a community property state, nonfiling spouse for a debt for necessities, nonmarital partner, or joint contractor. You must also list those codebtors here. In addition, you must list the name and address of any spouse or former spouse who lived with you in a community property state (or Puerto Rico) during the eight-year period immediately preceding your bankruptcy filing. (To remind you, the community property states are Alaska, Arizona, California, Idaho, Louisiana, Nevada, New Mexico, Texas, Washington, and Wisconsin.) If you are married but filing separately, include all names used by your spouse during the eight-year period.

In Chapter 7 bankruptcy, your codebtors will be wholly responsible for your debts, unless they, too, declare bankruptcy.

Below are a sample completed Schedule H and line-by-line instructions.

In re and **Case No.** Follow instructions for Schedule A.

Check this box if debtor has no codebtors. Check this box if it applies; otherwise, complete the form.

Name and Address of Codebtor. List the name and complete address (including zip code) of each codebtor. If the codebtor is a nonfiling, current spouse, put all names by which that person was known during the previous eight years.

If the creditor is a child, list the child's initials and the name and address of the child's parent or guardian. For example, "A.B., a minor child, by John Doe, Guardian, 111 Alabama Avenue, San Francisco, CA 94732." Don't state the child's name.

Name and Address of Creditor. List the name and address of each creditor (as listed on Schedule D, E, or F) to which each codebtor is indebted.

> EXAMPLE: Tom Martin cosigned three different loans—with three different banks—for debtor Jessica Green, a sole proprietor who is filing for bankruptcy. In the first column, Jessica lists Tom Martin as a codebtor. In the second, Jessica lists each of the three banks.

FOR MARRIED COUPLES

If you are married and filing alone. If you live in a community property state, your spouse may be a codebtor for most of the debts you listed in Schedules D, E, and F. In these states, most debts incurred by one spouse legally are owed by both spouses (even though creditors seldom go after a nonfiling spouse for debts that are only in the filing spouse's name). In this event, don't relist all the creditors in the second column. Simply write "all creditors listed in Schedules D, E, and F, except:" and then list any creditors who you alone owe.

If you lived with a former spouse in a community property state or Puerto Rico in the eight-year period prior to filing, list his or her name and address.

Schedule I—Current Income of Individual Debtor(s)

In this schedule, you calculate your actual current income (not your average monthly income in the six months before you file, which you'll have to calculate in Form 22A, below).

Directly below are a sample completed Schedule I and line-by-line instructions. If you're married and filing jointly, you must fill in information for both spouses.

In re and **Case No.** Follow the instructions for Schedule A.

Debtor's Marital Status. Enter your marital status. Your choices are single, married, separated (you aren't living with your spouse and plan never to again), widowed, or divorced. You are divorced only if you have received a final judgment of divorce from a court.

Dependents of Debtor and Spouse. List all people, according to their relationship with you (son, daughter, and so on), for whom you and your spouse provide at least 50% of support. There is no need to list their names. This list may include your children, your spouse's children, your parents, other relatives, and domestic partners. It does not include your spouse.

Sample Schedule I

B6I (Official Form 6I) (12/07)

In re **Annie Justine Kaye** Case No. ____________
Debtor(s)

SCHEDULE I - CURRENT INCOME OF INDIVIDUAL DEBTOR(S)

The column labeled "Spouse" must be completed in all cases filed by joint debtors and by every married debtor, whether or not a joint petition is filed, unless the spouses are separated and a joint petition is not filed. Do not state the name of any minor child. The average monthly income calculated on this form may differ from the current monthly income calculated on Form 22A, 22B, or 22C.

Debtor's Marital Status:	DEPENDENTS OF DEBTOR AND SPOUSE	
	RELATIONSHIP(S):	AGE(S):
Divorced	**Daughter**	**two**

Employment:	DEBTOR	SPOUSE
Occupation		
Name of Employer		
How long employed		
Address of Employer		

INCOME: (Estimate of average or projected monthly income at time case filed)	DEBTOR	SPOUSE
1. Monthly gross wages, salary, and commissions (Prorate if not paid monthly)	$ **0.00**	$ **N/A**
2. Estimate monthly overtime	$ **0.00**	$ **N/A**
3. SUBTOTAL	$ **0.00**	$ **N/A**
4. LESS PAYROLL DEDUCTIONS		
a. Payroll taxes and social security	$ **0.00**	$ **N/A**
b. Insurance	$ **0.00**	$ **N/A**
c. Union dues	$ **0.00**	$ **N/A**
d. Other (Specify): ____________	$ **0.00**	$ **N/A**
____________	$ **0.00**	$ **N/A**
5. SUBTOTAL OF PAYROLL DEDUCTIONS	$ **0.00**	$ **N/A**
6. TOTAL NET MONTHLY TAKE HOME PAY	$ **0.00**	$ **N/A**
7. Regular income from operation of business or profession or farm (Attach detailed statement)	$ **3,000.00**	$ **N/A**
8. Income from real property	$ **0.00**	$ **N/A**
9. Interest and dividends	$ **0.00**	$ **N/A**
10. Alimony, maintenance or support payments payable to the debtor for the debtor's use or that of dependents listed above	$ **500.00**	$ **N/A**
11. Social security or government assistance (Specify): ____________	$ **0.00**	$ **N/A**
____________	$ **0.00**	$ **N/A**
12. Pension or retirement income	$ **0.00**	$ **N/A**
13. Other monthly income (Specify): ____________	$ **0.00**	$ **N/A**
____________	$ **0.00**	$ **N/A**
14. SUBTOTAL OF LINES 7 THROUGH 13	$ **3,500.00**	$ **N/A**
15. AVERAGE MONTHLY INCOME (Add amounts shown on lines 6 and 14)	$ **3,500.00**	$ **N/A**
16. COMBINED AVERAGE MONTHLY INCOME: (Combine column totals from line 15)	$ **3,500.00**	

(Report also on Summary of Schedules and, if applicable, on Statistical Summary of Certain Liabilities and Related Data)

17. Describe any increase or decrease in income reasonably anticipated to occur within the year following the filing of this document:
I will be closing my business and will have no source of income until I can find employment. I plan to open a new business when conditions improve.

Employment. Provide the requested employment information. If you have more than one employer, enter "See continuation sheet" just below the box containing the employment information, then complete a continuation sheet. If you are self-employed or operate a sole proprietor business, or you are retired, unemployed, or disabled, enter the appropriate words in the blank for "occupation."

Items 1–3. Enter your estimated monthly gross income from regular employment, before any payroll deductions are taken. In the second blank, put your estimated monthly overtime pay. Add them together and enter the subtotal in the third blank. If your only income is from your business, leave these lines blank.

Three Different Income Figures

The bankruptcy law that went into effect in October 2005 produces a number of strange results. One of these is that you will report three different income figures: the "current monthly income" figure in Form 22A, the actual income you report here, and the annual income figures you report in your Statement of Financial Affairs (see below).

Schedule I explicitly states that the income you report there will likely be different from what you report as your current monthly income on Form 22A. That's because the income you report on Form 22A is your average gross income for the six months before you file, but the income you report here is the actual net income you expect to be receiving every month going forward. If, for example, your business income started to plummet a couple of months ago, your income will be lower on this form than what you reported on Form 22A.

CAUTION

Make sure the numbers add up. As you juggle these income and deduction numbers, remember that you need to use a monthly amount. This means you may need to convert the numbers on your pay stub or other documents if you're paid weekly, every two weeks, or twice a month. The most commonly required conversion is from payment every two weeks to a monthly payment. You do this by dividing your biweekly payment in half and then multiplying by 4.3. If your business income is sporadic, you may have to total your annual income, then divide by 12.

Item 4: Payroll Deductions. In the four blanks, enter the deductions taken from your gross salary. The deductions listed are the most common ones, but you may have others to report. Other possible deductions are state disability taxes, wages withheld or garnished for child support, credit union payments, or perhaps payments on a student loan or a car. Again, if your only income is from your business, you may not have anything to enter here or for Items 5 and 6.

Item 5: Subtotal of Payroll Deductions. Add your payroll deductions and enter the subtotal.

Item 6: Total Net Monthly Take Home Pay. Subtract your payroll deductions subtotal from your income subtotal.

Item 7: Regular income from operation of business or profession or farm. If you are self-employed or operate a sole proprietorship, enter your monthly gross income from your business here. If it's been fairly steady for at least one calendar year, divide your gross income amount from your most recent tax return (IRS Schedule C, *Profit or Loss From Business*) by 12 to come up with a monthly amount. If your income hasn't been steady for at least a year, enter the average monthly gross income from your business or profession over the past three months. In either case, you must attach a detailed statement of your income (you can use your IRS Schedule C). You'll be able to account for your business expenses on Schedule J, covered below.

Item 8: Income from real property. Enter your monthly income from real estate rentals, leases, or licenses (such as mineral exploration, oil, and the like).

Item 9: Interest and dividends. Enter the average estimated monthly interest you receive from bank or security deposits and other investments, such as stocks.

Item 10: Alimony, maintenance, or support payments payable to the debtor for the debtor's use or that of dependents listed above. Enter the average monthly amount you receive for your support (alimony, spousal support, or maintenance) or for your children (child support).

Item 11: Social security or government assistance. Enter the total monthly amount you receive in Social Security, SSI, public assistance, disability payments, veterans' benefits, unemployment compensation, workers' compensation, or any other government benefit. If you receive food stamps, include their monthly value. Specify the source of the benefits.

Item 12: Pension or retirement income. Enter the total monthly amount of all pension, annuity, IRA, Keogh, or other retirement benefits you currently receive.

Item 13: Other monthly income. Specify any other income (such as royalty payments or payments from a trust) you receive on a regular basis, and enter the monthly amount here. You may have to divide by three, six, or 12 if you receive the payments quarterly, semiannually, or annually.

Item 14: Subtotal of Lines 7 through 13. Add up your additional income (Items 7 through 13).

Item 15: Average Monthly Income. Add Items 6 and 14 and list the total here.

Item 16: Combined Average Monthly Income. If you are filing jointly, combine your total from Item 15 with your spouse's total from Item 15.

Item 17: Describe any increase or decrease in income reasonably anticipated to occur within the year following the filing of this document. If you indicate that you will soon have a significantly higher income, you might face a motion from the U.S. Trustee seeking to force you into Chapter 13 if the increase would allow you to repay a substantial portion of your unsecured debt (25% or more) over three to five years. In most cases, the increase is due to a scheduled promotion or raise in employment income, not an anticipated increase in business income (after all, nothing is certain in business). Whatever the cause, you must disclose anticipated future income changes here. Of course, if your income is due to decrease any time soon, you should use this part of the form to indicate that as well.

Schedule J—Current Expenditures of Individual Debtor(s)

In this form, you must list your monthly expenses. This includes both your family's personal expenses (even if you're married and filing alone) and the expenses of your sole proprietorship business. (If your business is a separate entity, don't include its expenses here.) Be complete and accurate.

Expenditures for items the trustee considers luxuries may not be considered reasonable and may be disregarded for the purpose of deciding whether you should be allowed to file a Chapter 7 bankruptcy or instead be limited to Chapter 13. For instance, the trustee may disregard lavish entertainment expenses, a lease on premises that are clearly more upscale than your business requires, or payments on expensive cars or investment properties. If this happens, you may not be allowed to use Chapter 7 bankruptcy because your disposable income (income after deducting reasonable expenses) is considered too high. However, reasonable business expenses and expenses for housing, utilities, food, medical care, clothing, education, and transportation will be counted. And you should include them all: the higher your reasonable expenses, the less likely the trustee is to challenge your eligibility to use Chapter 7. Be ready to support larger expense amounts with bills, receipts, and canceled checks.

> EXAMPLE 1: Joe owes $100,000 (excluding his mortgage and car), earns $4,000 a month, and spends $3,600 a month for the other items listed on Schedule J, including payments on a midpriced car and a moderately priced family home. Joe would probably be allowed

to proceed with a Chapter 7 bankruptcy because his monthly disposable income ($400) wouldn't put much of a dent in his $100,000 debt load, even over a five-year period.

EXAMPLE 2: Same facts, except that Joe's Schedule J expenses total only $2,200 a month. In this case, the court might rule that because Joe has $1,800 a month in disposable income, he could pay off most of his $100,000 debt load over a three- to five-year period, either informally or under a Chapter 13 repayment plan. The court could dismiss Joe's Chapter 7 bankruptcy petition or pressure him to convert it to Chapter 13 bankruptcy.

EXAMPLE 3: Same facts as Example 2, but Joe is incurably ill and will soon have to quit working. The court will more than likely allow him to proceed with a Chapter 7 bankruptcy.

Review the sample completed Schedule J, below, and the guidelines for completing it.

CAUTION

Another reason to be accurate. Creditors sometimes try to use the information on these forms to prove that you committed fraud when you applied for credit. If a creditor can prove that you lied on a credit application, the debt may survive bankruptcy. (See Ch. 11 for more information.) If being accurate on this form will substantially contradict information you previously gave a creditor, see a bankruptcy attorney before filing for bankruptcy.

In re and **Case No.** Follow the instructions for Schedule A.

Check this box if a joint petition is filed and debtor's spouse maintains a separate household. If you and your spouse are jointly filing for bankruptcy but maintain separate households (for example, you've recently separated), check this box and make sure that each of you fills out a separate Schedule J.

Dismissal for "Abuse"

As explained in Ch. 2, the new bankruptcy law (known as BAPCPA) created an eligibility requirement called the "means test" to determine who qualifies for Chapter 7 bankruptcy. Debtors who have a majority of consumer debts (as compared to business debts) and whose "current monthly income"—their average income over the six months before they filed for bankruptcy—exceeds their state's median income must take the means test. In the means test, debtors calculate their disposable income by subtracting certain allowable expenses (in amounts set by the IRS) from their current monthly income. If they have enough disposable income to fund a Chapter 13 repayment plan, their Chapter 7 case will be a "presumed abuse" of the bankruptcy laws and will be dismissed or converted to Chapter 13.

If you either pass the means test or don't have to take it at all, your case won't be a presumed abuse. However, the court can still find that allowing you to use Chapter 7 would be an abuse of the bankruptcy process if all of the circumstances show that you could afford a repayment plan. The great majority of courts to rule on this issue have been willing to dismiss Chapter 7 cases or convert them to Chapter 13 if the debtor's Schedule I and Schedule J show that the debtor has significantly more income than expenses (or has luxury expenses that the court excludes when determining the debtor's disposable income). A few courts have found that debtors who either pass or don't have to take the means test are automatically entitled to use Chapter 7, no matter what their Schedule I and Schedule J say.

Because the law on abuse is still unsettled, we suggest that you be very cautious if your expenses include payments for luxury items. If your total net income exceeds your expenses on Schedule J by more than a couple of hundred dollars for any reason, you may want to talk to a bankruptcy lawyer before filing.

Sample Schedule J

B6J (Official Form 6J) (12/07)

In re **Annie Justine Kaye** Case No. ______
Debtor(s)

SCHEDULE J - CURRENT EXPENDITURES OF INDIVIDUAL DEBTOR(S)

Complete this schedule by estimating the average or projected monthly expenses of the debtor and the debtor's family at time case filed. Prorate any payments made bi-weekly, quarterly, semi-annually, or annually to show monthly rate. The average monthly expenses calculated on this form may differ from the deductions from income allowed on Form 22A or 22C.

☐ Check this box if a joint petition is filed and debtor's spouse maintains a separate household. Complete a separate schedule of expenditures labeled "Spouse."

1. Rent or home mortgage payment (include lot rented for mobile home)	$ 800.00
a. Are real estate taxes included? Yes ___ No **X**	
b. Is property insurance included? Yes ___ No **X**	
2. Utilities: a. Electricity and heating fuel	$ 150.00
b. Water and sewer	$ 150.00
c. Telephone	$ 100.00
d. Other **See Detailed Expense Attachment**	$ 115.00
3. Home maintenance (repairs and upkeep)	$ 0.00
4. Food	$ 200.00
5. Clothing	$ 50.00
6. Laundry and dry cleaning	$ 40.00
7. Medical and dental expenses	$ 50.00
8. Transportation (not including car payments)	$ 150.00
9. Recreation, clubs and entertainment, newspapers, magazines, etc.	$ 25.00
10. Charitable contributions	$ 0.00
11. Insurance (not deducted from wages or included in home mortgage payments)	
a. Homeowner's or renter's	$ 100.00
b. Life	$ 0.00
c. Health	$ 0.00
d. Auto	$ 200.00
e. Other	$ 0.00
12. Taxes (not deducted from wages or included in home mortgage payments) (Specify)	$ 0.00
13. Installment payments: (In chapter 11, 12, and 13 cases, do not list payments to be included in the plan)	
a. Auto	$ 300.00
b. Other	$ 0.00
c. Other	$ 0.00
14. Alimony, maintenance, and support paid to others	$ 0.00
15. Payments for support of additional dependents not living at your home	$ 0.00
16. Regular expenses from operation of business, profession, or farm (attach detailed statement)	$ 1,500.00
17. Other **Child Care**	$ 400.00
Other	$ 0.00
18. AVERAGE MONTHLY EXPENSES (Total lines 1-17. Report also on Summary of Schedules and, if applicable, on the Statistical Summary of Certain Liabilities and Related Data.)	$ 4,330.00

19. Describe any increase or decrease in expenditures reasonably anticipated to occur within the year following the filing of this document:

I'll be closing my store when I file my bankrutpcy petition and will no longer be responsible for my lease or other business expenses. I hope to find a new place to operate my business at lesser expense and have several good leads. Until I find employment and/or open a new business I'll not have child care expenses.

20. STATEMENT OF MONTHLY NET INCOME

a.	Average monthly income from Line 15 of Schedule I	$ 3,500.00
b.	Average monthly expenses from Line 18 above	$ 4,330.00
c.	Monthly net income (a. minus b.)	$ -830.00

Items 1–17. For each listed item, fill in your monthly expenses. If you make some payments biweekly, quarterly, semiannually, or annually, prorate them to show your monthly payment. Here are some pointers:

- Do not list payroll deductions you listed on Schedule I.
- Include in your figures payments you make for your dependents' expenses as long as those expenses are reasonable and necessary for the dependents' support.
- **Utilities—Other:** This includes garbage, Internet, and cable TV service for your personal use (utilities for your business should be listed under "Business expenses," below).
- **Installment payments—Other:** In this blank, put the amount of any installment payments you are making on a secured debt or a debt you plan on reaffirming. Do not include payments you have been making on a credit card or other debt that does not involve collateral and that you plan to discharge in your bankruptcy. Installment payments related to your business go under "Business expenses," below.
- **Business expenses:** List all of your business expenses here; your gross income from your business goes on Schedule I. This means your net business income can be calculated subtracting the business expenses on Schedule J from the gross income on Schedule I.

Item 18. Average Monthly Expenses. Total up all your monthly expenses.

Item 19. Describe any increase or decrease in expenditures reasonably anticipated to occur within the year following the filing of this document. For instance, if you plan to pay off a car note during the coming year, indicate that fact.

Item 20. Statement of Monthly Net Income. Deduct your total expenses on Line 18 from your total income on Line 15 of Schedule I. If you have two totals on Line 15 (one for you and one for your spouse), subtract your expenses from the combined total on Line 16. This will show at a glance whether you have significantly more income than expenses.

Summary of Schedules

This form helps the bankruptcy trustee and judge get a quick look at your bankruptcy filing. Below are a completed Summary of Schedules and line-by-line instructions.

Court Name. Copy this information from Form 1—Voluntary Petition.

In re and **Case No.** Follow the instructions for Schedule A.

Name of Schedule. This lists the schedules. Don't add anything.

Attached (Yes/No). You should have completed all of the schedules, so type "Yes" in this column for each schedule, even if you added no information.

No. of Sheets. Enter the number of pages you completed for each schedule. Remember to count continuation pages. Enter the total at the bottom of the column.

Assets, Liabilities, Other. For each column—Assets, Liabilities, and Other—copy the totals from Schedules A, B, D, E, F, I, and J and enter them where indicated. Add up the amounts in the Assets and Liabilities columns and enter their totals at the bottom. (Once you've completed this form, you can go back and fill in the "Statistical/Administrative Information" section on Form 1—Voluntary Petition.)

Statistical Summary of Certain Liabilities and Related Data

This form asks you to list information from your other bankruptcy paperwork. Fill in the blanks using your completed schedules. You will need to come back to this form to fill in your current monthly income after completing Form 22A (instructions for this form are below).

Sample Summary of Schedules

B6 Summary (Form 6 - Summary) (12/07)

United States Bankruptcy Court
State of Anonymous

In re **Annie Justine Kaye**, Debtor(s) — Case No. ____ Chapter **7**

SUMMARY OF SCHEDULES

Indicate as to each schedule whether that schedule is attached and state the number of pages in each. Report the totals from Schedules A, B, D, E, F, I, and J in the boxes provided. Add the amounts from Schedules A and B to determine the total amount of the debtor's assets. Add the amounts of all claims from Schedules D, E, and F to determine the total amount of the debtor's liabilities. Individual debtors also must complete the "Statistical Summary of Certain Liabilities and Related Data" if they file a case under chapter 7, 11, or 13.

NAME OF SCHEDULE	ATTACHED (YES/NO)	NO. OF SHEETS	ASSETS	LIABILITIES	OTHER
A - Real Property	Yes	1	$0.00		
B - Personal Property	Yes	4	$63,825.00		
C - Property Claimed as Exempt	Yes	3			
D - Creditors Holding Secured Claims	Yes	1		$33,000.00	
E - Creditors Holding Unsecured Priority Claims (Total of Claims on Schedule E)	Yes	2		$4,000.00	
F - Creditors Holding Unsecured Nonpriority Claims	Yes	3		$101,350.00	
G - Executory Contracts and Unexpired Leases	Yes	1			
H - Codebtors	Yes	1			
I - Current Income of Individual Debtor(s)	Yes	1			$3,500.00
J - Current Expenditures of Individual Debtor(s)	Yes	2			$4,330.00
TOTAL		19	$63,825.00	$138,350.00	

Sample Statistical Summary of Certain Liabilities and Related Data

Form 6 - Statistical Summary (12/07)

United States Bankruptcy Court
Northern District of California

In re Annie Justine Kaye Debtor(s)

Case No. ______
Chapter 7

STATISTICAL SUMMARY OF CERTAIN LIABILITIES AND RELATED DATA (28 U.S.C. § 159)

If you are an individual debtor whose debts are primarily consumer debts, as defined in § 101(8) of the Bankruptcy Code (11 U.S.C. § 101(8)), filing a case under chapter 7, 11 or 13, you must report all information requested below.

☒ Check this box if you are an individual debtor whose debts are NOT primarily consumer debts. You are not required to report any information here.

This information is for statistical purposes only under 28 U.S.C. § 159.

Summarize the following types of liabilities, as reported in the Schedules, and total them.

Type of Liability	Amount
Domestic Support Obligations (from Schedule E)	$
Taxes and Certain Other Debts Owed to Governmental Units (from Schedule E)	$
Claims for Death or Personal Injury While Debtor Was Intoxicated (from Schedule E) (whether disputed or undisputed)	$
Student Loan Obligations (from Schedule F)	$
Domestic Support, Separation Agreement, and Divorce Decree Obligations Not Reported on Schedule E	$
Obligations to Pension or Profit-Sharing, and Other Similar Obligations (from Schedule F)	$
TOTAL	$

State the following:

Average Income (from Schedule I, Line 16)	$
Average Expenses (from Schedule J, Line 18)	$
Current Monthly Income (from Form 22A Line 12; OR, Form 22B Line 11; OR, Form 22C Line 20)	$

State the following:

1. Total from Schedule D, "UNSECURED PORTION, IF ANY" column		$
2. Total from Schedule E, "AMOUNT ENTITLED TO PRIORITY" column.	$	
3. Total from Schedule E, "AMOUNT NOT ENTITLED TO PRIORITY, IF ANY" column		$
4. Total from Schedule F		$
5. Total of non-priority unsecured debt (sum of 1, 3, and 4)		$

Declaration Concerning Debtor's Schedules

In this form, you are required to swear that everything you have said on your schedules is true and correct. Deliberate lying is a major sin in bankruptcy and could cost you your bankruptcy discharge, a fine of up to $500,000, and up to five years in prison.

Below is a completed Declaration with instructions.

In re and **Case No.** Follow the instructions for Schedule A.

Declaration Under Penalty of Perjury by Individual Debtor. Enter the total number of pages in your schedules (the number on the Summary of Schedules plus one). Enter the date and sign the form. If you are filing jointly, be sure that your spouse signs and dates the form.

Declaration and Signature of Non-Attorney Bankruptcy Petition Preparer (BPP). If a BPP typed your forms, have that person complete this section. Otherwise, type "N/A" anywhere in the box.

Declaration Under Penalty of Perjury on Behalf of Corporation or Partnership. Enter "N/A" anywhere in this blank.

Form 7—Statement of Financial Affairs

This form gives information about your recent financial transactions, such as payments to creditors, sales or other transfers of property, gifts, losses, and litigation. Under certain circumstances, the trustee may be entitled to take back property that you transferred to others prior to filing for bankruptcy, and sell it for the benefit of your unsecured creditors.

The questions on the form are, for the most part, self-explanatory. Spouses filing jointly may combine their answers and complete only one form.

Sample Declaration Concerning Debtor's Schedules

B6 Declaration (Official Form 6 - Declaration). (12/07)

United States Bankruptcy Court
State of Anonymous

In re **Annie Justine Kaye** Debtor(s) Case No. ______ Chapter **7**

DECLARATION CONCERNING DEBTOR'S SCHEDULES

DECLARATION UNDER PENALTY OF PERJURY BY INDIVIDUAL DEBTOR

I declare under penalty of perjury that I have read the foregoing summary and schedules, consisting of **21** sheets, and that they are true and correct to the best of my knowledge, information, and belief.

Date ______________ Signature ______________
Annie Justine Kaye
Debtor

Penalty for making a false statement or concealing property: Fine of up to $500,000 or imprisonment for up to 5 years or both. 18 U.S.C. §§ 152 and 3571.

If you have no information for a particular item, check the "None" box. If you fail to answer a question and don't check "None," you will have to amend your papers—that is, file a corrected form—after you file. Add continuation sheets if necessary.

A completed Statement of Financial Affairs and instructions follow.

Court Name. Copy this information from Form 1—Voluntary Petition.

In re and **Case No.** Follow the instructions for Schedule A.

Definitions. The Statement of Financial Affairs starts off with definitions that are important to small business owners.

In business. You are likely to be considered "in business." In addition to debtors that are business entities (corporations, LLCs, and partnerships), individuals are "in business" if they are, or have been in the past six years:

- an officer, director, managing executive, or owner of 5% or more of the voting or equity securities of a corporation
- a partner of a partnership (other than a limited partner), or
- a sole proprietor or self-employed person, whether full time or part time.

You will also be considered to be "in business" if you are engaged in a trade, business, or other activity, other than as an employee, to supplement your income from primary employment (for instance, you have a job as a computer network coordinator and do some consulting on the side). This "in business" definition is especially important when responding to Item 3(b) and Items 18 and beyond.

Insider. "Insiders" include relatives of any degree, your general partners and their relatives, and corporations or LLCs of which you are an officer, director, or person in control. This definition determines the length of the look-back period for transactions. As explained in Ch. 5, the trustee can undo certain transactions you've engaged in with an insider in the previous year, to get the money or property back for your bankruptcy estate. For transactions with non-insiders, the look-back period is only three months.

1. Income from employment or operation of business. Enter your gross income for this year and for the previous two years. Your gross income means the total income before any amounts are subtracted: taxes, payroll deductions, or business expenses. Make sure the amounts you provide here are consistent with the income disclosed on the tax return you provided to the trustee. For example, if you claim $50,000 gross income from a business for the previous year on this form, your tax return for that year should be in the same ballpark.

2. Income other than from employment or operation of business. Include interest, dividends, royalties, workers' compensation, other government benefits, and all other money you have received from sources other than your job or business during the last two years. Provide the source of each amount, the dates received, and the reason you received the money so that the trustee can verify it if he or she desires. Again, make sure the amounts you provide here are consistent with the income disclosed on the tax return you provided to the trustee.

3. Payments to creditors. Here you list payments you've recently made to creditors. There are three categories of payments that must be disclosed in this section:

a. payments made to creditors; only for debtors whose debts are primarily (more than 50%) consumer debts
b. payments made to creditors; only for debtors whose debts are primarily (more than 50%) business debts, and
c. payments made to creditors who are insiders; for all debtors.

Here's how to fill out these sections:

a. **Individual or joint debtor(s) with primarily consumer debts.** If your debts are primarily consumer debts—that is, more than 51% of the amount you owe was incurred for consumer, not business reasons—list

Sample Statement of Financial Affairs—page 1

B7 (Official Form 7) (12/07)

United States Bankruptcy Court
State of Anonymous

In re **Annie Justine Kaye** Debtor(s)

Case No. ______
Chapter **7**

STATEMENT OF FINANCIAL AFFAIRS

This statement is to be completed by every debtor. Spouses filing a joint petition may file a single statement on which the information for both spouses is combined. If the case is filed under chapter 12 or chapter 13, a married debtor must furnish information for both spouses whether or not a joint petition is filed, unless the spouses are separated and a joint petition is not filed. An individual debtor engaged in business as a sole proprietor, partner, family farmer, or self-employed professional, should provide the information requested on this statement concerning all such activities as well as the individual's personal affairs. To indicate payments, transfers and the like to minor children, state the child's initials and the name and address of the child's parent or guardian, such as "A.B., a minor child, by John Doe, guardian." Do not disclose the child's name. See, 11 U.S.C. § 112; Fed. R. Bankr. P. 1007(m).

Questions 1 - 18 are to be completed by all debtors. Debtors that are or have been in business, as defined below, also must complete Questions 19 - 25. **If the answer to an applicable question is "None," mark the box labeled "None."** If additional space is needed for the answer to any question, use and attach a separate sheet properly identified with the case name, case number (if known), and the number of the question.

DEFINITIONS

"In business." A debtor is "in business" for the purpose of this form if the debtor is a corporation or partnership. An individual debtor is "in business" for the purpose of this form if the debtor is or has been, within six years immediately preceding the filing of this bankruptcy case, any of the following: an officer, director, managing executive, or owner of 5 percent or more of the voting or equity securities of a corporation; a partner, other than a limited partner, of a partnership; a sole proprietor or self-employed full-time or part-time. An individual debtor also may be "in business" for the purpose of this form if the debtor engages in a trade, business, or other activity, other than as an employee, to supplement income from the debtor's primary employment.

"Insider." The term "insider" includes but is not limited to: relatives of the debtor; general partners of the debtor and their relatives; corporations of which the debtor is an officer, director, or person in control; officers, directors, and any owner of 5 percent or more of the voting or equity securities of a corporate debtor and their relatives; affiliates of the debtor and insiders of such affiliates; any managing agent of the debtor. 11 U.S.C. § 101.

---

1. Income from employment or operation of business

None ☐

State the gross amount of income the debtor has received from employment, trade, or profession, or from operation of the debtor's business, including part-time activities either as an employee or in independent trade or business, from the beginning of this calendar year to the date this case was commenced. State also the gross amounts received during the **two years** immediately preceding this calendar year. (A debtor that maintains, or has maintained, financial records on the basis of a fiscal rather than a calendar year may report fiscal year income. Identify the beginning and ending dates of the debtor's fiscal year.) If a joint petition is filed, state income for each spouse separately. (Married debtors filing under chapter 12 or chapter 13 must state income of both spouses whether or not a joint petition is filed, unless the spouses are separated and a joint petition is not filed.)

AMOUNT	SOURCE
$17,500.00	**XX through XX 20XX from operation of business**
$23,000.00	**20XX from operation of business**
$30,000.00	**20XX from operation of business**

payments made to a regular creditor that total more than $600, if the payment was made:

- to repay all or part a loan, installment purchase, or other debt, and
- during the 90 days before you filed your bankruptcy petition.

If you have made payments exceeding $600 during that 90-day period to satisfy a domestic support obligation (child support or alimony), identify that payment with an asterisk. Include payments made as part of a creditor repayment plan negotiated by an approved budget and credit counseling agency.

b. **Debtor whose debts are not primarily consumer debts.** If your debts are primarily business debts (which is often but not always true of small business owners), list any payments or other transfers you made within 90 days of filing that total $5,475 or more to any one creditor.

c. **All debtors.** List all payments or other transfers made to an insider creditor, if the payments or transfers were made within one year before you filed your bankruptcy petition. Include alimony and child support payments.

The basic purpose of these questions is to find out whether you have preferred any creditor over others. As explained in Ch. 5, the trustee can demand that a creditor who received a preference payment return the money so the trustee can use it to pay your other unsecured creditors. The trustee may ask you to produce written evidence of any payments you list here, such as copies of canceled checks, check stubs, or bank statements.

CAUTION

Don't use your tax refund to repay a debt to an insider. Many people use their tax refund to repay a loan from a relative without realizing that the payment may count as a preference that the trustee can take back. If the exemptions available to you provide protection for the refund, the better strategy is to hang on to the money, declare it on Schedule B, and claim it as exempt on Schedule C. Then, after your bankruptcy, you can do what you want with it. If you've already repaid a loan to a relative, perhaps the relative can return the money and you can exempt it as described above. If the money is gone, your relative can reject the trustee's demand to return the money and say, in effect, "Sue me." For amounts less than $1,000 or so, it's unlikely that the trustee will sue; the expense will likely outweigh whatever the trustee could recover. But you never know.

4. Suits and administrative proceedings, executions, garnishments and attachments.

a. **List all suits ....** Include all court actions that you are currently involved in or that you were involved in during the year before filing. Court actions include personal injury cases, small claims actions, contract disputes, divorces, paternity actions, support or custody modification actions, and the like. Include:

   - **Caption of suit and case number.** The caption is the case title (such as Carrie Edwards v. Ginny Jones). The case number is assigned by the court clerk and appears on the first page of any court-filed paper.
   - **Nature of proceeding.** A phrase, or even a one-word description, is sufficient. For example, "suit by debtor for compensation for damages to debtor's car caused by accident," "small claims case by debtor for unpaid invoices from client," "divorce."
   - **Court or agency and location.** This information is on any summons you received or prepared.
   - **Status or disposition.** State whether the case is awaiting trial, pending a decision, on appeal, or finished.

b. **Describe all property ....** If, at any time during the year before you filed for bankruptcy, your wages, real estate, or personal property were taken from you

Sample Statement of Financial Affairs—page 2

2

2. Income other than from employment or operation of business

None ☐ State the amount of income received by the debtor other than from employment, trade, profession, or operation of the debtor's business during the **two years** immediately preceding the commencement of this case. Give particulars. If a joint petition is filed, state income for each spouse separately. (Married debtors filing under chapter 12 or chapter 13 must state income for each spouse whether or not a joint petition is filed, unless the spouses are separated and a joint petition is not filed.)

AMOUNT	SOURCE
$12,000.00	**Child support from Ex-husband for previous two years ($6000 a year)**

3. Payments to creditors

None ☒ ***Complete a. or b., as appropriate, and c.***

a. *Individual or joint debtor(s) with primarily consumer debts.* List all payments on loans, installment purchases of goods or services, and other debts to any creditor made within **90 days** immediately preceding the commencement of this case unless the aggregate value of all property that constitutes or is affected by such transfer is less than $600. Indicate with an (*) any payments that were made to a creditor on account of a domestic support obligation or as part of an alternative repayment schedule under a plan by an approved nonprofit budgeting and creditor counseling agency. (Married debtors filing under chapter 12 or chapter 13 must include payments by either or both spouses whether or not a joint petition is filed, unless the spouses are separated and a joint petition is not filed.)

NAME AND ADDRESS OF CREDITOR	DATES OF PAYMENTS	AMOUNT PAID	AMOUNT STILL OWING

None ☒ b. *Debtor whose debts are not primarily consumer debts:* List each payment or other transfer to any creditor made within **90 days** immediately preceding the commencement of the case unless the aggregate value of all property that constitutes or is affected by such transfer is less than $5,475. If the debtor is an individual, indicate with an asterisk (*) any payments that were made to a creditor on account of a domestic support obligation or as part of an alternative repayment schedule under a plan by an approved nonprofit budgeting and creditor counseling agency. (Married debtors filing under chapter 12 or chapter 13 must include payments by either or both spouses whether or not a joint petition is filed, unless the spouses are separated and a joint petition is not filed.)

NAME AND ADDRESS OF CREDITOR	DATES OF PAYMENTS/ TRANSFERS	AMOUNT PAID OR VALUE OF TRANSFERS	AMOUNT STILL OWING

None ☒ c. *All debtors:* List all payments made within **one year** immediately preceding the commencement of this case to or for the benefit of creditors who are or were insiders. (Married debtors filing under chapter 12 or chapter 13 must include payments by either or both spouses whether or not a joint petition is filed, unless the spouses are separated and a joint petition is not filed.)

NAME AND ADDRESS OF CREDITOR AND RELATIONSHIP TO DEBTOR	DATE OF PAYMENT	AMOUNT PAID	AMOUNT STILL OWING

4. Suits and administrative proceedings, executions, garnishments and attachments

None ☐ a. List all suits and administrative proceedings to which the debtor is or was a party within **one year** immediately preceding the filing of this bankruptcy case. (Married debtors filing under chapter 12 or chapter 13 must include information concerning either or both spouses whether or not a joint petition is filed, unless the spouses are separated and a joint petition is not filed.)

CAPTION OF SUIT AND CASE NUMBER	NATURE OF PROCEEDING	COURT OR AGENCY AND LOCATION	STATUS OR DISPOSITION
Jones v. Kay and Annie's Beauty Accessories, Case #23456	**Personal injury case for damages arising from faulty product, case filed XX/XX**	**Court of Common Pleas for the State of AA, Freshstart, AA**	**Case filed, awaiting preliminary scheduling.**

None ☒ b. Describe all property that has been attached, garnished or seized under any legal or equitable process within **one year** immediately preceding the commencement of this case. (Married debtors filing under chapter 12 or chapter 13 must include information concerning property of either or both spouses whether or not a joint petition is filed, unless the spouses are separated and a joint petition is not filed.)

NAME AND ADDRESS OF PERSON FOR WHOSE BENEFIT PROPERTY WAS SEIZED	DATE OF SEIZURE	DESCRIPTION AND VALUE OF PROPERTY

under the authority of a court order to pay a debt, enter the requested information. If you don't know the exact date, put "on or about" and the approximate date.

5. Repossessions, foreclosures and returns. If, at any time during the year before you filed for bankruptcy, a creditor repossessed or foreclosed on property you had bought and were making payments on, or had pledged as collateral for a loan, give the requested information. For instance, if your car, boat, video equipment, or inventory was repossessed because you defaulted on your payments, describe it here. Also, if you voluntarily returned property to a creditor because you couldn't keep up the payments, enter that here.

6. Assignments and receiverships.

a. **Describe any assignments ....** If, at any time during the 120 days (four months) before you filed for bankruptcy, you assigned (legally transferred) your right to receive benefits, or any type of property, to a creditor to pay a debt, list it here. Examples include assigning a percentage of your wages to a creditor for several months or assigning a portion of a personal injury award to an attorney. The assignee is the person to whom the assignment was made, such as the creditor or attorney. The terms of the assignment should be given briefly—for example, "wages assigned to Snorkle's Store to satisfy debt of $500." If you made an assignment for the benefit of creditors (ABC) within the previous four months, you should disclose the details here (what was assigned, to whom, and so on). (ABCs are covered in Ch. 3.)

b. **List all property ....** Identify all of your property that has been in the hands of a court-appointed receiver, custodian, or other official during the year before you filed for bankruptcy. If you've made child support payments directly to a court, and the court in turn paid your child's other parent, list those payments here.

7. Gifts. Provide the requested information about gifts you've made in the past year. The bankruptcy court and trustee want this information to make sure you haven't improperly unloaded any property before filing for bankruptcy. List all charitable donations of more than $100 and gifts to family members of more than $200.

You don't have to list gifts to family members that are "ordinary and usual," such as reasonably priced birthday gifts, but it can be difficult to know which gifts are ordinary and usual. The best test is whether someone outside of the family might think the gift was unusual under the circumstances. If so, list it.

Forgiving a loan is also a gift, as is charging interest substantially below the market rate for a personal loan. Other gifts include giving a car or prepaid trip to a business associate.

8. Losses. Provide the requested information for losses from theft, fire, or gambling. If the loss was for an exempt item, most states let you keep the insurance proceeds up to the limit of the exemption. (See Appendix A.) If the item was not exempt, the trustee is entitled to the proceeds. In either case, list any proceeds you've received or expect to receive. If you experience a loss after you file, you should promptly amend your papers, as this question applies to losses both before you file and afterward.

9. Payments related to debt counseling or bankruptcy. If you paid an improperly high fee to an attorney, bankruptcy petition preparer, debt consultant, or debt consolidator, the trustee may try to get some of it back to distribute to your creditors. Be sure to list all payments someone else made on your behalf, as well as payments you made directly.

10. Other transfers.

a. **List all other property, other ....** List all real and personal property that you've sold or given to someone else during the two-year period before filing for bankruptcy. Some examples are selling or abandoning (junking) a car, pledging your house as

Sample Statement of Financial Affairs—page 3

3

5. Repossessions, foreclosures and returns

None ☐ List all property that has been repossessed by a creditor, sold at a foreclosure sale, transferred through a deed in lieu of foreclosure or returned to the seller, within **one year** immediately preceding the commencement of this case. (Married debtors filing under chapter 12 or chapter 13 must include information concerning property of either or both spouses whether or not a joint petition is filed, unless the spouses are separated and a joint petition is not filed.)

NAME AND ADDRESS OF CREDITOR OR SELLER	DATE OF REPOSSESSION, FORECLOSURE SALE, TRANSFER OR RETURN	DESCRIPTION AND VALUE OF PROPERTY
ABC Mortgage Co. **XXX P. St.** **Freshstart, AA 99999**	**02/XX**	**Home foreclosed, value of property $250,000, amount owed $500,000**

6. Assignments and receiverships

None ☒ a. Describe any assignment of property for the benefit of creditors made within **120 days** immediately preceding the commencement of this case. (Married debtors filing under chapter 12 or chapter 13 must include any assignment by either or both spouses whether or not a joint petition is filed, unless the spouses are separated and a joint petition is not filed.)

NAME AND ADDRESS OF ASSIGNEE	DATE OF ASSIGNMENT	TERMS OF ASSIGNMENT OR SETTLEMENT

None ☒ b. List all property which has been in the hands of a custodian, receiver, or court-appointed official within **one year** immediately preceding the commencement of this case. (Married debtors filing under chapter 12 or chapter 13 must include information concerning property of either or both spouses whether or not a joint petition is filed, unless the spouses are separated and a joint petition is not filed.)

NAME AND ADDRESS OF CUSTODIAN	NAME AND LOCATION OF COURT CASE TITLE & NUMBER	DATE OF ORDER	DESCRIPTION AND VALUE OF PROPERTY

7. Gifts

None ☒ List all gifts or charitable contributions made within **one year** immediately preceding the commencement of this case except ordinary and usual gifts to family members aggregating less than $200 in value per individual family member and charitable contributions aggregating less than $100 per recipient. (Married debtors filing under chapter 12 or chapter 13 must include gifts or contributions by either or both spouses whether or not a joint petition is filed, unless the spouses are separated and a joint petition is not filed.)

NAME AND ADDRESS OF PERSON OR ORGANIZATION	RELATIONSHIP TO DEBTOR, IF ANY	DATE OF GIFT	DESCRIPTION AND VALUE OF GIFT

8. Losses

None ☒ List all losses from fire, theft, other casualty or gambling within **one year** immediately preceding the commencement of this case **or since the commencement of this case.** (Married debtors filing under chapter 12 or chapter 13 must include losses by either or both spouses whether or not a joint petition is filed, unless the spouses are separated and a joint petition is not filed.)

DESCRIPTION AND VALUE OF PROPERTY	DESCRIPTION OF CIRCUMSTANCES AND, IF LOSS WAS COVERED IN WHOLE OR IN PART BY INSURANCE, GIVE PARTICULARS	DATE OF LOSS

security (collateral) for a loan, granting an easement on real estate, donating unsold inventory, or trading property. Also, describe any transfer within the past year to your ex-spouse as part of a marital settlement agreement. If you are filing alone, describe gifts to your current spouse made during that same period.

Don't include any gifts you listed in Item 7. Also, don't list property you've parted with as a regular part of your business or financial affairs. For example, if you operate a mail order book business, don't list the books you sold during the past year. Similarly, don't put down payments for regular goods and services, such as your phone bill, utilities, or rent. The idea is to disclose transfers of property that might legally belong in your bankruptcy estate.

CAUTION

Earlier transfers may also be in question. The Statement of Financial Affairs asks about transfers made during the previous two years only. However, you may be questioned at your creditors' meeting about transfers occurring four or five years ago. In most states, the law prohibits fraudulent transfers of property going back that long, and the trustee may decide to chase down such transfers if the circumstances seem fishy and the money is significant. (See Ch. 5 for more on state fraudulent transfer laws.)

EXAMPLE 1: John has accumulated a collection of junked classic cars and runs a business reselling the cars to restoration hobbyists. Within the past year, John has sold three of the cars for a total of $20,000. Because this is part of John's regular business, he needn't report the sales here. However, as a sole proprietor, John will be completing questions 18 through 20.

EXAMPLE 2: Within the year before filing for bankruptcy, Louise, a freelance Web designer, sold a vintage Jaguar E-type for $17,000. Because this isn't part of her business, Louise should list this sale here.

b. **List all property transferred ....** List all transfers of your own property that you have made in the previous ten years to an irrevocable trust that lists you as a beneficiary. These types of trusts—referred to as self-settled trusts—are commonly used by wealthy people to shield their assets from creditors and by disabled people to preserve their right to receive government benefits. In bankruptcy, however, assets placed in a self-settled trust will be considered nonexempt. There is an exception that applies to assets placed in certain special needs trusts. (*In re Schultz*, 368 B.R. 832 (D. Minn. 2007).) If you are the beneficiary of a self-settled trust, you should talk to a bankruptcy attorney before filing.

11. Closed financial accounts. Provide information for each account in your name or for your benefit that was closed or transferred to someone else during the past year.

12. Safe deposit boxes. Provide information for each safe deposit box you've had within the past year.

13. Setoffs. A setoff is when a creditor, often a bank, uses money in a customer's account to pay a debt owed to the creditor by that customer. For example, many credit unions tie loans to the borrower's savings and checking accounts, so that any default on the loan can be deducted from those accounts. Setoffs are not covered by the automatic stay. When you file for bankruptcy, the credit union can freeze your deposit accounts and recover at least part of the loan. Here, list any setoffs that your creditors have made during the previous 90 days.

14. Property held for another person. Describe all the property you've borrowed from someone else or

Sample Statement of Financial Affairs—page 4

4

9. Payments related to debt counseling or bankruptcy

None ☐ List all payments made or property transferred by or on behalf of the debtor to any persons, including attorneys, for consultation concerning debt consolidation, relief under the bankruptcy law or preparation of the petition in bankruptcy within **one year** immediately preceding the commencement of this case.

NAME AND ADDRESS OF PAYEE	DATE OF PAYMENT, NAME OF PAYOR IF OTHER THAN DEBTOR	AMOUNT OF MONEY OR DESCRIPTION AND VALUE OF PROPERTY
Affordable Attorney Advice **XXX Y St.** **Freshstart, AA 99999**	**02/XX**	**$250 for consultation on bankruptcy options**

10. Other transfers

None ☐ a. List all other property, other than property transferred in the ordinary course of the business or financial affairs of the debtor, transferred either absolutely or as security within **two years** immediately preceding the commencement of this case. (Married debtors filing under chapter 12 or chapter 13 must include transfers by either or both spouses whether or not a joint petition is filed, unless the spouses are separated and a joint petition is not filed.)

NAME AND ADDRESS OF TRANSFEREE, RELATIONSHIP TO DEBTOR	DATE	DESCRIBE PROPERTY TRANSFERRED AND VALUE RECEIVED
Benedict Kaye **XXX T St.** **Freshstart, AA 99999** **Nephew**	**05/XX**	**I gave my old dirt bike to my nephew Benedict Kaye for his last birthday. The dirtbike was valued at approximately $400 at the time of the transfer although I doubt I could have sold it for that.**

None ☒ b. List all property transferred by the debtor within **ten years** immediately preceding the commencement of this case to a self-settled trust or similar device of which the debtor is a beneficiary.

NAME OF TRUST OR OTHER DEVICE	DATE(S) OF TRANSFER(S)	AMOUNT OF MONEY OR DESCRIPTION AND VALUE OF PROPERTY OR DEBTOR'S INTEREST IN PROPERTY

11. Closed financial accounts

None ☐ List all financial accounts and instruments held in the name of the debtor or for the benefit of the debtor which were closed, sold, or otherwise transferred within **one year** immediately preceding the commencement of this case. Include checking, savings, or other financial accounts, certificates of deposit, or other instruments; shares and share accounts held in banks, credit unions, pension funds, cooperatives, associations, brokerage houses and other financial institutions. (Married debtors filing under chapter 12 or chapter 13 must include information concerning accounts or instruments held by or for either or both spouses whether or not a joint petition is filed, unless the spouses are separated and a joint petition is not filed.)

NAME AND ADDRESS OF INSTITUTION	TYPE OF ACCOUNT, LAST FOUR DIGITS OF ACCOUNT NUMBER, AND AMOUNT OF FINAL BALANCE	AMOUNT AND DATE OF SALE OR CLOSING
Freshstart Cmmunity Bank **XXX O St.** **Freshstart, AA 99999**	**Personal savings account, final balance $400, Acct # XXXX**	**XX/XX**

12. Safe deposit boxes

None ☒ List each safe deposit or other box or depository in which the debtor has or had securities, cash, or other valuables within **one year** immediately preceding the commencement of this case. (Married debtors filing under chapter 12 or chapter 13 must include boxes or depositories of either or both spouses whether or not a joint petition is filed, unless the spouses are separated and a joint petition is not filed.)

NAME AND ADDRESS OF BANK OR OTHER DEPOSITORY	NAMES AND ADDRESSES OF THOSE WITH ACCESS TO BOX OR DEPOSITORY	DESCRIPTION OF CONTENTS	DATE OF TRANSFER OR SURRENDER, IF ANY

that you are storing or holding in trust for someone else. Examples include property you're holding as executor or administrator of an estate and funds in an irrevocable trust held for someone else as beneficiary, but controlled by you as trustee. This type of property is not part of your bankruptcy estate. However, you must disclose these funds so the trustee is aware of them and can ask for more details. (Some people dishonestly describe all of their property as being in trust or otherwise belonging to someone else, hoping to avoid having to give it to the trustee. Disclosures in this part of the Statement of Financial Affairs allow the trustee to explore this possibility.)

If You Are Listed on Someone Else's Account

In the instructions for completing Schedule B, we explained that you should list any bank accounts you have been added to for money management purposes. Here, you should describe the account, explain (as you did on Schedule B) that you are on the account only to manage it for your relative, and state that the money in the account belongs to the relative, not to you.

A trustee who becomes interested in property you describe here may invoke several court procedures designed to get more information. However, it is unlikely that the trustee will invade your house to seize the property. If you can establish that the property truly belongs to someone else—by producing the trust document, for example—you needn't worry about losing it in your bankruptcy case.

> EXAMPLE: You are renting an unfurnished apartment owned by a friend. The friend has left a valuable baby grand piano in your care. If and when you decide to move, you have agreed to place the piano in storage for your friend. Because you don't own the piano, but rather are taking care of it for your friend, you would describe it here.

15. Prior address of debtor. If you have moved within the three years before you file for bankruptcy, list all of your residences within those three years.

16. Spouses and former spouses. If you lived in a community property state (or Puerto Rico) within eight years prior to filing for bankruptcy, list the name of your spouse and of any former spouses who lived with you in the community property state. (To remind you, community property states are Alaska, Arizona, California, Idaho, Louisiana, Nevada, New Mexico, Texas, Washington, and Wisconsin.)

17. Environmental information. Few individuals will have much to say here. It's intended primarily for businesses that do business on polluted premises. Still, read the questions carefully and provide the requested information, if applicable.

18. Nature, location and name of business. Provide all of the information requested on line **a** for your business. As mentioned earlier, note that the definition of business is very broad: It includes not only sole proprietors, but anyone self-employed in a trade, profession, or other activity either full or part time—or involved in a business in which the debtor owned 5% or more of the voting or equity securities within the six-year period. It is very important that you answer this question completely so that the trustee will have a good idea of how you earned your money over the past six years and what you did with your business interests (if you are no longer in business).

If the majority of your business income for any one business comes from renting, leasing, or otherwise operating a single piece of real property (other than an apartment building with fewer than four units), include your business name and the address of the property on line b.

19. Books, records and financial statements.

a. **List all bookkeepers ....** Identify every person other than yourself—usually a bookkeeper or accountant—who was involved in the accounting of your business during the previous two years. If you were the only person involved in your business's accounting, check "None."

Sample Statement of Financial Affairs—page 5

5

13. Setoffs

None ☒ List all setoffs made by any creditor, including a bank, against a debt or deposit of the debtor within **90 days** preceding the commencement of this case. (Married debtors filing under chapter 12 or chapter 13 must include information concerning either or both spouses whether or not a joint petition is filed, unless the spouses are separated and a joint petition is not filed.)

NAME AND ADDRESS OF CREDITOR	DATE OF SETOFF	AMOUNT OF SETOFF

14. Property held for another person

None ☐ List all property owned by another person that the debtor holds or controls.

NAME AND ADDRESS OF OWNER	DESCRIPTION AND VALUE OF PROPERTY	LOCATION OF PROPERTY
Twenty Five Artisans Addresses available upon request Freshstart, AA 99999	**necklaces, earrings, scarves, pendents, theme T-shirts, etc., all held on consignment in my store.**	**Store at XXX Third St., Freshstart AA**

15. Prior address of debtor

None ☐ If the debtor has moved within **three years** immediately preceding the commencement of this case, list all premises which the debtor occupied during that period and vacated prior to the commencement of this case. If a joint petition is filed, report also any separate address of either spouse.

ADDRESS	NAME USED	DATES OF OCCUPANCY
XXX CCC St., Freshstart AA	**Annie Kaye**	**XX/XX to XX/XX**

16. Spouses and Former Spouses

None ☐ If the debtor resides or resided in a community property state, commonwealth, or territory (including Alaska, Arizona, California, Idaho, Louisiana, Nevada, New Mexico, Puerto Rico, Texas, Washington, or Wisconsin) within **eight years** immediately preceding the commencement of the case, identify the name of the debtor's spouse and of any former spouse who resides or resided with the debtor in the community property state.

NAME
Steven Kaye

17. Environmental Information.

For the purpose of this question, the following definitions apply:

"Environmental Law" means any federal, state, or local statute or regulation regulating pollution, contamination, releases of hazardous or toxic substances, wastes or material into the air, land, soil, surface water, groundwater, or other medium, including, but not limited to, statutes or regulations regulating the cleanup of these substances, wastes, or material.

"Site" means any location, facility, or property as defined under any Environmental Law, whether or not presently or formerly owned or operated by the debtor, including, but not limited to, disposal sites.

"Hazardous Material" means anything defined as a hazardous waste, hazardous substance, toxic substance, hazardous material, pollutant, or contaminant or similar term under an Environmental Law

None ☒ a. List the name and address of every site for which the debtor has received notice in writing by a governmental unit that it may be liable or potentially liable under or in violation of an Environmental Law. Indicate the governmental unit, the date of the notice, and, if known, the Environmental Law:

SITE NAME AND ADDRESS	NAME AND ADDRESS OF GOVERNMENTAL UNIT	DATE OF NOTICE	ENVIRONMENTAL LAW

None ☒ b. List the name and address of every site for which the debtor provided notice to a governmental unit of a release of Hazardous Material. Indicate the governmental unit to which the notice was sent and the date of the notice.

Sample Statement of Financial Affairs—page 6

SITE NAME AND ADDRESS	NAME AND ADDRESS OF GOVERNMENTAL UNIT	DATE OF NOTICE	ENVIRONMENTAL LAW

None ☒ c. List all judicial or administrative proceedings, including settlements or orders, under any Environmental Law with respect to which the debtor is or was a party. Indicate the name and address of the governmental unit that is or was a party to the proceeding, and the docket number.

NAME AND ADDRESS OF GOVERNMENTAL UNIT	DOCKET NUMBER	STATUS OR DISPOSITION

18 . Nature, location and name of business

None ☐ a. *If the debtor is an individual*, list the names, addresses, taxpayer identification numbers, nature of the businesses, and beginning and ending dates of all businesses in which the debtor was an officer, director, partner, or managing executive of a corporation, partner in a partnership, sole proprietor, or was self-employed in a trade, profession, or other activity either full- or part-time within **six years** immediately preceding the commencement of this case, or in which the debtor owned 5 percent or more of the voting or equity securities within **six years** immediately preceding the commencement of this case.

If the debtor is a partnership, list the names, addresses, taxpayer identification numbers, nature of the businesses, and beginning and ending dates of all businesses in which the debtor was a partner or owned 5 percent or more of the voting or equity securities, within **six years** immediately preceding the commencement of this case.

If the debtor is a corporation, list the names, addresses, taxpayer identification numbers, nature of the businesses, and beginning and ending dates of all businesses in which the debtor was a partner or owned 5 percent or more of the voting or equity securities within **six years** immediately preceding the commencement of this case.

NAME	LAST FOUR DIGITS OF SOCIAL-SECURITY OR OTHER INDIVIDUAL TAXPAYER-I.D. NO. (ITIN)/ COMPLETE EIN	ADDRESS	NATURE OF BUSINESS	BEGINNING AND ENDING DATES
Annie's Beauty Accessories	**XXXX XX-XXXXXX**	**XXX 7th St. Freshstart, AA 99999**	**Retail**	**XX/XX to Current**

None ☒ b. Identify any business listed in response to subdivision a., above, that is "single asset real estate" as defined in 11 U.S.C. § 101.

NAME	ADDRESS

The following questions are to be completed by every debtor that is a corporation or partnership and by any individual debtor who is or has been, within **six years** immediately preceding the commencement of this case, any of the following: an officer, director, managing executive, or owner of more than 5 percent of the voting or equity securities of a corporation; a partner, other than a limited partner, of a partnership, a sole proprietor or self-employed in a trade, profession, or other activity, either full- or part-time.

(An individual or joint debtor should complete this portion of the statement ***only*** *if the debtor is or has been in business, as defined above, within six years immediately preceding the commencement of this case. A debtor who has not been in business within those six years should go directly to the signature page.)*

19. Books, records and financial statements

None ☐ a. List all bookkeepers and accountants who within **two years** immediately preceding the filing of this bankruptcy case kept or supervised the keeping of books of account and records of the debtor.

NAME AND ADDRESS	DATES SERVICES RENDERED
Alan Accountant 5 Green St. Freshstart, AA 99999	**XX to XX**

None ☐ b. List all firms or individuals who within the **two years** immediately preceding the filing of this bankruptcy case have audited the books of account and records, or prepared a financial statement of the debtor.

Sample Statement of Financial Affairs—page 7

7

NAME	ADDRESS	DATES SERVICES RENDERED
Alan Accountant	**5 Green St. Freshstart, AA 99999**	**XX to XX**

None ☐ c. List all firms or individuals who at the time of the commencement of this case were in possession of the books of account and records of the debtor. If any of the books of account and records are not available, explain.

NAME	ADDRESS
Debtor	

None ☐ d. List all financial institutions, creditors and other parties, including mercantile and trade agencies, to whom a financial statement was issued by the debtor within **two years** immediately preceding the commencement of this case.

NAME AND ADDRESS	DATE ISSUED
XYZ Bank XXX D St. Freshstart, AA 99999	**XX/XX**

20. Inventories

None ☐ a. List the dates of the last two inventories taken of your property, the name of the person who supervised the taking of each inventory, and the dollar amount and basis of each inventory.

DATE OF INVENTORY	INVENTORY SUPERVISOR	DOLLAR AMOUNT OF INVENTORY (Specify cost, market or other basis)
XX/XX	**Debtor**	**$3000 (Inventory owned by Debtor at market value at time of inventory) (No inventory taken of items held for sale on consignment)**
XX/XX	**Debtor**	**$10,000 for items owned by Debtor at time of inventory (items held on consignment not part of inventory)**

None ☐ b. List the name and address of the person having possession of the records of each of the two inventories reported in a., above.

DATE OF INVENTORY	NAME AND ADDRESSES OF CUSTODIAN OF INVENTORY RECORDS
XX/XX	**Debtor XXXX First St. Freshstart, AA 99999**
XX/XX	**Debtor XXXX First St. Freshstart, AA 99999**

21 . Current Partners, Officers, Directors and Shareholders

None ☒ a. If the debtor is a partnership, list the nature and percentage of partnership interest of each member of the partnership.

NAME AND ADDRESS	NATURE OF INTEREST	PERCENTAGE OF INTEREST

None ☒ b. If the debtor is a corporation, list all officers and directors of the corporation, and each stockholder who directly or indirectly owns, controls, or holds 5 percent or more of the voting or equity securities of the corporation.

NAME AND ADDRESS	TITLE	NATURE AND PERCENTAGE OF STOCK OWNERSHIP

Sample Statement of Financial Affairs—page 8

8

22 . Former partners, officers, directors and shareholders

None ☒ a. If the debtor is a partnership, list each member who withdrew from the partnership within **one year** immediately preceding the commencement of this case.

NAME	ADDRESS	DATE OF WITHDRAWAL

None ☒ b. If the debtor is a corporation, list all officers, or directors whose relationship with the corporation terminated within **one year** immediately preceding the commencement of this case.

NAME AND ADDRESS	TITLE	DATE OF TERMINATION

23 . Withdrawals from a partnership or distributions by a corporation

None ☒ If the debtor is a partnership or corporation, list all withdrawals or distributions credited or given to an insider, including compensation in any form, bonuses, loans, stock redemptions, options exercised and any other perquisite during **one year** immediately preceding the commencement of this case.

NAME & ADDRESS OF RECIPIENT, RELATIONSHIP TO DEBTOR	DATE AND PURPOSE OF WITHDRAWAL	AMOUNT OF MONEY OR DESCRIPTION AND VALUE OF PROPERTY

24. Tax Consolidation Group.

None ☒ If the debtor is a corporation, list the name and federal taxpayer identification number of the parent corporation of any consolidated group for tax purposes of which the debtor has been a member at any time within **six years** immediately preceding the commencement of the case.

NAME OF PARENT CORPORATION	TAXPAYER IDENTIFICATION NUMBER (EIN)

25. Pension Funds.

None ☒ If the debtor is not an individual, list the name and federal taxpayer identification number of any pension fund to which the debtor, as an employer, has been responsible for contributing at any time within **six years** immediately preceding the commencement of the case.

NAME OF PENSION FUND	TAXPAYER IDENTIFICATION NUMBER (EIN)

DECLARATION UNDER PENALTY OF PERJURY BY INDIVIDUAL DEBTOR

I declare under penalty of perjury that I have read the answers contained in the foregoing statement of financial affairs and any attachments thereto and that they are true and correct.

Date ______________________ Signature ______________________________
Annie Justine Kaye
Debtor

Penalty for making a false statement: Fine of up to $500,000 or imprisonment for up to 5 years, or both. 18 U.S.C. §§ 152 and 3571

b. **List all firms ....** If your books weren't audited during the past two years, check "None." Otherwise, fill in the requested information.

c. **List all firms ....** Usually, you, your bookkeeper, your accountant, an ex-business associate, or possibly an ex-mate will have business records. If any are missing, explain (you'll be better off if the loss of your records was beyond your control).

d. **List all financial ....** You most likely prepared a financial statement if you applied to a bank for a loan or line of credit for your business or in your own name. If you're self-employed and applied for a personal loan to purchase a car or house, you probably submitted a financial statement as evidence of your ability to repay. Such statements include:
   - balance sheets (these compare assets with liabilities)
   - profit and loss statements (these compare income with expenses), and
   - financial statements (these provide an overall financial description of a business).

CAUTION

If you haven't kept adequate business records, talk to an attorney. If the trustee wants to see records of your business activity and you come up empty, the trustee may challenge your right to a bankruptcy discharge on the ground that your failure to keep adequate records demonstrates bad faith. Whether your business records are so bad that your discharge is at risk is something that only a bankruptcy attorney familiar with your court can answer. Also, an attorney may be able to help you reconstruct records that would be satisfactory to the trustee.

20. Inventories. If you have an inventory, fill in the information requested in items a and b. If your business doesn't have an inventory (many service business don't), check "None." If your business deals in products, but you are primarily the middle person or original manufacturer, put "no inventory required" or "materials purchased for each order as needed."

21 through 25. These items are intended for filers who are business entities—such as a partnership, corporation, or limited liability company. This book is designed for individual filers—that is owners of small businesses—so you should be able to check "None" for each of these items.

Declaration Under Penalty of Perjury by Individual Debtor. Sign and date this section. If you're filing jointly, be sure your spouse dates and signs it as well.

If completed on behalf of a partnership or corporation. Type "N/A."

Certification and Signature of Non-Attorney Bankruptcy Petition Preparer. If a BPP typed your forms, have that person complete this section. Otherwise, type "N/A" anywhere in the box.

Be sure to insert the number of continuation pages you attached (if any).

Form 8—Chapter 7 Individual Debtor's Statement of Intention

This form is very important if you owe any secured debts (Schedule D), or you are a party to any ongoing contracts, loans, or unexpired leases (Schedule G). This is where you tell the trustee and your secured creditors how you want to handle each of your secured debts. Briefly, you may:

- reaffirm the debt, and keep the collateral under a reaffirmation agreement that will continue your liability for the debt despite your bankruptcy
- redeem the debt by buying the collateral at its replacement value, or
- voluntarily surrender the collateral.

These options were discussed in detail in Ch. 8; return to that chapter now if you want more guidance on your options here.

As explained in our discussion of Schedule G above, your trustee gets first crack at any leases and contracts to which you are a party, for up to 60 days after your filing date. If they have any intrinsic value, the trustee may take them over, sell them, and distribute the proceeds among your unsecured creditors. However, in your Statement of Intention, you should indicate how you'd like each lease or contract to be handled if the trustee isn't interested. For example, if you have leased equipment for your business, you can indicate on this form that you want to assume the lease (provided your creditor agrees) and continue on with your business after your bankruptcy. If you want to walk away from a lease or contract, you can indicate your intent to reject it.

Under 11 U.S.C. § 365p, you must provide the lessor (the leasing company) with written notice that you intend to assume the lease (if the trustee doesn't sell it). You do this by sending the lessor a copy of the Statement of Intention. The statute gives the lessor the option to agree to the assumption and notify you of any conditions you must meet (for example, catching up on your payments, if you're behind). The lessor is very likely to let you assume the lease; the alternative would be for you to walk away without any penalty.

CAUTION

Check your mileage on a leased car. Before you decide to assume a car lease, check your mileage. If your mileage substantially exceeds the limit in your lease and you plan on turning your car in when the lease is up, think again about whether it makes sense to keep the car. You may be better off letting it go now and getting out from under the excess-mileage charges.

FOR MARRIED COUPLES

If you are married. If you're filing jointly, complete only one form, even though it says "Individual Debtor's Statement of Intention."

Below is a completed Statement of Intention and instructions.

Court Name. Copy this information from Form 1—Voluntary Petition.

In re and **Case No.** Follow the instructions for Schedule A.

Chapter. Type in "7"

Part A—Debts secured by property of the estate. Here, you list each of your secured debts and indicate what you plan to do with the property securing the debt (the collateral). The form provides space to list three secured property items; if you have more, attach extra sheets. For each piece of property, you must list the creditor's name and describe the property, as you did on Schedule D. Then, you must check the appropriate box to indicate whether you are surrendering the property (giving it back to lender) or retaining it.

The next choices are more difficult. If you plan to enter into a reaffirmation agreement with the lender, check the "reaffirm the debt" box. If you are able to redeem the property by paying the creditor the lesser of what you owe or the replacement value of the property, check that box. (But few debtors can afford this option.) If there is equity in the property and you qualify to "avoid the lien" because it impairs an exemption, check the "other" box and write "avoid the lien" in the blank space. (All of these options are covered in detail in Ch. 8.)

In some cases involving secured personal property such as a car or business equipment, your lender will not require you to reaffirm the loan but rather will let you keep the property as long as you remain current on the payments. If this is your lender's choice, you can check the "other" box and put "Debtor will retain collateral and continue to make regular payments."

If you are moving to avoid a lien, check the "claimed as exempt" box. Also, if you have any equity in the property securing the debt (that is, the property is worth more than you owe), check the "exempt" box. If you are underwater on the property (you owe more than it's worth), check the "not claimed as exempt" box; you have no equity to protect with an exemption.

Sample Statement of Intention—page 1

B8 (Form 8) (12/08)

United States Bankruptcy Court
State of Anonymous

In re **Annie Justine Kaye** Debtor(s)

Case No. ____________
Chapter **7**

CHAPTER 7 INDIVIDUAL DEBTOR'S STATEMENT OF INTENTION

PART A - Debts secured by property of the estate. (Part A must be fully completed for **EACH** debt which is secured by property of the estate. Attach additional pages if necessary.)

Property No. 1	
Creditor's Name: **Freshstart Credit Union**	**Describe Property Securing Debt:** **2009 Honda Accord** **Location: XXXX First St., Freshstart AA**

Property will be (check one):
☐ Surrendered ☒ Retained

If retaining the property, I intend to (check at least one):
☐ Redeem the property
☒ Reaffirm the debt
☐ Other. Explain ____________ (for example, avoid lien using 11 U.S.C. § 522(f)).

Property is (check one):
☐ Claimed as Exempt ☒ Not claimed as exempt

Reaffirming a Mortgage

Bankruptcy professionals often advise against reaffirming a mortgage because it will leave you with a large debt after your bankruptcy case is over. If you don't reaffirm, there are some consequences. Your lender won't report your continued payments on the mortgage to the credit reporting agencies, so your payments won't help you rehabilitate your credit. Also, you may not be able to modify your mortgage unless you reaffirm, because many mortgage servicers take the position that once your bankruptcy filing wipes out the promissory note, there's nothing left to modify. Generally speaking, however, it's a better idea to finish your modification efforts before filing for bankruptcy—and to avoid reaffirming your mortgage.

There are exceptions to this general rule, however. If you are facing foreclosure and using bankruptcy as a strategic maneuver to increase the amount of time you can remain in your home without making any payments, reaffirmation makes more sense. If you surrender the house in your Statement of Intention, or don't indicate how you want to handle your mortgage, the lender may immediately foreclose on the mortgage after your bankruptcy without further complying with your state's rules regarding foreclosure. As a result, you may be kicked out of your home months earlier than would otherwise be the case.

And, as explained in Ch. 8, some courts may require you to either redeem or reaffirm if you want to keep the property. In other words, these courts don't recognize the "ride-through" option.

In these situations, you may want to reaffirm your mortgage to buy yourself more time. This means you would still owe the lender after your bankruptcy. But if you live in what's called a "nonrecourse" state, this shouldn't be a disadvantage. In nonrecourse states, the lender cannot collect a deficiency judgment on a first mortgage. If the house is worth less than the mortgage, the lender must accept the home's value as payment in full. If your state allows collection of deficiencies on second mortgages, however—which almost all states do—you'll still be on the hook for that debt. As you can see, reaffirming a mortgage as a strategy to gain more time in your home can be tricky; you should consult with a lawyer if you're planning to go this route.

Part B—Personal property subject to unexpired leases. In the first box, list the name of the creditor (lessor). In the middle box, describe the leased property as you did on Schedule G. In the third box, indicate whether you want the lease to continue after bankruptcy the same as before (check Yes) or whether you want to walk away from the lease (check No).

Sign and date the form. Even if you have no secured debts or leases to include, you must file the form with your signature and the date.

CAUTION

Save up those monthly payments. Some secured creditors will not accept payments while your bankruptcy case is open, but will expect you to get current after the bankruptcy discharge, when the automatic stay is no longer in place. If a creditor refuses your payments during bankruptcy, be sure to save the money so you'll be able to get current on your payments for the property you intend to keep.

Sample Statement of Intention—page 2

B8 (Form 8) (12/08) Page 2

Property No. 2	
Creditor's Name: **Freshstart Credit Union**	**Describe Property Securing Debt:** **01 23 Foot Travel Trailer** **Location: XXXX First St., Freshstart AA**

Property will be (check one):
☒ Surrendered ☐ Retained

If retaining the property, I intend to (check at least one):
☐ Redeem the property
☐ Reaffirm the debt
☐ Other. Explain ________________ (for example, avoid lien using 11 U.S.C. § 522(f)).

Property is (check one):
☐ Claimed as Exempt ☒ Not claimed as exempt

PART B - Personal property subject to unexpired leases. (All three columns of Part B must be completed for each unexpired lease. Attach additional pages if necessary.)

Property No. 1		
Lessor's Name: **Beauty Products Leasing Co.**	**Describe Leased Property:** **Laser skin treatment machine. Lease for five year period that expries on 2013**	Lease will be Assumed pursuant to 11 U.S.C. § 365(p)(2): ☐ YES ☒ NO

Property No. 2		
Lessor's Name: **Rural Industries Leasing Service**	**Describe Leased Property:** **Five year lease on business property. Four months behind and three years to go**	Lease will be Assumed pursuant to 11 U.S.C. § 365(p)(2): ☐ YES ☒ NO

I declare under penalty of perjury that the above indicates my intention as to any property of my estate securing a debt and/or personal property subject to an unexpired lease.

Date ______________________ Signature ______________________________

Annie Justine Kaye
Debtor

Credit Card Debts

If you owe money on a bank, home improvement, or department store credit card, and you want to keep the card through bankruptcy, contact the bank or store before you file. If you offer to reaffirm the debt, some banks or stores may let you keep the credit card and steeply cut the debt. If you do reaffirm it, list it on the Statement of Intention, even though it isn't really a secured debt. But think twice before you reaffirm credit card debt. If you don't reaffirm the debt, it will be discharged in bankruptcy—giving you the fresh start that is, after all, the purpose of the process.

Signature. Date and sign the form. If you're married and filing jointly, your spouse must also date and sign the form.

Certification of Non-Attorney Bankruptcy Petition Preparer. If a BPP typed your forms, have that person complete this section. Otherwise, type "N/A" anywhere in the box.

Form 21—Statement of Social Security Number

This form requires you to list your full Social Security number. It will be available to your creditors and the trustee but, to protect your privacy, it will not be part of your regular bankruptcy case file.

Form 22A—Statement of Current Monthly Income and Means-Test Calculation

SKIP AHEAD

Debtors whose debts are primarily business debts can skip ahead. This form is only for debtors whose debts are primarily consumer debts. If more than 50% of your debt load is attributable to the operation of a business, you are a business debtor and need not complete the entire form. Simply check the box on Line 1b and complete the verification. When making this determination, remember that home mortgages count as consumer debt and tax debts count as business debts. As a general rule, people with home mortgages often owe more consumer debt than business debt.

This form helps the U.S. Trustee decide whether your income and expenses qualify you to file for Chapter 7 bankruptcy, or whether you will have to use Chapter 13.

As discussed in Ch. 2, if your current monthly income is above your state's median income, you will have to take the means test. Parts II and III of this form are where you calculate your current monthly income; if it exceeds the state median (which is rare), you'll have to fill out the means test beginning with Part IV.

RESOURCE

Prefer to let your computer crunch the numbers? Rather than completing the means test form by hand, you can use an online calculator to run the numbers for you. You'll find an excellent free calculator (as well as a treasure trove of bankruptcy information and resources) at www.legalconsumer.com. Just click on the means test link, enter your zip code number, and away you go.

If You Fail the Means Test

If the information you provide on this form shows that your income exceeds the state median, and is sufficient to propose a Chapter 13 plan according to the guidelines set out in the form, your Chapter 7 filing will be presumed abusive, and the U.S. Trustee will ask the court to either dismiss your Chapter 7 filing or, with your consent, convert your case to a Chapter 13 case. If this happens to you, we highly recommend that you obtain the services of an attorney

Below is a completed Statement of Current Monthly Income and Means-Test Calculation, with instructions.

In re and **Case No.** Follow the instructions for Schedule A.

The presumption arises. Don't check any of these boxes for now. You will decide which box to check later, after you figure out whether you have to take the means test and, if so, whether you pass it.

Part I. Exclusion for Disabled Veterans and Non-Consumer Debtors

Line 1a. If all of the facts in the "Declaration of Disabled Veteran" are true of your situation, check the appropriate box and sign the verification in Part VIII. To qualify for this exclusion, you must have a disability rating of at least 30%, and more than half of your debt must have been incurred while you were either on active duty or performing homeland defense activity. If you qualify for the veteran's exclusion, you don't have to calculate your current income or take the means test on this form; you are automatically eligible to use Chapter 7.

Line 1b. If the majority of your debt comes from running a business, check this box. As mentioned, those who have primarily nonconsumer (business) debts don't have to take the means test and are free to use Chapter 7 if they wish. If the majority of your debts are for non-business-related purposes, you must take the means test to see whether you can file for Chapter 7 bankruptcy. (See Ch. 2 for more information on which debts go in each category.)

Line 1c. The law provides a temporary exclusion from taking the means test for National Guard members who were called to active duty after September 11, 2001 for at least 90 days. The exclusion period lasts for 540 days after the 90-day active duty. If you fit this category, complete the "Declaration of Reservists and National Guard Members," check the box at the top of the form marked "The presumption is temporarily inapplicable," and sign and date the form at the end.

Part II. Calculation of Monthly Income for § 707(b)(7) Exclusion

Line 2a. If you are unmarried, check this box and follow the instructions (complete only Lines 3 through 11 in column A).

Line 2b. If you are married but filing separately because you have separate households, check this box and complete only Lines 3 through 11 in Column A. If you check this box, you are declaring, under penalty of perjury, that you are legally separated under the laws of your state or that you are living separately for reasons other than to qualify for Chapter 7 bankruptcy.

Many couples live separately but have not yet filed for a legal separation or divorce. If you are in this situation, you can't check the 2b box. Instead, you'll have to include your spouse's income in your current monthly income, which may temporarily put you over the top. Not to worry. On Line 17, you are allowed to deduct any of your spouse's income that isn't actually available to you, which should solve the problem.

Line 2c. If you are married but filing separately for reasons other than those stated in Line 2b, check this box and complete Lines 3 through 11 in Columns A and B.

Line 2d. If you are married and filing jointly, check this box and complete Lines 3 through 11 in Columns A and B.

CAUTION

Use the right figures. All figures you enter in Lines 3 through 11 must be averages of the six-month period that ends on the last day of the month before you file. For instance, if you file on September 9, the six-month period ends on August 31. If the amounts are the same for each of those six months (for example, because you've held the same job and worked the same amount of hours during that period), then use those amounts. If the amounts vary, add up everything you've earned in that category for the six-month period, then divide the total by six to get a monthly average. You should include all gross income you actually received during the six-month period, even if you earned it or became entitled

Sample Statement of Current Monthly Income and Means Test Calculation—page 1

B22A (Official Form 22A) (Chapter 7) (12/08)

In re **Annie Justine Kaye**
Debtor(s)

Case Number: ____________
(If known)

According to the information required to be entered on this statement (check one box as directed in Part I, III, or VI of this statement):

☐ **The presumption arises.**

■ **The presumption does not arise.**

☐ **The presumption is temporarily inapplicable.**

CHAPTER 7 STATEMENT OF CURRENT MONTHLY INCOME AND MEANS-TEST CALCULATION

In addition to Schedules I and J, this statement must be completed by every individual chapter 7 debtor, whether or not filing jointly. Unless the exclusion in Line 1C applies, joint debtors may complete a single statement. If the exclusion in Line 1C applies, each joint filer must complete a separate statement.

Part I. MILITARY AND NON-CONSUMER DEBTORS	
1A	**Disabled Veterans.** If you are a disabled veteran described in the Declaration in this Part IA, (1) check the box at the beginning of the Declaration, (2) check the box for "The presumption does not arise" at the top of this statement, and (3) complete the verification in Part VIII. Do not complete any of the remaining parts of this statement. ☐ **Declaration of Disabled Veteran.** By checking this box, I declare under penalty of perjury that I am a disabled veteran (as defined in 38 U.S.C. § 3741(1)) whose indebtedness occurred primarily during a period in which I was on active duty (as defined in 10 U.S.C. § 101(d)(1)) or while I was performing a homeland defense activity (as defined in 32 U.S.C. §901(1)).
1B	**Non-consumer Debtors.** If your debts are not primarily consumer debts, check the box below and complete the verification in Part VIII. Do not complete any of the remaining parts of this statement. ■ **Declaration of non-consumer debts.** By checking this box, I declare that my debts are not primarily consumer debts.
1C	**Reservists and National Guard Members; active duty or homeland defense activity.** Members of a reserve component of the Armed Forces and members of the National Guard who were called to active duty (as defined in 10 U.S.C. § 101(d)(1)) after September 11, 2001, for a period of at least 90 days, or who have performed homeland defense activity (as defined in 32 U.S.C. § 901(1)) for a period of at least 90 days, are excluded from all forms of means testing during the time of active duty or homeland defense activity and for 540 days thereafter (the "exclusion period"). If you qualify for this temporary exclusion, (1) check the appropriate boxes and complete any required information in the Declaration of Reservists and National Guard Members below, (2) check the box for "The presumption is temporarily inapplicable" at the top of this statement, and (3) complete the verification in Part VIII. **During your exclusion period you are not required to complete the balance of this form, but you must complete the form no later than 14 days after the date on which your exclusion period ends, unless the time for filing a motion raising the means test presumption expires in your case before your exclusion period ends.** ☐ **Declaration of Reservists and National Guard Members.** By checking this box and making the appropriate entries below, I declare that I am eligible for a temporary exclusion from means testing because, as a member of a reserve component of the Armed Forces or the National Guard a. ☐ I was called to active duty after September 11, 2001, for a period of at least 90 days and ☐ I remain on active duty /or/ ☐ I was released from active duty on _____, which is less than 540 days before this bankruptcy case was filed; OR b. ☐ I am performing homeland defense activity for a period of at least 90 days /or/ ☐ I performed homeland defense activity for a period of at least 90 days, terminating on _____, which is less than 540 days before this bankruptcy case was filed.

Sample Statement of Current Monthly Income and Means Test Calculation—page 2

B22A (Official Form 22A) (Chapter 7) (12/08) **2**

Part II. CALCULATION OF MONTHLY INCOME FOR § 707(b)(7) EXCLUSION			
2	**Marital/filing status.** Check the box that applies and complete the balance of this part of this statement as directed. a. ☐ Unmarried. **Complete only Column A ("Debtor's Income") for Lines 3-11.** b. ☐ Married, not filing jointly, with declaration of separate households. By checking this box, debtor declares under penalty of perjury: "My spouse and I are legally separated under applicable non-bankruptcy law or my spouse and I are living apart other than for the purpose of evading the requirements of § 707(b)(2)(A) of the Bankruptcy Code." **Complete only column A ("Debtor's Income") for Lines 3-11.** c. ☐ Married, not filing jointly, without the declaration of separate households set out in Line 2.b above. **Complete both Column A ("Debtor's Income") and Column B ("Spouse's Income") for Lines 3-11.** d. ☐ Married, filing jointly. **Complete both Column A ("Debtor's Income") and Column B ("Spouse's Income") for Lines 3-11.**		
	All figures must reflect average monthly income received from all sources, derived during the six calendar months prior to filing the bankruptcy case, ending on the last day of the month before the filing. If the amount of monthly income varied during the six months, you must divide the six-month total by six, and enter the result on the appropriate line.	**Column A** **Debtor's Income**	**Column B** **Spouse's Income**
3	**Gross wages, salary, tips, bonuses, overtime, commissions.**	$	$
4	**Income from the operation of a business, profession or farm.** Subtract Line b from Line a and enter the difference in the appropriate column(s) of Line 4. If you operate more than one business, profession or farm, enter aggregate numbers and provide details on an attachment. Do not enter a number less than zero. **Do not include any part of the business expenses entered on Line b as a deduction in Part V.** | | | Debtor | Spouse | | a. | Gross receipts | $ | $ | | b. | Ordinary and necessary business expenses | $ | $ | | c. | Business income | Subtract Line b from Line a | |	$	$
5	**Rents and other real property income.** Subtract Line b from Line a and enter the difference in the appropriate column(s) of Line 5. Do not enter a number less than zero. **Do not include any part of the operating expenses entered on Line b as a deduction in Part V.** | | | Debtor | Spouse | | a. | Gross receipts | $ | $ | | b. | Ordinary and necessary operating expenses | $ | $ | | c. | Rent and other real property income | Subtract Line b from Line a | |	$	$
6	**Interest, dividends, and royalties.**	$	$
7	**Pension and retirement income.**	$	$
8	**Any amounts paid by another person or entity, on a regular basis, for the household expenses of the debtor or the debtor's dependents, including child support paid for that purpose.** Do not include alimony or separate maintenance payments or amounts paid by your spouse if Column B is completed.	$	$
9	**Unemployment compensation.** Enter the amount in the appropriate column(s) of Line 9. However, if you contend that unemployment compensation received by you or your spouse was a benefit under the Social Security Act, do not list the amount of such compensation in Column A or B, but instead state the amount in the space below: | Unemployment compensation claimed to be a benefit under the Social Security Act | Debtor $ | Spouse $ |	$	$
10	**Income from all other sources.** Specify source and amount. If necessary, list additional sources on a separate page. **Do not include alimony or separate maintenance payments paid by your spouse if Column B is completed, but include all other payments of alimony or separate maintenance.** Do not include any benefits received under the Social Security Act or payments received as a victim of a war crime, crime against humanity, or as a victim of international or domestic terrorism. | | | Debtor | Spouse | | a. | | $ | $ | | b. | | $ | $ | Total and enter on Line 10	$	$
11	**Subtotal of Current Monthly Income for § 707(b)(7).** Add Lines 3 thru 10 in Column A, and, if Column B is completed, add Lines 3 through 10 in Column B. Enter the total(s).	$	$

to receive it before the six-month period began. (*In re Burrell*, 399 B.R. 620 (Bkrtcy C.D. Ill., 2008).)

Line 3. Enter your average monthly earnings over the last six months from gross wages, salary, tips, bonuses, overtime, and commissions. ("Gross" means before any taxes, Social Security benefits, or other amounts are withheld.)

Line 4. Deduct your ordinary and necessary business operating expenses from your gross receipts and enter the difference here. While your gross income from employment determines whether you fall under the median income, it's your net business income that you use if you are in business. Be prepared in the course of your bankruptcy to produce records that support the net income figure you enter here.

Line 5. Enter your average monthly rental income for the six-month period (if you have any), and deduct ordinary and necessary operating expenses for that same period.

Line 6. Enter your average monthly income from interest, dividends, and royalties over the last six months.

Line 7. Here's where you include your average monthly pension and retirement income. Don't include Social Security retirement benefits.

Line 8. Enter the monthly average of any amounts regularly contributed by someone else to your household income. If you are filing separately but your spouse's income is included in Column B, don't include any contributions that your spouse makes to your household—his or her income is already being taken into account.

Line 9. Your average monthly unemployment compensation goes here. If you want, you can argue that unemployment compensation should be excluded under the general Social Security exclusion (see *In re Munger*, 370 B.R. 21 (D. Mass. 2007) and *In re Sorrell*, 359 B.R. 167 (S.D. Ohio 2007)) and omit it from Columns A and B. However, you'll need to enter the amount you receive in the boxes supplied for this purpose. The main trend in bankruptcy courts is to count unemployment insurance as income, but this issue is still up in the air. It's a good idea to include this income on your first draft of the form. If you fail the means test but would pass it without your unemployment, go ahead and exclude it and see what happens. Your court may not count unemployment insurance payments as income.

Line 10. Insert the average monthly amount you received from any other source. Do not include money or benefits received under the SSI, SSA, or TANF programs. These are Social Security benefits and are excluded from your current monthly income computation.

Line 11. Compute the subtotals for column A and B (if used). Remember, these subtotals should reflect an average monthly figure for all of the items you entered in Lines 3 through 10.

Line 12. Add the subtotals for columns A and B together. This is what the new bankruptcy law calls your "current monthly income." Because it's a six-month average, it might not match your actual monthly income at the time you file, especially if you've closed your business or become unable to work in the last six months.

Part III: Application of § 707(b)(7) Exclusion

This is where the rubber meets the road: In this part, you must compare the current monthly income figure you calculated in Part II with the median family income for your state. If your income is more than the median, you'll have to fill out the rest of the form—and you may be barred from using Chapter 7. If your income is equal to or less than the median, you can skip the rest of the form and file your Chapter 7 papers.

Line 13. Convert your monthly figure on Line 12 to an annual figure by multiplying it by 12. This is your current annual income.

Line 14. Enter the median income for your state and household size. The most recent state median income figures as of the date this book is published are in Appendix B. To make sure that you are using the most current figures, however, you should visit the U.S. Trustee's website, www.justicej.gov/ust, and

Sample Statement of Current Monthly Income and Means Test Calculation—page 3

B22A (Official Form 22A) (Chapter 7) (12/08) 3

12	**Total Current Monthly Income for § 707(b)(7).** If Column B has been completed, add Line 11, Column A to Line 11, Column B, and enter the total. If Column B has not been completed, enter the amount from Line 11, Column A.	$
	Part III. APPLICATION OF § 707(b)(7) EXCLUSION	
13	**Annualized Current Monthly Income for § 707(b)(7).** Multiply the amount from Line 12 by the number 12 and enter the result.	$
14	**Applicable median family income.** Enter the median family income for the applicable state and household size. (This information is available by family size at www.usdoj.gov/ust/ or from the clerk of the bankruptcy court.) a. Enter debtor's state of residence: ______ b. Enter debtor's household size: ______	$
15	**Application of Section 707(b)(7).** Check the applicable box and proceed as directed. ☐ **The amount on Line 13 is less than or equal to the amount on Line 14.** Check the box for "The presumption does not arise" at the top of page 1 of this statement, and complete Part VIII; do not complete Parts IV, V, VI or VII. ☐ **The amount on Line 13 is more than the amount on Line 14.** Complete the remaining parts of this statement.	

Complete Parts IV, V, VI, and VII of this statement only if required. (See Line 15.)

	Part IV. CALCULATION OF CURRENT MONTHLY INCOME FOR § 707(b)(2)	
16	**Enter the amount from Line 12.**	$
17	**Marital adjustment.** If you checked the box at Line 2.c, enter on Line 17 the total of any income listed in Line 11, Column B that was NOT paid on a regular basis for the household expenses of the debtor or the debtor's dependents. Specify in the lines below the basis for excluding the Column B income (such as payment of the spouse's tax liability or the spouse's support of persons other than the debtor or the debtor's dependents) and the amount of income devoted to each purpose. If necessary, list additional adjustments on a separate page. If you did not check box at Line 2.c, enter zero. a. ______ $ b. ______ $ c. ______ $ d. ______ $ Total and enter on Line 17	$
18	**Current monthly income for § 707(b)(2).** Subtract Line 17 from Line 16 and enter the result.	$
	Part V. CALCULATION OF DEDUCTIONS FROM INCOME	
	Subpart A: Deductions under Standards of the Internal Revenue Service (IRS)	
19A	**National Standards: food, clothing and other items.** Enter in Line 19A the "Total" amount from IRS National Standards for Food, Clothing and Other Items for the applicable household size. (This information is available at www.usdoj.gov/ust/ or from the clerk of the bankruptcy court.)	$
19B	**National Standards: health care.** Enter in Line a1 below the amount from IRS National Standards for Out-of-Pocket Health Care for persons under 65 years of age, and in Line a2 the IRS National Standards for Out-of-Pocket Health Care for persons 65 years of age or older. (This information is available at www.usdoj.gov/ust/ or from the clerk of the bankruptcy court.) Enter in Line b1 the number of members of your household who are under 65 years of age, and enter in Line b2 the number of members of your household who are 65 years of age or older. (The total number of household members must be the same as the number stated in Line 14b.) Multiply Line a1 by Line b1 to obtain a total amount for household members under 65, and enter the result in Line c1. Multiply Line a2 by Line b2 to obtain a total amount for household members 65 and older, and enter the result in Line c2. Add Lines c1 and c2 to obtain a total health care amount, and enter the result in Line 19B. **Household members under 65 years of age**: a1. Allowance per member ___; b1. Number of members ___; c1. Subtotal ___ **Household members 65 years of age or older**: a2. Allowance per member ___; b2. Number of members ___; c2. Subtotal ___	$
20A	**Local Standards: housing and utilities; non-mortgage expenses.** Enter the amount of the IRS Housing and Utilities Standards; non-mortgage expenses for the applicable county and household size. (This information is available at www.usdoj.gov/ust/ or from the clerk of the bankruptcy court).	$

click "Means Testing Information." Scroll down a bit for the link to the state median income figures.

Line 15. Do the math. If your income figure exceeds the state median, check the bottom box on Line 15 and continue to Part IV.

If your income does not exceed the median, check the top box on Line 15, and sign and date the form in Part VIII. Then, return to the first page of the form, where you should check the bottom box ("The presumption does not arise") in the top, right-hand corner.

TIP

Consider postponing your filing. If you conclude that you'll have to take the means test, think about whether your income will decrease in the next few months. If your spouse recently lost a high-paying job or your business receipts have really declined, for example, your average income over the past six months might look pretty substantial. But in a few months, when you average in your lower earnings, it will come down quite a bit—perhaps even to less than the state median. If so, you might want to delay your bankruptcy filing if you can.

Part IV. Calculation of Current Monthly Income for § 707(b)(2)

This is the beginning of the means test. With a couple of exceptions, the values you will be entering in the form are fairly straightforward. The purpose of the means test is to find out whether you have enough income to pay some of your unsecured, nonpriority debts over a five-year period. (Your unsecured, nonpriority debts are those you listed in Schedule F, above.)

Line 16. Enter the total from Line 12.

Line 17. If you checked the box on Line 2c (married, not filing jointly, and not making the declaration in Line 2b), you can subtract any portion of your spouse's income (as listed in Line 11, Column B) that was NOT regularly contributed to your household expenses or those of your dependents. For example, if Line 11, Column B shows that your nonfiling spouse has a monthly income of $2,000, but your spouse contributes only $400 a month to your household, you can enter $1,600 here.

Line 18. Subtract the amount on Line 17 from the amount on Line 16. Enter the total here.

Part V. Calculation of Deductions From Income

In this part, you will figure out what expenses you can deduct from your current monthly income. After you subtract all allowed expenses, you will be left with your monthly disposable income—the amount you would have left over, in theory, to pay into a Chapter 13 plan.

Subpart A: Deductions under Standards of the Internal Revenue Service (IRS)

If you have to complete this part of the form—that is, if your current monthly income exceeds the state median income—you are not allowed to subtract all of your actual expenses. Instead, you must calculate some of your expenses according to standards set by the IRS. (The IRS uses these standards to decide how much a delinquent taxpayer should have to give the agency each month to repay back taxes on an installment plan.)

Line 19A. Enter the total IRS National Standards for Food, Clothing, and Other Items for your family size and income level. This is the amount the IRS believes you should get to spend for food, clothing, household supplies, personal care, and miscellaneous other items. You can get these figures from www.justice.gov/ust. Click "Means Testing Information," then scroll down to the correct link. You also can get these figures from your court clerk.

Line 19B. Enter the amount you are allowed to claim for health expenses from the IRS National Standards for Out-of Pocket Health Care. You can find these figures at www.justice.gov/ust. Click "Means Testing Information," then scroll down to the appropriate link. As you'll see, you can claim more for household members who are at least 65 years old, which is reflected on the form. You'll also see that the total amount you can claim is quite small; if you spend more than you're allowed to claim here, you can claim it on Line 31.

Line 20A. Enter the amount of the IRS Housing and Utilities Standards, nonmortgage expenses for your county and family size. Get these figures from www.justice.gov/ust. Click "Means Testing Information," then scroll down to the IRS Housing and Utilities Standards section and enter your state in the drop-down menu. Find the figures for your county and family size, then enter the figure that appears under the heading "Non-Mortgage."

Line 20B. On Line **a**, enter the amount of the IRS Housing and Utility Standards, mortgage/rental expenses for your county and family size. These figures appear on the U.S. Trustee's website, on the same chart as nonmortgage expenses—follow the instructions for Line 20A, above.

On Line **b**, enter the average monthly payment for any debts secured by your home, including a mortgage, home equity loan, taxes, and insurance. The average monthly payment is the total of all amounts contractually due to each secured creditor in the five years after you file for bankruptcy, divided by 60.

On Line **c**, subtract Line **b** from Line **a**. This may turn out to be a negative figure—if so, enter a zero in the right-hand column. Later in the means test, you'll be able to add your average monthly payment back in as an expense.

Line 21. If your actual rental or mortgage expense is higher than that allowed by the IRS, you can claim an adjustment here. For instance, if the IRS mortgage/rental expense for a family of two is $550, you pay an actual rent of $900, and that amount is average for the area in which you live, enter the additional $350 here and explain why you should be able to subtract it (that you couldn't possibly find housing in your area for less, for example).

Line 22A. You are entitled to claim an expense here regardless of whether you actually have a car. First, indicate the number of cars for which you pay operating expenses or for which somebody else contributes to the operating expenses as part of the amount entered on Line 8. If you don't have a car, enter the amount listed under "Public Transportation" from the IRS Local Transportation Expense Standards. You can find these at www.justice.gov/ust; click "Means Testing Information" and scroll down to the appropriate link, where you will choose your region. If you indicated that you have one or two cars, enter the amount listed for your region (and sometimes, your city) under "Operating Costs" in the same chart.

Line 22B. If you have a car and also use public transportation, you may claim a public transportation expense here. Find the correct amount by following the instructions for Line 22A, above.

Line 23. These are your expenses for owning or leasing a car. On Line 23a, enter the IRS Local Transportation Standards for ownership of a first car. This amount is actually a national figure; currently, it is $489. To make sure you are using the most up-to-date numbers, use www.legalconsumer.com or check the website of the U.S. Trustee, www.justice.gov/ust. Click "Means Testing Information." Then scroll down to the Local Transportation Expense Standards drop-down menu and choose your region. The ownership figure is near the bottom of the page.

CAUTION

If you aren't making payments, you might face a challenge. A dispute exists over whether you can claim this expense if you aren't paying for or leasing a car. Some U.S. Trustees (and courts) insist that you can't claim the expense. However, the National Association for Consumer Bankruptcy Attorneys has filed briefs arguing that you should be able to, because old cars wear out, and you will need to lease or buy a new car sometime during the next five years. Currently, the courts are split,

Sample Statement of Current Monthly Income and Means Test Calculation—page 4

B22A (Official Form 22A) (Chapter 7) (12/08) 4

20B	**Local Standards: housing and utilities; mortgage/rent expense.** Enter, in Line a below, the amount of the IRS Housing and Utilities Standards; mortgage/rent expense for your county and household size (this information is available at www.usdoj.gov/ust/ or from the clerk of the bankruptcy court); enter on Line b the total of the Average Monthly Payments for any debts secured by your home, as stated in Line 42; subtract Line b from Line a and enter the result in Line 20B. **Do not enter an amount less than zero.** a. IRS Housing and Utilities Standards; mortgage/rental expense — $ b. Average Monthly Payment for any debts secured by your home, if any, as stated in Line 42 — $ c. Net mortgage/rental expense — Subtract Line b from Line a.	$
21	**Local Standards: housing and utilities; adjustment.** If you contend that the process set out in Lines 20A and 20B does not accurately compute the allowance to which you are entitled under the IRS Housing and Utilities Standards, enter any additional amount to which you contend you are entitled, and state the basis for your contention in the space below: ____________________	$
22A	**Local Standards: transportation; vehicle operation/public transportation expense.** You are entitled to an expense allowance in this category regardless of whether you pay the expenses of operating a vehicle and regardless of whether you use public transportation. Check the number of vehicles for which you pay the operating expenses or for which the operating expenses are included as a contribution to your household expenses in Line 8. ☐ 0 ☐ 1 ☐ 2 or more. If you checked 0, enter on Line 22A the "Public Transportation" amount from IRS Local Standards: Transportation. If you checked 1 or 2 or more, enter on Line 22A the "Operating Costs" amount from IRS Local Standards: Transportation for the applicable number of vehicles in the applicable Metropolitan Statistical Area or Census Region. (These amounts are available at www.usdoj.gov/ust/ or from the clerk of the bankruptcy court.)	$
22B	**Local Standards: transportation; additional public transportation expense.** If you pay the operating expenses for a vehicle and also use public transportation, and you contend that you are entitled to an additional deduction for you public transportation expenses, enter on Line 22B the "Public Transportation" amount from IRS Local Standards: Transportation. (This amount is available at www.usdoj.gov/ust/ or from the clerk of the bankruptcy court.)	$
23	**Local Standards: transportation ownership/lease expense; Vehicle 1.** Check the number of vehicles for which you claim an ownership/lease expense. (You may not claim an ownership/lease expense for more than two vehicles.) ☐ 1 ☐ 2 or more. Enter, in Line a below, the "Ownership Costs" for "One Car" from the IRS Local Standards: Transportation (available at www.usdoj.gov/ust/ or from the clerk of the bankruptcy court); enter in Line b the total of the Average Monthly Payments for any debts secured by Vehicle 1, as stated in Line 42; subtract Line b from Line a and enter the result in Line 23. **Do not enter an amount less than zero.** a. IRS Transportation Standards, Ownership Costs — $ b. Average Monthly Payment for any debts secured by Vehicle 1, as stated in Line 42 — $ c. Net ownership/lease expense for Vehicle 1 — Subtract Line b from Line a.	$
24	**Local Standards: transportation ownership/lease expense; Vehicle 2.** Complete this Line only if you checked the "2 or more" Box in Line 23. Enter, in Line a below, the "Ownership Costs" for "One Car" from the IRS Local Standards: Transportation (available at www.usdoj.gov/ust/ or from the clerk of the bankruptcy court); enter in Line b the total of the Average Monthly Payments for any debts secured by Vehicle 2, as stated in Line 42; subtract Line b from Line a and enter the result in Line 24. **Do not enter an amount less than zero.** a. IRS Transportation Standards, Ownership Costs — $ b. Average Monthly Payment for any debts secured by Vehicle 2, as stated in Line 42 — $ c. Net ownership/lease expense for Vehicle 2 — Subtract Line b from Line a.	$
25	**Other Necessary Expenses: taxes.** Enter the total average monthly expense that you actually incur for all federal, state and local taxes, other than real estate and sales taxes, such as income taxes, self employment taxes, social security taxes, and Medicare taxes. **Do not include real estate or sales taxes.**	$
26	**Other Necessary Expenses: involuntary deductions for employment.** Enter the total average monthly payroll deductions that are required for your employment, such as retirement contributions, union dues, and uniform costs. **Do not include discretionary amounts, such as voluntary 401(k) contributions.**	$

and the issue will likely have to be decided by the U.S. Supreme Court. In the meantime, if you aren't making payments on your car, the best approach is to first take the means test without including the ownership expense and see whether you pass. If you do, then there is no problem. However, if you need this expense to pass the test, include it (and be prepared to argue with your trustee). See Ch. 12 for help with bankruptcy research and www.legalconsumer.com for an up-to-date table of courts and cases addressing this issue.

On Line 23b, enter your average monthly payment (over the next five years) for all debts secured by your first car. For example, assume you have three years left to pay on the car and the monthly payment is $350. The total amount you will owe in the next five years is $12,600 (36 months times $350). If you spread that amount over the next five years—by dividing the total by 60, the number of months in five years—you'll see that you have an average monthly payment of $210.

On Line 23c, subtract Line 23b from Line 23a and enter the result in the column on the right. Later on, if necessary, you will be able to deduct your car payments to figure out whether you have disposable income for a Chapter 13 plan.

Line 24. Complete this item only if you have a second car (and checked the "2 or more" box in Line 23). Follow the instructions for Line 23 to enter the required figures for your second car.

Line 25. Enter the total average monthly expense that you actually incur for all taxes *other than real estate or sales taxes*. Examples of taxes that you enter here are income taxes, self-employment taxes, Social Security taxes, and Medicare taxes. You may need to convert the amounts you're paid to a monthly figure. Once you have figured out how much you pay each month for each type of tax, add them all together and enter them in the column on the right.

Converting Taxes to a Monthly Figure

If you are paid weekly, biweekly, or twice a month, you will have to convert the tax amounts on your pay stubs to a monthly amount. And, if you pay quarterly taxes (estimated income taxes, for example), you'll need to convert that figure as well. Here's how to do it:

- Weekly taxes: multiply by 4.3 to get a monthly amount.
- Biweekly taxes: divide by 2 to get a weekly amount, then multiply by 4.3.
- Bimonthly taxes: divide by 2.
- Quarterly taxes: divide by 3.

Line 26. Enter all of your mandatory payroll deductions here. Use the conversion rules set out above to arrive at average monthly deductions. Make sure you deduct only mandatory deductions (such as mandatory retirement contributions, union dues, and uniform costs). Contributions to a 401(k) should not be included, because they are voluntary.

Line 27. Enter any monthly payments you make for term life insurance. Do not enter payments for any other type of insurance, such as credit insurance, car insurance, renter's insurance, insurance on the lives of your dependents, or whole life insurance on your own life. (Whole life insurance is the type that allows you to borrow against the policy.)

Line 28. Enter the amount of any payments you make pursuant to a court order. Child support and alimony are the most common examples, but you may also have to pay to satisfy a court money judgment or a criminal fine. Do not include court-ordered payments toward a child support or alimony arrearage; only the payments you need to stay current should be entered here.

Line 29. Enter the total monthly amount that you pay for:

- education required by your employer to keep your job, and

- the total monthly amount you pay for the education of a physically or mentally challenged dependent child for whom no public education providing similar services is available. Include in this amount the actual costs of after-school enrichment educational services for a physically or mentally challenged child, and the actual education expenses you are paying in support of an individual educational plan.

Line 30. Enter the average monthly expense of child care (including baby-sitting, preschool, nursery school, and regular child care. If your employment (and therefore, your need for child care) is seasonal, add your child care costs up for the year and divide the total by 12. Do not equate education with child care. For instance, child care for a child who is of public education school age should only cover the hours before and after school.

Line 31. Enter the average monthly amount you pay for out-of-pocket health care expenses, but only to the extent it exceeds the amount you were allowed to claim on Line 19B. Do not include payments for health insurance or health savings accounts; those go on Line 34.

Line 32. Enter the average monthly expenses you pay for any communication devices that are necessary for the health and welfare of you or your dependents. Examples provided by the form are cell phones, pagers, call waiting, caller identification, and special long distance or Internet services. Virtually all of these devices arguably are necessary for the health and welfare of your family. However, some expenses might not be allowed (for example, cell phones you use for your business, or broadband Internet service). When in doubt, list the expense.

Line 33. Add the expenses you entered in Lines 19 through 32 and put the total in the column at the right.

Subpart B: Additional Living Expense Deductions

The expenses in this subpart are allowed by the Bankruptcy Code, in addition to the IRS expenses. However, you can't list an expense twice; if you already claimed it in subpart A or on Lines 4 or 5 in Section II (business expenses), don't list it again here.

Line 34. Here, list your reasonably necessary monthly expenses for health insurance, disability insurance, and health savings accounts (HSAs) on the lines provided. The form was revised in 2008 to clarify that you can list a "reasonable" expense whether you actually pay that amount each month or not. If, however, you pay less than the reasonable amount you list, you must indicate how much you actually spend each month on the additional line provided. If the U.S. Trustee or one of your creditors later wants to challenge your expense claims—for example, to argue that you really have more disposable income than the form indicates—they can use this information.

Line 35. Anything you spend to care for a member of your household or immediate family because of the member's age, illness, or disability can be deducted here. If your contributions are episodic—a wheelchair here, a vacation with a companion there—estimate your average monthly expense and enter it here.

CAUTION

Your response here could affect eligibility for government benefits. Expenses you list here could render the person you are assisting ineligible for Social Security or other government benefits. For example, if you state that you are spending $500 a month for the care of a relative, and that relative is receiving SSI, your relative might receive a lower benefit amount each month, to reflect your contribution. Despite this possible consequence, if you are making such expenditures, you are required to disclose them here. If you find yourself in this predicament, talk to a lawyer.

Line 36. The average monthly expense for security systems and any other method of protecting your family should be entered here.

Line 37. If your actual home energy costs exceed the figure you entered on Line 20A, enter the extra amount you spend here. As the form indicates, you

Sample Statement of Current Monthly Income and Means Test Calculation—page 5

B22A (Official Form 22A) (Chapter 7) (12/08) 5

27	**Other Necessary Expenses: life insurance.** Enter total average monthly premiums that you actually pay for term life insurance for yourself. **Do not include premiums for insurance on your dependents, for whole life or for any other form of insurance.**	$
28	**Other Necessary Expenses: court-ordered payments.** Enter the total monthly amount that you are required to pay pursuant to the order of a court or administrative agency, such as spousal or child support payments. **Do not include payments on past due obligations included in Line 44.**	$
29	**Other Necessary Expenses: education for employment or for a physically or mentally challenged child.** Enter the total average monthly amount that you actually expend for education that is a condition of employment and for education that is required for a physically or mentally challenged dependent child for whom no public education providing similar services is available.	$
30	**Other Necessary Expenses: childcare.** Enter the total average monthly amount that you actually expend on childcare - such as baby-sitting, day care, nursery and preschool. **Do not include other educational payments.**	$
31	**Other Necessary Expenses: health care.** Enter the total average monthly amount that you actually expend on health care that is required for the health and welfare of yourself or your dependents, that is not reimbursed by insurance or paid by a health savings account, and that is in excess of the amount entered in Line 19B. **Do not include payments for health insurance or health savings accounts listed in Line 34.**	$
32	**Other Necessary Expenses: telecommunication services.** Enter the total average monthly amount that you actually pay for telecommunication services other than your basic home telephone and cell phone service - such as pagers, call waiting, caller id, special long distance, or internet service - to the extent necessary for your health and welfare or that of your dependents. **Do not include any amount previously deducted.**	$
33	**Total Expenses Allowed under IRS Standards.** Enter the total of Lines 19 through 32.	$
	Subpart B: Additional Living Expense Deductions **Note: Do not include any expenses that you have listed in Lines 19-32**	
34	**Health Insurance, Disability Insurance, and Health Savings Account Expenses.** List the monthly expenses in the categories set out in lines a-c below that are reasonably necessary for yourself, your spouse, or your dependents. a. Health Insurance $ b. Disability Insurance $ c. Health Savings Account $ Total and enter on Line 34. **If you do not actually expend this total amount,** state your actual total average monthly expenditures in the space below: $	$
35	**Continued contributions to the care of household or family members.** Enter the total average actual monthly expenses that you will continue to pay for the reasonable and necessary care and support of an elderly, chronically ill, or disabled member of your household or member of your immediate family who is unable to pay for such expenses.	$
36	**Protection against family violence.** Enter the total average reasonably necessary monthly expenses that you actually incurred to maintain the safety of your family under the Family Violence Prevention and Services Act or other applicable federal law. The nature of these expenses is required to be kept confidential by the court.	$
37	**Home energy costs.** Enter the total average monthly amount, in excess of the allowance specified by IRS Local Standards for Housing and Utilities, that you actually expend for home energy costs. **You must provide your case trustee with documentation of your actual expenses, and you must demonstrate that the additional amount claimed is reasonable and necessary.**	$
38	**Education expenses for dependent children less than 18.** Enter the total average monthly expenses that you actually incur, not to exceed $137.50 per child, for attendance at a private or public elementary or secondary school by your dependent children less than 18 years of age. **You must provide your case trustee with documentation of your actual expenses, and you must explain why the amount claimed is reasonable and necessary and not already accounted for in the IRS Standards.**	$

may need to prove this extra expense to the trustee. Whether you need to provide proof will depend on the results of this means test. If the amount you enter here is the deciding factor in determining that you don't have enough disposable income to fund a Chapter 13 plan, proof will definitely be required.

Line 38. This item is for money you spend on your children's education. If your average monthly expense is $137.50 or more, put $137.50 in this blank; that's the maximum you can deduct. Remember not to list an amount twice; if you already listed an expense on Line 29 or 30, for example, don't repeat it here.

Line 39. Here, you can list the amount by which your actual expenses for food and clothing exceed the IRS allowance for these items as entered in Line 19. However, you cannot list more than 5% over the IRS allowance.

Line 40. If you have been making charitable contributions to an organization before your bankruptcy filing date, you can enter them here as long as the group is organized and operated exclusively for religious, charitable, scientific, literary, or educational purposes; to foster national or international amateur sports competition (but only if no part of its activities involve the provision of athletic facilities or equipment); or for the prevention of cruelty to children or animals. The organization also can't be disqualified from tax exemption status because of its political activities.

Line 41. Enter the total of Lines 34 through 40 in the column on the right.

Subpart C: Deductions for Debt Payment

Here, you deduct average monthly payments you will have to make on secured debts over the next five years. Once you complete this section, you can put all the numbers together to figure out whether you pass the means test.

Most courts to consider the issue have held that debtors are entitled to list all payments on secured debts they are contractually obligated to make, even if they aren't paying them. For example, if you haven't paid your mortgage for months or are even in foreclosure, these courts would allow you to list the required payments anyway as deductions against your income. Other courts won't allow this, however. If you don't know how your local bankruptcy court deals with this issue, don't include any payments you aren't actually making on your first round of calculations. If you pass the means test without these payments, great! If you need to deduct the payments to pass the means test, however, go back and include them; you may need to argue your side in front of the judge. (See Ch. 12 for suggestions on legal research; you can find citations to cases addressing this issue at www.legalconsumer.com.)

Line 42. List the average monthly payment you will have to make over the next five years to creditors that hold a secured interest in your property (for example, the mortgage holder on your house, a creditor holding your car note, or a business creditor who has a secured interest in your business equipment, inventory, or other assets). As explained in the instructions for Line 23, you can calculate this amount by figuring out the total amount you will owe over the next five years, then dividing that total by 60.

Line 43. Here, list the average monthly payments you would have to make to pay off any *past amounts* due to creditors for property that you must keep to support yourself or your dependents. Property necessary for support typically includes a car, your home, and any property you need for your employment. Past-due business obligations should not be listed here. Come up with the monthly figure you have to enter here by dividing the total amount you would have to pay by 60.

Line 44. List the average monthly amount you will have to pay for priority claims over the next five years. Your priority claims are all claims you listed earlier in Schedule E. Divide by 60 to arrive at the monthly average.

Line 45. Here, you must calculate the fee that the trustee would charge if you ended up in Chapter 13 bankruptcy. That fee would depend

Sample Statement of Current Monthly Income and Means Test Calculation—page 6

B22A (Official Form 22A) (Chapter 7) (12/08) **6**

39	**Additional food and clothing expense.** Enter the total average monthly amount by which your food and clothing expenses exceed the combined allowances for food and clothing (apparel and services) in the IRS National Standards, not to exceed 5% of those combined allowances. (This information is available at www.usdoj.gov/ust/ or from the clerk of the bankruptcy court.) **You must demonstrate that the additional amount claimed is reasonable and necessary.**	$
40	**Continued charitable contributions.** Enter the amount that you will continue to contribute in the form of cash or financial instruments to a charitable organization as defined in 26 U.S.C. § 170(c)(1)-(2).	$
41	**Total Additional Expense Deductions under § 707(b).** Enter the total of Lines 34 through 40	$

Subpart C: Deductions for Debt Payment

42	**Future payments on secured claims.** For each of your debts that is secured by an interest in property that you own, list the name of the creditor, identify the property securing the debt, and state the Average Monthly Payment, and check whether the payment includes taxes or insurance. The Average Monthly Payment is the total of all amounts scheduled as contractually due to each Secured Creditor in the 60 months following the filing of the bankruptcy case, divided by 60. If necessary, list additional entries on a separate page. Enter the total of the Average Monthly Payments on Line 42.	$

	Name of Creditor	Property Securing the Debt	Average Monthly Payment	Does payment include taxes or insurance?
a.			$	☐yes ☐no
			Total: Add Lines	

43	**Other payments on secured claims.** If any of debts listed in Line 42 are secured by your primary residence, a motor vehicle, or other property necessary for your support or the support of your dependents, you may include in your deduction 1/60th of any amount (the "cure amount") that you must pay the creditor in addition to the payments listed in Line 42, in order to maintain possession of the property. The cure amount would include any sums in default that must be paid in order to avoid repossession or foreclosure. List and total any such amounts in the following chart. If necessary, list additional entries on a separate page.	$

	Name of Creditor	Property Securing the Debt	1/60th of the Cure Amount
a.			$
			Total: Add Lines

44	**Payments on prepetition priority claims.** Enter the total amount, divided by 60, of all priority claims, such as priority tax, child support and alimony claims, for which you were liable at the time of your bankruptcy filing. **Do not include current obligations, such as those set out in Line 28.**	$
45	**Chapter 13 administrative expenses.** If you are eligible to file a case under Chapter 13, complete the following chart, multiply the amount in line a by the amount in line b, and enter the resulting administrative expense.	$

a.	Projected average monthly Chapter 13 plan payment.	$
b.	Current multiplier for your district as determined under schedules issued by the Executive Office for United States Trustees. (This information is available at www.usdoj.gov/ust/ or from the clerk of the bankruptcy court.)	x
c.	Average monthly administrative expense of Chapter 13 case	Total: Multiply Lines a and b

46	**Total Deductions for Debt Payment.** Enter the total of Lines 42 through 45.	$

Subpart D: Total Deductions from Income

47	**Total of all deductions allowed under § 707(b)(2).** Enter the total of Lines 33, 41, and 46.	$

Part VI. DETERMINATION OF § 707(b)(2) PRESUMPTION

48	**Enter the amount from Line 18 (Current monthly income for § 707(b)(2))**	$
49	**Enter the amount from Line 47 (Total of all deductions allowed under § 707(b)(2))**	$
50	**Monthly disposable income under § 707(b)(2).** Subtract Line 49 from Line 48 and enter the result.	$
51	**60-month disposable income under § 707(b)(2).** Multiply the amount in Line 50 by the number 60 and enter the result.	$

on how much you would be paying, through the trustee, to your secured and unsecured creditors. It's impossible to come up with a figure at this point in the form, so leave it blank for now.

You don't have to complete this section if you pass the means test without it. However, if you leave this blank on your initial pass through the form and your disposable income, from Line 51, is over the limit, follow these instructions to come up with a figure for Line 45:

Add Lines 42, 43, and 44.

Divide the total on Line 54 by 60 (for the average monthly payment you would have to make to pay down 25% of your unsecured debt over five years).

Add this number to the total of Lines 42, 43, and 44, and put the result on Line 45a. This is the average amount you would have to pay into a Chapter 13 plan to cover your secured debts, arrearages on those debts, priority debts, and 25% of your unsecured debts.

On Line 45b, enter the multiplier percentage from the U.S. Trustee's website for your state and district. Go to www.justice.gov/ust, click "Means Testing Information," scroll down to the section called "Administrative Expenses Multiplier" and click "Schedules," then scroll down to your district to get the percentage.

Multiply Line 45a by Line 45b and enter the result in the column on the right.

Line 46. Add Lines 42 through 45, and enter the total in the column on the right.

Subpart D: Total Deductions from Income.

Enter the total of Lines 33, 41, and 46 in the column at the right. This is the total amount you can subtract from your current monthly expenses to arrive at your disposable income.

Part VI: Determination of § 707(b)(2) Presumption

This is where you find out whether you received a passing grade on the means test.

Line 48. Enter the amount from Line 18 in the column on the right.

Line 49. Enter the amount from Line 47 in the column on the right.

Line 50. Subtract Line 49 from Line 48 and enter the result in the column on the right.

Line 51. Multiply the total from Line 50 by 60 (to find out how much disposable income you will have over the next five years, according to these figures). Enter the result in the column on the right.

Line 52. Here you must check one of three boxes. If the amount on Line 51 is less than $6,575, check the top box. This means that you don't have enough money left over to make a Chapter 13 plan feasible, so you can file for Chapter 7. If the total on Line 51 is more than $10,950, you have enough income to make a Chapter 13 plan feasible, and you probably won't be allowed to stay in Chapter 7. If your total is at least $6,575 but no more than $10,950, you will have to do a few more calculations to figure out where you fall.

If you checked the top box, go back to the first page and check the bottom box at the top, right-hand side of the page ("The presumption does not arise"). Then, complete the verification in Part VIII below.

If you checked the middle box, go back to Page One, check the top box ("The presumption arises"), and complete the verification in Part VIII.

If you checked the bottom box, continue on to Line 53.

Line 53. Enter the total nonpriority, unsecured debt that you entered in your Schedule F, above.

CAUTION

Don't double a debt for duplicate creditors. To get an accurate result here, you must make sure that you didn't duplicate the amount of any debt for which you have more than one creditor on Schedule F. If you did, go back and recalculate the total on your Schedule F, adding each debt only once even though you are listing two or more creditors for a specific debt (for instance the original debtor, a collection agency, and an attorney).

Sample Statement of Current Monthly Income and Means Test Calculation—page 7

B22A (Official Form 22A) (Chapter 7) (12/08) 7

52	**Initial presumption determination.** Check the applicable box and proceed as directed. ☐ **The amount on Line 51 is less than $6,575.** Check the box for "The presumption does not arise" at the top of page 1 of this statement, and complete the verification in Part VIII. Do not complete the remainder of Part VI. ☐ **The amount set forth on Line 51 is more than $10,950** Check the box for "The presumption arises" at the top of page 1 of this statement, and complete the verification in Part VIII. You may also complete Part VII. Do not complete the remainder of Part VI. ☐ **The amount on Line 51 is at least $6,575, but not more than $10,950.** Complete the remainder of Part VI (Lines 53 through 55).	
53	**Enter the amount of your total non-priority unsecured debt**	$
54	**Threshold debt payment amount.** Multiply the amount in Line 53 by the number 0.25 and enter the result.	$
55	**Secondary presumption determination.** Check the applicable box and proceed as directed. ☐ **The amount on Line 51 is less than the amount on Line 54.** Check the box for "The presumption does not arise" at the top of page 1 of this statement, and complete the verification in Part VIII. ☐ **The amount on Line 51 is equal to or greater than the amount on Line 54.** Check the box for "The presumption arises" at the top of page 1 of this statement, and complete the verification in Part VIII. You may also complete Part VII.	

Part VII. ADDITIONAL EXPENSE CLAIMS

56 **Other Expenses.** List and describe any monthly expenses, not otherwise stated in this form, that are required for the health and welfare of you and your family and that you contend should be an additional deduction from your current monthly income under § 707(b)(2)(A)(ii)(I). If necessary, list additional sources on a separate page. All figures should reflect your average monthly expense for each item. Total the expenses.

	Expense Description	Monthly Amount
a.		$
b.		$
c.		$
d.		$
	Total: Add Lines a, b, c, and d	$

Part VIII. VERIFICATION

57 I declare under penalty of perjury that the information provided in this statement is true and correct. *(If this is a joint case, both debtors must sign.)*

Date: ____________ Signature: ____________

Annie Justine Kaye
(Debtor)

Line 54. Multiply the amount on Line 53 by the number 0.25 and enter the result in the box on the right. This is equal to 25% of your total nonpriority, unsecured debt.

Line 55. Here, you determine whether the income you have left over (listed on Line 51) is sufficient to pay 25% of your unsecured, nonpriority debt (listed on Line 54). If Line 51 is less than Line 54, congratulations: You have passed the means test. Go back to the first page, check the bottom box at the top right-hand side of the page ("The presumption does not arise") and complete the verification in Part VIII below.

If Line 51 is greater than Line 54, you have failed the means test. The form instructs you to go back to the first page, check the top box at the top right-hand side of the page ("The presumption arises"), and complete the verification.

If you don't pass the means test, you can complete Part VII, in which you list additional expenses that were somehow not included in the earlier parts of the form. Those expenses will be taken into account by the U.S. Trustee as long as they don't duplicate earlier expenses and are reasonably necessary to support you and your family. In one case, for example, a married couple who filed jointly both had jobs in rural communities that required them to drive enormous distances. By documenting the travel expenses, which were not adequately covered in the means test transportation allowance, they were able to reduce their disposable income below the means test threshold. (*In re Batzkeil*, 349 B.R. 581 (N.D. Iowa 2006).)

If you have to check the "presumption arises" box, the U.S. Trustee will issue a notice and schedule a hearing at which the judge will be asked either to dismiss your case or convert it to Chapter 13. This is something that you probably don't want. What to do? Before completing Part VIII, we suggest that you go back over the form and carefully examine the expense items that aren't mandated by the IRS. Often, people underestimate their actual expenses. If you find that you underestimated one or more expenses, or left out an expense that is provided for in the form, make the adjustments and see whether you can get a passing grade. Because this form is so complex, we recommend that you go through it at least twice before arriving at your final figures.

SEE AN EXPERT

See a lawyer if the presumption arises and you want to stay in Chapter 7. If you have to check the box stating that the presumption (of abuse) arises, your Chapter 7 filing is in trouble. Unless you are willing to proceed under Chapter 13, or have your bankruptcy dismissed, we strongly suggest that you find a bankruptcy lawyer to help you.

Form 201A—Notice to Consumer Debtors Under § 342(b) of the Bankruptcy Code

This form, required by the revised bankruptcy law, gives you some information about credit counseling and the various chapters of bankruptcy available. It also warns you sternly of the consequences of lying on your bankruptcy papers, concealing assets, and failing to file the required forms on time.

You can find a blank copy of the form in Appendix C. You don't have to file it with your bankruptcy paperwork. Your signature on the bankruptcy petition indicates that you have received and read this notice. (Although there is a separate certification form—Form 201B—indicating that you have read and received this notice, you don't have to sign or file it unless you failed to sign the petition for some reason.)

Mailing Matrix

As part of your bankruptcy filing, you are required to submit a list of all of your creditors so the court can give them official notice of your bankruptcy. Called the "mailing matrix," this list must be prepared in a specific format prescribed by your local bankruptcy court. Your court may also require you to submit a declaration, or "verification," stating that your list is correct (as always, be sure to check your court's local rules). In a few courts, the form consists of boxes on a page in which you enter the names and addresses of your creditors. This is an artifact from the time when the trustee would use the form to prepare mailing labels.

Now, however, most courts ask you to submit the list on a computer disk in a particular word processing format, or at least submit a computer printout of the names so that they can be scanned. You should check with the bankruptcy court clerk or the court's local rules to learn the precise format. Then, take these steps:

Step 1: Make a list of all of your creditors, in alphabetical order. You can copy them from Schedules D, E, F, and H. Be sure to include cosigners and joint debtors. If, however, you and your spouse jointly incurred a debt and are filing jointly, don't include your spouse. Also include collection agencies, sheriffs, and attorneys who either have sued you or are trying to collect the debt. And, if you're seeking to discharge marital debts you assumed during a divorce, include both your ex-spouse and the creditors. Finally, if you have two or more debts owed to the same creditor at the same address, you can just list one.

Step 2: Make several copies of the mailing matrix form in Appendix C.

Step 3: If you are using the "box" format, enter your name and address in the top left-hand box on the sheet you designate as the first page. Then enter the names and addresses of each creditor, one per box and in alphabetical order (or in the order required by your local bankruptcy court). Use as many sheets as you need.

It is very important to be complete when preparing the matrix. If you leave a creditor off the matrix and the creditor does not find out about your bankruptcy by some other means, that debt may survive your bankruptcy—and you will have to pay it down the line. However, if you have no assets to be distributed (as is typically the case), the debt will still be discharged, unless the creditor could have successfully challenged the discharge had it known of your bankruptcy. See Ch. 11 for more information.

How to File Your Papers

Gather up all of the forms you have completed, as well as the documents you gathered at the beginning of this chapter. Make sure you have everything on the Bankruptcy Form Checklist and Bankruptcy Documents Checklist (you can find them in Appendix B). If you use a petition preparer, there will be several additional forms to file.

Basic Filing Procedures

Once you've got all of your papers together, follow these filing instructions.

Step 1: Put all your bankruptcy forms in the proper order.

Step 2: Check that you, and your spouse if you're filing a joint petition, have signed and dated each form where required.

Step 3: Make the required number of copies, plus one additional copy for you to keep just in case your papers are lost in the mail (if you file by mail). In addition, make:

- one extra copy of the Statement of Intention for each person listed on that form, and
- one extra copy of the Statement of Intention for the trustee.

Step 4: Unless the court clerk will hole-punch your papers when you file them, use a standard two-hole punch (copy centers have them) to punch the top center of your original set of bankruptcy papers. Don't staple any forms together.

Step 5: If you plan to mail your documents to the court, address a 9" × 12" envelope to yourself and affix adequate postage to handle one copy of all the paperwork. Although many people prefer to file by mail, we recommend that you personally take your papers to the bankruptcy court clerk if at all possible. Going to the court will give you a chance to correct minor mistakes on the spot.

Step 6: If you can pay the filing fee, clip or staple a money order to the petition, payable to the U.S. Trustee (courts won't accept a check). If you want to pay in installments, attach a completed Application and Order to Pay Filing Fee in Installments (Form 3A), plus any additional papers required by your court's local rules (see "Paying in Installments," below). If you have paid an attorney for help with your bankruptcy, you don't qualify for installment payments. If you don't think you can afford installment payments, you may be able to obtain a fee waiver. Use Form 3B (included in Appendix C) for this purpose. For both installment payments and fee waivers, you'll have to appear before the bankruptcy judge to justify your request.

Step 7: Take or mail the original and copies of all forms to the correct bankruptcy court.

Serving the Statement of Intention

The bankruptcy rules require you to serve (by mail) the Statement of Intention on each creditor listed on the statement. You have between 30 and 45 days to do this. We recommend you do it immediately so you don't forget. If you don't serve your Statement of Intention on time, the creditor can repossess the collateral. The trustee must also be served. The trustee's contact information will be provided either on the copy of your papers that the clerk returns to you or on the notice of filing you receive several days after you file.

Have a friend or relative (other than your spouse, if you are filing jointly) over the age of 18 mail, by first class, a copy of your Statement of Intention to the bankruptcy trustee and to all the creditors listed on that form. Be sure to keep the original.

On a Proof of Service by Mail (a copy is in Appendix C), enter the name and complete address of the trustee and all creditors to whom your friend or relative sent your Statement of Intention. Have that person sign and date the Proof of Service.

Paying in Installments

You can pay in up to four installments over 120 days if the judge approves. You can ask the judge to give you extra time for a particular installment, but all installments ultimately must be paid within 180 days after you file. You'll probably have to appear at a separate hearing a couple of weeks after you file to make your case for installment payments before the bankruptcy judge. If the judge refuses your request, you will be given some time to come up with the fees (probably ten days, perhaps longer). Because of this "appearance before the judge" requirement, many debtors prefer to raise the whole fee before filing and hopefully get through their entire bankruptcy without ever meeting up with the judge.

If you are applying to pay in installments, you must file a completed Form 3A (Application and Order to Pay Filing Fee in Installments) when you file your petition. You can find a blank copy of this form in Appendix C. You cannot apply for permission to pay in installments if you've paid an attorney to help you with your bankruptcy.

The application is easy to fill out. At the top, fill in the name of the court (this is on Form 1—Voluntary Petition), your name (and your spouse's name if you're filing jointly), and "7" in the blank after "Chapter." Leave the Case No. space blank. Then enter:

- the total filing fee you must pay: $299 (Item 1)
- the amount you propose to pay when you file the petition (Item 4, first blank)
- the number of additional installments you need (the total maximum is four), and
- the amount and date you propose for each installment payment (Item 4, second, third, and fourth blanks).

You (and your spouse, if you're filing jointly) must sign and date the application. Leave the rest blank. As mentioned, you may be required to appear for a hearing at which the judge will decide whether to approve or modify your application.

Waiver of Filing Fee

You also may apply to have your fees waived altogether by filing Form 3B. This form is fairly complex and asks for a lot of the information you've provided in the schedules completed earlier in this chapter. A blank copy of this form is in Appendix C and on the official U.S. Courts website at www.uscourts.gov. There is some doubt as to whether the courts will grant this benefit even if you qualify on economic grounds, but there is no harm in trying (other than perhaps having to take time off work to appear before the judge and justify your request). If you receive a waiver and it later turns out that you could pay the fee, the court can revoke your waiver (*In re Kauffman*, No. 06-10325 (D. Vt. 2006)).

Emergency Filing

If you want to file for bankruptcy in a hurry to get an automatic stay, you can accomplish that (in most places) by filing Form 1—Voluntary Petition, the mailing matrix, and Form 21 (Statement of Social Security Number). Some courts also require you to file a cover sheet and an Order Dismissing Chapter 7 Case, which will be processed if you don't file the rest of your papers within 14 days. (Bankruptcy Rule 1007(c).) If the bankruptcy court in your district requires this form, you can get it from the court (possibly on its website), a local bankruptcy attorney, or a bankruptcy petition preparer.

If you don't follow up by filing the additional documents within 14 days, your bankruptcy case will be dismissed. You can file again, if necessary. You'll have to ask the court to keep the automatic stay in effect once 30 days have passed after you file. (See Ch. 4.)

For an emergency filing, follow these steps:

Step 1: Check with the court to find out exactly what forms must be submitted for an emergency filing.

Step 2: Fill in Form 1—Voluntary Petition, including Exhibit D.

Step 3: On a mailing matrix (or whatever other form is required by your court), list all your creditors, as well as collection agencies, sheriffs, attorneys, and others who are seeking to collect debts from you.

Step 4: Fill in the Statement of Social Security number and any other papers the court requires.

Step 5: File the originals and the required number of copies, accompanied by your fee (or an application for payment of fee in installments) and a self-addressed envelope with the bankruptcy court. Keep copies of everything for your records.

Step 6: File all other required forms within 14 days. If you don't, your case will probably be dismissed.

After You File

Filing a bankruptcy petition has a dramatic effect on your creditors and your property.

The Automatic Stay

The instant you file for Chapter 7 bankruptcy, your creditors are subject to the automatic stay, as described in detail in Ch. 4. If you haven't read that chapter, now is the time to do it.

Property Ownership

When you file your bankruptcy papers, the trustee becomes the owner of all the property in your bankruptcy estate as of that date. (See Ch. 5 for an explanation of what's in your bankruptcy estate.) However, the trustee won't actually take physical control of the property. Most, if not all, of your property will be exempt, which means it will return to your legal possession after your bankruptcy is closed. If you have any questions about dealing with property after you file, ask the trustee or the trustee's staff.

While your bankruptcy is pending, do not throw out, give away, sell, or otherwise dispose of the property you owned as of your filing date—unless and until the bankruptcy trustee says otherwise. Even if all of your property is exempt, you are expected to hold on to it, in case the trustee or a creditor challenges your exemption claims.

What Happens to Business Property

If you are operating a business that has valuable property or inventory, you may have to shut down once you file your bankruptcy—at least temporarily—unless the trustee is willing to quickly assess the nature and value of your business assets. This shut-down period may last for a couple of months or even longer. On the other hand, if your business is service-oriented and lacks machines or inventory, you may be able to continue in business without interruption.

As a general rule, corporations and other business entities aren't part of a personal bankruptcy. However, if you (or you and your spouse) are the sole or majority owner of an entity, the trustee can legally "step into your shoes," vote your shares to dissolve the business, and sell off whatever inventory and assets you can't protect under your personal exemptions such as they are. Because it takes some time to assess business assets and go through the necessary corporate procedures, you would have to shut down your business at least while that process is going on. And if you aren't able to exempt your business assets, you'll probably have to shut down for good.

If some of your property is nonexempt, the trustee may ask you to turn it over. Or, the trustee may decide that the property is worth too little to bother with and abandon it. (Typically, the trustee doesn't let you know that property is abandoned, but once you receive your discharge, the property is legally considered abandoned.)

You are allowed to spend cash you had when you filed (declared on Schedule B) to make day-to-day purchases for necessities such as groceries, personal effects, and clothing. Just make sure you can account for what happened to that cash: You may need to reimburse the bankruptcy estate if the money wasn't exempt and the trustee disapproves your purchases.

In a Chapter 7 case, with a few exceptions, the trustee has no claim to property you acquire or income you earn after you file. You are free to spend it as you please. The exceptions are: property from an insurance settlement, marital settlement agreement, or inheritance that you become entitled to receive within 180 days after your filing date. (See Ch. 5.)

CHAPTER

10

Handling Your Case in Court

For most people, the Chapter 7 bankruptcy process is fairly straightforward. In fact, it proceeds pretty much on automatic pilot. The bankruptcy trustee decides what property you will have to surrender (if any), whether your papers pass muster, and, if not, what amendments you need to file. Ordinarily, you have few decisions to make.

This chapter tells you how to handle the routine procedures that move your bankruptcy case along, and how to deal with complications that may arise if any of the following occur:

- You or the trustee discovers an error in your papers.
- A creditor asks the court to lift the automatic stay.
- A creditor objects to the discharge of a particular debt.
- A creditor or the trustee objects to your claim that an item of property is exempt.
- The trustee demands that you turn over nonexempt property.
- You decide to dismiss your case or convert it to another type of bankruptcy, such as a Chapter 13 bankruptcy.
- Your case is dismissed, and you want to refile it and keep the protection of the automatic stay.

Some of these problems—fixing a simple error in your papers, for example—you can handle yourself. For more complicated problems, such as fighting a creditor in court about the discharge of a large debt or a disagreement as to whether property is exempt, you'll probably need a lawyer's help.

RESOURCE

If you're going to court. If you will have to appear before the bankruptcy judge, your first step should be to take a look at *Represent Yourself in Court,* by Paul Bergman and Sara Berman (Nolo). In addition to valuable information about handling federal court proceedings, this book has a special chapter on litigation in bankruptcy court.

Routine Bankruptcy Procedures

A routine Chapter 7 bankruptcy case takes three to six months from beginning to end and follows a series of predictable steps.

The Court Sends a Notice of Bankruptcy Filing

Shortly after you file for bankruptcy, the court sends an official notice to you and all of the creditors listed in your mailing matrix. This notice contains several crucial pieces of information.

Your Filing Date and Case Number

This information puts your creditors on notice that you have filed for bankruptcy and gives them a reference number to use when seeking information about your case.

Whether the Case Is an Asset Case or a No-Asset Case

When you filled in the bankruptcy petition, you had to check one of the following two boxes:

- ☐ Debtor estimates that funds will be available for distribution to unsecured creditors.
- ☐ Debtor estimates that, after any exempt property is excluded and administrative expenses paid, there will be no funds available for distribution to unsecured creditors.

The box you check determines the type of notice the court sends to your creditors. If you checked the first box, your case is known as an "asset case" and your creditors will be advised to file a claim describing what you owe them. If you checked the second box, your case will be known as a "no-asset" case and your creditors will be told to not file a claim. However, they will also be informed that they will have an opportunity to file a claim later if it turns out that there are assets available after all.

The Date of the Creditors' Meeting

The notice also sets a date for the meeting of creditors (also called the "341 meeting"), usually

How a Routine Chapter 7 Bankruptcy Proceeds

Step	Description	When It Happens
You begin your case by filing bankruptcy papers.	You file the petition and supporting schedules with the bankruptcy clerk, who scans them into the court records.	When you decide to do so. Once you file, your creditors are barred from taking collection actions.
The court notifies creditors that you have filed for bankruptcy.	A notice of your filing is mailed to you and your creditors, stating the date of the creditors' meeting and contact information for the trustee.	A few days after you file.
The court assigns a trustee to the case.	The trustee's job is to review your paperwork and take possession of any nonexempt property.	When the notice to creditors is mailed.
You provide your most recent tax return to the trustee.	You must give the trustee your most recent tax return but can black out sensitive information such as your Social Security number and date of birth.	At least seven days before the creditors' meeting.
The creditors' meeting is held.	Unless you are reaffirming a secured debt (which requires a hearing before a judge), the creditors' meeting is the only personal appearance you will make. The judge is not there and creditors seldom attend. The trustee questions you about your paperwork. Most meetings last only a few minutes.	Between 20 and 40 days after the date you file.
The means test is applied in appropriate cases.	The U.S. Trustee may start a process leading to dismissal or conversion of your case to Chapter 13 if your papers show that you have adequate income to fund a repayment plan.	The U.S. Trustee must file a statement within ten days after the creditors' meeting if it appears from the paperwork or information gleaned in the creditors' meeting that your income is more than the state median and you can't pass the means test.
Negotiations are held regarding nonexempt property, if any.	If you have nonexempt property, the trustee will give you a chance to buy it back. Otherwise, the trustee will require you to hand over the property so it can be sold for the benefit of your unsecured creditors.	Within 60 days after the meeting of creditors.
Secured property is dealt with.	If you owe money on property you want to keep, you must either redeem or reaffirm the debt unless the lender agrees to let you keep it as long as you remain current on your payments (the ride-through option).	Within 30 days after the creditors' meeting.
You attend budget counseling.	You must undergo personal financial management (budget) counseling before you can get your discharge.	Within 45 days after the creditors' meeting, you must certify that you completed counseling (Form 23).
The court holds a reaffirmation hearing.	If you sign and file a reaffirmation agreement and aren't represented by a lawyer, you must attend a court hearing. If the judge disapproves of the reaffirmation, you can still keep the property as long as you remain current on your payments.	Roughly 60 days after your creditors' meeting.
The court grants your discharge.	The court mails a notice of discharge that discharges all debts that can legally be discharged, unless the court has ruled otherwise in your bankruptcy case. The automatic stay is lifted at this time.	Roughly 90 days after you file.
Your case is closed	The trustee distributes any property collected from you to your unsecured creditors.	A few days or weeks after your discharge, or longer if the trustee believes that keeping the case open will add assets to your bankruptcy estate.

several weeks later. Mark this date carefully—it is very important for several reasons.

- You must attend the creditors' meeting; if you don't, your case can be dismissed (although you'll probably be given another opportunity to appear at a rescheduled meeting).
- Your creditors must file their claims (if it is an asset case) within 30 days after this meeting.
- Your creditors must file any objections they have to the discharge of their debts within 60 days after this meeting.

Contact Information for the Trustee

The notice of filing will also provide the name, address, and telephone number of the trustee assigned to your case. You probably won't receive the trustee's email address, even though almost all trustees prefer to communicate electronically. If you use email, call the trustee's office, get the trustee's email address, and communicate via email if possible. This is where you'll need to send a copy of your most recently filed federal tax return, as explained below.

Your Creditors Must Cease Most Collection Actions

The automatic stay goes into effect the moment you file your bankruptcy papers. The automatic stay prohibits most creditors and government support entities from taking any action to collect the debts you owe them until the court says otherwise.

There are some notable exceptions to the automatic stay, however. Even if you file for bankruptcy, the following proceedings can continue:

- A criminal case can proceed against you.
- A case to establish paternity or to establish, modify, or collect child support or alimony can go forward.
- A tax audit, the issuance of a tax deficiency notice, a demand for a tax return, the issuance of a tax assessment, and the demand for payment of such an assessment can all take place. The IRS cannot, however, record a lien or seize your property after you file for bankruptcy.
- Evictions from residential premises can go forward in some circumstances.

(Ch. 4 provides detailed information on the automatic stay, including which actions it does—and does not—prohibit.)

In addition, the bankruptcy court can lift the automatic stay for a particular creditor after notice and hearing—that is, allow the creditor to continue its collection efforts. (Lifting the automatic stay is covered in "Special Problems," below.)

Although the stay kicks in immediately, creditors won't know that they have to stop their collection efforts until they receive notice of your bankruptcy filing from the court. This official notice may take a week or more to reach your creditors. A lot can happen in a week, especially if you're facing an immediate foreclosure, repossession, or other emergency. That's why you might want to notify creditors of your bankruptcy filing right away. For instance, if you file for bankruptcy a couple of days before a foreclosure sale, the sale is legally barred by the automatic stay, even though the creditor hasn't received official notice of your filing yet. If you notify the creditor directly of your bankruptcy, the sale will be put on hold. If you don't, the sale may go through, but then will have to be put aside.

If you're facing immediate collection efforts, send your own notice to creditors (and bill collectors, landlords, or sheriffs about to enforce an eviction order). A sample letter notifying your creditors is shown below. You can also call your creditors. Be prepared to give your bankruptcy case number, the date you filed, and the name of the court in which you filed.

If a creditor tries to collect a debt in violation of the automatic stay, you can ask the bankruptcy court to hold the creditor in contempt of court and award you money damages. The procedures for making this request are beyond the scope of this book—and few debtors are likely to need them.

Because the penalties for willfully violating the automatic stay can be severe, most creditors play it safe and back off once they've heard that you've filed for bankruptcy.

Notice to Creditor of Filing for Bankruptcy

Lynn Adams
18 Orchard Park Blvd.
East Lansing, MI 48823

June 15, 20xx

Cottons Clothing Store
745 Main Street
Lansing, MI 48915

Dear Cottons Clothing:

On June 14, 20xx, I filed a voluntary petition under Chapter 7 of the U.S. Bankruptcy Code. The case number is 43-6736-91. I filed my case *in pro per*; no attorney is assisting me. Under 11 U.S.C. § 362(a), you may not:

- take any action against me or my property to collect any debt
- enforce any lien on my real or personal property
- repossess any property in my possession
- discontinue any service or benefit currently being provided to me, or
- take any action to evict me from where I live.

A violation of these prohibitions may be considered contempt of court and punished accordingly.

Very truly yours,
Lynn Adams
Lynn Adams

Attend the Meeting of Creditors

The meeting of creditors is conducted in an out-of-court hearing room, often in the courthouse or another federal building. The trustee conducts the meeting. Typically, the trustee will ask a few questions and try to resolve any ambiguities or omissions in your paperwork. Some trustees question debtors more closely about their bankruptcy papers than others. The trustee may want to see documentation of some of your figures, such as the value of a house or car; if you don't have this paperwork with you, the trustee will continue the meeting to another date to give you time to find the necessary documents. Typically, you won't have to appear at another meeting, but can submit these documents by mail.

Debtors who have been operating a business may come under closer scrutiny at the creditors' meeting if their record keeping was sloppy and the trustee can't readily determine how much money the business has been making (or losing). As a small business owner, your bankruptcy will go a lot smoother if you have a profit-and-loss statement (or something similar) that clearly depicts your business's economic activity. If you have a retail business or a business with significant assets (such as tangible goods or high accounts receivable), the trustee will likely order you to shut the business down at the creditors' meeting, if not before.

Even though it's called a creditors' meeting, few (if any) creditors typically show up. That doesn't let you off the hook, however: You—and your spouse, if filing jointly— must appear at the meeting. If you don't appear and you haven't notified the trustee in advance, you'll probably receive a letter from the trustee setting a new date and warning you that your case could be dismissed if you fail to show up again. You aren't legally entitled to this "second chance," however: Failing to show up for the first scheduled meeting might earn you a hearing before the judge where you'll have to explain yourself.

FOR MARRIED COUPLES

If you're married and filing jointly. Both you and your spouse must attend the first scheduled meeting of creditors. If you both attend but the meeting is continued to another date for a technical reason—to turn over certain papers to the trustee, for example—only one spouse may have to attend the follow-up meeting. Ask the trustee whether both of you have to come back, or whether one will do.

Preparing for the Creditors' Meeting

Some trustees send out a notice right after you file your case telling you what documents you'll have to bring to the creditors' meeting. You may be asked to bring copies of all documents that describe your debts and property, such as bills, deeds, contracts, and licenses. Some trustees also require you to bring financial records, such as tax returns (in addition to the one you filed with the court), checkbooks, and records for all businesses you have operated in the past six years. You have a right to redact (black out) all but the last four numbers of your Social Security number on any papers you submit. You can also redact the names of your minor children, full dates of birth, and full account numbers.

If your trustee doesn't tell you what to bring, you should plan to take a copy of every paper you've filed with the bankruptcy court. You should also bring the following:

- if you own real estate, documents showing the value of the property and how much you owe on mortgages and other loans
- business documents that you described in response to Items 19 (books, records and financial statements) and 20 (inventories) of your Statement of Financial Affairs; these records should cover the past two years
- evidence of your current income (if the wage stubs you already had to file don't provide this information or you had no wage stubs to begin with)
- statements from financial institutions for all of your deposit and investment accounts
- your most recent tax return (you are required to give this to the trustee at least seven days before the creditors' meeting, but bring it with you if you haven't given it to the trustee yet), and
- if you had to take the means test, proof of your monthly expenses.

If You Can't Appear

Sometimes, a person who has filed for bankruptcy cannot attend the creditors' meeting for a legitimate reason, such as a serious disability or illness. If that is true in your case, contact the U.S. Trustee's office for your district for information on how to proceed. The U.S. Trustee's office will make reasonable accommodations if you are unable to appear. For example, you may be able to provide the necessary information at another location (such as your home), before a notary public.

Some people become anxious at the prospect of answering a trustee's questions and consider having an attorney accompany them. But if you were completely honest in preparing your bankruptcy papers, and you are sufficiently familiar with your business's finances to answer any questions the trustee may have, there's no reason to have an attorney with you at the creditors' meeting. If the trustee asks tough questions, it is you, not the attorney, who will have to answer them. What's more, many trustees don't like it when debtors huddle with their attorney before answering a particular question, which means you'll be mostly on your own even if you pay a lawyer to accompany you to the meeting. Simply put, most attorneys who attend creditors' meetings don't say or do much at all.

If you may have been dishonest on the forms or with a creditor, you have attempted to unload some of your property before filing, or your business records are grossly inadequate, see a lawyer before you attend the creditors meeting (and preferably before you file your bankruptcy).

You can visit the hearing room where your district holds creditors' meetings (typically, the nearest federal building) and watch other meetings of creditors if you think that might help alleviate some anxiety. Just check with the U.S. Trustee's office in your district to find out when these meetings are held (see www.justice.gov/ust for contact information).

A day or so before the creditors' meeting, thoroughly review the papers you filed with the bankruptcy court. If you discover mistakes, make careful note of them. You'll probably have to correct your papers after the meeting, but that's an easy process. (Instructions are in "Amending Your Bankruptcy Papers," below.)

After reviewing your papers, go over the list of questions the trustee may ask (set out in "What Will the Trustee Ask You?" below). Despite the fact that these are "required" questions, few trustees ask all of them, and many trustees ask only one or two. Still, it's a good idea to be prepared to answer them all, if they relate to your situation.

At the beginning of the meeting, the trustee may ask you whether you have read the Statement of Information required by 11 U.S.C. § 342 (this is Form 201, which you signed and filed with your other papers). By reading this book, you have learned all the information on this form. Still, review it before the meeting, so you can tell the trustee that you've read it.

CAUTION

Don't forget your ID. You'll need identification at the creditors' meeting. Bring both a photo ID (such as a driver's license, passport, or identification card) and proof of your Social Security number from a third-party source (like a Social Security card, wage stub, retirement account statement, or passport).

The Routine Creditors' Meeting

Most creditors' meetings are quick and simple, even for small business owners. You appear in the designated meeting place at the date and time stated on the bankruptcy notice. A number of other people who have filed for bankruptcy will be there, too, for their own creditors' meetings. When your name is called, you'll be asked to sit or stand near the front of the meeting room. The trustee will swear you in and ask for your identification. At that point, many trustees look you in the eye and sternly ask whether everything in your papers is 100% true and correct. If you are uncertain about information in your papers or you have lied, the trustee is likely to pick up on your hesitancy and follow up with more questions that may make you uncomfortable. That's why it's so important that you:

- review your papers before filing them
- file amendments before the creditors' meeting if you discover any errors after you file (refer to "Amending Your Bankruptcy Papers," below)
- review your papers again shortly before the creditors' meeting, and
- volunteer any additional changes at the meeting before you are asked about them.

Then you can confidently answer "yes" to the trustee's first question.

The trustee will probably be most interested in:

- how you came up with a value for big ticket items, such as your home, car, or business assets
- anticipated tax refunds
- any possible right you may have to sue someone because of a recent accident or business loss
- reasons for inconsistencies in your paperwork or omitted information (such as answering "none" to the questions about clothing or bank accounts when it's obvious that you have either or both)
- recent large payments to creditors or relatives, and
- possible inheritances or insurance proceeds coming your way.

TIP

Ask to continue the creditors' meeting if you need to. You can usually change the date of your creditors' meeting if you can't make the date originally set. But what if you want to leave your creditors meeting once it has begun? For example, more than a few people have panic reactions in stressful situations. If this happens to you, you can pretty much count on the trustee to continue the meeting for a couple of weeks. In fact, you don't have to panic to want to continue the meeting; you may want an opportunity to talk to a lawyer about something that concerns you. Just ask for a continuance and there shouldn't be a problem.

If your answer to a trustee's question contradicts something you said in your bankruptcy papers, the trustee will have reason to suspect your entire case—and your bankruptcy may change from a routine procedure to an uphill battle. If you know that you have made mistakes, you should call them to the trustee's attention before the trustee raises the issue. If you are caught in a contradiction, immediately explain how it happened. Even if someone else prepared your papers for you, you can't use that as an excuse. You are responsible for the information in your papers, which is why you should thoroughly review them before appearing.

When the trustee is finished questioning you, any creditors who have appeared will have an opportunity to ask you questions. Most often, no creditors show up. If any do appear, they will probably be secured creditors who want to clarify your intentions regarding the collateral securing the debt. For example, if you've taken out a car loan and the car is the collateral, the creditor may ask whether you are going to reaffirm the debt or whether you might prefer to redeem the car at its replacement value. Also, if you obtained any cash advances or ran up credit card debts shortly before filing for bankruptcy, the credit card issuers may show up to question you about the circumstances and what you did with the proceeds. And, finally, a creditor might also ask for an explanation if information in your bankruptcy papers differs from what was on your credit application. When the creditors are through asking questions, the meeting will end. But don't lose any sleep about this part of the meeting; it's very rare for creditors to even show up.

Hold Your Head High

No matter how well you prepare for the creditors' meeting, you may feel nervous and apprehensive about coming face to face with the trustee (and possibly your creditors), to whom you've disclosed the intimate details of your finances over the last several years. You may feel angry with yourself and your creditors at having to be there. You may be embarrassed. You may think you're being perceived as a failure.

Nonsense. It takes courage to face your situation and deal firmly with it. Bankruptcy, especially when you're handling your own case without a lawyer, isn't an easy out. Try to see this as a turning point at which you're taking positive steps to improve your life. Go to the creditors' meeting proud that you've chosen to take control over your life and legal affairs.

Except in highly unusual situations (or if your business records are sufficiently sloppy to warrant intensive follow-up questioning), the trustee and any creditors should be finished questioning you in five minutes or less. In busy court districts, creditors' meetings often last no more than 90 seconds. When the trustee and creditors are done, the meeting will be concluded and you will be told you can leave. If you have no secured debts or nonexempt property, and neither you nor your creditors will be asking the court to rule on the dischargeability of a debt or the continuing effect of a lien, your case will effectively be over. No one will likely come to your house to inventory your property. No one will likely call your employer to confirm the information on your papers.

What Will the Trustee Ask You?

Technically, the trustee is *required* to ask the following questions at your creditors' meeting (although most don't):

- State your name and current address for the record.
- Have you read the Bankruptcy Information Sheet provided by the U.S. Trustee?
- Did you sign the petition, schedules, statements, and related documents you filed with the court? Did you read the petition, schedules, statements, and related documents before you signed them, and is the signature your own?
- Please provide your picture ID and Social Security number card for review.
- Are you personally familiar with the information contained in the petition, schedules, statements, and related documents?
- To the best of your knowledge, is the information contained in the petition, schedules, statements, and related documents true and correct?
- Are there any errors or omissions to bring to my or the court's attention at this time?
- Are all of your assets identified on the schedules?
- Have you listed all of your creditors on the schedules?
- Have you previously filed for bankruptcy? (If so, the trustee must obtain the case number and the discharge information to determine your discharge eligibility.)

The trustee may also ask additional questions, such as:

- Do you own or have any interest in any real estate?
- For property that you own: When did you purchase the property? How much did the property cost? What are the mortgages encumbering it? What do you estimate the present value of the property to be? Is that the whole value or your share? How did you arrive at that value?
- For property that you're renting: Have you ever owned the property where you live? Is the property owner in any way related to you?
- Have you made any transfers of any property, or given any property away, within the last two years (or a longer period if applicable under state law)? If so, what did you transfer? To whom was it transferred? What did you receive in exchange? What did you do with the funds?
- Does anyone hold property belonging to you? If so, who holds the property, and what is it? What is its value?
- Do you have a claim against anyone or any business? If there are large medical debts, are the medical bills from injury? Are you the plaintiff in any lawsuit? What is the status of each case, and who is representing you?
- Are you entitled to life insurance proceeds or an inheritance as a result of someone's death? If so, please explain the details. (If you become a beneficiary of anyone's estate within six months of the date your bankruptcy petition was filed, the trustee must be advised within ten days of the nature and extent of the property you will receive.)
- Does anyone owe you or your business money? If so, is the money collectible? Why haven't you collected it? Who owes the money, and where is that person?
- Have you made any large payments (more than $600) to anyone in the past year?
- Were your federal income tax returns filed on time? When was the last return filed? Do you have copies of your federal income tax returns? When you filed your petition, were you entitled to a tax refund from the federal or state government?
- Do you have a bank account, either checking or savings? If so, in what banks and what were the balances as of the date you filed your petition?
- When you filed your petition, did you have:
- any cash on hand

What Will the Trustee Ask You? (continued)

- any U.S. Savings Bonds
- any other stocks or bonds
- any certificates of deposit, or
- a safe deposit box in your name or in anyone else's name?
- Do you own an automobile? If so, what is the year, make, and value? Do you owe any money on it? Is it insured?
- Are you the owner of any cash value life insurance policies? If so, state the name of the company, face amount of the policy, cash surrender value (if any), and beneficiaries.
- Do you have any winning lottery tickets?
- Do you anticipate that you might acquire any property, cash or otherwise, as a result of a divorce or separation proceeding?
- Regarding any consumer debts secured by your property, have you filed the required Statement of Intention with respect to the exemption, retention, or surrender of that secured property? Please provide a copy of the statement to the trustee. Have you performed that intention?
- Have you been engaged in any other business during the last six years? If so, where and when? What happened to the assets of the business?

Depositions for Further Questioning

If the trustee has serious questions about your business, assets, or financial affairs that you were unable to answer to his or her satisfaction, the trustee may ask the court to order you to attend a deposition (called a "Rule 2004 proceeding"). In that proceeding, you will be questioned under oath about the issues that concern the trustee. While depositions are very rare in individual bankruptcy cases, they happen more often in cases involving small businesses that lack an adequate paper trail or clear records of recent business activities and income. If you are required to attend a Rule 2004 proceeding, you would be very well advised to hire an attorney to represent you. Although attorneys don't do much in a regular creditors' meeting, an attorney can play an important role in getting you safely through a deposition and on to your bankruptcy discharge.

Your bankruptcy case turns into a waiting game until the court sends you your notice of discharge and case closure. That should happen two to three months after your creditors' meeting.

Potential Problems at the Creditors' Meeting

If you or your papers give any indication that you own valuable nonexempt property, the trustee may question you about how you decided what it's worth. For instance, if you have valued your real estate at $150,000, and the trustee thinks it's worth a lot more, you will be asked how you came up with your number. Or, a creditor who's owed a lot of money may show up to grill you about the circumstances of the debt, hoping to show that you incurred the debt without intending to pay it, or by lying on a credit application, and that therefore it should survive bankruptcy. (See Ch. 11.)

You may also be closely questioned about the exemptions you claimed. Some trustees, who are usually attorneys, seem to believe that claiming exemptions requires legal expertise. If this happens to you, simply describe the process you went through in selecting your exemptions from Appendix A. If you consulted an attorney about exemptions or other issues, mention this also. This questioning won't affect your case unless the trustee disagrees with your exemption claims. Typically, the trustee's hidden agenda behind questions like these is to smoke out bankruptcy petition preparers who may have improperly provided you with legal advice (see Ch. 12 for more about bankruptcy petition preparers).

CAUTION

You're responsible for your paperwork, even if you used a bankruptcy petition preparer. You must provide the property valuation and other information in your bankruptcy papers. You cannot shift responsibility for the accuracy and thoroughness of your petition to the preparer, whose job is just to enter the information you supply. If you use a preparer, check all of your paperwork carefully before signing it and filing it with the court.

Make Sure the Creditors' Meeting Is "Closed"

The 30-day period in which the trustee and creditors may file objections to your exemption claims starts running when the creditors' meeting is finished or "closed." The meeting is officially closed—and the clock starts to run on objections—only when the trustee so notes in the court's docket. The trustee's oral statement alone at the creditors' meeting isn't enough to officially close the meeting. Check the court file to make sure that the trustee closed (or adjourned) the creditors' meeting, and follow up with the trustee if you don't see an entry like that. Otherwise, the 30-day period to file objections never starts to run, and the trustee and creditors will technically have an unlimited time to file objections.

Deal With Nonexempt Property

After the meeting of creditors, the trustee is supposed to collect all of your nonexempt property and have it sold to pay off your creditors. Normally, the trustee accepts the exemptions you claim on Schedule C and goes after only property you haven't claimed as exempt. If, however, the trustee or a creditor disagrees with an exemption you claimed and files a written objection with the bankruptcy court, the court will schedule a hearing. After listening to both sides, the judge will decide the issue. (See "Special Problems," below.)

If you really want to keep certain nonexempt items and you can raise some money, you may be able to pay the trustee for the property. The trustee, whose sole responsibility at this stage is to maximize what your creditors get paid, is interested only in how much money your property can produce, not in taking a particular item. So the trustee will probably be happy to accept cash instead of nonexempt property you want to keep.

> EXAMPLE: Maura files for Chapter 7 bankruptcy and claims her industrial coffee roaster as exempt. The trustee disagrees, and the judge rules that the coffee roaster is not exempt. To replace the coffee roaster on the open market will cost Maura about $7,000. The trustee determines that the coffee roaster would probably sell for $4,500 at an auction, and is willing to let Maura keep the coffee roaster if she can come up with $3,750, to avoid the cost of moving the coffee roaster, storing it, and selling it at auction.

The trustee may also be willing to let you keep nonexempt property if you volunteer to trade exempt property of equal value. For instance, the trustee might be willing to let Maura keep her nonexempt coffee roaster if she gives up her car, even though Maura could claim the car as exempt. Again, the trustee is interested in squeezing as many dollars as possible from the estate and usually won't care whether the money comes from exempt or nonexempt assets.

Deal With Secured Property

When you filed your Statement of Intention, you told the trustee and your creditors whether you wanted to keep the property securing the debt or give it to the creditor.

The law contradicts itself on the time limits for carrying out your intentions. Depending on which provision you believe, you have either 30 or 45 days after the date set for your first creditors' meeting to deal with your secured property. If you miss the deadline, the creditor can repossess the collateral—the automatic stay no longer applies (see Ch. 4). Because of these serious consequences, we strongly recommend that you follow through on your plans for secured property (as expressed on your Statement of Intention) within 30 days of the creditors' meeting, just in case the court enforces the earlier deadline. (Ch. 8 covers your options for dealing with secured property.)

Complete an Approved Debtor Education Course

After you file for bankruptcy but before you get your discharge, you must take a two-hour course in personal financial management. Known as "debtor education," or "pre-discharge" counseling, this course is typically offered by the same agencies that provide the credit counseling you must complete before you file. (You can find counseling agencies at www.justice.gov/ust; click "Credit Counseling and Debtor Education.") Like credit counseling, you can expect to pay about $50 or less for this course, and you can ask for a fee waiver if you can't afford the fee. Unlike credit counseling, which you can complete by phone, you are supposed to take your debtor education course in person or online.

Once you complete the counseling (and no later than 45 days after the first date set for your creditors' meeting), you must file Form 23 with the court to certify that you've met the requirement. (You'll find a copy of the form in Appendix C.) If you don't file this form on time, the court can close your case without granting you a discharge of your debts, which means your bankruptcy case was pointless. While it's possible to reopen your case to file the required form, it's obviously much easier to get the counseling and file the form as soon after you file your bankruptcy papers as possible.

You might be able to obtain a disability waiver of this counseling requirement—which means you wouldn't have to take it—if:

- you have a severe physical impairment
- you make a reasonable effort, despite the impairment, to participate in the counseling, and
- you are unable, because of your impairment, to meaningfully participate in the course.

(See *In re Hall*, 347 B.R. 532 (N.D. W.Va. 2006).) For example, in a case in which a married couple filed jointly, the judge waived the counseling requirement for the husband who was disabled by moderate Alzheimer's.

Attend a Discharge Hearing (If One Is Scheduled)

You may have to attend a brief court hearing at the end of your case, called a discharge hearing. At the hearing, the judge explains the effects of discharging your debts in bankruptcy and lectures you about staying clear of debt. You should receive a discharge order from the court within four weeks of the hearing. If you don't, call the trustee.

Most courts don't schedule a discharge hearing unless you signed and filed a reaffirmation agreement, in which case the court definitely will hold a hearing. At the hearing, the judge will determine whether reaffirmation would impose an undue hardship on you and whether it would be in your best interest to reaffirm the debt. You can find a complete explanation of the reaffirmation process—including what happens if the judge won't approve the agreement—in Ch 8.

Understand Your Discharge Order

About two or three months after the creditors' meeting, the court will send you a copy of your discharge order. On the back, it says that all debts you owed as of your filing date are discharged—unless they aren't. It then lists the types of debt that are not discharged. (A sample discharge order is below.) You will notice that the order does not refer to your debts or state which of your specific debts are or are not discharged. To get a handle on this crucial information, carefully read Ch. 11.

B18 (Official Form 18) (12/07)

United States Bankruptcy Court

_______________ District Of _______________

In re ______________________________, *[Set forth here all names including married, maiden, and trade names used by debtor within last 8 years.]* Debtor	)
	) Case No. _____________
Address ______________________________	)
______________________________	) Chapter 7
Last four digits of Social-Security or other Individual Taxpayer-Identification No(s)(if any).: ______________________	)
Employer Tax-Identification No(s).(EIN) [if any]:____________	)

DISCHARGE OF DEBTOR

It appearing that the debtor is entitled to a discharge, **IT IS ORDERED:** The debtor is granted a discharge under section 727 of title 11, United States Code, (the Bankruptcy Code).

Dated: ____________________

BY THE COURT

____

United States Bankruptcy Judge

SEE THE BACK OF THIS ORDER FOR IMPORTANT INFORMATION.

B18 (Official Form 18) (12/07) - Cont.

EXPLANATION OF BANKRUPTCY DISCHARGE IN A CHAPTER 7 CASE

This court order grants a discharge to the person named as the debtor. It is not a dismissal of the case and it does not determine how much money, if any, the trustee will pay to creditors.

Collection of Discharged Debts Prohibited

The discharge prohibits any attempt to collect from the debtor a debt that has been discharged. For example, a creditor is not permitted to contact a debtor by mail, phone, or otherwise, to file or continue a lawsuit, to attach wages or other property, or to take any other action to collect a discharged debt from the debtor. *[In a case involving community property:* There are also special rules that protect certain community property owned by the debtor's spouse, even if that spouse did not file a bankruptcy case.] A creditor who violates this order can be required to pay damages and attorney's fees to the debtor.

However, a creditor may have the right to enforce a valid lien, such as a mortgage or security interest, against the debtor's property after the bankruptcy, if that lien was not avoided or eliminated in the bankruptcy case. Also, a debtor may voluntarily pay any debt that has been discharged.

Debts that are Discharged

The chapter 7 discharge order eliminates a debtor's legal obligation to pay a debt that is discharged. Most, but not all, types of debts are discharged if the debt existed on the date the bankruptcy case was filed. (If this case was begun under a different chapter of the Bankruptcy Code and converted to chapter 7, the discharge applies to debts owed when the bankruptcy case was converted.)

Debts that are Not Discharged.

Some of the common types of debts which are not discharged in a chapter 7 bankruptcy case are:

a. Debts for most taxes;

b. Debts incurred to pay nondischargeable taxes;

c. Debts that are domestic support obligations;

d. Debts for most student loans;

e. Debts for most fines, penalties, forfeitures, or criminal restitution obligations;

f. Debts for personal injuries or death caused by the debtor's operation of a motor vehicle, vessel, or aircraft while intoxicated;

g. Some debts which were not properly listed by the debtor;

h. Debts that the bankruptcy court specifically has decided or will decide in this bankruptcy case are not discharged;

i. Debts for which the debtor has given up the discharge protections by signing a reaffirmation agreement in compliance with the Bankruptcy Code requirements for reaffirmation of debts; and

j. Debts owed to certain pension, profit sharing, stock bonus, other retirement plans, or to the Thrift Savings Plan for federal employees for certain types of loans from these plans.

This information is only a general summary of the bankruptcy discharge. There are exceptions to these general rules. Because the law is complicated, you may want to consult an attorney to determine the exact effect of the discharge in this case.

Make several photocopies of the discharge order and keep them in a safe place. Send them to creditors who attempt to collect their debt after your case is over or to credit reporting agencies that still list you as owing a discharged debt. (Ch. 11 covers postbankruptcy collection efforts.)

Amending Your Bankruptcy Papers

One of the helpful aspects of bankruptcy procedure is that you can amend any of your papers at any time before your final discharge (and perhaps even afterwards, although you'll have to reopen your case). This means that if you made a mistake on papers you've filed, you can correct it easily.

Despite this liberal amendment policy (as stated in Bankruptcy Rule 1009), some judges will not let you amend your exemption schedule after the deadline for creditors to object to the exemptions has passed (30 days after your creditors' meeting is closed). If you run into one of these judges, you'll need to talk to a bankruptcy attorney.

In most courts, you will have to pay to amend your bankruptcy papers only if you are amending Schedules D, E, or F to add a new creditor or change an address, because these changes require the court to make an additional mailing. The fee for this type of amendment is $26 as we go to press; ask the court clerk for the current amount.

If you become aware of debts or property that you should have included in your papers, amending your petition before you are called on the error will help you avoid any suspicion that you're trying to conceal things from the trustee. If you don't amend your papers after you discover this kind of information, your case may be dismissed or one or more debts may not be discharged if that new information comes to light.

Once your bankruptcy case is closed, you may be allowed to reopen your case and amend your papers to add an omitted creditor who tries to collect a debt. (See Ch. 11.)

Try to Get It Right the First Time

Too many changes can make you look dishonest, which can get your case dismissed and, if it seems you were hiding assets, investigated. The "Open Letter to Debtors and Their Counsel," below, gives a judge's negative view of amendments. Of course, if the facts have changed since you filed your petition, or you notice mistakes, you should amend. But the more accurate your papers are at the outset, the less likely your case will run into trouble.

Common Amendments

Even a simple change in one form may require changes to several other forms. Here are some of the more common reasons for amendments and the forms that you may need to amend. Exactly which forms you'll have to change depends on your court's rules. (Instructions for making the amendments are below.)

Add or Delete Exempt Property on Schedule C

If you want to add or delete property from your list of exemptions, you must file an amended Schedule C. You may also need to change other schedules, depending on the omission:

- Schedule A, if the property is real estate and you didn't list it there
- Schedule B, if the property is personal property and you didn't list it there
- Schedule D and Form 8—Chapter 7 Individual Debtor's Statement of Intention, if the property is collateral for a secured debt and isn't already listed
- Form 7—Statement of Financial Affairs, if any transactions regarding the property weren't described on that form, or
- Mailing Matrix, if the exempt item is tied to a particular creditor.

Open Letter to Debtors and Their Counsel

I have noticed a disturbing trend among debtors and their counsel to treat the schedules and statement of affairs as "working papers" which can be freely amended as circumstances warrant and need not contain the exact, whole truth.

Notwithstanding execution under penalty of perjury, debtors and their counsel seem to think that they are free to argue facts and values not contained in the schedules or even directly contrary to the schedules. Some debtors have felt justified signing a statement that they have only a few, or even a single creditor, in order to file an emergency petition, knowing full well that the statement is false.

Whatever your attitude is toward the schedules, you should know that as far as I am concerned they are the sacred text of any bankruptcy filing. There is no excuse for them not being 100% accurate and complete. Disclosure must be made to a fault. The filing of false schedules is a federal felony, and I do not hesitate to recommend prosecution of anyone who knowingly files a false schedule.

I have no idea where anyone got the idea that amendments can cure false schedules. The debtor has an obligation to correct schedules he or she knows are false, but amendment in no way cures a false filing. Any court may properly disregard [a] subsequent sworn statement at odds with previous sworn statements. I give no weight at all to amendments filed after an issue has been raised.

As a practical matter, where false statements or omissions have come to light due to investigation by a creditor or trustee, it is virtually impossible for the debtor to demonstrate good faith in a Chapter 13 case or entitlement to a discharge in a Chapter 7 case. I strongly recommend that any of you harboring a cavalier attitude toward the schedules replace it with a good healthy dose of paranoia.

Dated: September 10, 20xx

Alan Jaroslovsky

Alan Jaroslovsky
U.S. Bankruptcy Judge, N.D. Cal., Santa Rosa

Add or Delete Property on Schedule A or B

You may have forgotten to list some of your property on your schedules. Or, you may have received certain types of property after filing for bankruptcy. As explained in Ch. 5, the following property must be reported to the bankruptcy trustee if you receive it, or become entitled to receive it, within 180 days after filing for bankruptcy:

- property you inherit or become entitled to inherit
- property from a marital settlement agreement or divorce decree, and
- death benefits or life insurance policy proceeds.

If you have new property to report for any of these reasons, you may need to file amendments to:

- Schedule A, if the property is real estate
- Schedule B, if the property is personal property
- Schedule C, if the property was claimed as exempt and it's not, or you want to claim it as exempt
- Schedule D and Form 8—Chapter 7 Individual Debtor's Statement of Intention, if the property is collateral for a secured debt
- Form 7—Statement of Financial Affairs, if any transactions regarding the property haven't been described on that form, or
- The mailing matrix, if the item is tied to a particular creditor.

If your bankruptcy case is already closed, see Ch. 11.

Change Your Plans for Secured Property

If you've changed your plans for dealing with an item of secured property, you must file an amended Form 8 —Chapter 7 Individual Debtor's Statement of Intention.

Correct Your List of Creditors

To correct your list of creditors, you may need to amend:

- Schedule C, if the debt is secured and you plan to claim equity in the collateral as exempt
- Schedule D, if the debt is a secured debt
- Schedule E, if the debt is a priority debt (as defined in Ch. 9)
- Schedule F, if the debt is unsecured
- Form 7—Statement of Financial Affairs, if any transactions regarding the property haven't previously been described on that form, or
- Mailing Matrix, which contains the names and addresses of all your creditors.

If your bankruptcy case is already closed, see Ch. 11.

Add an Omitted Payment to a Creditor

If you didn't report payments you made to a creditor made within the last three months (or within the last year if the creditor was an insider, such as a business associate or a relative), you must amend your Form 7—Statement of Financial Affairs.

Add an Omitted Prefiling Transfer

If you didn't report a transfer of real or personal property that occurred within two years of your filing date, you must amend your Form 7—Statement of Financial Affairs.

How to File an Amendment

To amend your papers, follow the instructions in Appendix D, using the Amendment Cover Sheet provided.

Filing a Change of Address

If you move while your bankruptcy case is still open, you must give your new address to the court, the trustee, and your creditors. Appendix D includes a Notice of Change of Address form and instructions for filing it with the court.

Special Problems

Sometimes, complications arise in a bankruptcy—usually when a creditor files some type of motion, objects to the discharge of a debt, or challenges the entire bankruptcy case. If a creditor does this, the court will notify you by sending you a Notice of Motion or Notice of Objection. At that point, you may need to go to court yourself or get an attorney to help you. Here are some of the more common complications that may crop up.

You Failed the Means Test

If you didn't pass the means test (described in Chs. 2 and 9) but decided to file for Chapter 7 anyway, you may face a motion to dismiss or convert your case to a Chapter 13 bankruptcy.

Presumed Abuse

If you don't pass the means test, your Chapter 7 bankruptcy will be presumed to be an abuse of the bankruptcy system. A presumption means that the court will accept the allegation of abuse as true unless you can prove otherwise. You won't be allowed to proceed unless you can overcome the presumption of abuse by showing that special circumstances exist that justify your Chapter 7 filing. It's hard to prove that the special circumstances exception applies; courts rarely rule in favor of debtors on this issue.

To stop your Chapter 7 bankruptcy on the grounds of abuse, someone—a creditor, the trustee, or, most likely, the U.S. Trustee—must request a court hearing to dismiss or convert your case to Chapter 13 bankruptcy. The U.S. Trustee must file a statement, within ten days after your meeting of creditors, indicating whether your case should be considered a presumed abuse. (This statement is required only if your income is more than the state median; see Chs. 2 and 9 for more information.) Five days after the U.S. Trustee's statement is filed, the court must send it to all of your creditors, to inform them of the U.S. Trustee's decision and give them an opportunity to file a motion to dismiss or convert your case to Chapter 13 bankruptcy.

Within 30 days after filing this statement, the U.S. Trustee must either:

- file its own motion to dismiss or convert your case on grounds of abuse, or
- explain why a motion to convert or dismiss isn't appropriate (for example, because you passed the means test or special circumstances exist).

These duties and time limits apply only to the U.S. Trustee. If your income is more than the state median, your creditors can file a motion to dismiss or convert any time after you file, but no later than 60 days after the first date set for your meeting of creditors.

Defending a Motion to Dismiss or Convert

If the U.S. Trustee (or a trustee or a creditor, in some cases) files a motion to dismiss or convert your case on the basis of presumed abuse, you are entitled to notice of the hearing at least 20 days in advance. You will receive papers in the mail explaining the grounds for the motion and what you need to do to respond. Because abuse is presumed, you will bear the burden of proving that your filing really isn't abusive, and that you should be allowed to proceed.

There are three basic defenses to this type of motion:

- **You are exempt from the means test provisions because your debts were primarily business debts.** If you checked the appropriate box on your petition to indicate that your debts are primarily business debts, now is the time when you may be called on to prove it. In Ch. 2, we provide some general guidelines for separating consumer debts from business debts. With that material in front of you, review and recategorize all of your debts. If you conclude that you correctly characterized them as primarily business debts, you'll need to show the court how you came to that conclusion.
- **You didn't really fail the means test.** To defend yourself on this basis, you must be able to show that you actually passed the means test, and that the party bringing the motion to dismiss or convert your bankruptcy case misinterpreted the information you provided in Form 22A or misinterpreted the applicable law (for example, by including Social Security benefits in your current monthly income when the law says they should be excluded).
- **Special circumstances exist that allow you to pass the means test.** The new law gives a serious medical condition or a call to active duty in the armed forces as examples of special circumstances, but this isn't an exhaustive list. However, just showing that special circumstances exist isn't enough: You must also show that they justify additional expenses or adjustments to your current monthly income "for which there is no reasonable alternative."

To prove special circumstances, you must itemize each additional expense or adjustment of your income and provide:

- documentation for the expense or adjustment, and
- a detailed explanation of the special circumstances that make the expense or adjustment necessary and reasonable.

You will win only if the additional expenses or adjustments to your income enable you to pass the means test. (Ch. 9 explains how to make this calculation.)

> EXAMPLE: Maureen and Ralph have a child (Sarah) with severe autism. Sarah is making remarkable progress in her private school, for which Maureen and Ralph pay $1,000 a month. No equivalent school is available at a lower tuition. Under the means test guidelines, Maureen and Ralph are entitled to deduct only $150 a month from the income for private school expenses. If Maureen and Ralph were allowed to deduct

Motions to Dismiss for Abuse Under All the Circumstances

Even if you pass the means test on paper, your case can be dismissed if it appears that your Chapter 7 filing is an abuse of the bankruptcy code under "all the circumstances." In this context, "all the circumstances" means all of the facts before the judge. Motions to dismiss for this reason often focus on whether the debtor's claimed expenses are unnecessarily extravagant. For example, an Ohio bankruptcy court ruled that a mortgage expense on a $400,000 home and an expense for repayment of a 401(k) loan should not be allowed. Without those expenses, the debtors would have adequate income to fund a Chapter 13 plan, which made their case an abuse under all the circumstances. (*In Re Felske*, 385 B.R. 649 (N.D. Ohio 2008).)

The facts justifying dismissal of a Chapter 7 bankruptcy because of abuse under all the circumstances don't necessarily have to exist when you first file for bankruptcy. One appellate court ruled that a motion to dismiss may be based on events occurring anytime before the discharge, which typically occurs between three and four months after filing. (*In re Cortez*, 457 F.3d 448 (5th Cir. 2006).) So if, after you file for bankruptcy, you get a new job or win the lottery, or some other event happens while your case is pending that would enable you to proceed under Chapter 13, you may face a challenge to your Chapter 7 case. (See also *In re Henebury*, 361 B.R. 595 (S.D. Fla. 2007).)

If you face dismissal on this ground, you must explain why it's unlikely you could complete a Chapter 13 bankruptcy, or why expenses the trustee has challenged are necessary for you to get a fresh start. There is no clear test of what constitutes abuse under all the circumstances; it depends on how your judge views the situation. Fortunately, the U.S. Trustee (usually the party bringing these motions) must prove the abuse. If you pass the means test, your eligibility for Chapter 7 bankruptcy is presumed, and the trustee has to overcome that presumption.

the full $1,000 monthly tuition, they would easily pass the means test. By documenting Sarah's condition, the necessity for the extra educational expense, and the fact that moving her to a less expensive school would greatly undermine her progress, Maureen and Ralph would have a good chance of convincing the court to allow the $1,000 expense, which would overcome the presumption of abuse and allow them to use Chapter 7.

Bankruptcy courts have issued written decisions on a variety of special circumstance claims. If you need to prove special circumstances to pass the mean test, you will definitely want to check with a local attorney or do your own research to find out how bankruptcy court or the courts in your state have treated the special circumstances you're claiming. (See Ch. 12.) A frequently addressed issue is whether payments on nondischargeable student loans can be considered a special circumstance. While a few courts have held that they can be, more courts have gone the other way and ruled that student loan payments do not constitute special circumstances. (See, for example, *In re Champagne*, 389 B.R. 191 (Bkrtcy Kan. 2008) and *In re Pageau*, 383 B.R. 281 (S.D. Ind. 2008).)

Here are some cases in which the court has allowed a particular special circumstances claim, but remember that courts in your area may see the issue differently:

- unusually high transportation expenses (*In re Batzkiel*, 349 B.R. 581 (Bkrtcy N.D. Iowa 2006); *In re Turner*, 376 B.R. 370 (Bkrtcy D. N.H. 2007))
- mandatory repayment of 401(k) loan (*In re Lenton*, 358 B.R. 651 (Bkrtcy E.D. Pa. 2006))
- reduction in income (*In re Martin*, 371 B.R. 347 (Bkrtcy C.D. Ill. 2007) (diminished future availability of overtime hours); *In re Tamez*, No. 07-60047 (Bkrtcy W.D. Tex. 2007) (reduction in income due to voluntary job changes))

- wife's pregnancy, in a joint bankruptcy case (*In re Martin*, 371 B.R. 347 (Bkrtcy C.D. Ill. 2007))
- joint debtors who have two separate households (*In re Graham*, 363 B.R. 844 (Bkrtcy S.D. Ohio 2007); *In re Armstrong*, No. 06-31414 (Bkrtcy N.D. Ohio 2007))
- unusually high rent expenses (*In re Scarafiotti*, 375 B.R. 618 (Bkrtcy D. Colo. 2007)), and
- court-ordered child support payments (*In re Littman*, 370 B.R. 820 (Bkrtcy D. Idaho 2007)).

Most small business owners won't be able to claim special circumstances based on business expenses, because the means test already takes those expenses into account. When you calculate your current monthly income, you are allowed to subtract ordinary and necessary business expenses from your business income to come up with the total. If you have a business expense that's out of the ordinary and doesn't fit into any of the categories used in the means test, you could try to convince the judge to allow you to claim it as a special circumstance expense. (See, for example, *In re Turner*, 376 B.R. 370 (Bkrtcy D. N.H., 2007), in which the debtor was allowed to count his business mileage as a special circumstance, because he logged it separately from his personal mileage and had not already subtracted it as a reasonable and ordinary business expense when calculating his current monthly income.)

A Creditor Asks the Court to Lift the Automatic Stay

Your automatic stay lasts from the date you file your papers until the date you receive your bankruptcy discharge or the date your bankruptcy case is closed, whichever happens first. For example, assume you receive a discharge but the trustee keeps your case open in order to collect your pending tax refund or an inheritance you are due to receive in the future. In this situation, the automatic stay would not be in effect after your discharge, even though your case would still be open.

As long as the stay is in effect, most creditors must get permission from a judge to take any action against you or your property that might affect your bankruptcy estate. (See Ch. 4 for information on which creditors are affected by the stay and which are free to proceed with collection efforts despite the stay.) To get this permission, the creditor must file a request in writing called a "Motion to Lift the Stay." The court will schedule a hearing on this motion and send you written notice. You will have a certain period of time to file a written response. Even if you decide not to file a response, you may still be able to appear in court to argue that the stay shouldn't be lifted. Check your local rules on this point.

If you don't show up for the hearing—even if you filed a written response—the stay will probably be lifted as requested by the creditor, unless lifting the stay would potentially harm other creditors. For instance, if the creditor is seeking permission to repossess your car, and your equity in the car would produce some income for your unsecured creditors if sold by the trustee, the court may refuse to lift the stay whether or not you show up.

After hearing the motion, the judge will either rule "from the bench" (announce a decision right then and there), or "take it under submission" and mail a decision in a few days. A creditor can ask a judge to lift the stay within a week or two after you file, but a delay of several weeks to several months is more common.

Grounds for Lifting the Automatic Stay

The bankruptcy court may lift the automatic stay for several reasons:

- The activity being stayed is not a legitimate concern of the bankruptcy court. For instance, the court will let a child custody hearing proceed, because its outcome won't affect your economic situation.
- The activity being stayed is going to happen no matter what the bankruptcy court does.

For instance, if a lender shows the court that a mortgage foreclosure will ultimately occur, regardless of the bankruptcy filing, the court will usually lift the stay and let the foreclosure proceed (as long as the foreclosing entity can prove that it's the legal holder of the mortgage; see Ch. 7).

- The stay is harming the creditor's interest in property you own or possess. For example, if you've stopped making payments on a car and it's losing value, the court may lift the stay. That would allow the creditor to repossess the car now, unless you pay the creditor enough to cover the ongoing depreciation, at least until your case is closed.
- You have no ownership interest in the property sought by the creditor (ownership interests are explained just below). If you don't own some interest in property that a creditor wants, the court isn't interested in protecting the property—and won't hesitate to lift the stay. The most common example is when a month-to-month tenant files for bankruptcy to forestall an eviction. Because the tenancy has no monetary value, it is not considered to be property of the estate, and the stay will almost always be lifted.

Do You Have an Ownership Interest in the Property?

There are many kinds of ownership interests. You can own property outright. You can own the right to possess it sometime in the future. You can co-own it jointly with any number of other owners. You can own the right to possess it, while someone else actually owns legal title.

For most kinds of property, there's an easy way to tell if you have an ownership interest: If you would be entitled to receive any cash if the property were sold, you have an ownership interest.

For intangible property, however—property you can't see or touch, like intellectual property or rights under a rental agreement—it may be harder to show your ownership interest. This most often arises in cases involving contracts concerning residential real estate.

If you have a commercial lease when you file for bankruptcy, for example, most bankruptcy courts would consider it an ownership interest in the property because it could possibly be sold and assigned to another business. Most courts probably would not lift the stay to let a landlord go ahead with an eviction, regardless of the reason. But if the lease expired by its own terms before you filed—which converted your interest from a long-term "leasehold" to a month-to-month tenancy—most courts would rule that you have no ownership interest in the property and would lift the stay, allowing the eviction to go forward.

Another ownership interest is the contractual right to continued insurance coverage that an insured person has under an insurance policy. This means the automatic stay prevents insurance companies from canceling insurance policies.

Opposing a Request to Lift the Automatic Stay

Generally, a court won't lift the stay if you can show that it's necessary to preserve your property for yourself (if it's exempt) or for the benefit of your creditors (if it's not), or to maintain your general economic condition. You may also need to convince the court that the creditor's investment in the property will be protected while the bankruptcy is pending.

Here are some possible responses you can make if a creditor tries to get the stay lifted:

- **Repossession of cars or other personal property.** If the stay is preventing a creditor from repossessing business assets or personal property pledged as collateral, such as your car, equipment, or jewelry, the creditor will probably argue that the stay should be lifted because you might damage the collateral or because the collateral is depreciating (declining in value) while your bankruptcy case is pending. Your response should depend on the facts. If the property is still in good shape, be prepared to prove it to the judge.

If the property is worth more than you owe on it, you can argue that depreciation won't hurt the creditor, because the property could be repossessed later and sold for the amount of the debt or more. But if, as is common, you have little or no equity in the property, you'll need to propose a way to protect the creditor's interest while you keep the property (if you want it). One way to do this is to pay the creditor a cash security deposit to offset the expected depreciation (called "adequate assurance of payment").

If you intend to keep secured property, you can argue that lifting the stay would deprive you of your rights under the bankruptcy laws. For example, if you intend to redeem business equipment by paying its replacement value, the court should deny the motion to lift the stay until you have an opportunity to do so.

- **Utility disconnections.** For 20 days after you file your bankruptcy petition, a public utility—electric, gas, telephone, or water company—may not alter, refuse, or discontinue service to you or your business, or discriminate against you in any other way, solely on the basis of an unpaid debt or your bankruptcy filing. (11 U.S.C. § 366(a).) If your service was disconnected before you filed, the utility company must restore it within 20 days after you file for bankruptcy—without requiring a deposit—if you request it.

  Twenty days after the order to continue service, the utility is allowed to discontinue service unless you provide adequate assurance that your future bills will be paid. (11 U.S.C. § 366(b).) Usually, that means you'll have to come up with a security deposit. If you and the utility can't agree on the size of the deposit, the utility may cut off service, which means you'll need to get a lawyer and ask the bankruptcy court to have it reinstated. If the utility files a motion to lift the stay, argue at the hearing that your deposit is adequate.
- **Evictions.** Filing for bankruptcy has been a favorite tactic for some eviction defense clinics (legal housing clinics that help tenants fight eviction), which file a bare-bones bankruptcy petition to stop evictions even if the tenant's debts don't justify bankruptcy. Under the 2005 bankruptcy law amendments, the automatic stay doesn't apply if your landlord obtained a judgment for eviction before you filed for bankruptcy, or if the eviction is based on your endangerment of the property or use of illegal controlled substances on the premises. These exceptions are explained in Ch. 4.

The Trustee or a Creditor Disputes a Claimed Exemption

After the creditors' meeting, the trustee and creditors have 30 days to object to the exemptions you claimed. If the deadline passes and the trustee or a creditor wants to challenge an exemption, it's usually too late, even if the exemption statutes don't support the claimed exemption. (*Taylor v. Freeland and Kronz,* 503 U.S. 638 (1992).) The objections must be in writing and filed with the bankruptcy court. Copies must be served on the trustee, you, and your lawyer, if you have one.

In some cases, the trustee can object to an exemption after the 30-day period has passed. For instance, in one case the debtor stated that the value of certain stock options was unknown and used a $4,000 or so wildcard exemption to cover the value, whatever it was. Eight months after the bankruptcy case was closed, the trustee asked the debtor what happened to the stock options. As it happened, they had been cashed out for nearly $100,000. The trustee sought to have the case reopened to recover the excess value. The debtor argued that the 30-day period prevented a reexamination of the exemption claim. The issue was ultimately decided in favor of the trustee. The court found that the debtor's use of the term "unknown" relieved the trustee of the obligation to challenge the exemption claim within the 30-day limit. If, on the other hand, the debtor had listed a specific value for the options, the trustee's duty to file an objection within the deadline would have been triggered. (*In re Wick*, 276 F.3d 412 (8th Cir. 2002).)

Reasons for Objecting to Exemptions

The most common reasons trustees and creditors object to exemptions are:

- You aren't eligible to use the state exemptions you claimed. Under the 2005 bankruptcy law, you may use a state's exemptions only if you have made that state your domicile (your true home) for at least two years before filing. If you haven't been domiciled in your current state for at least two years, you must use the exemptions for the state where you were living for the better part of the 180-day period ending two years before you filed for bankruptcy. (See Ch. 6 for more on these rules, and Ch. 7 for more on the stricter rules that apply to homestead exemptions.)
- The claimed item isn't exempt under the law. For example, a plumber who lives in New Jersey and selects his state exemptions might try to exempt his plumbing tools under the "goods and chattels" exemption. The trustee and creditors are likely to object on the ground that these are work tools rather than goods and chattels, and New Jersey has no "tools of trade" exemption.
- Within ten years before filing for bankruptcy, you sold nonexempt property and purchased exempt property to hinder, delay, or cheat your creditors.
- Property you claimed as exempt is worth more than you say it is. If the property's true replacement value is higher than the exemption limit for that item, the item can be sold and the excess over the exemption limit distributed to your creditors (assuming you don't buy the property back from the trustee at a negotiated price).

EXAMPLE: In Connie's state, tools of the trade are exempt up to $6,000. Connie, a general contractor, values her tools at $2,000 and her truck at $4,000, which means they fit within the $6,000 total exempt amount. A creditor objects to Connie's valuation of the truck, claiming that it's worth $8,000 by itself. If the creditor prevails, Connie would have to surrender the truck to the trustee. She'd get the first $4,000 (the exempt amount of the truck's sale price). Or, Connie could keep the truck if she gave the trustee a negotiated amount of cash (perhaps $2,000 or so) or other property of equivalent value.

- You and your spouse have doubled an exemption where doubling isn't permitted.

EXAMPLE: David and Marylee, a married couple, file for bankruptcy using California's System 1 exemptions. Each claims a $2,550 exemption in their family car, for a total of $5,100. California bars a married couple from doubling the System 1 automobile exemption. They can claim only $2,550.

Responding to Objections

When objection papers are filed, the court schedules a hearing. The creditor or trustee must prove to the bankruptcy court that the exemption is improper. You don't have to prove anything. In fact, you don't have to respond to the objection or show up at the hearing unless the court orders, or local rules require, that you do so. Of course, you can—and probably should—either file a response or show up at the hearing to defend your claim of a legitimate exemption. If you don't show up, the bankruptcy judge will decide on the basis of the paperwork filed by the objecting party and the applicable laws, which most often means you'll lose, especially if the trustee or an attorney is objecting.

A Creditor Objects to the Discharge of a Debt

There are a variety of reasons a creditor may object to the discharge of a debt. The most common are:

- the creditor believes you made fraudulent statements to obtain the loan or credit in the first place
- the debt or obligation arose from your willful and malicious act (such as assault or libel), or
- you violated a duty of trust or embezzled funds from your employer or co-owned company.

See Ch. 11 for more on these and other potential grounds for objecting to the discharge of a debt.

A Creditor or the Trustee Objects to Your Bankruptcy Discharge

In some situations, a creditor or the trustee can object to your entire discharge. If an objection like this is granted, none of your debts would be discharged. In small business bankruptcies, this type of objection may be based on the business owner's failure to keep adequate records. For instance, under 11 U.S.C. § 727 (a)(3), a bankruptcy discharge may be denied if the debtor's failure to keep or preserve books or records makes it impossible to determine the debtor's true financial condition.

Although the creditor or trustee has the burden of proving the failure to keep adequate records, the debtor is required to provide adequate records if called on to do so. A creditor is not required to sift through a pile of documents and attempt to reconstruct the debtor's business affairs.

In considering an inadequate records objection, the court may consider:

- the complexity and volume of the business
- the amount of the debtor's obligations
- whether the debtor was at fault in failing to keep adequate records
- the debtor's education, business experience, and sophistication
- customary business practices for record keeping in the debtor's type of business
- the degree of accuracy disclosed by the debtor's existing books and records
- the extent of any egregious conduct on the debtor's part, and
- the debtor's courtroom demeanor.

For a good discussion of how this objection works, see *In re Moreo*, Case No. 07-71258-478 (Bankr E.D. N.Y. 2009).

You Want to Get Back Exempt Property Taken by a Creditor

You may have filed for bankruptcy after a creditor:

- repossessed collateral (such as a car) under a security agreement, or
- seized some of your property as part of a judgment collection action.

If so, you should have described the event in your Statement of Financial Affairs, which you filed along with your bankruptcy petition and schedules. Repossessions are difficult to undo, because they occur under a contract that you voluntarily entered into. However, property seized to satisfy a judgment can be pulled back into your bankruptcy estate if the seizure occurred within the three months before you filed. If the property is not exempt (or at least some of it is not exempt), the trustee may go after it so that it can be sold for the benefit of your unsecured creditors. If the property is exempt (meaning you are entitled to keep it), you can go after it yourself. However, you'll have to file a formal complaint in the bankruptcy court against the creditor.

The process for getting the bankruptcy judge to order property returned to you is complex; you'll probably need the assistance of an attorney. Given the cost of attorneys, it's seldom worth your while to go after this type of property unless it is worth a lot or has great sentimental value. Keep in mind that most property is only exempt up to a certain value. Thus, even if you get the property back, the trustee may decide to sell it, in which case you'll receive only the exempt amount from the proceeds.

Recapturing Garnished Funds

When funds are garnished to pay a judgment, the garnishing agent typically holds on to the money over several pay periods before giving it to the creditor. If you file for bankruptcy while the agent is holding funds, they will be put in an escrow account pending further notice from the bankruptcy trustee. If you are able to claim the funds as exempt, the bankruptcy trustee will "abandon" any claim to the funds, and you will be entitled to receive them when the trustee files a notice of abandonment or your bankruptcy case is over.

Some trustees notify the garnishing agent that they have abandoned their claim to the funds; others don't send any notice, but simply allow the funds to be abandoned automatically when your case is closed. If your trustee doesn't send a notice, you should send your own letter to the garnishing agent explaining that you claimed the funds as exempt, the bankruptcy trustee abandoned the funds by not asserting jurisdiction over them during your bankruptcy, and you are now the rightful owner of the funds. This will usually do the trick. If not, you'll have to obtain a court order either by filing a complaint against the garnishing agent or by filing a motion (courts follow different procedures in this situation).

You Want to Dismiss Your Case

If you change your mind after you file for bankruptcy, you can ask the court to dismiss your case. Common reasons for wanting to dismiss a case include the following:

- You discover that a major debt you thought was dischargeable isn't. You don't have enough other debts to justify your bankruptcy case.
- You realize that an item of property you thought was exempt isn't. You don't want to lose it in bankruptcy.
- You come into a sum of money and can afford to pay your debts.
- You realize that you have more property in your estate than you thought and decide that you don't have to file for bankruptcy after all.
- Your bankruptcy case turns out to be more complex than you originally thought. You need a lawyer, but you don't have the money to hire one.
- You made transfers before filing for bankruptcy, you learn that these transfers will likely be undone by the trustee, and you want to avoid that result.
- You learn that the trustee will require you to close your business, and you won't be able to survive under those conditions.
- The emotional stress of bankruptcy is too much for you.

It is within the court's discretion to dismiss your case. That means the court can grant or refuse the dismissal. How courts make this decision varies from district to district. In some districts, dismissing a case is next to impossible if your bankruptcy estate has assets that can be sold for the benefit of your creditors. However, if you have few assets the trustee could take and no creditor objects to the dismissal, you may have better luck getting it dismissed.

If you want to dismiss your case, you must file a request with the court. Instructions on how to do this are in Appendix D. Depending on how receptive your local bankruptcy court is to dismissal, you may need the help of a lawyer.

You Want to Reopen Your Case

At several places in this book, we've suggested that you might have to reopen your case (for example, to file a motion to avoid a lien you didn't include on your papers, or to file Form 23 proving that you completed budget counseling). To reopen your case, you must file what's called an "ex parte motion." This simply means that you don't have to provide formal notice to the other parties in your case. Instead, you just have to prepare and file your request and an accompanying order, and demonstrate that you have given written notice of your motion to the trustee and the U.S. Trustee. You don't have to schedule a hearing; the judge will consider your request and either grant or deny it based solely on your paperwork. In Appendix D, we provide the forms necessary to ask the court to reopen your case to allow you to file Form 23, and to ask the court for a discharge.

CHAPTER

11

After Your Bankruptcy

Congratulations! After you receive your final discharge, you can get on with your life and enjoy the fresh start that bankruptcy offers. Of course, you'll want to understand your discharge: which debts are cancelled and which may still be hanging around.

Some debts are virtually always discharged in Chapter 7 bankruptcy; others always survive a bankruptcy case. There are also debts that could go either way, depending on the circumstances. For example, certain debts—such as student loans—will not be discharged unless you prove that they should be. Other debts—such as debts you allegedly incurred through fraud (lying on a credit application, for example)—will be discharged unless the creditor proves that they should not be. We explain all of these nuances below, including information on what you'll need to prove to get the debt discharged.

This chapter also covers some issues you might face after your bankruptcy case is closed. For example, what happens if a creditor tries to collect a debt that was discharged in your bankruptcy case, or you are denied a job because you filed for bankruptcy? We explain how to handle some of these situations below.

What Happens to Your Debts in a Chapter 7 Bankruptcy

In a personal Chapter 7 bankruptcy, certain types of debts are discharged for the purpose of giving you a fresh start. Not all debts are discharged, however. Some debts survive the bankruptcy process—they remain valid and collectable, just as they were before you filed for bankruptcy.

When granting your final discharge, the bankruptcy court doesn't specify which of your debts have been discharged. Instead, you receive a standard form from the court stating that you have received a discharge. (A copy appears in Chapter 10.) This section will help you figure out which of your debts are discharged and which debts may survive.

Here's the lay of the land:

- Certain kinds of debts are always discharged in bankruptcy, except in rare circumstances.
- Some types of debts are never discharged in bankruptcy. Examples include back child support and recent income tax debts.
- Some types of debts (such as student loans) are not discharged unless you can prove your case is an exception.
- Some types of debts are discharged unless the creditor comes to court and successfully objects to the discharge.

Debts Your Creditors Claim Are Nondischargeable

Some of your creditors may claim that the debts you owe them cannot be wiped out in bankruptcy. For example, computer leases—for software and hardware—often contain clauses stating that if you're unable to complete the lease period, you can't eliminate the balance of the debt in bankruptcy. Don't fall for these arguments. The only debts you can't discharge in bankruptcy are the ones specifically listed in Bankruptcy Code Section 523 as nondischargeable—and we'll describe them in this chapter. Don't let your creditors intimidate you into thinking otherwise.

Debts That Will Be Discharged in Bankruptcy

Certain types of debts will be cancelled—that is, you will no longer be responsible for repaying them—when you receive your Chapter 7 discharge. The bankruptcy trustee will divide your nonexempt assets (if you have any) among your creditors, and then the court will discharge any amount that remains unpaid at the end of your case.

Credit Card Debts

Without a doubt, the vast majority of people who file for bankruptcy are trying to get rid of credit card debts. Happily for these filers, most bankruptcies succeed in this mission. With a few rare exceptions in cases involving fraud or luxury purchases immediately prior to your bankruptcy (outlined in "Debts That Survive Chapter 7 Bankruptcy," below), credit card debts are wiped out in bankruptcy.

Obligations Under Leases and Contracts

Increasingly in our society, things are leased rather than owned. And most leases have severe penalty clauses that kick in if you are unable to make the monthly payments or do something else the lease requires you to do.

Business debtors frequently enter into contracts, including contracts to sell real estate, buy a business, deliver merchandise, or provide certain benefits to employees. If you can't complete a contract or want to terminate it for any reason, the other party may want to force you to hold up your end of the deal, and may sue you for damages.

Contractual obligations and liabilities are usually discharged in bankruptcy. Filing for bankruptcy almost always converts your lease or contractual obligation into a dischargeable debt, unless the trustee believes the lease or contract could be sold to raise money for your creditors or the court finds that you've filed for bankruptcy precisely for the purpose of getting out of a personal services contract (such as a recording contract).

Loans and Promissory Notes

Money you borrow in exchange for a promissory note (or even a handshake and an oral promise to pay the money back) is almost always dischargeable in bankruptcy. As with any debt, however, the court may refuse to discharge a loan debt if the creditor can prove that you acted fraudulently. (See "Debts That Survive Chapter 7 Bankruptcy," below.) But that almost never happens.

Business Accounts

If your business is a sole proprietorship, you may enter bankruptcy owing employees, suppliers, utility companies, advertising agencies, a commercial landlord, and more. With some exceptions (outlined in "Debts That Survive Chapter 7 Bankruptcy," below), all of your business debts will be wiped out in bankruptcy. Certain debts owed to employees will be paid first—as priority debts—if your bankruptcy estate has any nonexempt property. Any portion of these debts that isn't paid from the proceeds of your nonexempt property will be discharged at the end of your case. As noted below, however, debts you owe to the IRS for your share of an employee's taxes may not be discharged; you'll continue to owe them after your bankruptcy.

Medical Bills

Many people who file for bankruptcy got into financial trouble because of medical bills. Some 40 million Americans have no medical insurance or other access to affordable medical care and rely on emergency rooms for their primary care. Many more millions of working Americans either have inadequate insurance or can't afford the plans available to them.

Luckily, bankruptcy provides an out: Your medical bills will be discharged at the end of your bankruptcy case. In fact, billions of dollars in medical bills are discharged in bankruptcy every year.

Lawsuit Judgments

Most civil court cases are about money. If someone wins one of these lawsuits against you, the court issues a judgment ordering you to pay. If you don't come up with the money voluntarily, the judgment holder is entitled to collect it by, for example, grabbing your bank account, levying your wages, collecting proceeds from your till as they come in (if you have a retail business), putting levies on your accounts receivable, or placing a lien on your home or business assets.

Money judgments are almost always dischargeable in bankruptcy, no matter what circumstances led to the lawsuit in the first place or when the judgment was obtained. There are a couple of exceptions (discussed in "Debts That Survive Chapter 7 Bankruptcy," below), but in the vast majority of cases, money judgments are discharged. Even liens on your home arising from a court money judgment can be cancelled if they interfere with your homestead exemption. (See Ch. 7 for more on how bankruptcy affects a judicial lien on your home.)

Debts Arising From Car Accidents

Car accidents usually result in property damage and sometimes in personal injuries. Often, the driver who was responsible for the accident is insured and doesn't have to pay personally for the damage or injury. Sometimes, however, the driver who was at fault either has no insurance or has insurance that doesn't cover everything. In that situation, the driver is financially responsible for the harm.

If the accident was the result of the debtor's negligence—careless driving or failing to drive in a prudent manner—the debt arising from the accident can be discharged in bankruptcy. The debt might also qualify for discharge even if it resulted from reckless driving. If, however, the accident was the result of the driver's willful and malicious act (defined in "Debts Not Dischargeable in Bankruptcy If the Creditor Successfully Objects," below) or the result of drunk driving that causes personal injury, it will not be discharged in bankruptcy.

Other Obligations

The sections above outline the most common debts that are discharged in bankruptcy, but this isn't an exhaustive list. Any obligation or debt will be discharged unless it fits within one of the exceptions discussed in "Debts That Survive Chapter 7 Bankruptcy," below. Even if you aren't sure whether you owe a debt, you should list it in your bankruptcy case to make sure it gets discharged.

Debts That Survive Chapter 7 Bankruptcy

Under bankruptcy law, there are several categories of debt that are "not dischargeable" in Chapter 7 (that is, you will still owe them after your bankruptcy is final):

- Some debts can't be discharged under any circumstances.
- Some will not be discharged unless you convince the court that the debts fit within a narrow exception to the rule.
- Some will not be discharged, but only if the creditor convinces the court that they shouldn't be.

Are Secured Debts Dischargeable?

If you have a debt secured by collateral, bankruptcy eliminates your personal liability for the underlying debt—that is, the creditor can't sue you to collect the debt itself. But bankruptcy doesn't eliminate the creditor's hold, or "lien," on the property that served as collateral under the contract. The same is true of secured debts that you haven't entered into voluntarily, often arising as a result of a lawsuit judgment or an enforcement action by the IRS on taxes that are old enough to be discharged (covered below). In these cases, too, bankruptcy gets rid of the underlying debt, but may not eliminate a lien placed on your property by the IRS or a judgment creditor.

Debts Not Dischargeable Under Any Circumstances

There are certain debts that bankruptcy doesn't affect at all: You will continue to owe them just as if you had never filed.

Certain Tax Debts

While regular income tax debts are dischargeable if they are old enough and meet some other requirements (discussed in "Debts Not Dischargeable Unless You Can Prove That an Exception Applies," below), other types of tax debts are frequently not dischargeable. The rules depend on the type of tax.

- **Fraudulent income taxes.** You cannot discharge debts for income taxes if you didn't file a return or you intentionally avoided your tax obligations. (Returns filed on your behalf by the IRS don't count as "filed by you" and therefore aren't eligible for discharge.)
- **Property taxes.** Property taxes aren't dischargeable unless they became due more than a year before you file for bankruptcy. Even if your personal liability to pay the property tax is discharged, however, the tax lien on your property will remain. From a practical standpoint, the discharge won't help you much, because you'll have to pay off the lien before you can sell the property with clear title. In fact, you may even face a foreclosure action by the property tax creditor if you take too long to come up with the money. In foreclosures and short sales, the taxes are typically paid off as part of the process, leaving you with no liability once the property is sold.
- **Trust fund taxes.** Taxes that have been collected from employees to be paid to a taxing agency, as well as taxes that have been collected from customers under a sales or use tax, are known as "trust fund taxes." They are not dischargeable. Even if the taxes are owed by a business entity, the principals of the entity—its owners and officers—will be held personally responsible for them. The penalties on nonpayment of trust fund taxes can be significant, so you should try to pay them off as quickly as possible.

Debts for Loans From a Retirement Plan

If you've borrowed from your 401(k) or other retirement plan that is qualified under IRS rules for tax-deferred status, you'll be stuck with that debt. Bankruptcy does not discharge 401(k) loans. Why not? Because only debts you owe to another person or entity can be discharged in bankruptcy. A 401(k) loan is money you borrowed from yourself. (You can, however, discharge a loan from a retirement plan in Chapter 13 bankruptcy.)

Domestic Support Obligations (Alimony and Child Support)

Debts defined as "domestic support obligations" are not dischargeable. Domestic support obligations are child support, alimony, and any other debt that is in the nature of alimony, maintenance, or support. For example, one spouse may have agreed to pay some of the other spouse's or the children's future living expenses (shelter, clothing, health insurance, and transportation) in exchange for a lower support obligation. The obligation to pay future living expenses may be treated as support owed to the other spouse—and be nondischargeable—even though no court ordered it.

If one spouse is responsible for paying the other spouse's attorney fees, numerous courts have held that this is a debt in nature of support. However, what one spouse owes to his or her own lawyer is not in the nature of support and can be discharged. (See *In re Rios*, 901 F.2d 71 (7th Cir. 1990); see also *In re Chase*, 372 B.R. 133 (S.D. N.Y. 2007), in which the court rejected the debtor's attorney's many arguments as to why his fees should survive bankruptcy, including claims of fraud and false pretenses.)

To be nondischargeable under this section, a domestic support obligation must have been established—or be capable of becoming established—in:

- a separation agreement, divorce decree, or property settlement agreement
- an order of a court authorized by law to impose support obligations, or

- a determination by a child support enforcement agency or other government unit that is legally authorized to impose support obligations.

A support obligation that has been assigned to a private entity for reasons other than collection (for example, as collateral for a loan) is dischargeable. This exception rarely applies, however: Almost all assignments of support to government or private entities are made for the purpose of collecting the support.

Other Debts Owed to a Spouse, Former Spouse, or Child

Under the old bankruptcy law, debts owed to a spouse or child, other than support that arose from a divorce or separation, were discharged unless the spouse or child appeared in court to object to the discharge. Under the 2005 bankruptcy law, this category of debt is now automatically nondischargeable if owed directly to the child or ex-spouse. The most common of these types of debts is when one spouse agrees to assume responsibility for marital debt or promises to pay the other spouse in exchange for his or her share of the family home. These types of obligations will now be nondischargeable if they are owed to a spouse, former spouse, or child, and arose out of "a divorce or separation or in connection with a separation agreement, divorce decree, or other order of a court of record, or a determination made in accordance with State or territorial law by a governmental unit." (11 U.S.C. § 523 (15).)

Importantly, your obligation to pay debts like these is discharged in respect to the creditor. If the creditor tries to collect the debt from your former spouse, however, your former spouse can go after you for repayment because your obligation to him or her cannot be discharged. In other words, even though the creditor cannot collect from you directly, the creditor may still have a right to collect from your ex—who still has a right to collect from you.

Note that this rule doesn't apply to debts arising from a separation agreement between domestic partners. This is one example of many as to why civil unions do not provide the same benefits as marriage.

Fines, Penalties, and Restitution

You can't discharge fines, penalties, or restitution that a federal, state, or local government has imposed to punish you for violating a law. Examples include:

- fines or penalties imposed under federal election law
- charges imposed for time spent in a court jail (*In re Donohue*, No. 05-01651 (N.D. Iowa 2006))
- fines for infractions, misdemeanors, or felonies
- fines imposed by a judge for contempt of court
- fines imposed by a government agency for violating agency regulations
- surcharges imposed by a court or agency for enforcement of a law
- restitution you are ordered to pay to victims in federal criminal cases, and
- debts owed to a bail bond company as a result of bond forfeiture.

However, one court has held that a restitution obligation imposed on a minor in a juvenile court proceeding can be discharged, because it isn't punitive in nature. (*In re Sweeney*, 341 B.R. 35 (10th Cir. BAP 2006).)

Court Fees

If you are a prisoner, you can't discharge a fee imposed by a court for filing a case, motion, complaint, or appeal, or for other costs and expenses assessed for that court filing, even if you claimed that you were unable to afford the fees. (You can discharge these types of fees in Chapter 13, however.)

Intoxicated Driving Debts

If you kill or injure someone while you are driving and are illegally intoxicated by alcohol or drugs, any debts resulting from the incident aren't dischargeable. Even if a judge or jury finds you liable but doesn't specifically find that you were intoxicated, the debt may still be nondischargeable. The judgment against you won't be discharged if the bankruptcy court (or a state court in a judgment collection action) determines that you were, in fact, intoxicated.

Note that this rule applies only to personal injuries: Debts for property damage resulting from your intoxicated driving are dischargeable.

> EXAMPLE: Christian was in a car accident in which he injured Ellen and damaged her car. He was convicted of driving under the influence. Several months later, Christian filed for bankruptcy and listed Ellen as a creditor. After the bankruptcy case was over, Ellen sued Christian, claiming that the debt wasn't discharged because Christian was driving while intoxicated. (She didn't have to file anything in the bankruptcy proceeding.) If Ellen shows that Christian was illegally intoxicated under his state's laws, she will be able to pursue her personal injury claim against him. She is barred, however, from trying to collect for the damage to her car.

Condominium, Cooperative, and Homeowners' Association Fees

You cannot discharge fees assessed after your bankruptcy filing date by a membership association for a condominium, housing cooperative, or lot in a homeownership association if you or the trustee have an ownership interest in the condominium, cooperative, or lot. As a practical matter, this means that any fees that become due after you file for Chapter 7 bankruptcy will survive the bankruptcy, but fees you owed prior to filing will be discharged.

Debts You Couldn't Discharge in a Previous Bankruptcy

If a bankruptcy court dismissed a previous bankruptcy case because of your fraud or other bad acts (for instance, misfeasance or failure to cooperate with the trustee), you cannot discharge any debts that you tried to discharge in that earlier bankruptcy. (This rule doesn't affect debts you incurred after filing the earlier bankruptcy case.)

> EXAMPLE: You filed for Chapter 7 bankruptcy in 2004, during a really rough time in your life. You had received an earlier Chapter 7 discharge in a case filed in 1998, which made you ineligible to file for Chapter 7 again before 2006, so you used a phony Social Security number when you filed in 2004. The court quickly discovered your ruse and dismissed your case. Luckily for you, you were not prosecuted for fraud. In 2010, you want to file a Chapter 7 case again. You can, because eight years have passed since your 1998 bankruptcy case was filed. Because of your dishonesty, however, you won't be able to discharge any of the debts you listed in your 2004 case.

Debts Not Dischargeable Unless You Can Prove That an Exception Applies

Some debts are not dischargeable in Chapter 7 unless you show the bankruptcy court that the debt should be discharged because it falls within an exception. To get this type of debt discharged, you can take one of two courses of action:

- While your case is open, ask the bankruptcy court to rule that the debt should be discharged. To do this, you have to file and serve a "Complaint to Determine Dischargeability of a Debt," and then show, in court, that your debt isn't covered by the general rule. (The grounds and procedures for getting such debts discharged are discussed in "Disputes Over Dischargeability," below; forms can be found in Appendix D.) If you succeed, the court will rule that the debt is discharged, and the creditor won't be allowed to collect it after bankruptcy.

- In the alternative, you may decide not to take any action during your bankruptcy. If the creditor attempts to collect after your case is closed, you can try to reopen your bankruptcy and raise the issue then (by bringing a contempt motion or by filing a complaint, as explained above). Or, you can wait until the creditor sues you over the debt—or, if you've already lost a lawsuit, until the creditor tries to collect on the judgment—and then argue in state court that the debt has been discharged.

The advantage of not raising the issue in the bankruptcy court is that you avoid the hassle of litigating the issue. And the problem may never come up again if the creditor doesn't sue you. The down side to this strategy is that questions about whether the debt has been discharged will be left hanging over your head after your bankruptcy case is over.

As a general rule, you are better off litigating issues of dischargeability in the bankruptcy court—either during or after your bankruptcy—because bankruptcy courts tend to tilt in the interest of giving the debtor a fresh start, and may be more willing to give you the benefit of the doubt.

If your creditor is a federal or state taxing agency or a student loan creditor, you are probably better off raising the issue during your bankruptcy. On the other hand, you might be better off not raising the issue in your bankruptcy case if you're up against an individual creditor whose claim is not big enough to justify hiring a lawyer. These creditors are probably less likely to pursue you—or even know that they can—after your bankruptcy is over.

Student Loans

Under the old law, student loans made by nonprofit organizations were not dischargeable unless the debtor could show undue hardship. The 2005 law extends the "undue hardship" rule to virtually all student loans, whether made by nonprofit or commercial entities.

Specifically, in addition to loans provided by a nonprofit or government institution, the new law provides that any other "qualified educational loan" will not be discharged in bankruptcy unless the debtor shows undue hardship. The Internal Revenue Code (Section 221(d)(1)) defines a qualified educational loan as:

"any indebtedness incurred by the taxpayer solely to pay qualified higher education expenses—

"(A) which are incurred on behalf of the taxpayer, the taxpayer's spouse, or any dependent of the taxpayer as of the time the indebtedness was incurred,

"(B) which are paid or incurred within a reasonable period of time before or after the indebtedness is incurred, and

"(C) which are attributable to education furnished during a period during which the recipient was an eligible student."

Debts taken on to refinance qualified educational loans also fall within this definition.

There may be some legal developments as courts interpret this new language, but generally it means that just about any type of debt incurred for higher education expenses will not be dischargeable unless you can show undue hardship.

To discharge your student loan on the basis of undue hardship, you must file a separate action in the bankruptcy court (a "Complaint to Determine Dischargeability of Student Loan") and obtain a court ruling in your favor on this issue. Succeeding in an action to discharge a student loan debt typically requires the services of an attorney, although it's possible to do it yourself if you're willing to put in the time. (See "Disputes Over Dischargeability," below.)

Special Rules for HEAL and PLUS Loans

The federal Health Education Assistance Loans (HEAL) Act, not bankruptcy law, governs HEAL loans. Under the HEAL Act, to discharge a loan, you must show that the loan became due more than seven years ago, and that repaying it would not merely be a hardship, but would impose an "unconscionable burden" on your life.

Parents can get Parental Loans for Students (PLUS Loans) to finance a child's education. Even though the parent does not receive the education, the loan is treated like any other student loan if the parent files for bankruptcy. The parent must meet the undue hardship test to discharge the loan.

When determining whether undue hardship exists, courts use one of two tests (depending on where the court is located). Courts look at either:

- the three factors listed below (these come from a case called *Brunner v. New York State Higher Education Services, Inc.*, 46 B.R. 752 (S.D. N.Y. 1985), aff'd, 831 F.2d 395 (2nd Cir. 1987)), or
- the totality of the circumstances, which essentially means the court will consider all of the facts it deems relevant in deciding whether undue hardship exists.

The vast majority of courts use the *Brunner* three-factor test. You must show that all three factors tilt in your favor in order to demonstrate undue hardship. The factors are:

- **Poverty.** Based on your current income and expenses, you cannot maintain a minimal standard of living and repay the loan. The court must consider your current and future employment and income (or your employment and income potential), education, and skills; how marketable your skills are; your health; and your family support obligations.
- **Persistence.** It's not enough that you can't repay your loan right now. You must also show that your current financial condition is likely to continue for a significant part of the repayment period. In one recent case, for example, a debtor with bipolar disorder lost her job as a result of stopping her medication. Because her history demonstrated that she could remain employed as long as she took her medication, however, the court found that her economic condition would not necessarily persist—and rejected her undue hardship claim. (*In re Kelly*, 351 B.R. 45 (E.D. N.Y. 2006).)
- **Good faith.** You must prove that you've made a good-faith effort to repay the debt. Someone who files for bankruptcy immediately after getting out of school or after the period for paying back the loan begins will not fare well in court. Nor will someone who hasn't tried hard to find work. And, if you haven't made any payments, you should be able to show that you took your obligations seriously enough to obtain a deferment or forbearance. (See *In re Kitterman*, 349 B.R. 775 (W.D. Ky. 2006), in which the court found that the debtor's failure to reapply for a deferment after his first request was denied showed his lack of good faith.)

Generally, courts look for reasons to deny student loan discharges. However, if you are older (at least 50 years old), you are likely to remain poor, and you have a history of doing your best to pay off your loan, you may be able to obtain a discharge.

In some cases, courts have found that it would be an undue hardship to repay the entire loan and have relieved the debtor of a portion of the debt. Other courts take the position that it's an all-or-nothing proposition: Either the entire loan is discharged or none of it is discharged.

Different Rules Apply Out West

If you try to discharge your student loans in one of the federal courts that make up the 9th Circuit Court of Appeals (which includes Alaska, Arizona, California, Hawaii, Idaho, Montana, Nevada, Oregon, Utah, and Washington), a much wider variety of factors might be considered. Circumstances that could potentially allow a discharge include:

- The debtor or debtor's dependent has a serious mental or physical disability, which prevents employment or advancement.
- The debtor has an obligation to care for dependents.
- The debtor has a lack of, severely limited, or poor quality education.
- The debtor has a lack of usable or market-able job skills.
- The debtor is underemployed.
- The debtor's income potential in his or her chosen field has maxed out, and the debtor has no more lucrative job skills.
- The debtor has limited work years remaining in which to pay back the loan.
- The debtor's age or other factors prevent retraining or relocation as a means of earning more to repay the loan.
- The debtor lacks assets that could be used to repay the loan.
- The debtor's potentially increasing expenses outweigh any potential appreciation in the debtor's assets or increases in the debtor's income.
- The debtor lacks better financial options elsewhere.

See *Educational Credit Management Corp. v. Nys*, 446 F.3d 938 (9th Cir. 2006).

SEE AN EXPERT

Consult with a lawyer about discharging your loan. There are dozens of court cases that interpret the three factors from the *Brunner* case or explain what the "totality of the circumstances" include. Debtors lose most of these cases, but sometimes they win. If you are filing for bankruptcy and you have substantial student loan debt, you should talk to an attorney who is knowledgeable on these issues.

Can Your School Withhold Your Transcript?

If you don't pay back loans obtained directly from your college, the school can withhold your transcript. But if you file for bankruptcy and receive a discharge of the loan, the school can no longer withhold your records. (*In re Gustafson*, 111 B.R. 282 (9th Cir. BAP 1990).) In addition, while your bankruptcy case is pending, the school cannot withhold your transcript, even if the court eventually rules your school loan nondischargeable. (*Loyola University v. McClarty*, 234 B.R. 386 (E.D. La. 1999).)

Regular Income Taxes

People who are considering bankruptcy because of tax problems are almost always concerned about income taxes they owe to the IRS or the state equivalent. There is a myth afoot that income tax debts can never be discharged in bankruptcy. This is not true, however, if the debt is relatively old and you can meet several other conditions. Tax debts that qualify under these rules are technically discharged; however, the IRS may continue to try to collect the debt until you file a complaint in the bankruptcy court to determine dischargeability of the debt and receive an order from the court that the debt is discharged.

Income tax debts are dischargeable if you meet all of these conditions:

- You filed a legitimate (nonfraudulent) tax return for the tax year or years in question.

If the IRS completes a Substitute for Return on your behalf that you neither sign nor consent to, your return is not considered filed. (See *In re Bergstrom,* 949 F.2d 341 (10th Cir. 1991).)

- The debt stems from a tax return (not a Substitute for Return) that you actually filed at least two years before you filed for bankruptcy.
- The tax return for the liability you wish to discharge was first due at least three years before you filed for bankruptcy. (If you get an extension on the filing date, the three-year period begins on the extended due date, not the original due date.)
- The IRS or state taxing agency has not assessed your liability for the taxes within the 240 days before you filed for bankruptcy.

You're probably safe if you do not receive a formal notice of assessment of federal taxes from the IRS within that 240-day period. If you're unsure of the assessment date, consider seeing a tax lawyer—but don't rely on the IRS for the date. If the IRS gives you the wrong date—telling you that the 240 days have elapsed—the IRS won't be held to it if it turns out to be wrong. (See, for example, *In re Howell,* 120 B.R. 137 (9th Cir. BAP 1990).) Under the 2005 bankruptcy law, the 240-day period is extended by the period of time collections were suspended because you were negotiating with the IRS for an offer in compromise or because of a previous bankruptcy.

EXAMPLE: Fred filed a tax return in August 2009 for the 2008 tax year. In March

Willful Evasion of Tax

The IRS views certain facts as red flags of possible willful tax evasion. They include:

- membership in a tax protest organization
- a pattern of unfiled returns
- filing a fraudulent, frivolous, blank, or incomplete return
- repeatedly understating income or overstating deductions on returns
- serial failure to pay taxes
- concealing, giving away, or trading away valuable assets or transferring title
- selling assets way below fair value (especially to insiders)
- setting up abusive trust or sham tax shelter and transferring assets to it
- creating a corporation and transferring assets to it
- changing bank or bank account frequently
- closing bank account and conducting business in cash only
- adding another person's name to bank account
- depositing income in another's bank account
- using a foreign bank account
- changing name or spelling of name; changing Social Security number
- an altercation with a revenue officer
- engaging in money laundering
- withdrawing cash from bank and hiding it
- claiming incorrect number of exemptions on tax return
- purchasing property in someone else's name
- refusing to cooperate with a revenue officer or deliberately obstructing audit or investigation.
- losing, concealing, or destroying financial documents
- maintaining inadequate records
- concealing actual residence address or business address
- trading valuable assets for less valuable assets
- devising clever schemes (such as divorcing your wife, directing all income to her, and renting a room in her house), and
- living a lavish lifestyle knowing that delinquent taxes had not been paid.

2011, the IRS audited Fred's 2008 return and assessed a tax due of $8,000. In May 2012, Fred files for bankruptcy. The taxes that Fred wishes to discharge were for tax year 2008. The return for those taxes was due on April 15, 2009, more than three years prior to Fred's filing date. The tax return was filed in August 2009, more than two years before Fred's bankruptcy filing date, and the assessment date of March 2011 was more than 240 days before the filing date. Fred can discharge those taxes.

- You didn't willfully evade payment of a tax. What constitutes willful tax evasion is a subjective matter, depending on the view of the IRS personnel making the judgment. See "Willful Evasion of Tax," above, for a list of factors that may cause the IRS to suspect willful tax evasion.

TIP

Get an account transcript to make sure you've got the dates right. If you want to make sure you have met all the requirements to get a tax debt discharged, you can obtain an account transcript from the IRS. To find out how, visit www.irs.gov and type "account transcript" in the search box.

If you meet each of these five requirements, your personal liability for the taxes should be discharged. However, any lien placed on your property by the taxing authority will remain after your bankruptcy. The result is that the taxing authority can't go after your bank account or wages, but you'll have to pay off the lien before you can sell your real estate with a clear title.

Penalties and interest on taxes that are dischargeable are also dischargeable. If the underlying tax debt is nondischargeable, courts are split as to whether you can discharge the penalties or not.

EXAMPLE: Jill failed to file a tax return for 2005. In 2009, the IRS discovers Jill's failure and in January 2011 assesses taxes of $5,000 and penalties and interest of $12,000. Jill files for bankruptcy in January 2012. Because Jill didn't file a return for 2005, she can't discharge the tax, even though it became due more than three years past (and more than 240 days have elapsed since the taxes were assessed). Jill may be able to discharge the IRS penalties for failure to file a tax return and failure to pay the tax. Or course, the IRS is likely to argue that she cannot discharge the penalties, and some courts will agree.

If You Borrow Money to Pay Nondischargeable Debts

Debts incurred to pay nondischargeable taxes will also be nondischargeable. If you borrowed money or used your credit card to pay taxes that would otherwise not be discharged, you can't eliminate that loan or credit card debt in a Chapter 7 bankruptcy. In other words, you can't turn a nondischargeable tax debt into a dischargeable tax debt by putting it on your credit card. This is true for any type of nondischargeable tax owed to a governmental agency.

However, credit card companies may not come after you for this type of debt. Even if a debt is not dischargeable under this rule, the creditors may not know it. In many Chapter 7 bankruptcy cases, credit card lenders don't scrutinize their records to find out exactly what you paid for with a particular card. Even if you did use the card to pay a tax, the underlying tax debt would have to be nondischargeable (which would require some analysis by the credit card entity's staff).

On the other hand, if you obtained a loan for the specific purpose of paying a tax, you can count on the lender knowing this rule and relying on it to continue its collection efforts after your bankruptcy.

Debts you take on to pay nondischargeable debts can be discharged in Chapter 13 bankruptcy. See Ch. 3 for more information on debts that are dischargeable only in Chapter 13.

Debts Not Dischargeable in Bankruptcy If the Creditor Successfully Objects

Four types of debts may survive Chapter 7 bankruptcy if, and only if:

- the creditor files a formal objection—called a Complaint to Determine Dischargeability —during the bankruptcy proceedings, and
- the creditor proves that the debt fits into one of the categories discussed below.

TIP

Creditors might not bother to object. Even though bankruptcy rules give creditors the right to object to the discharge of certain debts, many creditors—and their attorneys—don't fully understand this right. Even a creditor who knows the score might sensibly decide to write off the debt rather than contesting it. It can cost a lot to bring a dischargeability action (as this type of case is known). If the debt isn't huge, a cost benefit analysis might show that it will be cheaper to forgo collecting the debt than to fight about it in court.

Debts Arising From Fraud

In order for a creditor to prove that one of your debts should survive bankruptcy because you incurred it through fraud, the debt must fit one of the categories below.

Debts from intentionally fraudulent behavior. If a creditor can show that a debt resulted from your dishonest act, and that the debt wouldn't have arisen had you been honest, the court probably will not let you discharge the debt. Here are some examples:

- You rented or borrowed an expensive item and claimed it was yours, so you could use it as collateral to get a loan.
- You got a loan by telling the lender you'd pay it back when you had no intention of doing so.
- You wrote a check against insufficient funds but assured the merchant that the check was good.
- You wrote a check for something and stopped payment on it, even though you kept the item.

For this type of debt to be nondischargeable, your deceit must be intentional, and the creditor must have relied on your deceit in extending credit. Again, these are facts that the creditor has to prove before the debt will be ruled nondischargeable by the court.

Debts from a false written statement about your financial condition. If a creditor proves that you incurred a debt by making a false written statement, the debt isn't dischargeable. Here are the rules:

- The false statement must be written—for instance, made on a credit application, rental application, resume, or balance sheet.
- The false statement must have been "material"—that is, it was a potentially significant factor in the creditor's decision to extend you credit. The two most common types of materially false statements are omitting debts and overstating income.
- The false statement must relate to your financial condition or the financial condition of an "insider"—a person close to you or a business entity with which you're associated.
- The creditor must have relied on the false statement, and the reliance must have been reasonable.
- You must have intended to deceive the creditor. This is extremely hard for the creditor to prove based simply on your behavior. The creditor would have to show outrageous behavior on your part, such as adding a "0" to your income (claiming you make $180,000 rather than $18,000) on a credit application.

Recent debts for luxuries. If you run up more than $550 in debt to any one creditor for luxury goods or services within the 90 days before you file for bankruptcy, the law presumes that your intent was fraudulent regarding those charges. Therefore, the charges will survive your bankruptcy unless you prove that your intent wasn't fraudulent. "Luxury goods and services" do not include things that are reasonably necessary for the support and maintenance of you and your dependents (what that means is decided on a case-by-case basis).

Recent cash advances. If you get cash advances from any one creditor totaling more than $825 under an open-ended consumer credit plan within the 70 days before you file for bankruptcy, the debt is nondischargeable. "Open-ended" means there's no date when the debt must be repaid, but rather, as with most credit cards, you may take forever to repay the debt as long as you pay a minimum amount each month.

Debts Arising From Debtor's Willful and Malicious Acts

If the act that caused the debt was willful *and* malicious (that is, you intended to inflict a specific injury to a person or property), the debt isn't dischargeable if the creditor successfully objects. However, perhaps because they don't know their rights, creditors often don't object in this situation.

Generally, crimes involving intentional injury to people or damage to property are considered willful and malicious acts. Examples are assaults, rape, intentionally setting fire to a house (arson), or vandalism.

Your liability for personal injury or property damage the victim sustained in these types of cases will almost always be ruled nondischargeable—but (once again) only if the victim-creditor objects during your bankruptcy case. Other acts that would typically be considered to be willful and malicious include:

- kidnapping
- deliberately causing extreme anxiety, fear, or shock
- libel or slander, and
- illegal acts by a landlord to evict a tenant, such as removing a door or changing the locks.

Debts From Embezzlement, Larceny, or Breach of Fiduciary Duty

A debt incurred as a result of embezzlement, larceny, or breach of fiduciary duty is not dischargeable if the creditor successfully objects to its discharge.

"Embezzlement" means taking property entrusted to you for another and using it for yourself. "Larceny" is another word for theft. "Breach of fiduciary duty" is the failure to live up to a duty of trust you owe someone, based on a relationship where you're required to manage property or money for another, or a relationship that is close and confidential. Common fiduciary relationships include those between:

- spouses
- business partners
- corporations and LLCs and their officers
- business entities and their creditors
- attorney and client
- estate executor and beneficiary
- in-home caregiver and recipient of services, and
- guardian and ward.

Debts or Creditors You Don't List

In your bankruptcy paperwork, you must list all of your creditors and provide their most current addresses. This gives the court some assurance that everyone who needs to know about your bankruptcy will receive notice. As long as you do your part, the debt will be discharged (as long as it's otherwise dischargeable under the rules), even if the official notice fails to reach the creditor for some reason beyond your control. For example, if your notice doesn't get to the creditor because the post office errs or the creditor moves without leaving a forwarding address, that won't count against you.

Suppose, however, that you forget to list a creditor on your bankruptcy papers or carelessly misstate a creditor's identity or address. In that situation, the court's notice may not reach the creditor and the debt may not be discharged. Here are the rules:

- If the creditor knew or should have known of your bankruptcy through other means, such as a letter or phone call from you, the debt will be discharged even though the creditor wasn't listed. In this situation, the creditor should have taken steps to protect its interests, even though it didn't receive formal notice from the court.
- If all of your assets are exempt—that is, you have a no-asset case—the debt will be discharged unless the debt is non-dischargeable in any circumstances. In this situation, the creditor wouldn't have benefited from receiving notice because there is no property to distribute. However, if the lack of notice deprives a creditor of the opportunity to successfully object to the discharge by filing a complaint in the bankruptcy court (such as for a fraudulent debt), the debt may survive your bankruptcy.

Disputes Over Dischargeability

If your debt is not one that's automatically discharged, there may be a dispute over whether the debt should survive your bankruptcy. For example, if the debt will survive bankruptcy unless the judge orders otherwise, the burden is on you to file and litigate a Complaint to Determine Dischargeability. Or, if the debt will be discharged unless the judge orders otherwise, the creditor must prove that the debt should not be discharged, and you might have to defend yourself in court against the creditor's Complaint to Determine Dischargeability.

Complaints to Determine Dischargeability

If you want to have a student loan or tax debt wiped out (if the IRS doesn't recognize your right to discharge it), you will have to prove to the court that you meet all of the requirements for discharge. To do this, you must file a formal complaint with the bankruptcy court. Generally, you can file your complaint any time after you file for bankruptcy. Some courts may impose their own deadlines, however, so check your court's local rules.

Suppose, for example, that you want to have a student loan discharged. As discussed above, you will have to prove that it would be an undue hardship to repay the loan. You will file at least two forms: a Complaint to Determine Dischargeability, stating the facts that make repayment an undue hardship, and a proof of service, showing that you served the complaint on the affected creditor and the trustee.

CAUTION

Get help from a lawyer if you need it. Before you charge off into court, here is a heartfelt warning: Embarking upon litigation in the bankruptcy court can be quite a challenge if you don't have help from someone who has experience in the field. At the very least, you'll want to obtain a copy of *Represent Yourself in Court*, by Paul Bergman and Sara Berman (Nolo), and maybe consult with a bankruptcy lawyer from time to time to get your bearings. If your case is fairly straightforward—for example, a medical or similar condition is keeping you from working enough to pay your student loan—you may be able to proceed on your own. However, some people find it stressful or uncomfortable to discuss their own medical or other problems in court. If you think this might be difficult for you, consider filing your own bankruptcy case and hiring a lawyer to handle only this procedure.

Creditor Objections to Discharges

If you are defending against a creditor's claim that a debt should not be discharged, you and the trustee will be served with a copy of the complaint. To defend against the objection, you must file a written response within a specified time limit, respond to any requests for information that the creditor sends you, and be prepared to present your case in court through declarations (written statements under oath) and possibly live witnesses.

If the debt is one of the types that will be discharged unless the creditor objects, the creditor has the burden of proving that the debt fits within the specified category. For instance, if the creditor claims that the debt arose from a "willful and malicious injury" you caused, the creditor will have to prove that your actions were willful and malicious. Similarly, if the creditor is arguing that a particular debt arose from your fraudulent acts, the creditor will have to prove that all the required elements of fraud were present. Absent this type of specific proof, the bankruptcy court will reject the creditor's lawsuit and maybe even award you attorneys' fees (if you use an attorney).

Keep in mind, however, that if you plead guilty to a criminal charge involving fraud, a document from the court showing your conviction may be all that's necessary to convince the judge to rule the debt nondischargeable. A no-contest plea, on the other hand, would not have the same effect, because that type of plea can't be used as evidence in a later civil case (such as a bankruptcy case).

In a civil case that resulted in a judgment prior to the bankruptcy filing, the judgment can sometimes determine the outcome of the Complaint to Determine Dischargeability. This will depend on whether the civil court (or jury) made specific findings of misconduct that meet the requirements set out above (for example, for fraud).

> EXAMPLE: Ben sues Francis in civil court for breach of contract. The jury finds that Francis owes Ben $10,000 for failing to repay a loan, Francis made deliberate and fraudulent misrepresentations with the intent to trick Ben into lending the money in the first place, and Ben is entitled to punitive damages because of these fraudulent statements. Francis files for bankruptcy and tries to discharge this debt. Because the jury found that Francis committed fraud of the type that precludes the discharge of the debt in bankruptcy, however, the bankruptcy judge honors the prior judgment and rules that the debt cannot be discharged.

The fact that the creditor has the burden of proof in this type of case doesn't mean that you should sit back and do nothing. You should be prepared with proof of your own to show that the creditor's allegations in the complaint are not true (unless, of course, you already admitted your guilt in a prior case).

Objections on the Basis of Credit Card Fraud

These days, the creditors most likely to object to the discharge of a debt are credit card issuers. Except for charges made shortly before filing for bankruptcy, there are few specific rules about what constitutes credit card fraud in bankruptcy. But courts are looking to the following factors to determine fraud:

- **Timing.** A short time between incurring the charges and filing for bankruptcy may suggest fraudulent intent.
- **Manipulation of the system.** Incurring more debt after consulting with an attorney may lead a judge to conclude that you ran up your debts in anticipation of your bankruptcy filing.
- **Amount.** Recent charges of more than $550 for luxuries will be presumed to be fraudulent.
- **Crafty use of the card.** Multiple charges under $50 (to avoid preclearance of the charge by the credit card issuer) when you've reached your credit limit will start to look like fraud.
- **Deliberate misuse.** Charges after the card issuer has ordered you to return the card or sent several "past due" notices don't look good.
- **Last-minute sprees.** Changes in the way you use the card (for instance, much travel after a sedentary life), charges for luxuries, and multiple charges on the same day could lead to problems.

- **Bad-faith use.** Charges made when you were clearly insolvent and unable to make the required minimum payment (for instance, because you lost your job and had no other income or savings) are a no-no. Banks claim that insolvency is evidenced by any of the following:
  - A notation in the customer's file that the customer has met with an attorney (perhaps because the customer told the creditor he or she was considering bankruptcy and had talked to an attorney about it).
  - A rapid increase in spending, followed by 60–90 days without activity.
  - The date noted on any attorney's fee statement, if the customer consults a lawyer for help with a bankruptcy.

Of course, the mere fact that a creditor challenges your discharge of a credit card debt

Questions for Credit Card Companies

If you are facing a dischargeability action over a credit card debt, you'll have an opportunity to send written questions (called interrogatories) to the company, to be answered under oath. Here are some you might considering asking:

- You (the card issuer) have alleged that the debtor obtained funds from you by false pretenses and false representations. Please state with particularity the nature of the false pretenses and false representations.
- State all steps taken by you, the card issuer, to determine the creditworthiness of the debtor.
- Identify all means that you, the card issuer, used to verify the debtor's income, expenses, assets, or liabilities. Identify any documents obtained in the verification process.
- Identify your general policies concerning the decision to grant credit and how those policies were applied to the debtor.
- You have alleged that at the time the debtor obtained credit from you, the debtor did not intend to repay it. State all facts in your possession to support this allegation.
- Identify all credit policies you allege were violated by the debtor. State how such policies were communicated to the debtor, and identify all documents that contained those policies.
- Identify the dates on which you claim any of the following events occurred:
  - The debtor consulted a bankruptcy attorney.
  - The debtor had a reduction in income.
  - The debtor formed the intent not to repay this debt.
  - The debtor violated the terms of the credit agreement.
  - State whether you believe that every user of a credit card who does not later repay the debt has committed fraud.
  - If the answer to the preceding question is no, state all facts that give rise to allegations of fraud in this debtor's use of the card.

After receiving a list of questions like these, the credit card issuer is likely to conclude that you are serious about defending yourself. It might even withdraw its complaint.

If you want to read cases supporting the debtor's position when a credit card issuer claims fraud, visit a law library or search the Internet for some of these cases:

- *In re Hearn*, 211 B.R. 774 (N.D. Ga. 1997)
- *In re Etto*, 210 B.R. 734 (N.D. Ohio 1997)
- *In re Hunter*, 210 B.R. 212 (M.D. Fla. 1997)
- *In re Davis*, 176 B.R. 118 (W.D. N.Y. 1994)
- *In re Kitzmiller*, 206 B.R. 424 (N.D. W.Va. 1997)
- *In re Christensen*, 193 B.R. 863 (N.D. Ill. 1996)
- *In re Chinchilla*, 202 B.R. 1010 (S.D. Fla. 1996)
- *In re Grayson*, 199 B.R. 397 (W.D. Mo. 1996), and
- *In re Vianese*, 195 B.R. 572 (N.D. N.Y. 1995).

For tips on doing your own legal research, see "Legal Research" in Ch. 12.

doesn't mean the creditor will win in court. In most of these cases, the creditor files a standard 15- to 20-paragraph form complaint, which states conclusions without supporting facts. The creditor rarely attaches account statements, but only a printout of the charges to which it is objecting.

Some very sophisticated debtors may be able to represent themselves in this type of case. If you decide to do this, you'll need lots of time to familiarize yourself with general litigation procedures and strategies, as well as the bankruptcy cases in your district that deal with this issue. (Start by getting a copy of *Represent Yourself in Court*, by Paul Bergman and Sara Berman (Nolo).) Allegations of fraud should make you seriously consider consulting an attorney. If a creditor challenges discharge of a debt by claiming you engaged in fraud, but the judge finds in your favor, the judge may order the creditor to reimburse you for the money you spent on attorneys' fees.

Issues That May Arise After Your Bankruptcy

Even after your bankruptcy case is closed, there may still be one or two issues you need to deal with. For example, you may need to take action if:

- You receive or discover new nonexempt property.
- A creditor tries to collect a nondischargeable debt.
- A creditor tries to collect a debt that has been discharged in your bankruptcy.
- A creditor or the trustee asks the court to revoke your discharge in your bankruptcy.
- A government agency or private employer discriminates against you because of your bankruptcy.

This section explains how these events typically unfold, and how you can respond to them. But don't worry too much: Very few people face these circumstances. If you were complete and honest in your paperwork, it's very unlikely that you'll run into any postbankruptcy problems.

Newly Acquired or Discovered Property

If you omit property from your bankruptcy papers, or you acquire certain kinds of property soon after you file, the trustee may reopen your case after your discharge (if the trustee learns about the property). The trustee probably won't take action unless the property is nonexempt and is valuable enough to justify reopening the case, seizing and selling the property, and distributing the proceeds among your creditors. Even if the property you acquire or discover after discharge is of little value, however, you should still tell the trustee about it. Even if you think the assets don't justify reopening the case, that's the trustee's decision, not yours.

Notifying the Trustee

It's your legal responsibility to notify the bankruptcy trustee if either of the following is true:

- Within 180 days of filing for bankruptcy, you receive or become entitled to receive certain types of property that belong in your bankruptcy estate.
- You discover that you failed to disclose nonexempt property in your bankruptcy papers.

Newly Acquired Property

If you receive, or become entitled to receive, certain types of property within 180 days after your bankruptcy filing date, you must report it to the trustee, even if you think the property is exempt or your case is already closed. If you don't report it and the trustee learns of your acquisition, the trustee could ask the court to revoke your discharge. (See "Attempts to Revoke Your Discharge," below.) You must report:

- an inheritance (property you receive, or become entitled to receive, because of someone's death)
- property from a divorce settlement, or
- proceeds of a life insurance policy or death benefit plan. (11 U.S.C. § 541(a)(5).)

These categories of property are discussed in more detail in Ch. 5.

To report this property to the trustee, use the form called Supplemental Schedule for Property Acquired After Bankruptcy Discharge. A blank copy and instructions are in Appendix D.

Property Not Listed in Your Papers

If, after your bankruptcy case is closed, you discover some property that you should have listed in your bankruptcy papers, you don't need to file any documents with the court. You must, however, notify the trustee. Here is a sample letter:

Letter to Trustee

1900 Wishbone Place
Wilkes-Barre, PA 18704

October 22, 20xx

Francine J. Chen
Trustee of the Bankruptcy Court
217 Federal Building
197 S. Main St.
Wilkes-Barre, PA 18701

Dear Ms. Chen:

I've just discovered that I own some property I didn't know of while my bankruptcy case was open. Apparently, when I was a child I inherited a bank account from my uncle, the proceeds of which were supposed to be turned over to me when I turned 21. Although I turned 21 eight years ago, for some unknown reason I never got the money.

The account, #2424-5656-08 in the Bank of New England, 1700 Minuteman Plaza, Boston, MA 02442, has a balance of $4,975.19. As you know, I opted for the federal exemptions in my case and do not own a home. I believe this property would be exempt under 11 U.S.C. § 522(d)(5). Please let me know how you intend to proceed.

Sincerely,
Ondine Wallace
Ondine Wallace

CAUTION

Omitting property could put your discharge at risk. If the trustee believes you intentionally omitted the property from your petition, the trustee can get your case reopened and attempt to cancel your discharge. If it would appear to a neutral person that your omission could have been deliberate, consult with a bankruptcy lawyer before talking to the trustee.

Reopening Your Bankruptcy Case

If any of the new or newly discovered property is valuable and nonexempt, the trustee may try to reopen your case, take the property, and have it sold to pay your creditors. As noted above, the trustee will probably do this if it looks like the profit from selling the property will be large enough to offset the cost of reopening your bankruptcy case and administering the sale.

To get to these new assets, the trustee files a motion to reopen the case. Judges usually grant these motions, unless they think too much time has passed or the property isn't valuable enough to justify reopening. How much time constitutes "too much time" varies with the facts of the case. Once the case is reopened, the trustee asks the court for authorization to sell the new assets and distribute the proceeds.

CAUTION

Get help if you're fighting the trustee's attempt to reopen your case. If you can bear to lose the property, consider consenting to what the trustee wants. But if your discharge or valuable property is at stake, consult a bankruptcy lawyer. You could oppose the motion to reopen on your own, but you will need to do a lot of legal research. (See Ch. 12 for tips on lawyers and research.)

Newly Discovered Creditors

Perhaps you inadvertently failed to list a particular creditor on your schedule. As we pointed out in Ch. 10, you can always amend your paperwork if you discover the omission while your bankruptcy case is still open. But suppose you don't become aware of your omission until your bankruptcy is closed. Does that mean that the debt survives your bankruptcy? Not at all. If the creditor had actual knowledge of your bankruptcy, then it's the same as if the creditor were actually listed in your papers.

Even if the omitted creditor didn't have actual knowledge or you lost track of one or more creditors and had no way to identify them in your bankruptcy schedules, the the debt will probably be considered discharged. If yours was a no-asset case (that is, all of your property was exempt), the debt is considered discharged unless, by being left out, your creditor lost the opportunity to contest the discharge on the ground that the debt was caused by your fraudulent or embezzling behavior, or by a willful and malicious act (such as assault or libel). It is often possible to reopen the bankruptcy and let the bankruptcy judge rule on whether the debt is, in fact, dischargeable. If the creditor sues you in state court for a judgment, you could argue the issue in that court or have the case removed to bankruptcy court.

If yours was an asset case—that is, at some point in your case, your unsecured creditors received some property from your bankruptcy estate—your situation is more difficult. Your nonexempt assets were already distributed to your other unsecured creditors, so the omitted creditor would be unfairly discriminated against if the debt were discharged. If the debt is a large one, you might want to hire a lawyer to reopen the case and argue that the debt should be discharged due to your particular circumstances.

Postbankruptcy Attempts to Collect Debts

After bankruptcy, creditors whose debts haven't been discharged are entitled to be paid. Creditors whose debts have been discharged may not pursue the debt further. But it isn't always clear into which category a creditor falls. The bankruptcy court doesn't give you an itemized list of your debts, indicating which have been discharged and which have not. Instead, your final discharge paper merely explains the types of debts that are discharged in general terms. Because of this lack of specificity, it can be tough to figure out whether a particular debt has been wiped out.

How do you know which debts have been discharged and which debts must still be paid? Here's the general rule: All the debts you listed in your bankruptcy papers are discharged unless a creditor successfully objected to the discharge of a particular debt in the bankruptcy court, or the debt falls in one of the following categories discussed earlier in this chapter.

Even if a debt is not listed in your bankruptcy papers, it will be considered discharged if yours was a no-asset case—unless the creditor could have successfully challenged the discharge in bankruptcy court if the creditor were properly notified of your case.

Even if you think some of your debts weren't discharged in bankruptcy, the creditors may never try to collect. Many creditors believe that bankruptcy cuts off their rights, period; even attorneys often don't understand that some debts survive bankruptcy.

If a creditor does try to collect a debt after your bankruptcy discharge, write to the creditor and state that your debts were discharged. Unless you're absolutely certain that the debt wasn't discharged—for example, a student loan for which the court denied your hardship request—this is a justifiable position for you to take.

Letter to Creditor

388 Elm Street
Oakdale, WY 95439

March 18, 20xx

Bank of Wyoming
18th and "J" Streets
Cheyenne, WY 98989

To Whom It May Concern:

I've received numerous letters from your bank claiming that I owe $6,000 for charges between September 1997 and September 1999. I received a bankruptcy discharge of my debts on February 1, 20xx. I enclose a copy of the discharge for your reference.

Sincerely,

Brenda Woodruff
Brenda Woodruff

If the creditor ignores your letter and continues collection efforts, there are other ways to respond:

- **Amend your bankruptcy papers.** Remember that an unlisted debt is discharged in a no-asset case, unless the creditor was deprived of a chance to oppose the debt's discharge. If the court allows it, you can reopen the bankruptcy, amend your papers to list the debt, and then see what the creditor does.
- **Do nothing.** The creditor knows you've just been through bankruptcy, have little or no nonexempt property, and probably have no way to pay the debt, especially all at once. Thus, if you don't respond to collection efforts, the creditor may decide to leave you alone, at least for a while.
- **Try to get judgments wiped out.** If a creditor sued you and won before you filed for bankruptcy, the creditor may try to collect on that judgment, unless you can convince a state court that the judgment was discharged in bankruptcy. Creditors can try to enforce judgments years later, so it's a good idea to reopen your bankruptcy case now and ask the judge to rule that the judgment is discharged. (See Ch. 10 for information on reopening your case.)
- **Negotiate.** Try to negotiate for a lower balance or a payment schedule that works for you. Again, the creditor knows you've just been through bankruptcy and may be willing to compromise.
- **Defend in court.** If the creditor sues you for the debt, you can raise any defenses you have to the debt itself.

  EXAMPLE: The Department of Education sued Edna for failing to pay back a student loan she received. Edna refused to make the payments because the trade school she gave the money to went out of business before classes even began. Because this is one of the few valid defenses to the collection of a student loan, Edna should respond to the lawsuit and assert her defense.

- **Protest a garnishment or other judgment collection effort.** A creditor who has sued you and won a court judgment for a nondischargeable debt is likely to try to take (garnish) your wages or other property to satisfy the judgment. But the creditor can't take it all. What was exempt during your bankruptcy is still exempt. Nonetheless, if you are employed, the creditor can still request that 25% of your wages be taken out of each paycheck. If the debt was for child support or alimony, the creditor can take even more: up to 60% if you don't currently support anyone and up to 50% if you do. Those amounts may increase by 5% if you haven't paid child support in more than 12 weeks.

  Soon after the garnishment—or, in some states, before—the state court must notify you of the garnishment, what's exempt under your state's laws, and how you can protest. You can protest a garnishment if it isn't justified or causes you hardship. To protest, you'll have to file a document in the state court. That document goes by different names in different states. In New York, for example, it's called a Discharge of Attachment; in California, it's a Claim of Exemption. If you do protest, the state court must hold a hearing within a reasonable time, where you can present evidence as to why the court should not enforce the garnishment. The court may not agree, but it's certainly worth a try.

Protesting a wage garnishment is usually a relatively straightforward procedure. Because states are required to tell you how to proceed, you'll probably be able to handle it without the assistance of a lawyer.

Most states also have procedures for objecting to other types of property garnishments, such as a levy of a bank account. You'll have to do a bit of research at a law library to learn the exact protest procedure, which is generally similar to the one for protesting a wage garnishment. (See Ch. 12 for tips on doing your own research.)

Dealing With Difficult Debts After Bankruptcy

For some debts, such as taxes, child support, and alimony, exempt property may be taken, and a garnishment protest will do little good. Don't be surprised if the U.S. Treasury Department initially garnishes nearly 100% of your wages to pay back federal income taxes. The best strategy here is to attempt to negotiate the amount down, not to fight the taxing agency's right to garnish in the first place.

Attempts to Collect Clearly Discharged Debts

If a creditor tries to collect a debt that clearly was discharged in your bankruptcy, you should respond at once with a letter like the one shown below. Again, you can assume a debt was discharged if you listed it in your bankruptcy papers, the creditor didn't successfully object to its discharge, and it doesn't fall into one of the nondischargeable categories listed above. And, if yours was a no-asset case, you can assume the debt was discharged even if the debt wasn't listed. If you live in a community property state and your spouse filed alone, your creditors will likely also treat your share of the community debts as discharged.

Letter to Creditor

1905 Fifth Road
N. Miami Beach, FL 35466

March 18, 20xx

Bank of Miami
2700 Finances Hwy
Miami, FL 36678

To Whom It May Concern:

I've been contacted once by letter and once by phone by Rodney Moore of your bank. Mr. Moore claims that I owe $4,812 on Visa account number 1234 567 890 123.

As you're well aware, this debt was discharged in bankruptcy on February 1, 20xx. Thus, your collection efforts violate federal law, 11 U.S.C. § 524. If they continue, I won't hesitate to pursue my legal rights, including bringing a lawsuit against you for harassment.

Sincerely,
Dawn Schaffer
Dawn Schaffer

If a debt was discharged, the law prohibits creditors from filing a lawsuit, sending you collection letters, calling you, withholding credit, and threatening to file or actually filing a criminal complaint against you.

If the collection efforts don't immediately stop, you'll likely need the assistance of a lawyer to write the creditor again and, if that doesn't work, to sue the creditor for harassment. If the creditor sues you over the debt, you'll want to raise the discharge as a defense and sue the creditor yourself to stop the illegal collection efforts. The bankruptcy court has the power to hold the creditor in contempt of court. The court may also fine the creditor for the humiliation, inconvenience, and anguish you suffered, and order the creditor to pay your attorneys' fees. (See, for example, *In re Barbour,* 77 B.R. 530 (E.D. N.C. 1987), where the court fined a creditor $900 for attempting to collect a discharged debt.)

You can bring a lawsuit to stop collection efforts in state court or in the bankruptcy court. Bankruptcy courts are often more familiar with the prohibitions against collection and may be more sympathetic to you. If the creditor sues you (almost certainly in state court), you or your attorney can file papers requesting that the case be transferred to the bankruptcy court.

Attempts to Revoke Your Discharge

In rare instances, a trustee or creditor may ask the bankruptcy court to revoke the discharge of *all* your debts. If the trustee or a creditor attempts to revoke your discharge, consult a bankruptcy attorney. (See Ch. 12 for tips on finding a lawyer.)

Your discharge can be revoked only if the creditor or trustee proves one of the following:

- You obtained the discharge through fraud that the trustee or creditor discovered after your discharge.
- You intentionally didn't tell the trustee that you acquired property from an inheritance, a divorce settlement, or a life insurance policy or death benefit plan within 180 days after you filed for bankruptcy.
- You deliberately failed to report property that you had when you filed (for example, a commission that was due but not yet paid when you filed).
- Before your case was closed, you refused to obey an order of the bankruptcy court or, for a reason other than the privilege against self-incrimination, you refused to answer an important question asked by the court.

For the court to revoke your discharge on the basis of fraud, the trustee or creditor must file a complaint within one year of your discharge. For the court to revoke your discharge on the basis of your fraudulent failure to report property or your refusal to obey an order or answer a question, the complaint must be filed either within one year of your discharge or before your case is closed, whichever is later. You're entitled to receive a copy of the complaint and to respond, and the court must hold a hearing on the matter before deciding whether to revoke your discharge.

If your discharge is revoked, you'll owe your debts, just as if you'd never filed for bankruptcy. Any payment your creditors received from the trustee, however, will be credited against what you owe.

When the Trustee Keeps Your Bankruptcy Case Open

Most Chapter 7 bankruptcy cases are closed shortly after the discharge has been issued. However, in some situations the bankruptcy trustee may keep your case open for a lengthy period of time. This might happen, for instance, if:

- **Your business continues to produce income.** Because your sole proprietorship business is part of your bankruptcy estate, the income it produces as a result of activities conducted prior to your bankruptcy filing is also part of your bankruptcy estate (including accounts receivable owed as of the bankruptcy filing date). However, income earned after your filing date is not part of your bankruptcy estate.

EXAMPLE: Phil operates an organic pear farm as a sole proprietor. Shortly after he sells his crop for $30,000, the buyer of the pears files for Chapter 11 bankruptcy, and Phil isn't paid when he expected to be. Because Phil borrowed the money to produce the crop in the first place, and because he is overwhelmed with other personal and business debts, Phil files for Chapter 7 bankruptcy. While the farm and Phil's personal property are all protected under California exemption laws, the $30,000 Phil had coming from the buyer is not. Phil receives his Chapter 7 discharge in a timely manner (60 days after the creditors' meeting), but the trustee keeps his case open in the hopes that he can recover some part of the money due Phil from the pear buyer's Chapter 11 bankruptcy estate. Once the trustee decides that he's gotten as much as he can from the buyer's Chapter 11 estate, he closes Phil's case.

- **Property you have is likely to appreciate in the short term.** Back in the days of rapidly rising real estate prices, trustees and courts took the position that the trustee was entitled to the amount by which property appreciated while the case was open. For example, if the debtor's equity in his or her home was fully exempt when the debtor filed for bankruptcy, but the debtor's home appreciated in value by $20,000 during the bankruptcy proceedings, the trustee would likely argue that any nonexempt appreciation belonged to the bankruptcy estate, not the debtor. Although this scenario has become less likely, it could arise once the real estate market begins to improve.

EXAMPLE: When Laverne files for Chapter 7 bankruptcy in 2011, she owns a house valued at $300,000. Laverne owes approximately $250,000 (on a first mortgage for $175,000 and second mortgage for $75,000), leaving her with $50,000 equity in the house. The exemption laws available to Laverne allow her to exempt $50,000 for any home she is living in, so Laverne doesn't worry about losing her house in bankruptcy; all of her equity in the house is protected when she files for bankruptcy. As it turns out, however, property in Laverne's neighborhood is appreciating by 15% a year (which started in late 2010). Instead of closing Laverne's case on schedule, the trustee keeps Laverne's case open for an additional year, and then sells the house for $350,000. After the lienholders are paid off and Laverne is given a check for her exemption claim ($50,000), the trustee makes off with $50,000, less the costs of sale.

- **The trustee tries to "reverse pierce" the corporate veil and collect personal debts from your corporation or LLC.** The trustee may be able to access assets in a corporation, LLC, or partnership in extreme circumstances, even if the business has more than one owner. When one person, or a small group of related or closely associated people, have complete control over a corporation or LLC, and the corporation or LLC has been used in questionable ways (perhaps it has recklessly borrowed and lost money or perpetrated financial fraud), a trustee can try to "reverse pierce" the corporation's or LLC's veil of liability protection—similar to the "piercing of a corporate veil" discussed in Ch. 1. In this situation, the separate nature of the corporation or LLC won't protect it from your personal debts. If personal and business funds were commingled, the corporation or LLC was inadequately capitalized, or corporate or LLC formalities were neglected, the trustee might be able to dissolve the business and sell the assets attributable to the bankruptcy filer in order to pay off the bankruptcy filer's creditors. This is fairly rare and reserved for situations where the corporation or LLC has committed fraud.

Although debtors are always notified of their discharge, they seldom receive notice that their case is closed. Check with the court about a month after you get your discharge to see whether your case is closed. If it isn't, send the trustee a letter demanding that it be closed. While the trustee isn't required to go along with your request, you will have put it on record that your case is open and you believe it should be closed. At the very least, this will require the trustee to justify keeping your case open. In some cases, attorneys have actually sought and obtained a court order requiring closure of the case.

Postbankruptcy Discrimination

Although declaring bankruptcy has serious consequences, it might not be as bad as you think. There are laws that will protect you from most types of postbankruptcy discrimination by the government and by private employers.

Government Discrimination

All federal, state, and local governmental units are prohibited from denying, revoking, suspending, or refusing to renew a license, permit, charter, franchise, or other similar grant solely because you filed for bankruptcy. (11 U.S.C. § 525(a).) This law provides important protections, but it does not insulate debtors from all adverse consequences of filing for bankruptcy. Lenders, for example, can consider your bankruptcy filing when reviewing an application for a government loan or extension of credit. (See, for example, *Watts v. Pennsylvania Housing Finance Co.*, 876 F.2d 1090 (3rd Cir. 1989), and *Toth v. Michigan State Housing Development Authority*, 136 F.3d 477 (6th Cir. 1998).) Still, the government cannot use your bankruptcy as a reason to:

- deny you a contract, such as a contract for a construction project
- deny you or refuse to renew your state liquor license
- deny you a job or fire you
- deny you or terminate your public benefits
- evict you from public housing (although if you have a Section 8 voucher, you may not be protected)
- withhold your college transcript, or
- deny you a driver's license.

In addition, lenders may not exclude you from government-guaranteed student loan programs. (11 U.S.C. § 525(c).)

In general, once any government-related debt has been discharged, all acts against you that arise out of that debt also must end. If, for example, you lost your driver's license because you didn't pay a court judgment resulting from a car accident, you must be granted a license once the debt is discharged. If your license was also suspended because you didn't have insurance, you may not get your license back until you meet the requirements set forth in your state's financial responsibility law.

If, however, the judgment wasn't discharged, you can still be denied your license until you pay up. If you and the government disagree about whether or not the debt was discharged, see "Postbankruptcy Attempts to Collect Debts," above.

Keep in mind that only government denials based on your bankruptcy are prohibited. You may be denied a loan, job, contract, bid, or apartment for reasons unrelated to the bankruptcy. This includes denials for reasons related to your future creditworthiness—for example, because the government concludes you won't be able to repay a Small Business Administration loan.

Nongovernment Discrimination

Private employers may not fire you or otherwise discriminate against you solely because you filed for bankruptcy. (11 U.S.C. § 525(b).) While the law expressly prohibits employers from firing you, most courts to consider the issue have concluded that the law doesn't protect debtors from discrimination in hiring. In other words, an employer may legally refuse to hire you because of your bankruptcy.

Unfortunately, other forms of discrimination in the private sector aren't illegal. If you seek to rent an apartment and the landlord does a credit check, sees your bankruptcy, and refuses to rent to you, there's not much you can do other than try to show that you'll pay your rent and be a responsible tenant. It's often helpful if you can prepay your rent for a few months, or, if it is permitted under your state's laws, provide a bigger security deposit. (However, if you file for bankruptcy in the midst of a lease, your landlord cannot use this as grounds to evict you before the lease term is up.)

If a private employer refuses to hire you because of a poor credit history—not because you filed for bankruptcy—you may have little recourse.

If you suffer illegal discrimination because of your bankruptcy, you can sue in state court or in the bankruptcy court. You'll probably need the assistance of an attorney.

Reestablishing Credit

Many small businesses cannot function without credit. And, especially if you're a sole proprietor, you'll need to have good personal credit to obtain business credit. There are no magic solutions to rebuilding your personal credit after bankruptcy. However, history shows that the most reliable strategy is to reestablish some type of credit, use it wisely (and pay it off each month), and then slowly take on more credit and increase your credit limits on existing accounts.

In the past, it took at least two years to rebuild your personal credit sufficiently to qualify for a car loan, and four to five years before you could get a home loan. This may change in the future depending on how Congress and the credit markets respond to our current economic climate. For extensive information on rebuilding personal credit, see *Credit Repair*, by Robin Leonard and John Lamb (Nolo).

CHAPTER

12

Help Beyond the Book

We've tried to provide all of the information small business owners will need to handle their own Chapter 7 personal bankruptcies. As we've noted throughout the book, however, there are situations in which you may need more information or advice than this book provides. If we addressed every possible scenario, this book would be thousands of pages long; in fact, the leading bankruptcy treatise that bankruptcy lawyers use to look up the answers to their questions comes in a 17-volume set—and that doesn't include the appendixes!

If you have a question or complication that isn't addressed in this book, there are a number of other places you can go for help, including:

- bankruptcy petition preparers, when you're ready to file for bankruptcy, but need assistance in typing the forms and organizing them for filing in your district
- lawyers, when you want information, advice, or legal representation, and
- law libraries and the Internet, when you want to do your own research on issues raised in the course of your bankruptcy.

Information and Advice From the Authors

You can find more bankruptcy information—and updates for this book—at Nolo's website, www.nolo.com. In addition, Albin Renauer, coauthor of Nolo's book *How to File for Chapter 7 Bankruptcy* (for consumers), has created an information-rich website at www.legalconsumer.com. This site provides valuable resources, includes up-to-date exemption laws, a means-test calculator, help finding bankruptcy forms online, and much more—and it's all free.

Before we discuss each of these resources in more detail, here's a general piece of advice: Maintain control of your case whenever possible. By getting this book and filing for Chapter 7 bankruptcy, you've taken responsibility for your own legal affairs. If you decide to get help from others, shop around until you find someone who respects your efforts as a self-helper and recognizes your right to participate in the case as a valuable partner.

Debt Relief Agencies

Any person, business, or organization that you pay or otherwise compensate for help with your bankruptcy is considered a debt relief agency—and must identify itself as such. The two main types of debt relief agencies are lawyers and bankruptcy petition preparers (BPPs). Credit counseling agencies and budget counseling agencies are not debt relief agencies. Nor are:

- employers or employees of debt relief agencies (for instance, legal secretaries)
- nonprofit organizations that have federal 501(c)(3) tax-exempt status
- any creditor who works with you to restructure your debt
- banks, credit unions, and other deposit institutions, or
- an author, publisher, distributor, or seller of works subject to copyright protection when acting in that capacity (in other words, Nolo and the stores that sell its books aren't debt relief agencies).

This section explains what the 2005 bankruptcy law requires of debt relief agencies generally (that is, bankruptcy lawyers and BPPs), so you'll know what you can expect for your money.

Mandatory Contract

Within five days after a debt relief agency assists you, it (or he or she) must enter into a contract with you that explains, clearly and conspicuously:

- what services the agency will provide
- what the agency will charge for the services, and
- the terms of payment.

The agency must give you a copy of the completed, signed contract.

Mandatory Disclosures and Notices

Debt relief agencies must inform you, in writing, that:

- All information you are required to provide in your bankruptcy papers must be complete, accurate, and truthful.
- You must completely and accurately disclose your assets and liabilities in the documents you file to begin your case.
- You must undertake a reasonable inquiry to establish the replacement value of any item you plan to keep, before you provide that value on your forms.
- Your current monthly income, the amounts you provide in the means test, and your computation of projected disposable income (in a Chapter 13 case), as stated in your bankruptcy papers, must be based on a reasonable inquiry into their accuracy.
- Your case may be audited, and your failure to cooperate in the audit may result in dismissal of your case or some other sanction, including a possible criminal penalty.

In addition to these stark warnings—which most debt relief agencies would rather not have to give—a debt relief agency must also give you a general notice regarding some basic bankruptcy requirements and your options for help in filing and pursuing your case. Below is the notice that you can expect to receive from any debt relief agency within three business days after the agency first offers to provide you with services. Failure to give you this notice—in a timely manner—can land the agency in big trouble.

Finally, every debt relief agency has to give you some plain-English written information about the basic tasks associated with most bankruptcies, such as how to deal with secured debts and choose exemptions. Ideally, debt relief agencies would freely distribute this book, which has all of the information required (and much more, of course).

Restrictions on Debt Relief Agencies

Under the law, a debt relief agency may not:

- fail to perform any service that the agency told you it would perform in connection with your bankruptcy case
- counsel you to make any statement in a document that is untrue and misleading or that the agency should have known was untrue or misleading, or
- advise you to incur more debt in order to pay for the agency's services (for instance, accepting a credit card or steering you to a cash advance business).

Any contract that doesn't comply with the requirements for debt relief agencies may not be enforced against you. A debt relief agency is liable to you for costs and fees, including legal fees, if the agency negligently or intentionally:

- fails to comply with the new law's restrictions on debt relief agencies, or
- fails to file a document that results in dismissal of your case or conversion to another bankruptcy chapter.

In sum, debt relief agencies are on the hook if they are negligent in performing the services required by the bankruptcy law or other services they have agreed to provide.

Bankruptcy Petition Preparers

Even though you should be able to handle routine bankruptcy procedures yourself, you may want someone familiar with the bankruptcy forms and courts in your area to use a computer to enter your data in the official forms and print them out for filing with the court. For this level of assistance—routine form preparation and organization—consider using a bankruptcy petition preparer (BPP).

Sample Notice From Debt Relief Agency

IMPORTANT INFORMATION ABOUT BANKRUPTCY ASSISTANCE SERVICES FROM AN ATTORNEY OR BANKRUPTCY PETITION PREPARER.

If you decide to seek bankruptcy relief, you can represent yourself, you can hire an attorney to represent you, or you can get help in some localities from a bankruptcy petition preparer who is not an attorney. THE LAW REQUIRES AN ATTORNEY OR BANKRUPTCY PETITION PREPARER TO GIVE YOU A WRITTEN CONTRACT SPECIFYING WHAT THE ATTORNEY OR BANKRUPTCY PETITION PREPARER WILL DO FOR YOU AND HOW MUCH IT WILL COST. Ask to see the contract before you hire anyone.

The following information helps you understand what must be done in a routine bankruptcy case to help you evaluate how much service you need. Although bankruptcy can be complex, many cases are routine. Before filing a bankruptcy case, either you or your attorney should analyze your eligibility for different forms of debt relief available under the Bankruptcy Code and which form of relief is most likely to be beneficial for you. Be sure you understand the relief you can obtain and its limitations.

To file a bankruptcy case, documents called a Petition, Schedules and Statement of Financial Affairs, as well as in some cases a Statement of Intention need to be prepared correctly and filed with the bankruptcy court. You will have to pay a filing fee to the bankruptcy court. Once your case starts, you will have to attend the required first meeting of creditors where you may be questioned by your creditors.

If you choose to file a chapter 7 case, you may be asked by a creditor to reaffirm a debt. You may want help deciding whether to do so. A creditor is not permitted to coerce you into reaffirming your debts.

If you choose to file a chapter 13 case in which you repay your creditors what you can afford over 3 to 5 years, you may also want help with preparing your chapter 13 plan and with the confirmation hearing on your plan which will be before a bankruptcy judge.

If you select another type of relief under the Bankruptcy Code other than chapter 7 or chapter 13, you will want to find out what should be done from someone familiar with that type of relief.

Your bankruptcy case may also involve litigation. You are generally permitted to represent yourself in litigation in bankruptcy court, but only attorneys, not bankruptcy petition preparers, can give you legal advice.

What a Bankruptcy Petition Preparer Can Do for You

BPPs are very different from lawyers. BPPs are prohibited from giving you legal advice, which under 11 U.S.C. § 110(e) includes information such as:

- whether to file a bankruptcy petition or which chapter (7, 11, 12, or 13) is appropriate
- whether your debts will be discharged under a particular chapter of bankruptcy
- whether you will be able to hang on to your home or other property if you file under a particular chapter (that is, which exemptions you should choose)
- information about the tax consequences of a case brought under a particular chapter or whether tax claims in your case can be discharged
- whether you should offer to repay or agree to reaffirm a debt
- how to characterize the nature of your interest in property or debts, and
- information about bankruptcy procedures and rights.

Fees

All fees charged by debt relief agencies are reviewed by the U.S. Trustee for reasonableness. However, unlike lawyers' fees, which can vary widely according to the circumstances, a BPP's fees usually are subject to a strict cap, somewhere between $125 and $200, depending on the district. The rationale offered by the U.S. Trustee for this cap—and by the courts that have upheld it—is that BPP fees can be set according to what general typists charge per page in the community. Because BPPs aren't supposed to be doing anything other than "typing" the forms, the argument goes, they shouldn't be able to charge the rates professional services can command.

Rates allowed for BPPs are far less than lawyers charge. For that reason, BPPs are a good choice for people who want some help getting their forms typed and organized in a way that will sail past the court clerk and satisfy the trustee. Because BPPs can't provide legal advice, however, you are responsible for getting the information you need to make important choices and comply with the basic bankruptcy procedures.

How Bankruptcy Petition Preparers Are Regulated

Anyone can be a BPP. Yes, anyone. There is nothing in the bankruptcy code that requires BPPs to have any particular level of education, training, or experience. Unlike most other jobs, a prison record is no handicap to becoming a BPP. How, then, are BPPs regulated? Regulation is provided by the U.S. Trustee's office, which reviews all bankruptcy petitions prepared by a BPP. BPPs must provide their name, address, telephone number, and Social Security number on the bankruptcy petition, as well as on every other bankruptcy document they prepare. The U.S. Trustee uses this information to keep tabs on BPPs.

BPPs are also regulated at the creditors' meeting, where the bankruptcy trustee can ask you about the manner in which the BPP conducts his or her business. For instance, if you are representing yourself, the trustee might ask how you got the information necessary to choose your exemptions (see Ch. 6) or how you decided which bankruptcy chapter to use.

If the BPP provided you with this information, the trustee may refer the case to the U.S. Trustee's office, and the BPP will be hauled into court to explain why he or she violated the rules against giving legal advice. The BPP may be forced to return the fee you paid and may even be banned from practicing as a BPP, if it's not the first offense. In some circumstances, the BPP may even be forced to pay you up to $2,000 for their transgression, as explained below. None of this will have any effect on your case, however, other than the inconvenience of being dragged into court and the possibility of being awarded damages.

Can BPPs Give You Written Information?

Under the Bankruptcy Code, BPPs are supposed to prepare your bankruptcy forms under your direction. This means you are supposed to tell the BPP which exemptions you will use, whether you will file under Chapter 7 or Chapter 13, how you will handle your secured debts (car note, mortgage), and how much your property is worth. That's fine in theory, but unless you have the benefit of this book or another source of legal information, there is no way you would have adequate bankruptcy expertise to direct the BPP at this level of detail. In an attempt to bridge this gap, many BPPs hand their customers written materials that contain all the information their customers need to direct the case. Unfortunately, giving a customer written legal information about bankruptcy has itself been held to be the unauthorized practice of law in many states (California is an important exception).

BPPs can be fined for certain actions and inactions spelled out in the bankruptcy code (11 U.S.C. § 110). These are:

- failing to put their name, address, and Social Security number on your bankruptcy petition
- failing to give you a copy of your bankruptcy documents when you sign them
- using the word "legal" or any similar term in advertisements, or advertising under a category that includes such terms, and
- accepting court filing fees from you. You must pay the filing fee to the court yourself or, in some districts, give the BPP a cashier's check made out to the court.

Finally, under the revised law, BPPs must submit a statement under oath with each petition they prepare stating how much you paid them in the previous 12 months and any fees you owe them but haven't yet paid. If they charge more than the permitted amount, they will be ordered to return the excess fees to you.

If a BPP engages in any fraudulent act in your case or fails to comply with the rules governing their behavior listed above, they may be required to return your entire fee and pay a $500 fine for each transgression. If they engage in serious fraud, they may be fined up to $2,000 and three times your fee, and even be ordered to stop providing BPP services. Simply put, fraudulent BPPs (those who would take your money without providing promised services or counsel you to play fast and loose with the bankruptcy system) are likely to be weeded out in a hurry.

How to Find Bankruptcy Petition Preparers

Although BPP services are available here and there, you are much more likely to find a BPP if you live on the West Coast. The best way to find a reputable BPP in your area is to get a recommendation from someone who has used a particular BPP and been satisfied with his or her work.

BPPs sometimes advertise in classified sections of local newspapers and in the yellow pages. You may have to look hard to spot their ads, however, because they go by different names in different states. In California, your best bet is to find a legal document assistant (the official name given to independent paralegals in California) who also provides BPP services. (Check the website maintained by the California Association of Legal Document Assistants (www.calda.org).) In Arizona, hunt for a legal document preparer. In other states, especially Florida, search for paralegals who directly serve the public (often termed independent paralegals or legal technicians). You can also look for BPPs in your area at www.legalconsumer.com.

Combining Lawyers and Bankruptcy Petition Preparers

In California, it is possible to use a BPP to grind out your paperwork, and a lawyer to provide you with all the legal savvy you need to direct your own case. Under this arrangement, you are still representing yourself, but you are combining legal and secretarial resources to get the job done. The attorney is providing what is known as an unbundled legal service: The attorney performs a discrete task (providing some legal advice, for example) rather than the whole enchilada we know as "legal representation." For instance, for a one-time flat fee, the Affordable Attorney Advice service operated by Stephen Elias (a coauthor of this book) provides legal information and advice over the phone to California small business owners filing for Chapter 7 bankruptcy with the assistance of a BPP. The contract for, and information about, this service can be obtained directly from most California BPPs.

A Bankruptcy Petition Preparer Cannot Represent You

If you decide to use a BPP, remember that you are representing yourself and are responsible for the outcome of your case. This means that you must not only learn your rights under the bankruptcy law and understand the proper procedures to be followed, but also accept responsibility for correctly and accurately filling in the bankruptcy petition and schedules. If, for example, you lose your home because it turned out to be worth much more than you thought, and the homestead exemption available to you didn't cover your equity, you can't blame the BPP. Nor can you blame the BPP if the trustee takes your business assets or shuts your business down while trying to figure out what you own and whether it can be taken for your creditors. Unless you hire a lawyer to represent you, you are solely responsible for acquiring the information necessary to competently pursue your case—and, as a small business owner, you will probably need more information than the typical Chapter 7 bankruptcy filer.

Bankruptcy Lawyers

Bankruptcy lawyers (a type of debt relief agency under the new law) are regular lawyers who specialize in handling bankruptcy cases. Before 2005, it was usually possible to find an affordable bankruptcy lawyer who would provide at least a minimal level of representation throughout your case. However, for the reasons discussed below, lawyers are charging a lot more to represent clients in bankruptcies filed under the 2005 Bankruptcy Abuse Prevention and Consumer Protection Act (BAPCPA).

When You May Need a Lawyer

With the help of this book, your Chapter 7 bankruptcy should sail through without a hitch. However, there are some situations in which you may need some help from a bankruptcy lawyer:

- Your average gross income during the six months before you file is more than your state's median income, and it looks like you won't be able to pass the means test. (See Ch. 2 and Ch. 9 for more information on these calculations.)
- You want to continue operating your business during your bankruptcy case, but the trustee wants to shut you down and liquidate your business.
- You are the sole or majority owner of a corporation or an LLC, and you need information on what will happen to the company's assets if you file a personal Chapter 7 bankruptcy case.
- You want to get rid of a student loan or income tax debt that won't be wiped out in bankruptcy unless you convince a court that it should be discharged.
- A creditor files a lawsuit in the bankruptcy court claiming that one of your debts should survive your bankruptcy because you incurred it through fraud or other misconduct.

- The trustee seeks to have your whole bankruptcy dismissed because you didn't give honest and complete answers to questions about your assets, liabilities, and economic transactions.
- The U.S. Trustee asks the court to dismiss your case—or force you into Chapter 13—because your income is high enough to fund a Chapter 13 repayment plan, or because the trustee believes that your filing is an abuse of the Chapter 7 bankruptcy process for other reasons.
- You have recently given away or sold valuable property for substantially less than it is worth.
- You went on a recent buying spree with your credit card (especially if you charged more than $550 on luxury goods within the past 90 days or obtained a cash advance of more than $850 in the past 70 days).
- You want help negotiating with a creditor or the bankruptcy court, and the amount involved justifies hiring a bankruptcy lawyer to assist you.
- You have a large lien on your property because of a court judgment against you, and you want to remove the lien in your bankruptcy case.
- A creditor is asking the court to allow it to proceed with its collection action despite your bankruptcy filing (for instance, a creditor wants to foreclose on your house because you are behind on your mortgage payments).
- You are being evicted by your landlord because you have fallen behind on your rent or lease payments.

Even if you aren't facing one of these complications, you may still want a lawyer's help. If you find the thought of going through the process overwhelming, a lawyer can take charge of your case and relieve you of the responsibility to get everything done. The lawyer can accompany you to the creditor's meeting, work with you to make sure that your documents are complete and accurate, get all your paperwork filed on time, and generally handle all of the little details that go into a successful bankruptcy case. Although representation comes at a price—which can be considerable, especially for business owners—you will have the peace of mind of knowing that someone is watching your back. While we obviously believe that many small business owners can handle their own Chapter 7 bankruptcies, it isn't right for everyone, especially if your previous business transactions are complex or your business will have to close down once you file for Chapter 7 bankruptcy. Or, you may have other significant sources of stress in your life or just not feel up to handling it all by yourself.

Full-Service Lawyer Representation

In a general sense, a lawyer represents you if you contract with the lawyer to handle some or all of your bankruptcy case. There are two types of representation—the type where you hire a lawyer to assume complete responsibility for your bankruptcy, and the type where you represent yourself but hire a lawyer to handle one particular aspect of your bankruptcy case. We refer to the first type of representation as "full-service representation" and the second type of representation as "unbundled services" (discussed below).

When providing full-service representation, a bankruptcy lawyer is responsible for making sure that all of your paperwork is filed on time and that the information in your paperwork is accurate. These duties require the lawyer to review various documents—for instance, your business records, business and personal credit reports, tax returns, and home value appraisal—to make sure both that your paperwork is accurate and that you are filing for bankruptcy under the appropriate chapter. Under the new law, if your paperwork is inaccurate or you filed under Chapter 7 bankruptcy when you should have filed under Chapter 13, the lawyer can be fined a hefty amount and be required to return your fees.

In exchange for their basic fee, full-service bankruptcy lawyers typically are obligated under their contracts to provide the routine services associated with a Chapter 7 bankruptcy. Their contracts also typically provide for additional fees for nonroutine work (See "Fees" below.)

Sometimes, a case appears to be simple at the beginning but starts looking more complicated later on. In that event, you might start out representing yourself but later decide to hire an attorney to handle a tricky issue that arises.

Unbundled Services

Although many people represent themselves because they simply can't afford full-attorney representation, they still may need to hire a lawyer to help out with some aspect of the case. When lawyers do specific jobs at a client's request but don't contract for full-service representation in the underlying case, they are providing an unbundled service. For example, you may be able to hire an attorney to handle a specific procedure—such as to defend against a motion for relief from stay—while you handle the main part of the bankruptcy yourself. This may require some shopping around; not all lawyers are willing to offer unbundled services.

Few court cases discuss the boundaries of unbundled services. Some courts have held that attorneys can't "ghostwrite" legal documents for nonlawyers—because that would be a type of fraud on the court—but the issue has not been decided in most states. Also, nothing prevents a lawyer from appearing for you in a limited capacity and putting his or her own name on associated documents.

Lawyers providing unbundled services usually charge an hourly fee. As a general rule, you should bring an attorney into the case for an unbundled service only if a dispute involves something valuable enough to justify the attorney's fees. If a creditor objects to the discharge of a $500 debt, and it will cost you $400 to hire an attorney, you may be better off trying to handle the matter yourself, even though this increases the risk that the creditor will win. If, however, the dispute is worth $1,000 and the attorney will charge $200, hiring the attorney makes better sense.

Unfortunately, many bankruptcy attorneys do not like to appear or do paperwork on a piecemeal basis. Justified or not, these attorneys believe that by doing a little work for you, they might be on the hook if something goes wrong in another part of your case—that is, if they are in for a penny, they are in for a pound. Also, the bar associations of some states frown on unbundled services on ethical grounds. On the other hand, a number of other state bar associations are starting to encourage their attorneys to offer unbundled services simply because so many people—even middle-income people—are unable to afford full representation.

Bankruptcy Consultants

Many small business owners will be able to represent themselves with this book as their main source of information. As explained throughout this book, this will depend on how complex your business transactions have been over the past several years, how you have structured your business, and the type of business you operate. Fortunately, in many cases, it's still just a matter of knowing what to put on the forms and which forms to file. For many people, however, a book just won't do the trick, no matter how well written and complete: They want to talk to a human being. Because of unauthorized practice laws and restrictions in the bankruptcy law, however, there is only one kind of human being who is authorized to answer your questions about bankruptcy law and procedure: a lawyer.

Fortunately, there are lawyers who provide bankruptcy consultations (a category of unbundled service) for a transaction fee (for example, a $100 flat rate) or a fee based on the amount of time your call takes (for example, $3 a minute). There are also free consultations offered by private attorneys and bar associations. Similar services—free and paid—

are available on the Internet. To find a telephonic or online consultation service, in addition to those mentioned here, go to your favorite search engine and look for bankruptcy legal advice telephone or Internet. Internet lawyer directories are another good resource. For example, Nolo's online lawyer directory, at www.nolo.com/ldir/findlawyer.do, provides detailed information about each lawyer's practice and philosophy, including the bankruptcy lawyer's willingness to consult with self-helpers.

Even if you are using this book and hiring a BPP to help with your paperwork, you may wish to talk to a lawyer to get the information you need to make your choices and tell the BPP what you want in your papers. For instance, a BPP can't choose your exemptions for you, because that would be considered the practice of law—something only lawyers can do. However, a lawyer can help you decide which exemptions to pick so you can tell the BPP what to put in the form that lists your exemptions.

As with other debt relief agencies, lawyers offering telephonic services are considered debt relief agencies and will have to offer you a contract detailing their services and provide the other notices described above.

How to Find a Bankruptcy Lawyer

Where there's a bankruptcy court, there are bankruptcy lawyers. They're listed in the yellow pages under "Attorneys" and often advertise in newspapers. You should use an experienced bankruptcy lawyer, not a general practitioner, to handle or advise you on matters associated with bankruptcy.

There are several ways to find the best bankruptcy lawyer for your job:

- **Personal referrals.** This is your best approach. If you know someone who was pleased with the services of a bankruptcy lawyer, call that lawyer first.
- **Bankruptcy petition preparers.** If there's a BPP in your area, he or she may know some bankruptcy attorneys who are both competent and sympathetic to self-helpers. It is here that you are most likely to find a good referral to attorneys who are willing to deliver unbundled services, including advice over the telephone.
- **Legal aid.** Legal aid offices are partially funded by the federal Legal Services Corporation and offer legal assistance in many areas. A few offices do bankruptcies, although most do not. To qualify for legal aid, you must have a very low income.
- **Legal clinic.** Many law schools sponsor legal clinics and provide free legal advice to consumers. Some legal clinics have the same income requirements as legal aid; others offer free services to low- and moderate-income people.
- **Group legal plans.** If you're a member of a plan that provides free or low-cost legal assistance and the plan covers bankruptcies, make that your first stop in looking for a lawyer.
- **Lawyer-referral panels.** Most county bar associations will give you the names of bankruptcy attorneys who practice in your area. But bar associations may not provide much screening. Take the time to check out the credentials and experience of the person to whom you're referred.
- **Internet directories.** Both bar associations and private companies provide lists of bankruptcy lawyers on the Internet, with a lot more information about the lawyer than you're likely to get in a yellow pages ad. A good place to start is Nolo's lawyer's directory, www.nolo.com/ldir/findlawyer.do

Fees

For a Chapter 7 bankruptcy involving a small business, a full-service lawyer will likely charge you somewhere between $2,000 and $3,000 (plus the $299 filing fee), depending on the state you are filing in, whether you are in a rural or urban setting, and the complexity of your case. You will almost always have to pay the attorney in full before the attorney will file your case: Once you file your Chapter 7 bankruptcy, any money you owe the attorney is discharged along with your other dischargeable unsecured debts.

On your bankruptcy papers, you must state the amount you are paying your bankruptcy lawyer. Because every penny you pay to a bankruptcy lawyer is a penny not available to your creditors (at least in theory), the court has the legal authority to make the attorney justify his or her fee. This rarely happens, however, because attorneys know the range of fees generally allowed by local bankruptcy judges, and set their fees accordingly. This means that you probably won't find much variation in the amounts charged by lawyers in your area (although it never hurts to shop around).

The scope and range of services that the attorney promises you in return for your initial fee will be listed in what's called a Rule 2016 Attorney Fee Disclosure Form. This form is filed as part of your bankruptcy papers. In the typical Chapter 7 case, the attorney's fee will include the routine tasks associated with a bankruptcy filing, such as counseling, preparing and filing the necessary bankruptcy forms, negotiating reaffirmation and other agreements with your secured creditors, and attending the creditors' meeting. Any task not included in the Rule 2016 disclosure form is subject to a separate fee.

If your case will likely require more attorney time than the basic fee covers, you may—and probably will—be charged extra, according to the attorney's hourly fee or other criteria he or she uses. A typical bankruptcy attorney charges between $200 and $300 an hour (rural and urban) and would charge a minimum of roughly $400 to $600 for a court appearance. If they see the extra work coming, many attorneys will add these fees to their standard fee and require you to pay it all in advance. For instance, if the attorney's standard fee is $1,000, but the attorney sees extra work down the line, you may be charged $2,000 or more in anticipation of the extra work.

Other attorneys will happily just charge you their standard fee up front and wait until after you file to charge you for the extra work. Because these fees are earned after your bankruptcy filing, they won't be discharged in your bankruptcy and the attorney need not collect them up front. However the attorney charges you, you are protected against fee gouging. An attorney must file a supplemental Rule 2016 form to obtain the court's permission for any fees charged for work after your bankruptcy filing.

What to Look for in a Lawyer

No matter how you find a lawyer, these three suggestions will help you make sure you have the best possible working relationship.

First, fight any urge you may have to surrender to, or be intimidated by, the lawyer. You should be the one who decides what you feel comfortable doing about your legal and financial affairs. Keep in mind that you're hiring the lawyer to perform a service for you, so shop around if the price or personality isn't right.

Second, make sure you have good chemistry with any lawyer you hire. When making an appointment, ask to talk directly to the lawyer. If you can't, this may give you a hint as to how accessible he or she is. Of course, if you're told that a paralegal will be handling the routine aspects of your case under the supervision of a lawyer, you may be satisfied with that arrangement. If you do talk directly to a lawyer, ask some specific questions. Do you get clear, concise answers? If not, try someone else. Also, pay attention to how the lawyer responds to your knowledge. If you've read this book, you're already better informed than most clients (and some lawyers are threatened by clients who have done their homework).

Finally, once you find a lawyer you like, make an hour-long appointment to discuss your situation fully. The lawyer or a paralegal in the lawyer's office will tell you what to bring to the meeting, if anything (if not, be sure to ask ahead of time). Some lawyers will want to see a recent credit report and tax return, while others will send you a questionnaire to complete prior to your visit. Depending on the circumstances, you may also be asked to bring your bills and documents pertaining to your home and other real estate you own. Some lawyers prefer not to deal with details during the first visit, and will simply ask you to come as you are.

Your main goal at the initial conference is to find out what the lawyer recommends in your particular case and how much it will cost. Go home and think about the lawyer's suggestions. If they don't make sense or you have other reservations, call someone else.

TIP

Look for a member of the National Association of Consumer Bankruptcy Attorneys. Because of the massive changes enacted by the 2005 bankruptcy law (BAPCPA), you will want to find an attorney who has a means of keeping up to date and communicating with other bankruptcy lawyers. Membership in the National Association of Consumer Bankruptcy Attorneys (NACBA) is a good sign that your lawyer will be tuned in to the nuances of the BAPCPA and how courts are interpreting its provisions. Lawyers in this group typically represent consumers rather than businesses, but most know how to handle the business aspects of a personal Chapter 7 bankruptcy case brought by a small business owner. Of course, if you can find a bankruptcy lawyer who specializes in small business bankruptcies, so much the better.

Legal Research

Legal research can vary from the very simple to the hopelessly complex. In this section, we are staying on the simple side. If you would like to learn more about legal research or if you find that our suggestions come up a bit short in your particular case, we recommend that you obtain a copy of *Legal Research: How to Find & Understand the Law*, by Stephen Elias and the Editors of Nolo (Nolo), which provides a plain-English tutorial on legal research in the law library and on the Internet.

Sources of Bankruptcy Law

Bankruptcy law comes from a variety of sources:

- federal bankruptcy statutes passed by Congress
- federal rules about bankruptcy procedure issued by a federal judicial agency
- local rules issued by individual bankruptcy courts
- federal and bankruptcy court cases applying bankruptcy laws to specific disputes
- laws (statutes) passed by state legislatures that define the property you can keep in bankruptcy, and
- state court cases interpreting state exemption statutes.

Not so long ago, you would have had to visit a law library to find these resources. Now you can find most of them on the Internet. However, if you are able to visit a decent-sized law library, your research will be the better for it. Using actual books allows you to more easily find and read relevant court interpretations of the underlying statutes and rules—which can be crucial to getting a clear picture of what the laws and rules really mean.

There is another important reason to visit the law library, if possible. While you can find superficial discussions and overviews of various aspects of bankruptcy on the Internet, you'll find in-depth encyclopedias and treatises in the law library that delve into every aspect of bankruptcy. In other words, you can find not only the law itself, but also what the experts have to say about all the picky little issues that have arisen over the years. Also, books in a law library are almost always subjected to a rigorous quality control process—as is this book—whereas you never know what you're getting on the Internet. To avoid getting lost in cyberspace, follow our suggestions below for researching bankruptcy law online and avoid the temptation to settle for the first hit in a Google search.

Below, we show you how to get to the resources you'll most likely be using, whether you are doing your research on the Internet or in the law library.

Bankruptcy Background Materials: Overviews, Encyclopedias, and Treatises

Before digging into the primary law sources (statutes, rules, cases, and so on that we discuss below), you may want to do some background reading to get a firm grasp of your issue or question.

The Internet

A number of Internet sites contain large collections of articles written by experts about various aspects of bankruptcy. Good starting places are Nolo's website, www.nolo.com, and www.legalconsumer.com, which offer lots of information and resources.

The Law Library

Providing you with a good treatise or encyclopedia discussion of bankruptcy is where the law library shines. This type of resource is not typically available online unless you find a way to access the expensive legal databases—Westlaw and Lexis—marketed almost exclusively to lawyers. Many law libraries subscribe to either Westlaw or Lexis and provide these services for free to their patrons.

Collier on Bankruptcy

It's a good idea to get an overview of your subject before trying to find a precise answer to a precise question. The best way to do this is to find a general commentary on your subject by a bankruptcy expert. For example, if you want to find out whether a particular debt will be discharged in bankruptcy, you should start by reading a general discussion about the type of debt you're dealing with. Or, if you don't know whether you're entitled to claim certain property as exempt, a good overview of your state's exemptions would get you started on the right track.

The most complete source of this type of background information is a set of books known as *Collier on Bankruptcy*, by Lawrence P. King, et al. (Matthew Bender). It's available in most law libraries. *Collier* is both incredibly thorough and meticulously up to date; semiannual supplements, with all the latest developments, are in the front of each volume. In addition to commentary on every aspect of bankruptcy law, *Collier* contains the bankruptcy statutes, rules, and exemption lists for every state.

Collier is organized according to the bankruptcy statutes. This means that the quickest way to find information in it is to know which statute best addresses the issue you're researching. (See the Bankruptcy Code sections set out below.) If you still can't figure out the governing statute, start with the *Collier* subject matter index. Be warned, however, that the index can be difficult to use because it contains a lot of bankruptcy jargon you may be unfamiliar with. The glossary at the back of this book will be a big help. In addition, an assortment of legal dictionaries will be available in the library.

Bankruptcy (National Edition) published by The Rutter Group

This four-volume set authored by Kathleen P. March, Esq., and Judge Alan M. Ahart provides nice crisp treatments of all the pesky little issues that can arise in a bankruptcy case. Because of its relatively low cost (at least from a library's standpoint; it goes for $495), you are more likely to be able to find it in small county and court law libraries.

Foreclosure Resources

If you are facing foreclosure, you'll definitely want to look at *The Foreclosure Survival Guide,* by Stephen Elias (Nolo). This book explains the options available to you, then walks you through the necessary steps for handling your particular situation. If you are looking for a more comprehensive resource written primarily for lawyers, you can't do better than *Foreclosures*, by John Rao, Odette Williamson, and Tara Twomey (National Consumer Law Center). While the book is pricey ($110), it is cheap compared to the consequences of losing your home or hiring a lawyer to represent you. Even if you do hire a lawyer, you can benefit from having your own independent source of information. You can order a copy online at www.nclc.org.

For about half the price of its larger *Foreclosure* publication, the National Consumer Law Center (NCLC) offers a helpful resource titled *Foreclosure Prevention Counseling*, available through the NCLC Foreclosure Prevention Resource Center at www.consumerlaw.org/fprc.

Other Background Resources

Many libraries carry a legal encyclopedia called *American Jurisprudence*, 2nd Series. The article on bankruptcy has an extensive table of contents, and the entire encyclopedia has an index. This should help you zero in on useful material. Some large and well-stocked law libraries also carry a looseleaf publication known as the Commerce Clearing House (CCH) *Bankruptcy Law Reporter* (BLR). In this publication, you can find all three primary source materials relating to bankruptcy: statutes, rules, and cases.

If you are looking for information on adversary proceedings (such as how to defend against a creditor's challenge to the dischargeability of a debt), turn to *Represent Yourself in Court*, by Paul Bergman and Sara J. Berman (Nolo). It has an entire chapter on representing yourself in adversary proceedings in bankruptcy court. If you need information on court procedures or the local rules of a specific court, consult the *Collier Bankruptcy Practice Manual*.

Finding Federal Bankruptcy Statutes

Title 11 of the United States Code contains all the statutes that govern your bankruptcy.

The Internet

If you are using the Internet, go to the Legal Information Institute of Cornell University Law School, www.law.cornell.edu. Cornell lets you browse laws by subject matter and also offers a keyword search. To help you in your browsing, below is a table setting out the various subject matter sections of the U.S. Code that apply to bankruptcy.

How to Use Law Libraries

Law libraries that are open to the public are most often found in and around courthouses. Law schools also frequently admit the public at least some of the time (not, typically, during exam time, over the summer, or during other breaks in the academic year).

If you're using a library as a member of the public, find a way to feel at home, even if it seems that the library is run mostly to serve members of the legal community. Almost without exception, law libraries come with law librarians. The law librarians will be helpful as long as you ask them the right questions. For example, the law librarians will help you find specific library resources (for instance, where you can find the federal bankruptcy statutes or rules), but they normally won't teach you the ins and outs of legal research. Nor will they give an opinion about what a law means, how you should deal with the court, or how your particular question should be answered. For instance, if you want to find a state case interpreting a particular exemption, the law librarian will show you where your state code is located on the shelves and may even point out the volumes that contain the exemptions. The librarian won't, however, help you interpret the exemption, apply the exemption to your specific facts, or tell you how to raise the exemption in your bankruptcy case. Nor is the librarian likely to tell you what additional research steps you can or should take. When it comes to legal research in the law library, self help is the order of the day.

Bankruptcy Code Sections (11 U.S.C.)

§ 101	Definitions
§ 109	Who May File for Which Type of Bankruptcy; Credit Counseling Requirements
§ 110	Rules for Bankruptcy Petition Preparers
§ 111	Budget and Credit Counseling Agencies
§ 302	Who Can File Joint Cases
§ 326	How Trustees Are Compensated
§ 332	Consumer Privacy Ombudsmen
§ 341	Meeting of Creditors
§ 342	Notice of Creditors' Meeting; Informational Notice to Debtors; Requirements for Notice by Debtors
§ 343	Examination of Debtor at Creditors' Meeting
§ 348	Converting From One Type of Bankruptcy to Another
§ 349	Dismissing a Case
§ 350	Closing and Reopening a Case
§ 362	The Automatic Stay
§ 365	How Leases and Executory Contracts Are Treated in Bankruptcy
§ 366	Continuing or Reconnecting Utility Service
§ 501	Filing of Creditors' Claims
§ 506	Allowed Secured Claims and Lien Avoidance
§ 507	Priority Claims
§ 521	Paperwork Requirements and Deadlines
§ 522	Exemptions; Residency Requirements for Homestead Exemption; Stripping Liens From Property
§ 523	Nondischargeable Debts
§ 524	Effect of Discharge and Reaffirmation of Debts
§ 525	Prohibited Postbankruptcy Discrimination
§ 526	Restrictions on Debt Relief Agencies
§ 527	Required Disclosures by Debt Relief Agencies
§ 528	Requirements for Debt Relief Agencies
§ 541	What Property Is Part of the Bankruptcy Estate
§ 547	Preferences
§ 548	Fraudulent Transfers
§ 554	Trustee's Abandonment of Property in the Bankruptcy Estate
§ 707	The Means Test; Dismissal for Abuse; Conversion From Chapter 7 to Chapter 13
§ 722	Redemption of Liens on Personal Property
§ 727	Chapter 7 Discharge; Financial Management Counseling Requirements

The Law Library

Virtually every law library has at least one complete set of the annotated United States Code ("annotated" means that each statute is followed by citations and summaries of cases interpreting that provision). If you already have a citation to the statute you are seeking, you can use the citation to find the statute. However, if you have no citation—which is frequently the case—you can use either the index to Title 11 (the part of the Code that applies to bankruptcy) or the table we set out just above, which matches various issues that are likely to interest you with specific sections of Title 11.

Once you have found and read the statute, you can browse the one-paragraph summaries of written opinions issued by courts that have interpreted that particular statute. You will be looking to see whether a court has addressed your particular issue. If so, you can find and read the entire case in the law library. Reading what a judge has had to say about the statute regarding facts similar to yours is an invaluable guide to understanding how a judge is likely to handle the issue in your case, although when and where the case was decided may be important.

Finding the Federal Rules of Bankruptcy Procedure (FRBP)

The Federal Rules of Bankruptcy Procedure govern what happens if an issue is contested in the bankruptcy court. They also apply to certain routine bankruptcy procedures, such as deadlines for filing paperwork. Because most cases sail through the court without any need for the bankruptcy judge's intervention, you may not need to be familiar with these rules. However, certain types of creditor actions in the bankruptcy court must proceed by way of a regular lawsuit conducted under both these rules and the Federal Rules of Civil Procedure—for example, complaints to determine dischargeability of a debt (see Chapter 10). If you are representing yourself in such a lawsuit, you'll want to know these rules and look at the cases interpreting them. Any law library will have these rules. Your bankruptcy court's website will also have a link to the rules, as does www.law.cornell.edu.

Finding Local Court Rules

Every bankruptcy court operates under a set of local rules that govern how it does business and what is expected of the parties who use it. Throughout this book, we have cautioned you to read the rules for your particular court so that your dealings with the court will go smoothly—and so you won't end up getting tossed out of court if you become involved in litigation, such as an action to determine the dischargeability of a debt or a creditor's motion to lift the automatic stay.

Your bankruptcy court clerk's office will have the local rules available for you. Most courts also post their local rules on their own websites. To find the website for your court, take these steps:

Step 1: Go to www.uscourts.gov/links.html.

Step 2: Click the number on the map that is closest to where you live.

Step 3: Browse the list until you find your court and click on it.

Step 4: Click on the local rules link.

Court websites usually contain other helpful information as well, including case information, official and local bankruptcy forms, court guidelines (in addition to the local rules), information for lawyers and BPPs, information about the court and its judges, and the court calendar.

At the law library, the *Collier Bankruptcy Practice Manual* has the local rules for most (if not all) of the nation's bankruptcy courts.

Finding Federal Court Bankruptcy Cases

Court opinions are vital to understanding how a particular law might apply to your individual case. The following levels of federal courts issue bankruptcy-related opinions:

- the U.S. Supreme Court
- the U.S. Courts of Appeals
- the Bankruptcy Appellate Panels
- the U.S. District Courts, and
- the bankruptcy courts.

Most bankruptcy-related opinions are, not surprisingly, issued by the bankruptcy courts. By comparison, very few bankruptcy opinions come out of the U.S. Supreme Court. The other courts are somewhere in the middle.

The Internet

Depending on the date the case was decided, U.S. Supreme Court decisions and U.S. Court of Appeals decisions are available for free on the Internet (discussed below). For $13.95 a month, you can also subscribe to VersusLaw (at www.versuslaw.com), which provides U.S. Court of Appeals cases for an earlier period than you can get for free—often back to 1925. VersusLaw doesn't require you to sign a long-term contract. So, one payment of $13.95 gets you a month's worth of research. Not too shabby. VersusLaw also publishes many U.S. District Court cases on its website.

Opinions by the bankruptcy courts are not yet systematically available over the Internet, unless you subscribe to one of the databases described below. However, more often than not, a Google search will drum up some recently decided cases (typically because they appear on the court's website or in a bankruptcy blog).

U.S. Supreme Court. Google now has all Supreme Court cases available online. Under "Advanced Search" on the Google home page, choose "Google Scholar." Then select "Legal opinions and journals" and type in a case name. If you don't know the case name and you don't have a citation, enter some relevant words relating to your issue and see what you pull up.

U.S. Court of Appeals. Google now has federal appeals cases going back to 1925. Under "Advanced Search" on the Google home page, choose "Google Scholar." Then simply select "Legal opinions and journals" and type in a case name.

Again, if you are looking for a case decided prior to 1925, your best bet is to sign up for VersusLaw, described just above.

U.S. District Court and Bankruptcy Court. Cases reported by the bankruptcy courts may not be available to you online unless you subscribe to Westlaw, Lexis, or FastCase (www.fastcase.com). However, if you know the name of a particular case, a Google search might lead you to a court's website, where judges frequently post their decisions.

The Law Library

U.S. Supreme Court cases are published in three different book series:

- Supreme Court Reports
- Supreme Court Reporter, and
- Supreme Court Lawyer's Edition.

Some law libraries carry all three of these publications; others have only one. The cases are the same, but each series has different editorial enhancements.

U.S. Court of Appeals cases are published in the Federal Reporter (abbreviated simply as "F."). Most law libraries, large and small, carry this series.

Many U.S. District Court cases are published in the Federal Supplement (F.Supp), a series available in most law libraries.

Written opinions of bankruptcy judges, and related appeals, are published in the Bankruptcy Reporter (B.R.), available in most mid- to large-sized libraries. To accurately understand how your bankruptcy court is likely to interpret the laws in your particular case, sooner or later you will need access to the Bankruptcy Reporter.

State Statutes

The secret to understanding what property you can keep frequently lies in the exemptions that your state allows you to claim. These exemptions are found in your state's statutes.

The Internet

Every state has its statutes online, including its exemption statutes. This means that you can read your state's exemption statutes for yourself. Follow these steps:

Step 1: Go to Appendix A. At the top of your state's exemption table, you'll see a general reference to the collection of state laws for your state that contain the exemption statutes.

Step 2: Go to www.nolo.com; select "Legal Research."

Step 3: Select "State Laws," then find your state.

Step 4: Locate the collection of statutes mentioned in Appendix A.

Step 5: Use the exemption citation to the far right of your state's exemption table to search for the statute.

The Law Library

Your law library will have your state's statutes in book form, usually referred to as your state's code, annotated statutes, or compiled laws. Use Appendix A in this book to find a reference to the exemption statute you want to read, then use that reference to locate the exemption statute in the code. Once you find and read the statute, you can browse the summaries of court opinions interpreting the statute and, if you wish, read the cases in their entirety.

Alternatively, if your library has a copy of *Collier on Bankruptcy* or *Bankruptcy* by the Rutter Group (see above), you can find the exemptions for your state, accompanied by annotations summarizing state court interpretations.

State Court Cases

State courts are sometimes called on to interpret exemption statutes. If a court has interpreted the statute in which you are interested, you'll definitely want to chase down the relevant case and read it for yourself.

The Internet

Google now has state court cases going back to 1950. Under "Advanced Search" on the Google home page, choose "Google Scholar." Then select "Legal opinions and journals" and type in a case name.

In addition, all states make their more recent cases available free on the Internet—though usually not as far back as Google. To find these cases for your state:

Step 1: Go to www.law.cornell.edu/opinions.html#state.

Step 2: Click on your state.

Step 3: Locate the link to the court opinions for your state. This may be one link, or there may be separate links for your state's supreme court and your state's courts of appeal (the lower trial courts seldom publish their opinions, so you probably won't be able to find them).

If you want to go back to an earlier case (before 1950), consider subscribing to VersusLaw at www.versuslaw.com. As mentioned earlier, you don't have to sign a long-term contract.

The Law Library

Your law library will have a collection of books that contain opinions issued by your state's courts. If you have a citation, you can go right to the case. If you don't have a citation, you'll need to use a digest to find relevant bankruptcy cases. Finding cases by subject matter is a little too advanced for this brief summary. See *Legal Research: How to Find & Understand the Law,* by Stephen Elias and the Editors of Nolo (Nolo), for more help.

Other Helpful Resources

One very helpful bankruptcy website is maintained by the Office of the United States Trustee, at www.justice.gov/ust. This site provides lists of approved credit and financial management counseling agencies, median income figures for every state, the IRS national, regional, and local expenses you will need to complete the means test, and all of the forms you will need to file, in fill-in-the-blanks, PDF format. You can also download official bankruptcy forms from www.uscourts.gov/bkforms/index.html. However, this site doesn't include required local forms; for those, you'll have to visit your court or its website.

As part of the bankruptcy process, you are required to give the replacement (retail) value for all of the property you list in Schedule A (real property) and Schedule B (personal property). These figures are also the key to figuring out which of your property is exempt. Here are some tips on finding these values:

- **Cars:** Use the *Kelley Blue Book*, at www.kbb.com, or the website of the National Auto Dealers Association, www.nada.com.
- **Other personal property:** Check prices on eBay, www.ebay.com, or craigslist.
- **Homes:** Check the prices for which comparable homes have sold in the recent past. For a modest fee, you can get details on comparable homes, including sales history, number of bedrooms and baths, square footage, and property tax

information, at www.smarthomebuy.com. Less detailed information (purchase price, sales date, and address) is available free from sites like www.zillow.com, www.homevalues.com, www.domania.com, www.homeradar.com, and http://list.realestate.yahoo.com/re/homevalues.

Appendixes

APPENDIX

A

State and Federal Exemption Charts

The charts in this appendix summarize the laws that determine how much property debtors can keep when they file for Chapter 7 bankruptcy. As you will see, the charts are divided into categories of property, such as insurance, personal property, and wages. Following each exemption, we list the numerical citation to the state statute that includes the exemption. You'll need this information to complete your bankruptcy forms, as explained in Ch. 6.

The states are listed alphabetically, followed by the federal exemptions. (We also note the states that allow you to choose between the federal and state bankruptcy exemptions—see Ch. 3 for more information.)

RELATED TOPIC

Need help understanding a term? Many of the categories, types of property, and other terms used in these charts are defined in the Glossary, which you'll find right before this appendix.

Doubling

When married couples file for bankruptcy jointly, federal law and the laws of many states allow each person to claim the full amount of an exemption. (11 U.S.C. § 522.) Because these couples get to claim twice the amount available to those who file alone, this practice is informally known as "doubling."

Not all states allow doubling, however. And some states allow married filers to double only certain exemptions (for example, they can double personal property exemptions but not the homestead exemption). In the charts that follow, we indicate exemptions that cannot be doubled (and states that don't allow doubling at all). Unless you see a note stating that you cannot double, assume that you can.

CAUTION

These charts provide general information only. There are exceptions to state exemption laws that are much too detailed to include here. For example, even if an item is listed as exempt in one of these charts, you might have to give it up to pay a child support or tax debt. Consider doing further legal research or consulting an attorney about the exemptions you plan to claim, particularly if you anticipate—or are facing—a challenge to the value or types of property you want to keep. And, if valuable or cherished property is at stake, you may want to consult a local lawyer or accountant who is experienced in asset protection strategies.

Residency Requirements for Claiming State Exemptions

Prior to the new bankruptcy law, filers could use the exemptions of the state where they lived when they filed for bankruptcy. Under the new rules, however, some filers will have to use the exemptions of the state where they *used* to live. Congress was concerned about people gaming the system by moving to states with liberal exemptions just to file for bankruptcy. As a result, filers must now meet certain residency requirements before they can use a state's exemption system.

Here is a summary of these new rules:

- If you have been domiciled (that is, made your permanent home) in your current state for at least two years, you can use that state's exemptions.
- If you have been domiciled in your current state for more than 91 days but less than two years, you must use the exemptions of the state where you lived for the greater part of the 180-day period immediately prior to the two-year period preceding your filing.
- If you have been domiciled in your current state for less than 91 days, you can either

file in the state where you lived immediately before (as long as you lived there for at least 91 days) or wait until you have logged 91 days in your new home and file in your current state. Once you figure out where you can file, you'll need to use whatever exemptions are available to you according to the rules set out above.

- If the state you are filing in offers a choice between the state and federal bankruptcy exemptions, you can use the federal exemption list regardless of how long you've been living in the state.
- If these rules deprive you of the right to use *any* state's exemptions, you can use the federal exemption list. For example, some states allow their exemptions to be used only by current state residents, which might leave former residents who haven't lived in their new home state for at least two years without any available state exemptions.

For more detailed information and examples, see Ch. 3.

A longer residency requirement applies to homestead exemptions: If you acquired a home in your current state within the 40 months before you file for bankruptcy (and you didn't purchase it with the proceeds from selling another home in that state), your homestead exemption will be subject to a cap of $136,875, even if the state homestead exemption available to you is larger. For detailed information on homestead exemptions, see Ch. 4.

Retirement Accounts

Under the 2005 bankruptcy law, virtually all types of tax-exempt retirement accounts are exempt in bankruptcy, whether you use the state or federal exemptions. You can exempt 401(k)s, 403(b)s, profit-sharing and money purchase plans, IRAs (including Roth, SEP, and SIMPLE IRAs), and defined-benefit plans.

These exemptions are unlimited—that is, the entire account is exempt, regardless of how much money is in it—except in the case of traditional and Roth IRAs. For these types of IRAs only, the exemption is limited to a total value of $1,095,000 per person (this figure will be adjusted every three years for inflation). If you have more than one traditional or Roth IRA, you don't get to exempt $1,095,000 per account; your total exemption, no matter how many accounts you have, is $1,095,000.

If you are using the federal bankruptcy exemptions, you can find this new retirement account provision at 11 U.S.C. § 522(d)(12). If you are using state exemptions, cite 11 U.S.C. § 522(b)(3)(C) as the applicable exemption when you complete your bankruptcy papers.

Alabama

Federal bankruptcy exemptions not available. All law references are to Alabama Code unless otherwise noted.

ASSET	EXEMPTION	LAW
homestead	Real property or mobile home to $5,000; property cannot exceed 160 acres	6-10-2
	Must record homestead declaration before attempted sale of home	6-10-20
insurance	Annuity proceeds or avails to $250 per month	27-14-32
	Disability proceeds or avails to an average of $250 per month	27-14-31
	Fraternal benefit society benefits	27-34-27
	Life insurance proceeds or avails	6-10-8; 27-14-29
	Life insurance proceeds or avails if clause prohibits proceeds from being used to pay beneficiary's creditors	27-15-26
	Mutual aid association benefits	27-30-25
pensions	Tax-exempt retirement accounts, including 401(k)s, 403(b)s, profit-sharing and money purchase plans, SEP and SIMPLE IRAs, and defined-benefit plans	11 U.S.C. § 522(b)(3)(C)
	Traditional and Roth IRAs to $1,095,000 per person	11 U.S.C. § 522(b)(3)(C); (n)
	IRAs & other retirement accounts	19-3B-508
	Judges (only payments being received)	12-18-10(a),(b)
	Law enforcement officers	36-21-77
	Spendthrift trusts (with exceptions)	19-3B-501 to 503
	State employees	36-27-28
	Teachers	16-25-23
personal property	Books of debtor & family	6-10-6
	Burial place for self & family	6-10-5
	Church pew for self & family	6-10-5
	Clothing of debtor & family	6-10-6
	Family portraits or pictures	6-10-6
public benefits	Aid to blind, aged, disabled; & other public assistance	38-4-8
	Crime victims' compensation	15-23-15(e)
	Southeast Asian War POWs' benefits	31-7-2
	Unemployment compensation	25-4-140
	Workers' compensation	25-5-86(b)
tools of trade	Arms, uniforms, equipment that state military personnel are required to keep	31-2-78
wages	With respect to consumer loans, consumer credit sales, & consumer leases, 75% of weekly net earnings or 30 times the federal minimum hourly wage; all other cases, 75% of earned but unpaid wages; bankruptcy judge may authorize more for low-income debtors	5-19-15; 6-10-7
wildcard	$3,000 of any personal property, except wages	6-10-6

Alaska

Alaska law states that only the items found in Alaska Statutes §§ 9.38.010, 9.38.015(a), 9.38.017, 9.38.020, 9.38.025, and 9.38.030 may be exempted in bankruptcy. In *In re McNutt*, 87 B.R. 84 (9th Cir. 1988), however, an Alaskan debtor used the federal bankruptcy exemptions. All law references are to Alaska Statutes unless otherwise noted.

Alaska exemption amounts are adjusted regularly by administrative order. Current amounts are found at 8 Alaska Admin. Code tit. 8, § 95.030.

ASSET	EXEMPTION	LAW
homestead	$70,200 (joint owners may each claim a portion, but total can't exceed $70,200)	09.38.010(a)
insurance	Disability benefits	09.38.015(b); 09.38.030(e)(1),(5)
	Fraternal benefit society benefits	21.84.240
	Life insurance or annuity contracts, total avails to $13,000	09.38.025
	Medical, surgical, or hospital benefits	09.38.015(a)(3)
miscellaneous	Alimony, to extent wages exempt	09.38.030(e)(2)
	Child support payments made by collection agency	09.38.015(b)
	Liquor licenses	09.38.015(a)(7)
	Property of business partnership	09.38.100(b)
pensions	Tax-exempt retirement accounts, including 401(k)s, 403(b)s, profit-sharing and money purchase plans, SEP and SIMPLE IRAs, and defined-benefit plans	11 U.S.C. § 522(b)(3)(C)
	Traditional and Roth IRAs to $1,095,000 per person	11 U.S.C. § 522(b)(3)(C); (n)
	Elected public officers (only benefits building up)	09.38.015(b)
	ERISA-qualified benefits deposited more than 120 days before filing bankruptcy	09.38.017
	Judicial employees (only benefits building up)	09.38.015(b)
	Public employees (only benefits building up)	09.38.015(b); 39.35.505
	Roth & traditional IRAs, medical savings accounts	09.38.017(e)(3)
	Teachers (only benefits building up)	09.38.015(b)
	Other pensions, to extent wages exempt (only payments being received)	09.38.030(e)(5)
personal property	Books, musical instruments, clothing, family portraits, household goods, & heirlooms to $3,900 total	09.38.020(a)
	Building materials	34.35.105
	Burial plot	09.38.015(a)(1)
	Cash or other liquid assets to $1,820; for sole wage earner in household, $2,860 (restrictions apply—see *wages*)	09.38.030(b)
	Deposit in apartment or condo owners' association	09.38.010(e)
	Health aids needed	09.38.015(a)(2)
	Jewelry to $1,300	09.38.020(b)
	Money held in mortgage escrow accounts after July 1, 2008	09.38.015(e)
	Motor vehicle to $3,900; vehicle's market value can't exceed $26,000	09.38.020(e)
	Personal injury recoveries, to extent wages exempt	09.38.030(e)(3)
	Pets to $1,300	09.38.020(d)
	Proceeds for lost, damaged, or destroyed exempt property	09.38.060
	Tuition credits under an advance college tuition payment contract	09.38.015(a)(8)
	Wrongful death recoveries, to extent wages exempt	09.38.030(e)(3)

public benefits	Adult assistance to elderly, blind, disabled	47.25.550
	Alaska benefits for low-income seniors	09.38.015(a)(11)
	Alaska longevity bonus	09.38.015(a)(5)
	Crime victims' compensation	09.38.015(a)(4)
	Federally exempt public benefits paid or due	09.38.015(a)(6)
	General relief assistance	47.25.210
	Senior care (prescription drug) benefits	09.38.015(a)(10)
	20% of permanent fund dividends	43.23.065
	Unemployment compensation	09.38.015(b); 23.20.405
	Workers' compensation	23.30.160
tools of trade	Implements, books, & tools of trade to $3,640	09.38.020(c)
wages	Weekly net earnings to $456; for sole wage earner in a household, $716; if you don't receive weekly or semimonthly pay, you can claim $1,820 in cash or liquid assets paid any month; for sole wage earner in household, $2,860	9.38.030(a),(b); 9.38.050(b)
wildcard	None	

Arizona

Federal bankruptcy exemptions not available. All law references are to Arizona Revised Statutes unless otherwise noted.

ASSET	EXEMPTION	LAW
homestead	Real property, an apartment, or mobile home you occupy to $150,000; sale proceeds exempt 18 months after sale or until new home purchased, whichever occurs first (husband & wife may not double)	33-1101(A)
	May record homestead declaration to clarify which one of multiple eligible parcels is being claimed as homestead	33-1102
insurance	Fraternal benefit society benefits	20-877
	Group life insurance policy or proceeds	20-1132
	Health, accident, or disability benefits	33-1126(A)(4)
	Life insurance cash value or proceeds, or annuity contract if owned at least two years and beneficiary is dependent family member	33-1126(A)(6); 20-1131(D)
	Life insurance proceeds to $20,000 if beneficiary is spouse or child	33-1126(A)(1)
miscellaneous	Alimony, child support needed for support	33-1126(A)(3)
	Minor child's earnings, unless debt is for child	33-1126(A)(2)
pensions *see also wages*	Tax-exempt retirement accounts, including 401(k)s, 403(b)s, profit-sharing and money purchase plans, SEP and SIMPLE IRAs, and defined-benefit plans	11 U.S.C. § 522(b)(3)(C)
	Traditional and Roth IRAs to $1,095,000 per person	11 U.S.C. § 522(b)(3)(C); (n)
	Board of regents members, faculty & administrative officers under board's jurisdiction	15-1628(I)
	District employees	48-227
	ERISA-qualified benefits deposited over 120 days before filing	33-1126(B)
	IRAs & Roth IRAs	33-1126(B); *In re Herrscher,* 121 B.R. 29 (D. Ariz. 1989)
	Firefighters	9-968
	Police officers	9-931
	Rangers	41-955
	State employees' retirement & disability	38-792; 38-797.11
personal property *husband & wife may double all personal property*	2 beds & bedding; 1 living room chair per person; 1 dresser, table, lamp; kitchen table; dining room table & 4 chairs (1 more per person); living room carpet or rug; couch; 3 lamps; 3 coffee or end tables; pictures, paintings, personal drawings, family portraits; refrigerator, stove, washer, dryer, vacuum cleaner; TV, radio, stereo, alarm clock to $4,000 total	33-1123
	Bank deposit to $150 in one account	33-1126(A)(9)
	Bible; bicycle; sewing machine; typewriter; burial plot; rifle, pistol, or shotgun to $500 total	33-1125
	Books to $250; clothing to $500; wedding & engagement rings to $1,000; watch to $100; pets, horses, milk cows, & poultry to $500; musical instruments to $250	33-1125
	Food & fuel to last 6 months	33-1124
	Funeral deposits to $5,000	32-1391.05(4)
	Health aids	33-1125(9)
	Motor vehicle to $5,000 ($10,000, if debtor is physically disabled)	33-1125(8)
	Prepaid rent or security deposit to $1,000 or 1½ times your rent, whichever is less, in lieu of homestead	33-1126(C)
	Proceeds for sold or damaged exempt property	33-1126(A)(5),(8)
	Wrongful death awards	12-592
public benefits	Unemployment compensation	23-783(A)
	Welfare benefits	46-208
	Workers' compensation	23-1068(B)
tools of trade *husband & wife may double*	Arms, uniforms, & accoutrements of profession or office required by law	33-1130(3)
	Farm machinery, utensils, seed, instruments of husbandry, feed, grain, & animals to $2,500 total	33-1130(2)
	Library & teaching aids of teacher	33-1127
	Tools, equipment, instruments, & books to $2,500	33-1130(1)
wages	75% of earned but unpaid weekly net earnings or 30 times the federal minimum hourly wage; 50% of wages for support orders; bankruptcy judge may authorize more for low-income debtors	33-1131
wildcard	None	

Arkansas

Federal bankruptcy exemptions available. All law references are to Arkansas Code Annotated unless otherwise noted.

Note: *In re Holt*, 894 F.2d 1005 (8th Cir. 1990) held that Arkansas residents are limited to exemptions in the Arkansas Constitution. Statutory exemptions can still be used within Arkansas for nonbankruptcy purposes, but they cannot be claimed in bankruptcy.

ASSET	EXEMPTION	LAW
homestead *choose Option 1 or 2*	1. For married person or head of family: unlimited exemption on real or personal property used as residence to ¼ acre in city, town, or village, or 80 acres elsewhere; if property is between ¼–1 acre in city, town, or village, or 80–160 acres elsewhere, additional limit is $2,500; homestead may not exceed 1 acre in city, town, or village, or 160 acres elsewhere (husband & wife may not double)	Constitution 9-3; 9-4, 9-5; 16-66-210; 16-66-218(b)(3), (4); *In re Stevens*, 829 F.2d 693 (8th Cir. 1987)
	2. Real or personal property used as residence to $800 if single; $1,250 if married	16-66-218(a)(1)

insurance	Annuity contract	23-79-134
	Disability benefits	23-79-133
	Fraternal benefit society benefits	23-74-403
	Group life insurance	23-79-132
	Life, health, accident, or disability cash value or proceeds paid or due to $500	16-66-209; Constitution 9-1, 9-2; *In re Holt*, 894 F.2d 1005 (8th Cir. 1990)
	Life insurance proceeds if clause prohibits proceeds from being used to pay beneficiary's creditors	23-79-131
	Life insurance proceeds or avails if beneficiary isn't the insured	23-79-131
	Mutual assessment life or disability benefits to $1,000	23-72-114
	Stipulated insurance premiums	23-71-112
pensions	Tax-exempt retirement accounts, including 401(k)s, 403(b)s, profit-sharing and money purchase plans, SEP and SIMPLE IRAs, and defined-benefit plans	11 U.S.C. § 522(b)(3)(C)
	Traditional and Roth IRAs to $1,095,000 per person	11 U.S.C. § 522(b)(3)(C); (n)
	Disabled firefighters	24-11-814
	Disabled police officers	24-11-417
	Firefighters	24-10-616
	IRA deposits to $20,000 if deposited over 1 year before filing for bankruptcy	16-66-218(b)(16)
	Police officers	24-10-616
	School employees	24-7-715
	State police officers	24-6-205; 24-6-223
personal property	Burial plot to 5 acres, if choosing federal homestead exemption (Option 2)	16-66-207; 16-66-218(a)(1)
	Clothing	Constitution 9-1, 9-2
	Motor vehicle to $1,200	16-66-218(a)(2)
	Prepaid funeral trusts	23-40-117
	Wedding rings	16-66-219
public benefits	Crime victims' compensation	16-90-716(e)
	Unemployment compensation	11-10-109
	Workers' compensation	11-9-110
tools of trade	Implements, books, & tools of trade to $750	16-66-218(a)(4)
wages	Earned but unpaid wages due for 60 days; in no event less than $25 per week	16-66-208; 16-66-218(b)(6)
wildcard	$500 of any personal property if married or head of family; $200 if not married	Constitution 9-1, 9-2; 16-66-218(b)(1),(2)

California—System 1

Federal bankruptcy exemptions not available. California has two systems; you must select one or the other. All law references are to California Code of Civil Procedure unless otherwise noted. Many exemptions do not apply to claims for child support.

Note: California's exemption amounts are no longer updated in the statutes themselves. California Code of Civil Procedure Section 740.150 deputized the California Judicial Council to update the exemption amounts every three years. (The next revision will be in 2010.) As a result, the amounts listed in this chart will not match the amounts that appear in the cited statutes. The current exemption amounts can be found on the California Judicial Council website, www.courtinfo.ca.gov/forms/exemptions.htm.

ASSET	EXEMPTION	LAW
homestead	Real or personal property you occupy including mobile home, boat, stock cooperative, community apartment, planned development, or condo to $75,000 if single & not disabled; $100,000 for families if no other member has a homestead (if only one spouse files, may exempt one-half of amount if home held as community property & all of amount if home held as tenants in common); $175,000 if 65 or older, or physically or mentally disabled; $175,000 if 55 or older, single, & earn gross annual income under $15,000 or married & earn gross annual income under $20,000 & creditors seek to force the sale of your home; forced sale proceeds received exempt for 6 months after (husband & wife may not double); separated married debtor may claim homestead in community property homestead occupied by other spouse	704.710; 704.720; 704.730; *In re McFall*, 112 B.R. 336 (9th Cir. BAP 1990)
	May file homestead declaration to protect exemption amount from attachment of judicial liens and to protect proceeds of voluntary sale for 6 months	704.920
insurance	Disability or health benefits	704.130
	Fidelity bonds	Labor 404
	Fraternal benefit society benefits	704.170
	Fraternal unemployment benefits	704.120
	Homeowners' insurance proceeds for 6 months after received, to homestead exemption amount	704.720(b)
	Life insurance proceeds if clause prohibits proceeds from being used to pay beneficiary's creditors	Ins. 10132; Ins. 10170; Ins. 10171
	Matured life insurance benefits needed for support	704.100(c)
	Unmatured life insurance policy cash surrender value completely exempt; loan value exempt to $10,775	704.100(b)
miscellaneous	Business or professional licenses	695.060
	Inmates' trust funds to $1,350 (husband & wife may not double)	704.090
	Property of business partnership	Corp. 16501-04
pensions	Tax-exempt retirement accounts, including 401(k)s, 403(b)s, profit-sharing and money purchase plans, SEP and SIMPLE IRAs, and defined-benefit plans	11 U.S.C. § 522(b)(3)(C)
	Traditional and Roth IRAs to $1,095,000 per person	11 U.S.C. § 522(b)(3)(C); (n)
	County employees	Gov't 31452
	County firefighters	Gov't 32210
	County peace officers	Gov't 31913
	Private retirement benefits, including IRAs & Keoghs	704.115
	Public employees	Gov't 21255
	Public retirement benefits	704.110

personal property	Appliances, furnishings, clothing, & food	704.020
	Bank deposits from Social Security Administration to $2,700 ($4,050 for husband & wife); unlimited if SS funds are not commingled with other funds	704.080
	Bank deposits of other public benefits to $1,350 ($2,025 for husband & wife)	
	Building materials to repair or improve home to $2,700 (husband & wife may not double)	704.030
	Burial plot	704.200
	Funds held in escrow	Fin. 17410
	Health aids	704.050
	Jewelry, heirlooms, & art to $6,750 total (husband & wife may not double)	704.040
	Motor vehicles to $2,550, or $2,550 in auto insurance for loss or damages (husband & wife may not double)	704.010
	Personal injury & wrongful death causes of action	704.140(a); 704.150(a)
	Personal injury & wrongful death recoveries needed for support; if receiving installments, at least 75%	704.140(b),(c),(d); 704.150(b),(c)
public benefits	Aid to blind, aged, disabled; public assistance	704.170
	Financial aid to students	704.190
	Relocation benefits	704.180
	Unemployment benefits	704.120
	Union benefits due to labor dispute	704.120(b)(5)
	Workers' compensation	704.160
tools of trade	Tools, implements, materials, instruments, uniforms, one commercial vehicle, books, furnishings, & equipment to $6,750 total ($13,475 total if used by both spouses in same occupation)	704.060
	Commercial vehicle (Vehicle Code § 260) to $4,850 ($9,700 total if used by both spouses in same occupation) (this counts toward total tools of trade exemption)	704.060
wages	Minimum 75% of wages paid within 30 days prior to filing	704.070
	Public employees' vacation credits; if receiving installments, at least 75%	704.113
wildcard	None	

California—System 2

Refer to the notes for California—System 1, above.

Note: Married couples may not double any exemptions. (*In re Talmadge*, 832 F.2d 1120 (9th Cir. 1987); *In re Baldwin*, 70 B.R. 612 (9th Cir. BAP 1987).)

ASSET	EXEMPTION	LAW
homestead	Real or personal property, including co-op, used as residence to $20,725; unused portion of homestead may be applied to any property	703.140(b)(1)
insurance	Disability benefits	703.140(b)(10)(C)
	Life insurance proceeds needed for support of family	703.140(b)(11)(C)
	Unmatured life insurance contract accrued avails to $11,075	703.140(b)(8)
	Unmatured life insurance policy other than credit	703.140(b)(7)
miscellaneous	Alimony, child support needed for support	703.140(b)(10)(D)
pensions	Tax-exempt retirement accounts, including 401(k)s, 403(b)s, profit-sharing and money purchase plans, SEP and SIMPLE IRAs, and defined-benefit plans	11 U.S.C. § 522(b)(3)(C)
	Traditional and Roth IRAs to $1,095,000 per person	11 U.S.C. § 522(b)(3)(C); (n)
	ERISA-qualified benefits needed for support	703.140(b)(10)(E)
personal property	Animals, crops, appliances, furnishings, household goods, books, musical instruments, & clothing to $525 per item	703.140(b)(3)
	Burial plot to $20,725, in lieu of homestead	703.140(b)(1)
	Health aids	703.140(b)(9)
	Jewelry to $1,350	703.140(b)(4)
	Motor vehicle to $3,300	703.140(b)(2)
	Personal injury recoveries to $20,725 (not to include pain & suffering; pecuniary loss)	703.140(b)(11)(D),(E)
	Wrongful death recoveries needed for support	703.140(b)(11)(B)
public benefits	Crime victims' compensation	703.140(b)(11)(A)
	Public assistance	703.140(b)(10)(A)
	Social Security	703.140(b)(10)(A)
	Unemployment compensation	703.140(b)(10)(A)
	Veterans' benefits	703.140(b)(10)(B)
tools of trade	Implements, books, & tools of trade to $2,075	703.140(b)(6)
wages	None (use federal nonbankruptcy wage exemption)	
wildcard	$1,100 of any property	703.140(b)(5)
	Unused portion of homestead or burial exemption of any property	703.140(b)(5)

Colorado

Federal bankruptcy exemptions not available. All law references are to Colorado Revised Statutes unless otherwise noted.

ASSET	EXEMPTION	LAW
homestead	Real property, mobile home, manufactured home, or house trailer you occupy to $60,000; $90,000 if owner, spouse, or dependent is disabled or at least 60 years old; sale proceeds exempt 2 years after received	38-41-201; 38-41-201.6; 38-41-203; 38-41-207; *In re Pastrana*, 216 B.R. 948 (D. Colo., 1998)
	Spouse or child of deceased owner may claim homestead exemption	38-41-204
insurance	Disability benefits to $200 per month; if lump sum, entire amount exempt	10-16-212
	Fraternal benefit society benefits	10-14-403
	Group life insurance policy or proceeds	10-7-205
	Homeowners' insurance proceeds for 1 year after received, to homestead exemption amount	38-41-209
	Life insurance cash surrender value to $50,000, except contributions to policy within past 48 months	13-54-102(1)(l)
	Life insurance proceeds if clause prohibits proceeds from being used to pay beneficiary's creditors	10-7-106

miscellaneous	Child support or domestic support obligation	13-54-102(u) 13-54-102.5
	Property of business partnership	7-60-125
pensions *see also wages*	Tax-exempt retirement accounts, including 401(k)s, 403(b)s, profit-sharing and money purchase plans, SEP and SIMPLE IRAs, and defined-benefit plans	11 U.S.C. § 522(b)(3)(C)
	Traditional and Roth IRAs to $1,095,000 per person	11 U.S.C. § 522(b)(3)(C); (n)
	ERISA-qualified benefits, including IRAs & Roth IRAs	13-54-102(1)(s)
	Firefighters & police officers	31-30.5-208; 31-31-203
	Public employees' pensions, deferred compensation, & defined contribution plans	24-51-212
	Teachers	22-64-120
	Veteran's pension for veteran, spouse, or dependents if veteran served in war or armed conflict	13-54-102(1)(h); 13-54-104
personal property	1 burial plot per family member	13-54-102(1)(d)
	Clothing to $1,500	13-54-102(1)(a)
	Food & fuel to $600	13-54-102(1)(f)
	Health aids	13-54-102(1)(p)
	Household goods to $3,000	13-54-102(1)(e)
	Jewelry & articles of adornment to $2,000	13-54-102(1)(b)
	Motor vehicles or bicycles used for work to $5,000; $10,000 if used by a debtor or by a dependent who is disabled or 60 or over	13-54-102(j)(I), (II)
	Personal injury recoveries	13-54-102(1)(n)
	Family pictures & books to $1,500	13-54-102(1)(c)
	Proceeds for damaged exempt property	13-54-102(1)(m)
	Security deposits	13-54-102(1)(r)
public benefits	Aid to blind, aged, disabled; public assistance	26-2-131
	Crime victims' compensation	13-54-102(1)(q); 24-4.1-114
	Disability benefits to $3,000	13-54-102(v)
	Earned income tax credit or refund	13-54-102(1)(o)
	Unemployment compensation	8-80-103
	Veteran's benefits for veteran, spouse, or child if veteran served in war or armed conflict	13-54-102(1)(h)
	Workers' compensation	8-42-124
tools of trade	Livestock or other animals, machinery, tools, equipment, & seed of person engaged in agriculture, to $50,000 total	13-54-102(1)(g)
	Professional's library to $3,000 (if not claimed under other tools of trade exemption)	13-54-102(1)(k)
	Stock in trade, supplies, fixtures, tools, machines, electronics, equipment, books, & other business materials, to $20,000 total	13-54-102(1)(i)
	Military equipment personally owned by members of the National Guard	13-54-102(1)(h.5)
wages	Minimum 75% of weekly net earnings or 30 times the federal or state minimum wage, whichever is greater, including pension & insurance payments	13-54-104
wildcard	None	

Connecticut

Federal bankruptcy exemptions available. All law references are to Connecticut General Statutes Annotated unless otherwise noted.

ASSET	EXEMPTION	LAW
homestead	Real property, including mobile or manufactured home, to $75,000; applies only to claims arising after 1993, but to $125,000 in the case of a money judgment arising out of services provided at a hospital	52-352a(e); 52-352b(t)
insurance	Disability benefits paid by association for its members	52-352b(p)
	Fraternal benefit society benefits	38a-637
	Health or disability benefits	52-352b(e)
	Life insurance proceeds if clause prohibits proceeds from being used to pay beneficiary's creditors	38a-454
	Life insurance proceeds or avails	38a-453
	Unmatured life insurance policy avails to $4,000 if beneficiary is dependent	52-352b(s)
miscellaneous	Alimony, to extent wages exempt	52-352b(n)
	Child support	52-352b(h)
	Farm partnership animals & livestock feed reasonably required to run farm where at least 50% of partners are members of same family	52-352d
pensions	Tax-exempt retirement accounts, including 401(k)s, 403(b)s, profit-sharing and money purchase plans, SEP and SIMPLE IRAs, and defined-benefit plans	11 U.S.C. § 522(b)(3)(C)
	Traditional and Roth IRAs to $1,095,000 per person	11 U.S.C. § 522(b)(3)(C); (n)
	ERISA-qualified benefits, including IRAs, Roth IRAs, & Keoghs, to extent wages exempt	52-321a; 52-352b(m)
	Medical savings account	52-321a
	Municipal employees	7-446
	State employees	5-171; 5-192w
	Teachers	10-183q
personal property	Appliances, food, clothing, furniture, bedding	52-352b(a)
	Burial plot	52-352b(c)
	Health aids needed	52-352b(f)
	Motor vehicle to $3,500	52-352b(j)
	Proceeds for damaged exempt property	52-352b(q)
	Residential utility & security deposits for 1 residence	52-3252b(l)
	Spendthrift trust funds required for support of debtor & family	52-321(d)
	Transfers to a licensed debt adjuster	52-352b(u)
	Tuition savings accounts	52-321a(E)
	Wedding & engagement rings	52-352b(k)
public benefits	Crime victims' compensation	52-352b(o); 54-213
	Public assistance	52-352b(d)
	Social Security	52-352b(g)
	Unemployment compensation	31-272(c); 52-352b(g)
	Veterans' benefits	52-352b(g)
	Workers' compensation	52-352b(g)

tools of trade	Arms, military equipment, uniforms, musical instruments of military personnel	52-352b(i)
	Tools, books, instruments, & farm animals needed	52-352b(b)
wages	Minimum 75% of earned but unpaid weekly disposable earnings, or 40 times the state or federal hourly minimum wage, whichever is greater	52-361a(f)
wildcard	$1,000 of any property	52-352b(r)

Delaware

Federal bankruptcy exemptions not available. All law references are to Delaware Code Annotated (in the form title number-section number) unless otherwise noted.

Note: A single person may exempt no more than $25,000 total in all exemptions (not including retirement plans and principal residence); a husband & wife may exempt no more than $50,000 total (10-4914).

ASSET	EXEMPTION	LAW
homestead	Real property or manufactured home used as principal residence to $50,000 (spouses may not double)	10-4914(c)
	Property held as tenancy by the entirety may be exempt against debts owed by only one spouse	*In re Kelley*, 289 B.R. 38 (Bankr. D. Del. 2003)
insurance	Annuity contract proceeds to $350 per month	18-2728
	Fraternal benefit society benefits	18-6218
	Group life insurance policy or proceeds	18-2727
	Health or disability benefits	18-2726
	Life insurance proceeds if clause prohibits proceeds from being used to pay beneficiary's creditors	18-2729
	Life insurance proceeds or avails	18-2725
pensions	Tax-exempt retirement accounts, including 401(k)s, 403(b)s, profit-sharing and money purchase plans, SEP and SIMPLE IRAs, and defined-benefit plans	11 U.S.C. § 522(b)(3)(C)
	Traditional and Roth IRAs to $1,095,000 per person	11 U.S.C. § 522(b)(3)(C); (n)
	IRAs, Roth IRAs, & any other retirement plans	10-4915
	Kent County employees	9-4316
	Police officers	11-8803
	State employees	29-5503
	Volunteer firefighters	16-6653
personal property	Bible, books, & family pictures	10-4902(a)
	Burial plot	10-4902(a)
	Church pew or any seat in public place of worship	10-4902(a)
	Clothing, includes jewelry	10-4902(a)
	College investment plan account (limit for year before filing is $5,000 or average of past two years' contribution, whichever is more)	10-4916
	Principal and income from spendthrift trusts	12-3536
	Pianos & leased organs	10-4902(d)
	Sewing machines	10-4902(c)
public benefits	Aid to blind	31-2309
	Aid to aged, disabled; general assistance	31-513
	Crime victims' compensation	11-9011
	Unemployment compensation	19-3374
	Workers' compensation	19-2355
tools of trade	Tools of trade and/or vehicle necessary for employment to $15,000 each	10-4914(c)
	Tools, implements, & fixtures to $75 in New Castle & Sussex Counties; to $50 in Kent County	10-4902(b)
wages	85% of earned but unpaid wages	10-4913
wildcard	$500 of any personal property, except tools of trade, if head of family	10-4903

District of Columbia

Federal bankruptcy exemptions available. All law references are to District of Columbia Code unless otherwise noted.

ASSET	EXEMPTION	LAW
homestead	Any property used as a residence or co-op that debtor or debtor's dependent uses as a residence	15-501(a)(14)
	Property held as tenancy by the entirety may be exempt against debts owed by only one spouse	*Estate of Wall*, 440 F.2d 215 (D.C. Cir. 1971)
insurance	Disability benefits	15-501(a)(7); 31-4716.01
	Fraternal benefit society benefits	31-5315
	Group life insurance policy or proceeds	31-4717
	Life insurance payments	15-501(a)(11)
	Life insurance proceeds if clause prohibits proceeds from being used to pay beneficiary's creditors	31-4719
	Life insurance proceeds or avails	31-4716
	Other insurance proceeds to $200 per month, maximum 2 months, for head of family; else $60 per month	15-503
	Unmatured life insurance contract other than credit life insurance	15-501(a)(5)
miscellaneous	Alimony or child support	15-501(a)(7)
pensions *see also wages*	Tax-exempt retirement accounts, including 401(k)s, 403(b)s, profit-sharing and money purchase plans, SEP and SIMPLE IRAs, and defined-benefit plans	11 U.S.C. § 522(b)(3)(C)
	Traditional and Roth IRAs to $1,095,000 per person	11 U.S.C. § 522(b)(3)(C); (n)
	ERISA-qualified benefits, IRAs, Keoghs, etc. to maximum deductible contribution	15-501(b)(9)
	Any stock bonus, annuity, pension, or profit-sharing plan	15-501(a)(7)
	Judges	11-1570(f)
	Public school teachers	38-2001.17; 38-2021.17
personal property	Appliances, books, clothing, household furnishings, goods, musical instruments, pets to $425 per item or $8,625 total	15-501(a)(2)
	Cemetery & burial funds	43-111
	Cooperative association holdings to $50	29-928
	Food for 3 months	15-501(a)(12)
	Health aids	15-501(a)(6)

personal property (continued)	Higher education tuition savings account	47-4510
	Residential condominium deposit	42-1904.09
	All family pictures; all the family library to $400	15-501(a)(8)
	Motor vehicle to $2,575	15-501(a)(1)
	Payment, including pain & suffering, for loss of debtor or person depended on	15-501(a)(11)
	Uninsured motorist benefits	31-2408.01(h)
	Wrongful death damages	15-501(a)(11); 16-2703
public benefits	Aid to blind, aged, disabled; general assistance	4-215.01
	Crime victims' compensation	4-507(e); 15-501(a)(11)
	Social Security	15-501(a)(7)
	Unemployment compensation	51-118
	Veterans' benefits	15-501(a)(7)
	Workers' compensation	32-1517
tools of trade	Library, furniture, tools of professional or artist to $300	15-501(a)(13)
	Tools of trade or business to $1,625	15-501(a)(5)
	Mechanic's tools to $200	15-503(b)
	Seal & documents of notary public	1-1206
wages	Minimum 75% of earned but unpaid wages, pension payments; bankruptcy judge may authorize more for low-income debtors	16-572
	Nonwage (including pension & retirement) earnings to $200 per month for head of family; else $60 per month for a maximum of two months	15-503
	Payment for loss of future earnings	15-501(e)(11)
wildcard	Up to $850 in any property, plus up to $8,075 of unused homestead exemption	15-501(a)(3)

Florida

Federal bankruptcy exemptions not available. All law references are to Florida Statutes Annotated unless otherwise noted.

ASSET	EXEMPTION	LAW
homestead	Real or personal property including mobile or modular home to unlimited value; cannot exceed half acre in municipality or 160 acres elsewhere; spouse or child of deceased owner may claim homestead exemption	222.01; 222.02; 222.03; 222.05; Constitution 10-4 *In re Colwell*, 196 F.3d 1225 (11th Cir. 1999)
	May file homestead declaration	222.01
	Property held as tenancy by the entirety may be exempt against debts owed by only one spouse	*Havoco of America, Ltd. v. Hill*, 197 F.3d 1135 (11th Cir. 1999)
insurance	Annuity contract proceeds; does not include lottery winnings	222.14; *In re Pizzi*, 153 B.R. 357 (S.D. Fla. 1993)
	Death benefits payable to a specific beneficiary, not the deceased's estate	222.13
	Disability or illness benefits	222.18
	Fraternal benefit society benefits	632.619
	Life insurance cash surrender value	222.14
miscellaneous	Alimony, child support needed for support	222.201
	Damages to employees for injuries in hazardous occupations	769.05
pensions *see also wages*	Tax-exempt retirement accounts, including 401(k)s, 403(b)s, profit-sharing and money purchase plans, SEP and SIMPLE IRAs, and defined-benefit plans	11 U.S.C. § 522(b)(3)(C)
	Traditional and Roth IRAs to $1,095,000 per person	11 U.S.C. § 522(b)(3)(C); (n)
	County officers, employees	122.15
	ERISA-qualified benefits, including IRAs & Roth IRAs	222.21(2)
	Firefighters	175.241
	Police officers	185.25
	State officers, employees	121.131
	Teachers	238.15
personal property	Any personal property to $1,000 (husband & wife may double); to $4,000 if no homestead claimed	Constitution 10-4; *In re Hawkins*, 51 B.R. 348 (S.D. Fla. 1985)
	Federal income tax refund or credit	222.25
	Health aids	222.25
	Motor vehicle to $1,000	222.25
	Pre-need funeral contract deposits	497.56(8)
	Prepaid college education trust deposits	222.22(1)
	Prepaid hurricane savings accounts	222.22(4)
	Prepaid medical savings account deposits	222.22(2)
public benefits	Crime victims' compensation, unless seeking to discharge debt for treatment of injury incurred during the crime	960.14
	Public assistance	222.201
	Social Security	222.201
	Unemployment compensation	222.201; 443.051(2),(3)
	Veterans' benefits	222.201; 744.626
	Workers' compensation	440.22
tools of trade	None	
wages	100% of wages for heads of family up to $500 per week either unpaid or paid & deposited into bank account for up to 6 months	222.11
	Federal government employees' pension payments needed for support & received 3 months prior	222.21
wildcard	See personal property	

Georgia

Federal bankruptcy exemptions not available. All law references are to the Official Code of Georgia Annotated unless otherwise noted.

ASSET	EXEMPTION	LAW
homestead	Real or personal property, including co-op, used as residence to $10,000 (to $20,000 if married and debtor spouse is sole owner); up to $5,000 of unused portion of homestead may be applied to any property	44-13-100(a)(1); 44-13-100(a)(6); *In re Burnett*, 303 B.R. 684 (M.D. Ga. 2003)
insurance	Annuity & endowment contract benefits	33-28-7
	Disability or health benefits to $250 per month	33-29-15
	Fraternal benefit society benefits	33-15-62

insurance (continued)	Group insurance	33-30-10
	Proceeds & avails of life insurance	33-26-5; 33-25-11
	Life insurance proceeds if policy owned by someone you depended on, needed for support	44-13-100(a)(11)(C)
	Unmatured life insurance contract	44-13-100(a)(8)
	Unmatured life insurance dividends, interest, loan value, or cash value to $2,000 if beneficiary is you or someone you depend on	44-13-100(a)(9)
miscellaneous	Alimony, child support needed for support	44-13-100(a)(2)(D)
pensions	Tax-exempt retirement accounts, including 401(k)s, 403(b)s, profit-sharing and money purchase plans, SEP and SIMPLE IRAs, and defined-benefit plans	11 U.S.C. § 522(b)(3)(C)
	Traditional and Roth IRAs to $1,095,000 per person	11 U.S.C. § 522(b)(3)(C); (n)
	Employees of nonprofit corporations	44-13-100(a)(2.1)(B)
	ERISA-qualified benefits & IRAs	18-4-22
	Public employees	44-13-100(a)(2.1)(A); 47-2-332
	Payments from IRA necessary for support	44-13-100(a)(2)(F)
	Other pensions needed for support	18-4-22; 44-13-100(a)(2)(E); 44-13-100(a)(2.1)(C)
personal property	Animals, crops, clothing, appliances, books, furnishings, household goods, musical instruments to $300 per item, $5,000 total	44-13-100(a)(4)
	Burial plot, in lieu of homestead	44-13-100(a)(1)
	Compensation for lost future earnings needed for support to $7,500	44-13-100(a)(11)(E)
	Health aids	44-13-100(a)(10)
	Jewelry to $500	44-13-100(a)(5)
	Motor vehicles to $3,500	44-13-100(a)(3)
	Personal injury recoveries to $10,000	44-13-100(a)(11)(D)
	Wrongful death recoveries needed for support	44-13-100(a)(11)(B)
public benefits	Aid to blind	49-4-58
	Aid to disabled	49-4-84
	Crime victims' compensation	44-13-100(a)(11)(A)
	Local public assistance	44-13-100(a)(2)(A)
	Old age assistance	49-4-35
	Social Security	44-13-100(a)(2)(A)
	Unemployment compensation	44-13-100(a)(2)(A)
	Veterans' benefits	44-13-100(a)(2)(B)
	Workers' compensation	34-9-84
tools of trade	Implements, books, & tools of trade to $1,500	44-13-100(a)(7)
wages	Minimum 75% of earned but unpaid weekly disposable earnings, or 40 times the state or federal hourly minimum wage, whichever is greater, for private & federal workers; bankruptcy judge may authorize more for low-income debtors	18-4-20; 18-4-21
wildcard	$600 of any property	44-13-100(a)(6)
	Unused portion of homestead exemption to $5,000	44-13-100(a)(6)

Hawaii

Federal bankruptcy exemptions available. All law references are to Hawaii Revised Statutes unless otherwise noted.

ASSET	EXEMPTION	LAW
homestead	Head of family or over 65 to $30,000; all others to $20,000; property cannot exceed 1 acre; sale proceeds exempt for 6 months after sale (husband & wife may not double)	651-91; 651-92; 651-96
	Property held as tenancy by the entirety may be exempt against debts owed by only one spouse	*Security Pacific Bank v. Chang*, 818 F.Supp. 1343 (D. Haw. 1993)
insurance	Annuity contract or endowment policy proceeds if beneficiary is insured's spouse, child, or parent	431:10-232(b)
	Accident, health, or sickness benefits	431:10-231
	Fraternal benefit society benefits	432:2-403
	Group life insurance policy or proceeds	431:10-233
	Life insurance proceeds if clause prohibits proceeds from being used to pay beneficiary's creditors	431:10D-112
	Life or health insurance policy for spouse or child	431:10-234
miscellaneous	Property of business partnership	425-125
pensions	Tax-exempt retirement accounts, including 401(k)s, 403(b)s, profit-sharing and money purchase plans, SEP and SIMPLE IRAs, and defined-benefit plans	11 U.S.C. § 522(b)(3)(C)
	Traditional and Roth IRAs to $1,095,000 per person	11 U.S.C. § 522(b)(3)(C); (n)
	IRAs, Roth IRAs, and ERISA-qualified benefits deposited over 3 years before filing bankruptcy	651-124
	Firefighters	88-169
	Police officers	88-169
	Public officers & employees	88-91; 653-3
personal property	Appliances & furnishings	651-121(1)
	Books	651-121(1)
	Burial plot to 250 sq. ft. plus tombstones, monuments, & fencing	651-121(4)
	Clothing	651-121(1)
	Jewelry, watches, & articles of adornment to $1,000	651-121(1)
	Motor vehicle to wholesale value of $2,575	651-121(2)
	Proceeds for sold or damaged exempt property; sale proceeds exempt for 6 months after sale	651-121(5)
public benefits	Crime victims' compensation & special accounts created to limit commercial exploitation of crimes	351-66; 351-86
	Public assistance paid by Department of Health Services for work done in home or workshop	346-33
	Temporary disability benefits	392-29
	Unemployment compensation	383-163
	Unemployment work relief funds to $60 per month	653-4
	Workers' compensation	386-57

tools of trade	Tools, implements, books, instruments, uniforms, furnishings, fishing boat, nets, motor vehicle, & other property needed for livelihood	651-121(3)
wages	Prisoner's wages held by Department of Public Safety (except for restitution, child support, & other claims)	353-22.5
	Unpaid wages due for services of past 31 days	651-121(6)
wildcard	None	

Idaho

Federal bankruptcy exemptions not available. All law references are to Idaho Code unless otherwise noted.

ASSET	EXEMPTION	LAW
homestead	Real property or mobile home to $100,000; sale proceeds exempt for 6 months (husband & wife may not double)	55-1003; 55-1113
	Must record homestead exemption for property that is not yet occupied	55-1004
insurance	Annuity contract proceeds to $1,250 per month	41-1836
	Death or disability benefits	11-604(1)(a); 41-1834
	Fraternal benefit society benefits	41-3218
	Group life insurance benefits	41-1835
	Homeowners' insurance proceeds to amount of homestead exemption	55-1008
	Life insurance proceeds if clause prohibits proceeds from being used to pay beneficiary's creditors	41-1930
	Life insurance proceeds or avails for beneficiary other than the insured	11-604(d); 41-1833
	Medical, surgical, or hospital care benefits & amount in medical savings account	11-603(5)
	Unmatured life insurance contract, other than credit life insurance, owned by debtor	11-605(8)
	Unmatured life insurance contract interest or dividends to $5,000 owned by debtor or person debtor depends on	11-605(9)
miscellaneous	Alimony, child support	11-604(1)(b)
	Liquor licenses	23-514
pension *see also wages*	Tax-exempt retirement accounts, including 401(k)s, 403(b)s, profit-sharing and money purchase plans, SEP and SIMPLE IRAs, and defined-benefit plans	11 U.S.C. § 522(b)(3)(C)
	Traditional and Roth IRAs to $1,095,000 per person	11 U.S.C. § 522(b)(3)(C); (n)
	ERISA-qualified benefits	55-1011
	Firefighters	72-1422
	Government & private pensions, retirement plans, IRAs, Roth IRAs, Keoghs, etc.	11-604A
	Police officers	50-1517
	Public employees	59-1317
personal property	Appliances, furnishings, books, clothing, pets, musical instruments, 1 firearm, family portraits, & sentimental heirlooms to $500 per item, $5,000 total	11-605(1)
	Building materials	45-514
personal property (continued)	Burial plot	11-603(1)
	College savings program account	11-604A(4)(b)
	Crops cultivated on maximum of 50 acres, to $1,000; water rights to 160 inches	11-605(6)
	Health aids	11-603(2)
	Jewelry to $1,000	11-605(2)
	Motor vehicle to $5,000	11-605(3)
	Personal injury recoveries	11-604(1)(c)
	Proceeds for damaged exempt property for 3 months after proceeds received	11-606
	Wrongful death recoveries	11-604(1)(c)
public benefits	Aid to blind, aged, disabled	56-223
	Federal, state, & local public assistance	11-603(4)
	General assistance	56-223
	Social Security	11-603(3)
	Unemployment compensation	11-603(6)
	Veterans' benefits	11-603(3)
	Workers' compensation	72-802
tools of trade	Arms, uniforms, & accoutrements that peace officer, National Guard, or military personnel is required to keep	11-605(5)
	Implements, books, & tools of trade to $1,500	11-605(3)
wages	Minimum 75% of earned but unpaid weekly disposable earnings, or 30 times the federal hourly minimum wage, whichever is greater; pension payments; bankruptcy judge may authorize more for low-income debtors	11-207
wildcard	$800 in any tangible personal property	11-605(10)

Illinois

Federal bankruptcy exemptions not available. All law references are to Illinois Compiled Statutes Annotated unless otherwise noted.

ASSET	EXEMPTION	LAW
homestead	Real or personal property including a farm, lot, & buildings, condo, co-op, or mobile home to $15,000; sale proceeds exempt for 1 year	735-5/12-901; 735-5/12-906
	Spouse or child of deceased owner may claim homestead exemption	735-5/12-902
	Illinois recognizes tenancy by the entirety, with limitations	750-65/22; 765-1005/1c; *In re Gillissie*, 215 B.R. 370 (Bankr. N.D. Ill. 1998); *Great Southern Co. v. Allard*, 202 B.R. 938 (N.D. Ill. 1996).
insurance	Fraternal benefit society benefits	215-5/299.1a
	Health or disability benefits	735-5/12-1001(g)(3)
	Homeowners' proceeds if home destroyed, to $15,000	735-5/12-907
	Life insurance, annuity proceeds, or cash value if beneficiary is insured's child, parent, spouse, or other dependent	215-5/238; 735-5/12-1001(f)
	Life insurance proceeds to a spouse or dependent of debtor to extent needed for support	735-5/12-1001(f),(g)(3)
miscellaneous	Alimony, child support	735-5/12-1001(g)(4)
	Property of business partnership	805-205/25

pensions	Tax-exempt retirement accounts, including 401(k)s, 403(b)s, profit-sharing and money purchase plans, SEP and SIMPLE IRAs, and defined-benefit plans	11 U.S.C. § 522(b)(3)(C)
	Traditional and Roth IRAs to $1,095,000 per person	11 U.S.C. § 522(b)(3)(C); (n)
	Civil service employees	40-5/11-223
	County employees	40-5/9-228
	Disabled firefighters; widows & children of firefighters	40-5/22-230
	IRAs and ERISA-qualified benefits	735-5/12-1006
	Firefighters	40-5/4-135; 40-5/6-213
	General Assembly members	40-5/2-154
	House of correction employees	40-5/19-117
	Judges	40-5/18-161
	Municipal employees	40-5/7-217(a); 40-5/8-244
	Park employees	40-5/12-190
	Police officers	40-5/3-144.1; 40-5/5-218
	Public employees	735-5/12-1006
	Public library employees	40-5/19-218
	Sanitation district employees	40-5/13-805
	State employees	40-5/14-147
	State university employees	40-5/15-185
	Teachers	40-5/16-190; 40-5/17-151
personal property	Bible, family pictures, schoolbooks, & clothing	735-5/12-1001(a)
	Health aids	735-5/12-1001(e)
	Illinois College Savings Pool accounts invested more than 1 year before filing if below federal gift tax limit, or 2 years before filing if above	735-5/12-1001(j)
	Motor vehicle to $2,400	735-5/12-1001(c)
	Personal injury recoveries to $15,000	735-5/12-1001(h)(4)
	Pre-need cemetery sales funds, care funds, & trust funds	235-5/6-1; 760-100/4; 815-390/16
	Prepaid tuition trust fund	110-979/45(g)
	Proceeds of sold exempt property	735-5/12-1001
	Wrongful death recoveries	735-5/12-1001(h)(2)
public benefits	Aid to aged, blind, disabled; public assistance	305-5/11-3
	Crime victims' compensation	735-5/12-1001(h)(1)
	Restitution payments on account of WWII relocation of Aleuts & Japanese Americans	735-5/12-1001(12)(h)(5)
	Social Security	735-5/12-1001(g)(1)
	Unemployment compensation	735-5/12-1001(g)(1),(3)
	Veterans' benefits	735-5/12-1001(g)(2)
	Workers' compensation	820-305/21
	Workers' occupational disease compensation	820-310/21
tools of trade	Implements, books, & tools of trade to $1,500	735-5/12-1001(d)
wages	Minimum 85% of earned but unpaid weekly wages or 45 times the federal minimum hourly wage (or state minimum hourly wage, if higher); bankruptcy judge may authorize more for low-income debtors	740-170/4
wildcard	$4,000 of any personal property (does not include wages)	735-5/12-1001(b)

Indiana

Federal bankruptcy exemptions not available. All law references are to Indiana Statutes Annotated unless otherwise noted.

ASSET	EXEMPTION	LAW
homestead *see also wildcard*	Real or personal property used as residence to $15,000	34-55-10-2(c)(1)
	Property held as tenancy by the entirety may be exempt against debts incurred by only one spouse	34-55-10-2(c)(5); 32-17-3-1
insurance	Employer's life insurance policy on employee	27-1-12-17.1
	Fraternal benefit society benefits	27-11-6-3
	Group life insurance policy	27-1-12-29
	Life insurance policy, proceeds, cash value, or avails if beneficiary is insured's spouse or dependent	27-1-12-14
	Life insurance proceeds if clause prohibits proceeds to be used to pay beneficiary's creditors	27-2-5-1
	Mutual life or accident proceeds needed for support	27-8-3-23; *In re Stinnet*, 321 B.R. 477 (S.D. Ind. 2005)
miscellaneous	Property of business partnership	23-4-1-25
pensions	Tax-exempt retirement accounts, including 401(k)s, 403(b)s, profit-sharing and money purchase plans, SEP and SIMPLE IRAs, and defined-benefit plans	11 U.S.C. § 522(b)(3)(C)
	Traditional and Roth IRAs to $1,095,000 per person	11 U.S.C. § 522(b)(3)(C); (n)
	Firefighters	36-8-7-22 36-8-8-17
	Police officers	36-8-8-17; 10-12-2-10
	Public employees	5-10.3-8-9
	Public or private retirement benefits & contributions	34-55-10-2(c)(6)
	Sheriffs	36-8-10-19
	State teachers	5-10.4-5-14
personal property	Health aids	34-55-10-2(c)(4)
	Money in medical care savings account	34-55-10-2(c)(7)
	Spendthrift trusts	30-4-3-2
	$300 of any intangible personal property, except money owed to you	34-55-10-2(c)(3)
public benefits	Crime victims' compensation, unless seeking to discharge the debts for which the victim was compensated	5-2-6.1-38
	Unemployment compensation	22-4-33-3
	Workers' compensation	22-3-2-17
tools of trade	National Guard uniforms, arms, & equipment	10-16-10-3
wages	Minimum 75% of earned but unpaid weekly disposable earnings, or 30 times the federal hourly minimum wage; bankruptcy judge may authorize more for low-income debtors	24-4.5-5-105

wildcard	$8,000 of any real estate or tangible personal property	34-55-10-2(c)(2)

Iowa

Federal bankruptcy exemptions not available. All law references are to Iowa Code Annotated unless otherwise noted.

ASSET	EXEMPTION	LAW
homestead	May record homestead declaration	561.4
	Real property or an apartment to an unlimited value; property cannot exceed ½ acre in town or city, 40 acres elsewhere (husband & wife may not double)	499A.18; 561.2; 561.16
insurance	Accident, disability, health, illness, or life proceeds or avails	627.6(6)
	Disability or illness benefit	627.6(8)(c)
	Employee group insurance policy or proceeds	509.12
	Fraternal benefit society benefits	512B.18
	Life insurance proceeds if clause prohibits proceeds from being used to pay beneficiary's creditors	508.32
	Life insurance proceeds paid to spouse, child, or other dependent (limited to $10,000 if acquired within 2 years of filing for bankruptcy)	627.6(6)
	Upon death of insured, up to $15,000 total proceeds from all matured life, accident, health, or disability policies exempt from beneficiary's debts contracted before insured's death	627.6(6)
miscellaneous	Alimony, child support needed for support	627.6(8)(d)
	Liquor licenses	123.38
pensions *see also wages*	Tax-exempt retirement accounts, including 401(k)s, 403(b)s, profit-sharing and money purchase plans, SEP and SIMPLE IRAs, and defined-benefit plans	11 U.S.C. § 522(b)(3)(C)
	Traditional and Roth IRAs to $1,095,000 per person	11 U.S.C. § 522(b)(3)(C); (n)
	Disabled firefighters, police officers (only payments being received)	410.11
	Federal government pension	627.8
	Firefighters	411.13
	Other pensions, annuities, & contracts fully exempt; however, contributions made within 1 year prior to filing for bankruptcy not exempt to the extent they exceed normal & customary amounts	627.6(8)(e)
	Peace officers	97A.12
	Police officers	411.13
	Public employees	97B.39
	Retirement plans, Keoghs, IRAs, Roth IRAs, ERISA-qualified benefits	627.6(8)(f)
personal property	Bibles, books, portraits, pictures, & paintings to $1,000 total	627.6(3)
	Burial plot to 1 acre	627.6(4)
	Clothing & its storage containers, household furnishings, appliances, musical instruments, and other personal property to $7,000	627.6(5)
	Health aids	627.6(7)
	Jewelry to $2,000	627.6(1)(6)
personal property (continued)	Residential security or utility deposit, or advance rent, to $500	627.6(14)
	Rifle or musket; shotgun	627.6(2)
	One motor vehicle to $7,000	627.6(9)
	Wedding or engagement rings, limited to $7,000 if purchased after marriage and within last two years	627.6(1)(a)
	Wrongful death proceeds and awards needed for support of debtor and dependents	627.6(15)
public benefits	Adopted child assistance	627.19
	Aid to dependent children	239B.6
	Any public assistance benefit	627.6(8)(a)
	Social Security	627.6(8)(a)
	Unemployment compensation	627.6(8)(a)
	Veterans' benefits	627.6(8)(b)
	Workers' compensation	627.13
tools of trade	Farming equipment; includes livestock, feed to $10,000	627.6(11)
	National Guard articles of equipment	29A.41
	Nonfarming equipment to $10,000	627.6(10)
wages	Expected annual earnings — Amount NOT exempt per year $0 to $12,000 — $250 $12,000 to $16,000 — $400 $16,000 to $24,000 — $800 $24,000 to $35,000 — $1,000 $35,000 to $50,000 — $2,000 More than $50,000 — 10% Not exempt from spousal or child support	642.21
	Wages or salary of a prisoner	356.29
wildcard	$1,000 of any personal property, including cash	627.6(14)

Kansas

Federal bankruptcy exemptions not available. All law references are to Kansas Statutes Annotated unless otherwise noted.

ASSET	EXEMPTION	LAW
homestead	Real property or mobile home you occupy or intend to occupy to unlimited value; property cannot exceed 1 acre in town or city, 160 acres on farm	60-2301; Constitution 15-9
insurance	Cash value of life insurance; not exempt if obtained within 1 year prior to bankruptcy with fraudulent intent	60-2313(a)(7); 40-414(b)
	Disability & illness benefits	60-2313(a)(1)
	Fraternal life insurance benefits	60-2313(a)(8)
	Life insurance proceeds	40-414(a)
miscellaneous	Alimony, maintenance, & support	60-2312(b)
	Liquor licenses	60-2313(a)(6); 41-326
pensions	Tax-exempt retirement accounts, including 401(k)s, 403(b)s, profit-sharing and money purchase plans, SEP and SIMPLE IRAs, and defined-benefit plans	11 U.S.C. § 522(b)(3)(C)
	Traditional and Roth IRAs to $1,095,000 per person	11 U.S.C. § 522(b)(3)(C); (n)
	Elected & appointed officials in cities with populations between 120,000 & 200,000	13-14a10
	ERISA-qualified benefits	60-2308(b)

pensions (continued)	Federal government pension needed for support & paid within 3 months of filing for bankruptcy (only payments being received)	60-2308(a)
	Firefighters	12-5005(e); 14-10a10
	Judges	20-2618
	Police officers	12-5005(e); 13-14a10
	Public employees	74-4923; 74-49,105
	State highway patrol officers	74-4978g
	State school employees	72-5526
	Payment under a stock bonus, pension, profit-sharing, annuity, or similar plan or contract on account of illness, disability, death, age, or length of service, to the extent reasonably necessary for support	60-2312(b)
personal property	Burial plot or crypt	60-2304(d)
	Clothing to last 1 year	60-2304(a)
	Food & fuel to last 1 year	60-2304(a)
	Funeral plan prepayments	60-2313(a)(10); 16-310(d)
	Furnishings & household equipment	60-2304(a)
	Jewelry & articles of adornment to $1,000	60-2304(b)
	Motor vehicle to $20,000; if designed or equipped for disabled person, no limit	60-2304(c)
public benefits	Crime victims' compensation	60-2313(a)(7); 74-7313(d)
	General assistance	39-717(c)
	Social Security	60-2312(b)
	Unemployment compensation	60-2313(a)(4); 44-718(c)
	Veterans' benefits	60-2312(b)
	Workers' compensation	60-2313(a)(3); 44-514
tools of trade	Books, documents, furniture, instruments, equipment, breeding stock, seed, grain, & stock to $7,500 total	60-2304(e)
	National Guard uniforms, arms, & equipment	48-245
wages	Minimum 75% of disposable weekly wages or 30 times the federal minimum hourly wage per week, whichever is greater; bankruptcy judge may authorize more for low-income debtors	60-2310
wildcard	None	

Kentucky

Federal bankruptcy exemptions available. All law references are to Kentucky Revised Statutes unless otherwise noted.

ASSET	EXEMPTION	LAW
homestead	Real or personal property used as residence to $5,000; sale proceeds exempt	427.060; 427.090
insurance	Annuity contract proceeds to $350 per month	304.14-330
	Cooperative life or casualty insurance benefits	427.110(1)
	Fraternal benefit society benefits	427.110(2)
	Group life insurance proceeds	304.14-320
insurance (continued)	Health or disability benefits	304.14-310
	Life insurance policy if beneficiary is a married woman	304.14-340
	Life insurance proceeds if clause prohibits proceeds from being used to pay beneficiary's creditors	304.14-350
	Life insurance proceeds or cash value if beneficiary is someone other than insured	304.14-300
miscellaneous	Alimony, child support needed for support	427.150(1)
pensions	Tax-exempt retirement accounts, including 401(k)s, 403(b)s, profit-sharing and money purchase plans, SEP and SIMPLE IRAs, and defined-benefit plans	11 U.S.C. § 522(b)(3)(C)
	Traditional and Roth IRAs to $1,095,000 per person	11 U.S.C. § 522(b)(3)(C); (n)
	ERISA-qualified benefits, including IRAs, SEPs, & Keoghs deposited more than 120 days before filing	427.150
	Firefighters	67A.620; 95.878
	Police officers	427.120; 427.125
	State employees	61.690
	Teachers	161.700
	Urban county government employees	67A.350
personal property	Burial plot to $5,000, in lieu of homestead	427.060
	Clothing, jewelry, articles of adornment, & furnishings to $3,000 total	427.010(1)
	Health aids	427.010(1)
	Lost earnings payments needed for support	427.150(2)(d)
	Medical expenses paid & reparation benefits received under motor vehicle reparation law	304.39-260
	Motor vehicle to $2,500	427.010(1)
	Personal injury recoveries to $7,500 (not to include pain & suffering or pecuniary loss)	427.150(2)(c)
	Prepaid tuition payment fund account	164A.707(3)
	Wrongful death recoveries for person you depended on, needed for support	427.150(2)(b)
public benefits	Aid to blind, aged, disabled; public assistance	205.220(c)
	Crime victims' compensation	427.150(2)(a)
	Unemployment compensation	341.470(4)
	Workers' compensation	342.180
tools of trade	Library, office equipment, instruments, & furnishings of minister, attorney, physician, surgeon, chiropractor, veterinarian, or dentist to $1,000	427.040
	Motor vehicle of auto mechanic, mechanical, or electrical equipment servicer, minister, attorney, physician, surgeon, chiropractor, veterinarian, or dentist to $2,500	427.030
	Tools, equipment, livestock, & poultry of farmer to $3,000	427.010(1)
	Tools of nonfarmer to $300	427.030

wages	Minimum 75% of disposable weekly earnings or 30 times the federal minimum hourly wage per week, whichever is greater; bankruptcy judge may authorize more for low-income debtors	427.010(2),(3)
wildcard	$1,000 of any property	427.160

Louisiana

Federal bankruptcy exemptions not available. All law references are to Louisiana Revised Statutes Annotated unless otherwise noted.

ASSET	EXEMPTION	LAW
homestead	Property you occupy to $25,000 (if debt is result of catastrophic or terminal illness or injury, limit is full value of property as of 1 year before filing); cannot exceed 5 acres in city or town, 200 acres elsewhere (husband & wife may not double)	20:1(A)(1),(2),(3)
	Spouse or child of deceased owner may claim homestead exemption; spouse given home in divorce gets homestead	20:1(B)
insurance	Annuity contract proceeds & avails	22:647
	Fraternal benefit society benefits	22:558
	Group insurance policies or proceeds	22:649
	Health, accident, or disability proceeds or avails	22:646
	Life insurance proceeds or avails; if policy issued within 9 months of filing, exempt only to $35,000	22:647
miscellaneous	Property of minor child	13:3881(A)(3); Civil Code Art. 223
pensions	Tax-exempt retirement accounts, including 401(k)s, 403(b)s, profit-sharing and money purchase plans, SEP and SIMPLE IRAs, and defined-benefit plans	11 U.S.C. § 522(b)(3)(C)
	Traditional and Roth IRAs to $1,095,000 per person	11 U.S.C. § 522(b)(3)(C); (n)
	Assessors	11:1403
	Court clerks	11:1526
	District attorneys	11:1583
	ERISA-qualified benefits, including IRAs, Roth IRAs, & Keoghs, if contributions made over 1 year before filing for bankruptcy	13:3881; 20:33(1)
	Firefighters	11:2263
	Gift or bonus payments from employer to employee or heirs whenever paid	20:33(2)
	Judges	11:1378
	Louisiana University employees	11:952.3
	Municipal employees	11:1735
	Parochial employees	11:1905
	Police officers	11:3513
	School employees	11:1003
	Sheriffs	11:2182
	State employees	11:405
	Teachers	11:704
	Voting registrars	11:2033
personal property	Arms, military accoutrements; bedding; dishes, glassware, utensils, silverware (nonsterling); clothing, family portraits, musical instruments; bedroom, living room, & dining room furniture; poultry, 1 cow, household pets; heating & cooling equipment, refrigerator, freezer, stove, washer & dryer, iron, sewing machine	13:3881(A)(4)
	Cemetery plot, monuments	8:313
	Disaster relief insurance proceeds	13:3881(A)(7)
	Engagement & wedding rings to $5,000	13:3881(A)(5)
	Motor vehicle to $7,500	13:3881(A)(7)
	Motor vehicle modified for disability to $7,500	13:3881(A)(8)
	Spendthrift trusts	9:2004
public benefits	Aid to blind, aged, disabled; public assistance	46:111
	Crime victims' compensation	46:1811
	Earned income tax credit	13:3881 (A)(6)
	Unemployment compensation	23:1693
	Workers' compensation	23:1205
tools of trade	Tools, instruments, books, $7,500 of equity in a motor vehicle, one firearm to $500, needed to work	13:3881(A)(2)
wages	Minimum 75% of disposable weekly earnings or 30 times the federal minimum hourly wage per week, whichever is greater; bankruptcy judge may authorize more for low-income debtors	13:3881(A)(1)
wildcard	None	

Maine

Federal bankruptcy exemptions not available. All law references are to Maine Revised Statutes Annotated, in the form title number-section number, unless otherwise noted.

ASSET	EXEMPTION	LAW
homestead	Real or personal property (including cooperative) used as residence to $47,500; if debtor has minor dependents in residence, to $95,000; if debtor over age 60 or physically or mentally disabled, $95,000; proceeds of sale exempt for six months	14-4422(1)
insurance	Annuity proceeds to $450 per month	24-A-2431
	Death benefit for police, fire, or emergency medical personnel who die in the line of duty	25-1612
	Disability or health proceeds, benefits, or avails	14-4422(13)(A),(C); 24-A-2429
	Fraternal benefit society benefits	24-A-4118
	Group health or life policy or proceeds	24-A-2430
	Life, endowment, annuity, or accident policy, proceeds or avails	14-4422(14)(C); 24-A-2428
	Life insurance policy, interest, loan value, or accrued dividends for policy from person you depended on, to $4,000	14-4422(11)
	Unmatured life insurance policy, except credit insurance policy	14-4422(10)
miscellaneous	Alimony & child support needed for support	14-4422(13)(D)

pensions	Tax-exempt retirement accounts, including 401(k)s, 403(b)s, profit-sharing and money purchase plans, SEP and SIMPLE IRAs, and defined-benefit plans	11 U.S.C. § 522(b)(3)(C)
	Traditional and Roth IRAs to $1,095,000 per person	11 U.S.C. § 522(b)(3)(C); (n)
	ERISA-qualified benefits	14-4422(13)(E)
	Judges	4-1203
	Legislators	3-703
	State employees	5-17054
personal property	Animals, crops, musical instruments, books, clothing, furnishings, household goods, appliances to $200 per item	14-4422(3)
	Balance due on repossessed goods; total amount financed can't exceed $2,000	9-A-5-103
	Burial plot in lieu of homestead exemption	14-4422(1)
	Cooking stove; furnaces & stoves for heat	14-4422(6)(A),(B)
	Food to last 6 months	14-4422(7)(A)
	Fuel not to exceed 10 cords of wood, 5 tons of coal, or 1,000 gal. of heating oil	14-4422(6)(C)
	Health aids	14-4422(12)
	Jewelry to $750; no limit for one wedding & one engagement ring	14-4422(4)
	Lost earnings payments needed for support	14-4422(14)(E)
	Military clothes, arms, & equipment	37-B-262
	Motor vehicle to $5,000	14-4422(2)
	Personal injury recoveries to $12,500	14-4422(14)(D)
	Seeds, fertilizers, & feed to raise & harvest food for 1 season	14-4422(7)(B)
	Tools & equipment to raise & harvest food	14-4422(7)(C)
	Wrongful death recoveries needed for support	14-4422(14)(B)
public benefits	Maintenance under the Rehabilitation Act	26-1411-H
	Crime victims' compensation	14-4422(14)(A)
	Federal, state, or local public assistance benefits; earned income and child tax credits	14-4422(13)(A); 22-3180, 22-3766
	Social Security	14-4422(13)(A)
	Unemployment compensation	14-4422(13)(A),(C)
	Veterans' benefits	14-4422(13)(B)
	Workers' compensation	39-A-106
tools of trade	Books, materials, & stock to $5,000	14-4422(5)
	Commercial fishing boat, 5-ton limit	14-4422(9)
	One of each farm implement (& its maintenance equipment needed to harvest & raise crops)	14-4422(8)
wages	None (use federal nonbankruptcy wage exemption)	
wildcard	Unused portion of exemption in homestead to $6,000; or unused exemption in animals, crops, musical instruments, books, clothing, furnishings, household goods, appliances, tools of the trade, & personal injury recoveries	14-4422(16)
	$400 of any property	14-4422(15)

Maryland

Federal bankruptcy exemptions not available. All law references are to Maryland Code of Courts & Judicial Proceedings unless otherwise noted.

ASSET	EXEMPTION	LAW
homestead	None; however, property held as tenancy by the entirety is exempt against debts owed by only one spouse	*In re Birney*, 200 F.3d 225 (4th Cir. 1999)
insurance	Disability or health benefits, including court awards, arbitrations, & settlements	11-504(b)(2)
	Fraternal benefit society benefits	Ins. 8-431; Estates & Trusts 8-115
	Life insurance or annuity contract proceeds or avails if beneficiary is insured's dependent, child, or spouse	Ins. 16-111(a); Estates & Trusts 8-115
	Medical insurance benefits deducted from wages plus medical insurance payments to $145 per week or 75% of disposable wages	Commercial Law 15-601.1(3)
miscellaneous	Child support	11-504(b)(6)
	Alimony to same extent wages are exempt	11-504(b)(7)
pensions	Tax-exempt retirement accounts, including 401(k)s, 403(b)s, profit-sharing and money purchase plans, SEP and SIMPLE IRAs, and defined-benefit plans	11 U.S.C. § 522(b)(3)(C)
	Traditional and Roth IRAs to $1,095,000 per person	11 U.S.C. § 522(b)(3)(C); (n)
	ERISA-qualified benefits, including IRAs, Roth IRAs, & Keoghs	11-504(h)(1), (4)
	State employees	State Pers. & Pen. 21-502
personal property	Appliances, furnishings, household goods, books, pets, & clothing to $1,000 total	11-504(b)(4)
	Burial plot	Bus. Reg. 5-503
	Health aids	11-504(b)(3)
	Perpetual care trust funds	Bus. Reg. 5-603
	Prepaid college trust funds	Educ. 18-1913
	Lost future earnings recoveries	11-504(b)(2)
public benefits	Baltimore Police death benefits	Code of 1957 art. 24, 16-103
	Crime victims' compensation	Crim. Proc. 11-816(b)
	Unemployment compensation	Labor & Employment 8-106
	Workers' compensation	Labor & Employment 9-732
tools of trade	Clothing, books, tools, instruments, & appliances to $5,000	11-504(b)(1)
wages	Earned but unpaid wages, the greater of 75% or $145 per week; in Kent, Caroline, Queen Anne's, & Worcester Counties, the greater of 75% or 30 times federal minimum hourly wage	Commercial Law 15-601.1
wildcard	$6,000 in cash or any property, if claimed within 30 days of attachment or levy	11-504(b)(5)
	An additional $5,000 in real or personal property	11-504(f)

Massachusetts

Federal bankruptcy exemptions available. All law references are to Massachusetts General Laws Annotated, in the form title number-section number, unless otherwise noted.

ASSET	EXEMPTION	LAW
homestead	If statement of homestead is not in title to property, must record homestead declaration before filing bankruptcy	188-2
	Property held as tenancy by the entirety may be exempt against debt for nonnecessity owed by only one spouse	209-1
	Property you occupy or intend to occupy (including mobile home) to $500,000 (special rules if over 65 or disabled) (co-owners may not double)	188-1; 188-1A
	Spouse or children of deceased owner may claim homestead exemption	188-4
insurance	Disability benefits to $400 per week	175-110A
	Fraternal benefit society benefits	176-22
	Group annuity policy or proceeds	175-132C
	Group life insurance policy	175-135
	Life insurance or annuity contract proceeds if clause prohibits proceeds from being used to pay beneficiary's creditors	175-119A
	Life insurance policy if beneficiary is a married woman	175-126
	Life or endowment policy, proceeds, or cash value	175-125
	Medical malpractice self-insurance	175F-15
miscellaneous	Property of business partnership	108A-25
pensions *see also wages*	Tax-exempt retirement accounts, including 401(k)s, 403(b)s, profit-sharing and money purchase plans, SEP and SIMPLE IRAs, and defined-benefit plans	11 U.S.C. § 522(b)(3)(C)
	Traditional and Roth IRAs to $1,095,000 per person	11 U.S.C. § 522(b)(3)(C); (n)
	Credit union employees	171-84
	ERISA-qualified benefits, including IRAs & Keoghs to specified limits	235-34A; 246-28
	Private retirement benefits	32-41
	Public employees	32-19
	Savings bank employees	168-41; 168-44
personal property	Bank deposits to $125	235-34
	Beds & bedding; heating unit; clothing	235-34
	Bibles & books to $200 total; sewing machine to $200	235-34
	Burial plots, tombs, & church pew	235-34
	Cash for fuel, heat, water, or light to $75 per month	235-34
	Cash to $200 per month for rent, in lieu of homestead	235-34
	Cooperative association shares to $100	235-34
	Food or cash for food to $300	235-34
	Furniture to $3,000; motor vehicle to $700	235-34
	Moving expenses for eminent domain	79-6A
	Trust company, bank, or credit union deposits to $500	246-28A
	2 cows, 12 sheep, 2 swine, 4 tons of hay	235-34
public benefits	Aid to families with dependent children	118-10
	Public assistance	235-34
	Unemployment compensation	151A-36
	Veterans' benefits	115-5
	Workers' compensation	152-47
tools of trade	Arms, accoutrements, & uniforms required	235-34
	Fishing boats, tackle, & nets to $500	235-34
	Materials you designed & procured to $500	235-34
	Tools, implements, & fixtures to $500 total	235-34
wages	Earned but unpaid wages to $125 per week	246-28
wildcard	None	

Michigan

Federal bankruptcy exemptions available. All law references are to Michigan Compiled Laws Annotated unless otherwise noted.

Under Michigan law, bankruptcy exemption amounts are adjusted for inflation every three years (starting in 2005) by the Michigan Department of Treasury. These amounts have already been adjusted, so the amounts listed in the statutes are not current. You can find the current amounts at www.michigan.gov/documents/BankruptcyExemptions2005_141050_7.pdf or by searching Google for "Property Debtor in Bankruptcy May Exempt, Inflation Adjusted Amounts."

ASSET	EXEMPTION	LAW
homestead	Property held as tenancy by the entirety may be exempt against debts owed by only one spouse	600.5451(1)(o)
	Real property including condo to $34,450 ($51,650 if over 65 or disabled); property cannot exceed 1 lot in town, village, city, or 40 acres elsewhere; spouse or children of deceased owner may claim homestead exemption; spouses or unmarried co-owners may not double	600.5451(1)(n); *Vinson v. Dakmak*, 347 B.R. 620 (E.D. Mich. 2006)
insurance	Disability, mutual life, or health benefits	600.5451(1)(j)
	Employer-sponsored life insurance policy or trust fund	500.2210
	Fraternal benefit society benefits	500.8181
	Life, endowment, or annuity proceeds if clause prohibits proceeds from being used to pay beneficiary's creditors	500.4054
	Life insurance	500.2207
miscellaneous	Property of business partnership	449.25
pensions	Tax-exempt retirement accounts, including 401(k)s, 403(b)s, profit-sharing and money purchase plans, SEP and SIMPLE IRAs, and defined-benefit plans	11 U.S.C. § 522(b)(3)(C)
	Traditional and Roth IRAs to $1,095,000 per person	11 U.S.C. § 522(b)(3)(C); (n)
	ERISA-qualified benefits, except contributions within last 120 days	600.5451(1)(m)
	Firefighters, police officers	38.559(6); 38.1683
	IRAs & Roth IRAs, except contributions within last 120 days	600.5451(1)(l))
	Judges	38.2308; 38.1683
	Legislators	38.1057; 38.1683
	Probate judges	38.2308; 38.1683
	Public school employees	38.1346; 38.1683
	State employees	38.40; 38.1683

personal property	Appliances, utensils, books, furniture, & household goods to $525 each, $3,450 total	600.5451(1)(c)
	Building & loan association shares to $1,150 par value, in lieu of homestead	600.5451(1)(k)
	Burial plots, cemeteries	600.5451(1)(a)(vii)
	Church pew, slip, seat for entire family to $575	600.5451(1)(d)
	Clothing; family pictures	600.5451(1)(a)
	Food & fuel to last family for 6 months	600.5451(1)(b)
	Crops, animals, and feed to $2,300	600.5451(1)(e)
	1 motor vehicle to $3,175	600.5451(1)(g)
	Computer & accessories to $575	600.5451(1)(h)
	Household pets to $575	600.5451(1)(f)
	Professionally prescribed health aids	600.5451(a)
public benefits	Crime victims' compensation	18.362
	Social welfare benefits	400.63
	Unemployment compensation	421.30
	Veterans' benefits for Korean War veterans	35.977
	Veterans' benefits for Vietnam veterans	35.1027
	Veterans' benefits for WWII veterans	35.926
	Workers' compensation	418.821
tools of trade	Arms & accoutrements required	600.6023(1)(a)
	Tools, implements, materials, stock, apparatus, or other things needed to carry on occupation to $2,300 total	600.5451(1)(i)
wages	Head of household may keep 60% of earned but unpaid wages (no less than $15/week), plus $2/week per nonspouse dependent; if not head of household may keep 40% (no less than $10/week)	600.5311
wildcard	None	

Minnesota

Federal bankruptcy exemptions available. All law references are to Minnesota Statutes Annotated, unless otherwise noted.

Note: Section 550.37(4)(a) requires certain exemptions to be adjusted for inflation on July 1 of even-numbered years; this table includes all changes made through July 1, 2008. Exemptions are published on or before the May 1 issue of the Minnesota State Register, *www.comm.media.state.mn.us/bookstore/stateregister.asp*, or call the Minnesota Dept. of Commerce at 651-296-7977.

ASSET	EXEMPTION	LAW
homestead	Home & land on which it is situated to $300,000; if homestead is used for agricultural purposes, $750,000; cannot exceed ½ acre in city, 160 acres elsewhere (husband & wife may not double)	510.01; 510.02
	Manufactured home to an unlimited value	550.37 subd. 12
insurance	Accident or disability proceeds	550.39
	Fraternal benefit society benefits	64B.18
	Life insurance proceeds to $42,000 if beneficiary is spouse or child of insured, plus $10,500 per dependent	550.37 subd. 10
	Police, fire, or beneficiary association benefits	550.37 subd. 11
	Unmatured life insurance contract dividends, interest, or loan value to $8,400 if insured is debtor or person debtor depends on	550.37 subd. 23
miscellaneous	Earnings of minor child	550.37 subd. 15
pensions	Tax-exempt retirement accounts, including 401(k)s, 403(b)s, profit-sharing and money purchase plans, SEP and SIMPLE IRAs, and defined-benefit plans	11 U.S.C. § 522(b)(3)(C)
	Traditional and Roth IRAs to $1,095,000 per person	11 U.S.C. § 522(b)(3)(C); (n)
	ERISA-qualified benefits if needed for support, up to $63,000 in present value	550.37 subd. 24
	IRAs or Roth IRAs needed for support, up to $63,000 in present value	550.37 subd. 24
	Public employees	353.15; 356.401
	State employees	352.965 subd. 8; 356.401
	State troopers	352B.071; 356.401
personal property	Appliances, furniture, jewelry, radio, phonographs, & TV to $9,300 total	550.37 subd. 4(b)
	Bible & books	550.37 subd. 2
	Burial plot; church pew or seat	550.37 subd. 3
	Clothing, one watch, food, & utensils for family	550.37 subd. 4(a)
	Motor vehicle to $4,200 (up to $42,000 if vehicle has been modified for disability)	550.37 subd. 12(a)
	Personal injury recoveries	550.37 subd. 22
	Proceeds for damaged exempt property	550.37 subds. 9, 16
	Wedding rings to $2,572.50	550.37 subd. 4(c)
	Wrongful death recoveries	550.37 subd. 22
public benefits	Crime victims' compensation	611A.60
	Public benefits	550.37 subd. 14
	Unemployment compensation	268.192 subd. 2
	Veterans' benefits	550.38
	Workers' compensation	176.175
tools of trade *total (except teaching materials) can't exceed $13,000*	Farm machines, implements, livestock, produce, & crops	550.37 subd. 5
	Teaching materials of college, university, public school, or public institution teacher	550.37 subd. 8
	Tools, machines, instruments, stock in trade, furniture, & library to $15,000 total	550.37 subd. 6
wages	Minimum 75% of weekly disposable earnings or 40 times federal minimum hourly wage, whichever is greater	571.922
	Wages deposited into bank accounts for 20 days after depositing	550.37 subd. 13
	Wages paid within 6 months of returning to work after receiving welfare or after incarceration; includes earnings deposited in a financial institution in the last 60 days	550.37 subd. 14
wildcard	None	

Note: In cases of suspected fraud, the Minnesota constitution permits courts to cap exemptions that would otherwise be unlimited. (*In re Tveten*, 402 N.W.2d 551 (Minn. 1987); *In re Medill*, 119 B.R. 685 (Bankr. D. Minn. 1990); *In re Sholdan*, 217 F.3d 1006 (8th Cir. 2000).)

Mississippi

Federal bankruptcy exemptions not available. All law references are to Mississippi Code unless otherwise noted.

ASSET	EXEMPTION	LAW
homestead	May file homestead declaration	85-3-27; 85-3-31
	Mobile home does not qualify as homestead unless you own land on which it is located (see *personal property*)	*In re Cobbins*, 234 B.R. 882 (S.D. Miss. 1999)
	Property you own & occupy to $75,000; if over 60 & married or widowed may claim a former residence; property cannot exceed 160 acres; sale proceeds exempt	85-3-1(b)(i); 85-3-21; 85-3-23
insurance	Disability benefits	85-3-1(b)(ii)
	Fraternal benefit society benefits	83-29-39
	Homeowners' insurance proceeds to $75,000	85-3-23
	Life insurance proceeds if clause prohibits proceeds from being used to pay beneficiary's creditors	83-7-5; 85-3-11
pensions	Tax-exempt retirement accounts, including 401(k)s, 403(b)s, profit-sharing and money purchase plans, SEP and SIMPLE IRAs, and defined-benefit plans	11 U.S.C. § 522(b)(3)(C)
	Traditional and Roth IRAs to $1,095,000 per person	11 U.S.C. § 522(b)(3)(C); (n)
	ERISA-qualified benefits, IRAs, Keoghs deposited over 1 year before filing bankruptcy	85-3-1(e)
	Firefighters (includes death benefits)	21-29-257; 45-2-1
	Highway patrol officers	25-13-31
	Law enforcement officers' death benefits	45-2-1
	Police officers (includes death benefits)	21-29-257; 45-2-1
	Private retirement benefits to extent tax-deferred	71-1-43
	Public employees retirement & disability benefits	25-11-129
	State employees	25-14-5
	Teachers	25-11-201(1)(d)
	Volunteer firefighters' death benefits	45-2-1
personal property	Mobile home to $30,000	85-3-1(d)
	Personal injury judgments to $10,000	85-3-17
	Sale or insurance proceeds for exempt property	85-3-1(b)(i)
	State health savings accounts	85-3-1(g)
	Tangible personal property to $10,000: any items worth less than $200 each; furniture, dishes, kitchenware, household goods, appliances, 1 radio, 1 TV, 1 firearm, 1 lawn-mower, clothing, wedding rings, motor vehicles, tools of the trade, books, crops, health aids, domestic animals (does not include works of art, antiques, jewelry, or electronic entertainment equipment)	85-3-1(a)
	Tax-qualified § 529 education savings plans, including those under the Mississippi Prepaid Affordable College Tuition Program	85-3-1(f)
public benefits	Assistance to aged	43-9-19
	Assistance to blind	43-3-71
	Assistance to disabled	43-29-15
	Crime victims' compensation	99-41-23(7)
	Federal income tax refund to $5,000; earned income tax credit to $5,000; state tax refunds to $5,000	85-3-1(h); (i); (j); (k)
	Social Security	25-11-129
	Unemployment compensation	71-5-539
	Workers' compensation	71-3-43
tools of trade	*See personal property*	
wages	Earned but unpaid wages owed for 30 days; after 30 days, minimum 75% of earned but unpaid weekly disposable earnings or 30 times the federal hourly minimum wage, whichever is greater; bankruptcy judge may authorize more for low-income debtors	85-3-4
wildcard	$50,000 of any property, including deposits of money, available to Mississippi resident who is at least 70 years old; *also see personal property*	85-3-1(h)

Missouri

Federal bankruptcy exemptions not available. All law references are to Annotated Missouri Statutes unless otherwise noted.

ASSET	EXEMPTION	LAW
homestead	Property held as tenancy by the entirety may be exempt against debts owed by only one spouse	*In re Eads*, 271 B.R. 371 (Bankr. W.D. Mo. 2002)
	Real property to $15,000 or mobile home to $5,000 (joint owners may not double)	513.430(6); 513.475 *In re Smith*, 254 B.R. 751 (Bankr. W.D. Mo. 2000)
insurance	Assessment plan or life insurance proceeds	377.090
	Disability or illness benefits	513.430(10)(c)
	Fraternal benefit society benefits to $5,000, bought over 6 months before filing	513.430(8)
	Life insurance dividends, loan value, or interest to $150,000, bought over 6 months before filing	513.430(8)
	Stipulated insurance premiums	377.330
	Unmatured life insurance policy	513.430(7)
miscellaneous	Alimony, child support to $750 per month	513.430(10)(d)
	Property of business partnership	358.250
pensions	Tax-exempt retirement accounts, including 401(k)s, 403(b)s, profit-sharing and money purchase plans, SEP and SIMPLE IRAs, and defined-benefit plans	11 U.S.C. § 522(b)(3)(C)
	Traditional and Roth IRAs to $1,095,000 per person	11 U.S.C. § 522(b)(3)(C); (n)
	Employee benefit spendthrift trust	456.014
	Employees of cities with 100,000 or more people	71.207
	ERISA-qualified benefits, IRAs, Roth IRAs, & other retirement accounts needed for support	513.430(10)(e), (f)
	Firefighters	87.090; 87.365; 87.485

pensions (continued)	Highway & transportation employees	104.250
	Police department employees	86.190; 86.353; 86.1430
	Public officers & employees	70.695; 70.755
	State employees	104.540
	Teachers	169.090
personal property	Appliances, household goods, furnishings, clothing, books, crops, animals, & musical instruments to $3,000 total	513.430(1)
	Burial grounds to 1 acre or $100	214.190
	Health aids	513.430(9)
	Motor vehicle to $3,000	513.430(5)
	Wedding ring to $1,500 & other jewelry to $500	513.430(2)
	Wrongful death recoveries for person you depended on	513.430(11)
public benefits	Crime victim's compensation	595.025
	Public assistance	513.430(10)(a)
	Social Security	513.430(10)(a)
	Unemployment compensation	288.380(10)(l); 513.430(10)(c)
	Veterans' benefits	513.430(10)b)
	Workers' compensation	287.260
tools of trade	Implements, books, & tools of trade to $3,000	513.430(4)
wages	Minimum 75% of weekly earnings (90% of weekly earnings for head of family), or 30 times the federal minimum hourly wage, whichever is more; bankruptcy judge may authorize more for low-income debtors	525.030
	Wages of servant or common laborer to $90	513.470
wildcard	$1,250 of any property if head of family, else $600; head of family may claim additional $350 per child	513.430(3); 513.440

Montana

Federal bankruptcy exemptions not available. All law references are to Montana Code Annotated unless otherwise noted.

ASSET	EXEMPTION	LAW
homestead	Must record homestead declaration before filing for bankruptcy	70-32-105
	Real property or mobile home you occupy to $250,000; sale, condemnation, or insurance proceeds exempt for 18 months	70-32-104; 70-32-201; 70-32-213
insurance	Annuity contract proceeds to $350 per month	33-15-514
	Disability or illness proceeds, avails, or benefits	25-13-608(1)(d); 33-15-513
	Fraternal benefit society benefits	33-7-522
	Group life insurance policy or proceeds	33-15-512
	Hail insurance benefits	80-2-245
	Life insurance proceeds if clause prohibits proceeds from being used to pay beneficiary's creditors	33-20-120
insurance (continued)	Medical, surgical, or hospital care benefits	25-13-608(1)(f)
	Unmatured life insurance contracts	25-13-608(1)(k)
miscellaneous	Alimony, child support	25-13-608(1)(g)
pensions	Tax-exempt retirement accounts, including 401(k)s, 403(b)s, profit-sharing and money purchase plans, SEP and SIMPLE IRAs, and defined-benefit plans	11 U.S.C. § 522(b)(3)(C)
	Traditional and Roth IRAs to $1,095,000 per person	11 U.S.C. § 522(b)(3)(C); (n)
	IRAs & ERISA-qualified benefits deposited over 1 year before filing bankruptcy or up to 15% of debtor's gross annual income	31-2-106
	Firefighters	19-18-612(1)
	IRA & Roth IRA contributions & earnings made before judgment filed	25-13-608(1)(e)
	Police officers	19-19-504(1)
	Public employees	19-2-1004; 25-13-608(i)
	Teachers	19-20-706(2); 25-13-608(j)
	University system employees	19-21-212
personal property	Appliances, household furnishings, goods, animals with feed, crops, musical instruments, books, firearms, sporting goods, clothing, & jewelry to $600 per item, $4,500 total	25-13-609(1)
	Burial plot	25-13-608(1)(h)
	Cooperative association shares to $500 value	35-15-404
	Health aids	25-13-608(1)(a)
	Motor vehicle to $2,500	25-13-609(2)
	Proceeds from sale or for damage or loss of exempt property for 6 months after received	25-13-610
public benefits	Aid to aged, disabled needy persons	53-2-607
	Crime victims' compensation	53-9-129
	Local public assistance	25-13-608(1)(b)
	Silicosis benefits	39-73-110
	Social Security	25-13-608(1)(b)
	Subsidized adoption payments to needy persons	53-2-607
	Unemployment compensation	31-2-106(2); 39-51-3105
	Veterans' benefits	25-13-608(1)(c)
	Vocational rehabilitation to blind needy persons	53-2-607
	Workers' compensation	39-71-743
tools of trade	Implements, books, & tools of trade to $3,000	25-13-609(3)
	Uniforms, arms, & accoutrements needed to carry out government functions	25-13-613(b)
wages	Minimum 75% of earned but unpaid weekly disposable earnings, or 30 times the federal hourly minimum wage, whichever is greater; bankruptcy judge may authorize more for low-income debtors	25-13-614
wildcard	None	

Nebraska

Federal bankruptcy exemptions not available. All law references are to Revised Statutes of Nebraska unless otherwise noted.

ASSET	EXEMPTION	LAW
homestead	$60,000 for married debtor or head of household; cannot exceed 2 lots in city or village, 160 acres elsewhere; sale proceeds exempt 6 months after sale (husband & wife may not double)	40-101; 40-111; 40-113
	May record homestead declaration	40-105
insurance	Fraternal benefit society benefits to $100,000 loan value unless beneficiary convicted of a crime related to benefits	44-1089
	Life insurance proceeds and avails to $100,000	44-371
pensions *see also wages*	Tax-exempt retirement accounts, including 401(k)s, 403(b)s, profit-sharing and money purchase plans, SEP and SIMPLE IRAs, and defined-benefit plans	11 U.S.C. § 522(b)(3)(C)
	Traditional and Roth IRAs to $1,095,000 per person	11 U.S.C. § 522(b)(3)(C); (n)
	County employees	23-2322
	Deferred compensation of public employees	48-1401
	ERISA-qualified benefits including IRAs & Roth IRAs needed for support	25-1563.01
	Military disability benefits	25-1559
	School employees	79-948
	State employees	84-1324
personal property	Burial plot	12-517
	Clothing	25-1556(2)
	Crypts, lots, tombs, niches, vaults	12-605
	Furniture, household goods & appliances, household electronics, personal computers, books, & musical instruments to $1,500	25-1556(3)
	Health aids	25-1556(5)
	Medical or health savings accounts to $25,000	8-1, 131(2)(b)
	Perpetual care funds	12-511
	Personal injury recoveries	25-1563.02
	Personal possessions	25-1556
public benefits	Aid to disabled, blind, aged; public assistance	68-1013
	General assistance to poor persons	68-148
	Unemployment compensation	48-647
	Workers' compensation	48-149
tools of trade	Equipment or tools including a vehicle used in or for commuting to principal place of business to $2,400 (husband & wife may double)	25-1556(4); *In re Keller,* 50 B.R. 23 (D. Neb. 1985)
wages	Minimum 85% of earned but unpaid weekly disposable earnings or pension payments for head of family; minimum 75% of earned but unpaid weekly disposable earnings or 30 times the federal hourly minimum wage, whichever is greater, for all others; bankruptcy judge may authorize more for low-income debtors	25-1558
wildcard	$2,500 of any personal property except wages, in lieu of homestead	25-1552

Nevada

Federal bankruptcy exemptions not available. All law references are to Nevada Revised Statutes Annotated unless otherwise noted.

ASSET	EXEMPTION	LAW
homestead	Must record homestead declaration before filing for bankruptcy	115.020
	Real property or mobile home to $550,000 Husband and wife may not double	115.010; 21.090(1)(m)
insurance	Annuity contract proceeds to $350 per month	687B.290
	Fraternal benefit society benefits	695A.220
	Group life or health policy or proceeds	687B.280
	Health proceeds or avails	687B.270
	Life insurance policy or proceeds if annual premiums not over $1,000	21.090(1)(k); *In re Bower,* 234 B.R. 109 (Nev. 1999)
	Life insurance proceeds if you're not the insured	687B.260
miscellaneous	Alimony & child support	21.090(1)(s)
	Property of some business partnerships	87.250
	Security deposits for a rental residence, except landlord may enforce terms of lease or rental agreement	21.090(1)(n)
pensions	Tax-exempt retirement accounts, including 401(k)s, 403(b)s, profit-sharing and money purchase plans, SEP and SIMPLE IRAs, and defined-benefit plans	11 U.S.C. § 522(b)(3)(C)
	Traditional and Roth IRAs to $1,095,000 per person	11 U.S.C. § 522(b)(3)(C); (n)
	ERISA-qualified benefits, deferred compensation, SEP IRA, Roth IRA, or IRA to $500,000	21.090(1)(r)
	Public employees	286.670
personal property	Appliances, household goods, furniture, home & yard equipment to $12,000 total	21.090(1)(b)
	Books, works of art, musical instruments, & jewelry to $5,000	21.090(1)(a)
	Burial plot purchase money held in trust	689.700
	Funeral service contract money held in trust	689.700
	Health aids	21.090(1)(q)
	Interests in qualifying trusts	21.090(1)(cc)
	Keepsakes & pictures	21.090(1)(a)
	Metal-bearing ores, geological specimens, art curiosities, or paleontological remains; must be arranged, classified, cataloged, & numbered in reference books	21.100
	Mortgage impound accounts	645B.180
	Motor vehicle to $15,000; no limit on vehicle equipped for disabled person	21.090(1)(f),(o)
	1 gun	21.090(1)(i)
	Personal injury compensation to $16,500	21.090(1)(u)
	Restitution received for criminal act	21.090(1)(x)
	Stock in certain closely held corporations	21.090(1)(bb)
	Tax refunds derived from the earned income credit	21.090(1)(aa)
	Wrongful death awards to survivors	21.090(1)(v)

public benefits	Aid to blind, aged, disabled; public assistance	422.291
	Crime victim's compensation	21.090
	Industrial insurance (workers' compensation)	616C.205
	Public assistance for children	432.036
	Social Security retirement, disability, SSI, survivor benefits	21.090(1)(y)
	Unemployment compensation	612.710
	Vocational rehabilitation benefits	615.270
tools of trade	Arms, uniforms, & accoutrements you're required to keep	21.090(1)(j)
	Cabin or dwelling of miner or prospector; mining claim, cars, implements, & appliances to $4,500 total (for working claim only)	21.090(1)(e)
	Farm trucks, stock, tools, equipment, & seed to $4,500	21.090(1)(c)
	Library, equipment, supplies, tools, inventory, & materials to $10,000	21.090(1)(d)
wages	Minimum 75% of disposable weekly earnings or 30 times the federal minimum hourly wage per week, whichever is more; bankruptcy judge may authorize more for low-income debtors	21.090(1)(g)
wildcard	$1,000 of any personal property	21.090(1)(z)

New Hampshire

Federal bankruptcy exemptions available. All law references are to New Hampshire Revised Statutes Annotated unless otherwise noted.

ASSET	EXEMPTION	LAW
homestead	Real property or manufactured housing (& the land it's on if you own it) to $100,000	480:1
insurance	Firefighters' aid insurance	402:69
	Fraternal benefit society benefits	418:17
	Homeowners' insurance proceeds to $5,000	512:21(VIII)
miscellaneous	Jury, witness fees	512:21(VI)
	Property of business partnership	304-A:25
	Wages of minor child	512:21(III)
pensions	Tax-exempt retirement accounts, including 401(k)s, 403(b)s, profit-sharing and money purchase plans, SEP and SIMPLE IRAs, and defined-benefit plans	11 U.S.C. § 522(b)(3)(C)
	Traditional and Roth IRAs to $1,095,000 per person	11 U.S.C. § 522(b)(3)(C); (n)
	ERISA-qualified retirement accounts including IRAs & Roth IRAs	512:2 (XIX)
	Federally created pension (only benefits building up)	512:21(IV)
	Firefighters	102:23
	Police officers	103:18
	Public employees	100-A:26
personal property	Beds, bedding, & cooking utensils	511:2(II)
	Bibles & books to $800	511:2(VIII)
	Burial plot, lot	511:2(XIV)
	Church pew	511:2(XV)
	Clothing	511:2(I)
personal property (continued)	Cooking & heating stoves, refrigerator	511:2(IV)
	Domestic fowl to $300	511:2(XIII)
	Food & fuel to $400	511:2(VI)
	Furniture to $3,500	511:2(III)
	Jewelry to $500	511:2(XVII)
	Motor vehicle to $4,000	511:2(XVI)
	Proceeds for lost or destroyed exempt property	512:21(VIII)
	Sewing machine	511:2(V)
	1 cow, 6 sheep & their fleece, 4 tons of hay	511:2(XI); (XII)
	1 hog or pig or its meat (if slaughtered)	511:2(X)
public benefits	Aid to blind, aged, disabled; public assistance	167:25
	Unemployment compensation	282-A:159
	Workers' compensation	281-A:52
tools of trade	Tools of your occupation to $5,000	511:2(IX)
	Uniforms, arms, & equipment of military member	511:2(VII)
	Yoke of oxen or horse needed for farming or teaming	511:2(XII)
wages	50 times the federal minimum hourly wage per week	512:21(II)
	Deposits in any account designated a payroll account.	512:21(XI)
	Earned but unpaid wages of spouse	512:21(III)
wildcard	$1,000 of any property	511:2(XVIII)
	Unused portion of bibles & books, food & fuel, furniture, jewelry, motor vehicle, & tools of trade exemptions to $7,000	511:2(XVIII)

New Jersey

Federal bankruptcy exemptions available. All law references are to New Jersey Statutes Annotated unless otherwise noted.

ASSET	EXEMPTION	LAW
homestead	None, but survivorship interest of a spouse in property held as tenancy by the entirety is exempt from creditors of a single spouse	*Freda v. Commercial Trust Co. of New Jersey*, 570 A.2d 409 (N.J. 1990)
insurance	Annuity contract proceeds to $500 per month	17B:24-7
	Disability benefits	17:18-12
	Disability, death, medical, or hospital benefits for civil defense workers	App. A:9-57.6
	Disability or death benefits for military member	38A:4-8
	Group life or health policy or proceeds	17B:24-9
	Health or disability benefits	17:18-12; 17B:24-8
	Life insurance proceeds if clause prohibits proceeds from being used to pay beneficiary's creditors	17B:24-10
	Life insurance proceeds or avails if you're not the insured	17B:24-6b
pensions	Tax-exempt retirement accounts, including 401(k)s, 403(b)s, profit-sharing and money purchase plans, SEP and SIMPLE IRAs, and defined-benefit plans	11 U.S.C. § 522(b)(3)(C)
	Traditional and Roth IRAs to $1,095,000 per person	11 U.S.C. § 522(b)(3)(C); (n)

pensions (continued)	Alcohol beverage control officers	43:8A-20
	City boards of health employees	43:18-12
	Civil defense workers	App. A:9-57.6
	County employees	43:10-57; 43:10-105
	ERISA-qualified benefits for city employees	43:13-9
	Firefighters, police officers, traffic officers	43:16-7; 43:16A-17
	IRAs	*In re Yuhas*, 104 F.3d 612 (3d Cir. 1997)
	Judges	43:6A-41
	Municipal employees	43:13-44
	Prison employees	43:7-13
	Public employees	43:15A-53
	School district employees	18A:66-116
	State police	53:5A-45
	Street & water department employees	43:19-17
	Teachers	18A:66-51
	Trust containing personal property created pursuant to federal tax law, including 401(k) plans, IRAs, Roth IRAs, & higher education (529) savings plans	25:2-1; *In re Yuhas*, 104 F.3d 612 (3d Cir. 1997)
personal property	Burial plots	45:27-21
	Clothing	2A:17-19
	Furniture & household goods to $1,000	2A:26-4
	Personal property & possessions of any kind, stock or interest in corporations to $1,000 total	2A:17-19
public benefits	Old age, permanent disability assistance	44:7-35
	Unemployment compensation	43:21-53
	Workers' compensation	34:15-29
tools of trade	None	
wages	90% of earned but unpaid wages if annual income is less than 250% of federal poverty level; 75% if annual income is higher	2A:17-56
	Wages or allowances received by military personnel	38A:4-8
wildcard	None	

New Mexico

Federal bankruptcy exemptions available. All law references are to New Mexico Statutes Annotated unless otherwise noted.

ASSET	EXEMPTION	LAW
homestead	$60,000	42-10-9
insurance	Benevolent association benefits to $5,000	42-10-4
	Fraternal benefit society benefits	59A-44-18
	Life, accident, health, or annuity benefits, withdrawal or cash value, if beneficiary is a New Mexico resident	42-10-3
	Life insurance proceeds	42-10-5
miscellaneous	Ownership interest in unincorporated association	53-10-2
	Property of business partnership	54-1A-501
pensions	Tax-exempt retirement accounts, including 401(k)s, 403(b)s, profit-sharing and money purchase plans, SEP and SIMPLE IRAs, and defined-benefit plans	11 U.S.C. § 522(b)(3)(C)
pensions (continued)	Traditional and Roth IRAs to $1,095,000 per person	11 U.S.C. § 522(b)(3)(C); (n)
	Pension or retirement benefits	42-10-1; 42-10-2
	Public school employees	22-11-42A
personal property	Books & furniture	42-10-1; 42-10-2
	Building materials	48-2-15
	Clothing	42-10-1; 42-10-2
	Cooperative association shares, minimum amount needed to be member	53-4-28
	Health aids	42-10-1; 42-10-2
	Jewelry to $2,500	42-10-1; 42-10-2
	Materials, tools, & machinery to dig, drill, complete, operate, or repair oil line, gas well, or pipeline	70-4-12
	Motor vehicle to $4,000	42-10-1; 42-10-2
public benefits	Crime victims' compensation	31-22-15
	General assistance	27-2-21
	Occupational disease disablement benefits	52-3-37
	Unemployment compensation	51-1-37
	Workers' compensation	52-1-52
tools of trade	$1,500	42-10-1; 42-10-2
wages	Minimum 75% of disposable earnings or 40 times the federal hourly minimum wage, whichever is more; bankruptcy judge may authorize more for low-income debtors	35-12-7
wildcard	$500 of any personal property	42-10-1
	$5,000 of any real or personal property, in lieu of homestead	42-10-10

New York

Federal bankruptcy exemptions not available. All references are to Consolidated Laws of New York unless otherwise noted; Civil Practice Law & Rules are abbreviated C.P.L.R.

ASSET	EXEMPTION	LAW
homestead	Real property including co-op, condo, or mobile home, to $50,000	C.P.L.R. 5206(a); *In re Pearl*, 723 F.2d 193 (2nd Cir. 1983)
insurance	Annuity contract benefits due the debtor, if debtor paid for the contract; $5,000 limit if purchased within 6 months prior to filing & not tax-deferred	Ins. 3212(d); Debt. & Cred. 283(1)
	Disability or illness benefits to $400 per month	Ins. 3212(c)
	Life insurance proceeds & avails if the beneficiary is not the debtor, or if debtor's spouse has taken out policy	Ins. 3212(b)
	Life insurance proceeds left at death with the insurance company, if clause prohibits proceeds from being used to pay beneficiary's creditors	Est. Powers & Trusts 7-1.5(a)(2)

miscellaneous	Alimony, child support	C.P.L.R. 5205 (d)(3); Debt. & Cred. 282(2)(d)
	Property of business partnership	Partnership 51
pensions	Tax-exempt retirement accounts, including 401(k)s, 403(b)s, profit-sharing and money purchase plans, SEP and SIMPLE IRAs, and defined-benefit plans	11 U.S.C. § 522(b)(3)(C)
	Traditional and Roth IRAs to $1,095,000 per person	11 U.S.C. § 522(b)(3)(C); (n)
	ERISA-qualified benefits, IRAs, Roth IRAs, & Keoghs, & income needed for support	C.P.L.R. 5205(c); Debt. & Cred. 282(2)(e)
	Public retirement benefits	Ins. 4607
	State employees	Ret. & Soc. Sec. 10
	Teachers	Educ. 524
	Village police officers	Unconsolidated 5711-o
	Volunteer ambulance workers' benefits	Vol. Amb. Wkr. Ben. 23
	Volunteer firefighters' benefits	Vol. Firefighter Ben. 23
personal property	Bible, schoolbooks, other books to $50; pictures; clothing; church pew or seat; sewing machine, refrigerator, TV, radio; furniture, cooking utensils & tableware, dishes; food to last 60 days; stoves with fuel to last 60 days; domestic animal with food to last 60 days, to $450; wedding ring; watch to $35; exemptions may not exceed $5,000 total (including tools of trade & limited annuity)	C.P.L.R. 5205(a)(1)-(6); Debt. & Cred. 283(1)
	Burial plot without structure to ¼ acre	C.P.L.R. 5206(f)
	Cash (including savings bonds, tax refunds, bank & credit union deposits) to $2,500, or to $5,000 after exemptions for personal property taken, whichever amount is less (for debtors who do not claim homestead)	Debt. & Cred. 283(2)
	College tuition savings program trust fund	C.P.L.R. 5205(j)
	Electronic deposits of exempt property into bank account in last 45 days	C.P.L.R. 5205(l)(1)
	Health aids, including service animals with food	C.P.L.R. 5205(h)
	Lost future earnings recoveries needed for support	Debt. & Cred. 282(3)(iv)
	Motor vehicle to $2,400	Debt. & Cred. 282(1); *In re Miller*, 167 B.R. 782 (S.D. N.Y. 1994)
	Personal injury recoveries up to 1 year after receiving	Debt. & Cred. 282(3)(iii)
	Recovery for injury to exempt property up to 1 year after receiving	C.P.L.R. 5205(b)
	Savings & loan savings to $600	Banking 407
	Security deposit to landlord, utility company	C.P.L.R. 5205(g)
	Spendthrift trust fund principal, 90% of income if not created by debtor	C.P.L.R. 5205(c),(d)
	Wrongful death recoveries for person you depended on	Debt. & Cred. 282(3)(ii)
public benefits	Aid to blind, aged, disabled	Debt. & Cred. 282(2)(c)
	Crime victims' compensation	Debt. & Cred. 282(3)(i)
	Home relief, local public assistance	Debt. & Cred. 282(2)(a)
	Public assistance	Soc. Serv. 137
public benefits (continued)	Social Security	Debt. & Cred. 282(2)(a)
	Unemployment compensation	Debt. & Cred. 282(2)(a)
	Veterans' benefits	Debt. & Cred. 282(2)(b)
	Workers' compensation	Debt. & Cred. 282(2)(c); Work. Comp. 33, 218
tools of trade	Farm machinery, team, & food for 60 days; professional furniture, books, & instruments to $600 total	C.P.L.R. 5205(a),(b)
	Uniforms, medal, emblem, equipment, horse, arms, & sword of member of military	C.P.L.R. 5205(e)
wages	90% of earned but unpaid wages received within 60 days before & anytime after filing	C.P.L.R. 5205(d)
	90% of earnings from dairy farmer's sales to milk dealers	C.P.L.R. 5205(f)
	100% of pay of noncommissioned officer, private, or musician in U.S. or N.Y. state armed forces	C.P.L.R. 5205(e)
wildcard	None	

North Carolina

Federal bankruptcy exemptions not available. All law references are to General Statutes of North Carolina unless otherwise noted.

ASSET	EXEMPTION	LAW
homestead	Property held as tenancy by the entirety may be exempt against debts owed by only one spouse	*In re Chandler*, 148 B.R. 13 (E.D. N.C. 1992)
	Real or personal property, including co-op, used as residence to $35,000; $60,000 if 65 or older, property owned with spouse as tenants by the entirely or joint tenants with right of survivorship, and spouse has died; up to $5,000 of unused portion of homestead may be applied to any property	1C-1601(a)(1),(2)
insurance	Employee group life policy or proceeds	58-58-165
	Fraternal benefit society benefits	58-24-85
	Life insurance on spouse or children	1C-1601(a)(6); Const. Art. X § 5
miscellaneous	Alimony, support, separate maintenance, and child support necessary for support of debtor and dependents	1C-1601(a)(12)
	Property of business partnership	59-55
	Support received by a surviving spouse for 1 year, up to $10,000	30-15
pensions	Tax-exempt retirement accounts, including 401(k)s, 403(b)s, profit-sharing and money purchase plans, SEP and SIMPLE IRAs, and defined-benefit plans	11 U.S.C. § 522(b)(3)(C)
	Traditional and Roth IRAs to $1,095,000 per person	11 U.S.C. § 522(b)(3)(C); (n)
	Firefighters & rescue squad workers	58-86-90
	IRAs & Roth IRAs	1C-1601(a)(9)
	Law enforcement officers	143-166.30(g)
	Legislators	120-4.29
	Municipal, city, & county employees	128-31
	Retirement benefits from another state to extent exempt in that state	1C-1601(a)(11)
	Teachers & state employees	135-9; 135-95

personal property	Animals, crops, musical instruments, books, clothing, appliances, household goods & furnishings to $5,000 total; may add $1,000 per dependent, up to $4,000 total additional (all property must have been purchased at least 90 days before filing)	1C-1601(a)(4),(d)
	Burial plot to $18,500, in lieu of homestead	1C-1601(a)(1)
	College savings account established under 26 U.S.C. § 529 to $25,000, excluding certain contributions within prior year	1C-1601(a)(10)
	Health aids	1C-1601(a)(7)
	Motor vehicle to $3,500	1C-1601(a)(3)
	Personal injury & wrongful death recoveries for person you depended on	1C-1601(a)(8)
public benefits	Aid to blind	111-18
	Crime victims' compensation	15B-17
	Public adult assistance under work first program	108A-36
	Unemployment compensation	96-17
	Workers' compensation	97-21
tools of trade	Implements, books, & tools of trade to $2,000	1C-1601(a)(5)
wages	Earned but unpaid wages received 60 days before filing for bankruptcy, needed for support	1-362
wildcard	$5,000 of unused homestead or burial exemption	1C-1601(a)(2)
	$500 of any personal property	Constitution Art. X § 1

North Dakota

Federal bankruptcy exemptions not available. All law references are to North Dakota Century Code unless otherwise noted.

ASSET	EXEMPTION	LAW
homestead	Real property, house trailer, or mobile home to $100,000 (husband & wife may not double)	28-22-02(10); 47-18-01
insurance	Fraternal benefit society benefits Any unmatured life insurance contract, other than credit life insurance	26.1-15.1-18; 26.1-33-40; 28-22-03.1(4)
	Life insurance proceeds payable to deceased's estate, not to a specific beneficiary	26.1-33-40
	Life insurance surrender value to $8,000 per policy, if beneficiary is insured's dependent & policy was owned over 1 year before filing for bankruptcy; limit does not apply if more needed for support	28-22-03.1(5)
miscellaneous	Child support payments	14-09-09.31; 28-22-03.1(8)(d)
pensions	Tax-exempt retirement accounts, including 401(k)s, 403(b)s, profit-sharing and money purchase plans, SEP and SIMPLE IRAs, and defined-benefit plans	11 U.S.C. § 522(b)(3)(C)
	Traditional and Roth IRAs to $1,095,000 per person	11 U.S.C. § 522(b)(3)(C); (n)
	Disabled veterans' benefits, except military retirement pay	28-22-03.1(4)(d)
	ERISA-qualified benefits, IRAs, Roth IRAs, & Keoghs to $100,000 per plan; no limit if more needed for support; total of all accounts cannot exceed $200,000	28-22-03.1(7)
pensions	Public employees deferred compensation	54-52.2-06
(continued)	Public employees pensions	28-22-19(1)
personal property	One Bible or other religious text; schoolbooks; other books	28-22-02(4)
	Burial plots, church pew	28-22-02(2),(3)
	Wearing apparel to $5,000 and all clothing & family pictures	28-22-02(1),(5)
	Crops or grain raised by debtor on 160 acres where debtor resides	28-22-02(8)
	Food & fuel to last 1 year	28-22-02(6)
	Health aids	28-22-03.1(6)
	Insurance proceeds for exempt property	28-22-02(9)
	One motor vehicle to $2,950 (or $32,000 for vehicle that has been modified to accommodate owner's disability)	28-22-03.1(2)
	Personal injury recoveries to $15,000	28-22-03.1(4)(b)
	Wrongful death recoveries to $15,000	28-22-03.1(4)(a)
	Head of household not claiming crops or grain may claim $5,000 of any personal property	28-22-03
	Unmarried with no dependents not claiming crops or grain may claim $3,750 of any personal property	28-22-05
public benefits	Crime victims' compensation	28-22-03.1(4); 28-22-19(2)
	Old age & survivor insurance program benefits	52-09-22
	Public assistance	28-22-19(3)
	Social Security	28-22-03.1(8)(a)
	Unemployment compensation	52-06-30
	Veteran's disability benefits	28-22-03.1(8)(b)
	Workers' compensation	65-05-29
tools of trade	Books, tools, & implements of trade to $1,500	28-22-03.1(3)
wages	Minimum 75% of disposable weekly earnings or 40 times the federal minimum wage, whichever is more; bankruptcy judge may authorize more for low-income debtors	32-09.1-03
wildcard	$7,500 of any property in lieu of homestead	28-22-03.1(1)

Ohio

Federal bankruptcy exemptions not available. All law references are to Ohio Revised Code unless otherwise noted.

ASSET	EXEMPTION	LAW
homestead	Property held as tenancy by the entirety may be exempt against debts owed by only one spouse	*In re Pernus*, 143 B.R. 856 (N.D. Ohio 1992)
	Real or personal property used as residence to $20,000	2329.66(A)(1)(b)
insurance	Benevolent society benefits to $5,000	2329.63; 2329.66(A)(6)(a)
	Disability benefits needed for support	2329.66(A)(6)(e); 3923.19
	Fraternal benefit society benefits	2329.66(A)(6)(d); 3921.18
	Group life insurance policy or proceeds	2329.66(A)(6)(c); 3917.05
	Life, endowment, or annuity contract avails for your spouse, child, or dependent	2329.66(A)(6)(b); 3911.10

insurance (continued)	Life insurance proceeds for a spouse	3911.12
	Life insurance proceeds if clause prohibits proceeds from being used to pay beneficiary's creditors	3911.14
miscellaneous	Alimony, child support needed for support	2329.66(A)(11)
	Property of business partnership	1775.24; 2329.66(A)(14)
pensions	Tax-exempt retirement accounts, including 401(k)s, 403(b)s, profit-sharing and money purchase plans, SEP and SIMPLE IRAs, and defined-benefit plans	11 U.S.C. § 522(b)(3)(C)
	Traditional and Roth IRAs to $1,095,000 per person	11 U.S.C. § 522(b)(3)(C); (n)
	ERISA-qualified benefits needed for support	2329.66(A)(10)(b)
	Firefighters, police officers	742.47
	IRAs, Roth IRAs, & Keoghs needed for support	2329.66(A)(10)(c), (a)
	Public employees	145.56
	Public safety officers' death benefit	2329.66(A)(10)(a)
	Public school employees	3309.66
	State highway patrol employees	5505.22
	Volunteer firefighters' dependents	146.13
personal property	Animals, crops, books, musical instruments, appliances, household goods, furnishings, firearms, hunting & fishing equipment to $525 per item; jewelry to $1,350 for 1 or more items; $10,775 total	2329.66(A)(4)(b),(c),(d); *In re Szydlowski*, 186 B.R. 907 (N.D. Ohio 1995)
	Burial plot	517.09; 2329.66(A)(8)
	Cash, money due within 90 days, tax refund, bank, security, & utility deposits to $400 total	2329.66(A)(4)(a); *In re Szydlowski*, 186 B.R. 907 (N.D. Ohio 1995)
	Compensation for lost future earnings needed for support, received during 12 months before filing	2329.66(A)(12)(d)
	Cooking unit & refrigerator to $300 each	2329.66(A)(3)
	Health aids (professionally prescribed)	2329.66(A)(7)
	Motor vehicle to $3,225	2329.66(A)(2)(b)
	Personal injury recoveries to $20,200, received during 12 months before filing	2329.66(A)(12)(c)
	Tuition credit or payment	2329.66(A)(16)
	Wrongful death recoveries for person debtor depended on, needed for support, received during 12 months before filing	2329.66(A)(12)(b)
public benefits	Crime victim's compensation, received during 12 months before filing	2329.66(A)(12)(a); 2743.66(D)
	Disability assistance payments	2329.66(A)(9)(f); 5115.07
	Public assistance	2329.66(A)(9)(d); (e); 5107.75; 5108.08
	Unemployment compensation	2329.66(A)(9)(c); 4141.32
	Vocational rehabilitation benefits	2329.66(A)(9)(a); 3304.19
	Workers' compensation	2329.66(A)(9)(b); 4123.67
tools of trade	Implements, books, & tools of trade to $2,025	2329.66(A)(5)
wages	Minimum 75% of disposable weekly earnings or 30 times the federal hourly minimum wage, whichever is higher; bankruptcy judge may authorize more for low-income debtors	2329.66(A)(13)
wildcard	$1,075 of any property	2329.66(A)(18)

Oklahoma

Federal bankruptcy exemptions not available. All law references are to Oklahoma Statutes Annotated (in the form title number-section number), unless otherwise noted.

ASSET	EXEMPTION	LAW
homestead	Real property or manufactured home to unlimited value; property cannot exceed 1 acre in city, town, or village, or 160 acres elsewhere; $5,000 limit if more than 25% of total sq. ft. area used for business purposes; okay to rent homestead as long as no other residence is acquired	31-1(A)(1); 31-1(A)(2); 31-2
insurance	Annuity benefits & cash value	36-3631.1
	Assessment or mutual benefits	36-2410
	Fraternal benefit society benefits	36-2718.1
	Funeral benefits prepaid & placed in trust	36-6125
	Group life policy or proceeds	36-3632
	Life, health, accident, & mutual benefit insurance proceeds & cash value, if clause prohibits proceeds from being used to pay beneficiary's creditors	36-3631.1
	Limited stock insurance benefits	36-2510
miscellaneous	Alimony, child support	31-1(A)(19)
	Beneficiary's interest in a statutory support trust	6-3010
	Liquor license	37-532
	Property of business partnership	54-1-504
pensions	Tax-exempt retirement accounts, including 401(k)s, 403(b)s, profit-sharing and money purchase plans, SEP and SIMPLE IRAs, and defined-benefit plans	11 U.S.C. § 522(b)(3)(C)
	Traditional and Roth IRAs to $1,095,000 per person	11 U.S.C. § 522(b)(3)(C); (n)
	County employees	19-959
	Disabled veterans	31-7
	ERISA-qualified benefits, IRAs, Roth IRAs, Education IRAs, & Keoghs	31-1(A)(20), (24)
	Firefighters	11-49-126
	Judges	20-1111
	Law enforcement employees	47-2-303.3
	Police officers	11-50-124
	Public employees	74-923
	Tax-exempt benefits	60-328
	Teachers	70-17-109

personal property	Books, portraits, & pictures	31-1(A)(6)
	Burial plots	31-1(A)(4); 8-7
	Clothing to $4,000	31-1(A)(7)
	College savings plan interest	31-1A(24)
	Deposits in an IDA (Individual Development Account)	31-1A(22)
	Federal earned income tax credit	31-1(A)(23)
	Food & seed for growing to last 1 year	31-1(A)(17)
	Guns for household use to $2,000	31-1A(14)
	Health aids (professionally prescribed)	31-1(A)(9)
	Household & kitchen furniture; personal computer and related equipment	31-1(A)(3)
	Livestock for personal or family use: 5 dairy cows & calves under 6 months; 100 chickens; 20 sheep; 10 hogs; 2 horses, bridles, & saddles; forage & feed to last 1 year	31-1(A)(10),(11),(12),(15),(16),(17)
	Motor vehicle to $7,500	31-1(A)(13)
	Personal injury & wrongful death recoveries to $50,000	31-1(A)(21)
	Prepaid funeral benefits	36-6125(H)
	War bond payroll savings account	51-42
	Wedding and anniversary rings to $3,000	31-1(A)(8)
public benefits	Crime victims' compensation	21-142.13
	Public assistance	56-173
	Social Security	56-173
	Unemployment compensation	40-2-303
	Workers' compensation	85-48
tools of trade	Implements needed to farm homestead; tools, books, & apparatus to $10,000 total	31-1(A)(5); 31-1(C)
wages	75% of wages earned in 90 days before filing bankruptcy; bankruptcy judge may allow more if you show hardship	12-1171.1; 31-1(A)(18); 31-1.1
wildcard	None	

Oregon

Federal bankruptcy exemptions not available. All law references are to Oregon Revised Statutes unless otherwise noted.

ASSET	EXEMPTION	LAW
homestead	Prepaid rent & security deposit for renter's dwelling	*In re Casserino*, 379 F.3d 1069 (9th Cir. 2004)
	Real property of a soldier or sailor during time of war	408.440
	Real property you occupy or intend to occupy to $40,000 ($50,000 for joint owners); property cannot exceed 1 block in town or city or 160 acres elsewhere; sale proceeds exempt 1 year from sale if you intend to purchase another home or use sale proceeds for rent	18.395; 18.402; *In re Wynn*, 369 B.R. 605 (D. Or. 2007)
	Tenancy by entirety not exempt, but subject to survivorship rights of nondebtor spouse	*In re Pletz*, 225 B.R. 206 (D. Or. 1997)
insurance	Annuity contract benefits to $500 per month	743.049
	Fraternal benefit society benefits to $7,500	748.207; 18.348
	Group life policy or proceeds not payable to insured	743.047
insurance (continued)	Health or disability proceeds or avails	743.050
	Life insurance proceeds or cash value if you are not the insured	743.046; 743.047
miscellaneous	Alimony, child support needed for support	18.345(1)(i)
	Liquor licenses	471.292 (1)
pensions	Tax-exempt retirement accounts, including 401(k)s, 403(b)s, profit-sharing and money purchase plans, SEP and SIMPLE IRAs, and defined-benefit plans	11 U.S.C. § 522(b)(3)(C)
	Traditional and Roth IRAs to $1,095,000 per person	11 U.S.C. § 522(b)(3)(C); (n)
	ERISA-qualified benefits, including IRAs & SEPs; & payments to $7,500	18.358; 18.348
	Public officers', employees' pension payments to $7,500	237.980; 238.445; 18.348(2)
personal property	Bank deposits to $7,500; cash for sold exempt property	18.348; 18.345(2)
	Books, pictures, & musical instruments to $600 total	18.345(1)(a)
	Building materials for construction of an improvement	87.075
	Burial plot	65.870
	Clothing, jewelry, & other personal items to $1,800 total	18.345(1)(b)
	Compensation for lost earnings payments for debtor or someone debtor depended on, to extent needed	18.345(1)(L),(3)
	Domestic animals, poultry, & pets to $1,000 plus food to last 60 days	18.345(1)(e)
	Federal earned income tax credit	18.345(1)(n)
	Food & fuel to last 60 days if debtor is householder	18.345(1)(f)
	Furniture, household items, utensils, radios, & TVs to $3,000 total	18.345(1)(f)
	Health aids	18.345(1)(h)
	Higher education savings account to $7,500	348.863; 18.348(1)
	Motor vehicle to $3,000	18.345(1)(d),(3)
	Personal injury recoveries to $10,000	18.345(1)(k),(3)
	Pistol; rifle or shotgun (owned by person over 16) to $1,000	18.362
public benefits	Aid to blind to $7,500	411.706; 411.760; 18.348
	Aid to disabled to $7,500	411.706; 411.760; 18.348
	Civil defense & disaster relief to $7,500	401.405; 18.348
	Crime victims' compensation	18.345(1)(j)(A),(3); 147.325
	General assistance to $7,500	411.760; 18.348
	Injured inmates' benefits to $7,500	655.530; 18.348
	Medical assistance to $7,500	414.095; 18.348
	Old-age assistance to $7,500	411.706; 411.760; 18.348
	Unemployment compensation to $7,500	657.855; 18.348
	Veterans' benefits & proceeds of Veterans loans	407.125; 407.595; 18.348(m)
	Vocational rehabilitation to $7,500	344.580; 18.348
	Workers' compensation to $7,500	656.234; 18.348

tools of trade	Tools, library, team with food to last 60 days, to $3,000	18.345(1)(c),(3)
wages	75% of disposable wages or $170 per week, whichever is greater; bankruptcy judge may authorize more for low-income debtors	18.385
	Wages withheld in state employee's bond savings accounts	292.070
wildcard	$400 of any personal property not already covered by existing exemption	18.348(1)(o)

Pennsylvania

Federal bankruptcy exemptions available. All law references are to Pennsylvania Consolidated Statutes Annotated unless otherwise noted.

ASSET	EXEMPTION	LAW
homestead	None; however, property held as tenancy by the entirety may be exempt against debts owed by only one spouse	*In re Martin*, 269 B.R. 119 (M.D. Pa. 2001)
insurance	Accident or disability benefits	42-8124(c)(7)
	Fraternal benefit society benefits	42-8124(c)(1),(8)
	Group life policy or proceeds	42-8124(c)(5)
	Insurance policy or annuity contract payments where insured is the beneficiary, cash value or proceeds to $100 per month	42-8124(c)(3)
	Life insurance & annuity proceeds if clause prohibits proceeds from being used to pay beneficiary's creditors	42-8214(c)(4)
	Life insurance annuity policy cash value or proceeds if beneficiary is insured's dependent, child or spouse	42-8124(c)(6)
	No-fault automobile insurance proceeds	42-8124(c)(9)
miscellaneous	Property of business partnership	15-8342
pensions	Tax-exempt retirement accounts, including 401(k)s, 403(b)s, profit-sharing and money purchase plans, SEP and SIMPLE IRAs, and defined-benefit plans	11 U.S.C. § 522(b)(3)(C)
	Traditional and Roth IRAs to $1,095,000 per person	11 U.S.C. § 522(b)(3)(C); (n)
pensions	City employees	53-13445; 53-23572; 53-39383; 42-8124(b)(1)(iv)
	County employees	16-4716
	Municipal employees	53-881.115; 42-8124(b)(1)(vi)
	Police officers	53-764; 53-776; 53-23666; 42-8124(b)(1)(iii)
	Private retirement benefits to extent tax-deferred, if clause prohibits proceeds from being used to pay beneficiary's creditors; exemption limited to deposits of $15,000 per year made at least 1 year before filing (limit does not apply to rollovers from other exempt funds or accounts)	42-8124(b)(1)(vii), (viii),(ix)
	Public school employees	24-8533; 42-8124(b)(1)(i)
	State employees	71-5953; 42-8124(b)(1)(ii)
personal property	Bibles & schoolbooks	42-8124(a)(2)
	Clothing	42-8124(a)(1)
	Military uniforms & accoutrements	42-8124(a)(4); 51-4103
	Sewing machines	42-8124(a)(3)
public benefits	Crime victims' compensation	18-11.708
	Korean conflict veterans' benefits	51-20098
	Unemployment compensation	42-8124(a)(10); 43-863
	Veterans' benefits	51-20012; 20048; 20098; 20127
	Workers' compensation	42-8124(c)(2)
tools of trade	Seamstress's sewing machine	42-8124(a)(3)
wages	Earned but unpaid wages	42-8127
	Prison inmate's wages	61-1054
	Wages of victims of abuse	42-8127(f)
wildcard	$300 of any property, including cash, real property, securities, or proceeds from sale of exempt property	42-8123

Rhode Island

Federal bankruptcy exemptions available. All law references are to General Laws of Rhode Island unless otherwise noted.

ASSET	EXEMPTION	LAW
homestead	$300,000 in land & buildings you occupy or intend to occupy as a principal residence (husband & wife may not double)	9-26-4.1
insurance	Accident or sickness proceeds, avails, or benefits	27-18-24
	Fraternal benefit society benefits	27-25-18
	Life insurance proceeds if clause prohibits proceeds from being used to pay beneficiary's creditors	27-4-12
	Temporary disability insurance	28-41-32
miscellaneous	Earnings of a minor child	9-26-4(9)
	Property of business partnership	7-12-36
pensions	Tax-exempt retirement accounts, including 401(k)s, 403(b)s, profit-sharing and money purchase plans, SEP and SIMPLE IRAs, and defined-benefit plans	11 U.S.C. § 522(b)(3)(C)
	Traditional and Roth IRAs to $1,095,000 per person	11 U.S.C. § 522(b)(3)(C); (n)
	ERISA-qualified benefits	9-26-4(12)
	Firefighters	9-26-5
	IRAs & Roth IRAs	9-26-4(11)
	Police officers	9-26-5
	Private employees	28-17-4
	State & municipal employees	36-10-34
personal property	Beds, bedding, furniture, household goods, & supplies, to $9,600 total (husband & wife may not double)	9-26-4(3); *In re Petrozella*, 247 B.R. 591 (R.I. 2000)
	Bibles & books to $300	9-26-4(4)
	Burial plot	9-26-4(5)
	Clothing	9-26-4(1)

personal property (continued)	Consumer cooperative association holdings to $50	7-8-25
	Debt secured by promissory note or bill of exchange	9-26-4(7)
	Jewelry to $2,000	9-26-4 (14)
	Motor vehicles to $12,000	9-26-4 (13)
	Prepaid tuition program or tuition savings account	9-26-4 (15)
public benefits	Aid to blind, aged, disabled; general assistance	40-6-14
	Crime victims' compensation	12-25.1-3(b)(2)
	Family assistance benefits	40-5.1-15
	State disability benefits	28-41-32
	Unemployment compensation	28-44-58
	Veterans' disability or survivors' death benefits	30-7-9
	Workers' compensation	28-33-27
tools of trade	Library of practicing professional	9-26-4(2)
	Working tools to $1,500	9-26-4(2)
wages	Earned but unpaid wages due military member on active duty	30-7-9
	Earned but unpaid wages due seaman	9-26-4(6)
	Earned but unpaid wages to $50	9-26-4(8)(iii)
	Wages of any person who had been receiving public assistance are exempt for 1 year after going off of relief	9-26-4(8)(ii)
	Wages of spouse & minor children	9-26-4(9)
	Wages paid by charitable organization or fund providing relief to the poor	9-26-4(8)(i)
wildcard	$5,000	9-26-4(16)

South Carolina

Federal bankruptcy exemptions not available. All law references are to Code of Laws of South Carolina unless otherwise noted. (Amounts to be adjusted for inflation in 2010 (15-41-30(B).)

ASSET	EXEMPTION	LAW
homestead	Real property, including co-op, to $50,000	15-41-30(A)(1)
insurance	Accident & disability benefits	38-63-40(D)
	Benefits accruing under life insurance policy after death of insured, where proceeds left with insurance company pursuant to agreement; benefits not exempt from action to recover necessaries if parties agree	38-63-50
	Disability or illness benefits	15-41-30(A)(10)(C)
	Fraternal benefit society benefits	38-38-330
	Group life insurance proceeds; cash value to $50,000	38-63-40(C); 38-65-90
	Life insurance avails from policy for person you depended on to $4,000	15-41-30(A)(8)
	Life insurance proceeds from policy for person you depended on, needed for support	15-41-30(A)(12)(C)
insurance (continued)	Proceeds & cash surrender value of life insurance payable to beneficiary other than insured's estate & for the express benefit of insured's spouse, children, or dependents (must be purchased 2 years before filing)	38-63-40(A)
	Proceeds of life insurance or annuity contract	38-63-40(B)
	Unmatured life insurance contract, except credit insurance policy	15-41-30(A)(8)
miscellaneous	Alimony, child support	15-41-30(A)(10)(D)
	Property of business partnership	33-41-720
pensions	Tax-exempt retirement accounts, including 401(k)s, 403(b)s, profit-sharing and money purchase plans, SEP and SIMPLE IRAs, and defined-benefit plans	11 U.S.C. § 522(b)(3)(C)
	Traditional and Roth IRAs to $1,095,000 per person	11 U.S.C. § 522(b)(3)(C); (n)
	ERISA-qualified benefits; your share of the pension plan fund	15-41-30(10)(E),(13)
	Firefighters	9-13-230
	General assembly members	9-9-180
	IRAs & Roth IRAs needed for support	15-41-30(A)(12)
	Judges, solicitors	9-8-190
	Police officers	9-11-270
	Public employees	9-1-1680
personal property	Animals, crops, appliances, books, clothing, household goods, furnishings, musical instruments to $4,000 total	15-41-30(A)(3)
	Burial plot to $50,000, in lieu of homestead	15-41-30(1)
	Cash & other liquid assets to $5,000, in lieu of burial or homestead exemption	15-41-30(A)(5)
	College investment program trust fund	59-2-140
	Health aids	15-41-30(A)(10)
	Jewelry to $1,000	15-41-30(A)(4)
	Motor vehicle to $5,000	15-41-30(A)(2)
	Personal injury & wrongful death recoveries for person you depended on for support	15-41-30(A)(12)
public benefits	Crime victims' compensation	15-41-30(A)(12); 16-3-1300
	General relief; aid to aged, blind, disabled	43-5-190
	Local public assistance	15-41-30(A)(11)
	Social Security	15-41-30(A)(11)
	Unemployment compensation	15-41-30(A)(11)
	Veterans' benefits	15-41-30(A)(11)
	Workers' compensation	42-9-360
tools of trade	Implements, books, & tools of trade to $1,500	15-41-30(A)(6)
wages	None (use federal nonbankruptcy wage exemption)	15-41-30(A)(7)
wildcard	Up to $5,000 for any property from unused exemption amounts	

South Dakota

Federal bankruptcy exemptions not available. All law references are to South Dakota Codified Law unless otherwise noted.

ASSET	EXEMPTION	LAW
homestead	Gold or silver mine, mill, or smelter not exempt	43-31-5
	May file homestead declaration	43-31-6
	Real property to unlimited value or mobile home (larger than 240 sq. ft. at its base & registered in state at least 6 months before filing) to unlimited value; property cannot exceed 1 acre in town or 160 acres elsewhere; sale proceeds to $30,000 ($170,000 if over age 70 or widow or widower who hasn't remarried) exempt for 1 year after sale (husband & wife may not double)	43-31-1; 43-31-2; 43-31-3; 43-31-4; 43-45-3
	Spouse or child of deceased owner may claim homestead exemption	43-31-13
insurance	Annuity contract proceeds to $250 per month	58-12-6; 58-12-8
	Endowment, life insurance, policy proceeds to $20,000; if policy issued by mutual aid or benevolent society, cash value to $20,000	58-12-4
	Fraternal benefit society benefits	58-37A-18
	Health benefits to $20,000	58-12-4
	Life insurance proceeds, if clause prohibits proceeds from being used to pay beneficiary's creditors	58-15-70
	Life insurance proceeds to $10,000, if beneficiary is surviving spouse or child	43-45-6
pensions	Tax-exempt retirement accounts, including 401(k)s, 403(b)s, profit-sharing and money purchase plans, SEP and SIMPLE IRAs, and defined-benefit plans	11 U.S.C. § 522(b)(3)(C)
	Traditional and Roth IRAs to $1,095,000 per person	11 U.S.C. § 522(b)(3)(C); (n)
	City employees	9-16-47
	ERISA-qualified benefits, limited to income & distribution on $1,000,000	43-45-16
	Public employees	3-12-115
personal property	Bible, schoolbooks; other books to $200	43-45-2(4)
	Burial plots, church pew	43-45-2(2),(3)
	Cemetery association property	47-29-25
	Clothing	43-45-2(5)
	Family pictures	43-45-2(1)
	Food & fuel to last 1 year	43-45-2(6)
public benefits	Crime victim's compensation	23A-28B-24
	Public assistance	28-7A-18
	Unemployment compensation	61-6-28
	Workers' compensation	62-4-42
tools of trade	None	
wages	Earned wages owed 60 days before filing bankruptcy, needed for support of family	15-20-12
	Wages of prisoners in work programs	24-8-10
wildcard	Head of family may claim $6,000, or nonhead of family may claim $4,000 of any personal property	43-45-4

Tennessee

Federal bankruptcy exemptions not available. All law references are to Tennessee Code Annotated unless otherwise noted.

ASSET	EXEMPTION	LAW
homestead	$5,000; $7,500 for joint owners; $25,000 if at least one dependent is a minor child (if 62 or older, $12,500 if single; $20,000 if married; $25,000 if spouse is also 62 or older)	26-2-301
	2–15-year lease	26-2-303
	Life estate	26-2-302
	Property held as tenancy by the entirety may be exempt against debts owed by only one spouse, but survivorship right is not exempt	*In re Arango*, 136 B.R. 740 aff'd, 992 F.2d 611 (6th Cir. 1993); *In re Arwood*, 289 B.R. 889 (Bankr. E.D. Tenn. 2003)
	Spouse or child of deceased owner may claim homestead exemption	26-2-301
insurance	Accident, health, or disability benefits for resident & citizen of Tennessee	26-2-110
	Disability or illness benefits	26-2-111(1)(C)
	Fraternal benefit society benefits	56-25-1403
	Life insurance or annuity	56-7-203
miscellaneous	Alimony, child support owed for 30 days before filing for bankruptcy	26-2-111(1)(E)
	Educational scholarship trust funds & prepayment plans	49-4-108; 49-7-822
pensions	Tax-exempt retirement accounts, including 401(k)s, 403(b)s, profit-sharing and money purchase plans, SEP and SIMPLE IRAs, and defined-benefit plans	11 U.S.C. § 522(b)(3)(C)
	Traditional and Roth IRAs to $1,095,000 per person	11 U.S.C. § 522(b)(3)(C); (n)
	ERISA-qualified benefits, IRAs, & Roth IRAs	26-2-111(1)(D)
	Public employees	8-36-111
	State & local government employees	26-2-105
	Teachers	49-5-909
personal property	Bible, schoolbooks, family pictures, & portraits	26-2-104
	Burial plot to 1 acre	26-2-305; 46-2-102
	Clothing & storage containers	26-2-104
	Health aids	26-2-111(5)
	Health savings accounts	26-2-105
	Lost future earnings payments for you or person you depended on	26-2-111(3)
	Personal injury recoveries to $7,500; wrongful death recoveries to $10,000 ($15,000 total for personal injury, wrongful death, & crime victims' compensation)	26-2-111(2)(B),(C)
	Wages of debtor deserting family, in hands of family	26-2-109
public benefits	Aid to blind	71-4-117
	Aid to disabled	71-4-1112

public benefits (continued)	Crime victims' compensation to $5,000 (*see personal property*)	26-2-111(2)(A); 29-13-111
	Local public assistance	26-2-111(1)(A)
	Old-age assistance	71-2-216
	Relocation assistance payments	13-11-115
	Social Security	26-2-111(1)(A)
	Unemployment compensation	26-2-111(1)(A)
	Veterans' benefits	26-2-111(1)(B)
	Workers' compensation	50-6-223
tools of trade	Implements, books, & tools of trade to $1,900	26-2-111(4)
wages	Minimum 75% of disposable weekly earnings or 30 times the federal minimum hourly wage, whichever is more, plus $2.50 per week per child; bankruptcy judge may authorize more for low-income debtors	26-2-106,107
wildcard	$4,000 of any personal property including deposits on account with any bank or financial institution	26-2-103

Texas

Federal bankruptcy exemptions available. All law references are to Texas Revised Civil Statutes Annotated unless otherwise noted.

ASSET	EXEMPTION	LAW
homestead	Unlimited; property cannot exceed 10 acres in town, village, city or 100 acres (200 for families) elsewhere; sale proceeds exempt for 6 months after sale (renting okay if another home not acquired, Prop. 41.003)	Prop. 41.001; 41.002; Const. Art. 16 §§ 50, 51
	Must file homestead declaration, or court will file it for you & charge you for doing so	Prop. 41.005(f); 41.021 to 41.023
insurance	Church benefit plan benefits	1407a(6)
	Fraternal benefit society benefits	Ins. 885.316
	Life, health, accident, or annuity benefits, monies, policy proceeds, & cash values due or paid to beneficiary or insured	Ins. 1108.051
	Texas employee uniform group insurance	Ins. 1551.011
	Texas public school employees group insurance	Ins. 1575.006
	Texas state college or university employee benefits	Ins. 1601.008
miscellaneous	Alimony & child support	Prop. 42.001(b)(3)
	Higher education savings plan trust account	Educ. 54.709(e)
	Liquor licenses & permits	Alco. Bev. Code 11.03
	Prepaid tuition plans	Educ. 54.639
	Property of business partnership	6132b-5.01
pensions	Tax-exempt retirement accounts, including 401(k)s, 403(b)s, profit-sharing and money purchase plans, SEP and SIMPLE IRAs, and defined-benefit plans	11 U.S.C. § 522(b)(3)(C)
	Traditional and Roth IRAs to $1,095,000 per person	11 U.S.C. § 522(b)(3)(C); (n)
pensions (continued)	County & district employees	Gov't. 811.006
	ERISA-qualified government or church benefits, including Keoghs & IRAs	Prop. 42.0021
	Firefighters	6243e(5); 6243a-1(8.03); 6243b(15); 6243e(5); 6243e.1(1.04)
	Judges	Gov't. 831.004
	Law enforcement officers, firefighters, emergency medical personnel survivors	Gov't. 615.005
	Municipal employees & elected officials, state employees	6243h(22); Gov't. 811.005
	Police officers	6243d-1(17); 6243j(20); 6243a-1(8.03); 6243b(15); 6243d-1(17)
	Retirement benefits to extent tax-deferred	Prop. 42.0021
	Teachers	Gov't. 821.005
personal property *to $60,000 total for family, $30,000 for single adult (see also tools of trade)*	Athletic & sporting equipment, including bicycles	Prop. 42.002(a)(8)
	Bible or other book containing sacred writings of a religion (doesn't count toward $30,000 or $60,000 total)	Prop. 42.001(b)(4)
	Burial plots (exempt from total)	Prop. 41.001
	Clothing & food	Prop. 42.002(a)(2),(5)
	Health aids (exempt from total)	Prop. 42.001(b)(2)
	Health savings accounts	Prop. 42.0021
	Home furnishings including family heirlooms	Prop. 42.002(a)(1)
	Jewelry (limited to 25% of total exemption)	Prop. 42.002(a)(6)
	Pets & domestic animals plus their food: 2 horses, mules, or donkeys & tack; 12 head of cattle; 60 head of other livestock; 120 fowl	Prop. 42.002(a)(10),(11)
	1 two-, three- or four-wheeled motor vehicle per family member or per single adult who holds a driver's license; or, if not licensed, who relies on someone else to operate vehicle	Prop. 42.002(a)(9)
	2 firearms	Prop. 42.002(a)(7)
public benefits	Crime victims' compensation	Crim. Proc. 56.49
	Medical assistance	Hum. Res. 32.036
	Public assistance	Hum. Res. 31.040
	Unemployment compensation	Labor 207.075
	Workers' compensation	Labor 408.201
tools of trade *included in aggregate dollar limits for personal property*	Farming or ranching vehicles & implements	Prop. 42.002(a)(3)
	Tools, equipment (includes boat & motor vehicles used in trade), & books	Prop. 42.002(a)(4)
wages	Earned but unpaid wages	Prop. 42.001(b)(1)
	Unpaid commissions not to exceed 25% of total personal property exemptions	Prop. 42.001(d)
wildcard	None	

Utah

Federal bankruptcy exemptions not available. All law references are to Utah Code unless otherwise noted.

ASSET	EXEMPTION	LAW
homestead	Must file homestead declaration before attempted sale of home	78-23-4
	Real property, mobile home, or water rights to $20,000 if primary residence; $5,000 if not primary residence	78-23-3(1),(2),(4)
	Sale proceeds exempt for 1 year	78-23-3(5)(b)
insurance	Disability, illness, medical, or hospital benefits	78-23-5(1)(a)(iii)
	Fraternal benefit society benefits	31A-9-603
	Life insurance policy cash surrender value, excluding payments made on the contract within the prior year	78-23-5(a)(xiii)
	Life insurance proceeds if beneficiary is insured's spouse or dependent, as needed for support	78-23-5(a)(xi)
	Medical, surgical, & hospital benefits	78-23-5(1)(a)(iv)
miscellaneous	Alimony needed for support	78-23-5(1)(a)(vi)
	Child support	78-23-5(1)(a)(vi), (f),(k)
	Property of business partnership	48-1-22
pensions	Tax-exempt retirement accounts, including 401(k)s, 403(b)s, profit-sharing and money purchase plans, SEP and SIMPLE IRAs, and defined-benefit plans	11 U.S.C. § 522(b)(3)(C)
	Traditional and Roth IRAs to $1,095,000 per person	11 U.S.C. § 522(b)(3)(C); (n)
	ERISA-qualified benefits, IRAs, Roth IRAs, & Keoghs (benefits that have accrued & contributions that have been made at least 1 year prior to filing)	78-23-5(1)(a)(xiv)
	Other pensions & annuities needed for support	78-23-6(3)
	Public employees	49-11-612
personal property	Animals, books, & musical instruments to $500	78-23-8(1)(c)
	Artwork depicting, or done by, a family member	78-23-5(1)(a)(ix)
	Bed, bedding, carpets	78-23-5(1)(a)(viii)
	Burial plot	78-23-5(1)(a)(i)
	Clothing (cannot claim furs or jewelry)	78-23-5(1)(a)(viii)
	Dining & kitchen tables & chairs to $500	78-23-8(1)(b)
	Food to last 12 months	78-23-5(1)(a)(viii)
	Health aids	78-23-5(1)(a)(ii)
	Heirlooms to $500	78-23-8(1)(d)
	Motor vehicle to $2,500	78-23-8(3)
	Personal injury, wrongful death recoveries for you or person you depended on	78-23-5(1)(a)(x)
	Proceeds for sold, lost, or damaged exempt property	78-23-9
	Refrigerator, freezer, microwave, stove, sewing machine, washer & dryer	78-23-5(1)(a)(viii)
	Sofas, chairs, & related furnishings to $500	78-23-8(1)(a)
public benefits	Crime victims' compensation	63-25a-421(4)
	General assistance	35A-3-112
	Occupational disease disability benefits	34A-3-107
	Unemployment compensation	35A-4-103(4)(b)
	Veterans' benefits	78-23-5(1)(a)(v)
	Workers' compensation	34A-2-422
tools of trade	Implements, books, & tools of trade to $3,500	78-23-8(2)
	Military property of National Guard member	39-1-47
wages	Minimum 75% of disposable weekly earnings or 30 times the federal hourly minimum wage, whichever is more; bankruptcy judge may authorize more for low-income debtors	70C-7-103
wildcard	None	

Vermont

Federal bankruptcy exemptions available. All law references are to Vermont Statutes Annotated unless otherwise noted.

ASSET	EXEMPTION	LAW
homestead	Property held as tenancy by the entirety may be exempt against debts owed by only one spouse	*In re McQueen*, 21 B.R. 736 (D. Ver. 1982)
	Real property or mobile home to $75,000; may also claim rents, issues, profits, & outbuildings	27-101
	Spouse of deceased owner may claim homestead exemption	27-105
insurance	Annuity contract benefits to $350 per month	8-3709
	Disability benefits that supplement life insurance or annuity contract	8-3707
	Disability or illness benefits needed for support	12-2740(19)(C)
	Fraternal benefit society benefits	8-4478
	Group life or health benefits	8-3708
	Health benefits to $200 per month	8-4086
	Life insurance proceeds for person you depended on	12-2740(19)(H)
	Life insurance proceeds if clause prohibits proceeds from being used to pay beneficiary's creditors	8-3705
	Life insurance proceeds if beneficiary is not the insured	8-3706
	Unmatured life insurance contract other than credit	12-2740(18)
miscellaneous	Alimony, child support	12-2740(19)(D)
pensions	Tax-exempt retirement accounts, including 401(k)s, 403(b)s, profit-sharing and money purchase plans, SEP and SIMPLE IRAs, and defined-benefit plans	11 U.S.C. § 522(b)(3)(C)
	Traditional and Roth IRAs to $1,095,000 per person	11 U.S.C. § 522(b)(3)(C); (n)
	Municipal employees	24-5066
	Other pensions	12-2740(19)(J)
	Self-directed accounts (IRAs, Roth IRAs, Keoghs); contributions must be made 1 year before filing	12-2740(16)

pensions (continued)	State employees	3-476
	Teachers	16-1946
personal property	Appliances, furnishings, goods, clothing, books, crops, animals, musical instruments to $2,500 total	12-2740(5)
	Bank deposits to $700	12-2740(15)
	Cow, 2 goats, 10 sheep, 10 chickens, & feed to last 1 winter; 3 swarms of bees plus honey; 5 tons coal or 500 gal. heating oil, 10 cords of firewood; 500 gal. bottled gas; growing crops to $5,000; yoke of oxen or steers, plow & ox yoke; 2 horses with harnesses, halters, & chains	12-2740(6), (9)-(14)
	Health aids	12-2740(17)
	Jewelry to $500; wedding ring unlimited	12-2740(3),(4)
	Motor vehicles to $2,500	12-2740(1)
	Personal injury, lost future earnings, wrongful death recoveries for you or person you depended on	12-2740(19)(F), (G),(I)
	Stove, heating unit, refrigerator, freezer, water heater, & sewing machines	12-2740(8)
public benefits	Aid to blind, aged, disabled; general assistance	33-124
	Crime victims' compensation needed for support	12-2740(19)(E)
	Social Security needed for support	12-2740(19)(A)
	Unemployment compensation	21-1367
	Veterans' benefits needed for support	12-2740(19)(B)
	Workers' compensation	21-681
tools of trade	Books & tools of trade to $5,000	12-2740(2)
wages	Entire wages, if you received welfare during 2 months before filing	12-3170
	Minimum 75% of weekly disposable earnings or 30 times the federal minimum hourly wage, whichever is greater; bankruptcy judge may authorize more for low-income debtors	12-3170
wildcard	Unused exemptions for motor vehicle, tools of trade, jewelry, household furniture, appliances, clothing, & crops to $7,000	12-2740(7)
	$400 of any property	12-2740(7)

Virginia

Federal bankruptcy exemptions not available. All law references are to Code of Virginia unless otherwise noted.

ASSET	EXEMPTION	LAW
homestead	$5,000 plus $500 per dependent; rents & profits; sale proceeds exempt to $5,000 (unused portion of homestead may be applied to any personal property); exemption is $10,000 if over 65	*Cheeseman v. Nachman*, 656 F.2d 60 (4th Cir. 1981); 34-4; 34-18; 34-20
	May include mobile home	*In re Goad*, 161 B.R. 161 (W.D. Va. 1993)
	Must file homestead declaration before filing for bankruptcy	34-6
	Property held as tenancy by the entirety may be exempt against debts owed by only one spouse	*In re Bunker*, 312 F.3d 145 (4th Cir. 2002)
homestead (continued)	Surviving spouse may claim $15,000; if no surviving spouse, minor children may claim exemption	64.1-151.3
insurance	Accident or sickness benefits	38.2-3406
	Burial society benefits	38.2-4021
	Cooperative life insurance benefits	38.2-3811
	Fraternal benefit society benefits	38.2-4118
	Group life or accident insurance for government officials	51.1-510
	Group life insurance policy or proceeds	38.2-3339
	Industrial sick benefits	38.2-3549
	Life insurance proceeds	38.2-3122
miscellaneous	Property of business partnership	50-73.108
pensions *see also wages*	Tax-exempt retirement accounts, including 401(k)s, 403(b)s, profit-sharing and money purchase plans, SEP and SIMPLE IRAs, and defined-benefit plans	11 U.S.C. § 522(b)(3)(C)
	Traditional and Roth IRAs to $1,095,000 per person	11 U.S.C. § 522(b)(3)(C); (n)
	City, town, & county employees	51.1-802
	ERISA-qualified benefits to same extent permitted by federal bankruptcy law	34-34
	Judges	51.1-300
	State employees	51.1-124.4(A)
	State police officers	51.1-200
personal property	Bible	34-26(1)
	Burial plot	34-26(3)
	Clothing to $1,000	34-26(4)
	Family portraits & heirlooms to $5,000 total	34-26(2)
	Health aids	34-26(6)
	Household furnishings to $5,000	34-26(4a)
	Motor vehicle to $2,000	34-26(8)
	Personal injury causes of action & recoveries	34-28.1
	Pets	34-26(5)
	Prepaid tuition contracts	23-38.81(E)
	Wedding & engagement rings	34-26(1a)
public benefits	Aid to blind, aged, disabled; general relief	63.2-506
	Crime victims' compensation unless seeking to discharge debt for treatment of injury incurred during crime	19.2-368.12
	Payments to tobacco farmers	3.1-1111.1
	Unemployment compensation	60.2-600
	Workers' compensation	65.2-531
tools of trade	For farmer, pair of horses, or mules with gear; one wagon or cart, one tractor to $3,000; 2 plows & wedges; one drag, harvest cradle, pitchfork, rake; fertilizer to $1,000	34-27
	Tools, books, & instruments of trade, including motor vehicles, to $10,000, needed in your occupation or education	34-26(7)
	Uniforms, arms, equipment of military member	44-96

wages	Minimum 75% of weekly disposable earnings or 40 times the federal minimum hourly wage, whichever is greater; bankruptcy judge may authorize more for low-income debtors	34-29
wildcard	Unused portion of homestead or personal property exemption	34-13
	$10,000 of any property for disabled veterans	34-4.1

Washington

Federal bankruptcy exemptions available. All law references are to Revised Code of Washington Annotated unless otherwise noted.

ASSET	EXEMPTION	LAW
homestead	Must record homestead declaration before sale of home if property unimproved or home unoccupied	6.15.040
	Real property or manufactured home to $125,000; unimproved property intended for residence to $15,000 (husband & wife may not double)	6.13.010; 6.13.030
insurance	Annuity contract proceeds to $2,500 per month	48.18.430
	Disability proceeds, avails, or benefits	48.36A.180
	Fraternal benefit society benefits	48.18.400
	Group life insurance policy or proceeds	48.18.420
	Life insurance proceeds or avails if beneficiary is not the insured	48.18.410
miscellaneous	Child support payments	6.15.010(3)(d)
pensions	Tax-exempt retirement accounts, including 401(k)s, 403(b)s, profit-sharing and money purchase plans, SEP and SIMPLE IRAs, and defined-benefit plans	11 U.S.C. § 522(b)(3)(C)
	Traditional and Roth IRAs to $1,095,000 per person	11 U.S.C. § 522(b)(3)(C); (n)
	City employees	41.28.200; 41.44.240
	ERISA-qualified benefits, IRAs, Roth IRAs, & Keoghs	6.15.020
	Judges	2.10.180; 2.12.090
	Law enforcement officials & firefighters	41.26.053
	Police officers	41.20.180
	Public & state employees	41.40.052
	State patrol officers	43.43.310
	Teachers	41.32.052
	Volunteer firefighters	41.24.240
personal property	Appliances, furniture, household goods, home & yard equipment to $2,700 total for individual ($5,400 for community)	6.15.010(3)(a)
	Books to $1,500	6.15.010(2)
	Burial ground	68.24.220
	Burial plots sold by nonprofit cemetery association	68.20.120
	Clothing, no more than $1,000 in furs, jewelry, ornaments	6.15.010(1)
	Fire insurance proceeds for lost, stolen, or destroyed exempt property	6.15.030
	Food & fuel for comfortable maintenance	6.15.010(3)(a)
personal property (continued)	Health aids prescribed	6.15.010(3)(e)
	Keepsakes & family pictures	6.15.010(2)
	Motor vehicle to $2,500 total for individual (two vehicles to $5,000 for community)	6.15.010(3)(c)
	Personal injury recoveries to $16,150	6.15.010(3)(f)
	Tuition units purchased more than 2 years before	6.15.010(5)
public benefits	Child welfare	74.13.070
	Crime victims' compensation	7.68.070(10)
	General assistance	74.04.280
	Industrial insurance (workers' compensation)	51.32.040
	Old-age assistance	74.08.210
	Unemployment compensation	50.40.020
tools of trade	Farmer's trucks, stock, tools, seed, equipment, & supplies to $5,000 total	6.15.010(4)(a)
	Library, office furniture, office equipment, & supplies of physician, surgeon, attorney, clergy, or other professional to $5,000 total	6.15.010(4)(b)
	Tools & materials used in any other trade to $5,000	6.15.010(4)(c)
wages	Minimum 75% of weekly disposable earnings or 30 times the federal minimum hourly wage, whichever is greater; bankruptcy judge may authorize more for low-income debtors	6.27.150
wildcard	$2,000 of any personal property (no more than $200 in cash, bank deposits, bonds, stocks, & securities)	6.15.010(3)(b)

West Virginia

Federal bankruptcy exemptions not available. All law references are to West Virginia Code unless otherwise noted.

ASSET	EXEMPTION	LAW
homestead	Real or personal property used as residence to $25,000; unused portion of homestead may be applied to any property	38-10-4(a)
insurance	Fraternal benefit society benefits	33-23-21
	Group life insurance policy or proceeds	33-6-28
	Health or disability benefits	38-10-4(j)(3)
	Life insurance payments from policy for person you depended on, needed for support	38-10-4(k)(3)
	Unmatured life insurance contract, except credit insurance policy	38-10-4(g)
	Unmatured life insurance contract's accrued dividend, interest, or loan value to $8,000, if debtor owns contract & insured is either debtor or a person on whom debtor is dependent	38-10-4(h)
miscellaneous	Alimony, child support needed for support	38-10-4(j)(4)
pensions	Tax-exempt retirement accounts, including 401(k)s, 403(b)s, profit-sharing and money purchase plans, SEP and SIMPLE IRAs, and defined-benefit plans	11 U.S.C. § 522(b)(3)(C)
	Traditional and Roth IRAs to $1,095,000 per person	11 U.S.C. § 522(b)(3)(C); (n)
	ERISA-qualified benefits, IRAs needed for support	38-10-4(j)(5)
	Public employees	5-10-46
	Teachers	18-7A-30

personal property	Animals, crops, clothing, appliances, books, household goods, furnishings, musical instruments to $400 per item, $8,000 total	38-10-4(c)
	Burial plot to $25,000, in lieu of homestead	38-10-4(a)
	Health aids	38-10-4(i)
	Jewelry to $1,000	38-10-4(d)
	Lost earnings payments needed for support	38-10-4(k)(5)
	Motor vehicle to $2,400	38-10-4(b)
	Personal injury recoveries to $15,000	38-10-4(k)(4)
	Prepaid higher education tuition trust fund & savings plan payments	38-10-4(k)(6)
	Wrongful death recoveries for person you depended on, needed for support	38-10-4(k)(2)
public benefits	Aid to blind, aged, disabled; general assistance	9-5-1
	Crime victims' compensation	38-10-4(k)(1)
	Social Security	38-10-4(j)(1)
	Unemployment compensation	38-10-4(j)(1)
	Veterans' benefits	38-10-4(j)(2)
	Workers' compensation	23-4-18
tools of trade	Implements, books, & tools of trade to $1,500	38-10-4(f)
wages	Minimum 30 times the federal minimum hourly wage per week; bankruptcy judge may authorize more for low-income debtors	38-5A-3
wildcard	$800 plus unused portion of homestead or burial exemption, of any property	38-10-4(e)

Wisconsin

Federal bankruptcy exemptions available. All law references are to Wisconsin Statutes Annotated unless otherwise noted.

ASSET	EXEMPTION	LAW
homestead	Property you occupy or intend to occupy to $75,000; $150,000 for married couples filing jointly; sale proceeds exempt for 2 years if you intend to purchase another home (husband & wife may not double)	815.20
insurance	Federal disability insurance benefits	815.18(3)(ds)
	Fraternal benefit society benefits	614.96
	Life insurance proceeds for someone debtor depended on, needed for support	815.18(3)(i)(a)
	Life insurance proceeds held in trust by insurer, if clause prohibits proceeds from being used to pay beneficiary's creditors	632.42
	Unmatured life insurance contract (except credit insurance contract) if debtor owns contract & insured is debtor or dependents, or someone debtor is dependent on	815.18(3)(f)
	Unmatured life insurance contract's accrued dividends, interest, or loan value to $4,000 total, if debtor owns contract & insured is debtor or dependents, or someone debtor is dependent on	815.18(3)(f)
miscellaneous	Alimony, child support needed for support	815.18(3)(c)
	Property of business partnership	178.21(3)(c)
pensions	Tax-exempt retirement accounts, including 401(k)s, 403(b)s, profit-sharing and money purchase plans, SEP and SIMPLE IRAs, and defined-benefit plans	11 U.S.C. § 522(b)(3)(C)
pensions (continued)	Traditional and Roth IRAs to $1,095,000 per person	11 U.S.C. § 522(b)(3)(C); (n)
	Certain municipal employees	62.63(4)
	Firefighters, police officers who worked in city with population over 100,000	815.18(3)(ef)
	Military pensions	815.18(3)(n)
	Private or public retirement benefits	815.18(3)(j)
	Public employees	40.08(1)
personal property	Burial plot, tombstone, coffin	815.18(3)(a)
	College savings account or tuition trust fund	14.64(7); 14.63(8)
	Deposit accounts to $5,000	815.18(3)(k)
	Fire & casualty proceeds for destroyed exempt property for 2 years from receiving	815.18(3)(e)
	Household goods & furnishings, clothing, keepsakes, jewelry, appliances, books, musical instruments, firearms, sporting goods, animals, & other tangible personal property to $12,000 total	815.18(3)(d)
	Lost future earnings recoveries, needed for support	815.18(3)(i)(d)
	Motor vehicles to $4,000; unused portion of $12,000 personal property exemption may be added	815.18(3)(g)
	Personal injury recoveries to $50,000	815.18(3)(i)(c)
	Tenant's lease or stock interest in housing co-op, to homestead amount	182.004(6)
	Wages used to purchase savings bonds	20.921(1)(e)
	Wrongful death recoveries, needed for support	815.18(3)(i)(b)
public benefits	Crime victims' compensation	949.07
	Social services payments	49.96
	Unemployment compensation	108.13
	Veterans' benefits	45.03(8)(b)
	Workers' compensation	102.27
tools of trade	Equipment, inventory, farm products, books, & tools of trade to $15,000 total	815.18(3)(b)
wages	75% of weekly net income or 30 times the greater of the federal or state minimum hourly wage; bankruptcy judge may authorize more for low-income debtors	815.18(3)(h)
	Wages of county jail prisoners	303.08(3)
	Wages of county work camp prisoners	303.10(7)
	Wages of inmates under work-release plan	303.065(4)(b)
wildcard	None	

Wyoming

Federal bankruptcy exemptions not available. All law references are to Wyoming Statutes Annotated unless otherwise noted.

ASSET	EXEMPTION	LAW
homestead	Property held as tenancy by the entirety may be exempt against debts owed by only one spouse	*In re Anselmi*, 52 B.R. 479 (D. Wy. 1985)
	Real property you occupy to $10,000 or house trailer you occupy to $6,000	1-20-101; 102; 104

homestead (continued)	Spouse or child of deceased owner may claim homestead exemption	1-20-103
insurance	Annuity contract proceeds to $350 per month	26-15-132
	Disability benefits if clause prohibits proceeds from being used to pay beneficiary's creditors	26-15-130
	Fraternal benefit society benefits	26-29-218
	Group life or disability policy or proceeds, cash surrender & loan values, premiums waived, & dividends	26-15-131
	Individual life insurance policy proceeds, cash surrender & loan values, premiums waived, & dividends	26-15-129
	Life insurance proceeds held by insurer, if clause prohibits proceeds from being used to pay beneficiary's creditors	26-15-133
miscellaneous	Liquor licenses & malt beverage permits	12-4-604
pensions	Tax-exempt retirement accounts, including 401(k)s, 403(b)s, profit-sharing and money purchase plans, SEP and SIMPLE IRAs, and defined-benefit plans	11 U.S.C. § 522(b)(3)(C)
	Traditional and Roth IRAs to $1,095,000 per person	11 U.S.C. § 522(b)(3)(C); (n)
	Criminal investigators, highway officers	9-3-620
	Firefighters' death benefits	15-5-209
	Game & fish wardens	9-3-620
	Police officers	15-5-313(c)
	Private or public retirement funds & accounts	1-20-110
	Public employees	9-3-426
personal property	Bedding, furniture, household articles, & food to $2,000 per person in the home	1-20-106(a)(iii)
	Bible, schoolbooks, & pictures	1-20-106(a)(i)
	Burial plot	1-20-106(a)(ii)
	Clothing & wedding rings to $1,000	1-20-105
	Medical savings account contributions	1-20-111
	Motor vehicle to $2,400	1-20-106(a)(iv)
	Prepaid funeral contracts	26-32-102
public benefits	Crime victims' compensation	1-40-113
	General assistance	42-2-113(b)
	Unemployment compensation	27-3-319
	Workers' compensation	27-14-702
tools of trade	Library & implements of profession to $2,000 or tools, motor vehicle, implements, team & stock in trade to $2,000	1-20-106(b)
wages	Earnings of National Guard members	19-9-401
	Minimum 75% of disposable weekly earnings or 30 times the federal hourly minimum wage, whichever is more	1-15-511
	Wages of inmates in adult community corrections program	7-18-114
	Wages of inmates in correctional industries program	25-13-107
	Wages of inmates on work release	7-16-308
wildcard	None	

Federal Bankruptcy Exemptions

Married couples filing jointly may double all exemptions. All references are to 11 U.S.C. § 522. These exemptions were last adjusted in 2007. Every three years ending on April 1, these amounts will be adjusted to reflect changes in the Consumer Price Index. Debtors in the following states may select the federal bankruptcy exemptions:

Arkansas	Massachusetts	New Jersey	Texas
Connecticut	Michigan	New Mexico	Vermont
District of Columbia	Minnesota	Pennsylvania	Washington
Hawaii	New Hampshire	Rhode Island	Wisconsin
Kentucky			

ASSET	EXEMPTION	SUBSECTION
homestead	Real property, including co-op or mobile home, or burial plot to $20,200; unused portion of homestead to $10,125 may be applied to any property	(d)(1); (d)(5)
insurance	Disability, illness, or unemployment benefits	(d)(10)(C)
	Life insurance payments from policy for person you depended on, needed for support	(d)(11)(C)
	Life insurance policy with loan value, in accrued dividends or interest, to $10,775	(d)(8)
	Unmatured life insurance contract, except credit insurance policy	(d)(7)
miscellaneous	Alimony, child support needed for support	(d)(10)(D)
pensions	Tax exempt retirement accounts (including 401(k)s, 403(b)s, profit-sharing and money purchase plans, SEP and SIMPLE IRAs, and defined-benefit plans	(b)(3)(C)
	IRAs and Roth IRAs to $1,095,000 per person	(b)(3)(C)(n)
personal property	Animals, crops, clothing, appliances, books, furnishings, household goods, musical instruments to $525 per item, $10,775 total	(d)(3)
	Health aids	(d)(9)
	Jewelry to $1,350	(d)(4)
	Lost earnings payments	(d)(11)(E)
	Motor vehicle to $3,225	(d)(2)
	Personal injury recoveries to $20,200 (not to include pain & suffering or pecuniary loss)	(d)(11)(D)
	Wrongful death recoveries for person you depended on	(d)(11)(B)
public benefits	Crime victims' compensation	(d)(11)(A)
	Public assistance	(d)(10)(A)
	Social Security	(d)(10)(A)
	Unemployment compensation	(d)(10)(A)
	Veterans' benefits	(d)(10)(A)
tools of trade	Implements, books, & tools of trade to $2,025	(d)(6)
wages	None	
wildcard	$1,075 of any property	(d)(5)
	Up to $10,125 of unused homestead exemption amount, for any property	(d)(5)

Federal Nonbankruptcy Exemptions

These exemptions are available only if you select your state exemptions. You may use them for any exemptions in addition to those allowed by your state, but they cannot be claimed if you file using federal bankruptcy exemptions. All law references are to the United States Code.

ASSET	EXEMPTION	LAW
death & disability benefits	Government employees	5 § 8130
	Longshoremen & harbor workers	33 § 916
	War risk, hazard, death, or injury compensation	42 § 1717
retirement	Civil service employees	5 § 8346
	Foreign Service employees	22 § 4060
	Military Medal of Honor roll pensions	38 § 1562(c)
	Military service employees	10 § 1440
	Railroad workers	45 § 231m
	Social Security	42 § 407
	Veterans' benefits	38 § 5301
survivor's benefits	Judges, U.S. court & judicial center directors, administrative assistants to U.S. Supreme Court Chief Justice	28 § 376
	Lighthouse workers	33 § 775
	Military service	10 § 1450
miscellaneous	Indian lands or homestead sales or lease proceeds	25 § 410
	Klamath Indian tribe benefits for Indians residing in Oregon	25 §§ 543; 545
	Military deposits in savings accounts while on permanent duty outside U.S.	10 § 1035
	Military group life insurance	38 § 1970(g)
	Railroad workers' unemployment insurance	45 § 352(e)
	Seamen's clothing	46 § 11110
	Seamen's wages (while on a voyage) pursuant to a written contract	46 § 11109
	Minimum 75% of disposable weekly earnings or 30 times the federal minimum hourly wage, whichever is more; bankruptcy judge may authorize more for low-income debtors	15 § 1673

APPENDIX

B

Worksheets and Charts

Personal Property Checklist

Property Exemption Worksheet

Homeowners' Worksheet

Judicial Lien Worksheet

Bankruptcy Forms Checklist

Bankruptcy Documents Checklist

Median Family Income Chart

Personal Property Checklist

Cash on hand (include sources)

- ☐ In your home
- ☐ In your wallet
- ☐ Under your mattress

Deposits of money (include sources)

- ☐ Bank account
- ☐ Brokerage account (with stockbroker)
- ☐ Certificates of deposit (CDs)
- ☐ Credit union deposit
- ☐ Escrow account
- ☐ Money market account
- ☐ Money in a safe deposit box
- ☐ Savings and loan deposit

Security deposits

- ☐ Electric
- ☐ Gas
- ☐ Heating oil
- ☐ Security deposit on a rental unit
- ☐ Prepaid rent
- ☐ Rented furniture or equipment
- ☐ Telephone
- ☐ Water

Household goods, supplies, and furnishings

- ☐ Antiques
- ☐ Appliances
- ☐ Carpentry tools
- ☐ China and crystal
- ☐ Clocks
- ☐ Dishes
- ☐ Food (total value)
- ☐ Furniture (list every item; go from room to room so you don't miss anything)
- ☐ Gardening tools
- ☐ Home computer (for personal use)
- ☐ Iron and ironing board
- ☐ Lamps
- ☐ Lawn mower or tractor
- ☐ Microwave oven
- ☐ Patio or outdoor furniture
- ☐ Radios
- ☐ Rugs
- ☐ Sewing machine
- ☐ Silverware and utensils
- ☐ Small appliances
- ☐ Snow blower
- ☐ Stereo system
- ☐ Telephone and answering machines
- ☐ Televisions
- ☐ Vacuum cleaner
- ☐ Video equipment (VCR, camcorder)

Books, pictures, and other art objects; stamp, coin, and other collections

- ☐ Art prints
- ☐ Bibles
- ☐ Books
- ☐ Coins
- ☐ Collectibles (such as political buttons, baseball cards)
- ☐ Family portraits
- ☐ Figurines
- ☐ Original artworks
- ☐ Photographs
- ☐ Records, CDs, audiotapes
- ☐ Stamps
- ☐ Videotapes

Apparel

- ☐ Clothing
- ☐ Furs

Jewelry

- ☐ Engagement and wedding rings
- ☐ Gems
- ☐ Precious metals
- ☐ Watches

Firearms, sports equipment, and other hobby equipment

- ☐ Board games
- ☐ Bicycle
- ☐ Camera equipment
- ☐ Electronic musical equipment
- ☐ Exercise machine
- ☐ Fishing gear
- ☐ Guns (rifles, pistols, shotguns, muskets)
- ☐ Model or remote-controlled cars or planes
- ☐ Musical instruments
- ☐ Scuba diving equipment
- ☐ Ski equipment
- ☐ Other sports equipment
- ☐ Other weapons (swords and knives)

Interests in insurance policies

- ☐ Credit insurance
- ☐ Disability insurance
- ☐ Health insurance
- ☐ Homeowners' or renters' insurance
- ☐ Term life insurance
- ☐ Whole life insurance

Annuities

Pension or profit-sharing plans

- ☐ IRA
- ☐ Keogh
- ☐ Pension or retirement plan
- ☐ 401(k) plan

Stock and interests in incorporated and unincorporated companies

- ☐ Corporate shares
- ☐ Stock options
- ☐ LLC membership
- ☐ Sole proprietorship business

Interests in partnerships

- ☐ Limited partnership interest
- ☐ General partnership interest

Government and corporate bonds and other investment instruments

- ☐ Corporate bonds
- ☐ Municipal bonds
- ☐ Promissory notes
- ☐ U.S. savings bonds

Accounts receivable

- ☐ Accounts receivable from business
- ☐ Commissions already earned

Family support

- ☐ Alimony (spousal support, maintenance) due under court order
- ☐ Child support payments due under court order
- ☐ Payments due under divorce property settlement

Other debts for which the amount owed you is known and definite

- ☐ Disability benefits due
- ☐ Disability insurance due
- ☐ Judgments obtained against third parties you haven't yet collected
- ☐ Sick pay earned
- ☐ Social Security benefits due
- ☐ Tax refund due under returns already filed
- ☐ Vacation pay earned
- ☐ Wages due
- ☐ Workers' compensation due

Any special powers that you or another person can exercise for your benefit, other than those listed under "real estate"

- ☐ A right to receive, at some future time, cash, stock, or other personal property placed in an irrevocable trust
- ☐ Current payments of interest or principal from a trust
- ☐ General power of appointment over personal property

An interest in property due to another person's death

- ☐ Any interest as the beneficiary of a living trust, if the trustor has died
- ☐ Expected proceeds from a life insurance policy where the insured has died
- ☐ Inheritance from an existing estate in probate (the owner has died and the court is overseeing the distribution of the property), even if the final amount is not yet known

- ☐ Inheritance under a will that is contingent on one or more events occurring, but only if the owner has died

All other contingent claims and claims where the amount owed you is not known, including tax refunds, counterclaims, and rights to setoff claims (claims you think you have against a person, government, or corporation, but you haven't yet sued on)

- ☐ Claims against a corporation, government entity, or individual
- ☐ Potential tax refund on a return that is not yet filed

Patents, copyrights, and other intellectual property

- ☐ Copyrights
- ☐ Patents
- ☐ Trade secrets
- ☐ Trademarks
- ☐ Trade names

Licenses, franchises, and other general intangibles

- ☐ Building permits
- ☐ Business goodwill
- ☐ Cooperative association holdings
- ☐ Exclusive licenses
- ☐ Liquor licenses
- ☐ Nonexclusive licenses
- ☐ Patent licenses
- ☐ Professional licenses
- ☐ Customer lists

Automobiles and other vehicles

- ☐ Car
- ☐ Minibike or motor scooter
- ☐ Mobile or motor home if on wheels
- ☐ Motorcycle
- ☐ Recreational vehicle (RV)
- ☐ Trailer
- ☐ Truck
- ☐ Van

Boats, motors, and accessories

- ☐ Boat (canoe, kayak, rowboat, shell, sailboat, pontoon, yacht)
- ☐ Boat radar, radio, or telephone
- ☐ Outboard motor

Aircraft and accessories

- ☐ Aircraft
- ☐ Aircraft radar, radio, and other accessories

Office equipment, furnishings, and supplies

- ☐ Artwork in your office
- ☐ Computers, software, modems, printers
- ☐ Copier
- ☐ Fax machine
- ☐ Furniture
- ☐ Rugs
- ☐ Supplies
- ☐ Telephones
- ☐ Typewriters

Machinery, fixtures, equipment, and supplies used in business

- ☐ Equipment
- ☐ Fixtures
- ☐ Machinery
- ☐ Supplies
- ☐ Tools of your trade

Business inventory

Livestock, poultry, and other animals

- ☐ Birds
- ☐ Cats
- ☐ Dogs
- ☐ Fish and aquarium equipment
- ☐ Horses
- ☐ Other pets
- ☐ Livestock and poultry

Crops—growing or harvested

Farming equipment and implements

Farm supplies, chemicals, and feed

Other personal property of any kind not already listed

- ☐ Church pew
- ☐ Health aids (such as a wheelchair or crutches)
- ☐ Hot tub or portable spa
- ☐ Season tickets

Property Exemption Worksheet

1 Property	2 Replacement Value	3 Exemption	4 Statute No.
1. Cash on hand			
2. Checking/savings account, certificate of deposit, other bank accounts			
3. Security deposits held by utility companies, landlord			
4. Household goods, furniture, audio, video, and computer equipment			

Property 1	2 Replacement Value	3 Exemption	4 Statute No.

5. Books, pictures, art objects, records, compact discs, collectibles

6. Clothing

7. Furs and jewelry

8. Sports, photographic, and hobby equipment; firearms

1 Property	2 Replacement Value	3 Exemption	4 Statute No.

9. Interest in insurance policies—specify refund or cancellation value

10. Annuities

11. Interests in education savings plans

12. Interests in pension or profit-sharing plans

13. Stock and interests in incorporated/unincorporated business

14. Interests in partnerships/joint ventures

1 Property	2 Replacement Value	3 Exemption	4 Statute No.
15. Bonds			
16. Accounts receivable			
17. Alimony/family support to which you are entitled			
18. Other liquidated debts owed to you, including tax refunds			
19. Equitable or future interests or life estates			

1 Property	2 Replacement Value	3 Exemption	4 Statute No.
20. Interests in estate of decedent or life insurance plan or trust			
21. Other contingent/unliquidated claims, including tax refunds, counterclaims			
22. Patents, copyrights, other intellectual property			
23. Licenses, franchises			
24. Customer lists			
25. Automobiles, trucks, trailers, and accessories			
26. Boats, motors, accessories			
27. Aircraft, accessories			

1 Property	2 Replacement Value	3 Exemption	4 Statute No.
28. Office equipment, supplies			
29. Machinery, fixtures, etc., for business			
30. Inventory			

1 Property	2 Replacement Value	3 Exemption	4 Statute No.
31. Animals			
32. Crops—growing or harvested			
33. Farming equipment, implements			
34. Farm supplies, chemicals, feed			

1 Property	2 Replacement Value	3 Exemption	4 Statute No.

35. Other personal property of any kind not listed

Homeowners' Worksheet

Part I. Do you have any equity in your home?

1. Market value of your home .... $________________
2. Costs of sale (if unsure, put 5% of market value) .... $________________
3. Amount owed on all mortgages .... $________________
4. Amount of all liens on the property .... $________________
5. Total of Lines 2, 3, and 4 .... $________________
6. Your equity (Line 1 minus Line 5) .... $________________

   If Line 6 is less than zero, skip the rest of the worksheet. The trustee will have no interest in selling your home.

Part II. Is your property protected by an exemption?

7. Does the available homestead exemption protect your kind of dwelling?

   ☐ Yes. *Go on to Line 8.*

   ☐ No. *Enter $0 on Line 11, then continue on to Line 12.*

8. Do you have to file a "declaration of homestead" to claim the homestead exemption?

   ☐ Yes, but I have not filed it yet. *(You should. See instructions.)*

   ☐ Yes, and I have already filed it.

   ☐ No.

9. Is the homestead exemption based on lot size?

   ☐ No, it is based on equity alone. *Go to Line 10.*

   ☐ No, it is unlimited (true only of the exemptions for Washington, DC).

   If you are using the D.C. exemptions, you can stop here. Your home is protected.

   ☐ Yes. The exemption is limited to property of ____________ acres.

   If your property is smaller than this limit, you can stop here. Your home is protected. If your property exceeds this limit, see the instructions.

   ☐ Yes, but there is an equity limit as well. The exemption is limited to property of ____________ acres.

   If your property is smaller than this limit, go on to Line 10. If your property exceeds this limit, see the instructions.

10. Do you own the property with your spouse in "tenancy by the entirety"?

    ☐ Yes. *See the instructions and talk to a bankruptcy attorney to find out whether your house is fully protected.*

    ☐ No. *Go on to Line 11.*

11. Is the dollar amount of the homestead exemption limited?

 ☐ Yes. *Enter the dollar limit here:* $ ____________

 ☐ No dollar limit. *You can stop here. Your home is protected.*

12. Can you protect more equity with a wildcard exemption?

 ☐ Yes. *Enter the dollar amount here:* $ ____________

 ☐ No.

13. How much of your equity is protected?

 Total of Lines 11 and 12: $ ____________

 If the total exceeds $136,875 and you are subject to the cap on homestead exemptions, write "$136,875" on this line. See the instructions for more information.

14. Is your home fully protected?

 Subtract Line 13 from Line 6: $ ____________

 If this total is a negative number, your home is protected. If this total is a positive number, you have unprotected equity in your home, and the trustee might choose to sell it (or allow you to keep it in exchange for cash or exempt property roughly equal in value to your unprotected equity).

Judicial Lien Worksheet

1. Value of your home .... $ ________
2. Amount of first mortgage .... $ ________
3. Amount of other mortgages and home equity loans .... $ ________
4. Amount of tax liens .... $ ________
5. Amount of mechanics' liens .... $ ________
6. Total of Lines 2 through 5 .... $ ________
   (Total of all liens that are not judicial liens)

   If Line 6 is greater than Line 1, you can stop here—you can eliminate all judicial liens. Otherwise, go on to Line 7.
7. Line 1 minus Line 6 .... $ ________
   This is the amount of equity you can protect with an exemption.
8. Exemption amount .... $ ________

   If Line 8 is greater than Line 7 you can stop here—you can eliminate all judicial liens. Otherwise, go on to Line 9.
9. Line 7 minus Line 8 .... $ ________
   This is the amount of the judicial liens that you can't eliminate.
10. Amount of judicial liens .... $ ________

    If Line 9 is greater than Line 10, you can stop here—you cannot eliminate judicial liens from this property. Otherwise, go on to Line 11.
11. Line 10 minus Line 9 .... $ ________
    This is the portion of the judicial lien that you can eliminate.
    (Line 9 is the portion of judicial lien you cannot eliminate.)

Bankruptcy Forms Checklist

- ☐ Form 1—Voluntary Petition
- ☐ Form 3A (only if you are paying your filing fee in installments)
- ☐ Form 6, which consists of:
  - ☐ Schedule A—Real Property
  - ☐ Schedule B—Personal Property
  - ☐ Schedule C—Property Claimed as Exempt
  - ☐ Schedule D—Creditors Holding Secured Claims
  - ☐ Schedule E—Creditors Holding Unsecured Priority Claims
  - ☐ Schedule F—Creditors Holding Unsecured Nonpriority Claims
  - ☐ Schedule G—Executory Contracts and Unexpired Leases
  - ☐ Schedule H—Codebtors
  - ☐ Schedule I—Current Income of Individual Debtor(s)
  - ☐ Schedule J—Current Expenditures of Individual Debtor(s)
  - ☐ Summary of Schedules A through J
  - ☐ Declaration Concerning Debtor's Schedules
- ☐ Form 7—Statement of Financial Affairs
- ☐ Form 21—Statement of Social Security Number(s)
- ☐ Form 22C—Statement of Current Monthly Income and Disposable Income Calculation
- ☐ Form 201—Notice to Consumer Debtors Under § 342(b) of the Bankruptcy Code
- ☐ Mailing Matrix

Bankruptcy Documents Checklist

- ☐ Your Chapter 13 repayment plan
- ☐ Required local forms, if any
- ☐ Your most recent federal tax return (or a transcript of the return obtained from the IRS)
- ☐ Proof that you've filed your tax returns for the last four years with the IRS
- ☐ Your credit counseling certificate
- ☐ Any repayment plan that was developed during your credit counseling session
- ☐ Your pay stubs for the previous 60 days (along with any accompanying form your local court requires)

Median Family Income Chart

State	Family Size: 1 Earner	2 People	3 People	4 People *	State	Family Size: 1 Earner	2 People	3 People	4 People *
Alabama	$38,415	$48,075	$55,631	$65,311	**Montana**	$40,122	$52,497	$58,636	$65,827
Alaska	$52,130	$74,073	$77,544	$85,422	**Nebraska**	$40,352	$56,861	$63,702	$72,542
Arizona	$42,628	$56,894	$62,066	$69,452	**Nevada**	$46,316	$60,449	$67,052	$71,104
Arkansas	$33,531	$44,415	$48,721	$57,905	**New Hampshire**	$51,515	$64,204	$79,668	$93,926
California	$48,140	$64,878	$70,890	$79,477	**New Jersey**	$60,026	$72,000	$86,070	$103,261
Colorado	$47,253	$64,985	$69,977	$81,644	**New Mexico**	$36,773	$50,637	$50,637	$55,561
Connecticut	$58,529	$72,586	$86,643	$102,124	**New York**	$46,485	$58,109	$69,421	$82,457
Delaware	$46,414	$60,953	$70,075	$88,725	**North Carolina**	$38,794	$52,194	$56,930	$67,295
DC	$42,270	$68,892	$69,294	$69,294	**North Dakota**	$36,884	$54,662	$62,635	$75,140
Florida	$41,226	$52,259	$58,574	$69,009	**Ohio**	$41,873	$52,216	$61,772	$73,301
Georgia	$40,691	$55,258	$61,104	$68,502	**Oklahoma**	$39,068	$50,891	$54,522	$62,037
Hawaii	$55,418	$67,199	$77,539	$91,483	**Oregon**	$42,495	$56,019	$62,832	$72,667
Idaho	$39,625	$51,474	$52,765	$62,051	**Pennsylvania**	$44,555	$53,763	$67,757	$77,867
Illinois	$46,105	$60,052	$71,329	$81,465	**Rhode Island**	$45,222	$62,806	$76,846	$87,002
Indiana	$40,828	$52,554	$59,650	$70,873	**South Carolina**	$39,191	$51,374	$55,296	$65,655
Iowa	$40,061	$55,284	$64,372	$72,961	**South Dakota**	$36,844	$54,331	$63,153	$70,182
Kansas	$41,357	$57,767	$63,438	$72,610	**Tennessee**	$37,732	$49,110	$54,014	$64,228
Kentucky	$37,584	$45,653	$54,683	$64,459	**Texas**	$38,940	$55,859	$59,222	$66,381
Louisiana	$37,464	$48,287	$53,461	$66,256	**Utah**	$50,568	$56,932	$61,905	$69,990
Maine	$38,812	$50,912	$62,076	$70,374	**Vermont**	$41,742	$56,858	$65,326	$74,163
Maryland	$55,238	$73,061	$85,455	$101,803	**Virginia**	$48,362	$65,122	$74,151	$85,939
Massachusetts	$53,505	$69,451	$82,591	$99,648	**Washington**	$51,344	$64,158	$72,533	$82,716
Michigan	$43,611	$52,620	$61,737	$74,824	**West Virginia**	$39,275	$43,224	$51,836	$58,479
Minnesota	$45,262	$62,384	$75,073	$86,637	**Wisconsin**	$42,356	$57,405	$68,123	$80,530
Mississippi	$32,068	$42,758	$46,685	$58,518	**Wyoming**	$44,161	$59,830	$65,820	$76,964
Missouri	$39,645	$51,568	$60,371	$71,059	* Add $6,900 for each individual in excess of 4.				

APPENDIX C

Tear-Out Forms

Form 1—Voluntary Petition

Exhibit C to Voluntary Petition

Exhibit D to Voluntary Petition

Schedule A—Real Property

Schedule B—Personal Property

Schedule C—Property Claimed as Exempt

Schedule D—Creditors Holding Secured Claims

Schedule E—Creditors Holding Unsecured Priority Claims

Schedule F—Creditors Holding Unsecured Nonpriority Claims

Schedule G—Executory Contracts and Unexpired Leases

Schedule H—Codebtors

Schedule I—Current Income of Individual Debtors(s)

Schedule J—Current Expenditures of Individual Debtor(s)

Declaration Concerning Debtor's Schedules

Summary of Schedules and Statistical Summary of Certain Liabilities

Form 3A—Application to Pay Filing Fee in Installments and Order Approving Payment of Filing Fee in Installments

Form 3B—Application for Waiver of the Chapter 7 Filing Fee and Order on Debtor's Application of Waiver

Form 7—Statement of Financial Affairs

Form 8—Chapter 7 Individual Debtor's Statement of Intention

Form 16A—Caption

Form 20A—Notice of Motion or Objection

Form 21—Statement of Social Security Number(s)

Form 22A—Chapter 7 Statement of Current Monthly Income and Means-Test Calculation

Form 23—Debtor's Certification of Completion of Postpetition Instructional Course Concerning Personal Financial Management

Form 27—Reaffirmation Agreement Cover Sheet

Form 201—Notice to Consumer Debtors Under § 342(b) of the Bankruptcy Code

Form 240A—Reaffirmation Agreement

Form 240B—Motion for Approval of Reaffirmation Agreement

Form 240C—Order on Reaffirmation Agreement

Mailing Matrix

United States Bankruptcy Court

Voluntary Petition

Name of Debtor (if individual, enter Last, First, Middle):	Name of Joint Debtor (Spouse) (Last, First, Middle):
All Other Names used by the Debtor in the last 8 years (include married, maiden, and trade names):	All Other Names used by the Joint Debtor in the last 8 years (include married, maiden, and trade names):
Last four digits of Soc. Sec. or Indvidual-Taxpayer I.D. (ITIN) No./Complete EIN (if more than one, state all):	Last four digits of Soc. Sec. or Indvidual-Taxpayer I.D. (ITIN) No./Complete EIN (if more than one, state all):
Street Address of Debtor (No. and Street, City, and State): ZIP CODE	Street Address of Joint Debtor (No. and Street, City, and State): ZIP CODE
County of Residence or of the Principal Place of Business:	County of Residence or of the Principal Place of Business:
Mailing Address of Debtor (if different from street address): ZIP CODE	Mailing Address of Joint Debtor (if different from street address): ZIP CODE

Location of Principal Assets of Business Debtor (if different from street address above):

ZIP CODE

Type of Debtor
(Form of Organization)
(Check **one** box.)

- ☐ Individual (includes Joint Debtors) *See Exhibit D on page 2 of this form.*
- ☐ Corporation (includes LLC and LLP)
- ☐ Partnership
- ☐ Other (If debtor is not one of the above entities, check this box and state type of entity below.)

____

Nature of Business
(Check **one** box.)

- ☐ Health Care Business
- ☐ Single Asset Real Estate as defined in 11 U.S.C. § 101(51B)
- ☐ Railroad
- ☐ Stockbroker
- ☐ Commodity Broker
- ☐ Clearing Bank
- ☐ Other

Tax-Exempt Entity
(Check box, if applicable.)

- ☐ Debtor is a tax-exempt organization under Title 26 of the United States Code (the Internal Revenue Code).

Chapter of Bankruptcy Code Under Which the Petition is Filed (Check **one** box.)

- ☐ Chapter 7
- ☐ Chapter 9
- ☐ Chapter 11
- ☐ Chapter 12
- ☐ Chapter 13
- ☐ Chapter 15 Petition for Recognition of a Foreign Main Proceeding
- ☐ Chapter 15 Petition for Recognition of a Foreign Nonmain Proceeding

Nature of Debts
(Check one box.)

- ☐ Debts are primarily consumer debts, defined in 11 U.S.C. § 101(8) as "incurred by an individual primarily for a personal, family, or house-hold purpose."
- ☐ Debts are primarily business debts.

Filing Fee (Check one box.)

- ☐ Full Filing Fee attached.
- ☐ Filing Fee to be paid in installments (applicable to individuals only). Must attach signed application for the court's consideration certifying that the debtor is unable to pay fee except in installments. Rule 1006(b). See Official Form 3A.
- ☐ Filing Fee waiver requested (applicable to chapter 7 individuals only). Must attach signed application for the court's consideration. See Official Form 3B.

Chapter 11 Debtors

Check one box:

- ☐ Debtor is a small business debtor as defined in 11 U.S.C. § 101(51D).
- ☐ Debtor is not a small business debtor as defined in 11 U.S.C. § 101(51D).

Check if:

- ☐ Debtor's aggregate noncontingent liquidated debts (excluding debts owed to insiders or affiliates) are less than $2,190,000.

- -

Check all applicable boxes:

- ☐ A plan is being filed with this petition.
- ☐ Acceptances of the plan were solicited prepetition from one or more classes of creditors, in accordance with 11 U.S.C. § 1126(b).

Statistical/Administrative Information

THIS SPACE IS FOR COURT USE ONLY

- ☐ Debtor estimates that funds will be available for distribution to unsecured creditors.
- ☐ Debtor estimates that, after any exempt property is excluded and administrative expenses paid, there will be no funds available for distribution to unsecured creditors.

Estimated Number of Creditors

☐	☐	☐	☐	☐	☐	☐	☐	☐	☐
1-49	50-99	100-199	200-999	1,000-5,000	5,001-10,000	10,001-25,000	25,001-50,000	50,001-100,000	Over 100,000

Estimated Assets

☐	☐	☐	☐	☐	☐	☐	☐	☐	☐
$0 to $50,000	$50,001 to $100,000	$100,001 to $500,000	$500,001 to $1 million	$1,000,001 to $10 million	$10,000,001 to $50 million	$50,000,001 to $100 million	$100,000,001 to $500 million	$500,000,001 to $1 billion	More than $1 billion

Estimated Liabilities

☐	☐	☐	☐	☐	☐	☐	☐	☐	☐
$0 to $50,000	$50,001 to $100,000	$100,001 to $500,000	$500,001 to $1 million	$1,000,001 to $10 million	$10,000,001 to $50 million	$50,000,001 to $100 million	$100,000,001 to $500 million	$500,000,001 to $1 billion	More than $1 billion

Voluntary Petition *(This page must be completed and filed in every case.)*	Name of Debtor(s):	
All Prior Bankruptcy Cases Filed Within Last 8 Years (If more than two, attach additional sheet.)		
Location Where Filed:	Case Number:	Date Filed:
Location Where Filed:	Case Number:	Date Filed:
Pending Bankruptcy Case Filed by any Spouse, Partner, or Affiliate of this Debtor (If more than one, attach additional sheet.)		
Name of Debtor:	Case Number:	Date Filed:
District:	Relationship:	Judge:

Exhibit A

(To be completed if debtor is required to file periodic reports (e.g., forms 10K and 10Q) with the Securities and Exchange Commission pursuant to Section 13 or 15(d) of the Securities Exchange Act of 1934 and is requesting relief under chapter 11.)

☐ Exhibit A is attached and made a part of this petition.

Exhibit B

(To be completed if debtor is an individual whose debts are primarily consumer debts.)

I, the attorney for the petitioner named in the foregoing petition, declare that I have informed the petitioner that [he or she] may proceed under chapter 7, 11, 12, or 13 of title 11, United States Code, and have explained the relief available under each such chapter. I further certify that I have delivered to the debtor the notice required by 11 U.S.C. § 342(b).

X ______________________________

Signature of Attorney for Debtor(s) (Date)

Exhibit C

Does the debtor own or have possession of any property that poses or is alleged to pose a threat of imminent and identifiable harm to public health or safety?

☐ Yes, and Exhibit C is attached and made a part of this petition.

☐ No.

Exhibit D

(To be completed by every individual debtor. If a joint petition is filed, each spouse must complete and attach a separate Exhibit D.)

☐ Exhibit D completed and signed by the debtor is attached and made a part of this petition.

If this is a joint petition:

☐ Exhibit D also completed and signed by the joint debtor is attached and made a part of this petition.

Information Regarding the Debtor - Venue

(Check any applicable box.)

☐ Debtor has been domiciled or has had a residence, principal place of business, or principal assets in this District for 180 days immediately preceding the date of this petition or for a longer part of such 180 days than in any other District.

☐ There is a bankruptcy case concerning debtor's affiliate, general partner, or partnership pending in this District.

☐ Debtor is a debtor in a foreign proceeding and has its principal place of business or principal assets in the United States in this District, or has no principal place of business or assets in the United States but is a defendant in an action or proceeding [in a federal or state court] in this District, or the interests of the parties will be served in regard to the relief sought in this District.

Certification by a Debtor Who Resides as a Tenant of Residential Property

(Check all applicable boxes.)

☐ Landlord has a judgment against the debtor for possession of debtor's residence. (If box checked, complete the following.)

____

(Name of landlord that obtained judgment)

____

(Address of landlord)

☐ Debtor claims that under applicable nonbankruptcy law, there are circumstances under which the debtor would be permitted to cure the entire monetary default that gave rise to the judgment for possession, after the judgment for possession was entered, and

☐ Debtor has included with this petition the deposit with the court of any rent that would become due during the 30-day period after the filing of the petition.

☐ Debtor certifies that he/she has served the Landlord with this certification. (11 U.S.C. § 362(l)).

Voluntary Petition
(This page must be completed and filed in every case.)

Name of Debtor(s):

Signatures

Signature(s) of Debtor(s) (Individual/Joint)

I declare under penalty of perjury that the information provided in this petition is true and correct.
[If petitioner is an individual whose debts are primarily consumer debts and has chosen to file under chapter 7] I am aware that I may proceed under chapter 7, 11, 12 or 13 of title 11, United States Code, understand the relief available under each such chapter, and choose to proceed under chapter 7.
[If no attorney represents me and no bankruptcy petition preparer signs the petition] I have obtained and read the notice required by 11 U.S.C. § 342(b).

I request relief in accordance with the chapter of title 11, United States Code, specified in this petition.

X ______________________________
Signature of Debtor

X ______________________________
Signature of Joint Debtor

____
Telephone Number (if not represented by attorney)

____
Date

Signature of a Foreign Representative

I declare under penalty of perjury that the information provided in this petition is true and correct, that I am the foreign representative of a debtor in a foreign proceeding, and that I am authorized to file this petition.

(Check only **one** box.)

☐ I request relief in accordance with chapter 15 of title 11, United States Code. Certified copies of the documents required by 11 U.S.C. § 1515 are attached.

☐ Pursuant to 11 U.S.C. § 1511, I request relief in accordance with the chapter of title 11 specified in this petition. A certified copy of the order granting recognition of the foreign main proceeding is attached.

X ______________________________
(Signature of Foreign Representative)

____
(Printed Name of Foreign Representative)

____
Date

Signature of Attorney*

X ______________________________
Signature of Attorney for Debtor(s)

____
Printed Name of Attorney for Debtor(s)

____
Firm Name

____
Address

____

____

____
Telephone Number

____
Date

*In a case in which § 707(b)(4)(D) applies, this signature also constitutes a certification that the attorney has no knowledge after an inquiry that the information in the schedules is incorrect.

Signature of Debtor (Corporation/Partnership)

I declare under penalty of perjury that the information provided in this petition is true and correct, and that I have been authorized to file this petition on behalf of the debtor.

The debtor requests the relief in accordance with the chapter of title 11, United States Code, specified in this petition.

X ______________________________
Signature of Authorized Individual

____
Printed Name of Authorized Individual

____
Title of Authorized Individual

____
Date

Signature of Non-Attorney Bankruptcy Petition Preparer

I declare under penalty of perjury that: (1) I am a bankruptcy petition preparer as defined in 11 U.S.C. § 110; (2) I prepared this document for compensation and have provided the debtor with a copy of this document and the notices and information required under 11 U.S.C. §§ 110(b), 110(h), and 342(b); and, (3) if rules or guidelines have been promulgated pursuant to 11 U.S.C. § 110(h) setting a maximum fee for services chargeable by bankruptcy petition preparers, I have given the debtor notice of the maximum amount before preparing any document for filing for a debtor or accepting any fee from the debtor, as required in that section. Official Form 19 is attached.

____
Printed Name and title, if any, of Bankruptcy Petition Preparer

____
Social-Security number (If the bankruptcy petition preparer is not an individual, state the Social-Security number of the officer, principal, responsible person or partner of the bankruptcy petition preparer.) (Required by 11 U.S.C. § 110.)

____
Address

____

X ______________________________

____
Date

Signature of bankruptcy petition preparer or officer, principal, responsible person, or partner whose Social-Security number is provided above.

Names and Social-Security numbers of all other individuals who prepared or assisted in preparing this document unless the bankruptcy petition preparer is not an individual.

If more than one person prepared this document, attach additional sheets conforming to the appropriate official form for each person.

A bankruptcy petition preparer's failure to comply with the provisions of title 11 and the Federal Rules of Bankruptcy Procedure may result in fines or imprisonment or both. 11 U.S.C. § 110; 18 U.S.C. § 156.

Exhibit "C"

[If, to the best of the debtor's knowledge, the debtor owns or has possession of property that poses or is alleged to pose a threat of imminent and identifiable harm to the public health or safety, attach this Exhibit "C" to the petition.]

[Caption as in Form 16B]

Exhibit "C" to Voluntary Petition

1. Identify and briefly describe all real or personal property owned by or in possession of the debtor that, to the best of the debtor's knowledge, poses or is alleged to pose a threat of imminent and identifiable harm to the public health or safety (attach additional sheets if necessary):

....

....

....

....

2. With respect to each parcel of real property or item of personal property identified in question 1, describe the nature and location of the dangerous condition, whether environmental or otherwise, that poses or is alleged to pose a threat of imminent and identifiable harm to the public health or safety (attach additional sheets if necessary):

....

....

....

....

United States Bankruptcy Court

In re____________________________ Case No.____________

Debtor (if known)

EXHIBIT D - INDIVIDUAL DEBTOR'S STATEMENT OF COMPLIANCE WITH CREDIT COUNSELING REQUIREMENT

Warning: You must be able to check truthfully one of the five statements regarding credit counseling listed below. If you cannot do so, you are not eligible to file a bankruptcy case, and the court can dismiss any case you do file. If that happens, you will lose whatever filing fee you paid, and your creditors will be able to resume collection activities against you. If your case is dismissed and you file another bankruptcy case later, you may be required to pay a second filing fee and you may have to take extra steps to stop creditors' collection activities.

Every individual debtor must file this Exhibit D. If a joint petition is filed, each spouse must complete and file a separate Exhibit D. Check one of the five statements below and attach any documents as directed.

❒ 1. Within the 180 days **before the filing of my bankruptcy case**, I received a briefing from a credit counseling agency approved by the United States trustee or bankruptcy administrator that outlined the opportunities for available credit counseling and assisted me in performing a related budget analysis, and I have a certificate from the agency describing the services provided to me. *Attach a copy of the certificate and a copy of any debt repayment plan developed through the agency.*

❒ 2. Within the 180 days **before the filing of my bankruptcy case**, I received a briefing from a credit counseling agency approved by the United States trustee or bankruptcy administrator that outlined the opportunities for available credit counseling and assisted me in performing a related budget analysis, but I do not have a certificate from the agency describing the services provided to me. *You must file a copy of a certificate from the agency describing the services provided to you and a copy of any debt repayment plan developed through the agency no later than 14 days after your bankruptcy case is filed.*

❒ 3. I certify that I requested credit counseling services from an approved agency but was unable to obtain the services during the seven days from the time I made my request, and the following exigent circumstances merit a temporary waiver of the credit counseling requirement so I can file my bankruptcy case now. *[Summarize exigent circumstances here.]*

If your certification is satisfactory to the court, you must still obtain the credit counseling briefing within the first 30 days after you file your bankruptcy petition and promptly file a certificate from the agency that provided the counseling, together with a copy of any debt management plan developed through the agency. Failure to fulfill these requirements may result in dismissal of your case. Any extension of the 30-day deadline can be granted only for cause and is limited to a maximum of 15 days. Your case may also be dismissed if the court is not satisfied with your reasons for filing your bankruptcy case without first receiving a credit counseling briefing.

❒ 4. I am not required to receive a credit counseling briefing because of: *[Check the applicable statement.]* *[Must be accompanied by a motion for determination by the court.]*

❒ Incapacity. (Defined in 11 U.S.C. § 109(h)(4) as impaired by reason of mental illness or mental deficiency so as to be incapable of realizing and making rational decisions with respect to financial responsibilities.);

❒ Disability. (Defined in 11 U.S.C. § 109(h)(4) as physically impaired to the extent of being unable, after reasonable effort, to participate in a credit counseling briefing in person, by telephone, or through the Internet.);

❒ Active military duty in a military combat zone.

❒ 5. The United States trustee or bankruptcy administrator has determined that the credit counseling requirement of 11 U.S.C. § 109(h) does not apply in this district.

I certify under penalty of perjury that the information provided above is true and correct.

Signature of Debtor: ______________________

Date: ________________

In re ____, **Case No.** ______________________________
Debtor **(If known)**

SCHEDULE A - REAL PROPERTY

Except as directed below, list all real property in which the debtor has any legal, equitable, or future interest, including all property owned as a co-tenant, community property, or in which the debtor has a life estate. Include any property in which the debtor holds rights and powers exercisable for the debtor's own benefit. If the debtor is married, state whether the husband, wife, both, or the marital community own the property by placing an "H," "W," "J," or "C" in the column labeled "Husband, Wife, Joint, or Community." If the debtor holds no interest in real property, write "None" under "Description and Location of Property."

Do not include interests in executory contracts and unexpired leases on this schedule. List them in Schedule G - Executory Contracts and Unexpired Leases.

If an entity claims to have a lien or hold a secured interest in any property, state the amount of the secured claim. See Schedule D. If no entity claims to hold a secured interest in the property, write "None" in the column labeled "Amount of Secured Claim."

If the debtor is an individual or if a joint petition is filed, state the amount of any exemption claimed in the property only in Schedule C - Property Claimed as Exempt.

DESCRIPTION AND LOCATION OF PROPERTY	NATURE OF DEBTOR'S INTEREST IN PROPERTY	HUSBAND, WIFE, JOINT OR COMMUNITY	CURRENT VALUE OF DEBTOR'S INTEREST IN PROPERTY, WITHOUT DEDUCTING ANY SECURED CLAIM OR EXEMPTION	AMOUNT OF SECURED CLAIM
		Total➤		

(Report also on Summary of Schedules.)

B 6B (Official Form 6B) (12/07)

In re ______________________________, Case No. ______________________
Debtor (If known)

SCHEDULE B - PERSONAL PROPERTY

Except as directed below, list all personal property of the debtor of whatever kind. If the debtor has no property in one or more of the categories, place an "x" in the appropriate position in the column labeled "None." If additional space is needed in any category, attach a separate sheet properly identified with the case name, case number, and the number of the category. If the debtor is married, state whether the husband, wife, both, or the marital community own the property by placing an "H," "W," "J," or "C" in the column labeled "Husband, Wife, Joint, or Community." If the debtor is an individual or a joint petition is filed, state the amount of any exemptions claimed only in Schedule C - Property Claimed as Exempt.

Do not list interests in executory contracts and unexpired leases on this schedule. List them in Schedule G - Executory Contracts and Unexpired Leases.

If the property is being held for the debtor by someone else, state that person's name and address under "Description and Location of Property." If the property is being held for a minor child, simply state the child's initials and the name and address of the child's parent or guardian, such as "A.B., a minor child, by John Doe, guardian." Do not disclose the child's name. See, 11 U.S.C. §112 and Fed. R. Bankr. P. 1007(m).

TYPE OF PROPERTY	NONE	DESCRIPTION AND LOCATION OF PROPERTY	HUSBAND, WIFE, JOINT, OR COMMUNITY	CURRENT VALUE OF DEBTOR'S INTEREST IN PROPERTY, WITH-OUT DEDUCTING ANY SECURED CLAIM OR EXEMPTION
1. Cash on hand.				
2. Checking, savings or other financial accounts, certificates of deposit or shares in banks, savings and loan, thrift, building and loan, and homestead associations, or credit unions, brokerage houses, or cooperatives.				
3. Security deposits with public utilities, telephone companies, landlords, and others.				
4. Household goods and furnishings, including audio, video, and computer equipment.				
5. Books; pictures and other art objects; antiques; stamp, coin, record, tape, compact disc, and other collections or collectibles.				
6. Wearing apparel.				
7. Furs and jewelry.				
8. Firearms and sports, photographic, and other hobby equipment.				
9. Interests in insurance policies. Name insurance company of each policy and itemize surrender or refund value of each.				
10. Annuities. Itemize and name each issuer.				
11. Interests in an education IRA as defined in 26 U.S.C. § 530(b)(1) or under a qualified State tuition plan as defined in 26 U.S.C. § 529(b)(1). Give particulars. (File separately the record(s) of any such interest(s). 11 U.S.C. § 521(c).)				

In re ____,
Debtor

Case No. ____________________________
(If known)

SCHEDULE B - PERSONAL PROPERTY
(Continuation Sheet)

TYPE OF PROPERTY	NONE	DESCRIPTION AND LOCATION OF PROPERTY	HUSBAND, WIFE, JOINT, OR COMMUNITY	CURRENT VALUE OF DEBTOR'S INTEREST IN PROPERTY, WITH-OUT DEDUCTING ANY SECURED CLAIM OR EXEMPTION
12. Interests in IRA, ERISA, Keogh, or other pension or profit sharing plans. Give particulars.				
13. Stock and interests in incorporated and unincorporated businesses. Itemize.				
14. Interests in partnerships or joint ventures. Itemize.				
15. Government and corporate bonds and other negotiable and non-negotiable instruments.				
16. Accounts receivable.				
17. Alimony, maintenance, support, and property settlements to which the debtor is or may be entitled. Give particulars.				
18. Other liquidated debts owed to debtor including tax refunds. Give particulars.				
19. Equitable or future interests, life estates, and rights or powers exercisable for the benefit of the debtor other than those listed in Schedule A – Real Property.				
20. Contingent and noncontingent interests in estate of a decedent, death benefit plan, life insurance policy, or trust.				
21. Other contingent and unliquidated claims of every nature, including tax refunds, counterclaims of the debtor, and rights to setoff claims. Give estimated value of each.				

In re ______________________________,
Debtor

Case No. ______________________
(If known)

SCHEDULE B - PERSONAL PROPERTY

(Continuation Sheet)

TYPE OF PROPERTY	NONE	DESCRIPTION AND LOCATION OF PROPERTY	HUSBAND, WIFE, JOINT, OR COMMUNITY	CURRENT VALUE OF DEBTOR'S INTEREST IN PROPERTY, WITHOUT DEDUCTING ANY SECURED CLAIM OR EXEMPTION
22. Patents, copyrights, and other intellectual property. Give particulars.				
23. Licenses, franchises, and other general intangibles. Give particulars.				
24. Customer lists or other compilations containing personally identifiable information (as defined in 11 U.S.C. § 101(41A)) provided to the debtor by individuals in connection with obtaining a product or service from the debtor primarily for personal, family, or household purposes.				
25. Automobiles, trucks, trailers, and other vehicles and accessories.				
26. Boats, motors, and accessories.				
27. Aircraft and accessories.				
28. Office equipment, furnishings, and supplies.				
29. Machinery, fixtures, equipment, and supplies used in business.				
30. Inventory.				
31. Animals.				
32. Crops - growing or harvested. Give particulars.				
33. Farming equipment and implements.				
34. Farm supplies, chemicals, and feed.				
35. Other personal property of any kind not already listed. Itemize.				

__________continuation sheets attached Total➤ $

(Include amounts from any continuation sheets attached. Report total also on Summary of Schedules.)

B 6C (Official Form 6C) (12/07)

In re ____,
Debtor

Case No. ___________________________
(If known)

SCHEDULE C - PROPERTY CLAIMED AS EXEMPT

Debtor claims the exemptions to which debtor is entitled under:
(Check one box)
☐ 11 U.S.C. § 522(b)(2)
☐ 11 U.S.C. § 522(b)(3)

☐ Check if debtor claims a homestead exemption that exceeds $136,875.

DESCRIPTION OF PROPERTY	SPECIFY LAW PROVIDING EACH EXEMPTION	VALUE OF CLAIMED EXEMPTION	CURRENT VALUE OF PROPERTY WITHOUT DEDUCTING EXEMPTION

In re __________________________________, **Case No.** ______________________________
Debtor **(If known)**

SCHEDULE D - CREDITORS HOLDING SECURED CLAIMS

State the name, mailing address, including zip code, and last four digits of any account number of all entities holding claims secured by property of the debtor as of the date of filing of the petition. The complete account number of any account the debtor has with the creditor is useful to the trustee and the creditor and may be provided if the debtor chooses to do so. List creditors holding all types of secured interests such as judgment liens, garnishments, statutory liens, mortgages, deeds of trust, and other security interests.

List creditors in alphabetical order to the extent practicable. If a minor child is the creditor, state the child's initials and the name and address of the child's parent or guardian, such as "A.B., a minor child, by John Doe, guardian." Do not disclose the child's name. See, 11 U.S.C. §112 and Fed. R. Bankr. P. 1007(m). If all secured creditors will not fit on this page, use the continuation sheet provided.

If any entity other than a spouse in a joint case may be jointly liable on a claim, place an "X" in the column labeled "Codebtor," include the entity on the appropriate schedule of creditors, and complete Schedule H – Codebtors. If a joint petition is filed, state whether the husband, wife, both of them, or the marital community may be liable on each claim by placing an "H," "W," "J," or "C" in the column labeled "Husband, Wife, Joint, or Community."

If the claim is contingent, place an "X" in the column labeled "Contingent." If the claim is unliquidated, place an "X" in the column labeled "Unliquidated." If the claim is disputed, place an "X" in the column labeled "Disputed." (You may need to place an "X" in more than one of these three columns.)

Total the columns labeled "Amount of Claim Without Deducting Value of Collateral" and "Unsecured Portion, if Any" in the boxes labeled "Total(s)" on the last sheet of the completed schedule. Report the total from the column labeled "Amount of Claim Without Deducting Value of Collateral" also on the Summary of Schedules and, if the debtor is an individual with primarily consumer debts, report the total from the column labeled "Unsecured Portion, if Any" on the Statistical Summary of Certain Liabilities and Related Data.

☐ Check this box if debtor has no creditors holding secured claims to report on this Schedule D.

CREDITOR'S NAME AND MAILING ADDRESS INCLUDING ZIP CODE AND AN ACCOUNT NUMBER (*See Instructions Above.*)	CODEBTOR	HUSBAND, WIFE, JOINT, OR COMMUNITY	DATE CLAIM WAS INCURRED, NATURE OF LIEN , AND DESCRIPTION AND VALUE OF PROPERTY SUBJECT TO LIEN	CONTINGENT	UNLIQUIDATED	DISPUTED	AMOUNT OF CLAIM WITHOUT DEDUCTING VALUE OF COLLATERAL	UNSECURED PORTION, IF ANY
ACCOUNT NO.			VALUE $					
ACCOUNT NO.			VALUE $					
ACCOUNT NO.			VALUE $					
____ continuation sheets attached			Subtotal ► (Total of this page)				$	$
			Total ► (Use only on last page)				$	$
							(Report also on Summary of Schedules.)	(If applicable, report also on Statistical Summary of Certain Liabilities and Related Data.)

In re ______________________________, **Case No.** ______________________________
Debtor **(if known)**

SCHEDULE D - CREDITORS HOLDING SECURED CLAIMS

(Continuation Sheet)

CREDITOR'S NAME AND MAILING ADDRESS INCLUDING ZIP CODE AND AN ACCOUNT NUMBER (*See Instructions Above.*)	CODEBTOR	HUSBAND, WIFE, JOINT, OR COMMUNITY	DATE CLAIM WAS INCURRED, NATURE OF LIEN , AND DESCRIPTION AND VALUE OF PROPERTY SUBJECT TO LIEN	CONTINGENT	UNLIQUIDATED	DISPUTED	AMOUNT OF CLAIM WITHOUT DEDUCTING VALUE OF COLLATERAL	UNSECURED PORTION, IF ANY
ACCOUNT NO.			VALUE $					
ACCOUNT NO.			VALUE $					
ACCOUNT NO.			VALUE $					
ACCOUNT NO.			VALUE $					
ACCOUNT NO.			VALUE $					
Sheet no.______of______continuation sheets attached to Schedule of Creditors Holding Secured Claims			Subtotal (s)► (Total(s) of this page)				$	$
			Total(s) ► (Use only on last page)				$	$
							(Report also on Summary of Schedules.)	(If applicable, report also on Statistical Summary of Certain Liabilities and Related Data.)

In re ______________________________,
Debtor

Case No.______________
(if known)

SCHEDULE E - CREDITORS HOLDING UNSECURED PRIORITY CLAIMS

A complete list of claims entitled to priority, listed separately by type of priority, is to be set forth on the sheets provided. Only holders of unsecured claims entitled to priority should be listed in this schedule. In the boxes provided on the attached sheets, state the name, mailing address, including zip code, and last four digits of the account number, if any, of all entities holding priority claims against the debtor or the property of the debtor, as of the date of the filing of the petition. Use a separate continuation sheet for each type of priority and label each with the type of priority.

The complete account number of any account the debtor has with the creditor is useful to the trustee and the creditor and may be provided if the debtor chooses to do so. If a minor child is a creditor, state the child's initials and the name and address of the child's parent or guardian, such as "A.B., a minor child, by John Doe, guardian." Do not disclose the child's name. See, 11 U.S.C. §112 and Fed. R. Bankr. P. 1007(m).

If any entity other than a spouse in a joint case may be jointly liable on a claim, place an "X" in the column labeled "Codebtor," include the entity on the appropriate schedule of creditors, and complete Schedule H-Codebtors. If a joint petition is filed, state whether the husband, wife, both of them, or the marital community may be liable on each claim by placing an "H," "W," "J," or "C" in the column labeled "Husband, Wife, Joint, or Community." If the claim is contingent, place an "X" in the column labeled "Contingent." If the claim is unliquidated, place an "X" in the column labeled "Unliquidated." If the claim is disputed, place an "X" in the column labeled "Disputed." (You may need to place an "X" in more than one of these three columns.)

Report the total of claims listed on each sheet in the box labeled "Subtotals" on each sheet. Report the total of all claims listed on this Schedule E in the box labeled "Total" on the last sheet of the completed schedule. Report this total also on the Summary of Schedules.

Report the total of amounts entitled to priority listed on each sheet in the box labeled "Subtotals" on each sheet. Report the total of all amounts entitled to priority listed on this Schedule E in the box labeled "Totals" on the last sheet of the completed schedule. Individual debtors with primarily consumer debts report this total also on the Statistical Summary of Certain Liabilities and Related Data.

Report the total of amounts not entitled to priority listed on each sheet in the box labeled "Subtotals" on each sheet. Report the total of all amounts not entitled to priority listed on this Schedule E in the box labeled "Totals" on the last sheet of the completed schedule. Individual debtors with primarily consumer debts report this total also on the Statistical Summary of Certain Liabilities and Related Data.

☐ Check this box if debtor has no creditors holding unsecured priority claims to report on this Schedule E.

TYPES OF PRIORITY CLAIMS (Check the appropriate box(es) below if claims in that category are listed on the attached sheets.)

☐ **Domestic Support Obligations**

Claims for domestic support that are owed to or recoverable by a spouse, former spouse, or child of the debtor, or the parent, legal guardian, or responsible relative of such a child, or a governmental unit to whom such a domestic support claim has been assigned to the extent provided in 11 U.S.C. § 507(a)(1).

☐ **Extensions of credit in an involuntary case**

Claims arising in the ordinary course of the debtor's business or financial affairs after the commencement of the case but before the earlier of the appointment of a trustee or the order for relief. 11 U.S.C. § 507(a)(3).

☐ **Wages, salaries, and commissions**

Wages, salaries, and commissions, including vacation, severance, and sick leave pay owing to employees and commissions owing to qualifying independent sales representatives up to $10,950* per person earned within 180 days immediately preceding the filing of the original petition, or the cessation of business, whichever occurred first, to the extent provided in 11 U.S.C. § 507(a)(4).

☐ **Contributions to employee benefit plans**

Money owed to employee benefit plans for services rendered within 180 days immediately preceding the filing of the original petition, or the cessation of business, whichever occurred first, to the extent provided in 11 U.S.C. § 507(a)(5).

In re ____, **Case No.__________________________**

Debtor **(if known)**

☐ **Certain farmers and fishermen**

Claims of certain farmers and fishermen, up to $5,400* per farmer or fisherman, against the debtor, as provided in 11 U.S.C. § 507(a)(6).

☐ **Deposits by individuals**

Claims of individuals up to $2,425* for deposits for the purchase, lease, or rental of property or services for personal, family, or household use, that were not delivered or provided. 11 U.S.C. § 507(a)(7).

☐ **Taxes and Certain Other Debts Owed to Governmental Units**

Taxes, customs duties, and penalties owing to federal, state, and local governmental units as set forth in 11 U.S.C. § 507(a)(8).

☐ **Commitments to Maintain the Capital of an Insured Depository Institution**

Claims based on commitments to the FDIC, RTC, Director of the Office of Thrift Supervision, Comptroller of the Currency, or Board of Governors of the Federal Reserve System, or their predecessors or successors, to maintain the capital of an insured depository institution. 11 U.S.C. § 507 (a)(9).

☐ **Claims for Death or Personal Injury While Debtor Was Intoxicated**

Claims for death or personal injury resulting from the operation of a motor vehicle or vessel while the debtor was intoxicated from using alcohol, a drug, or another substance. 11 U.S.C. § 507(a)(10).

* Amounts are subject to adjustment on April 1, 2010, and every three years thereafter with respect to cases commenced on or after the date of adjustment.

____ continuation sheets attached

In re ____, **Case No.** ________________________________
Debtor **(if known)**

SCHEDULE E - CREDITORS HOLDING UNSECURED PRIORITY CLAIMS

(Continuation Sheet)

Type of Priority for Claims Listed on This Sheet

CREDITOR'S NAME, MAILING ADDRESS INCLUDING ZIP CODE, AND ACCOUNT NUMBER (*See instructions above.*)	CODEBTOR	HUSBAND, WIFE, JOINT, OR COMMUNITY	DATE CLAIM WAS INCURRED AND CONSIDERATION FOR CLAIM	CONTINGENT	UNLIQUIDATED	DISPUTED	AMOUNT OF CLAIM	AMOUNT ENTITLED TO PRIORITY	AMOUNT NOT ENTITLED TO PRIORITY, IF ANY
Account No.									
Account No.									
Account No.									
Account No.									
Sheet no. _____ of _____ continuation sheets attached to Schedule of Creditors Holding Priority Claims						Subtotals➤ (Totals of this page)	$	$	
						Total➤ (Use only on last page of the completed Schedule E. Report also on the Summary of Schedules.)	$		
						Totals➤ (Use only on last page of the completed Schedule E. If applicable, report also on the Statistical Summary of Certain Liabilities and Related Data.)		$	$

B 6F (Official Form 6F) (12/07)

In re ____, Debtor

Case No. ______________________ (if known)

SCHEDULE F - CREDITORS HOLDING UNSECURED NONPRIORITY CLAIMS

State the name, mailing address, including zip code, and last four digits of any account number, of all entities holding unsecured claims without priority against the debtor or the property of the debtor, as of the date of filing of the petition. The complete account number of any account the debtor has with the creditor is useful to the trustee and the creditor and may be provided if the debtor chooses to do so. If a minor child is a creditor, state the child's initials and the name and address of the child's parent or guardian, such as "A.B., a minor child, by John Doe, guardian." Do not disclose the child's name. See, 11 U.S.C. §112 and Fed. R. Bankr. P. 1007(m). Do not include claims listed in Schedules D and E. If all creditors will not fit on this page, use the continuation sheet provided.

If any entity other than a spouse in a joint case may be jointly liable on a claim, place an "X" in the column labeled "Codebtor," include the entity on the appropriate schedule of creditors, and complete Schedule H - Codebtors. If a joint petition is filed, state whether the husband, wife, both of them, or the marital community may be liable on each claim by placing an "H," "W," "J," or "C" in the column labeled "Husband, Wife, Joint, or Community."

If the claim is contingent, place an "X" in the column labeled "Contingent." If the claim is unliquidated, place an "X" in the column labeled "Unliquidated." If the claim is disputed, place an "X" in the column labeled "Disputed." (You may need to place an "X" in more than one of these three columns.)

Report the total of all claims listed on this schedule in the box labeled "Total" on the last sheet of the completed schedule. Report this total also on the Summary of Schedules and, if the debtor is an individual with primarily consumer debts, report this total also on the Statistical Summary of Certain Liabilities and Related Data..

☐ Check this box if debtor has no creditors holding unsecured claims to report on this Schedule F.

CREDITOR'S NAME, MAILING ADDRESS INCLUDING ZIP CODE, AND ACCOUNT NUMBER *(See instructions above.)*	CODEBTOR	HUSBAND, WIFE, JOINT, OR COMMUNITY	DATE CLAIM WAS INCURRED AND CONSIDERATION FOR CLAIM. IF CLAIM IS SUBJECT TO SETOFF, SO STATE.	CONTINGENT	UNLIQUIDATED	DISPUTED	AMOUNT OF CLAIM
ACCOUNT NO.							
ACCOUNT NO.							
ACCOUNT NO.							
ACCOUNT NO.							
						Subtotal➤	$
						Total➤ (Use only on last page of the completed Schedule F.) (Report also on Summary of Schedules and, if applicable, on the Statistical Summary of Certain Liabilities and Related Data.)	$

_____continuation sheets attached

In re ______________________________, **Debtor**

Case No. ______________________ **(if known)**

SCHEDULE F - CREDITORS HOLDING UNSECURED NONPRIORITY CLAIMS

(Continuation Sheet)

CREDITOR'S NAME, MAILING ADDRESS INCLUDING ZIP CODE, AND ACCOUNT NUMBER (See instructions above.)	CODEBTOR	HUSBAND, WIFE, JOINT, OR COMMUNITY	DATE CLAIM WAS INCURRED AND CONSIDERATION FOR CLAIM. IF CLAIM IS SUBJECT TO SETOFF, SO STATE.	CONTINGENT	UNLIQUIDATED	DISPUTED	AMOUNT OF CLAIM
ACCOUNT NO.							
ACCOUNT NO.							
ACCOUNT NO.							
ACCOUNT NO.							
ACCOUNT NO.							

Sheet no.______ of______ continuation sheets attached to Schedule of Creditors Holding Unsecured Nonpriority Claims

Subtotal➤ $

Total➤ $
(Use only on last page of the completed Schedule F.)
(Report also on Summary of Schedules and, if applicable on the Statistical Summary of Certain Liabilities and Related Data.)

In re ______________________________ ,
Debtor

Case No.______________________
(if known)

SCHEDULE G - EXECUTORY CONTRACTS AND UNEXPIRED LEASES

Describe all executory contracts of any nature and all unexpired leases of real or personal property. Include any timeshare interests. State nature of debtor's interest in contract, i.e., "Purchaser," "Agent," etc. State whether debtor is the lessor or lessee of a lease. Provide the names and complete mailing addresses of all other parties to each lease or contract described. If a minor child is a party to one of the leases or contracts, state the child's initials and the name and address of the child's parent or guardian, such as "A.B., a minor child, by John Doe, guardian." Do not disclose the child's name. See, 11 U.S.C. §112 and Fed. R. Bankr. P. 1007(m).

☐ Check this box if debtor has no executory contracts or unexpired leases.

NAME AND MAILING ADDRESS, INCLUDING ZIP CODE, OF OTHER PARTIES TO LEASE OR CONTRACT.	DESCRIPTION OF CONTRACT OR LEASE AND NATURE OF DEBTOR'S INTEREST. STATE WHETHER LEASE IS FOR NONRESIDENTIAL REAL PROPERTY. STATE CONTRACT NUMBER OF ANY GOVERNMENT CONTRACT.

In re ____ ,
Debtor

Case No. ________________________________
(if known)

SCHEDULE H - CODEBTORS

Provide the information requested concerning any person or entity, other than a spouse in a joint case, that is also liable on any debts listed by the debtor in the schedules of creditors. Include all guarantors and co-signers. If the debtor resides or resided in a community property state, commonwealth, or territory (including Alaska, Arizona, California, Idaho, Louisiana, Nevada, New Mexico, Puerto Rico, Texas, Washington, or Wisconsin) within the eight-year period immediately preceding the commencement of the case, identify the name of the debtor's spouse and of any former spouse who resides or resided with the debtor in the community property state, commonwealth, or territory. Include all names used by the nondebtor spouse during the eight years immediately preceding the commencement of this case. If a minor child is a codebtor or a creditor, state the child's initials and the name and address of the child's parent or guardian, such as "A.B., a minor child, by John Doe, guardian." Do not disclose the child's name. See, 11 U.S.C. §112 and Fed. R. Bankr. P. 1007(m).

☐ Check this box if debtor has no codebtors.

NAME AND ADDRESS OF CODEBTOR	NAME AND ADDRESS OF CREDITOR

B6I (Official Form 6I) (12/07)

In re ______________________________, **Case No.** ______________________________
Debtor **(if known)**

SCHEDULE I - CURRENT INCOME OF INDIVIDUAL DEBTOR(S)

The column labeled "Spouse" must be completed in all cases filed by joint debtors and by every married debtor, whether or not a joint petition is filed, unless the spouses are separated and a joint petition is not filed. Do not state the name of any minor child. The average monthly income calculated on this form may differ from the current monthly income calculated on Form 22A, 22B, or 22C.

Debtor's Marital Status:	DEPENDENTS OF DEBTOR AND SPOUSE	
	RELATIONSHIP(S):	AGE(S):

Employment:	DEBTOR	SPOUSE
Occupation		
Name of Employer		
How long employed		
Address of Employer		

INCOME: (Estimate of average or projected monthly income at time case filed)	DEBTOR	SPOUSE
1. Monthly gross wages, salary, and commissions (Prorate if not paid monthly)	$	$
2. Estimate monthly overtime	$	$
3. SUBTOTAL	$	$
4. LESS PAYROLL DEDUCTIONS		
a. Payroll taxes and social security	$	$
b. Insurance	$	$
c. Union dues	$	$
d. Other (Specify): ______________	$	$
5. SUBTOTAL OF PAYROLL DEDUCTIONS	$	$
6. TOTAL NET MONTHLY TAKE HOME PAY	$	$
7. Regular income from operation of business or profession or farm (Attach detailed statement)	$	$
8. Income from real property	$	$
9. Interest and dividends	$	$
10. Alimony, maintenance or support payments payable to the debtor for the debtor's use or that of dependents listed above	$	$
11. Social security or government assistance (Specify): ______________	$	$
12. Pension or retirement income	$	$
13. Other monthly income (Specify): ______________	$	$
14. SUBTOTAL OF LINES 7 THROUGH 13	$	$
15. AVERAGE MONTHLY INCOME (Add amounts on lines 6 and 14)	$	$
16. COMBINED AVERAGE MONTHLY INCOME: (Combine column totals from line 15)	$	

(Report also on Summary of Schedules and, if applicable, on Statistical Summary of Certain Liabilities and Related Data)

17. Describe any increase or decrease in income reasonably anticipated to occur within the year following the filing of this document:

____

B6J (Official Form 6J) (12/07)

In re ______________________________________, Case No. ______________________________
Debtor (if known)

SCHEDULE J - CURRENT EXPENDITURES OF INDIVIDUAL DEBTOR(S)

Complete this schedule by estimating the average or projected monthly expenses of the debtor and the debtor's family at time case filed. Prorate any payments made bi-weekly, quarterly, semi-annually, or annually to show monthly rate. The average monthly expenses calculated on this form may differ from the deductions from income allowed on Form22A or 22C.

☐ Check this box if a joint petition is filed and debtor's spouse maintains a separate household. Complete a separate schedule of expenditures labeled "Spouse."

1. Rent or home mortgage payment (include lot rented for mobile home) $ __________
 a. Are real estate taxes included? Yes ______ No ______
 b. Is property insurance included? Yes ______ No ______
2. Utilities: a. Electricity and heating fuel $ __________
 b. Water and sewer $ __________
 c. Telephone $ __________
 d. Other ______________________________ $ __________
3. Home maintenance (repairs and upkeep) $ __________
4. Food $ __________
5. Clothing $ __________
6. Laundry and dry cleaning $ __________
7. Medical and dental expenses $ __________
8. Transportation (not including car payments) $ __________
9. Recreation, clubs and entertainment, newspapers, magazines, etc. $ __________
10.Charitable contributions $ __________
11.Insurance (not deducted from wages or included in home mortgage payments)
 a. Homeowner's or renter's $ __________
 b. Life $ __________
 c. Health $ __________
 d. Auto $ __________
 e. Other ______________________________ $ __________
12. Taxes (not deducted from wages or included in home mortgage payments)
(Specify) ______________________________ $ __________
13. Installment payments: (In chapter 11, 12, and 13 cases, do not list payments to be included in the plan)
 a. Auto $ __________
 b. Other ______________________________ $ __________
 c. Other ______________________________ $ __________
14. Alimony, maintenance, and support paid to others $ __________
15. Payments for support of additional dependents not living at your home $ __________
16. Regular expenses from operation of business, profession, or farm (attach detailed statement) $ __________
17. Other ______________________________ $ __________
18. AVERAGE MONTHLY EXPENSES (Total lines 1-17. Report also on Summary of Schedules and, if applicable, on the Statistical Summary of Certain Liabilities and Related Data.) $ __________
19. Describe any increase or decrease in expenditures reasonably anticipated to occur within the year following the filing of this document:

20. STATEMENT OF MONTHLY NET INCOME
 a. Average monthly income from Line 15 of Schedule I $ __________
 b. Average monthly expenses from Line 18 above $ __________
 c. Monthly net income (a. minus b.) $ __________

In re ______________________________ ,
Debtor

Case No. ____________________
(if known)

DECLARATION CONCERNING DEBTOR'S SCHEDULES

DECLARATION UNDER PENALTY OF PERJURY BY INDIVIDUAL DEBTOR

I declare under penalty of perjury that I have read the foregoing summary and schedules, consisting of _____ sheets, and that they are true and correct to the best of my knowledge, information, and belief.

Date ____________________________ Signature: ________________________________
Debtor

Date ____________________________ Signature: ________________________________
(Joint Debtor, if any)

[If joint case, both spouses must sign.]

DECLARATION AND SIGNATURE OF NON-ATTORNEY BANKRUPTCY PETITION PREPARER (See 11 U.S.C. § 110)

I declare under penalty of perjury that: (1) I am a bankruptcy petition preparer as defined in 11 U.S.C. § 110; (2) I prepared this document for compensation and have provided the debtor with a copy of this document and the notices and information required under 11 U.S.C. §§ 110(b), 110(h) and 342(b); and, (3) if rules or guidelines have been promulgated pursuant to 11 U.S.C. § 110(h) setting a maximum fee for services chargeable by bankruptcy petition preparers, I have given the debtor notice of the maximum amount before preparing any document for filing for a debtor or accepting any fee from the debtor, as required by that section.

______________________________________ ______________________
Printed or Typed Name and Title, if any, of Bankruptcy Petition Preparer

Social Security No.
(Required by 11 U.S.C. § 110.)

If the bankruptcy petition preparer is not an individual, state the name, title (if any), address, and social security number of the officer, principal, responsible person, or partner who signs this document.

____
____
____
Address

X ______________________________________ ______________________
Signature of Bankruptcy Petition Preparer Date

Names and Social Security numbers of all other individuals who prepared or assisted in preparing this document, unless the bankruptcy petition preparer is not an individual:

If more than one person prepared this document, attach additional signed sheets conforming to the appropriate Official Form for each person.

A bankruptcy petition preparer's failure to comply with the provisions of title 11 and the Federal Rules of Bankruptcy Procedure may result in fines or imprisonment or both. 11 U.S.C. § 110; 18 U.S.C. § 156.

DECLARATION UNDER PENALTY OF PERJURY ON BEHALF OF A CORPORATION OR PARTNERSHIP

I, the ________________________ [the president or other officer or an authorized agent of the corporation or a member or an authorized agent of the partnership] of the ________________________ [corporation or partnership] named as debtor in this case, declare under penalty of perjury that I have read the foregoing summary and schedules, consisting of _____ sheets (*Total shown on summary page plus 1*), and that they are true and correct to the best of my knowledge, information, and belief.

Date ____________________________

Signature: ____

____
[Print or type name of individual signing on behalf of debtor.]

[An individual signing on behalf of a partnership or corporation must indicate position or relationship to debtor.]

Penalty for making a false statement or concealing property: Fine of up to $500,000 or imprisonment for up to 5 years or both. 18 U.S.C. §§ 152 and 3571.

United States Bankruptcy Court

In re ______________________________, Debtor

Case No. ______________

Chapter __________

SUMMARY OF SCHEDULES

Indicate as to each schedule whether that schedule is attached and state the number of pages in each. Report the totals from Schedules A, B, D, E, F, I, and J in the boxes provided. Add the amounts from Schedules A and B to determine the total amount of the debtor's assets. Add the amounts of all claims from Schedules D, E, and F to determine the total amount of the debtor's liabilities. Individual debtors also must complete the "Statistical Summary of Certain Liabilities and Related Data" if they file a case under chapter 7, 11, or 13.

NAME OF SCHEDULE	ATTACHED (YES/NO)	NO. OF SHEETS	ASSETS	LIABILITIES	OTHER
A - Real Property			$		
B - Personal Property			$		
C - Property Claimed as Exempt					
D - Creditors Holding Secured Claims				$	
E - Creditors Holding Unsecured Priority Claims (Total of Claims on Schedule E)				$	
F - Creditors Holding Unsecured Nonpriority Claims				$	
G - Executory Contracts and Unexpired Leases					
H - Codebtors					
I - Current Income of Individual Debtor(s)					$
J - Current Expenditures of Individual Debtors(s)					$
TOTAL			$	$	

B 6 Summary (Official Form 6 - Summary) (12/07)

United States Bankruptcy Court

In re ______________________________________,
Debtor

Case No. ____________________

Chapter ____________

STATISTICAL SUMMARY OF CERTAIN LIABILITIES AND RELATED DATA (28 U.S.C. § 159)

If you are an individual debtor whose debts are primarily consumer debts, as defined in § 101(8) of the Bankruptcy Code (11 U.S.C. § 101(8)), filing a case under chapter 7, 11 or 13, you must report all information requested below.

☐ Check this box if you are an individual debtor whose debts are NOT primarily consumer debts. You are not required to report any information here.

This information is for statistical purposes only under 28 U.S.C. § 159.

Summarize the following types of liabilities, as reported in the Schedules, and total them.

Type of Liability	Amount
Domestic Support Obligations (from Schedule E)	$
Taxes and Certain Other Debts Owed to Governmental Units (from Schedule E)	$
Claims for Death or Personal Injury While Debtor Was Intoxicated (from Schedule E) (whether disputed or undisputed)	$
Student Loan Obligations (from Schedule F)	$
Domestic Support, Separation Agreement, and Divorce Decree Obligations Not Reported on Schedule E	$
Obligations to Pension or Profit-Sharing, and Other Similar Obligations (from Schedule F)	$
TOTAL	$

State the following:

Average Income (from Schedule I, Line 16)	$
Average Expenses (from Schedule J, Line 18)	$
Current Monthly Income (from Form 22A Line 12; **OR**, Form 22B Line 11; **OR**, Form 22C Line 20)	$

State the following:

1. Total from Schedule D, "UNSECURED PORTION, IF ANY" column		$
2. Total from Schedule E, "AMOUNT ENTITLED TO PRIORITY" column.	$	
3. Total from Schedule E, "AMOUNT NOT ENTITLED TO PRIORITY, IF ANY" column		$
4. Total from Schedule F		$
5. Total of non-priority unsecured debt (sum of 1, 3, and 4)		$

B 3A (Official Form 3A) (12/07)

UNITED STATES BANKRUPTCY COURT

In re ______________________________________,
Debtor

Case No. ________________

Chapter ___________

APPLICATION TO PAY FILING FEE IN INSTALLMENTS

1. In accordance with Fed. R. Bankr. P. 1006, I apply for permission to pay the filing fee amounting to $__________ in installments.

2. I am unable to pay the filing fee except in installments.

3. Until the filing fee is paid in full, I will not make any additional payment or transfer any additional property to an attorney or any other person for services in connection with this case.

4. I propose the following terms for the payment of the Filing Fee.*

$ _______________ Check one ☐ With the filing of the petition, or
☐ On or before __________

$ _______________ on or before ______________________________

$ _______________ on or before ______________________________

$ _______________ on or before ______________________________

* The number of installments proposed shall not exceed four (4), and the final installment shall be payable not later than 120 days after filing the petition. For cause shown, the court may extend the time of any installment, provided the last installment is paid not later than 180 days after filing the petition. Fed. R. Bankr. P. 1006(b)(2).

5. I understand that if I fail to pay any installment when due, my bankruptcy case may be dismissed and I may not receive a discharge of my debts.

____
Signature of Attorney Date

____
Name of Attorney

____
Signature of Debtor Date
(In a joint case, both spouses must sign.)

____
Signature of Joint Debtor (if any) Date

DECLARATION AND SIGNATURE OF NON-ATTORNEY BANKRUPTCY PETITION PREPARER (See 11 U.S.C. § 110)

I declare under penalty of perjury that: (1) I am a bankruptcy petition preparer as defined in 11 U.S.C. § 110; (2) I prepared this document for compensation and have provided the debtor with a copy of this document and the notices and information required under 11 U.S.C. §§ 110(b), 110(h), and 342(b); (3) if rules or guidelines have been promulgated pursuant to 11 U.S.C. § 110(h) setting a maximum fee for services chargeable by bankruptcy petition preparers, I have given the debtor notice of the maximum amount before preparing any document for filing for a debtor or accepting any fee from the debtor, as required under that section; and (4) I will not accept any additional money or other property from the debtor before the filing fee is paid in full.

____
Printed or Typed Name and Title, if any, of Bankruptcy Petition Preparer

____
Social-Security No. (Required by 11 U.S.C. § 110.)

If the bankruptcy petition preparer is not an individual, state the name, title (if any), address, and social-security number of the officer, principal, responsible person, or partner who signs the document.

____

____
Address

x_________________________________
Signature of Bankruptcy Petition Preparer

____
Date

Names and Social-Security numbers of all other individuals who prepared or assisted in preparing this document, unless the bankruptcy petition preparer is not an individual:

If more than one person prepared this document, attach additional signed sheets conforming to the appropriate Official Form for each person.
A bankruptcy petition preparer's failure to comply with the provisions of title 11 and the Federal Rules of Bankruptcy Procedure may result in fines or imprisonment or both. 11 U.S.C. § 110; 18 U.S.C. § 156.

UNITED STATES BANKRUPTCY COURT

In re ______________________________________,
Debtor

Case No. ________________

Chapter __________

ORDER APPROVING PAYMENT OF FILING FEE IN INSTALLMENTS

☐ IT IS ORDERED that the debtor(s) may pay the filing fee in installments on the terms proposed in the foregoing application.

☐ IT IS ORDERED that the debtor(s) shall pay the filing fee according to the following terms:

$ __________________ Check one ☐ With the filing of the petition, or
☐ On or before ____________

$ __________________ on or before ____________________________________

$ __________________ on or before ____________________________________

$ __________________ on or before ____________________________________

☐ IT IS FURTHER ORDERED that until the filing fee is paid in full the debtor(s) shall not make any additional payment or transfer any additional property to an attorney or any other person for services in connection with this case.

BY THE COURT

Date: __________________

____
United States Bankruptcy Judge

APPLICATION FOR WAIVER OF THE CHAPTER 7 FILING FEE FOR INDIVIDUALS WHO CANNOT PAY THE FILING FEE IN FULL OR IN INSTALLMENTS

The court fee for filing a case under chapter 7 of the Bankruptcy Code is $299.

If you cannot afford to pay the full fee at the time of filing, you may apply to pay the fee in installments. A form, which is available from the bankruptcy clerk's office, must be completed to make that application. If your application to pay in installments is approved, you will be permitted to file your petition, generally completing payment of the fee over the course of four to six months.

If you cannot afford to pay the fee either in full at the time of filing or in installments, you may request a waiver of the filing fee by completing this application and filing it with the Clerk of Court. A judge will decide whether you have to pay the fee. By law, the judge may waive the fee only if your income is less than 150 percent of the official poverty line applicable to your family size and you are unable to pay the fee in installments. You may obtain information about the poverty guidelines at www.uscourts.gov or in the bankruptcy clerk's office.

Required information. Complete all items in the application, and attach requested schedules. Then sign the application on the last page. If you and your spouse are filing a joint bankruptcy petition, you both must provide information as requested and sign the application.

UNITED STATES BANKRUPTCY COURT

In re: ____________________
Debtor(s)

Case No. ____________________
(if known)

APPLICATION FOR WAIVER OF THE CHAPTER 7 FILING FEE FOR INDIVIDUALS WHO CANNOT PAY THE FILING FEE IN FULL OR IN INSTALLMENTS

Part A. Family Size and Income

1. Including yourself, your spouse, and dependents you have listed or will list on Schedule I (Current Income of Individual Debtors(s)), how many people are in your family? (Do not include your spouse if you are separated AND are not filing a joint petition.) __________

2. Restate the following information that you provided, or will provide, on Line 16 of Schedule I. Attach a completed copy of Schedule I, if it is available.

   Total Combined Monthly Income (Line 16 of Schedule I): $____________________

3. State the monthly net income, if any, of dependents included in Question 1 above. Do not include any income already reported in Item 2. If none, enter $0.

   $____________________

4. Add the "Total Combined Monthly Income" reported in Question 2 to your dependents' monthly net income from Question 3.

   $____________________

5. Do you expect the amount in Question 4 to increase or decrease by more than 10% during the next 6 months? Yes ___ No ___

   If yes, explain.

Part B. Monthly Expenses

6. EITHER (a) attach a completed copy of Schedule J (Schedule of Monthly Expenses), and state your total monthly expenses reported on Line 18 of that Schedule, OR (b) if you have not yet completed Schedule J, provide an estimate of your total monthly expenses.

   $____________________

7. Do you expect the amount in Question 6 to increase or decrease by more than 10% during the next 6 months? Yes ___ No ___
   If yes, explain.

Part C. Real and Personal Property

EITHER (1) attach completed copies of Schedule A (Real Property) and Schedule B (Personal Property), OR (2) if you have not yet completed those schedules, answer the following questions.

8. State the amount of cash you have on hand. $ ____________________

9. State below any money you have in savings, checking, or other accounts in a bank or other financial institution.

Bank or Other Financial Institution:	Type of Account such as savings, checking, CD:	Amount:
____________________	____________________	$________________
____________________	____________________	$________________

10. State below the assets owned by you. **Do not list ordinary household furnishings and clothing**.

Home	Address: ______________________ ______________________	Value: $ ______________ Amount owed on mortgages and liens: $ ______________
Other real estate	Address: ______________________ ______________________	Value: $ ______________ Amount owed on mortgages and liens: $ ______________
Motor vehicle	Model/Year: ______________ ______________________	Value: $ ______________ Amount owed: $ ______________
Motor vehicle	Model/Year: ______________ ______________________	Value: $ ______________ Amount owed: $ ______________
Other	Description______________ ______________________	Value: $ ______________ Amount owed: $ ______________

11. State below any person, business, organization, or governmental unit that owes you money and the amount that is owed.

Name of Person, Business, or Organization that Owes You Money	Amount Owed
______________________	$ ______________
______________________	$ ______________

Part D. Additional Information.

12. Have you paid an **attorney** any money for services in connection with this case, including the completion of this form, the bankruptcy petition, or schedules? Yes ___ No ___
If yes, how much have you paid? $ ______________

13. Have you promised to pay or do you anticipate paying an **attorney** in connection with your bankruptcy case? Yes ___ No ___
If yes, how much have you promised to pay or do you anticipate paying? $ ______________

14. Have you paid **anyone other than an attorney** (such as a bankruptcy petition preparer, paralegal, typing service, or another person) any money for services in connection with this case, including the completion of this form, the bankruptcy petition, or schedules? Yes ___ No ___
If yes, how much have you paid? $ ______________

15. Have you promised to pay or do you anticipate paying **anyone other than an attorney** (such as a bankruptcy petition preparer, paralegal, typing service, or another person) any money for services in connection with this case, including the completion of this form, the bankruptcy petition, or schedules?
Yes ___ No ___
If yes, how much have you promised to pay or do you anticipate paying? $ ______________

16. Has anyone paid an attorney or other person or service in connection with this case, on your behalf?
Yes ___ No ___

If yes, explain.

17. Have you previously filed for bankruptcy relief during the past eight years? Yes ___ No ___

Case Number (if known)	Year filed	Location of filing	Did you obtain a discharge? (if known)
________________	_______	______________	Yes ____ No ____ Don't know ____
________________	_______	______________	Yes ____ No ____ Don't know ____

18. Please provide any other information that helps to explain why you are unable to pay the filing fee in installments.

19. I (we) declare under penalty of perjury that I (we) cannot currently afford to pay the filing fee in full or in installments and that the foregoing information is true and correct.

Executed on: ____________________ ________________________________
Date Signature of Debtor

____________________ ________________________________
Date Signature of Codebtor

DECLARATION AND SIGNATURE OF BANKRUPTCY PETITION PREPARER (See 11 U.S.C. § 110)

I declare under penalty of perjury that: (1) I am a bankruptcy petition preparer as defined in 11 U.S.C. § 110; (2) I prepared this document for compensation and have provided the debtor with a copy of this document and the notices and information required under 11 U.S.C. §§ 110(b), 110(h), and 342(b); and (3) if rules or guidelines have been promulgated pursuant to 11 U.S.C. § 110(h) setting a maximum fee for services chargeable by bankruptcy petition preparers, I have given the debtor notice of the maximum amount before preparing any document for filing for a debtor or accepting any fee from the debtor, as required under that section.

____ ______________________

Printed or Typed Name and Title, if any, of Bankruptcy Petition Preparer Social-Security No. (Required by 11 U.S.C. §110.)

If the bankruptcy petition preparer is not an individual, state the name, title (if any), address, and social-security number of the officer, principal, responsible person, or partner who signs the document.

____

____

Address

x____ ________________

Signature of Bankruptcy Petition Preparer Date

Names and Social-Security numbers of all other individuals who prepared or assisted in preparing this document, unless the bankruptcy petition preparer is not an individual:

If more than one person prepared this document, attach additional signed sheets conforming to the appropriate Official Form for each person.

A bankruptcy petition preparer's failure to comply with the provisions of title 11 and the Federal Rules of Bankruptcy Procedure may result in fines or imprisonment or both. 11 U.S.C. § 110; 18 U.S.C. § 156.

UNITED STATES BANKRUPTCY COURT

In re: ____________________ Case No. ____________________
Debtor(s)

ORDER ON DEBTOR'S APPLICATION FOR WAIVER OF THE CHAPTER 7 FILING FEE

Upon consideration of the debtor's "Application for Waiver of the Chapter 7 Filing Fee," the court orders that the application be:

[ ] GRANTED.

This order is subject to being vacated at a later time if developments in the administration of the bankruptcy case demonstrate that the waiver was unwarranted.

[ ] DENIED.

The debtor shall pay the chapter 7 filing fee according to the following terms:

$ __________ on or before __________

$ __________ on or before __________

$ __________ on or before __________

$ __________ on or before __________

Until the filing fee is paid in full, the debtor shall not make any additional payment or transfer any additional property to an attorney or any other person for services in connection with this case.

IF THE DEBTOR FAILS TO TIMELY PAY THE FILING FEE IN FULL OR TO TIMELY MAKE INSTALLMENT PAYMENTS, THE COURT MAY DISMISS THE DEBTOR'S CASE.

[ ] SCHEDULED FOR HEARING.

A hearing to consider the debtor's "Application for Waiver of the Chapter 7 Filing Fee" shall be held on ____________________ at ________ am/pm at ____.
(address of courthouse)

IF THE DEBTOR FAILS TO APPEAR AT THE SCHEDULED HEARING, THE COURT MAY DEEM SUCH FAILURE TO BE THE DEBTOR'S CONSENT TO THE ENTRY OF AN ORDER DENYING THE FEE WAIVER APPLICATION BY DEFAULT.

BY THE COURT:

DATE: __________

____
United States Bankruptcy Judge

UNITED STATES BANKRUPTCY COURT

In re:_____ ____, Case No. ______________________________________
Debtor (if known)

STATEMENT OF FINANCIAL AFFAIRS

This statement is to be completed by every debtor. Spouses filing a joint petition may file a single statement on which the information for both spouses is combined. If the case is filed under chapter 12 or chapter 13, a married debtor must furnish information for both spouses whether or not a joint petition is filed, unless the spouses are separated and a joint petition is not filed. An individual debtor engaged in business as a sole proprietor, partner, family farmer, or self-employed professional, should provide the information requested on this statement concerning all such activities as well as the individual's personal affairs. To indicate payments, transfers and the like to minor children, state the child's initials and the name and address of the child's parent or guardian, such as "A.B., a minor child, by John Doe, guardian." Do not disclose the child's name. See, 11 U.S.C. §112 and Fed. R. Bankr. P. 1007(m).

Questions 1 - 18 are to be completed by all debtors. Debtors that are or have been in business, as defined below, also must complete Questions 19 - 25. **If the answer to an applicable question is "None," mark the box labeled "None."** If additional space is needed for the answer to any question, use and attach a separate sheet properly identified with the case name, case number (if known), and the number of the question.

DEFINITIONS

"In business." A debtor is "in business" for the purpose of this form if the debtor is a corporation or partnership. An individual debtor is "in business" for the purpose of this form if the debtor is or has been, within six years immediately preceding the filing of this bankruptcy case, any of the following: an officer, director, managing executive, or owner of 5 percent or more of the voting or equity securities of a corporation; a partner, other than a limited partner, of a partnership; a sole proprietor or self-employed full-time or part-time. An individual debtor also may be "in business" for the purpose of this form if the debtor engages in a trade, business, or other activity, other than as an employee, to supplement income from the debtor's primary employment.

"Insider." The term "insider" includes but is not limited to: relatives of the debtor; general partners of the debtor and their relatives; corporations of which the debtor is an officer, director, or person in control; officers, directors, and any owner of 5 percent or more of the voting or equity securities of a corporate debtor and their relatives; affiliates of the debtor and insiders of such affiliates; any managing agent of the debtor. 11 U.S.C. § 101.

---

1. Income from employment or operation of business

None ☐

State the gross amount of income the debtor has received from employment, trade, or profession, or from operation of the debtor's business, including part-time activities either as an employee or in independent trade or business, from the beginning of this calendar year to the date this case was commenced. State also the gross amounts received during the **two years** immediately preceding this calendar year. (A debtor that maintains, or has maintained, financial records on the basis of a fiscal rather than a calendar year may report fiscal year income. Identify the beginning and ending dates of the debtor's fiscal year.) If a joint petition is filed, state income for each spouse separately. (Married debtors filing under chapter 12 or chapter 13 must state income of both spouses whether or not a joint petition is filed, unless the spouses are separated and a joint petition is not filed.)

AMOUNT SOURCE

2. Income other than from employment or operation of business

None ☐

State the amount of income received by the debtor other than from employment, trade, profession, operation of the debtor's business during the **two years** immediately preceding the commencement of this case. Give particulars. If a joint petition is filed, state income for each spouse separately. (Married debtors filing under chapter 12 or chapter 13 must state income for each spouse whether or not a joint petition is filed, unless the spouses are separated and a joint petition is not filed.)

AMOUNT	SOURCE

3. Payments to creditors

Complete a. or b., as appropriate, and c.

None ☐

a. *Individual or joint debtor(s) with primarily consumer debts:* List all payments on loans, installment purchases of goods or services, and other debts to any creditor made within **90 days** immediately preceding the commencement of this case unless the aggregate value of all property that constitutes or is affected by such transfer is less than $600. Indicate with an asterisk (*) any payments that were made to a creditor on account of a domestic support obligation or as part of an alternative repayment schedule under a plan by an approved nonprofit budgeting and credit counseling agency. (Married debtors filing under chapter 12 or chapter 13 must include payments by either or both spouses whether or not a joint petition is filed, unless the spouses are separated and a joint petition is not filed.)

NAME AND ADDRESS OF CREDITOR	DATES OF PAYMENTS	AMOUNT PAID	AMOUNT STILL OWING

None ☐

b. *Debtor whose debts are not primarily consumer debts: List each payment or other transfer to any creditor made* within **90 days** immediately preceding the commencement of the case unless the aggregate value of all property that constitutes or is affected by such transfer is less than $5,475. If the debtor is an individual, indicate with an asterisk (*) any payments that were made to a creditor on account of a domestic support obligation or as part of an alternative repayment schedule under a plan by an approved nonprofit budgeting and credit counseling agency. (Married debtors filing under chapter 12 or chapter 13 must include payments and other transfers by either or both spouses whether or not a joint petition is filed, unless the spouses are separated and a joint petition is not filed.)

NAME AND ADDRESS OF CREDITOR	DATES OF PAYMENTS/ TRANSFERS	AMOUNT PAID OR VALUE OF TRANSFERS	AMOUNT STILL OWING

None

☐ c. *All debtors:* List all payments made within **one year** immediately preceding the commencement of this case to or for the benefit of creditors who are or were insiders. (Married debtors filing under chapter 12 or chapter 13 must include payments by either or both spouses whether or not a joint petition is filed, unless the spouses are separated and a joint petition is not filed.)

NAME AND ADDRESS OF CREDITOR AND RELATIONSHIP TO DEBTOR	DATE OF PAYMENT	AMOUNT PAID	AMOUNT STILL OWING

---

4. Suits and administrative proceedings, executions, garnishments and attachments

None

☐ a. List all suits and administrative proceedings to which the debtor is or was a party within **one year** immediately preceding the filing of this bankruptcy case. (Married debtors filing under chapter 12 or chapter 13 must include information concerning either or both spouses whether or not a joint petition is filed, unless the spouses are separated and a joint petition is not filed.)

CAPTION OF SUIT AND CASE NUMBER	NATURE OF PROCEEDING	COURT OR AGENCY AND LOCATION	STATUS OR DISPOSITION

None

☐ b. Describe all property that has been attached, garnished or seized under any legal or equitable process within **one year** immediately preceding the commencement of this case. (Married debtors filing under chapter 12 or chapter 13 must include information concerning property of either or both spouses whether or not a joint petition is filed, unless the spouses are separated and a joint petition is not filed.)

NAME AND ADDRESS OF PERSON FOR WHOSE BENEFIT PROPERTY WAS SEIZED	DATE OF SEIZURE	DESCRIPTION AND VALUE OF PROPERTY

---

5. Repossessions, foreclosures and returns

None

☐ List all property that has been repossessed by a creditor, sold at a foreclosure sale, transferred through a deed in lieu of foreclosure or returned to the seller, within **one year** immediately preceding the commencement of this case. (Married debtors filing under chapter 12 or chapter 13 must include information concerning property of either or both spouses whether or not a joint petition is filed, unless the spouses are separated and a joint petition is not filed.)

NAME AND ADDRESS OF CREDITOR OR SELLER	DATE OF REPOSSESSION, FORECLOSURE SALE, TRANSFER OR RETURN	DESCRIPTION AND VALUE OF PROPERTY

6. Assignments and receiverships

None ☐

a. Describe any assignment of property for the benefit of creditors made within **120 days** immediately preceding the commencement of this case. (Married debtors filing under chapter 12 or chapter 13 must include any assignment by either or both spouses whether or not a joint petition is filed, unless the spouses are separated and a joint petition is not filed.)

NAME AND ADDRESS OF ASSIGNEE	DATE OF ASSIGNMENT	TERMS OF ASSIGNMENT OR SETTLEMENT

None ☐

b. List all property which has been in the hands of a custodian, receiver, or court-appointed official within **one year** immediately preceding the commencement of this case. (Married debtors filing under chapter 12 or chapter 13 must include information concerning property of either or both spouses whether or not a joint petition is filed, unless the spouses are separated and a joint petition is not filed.)

NAME AND ADDRESS OF CUSTODIAN	NAME AND LOCATION OF COURT CASE TITLE & NUMBER	DATE OF ORDER	DESCRIPTION AND VALUE Of PROPERTY

7. Gifts

None ☐

List all gifts or charitable contributions made within **one year** immediately preceding the commencement of this case except ordinary and usual gifts to family members aggregating less than $200 in value per individual family member and charitable contributions aggregating less than $100 per recipient. (Married debtors filing under chapter 12 or chapter 13 must include gifts or contributions by either or both spouses whether or not a joint petition is filed, unless the spouses are separated and a joint petition is not filed.)

NAME AND ADDRESS OF PERSON OR ORGANIZATION	RELATIONSHIP TO DEBTOR, IF ANY	DATE OF GIFT	DESCRIPTION AND VALUE OF GIFT

8. Losses

None ☐

List all losses from fire, theft, other casualty or gambling within **one year** immediately preceding the commencement of this case **or since the commencement of this case**. (Married debtors filing under chapter 12 or chapter 13 must include losses by either or both spouses whether or not a joint petition is filed, unless the spouses are separated and a joint petition is not filed.)

DESCRIPTION AND VALUE OF PROPERTY	DESCRIPTION OF CIRCUMSTANCES AND, IF LOSS WAS COVERED IN WHOLE OR IN PART BY INSURANCE, GIVE PARTICULARS	DATE OF LOSS

9. Payments related to debt counseling or bankruptcy

None ☐

List all payments made or property transferred by or on behalf of the debtor to any persons, including attorneys, for consultation concerning debt consolidation, relief under the bankruptcy law or preparation of a petition in bankruptcy within **one year** immediately preceding the commencement of this case.

NAME AND ADDRESS OF PAYEE	DATE OF PAYMENT, NAME OF PAYER IF OTHER THAN DEBTOR	AMOUNT OF MONEY OR DESCRIPTION AND VALUE OF PROPERTY

---

10. Other transfers

None ☐

a. List all other property, other than property transferred in the ordinary course of the business or financial affairs of the debtor, transferred either absolutely or as security within **two years** immediately preceding the commencement of this case. (Married debtors filing under chapter 12 or chapter 13 must include transfers by either or both spouses whether or not a joint petition is filed, unless the spouses are separated and a joint petition is not filed.)

NAME AND ADDRESS OF TRANSFEREE, RELATIONSHIP TO DEBTOR	DATE	DESCRIBE PROPERTY TRANSFERRED AND VALUE RECEIVED

None ☐

b. List all property transferred by the debtor within **ten years** immediately preceding the commencement of this case to a self-settled trust or similar device of which the debtor is a beneficiary.

NAME OF TRUST OR OTHER DEVICE	DATE(S) OF TRANSFER(S)	AMOUNT OF MONEY OR DESCRIPTION AND VALUE OF PROPERTY OR DEBTOR'S INTEREST IN PROPERTY

---

11. Closed financial accounts

None ☐

List all financial accounts and instruments held in the name of the debtor or for the benefit of the debtor which were closed, sold, or otherwise transferred within **one year** immediately preceding the commencement of this case. Include checking, savings, or other financial accounts, certificates of deposit, or other instruments; shares and share accounts held in banks, credit unions, pension funds, cooperatives, associations, brokerage houses and other financial institutions. (Married debtors filing under chapter 12 or chapter 13 must include information concerning accounts or instruments held by or for either or both spouses whether or not a joint petition is filed, unless the spouses are separated and a joint petition is not filed.)

NAME AND ADDRESS OF INSTITUTION	TYPE OF ACCOUNT, LAST FOUR DIGITS OF ACCOUNT NUMBER, AND AMOUNT OF FINAL BALANCE	AMOUNT AND DATE OF SALE OR CLOSING

12. Safe deposit boxes

None ☐

List each safe deposit or other box or depository in which the debtor has or had securities, cash, or other valuables within **one year** immediately preceding the commencement of this case. (Married debtors filing under chapter 12 or chapter 13 must include boxes or depositories of either or both spouses whether or not a joint petition is filed, unless the spouses are separated and a joint petition is not filed.)

NAME AND ADDRESS OF BANK OR OTHER DEPOSITORY	NAMES AND ADDRESSES OF THOSE WITH ACCESS TO BOX OR DEPOSITORY	DESCRIPTION OF CONTENTS	DATE OF TRANSFER OR SURRENDER, IF ANY

13. Setoffs

None ☐

List all setoffs made by any creditor, including a bank, against a debt or deposit of the debtor within **90 days** preceding the commencement of this case. (Married debtors filing under chapter 12 or chapter 13 must include information concerning either or both spouses whether or not a joint petition is filed, unless the spouses are separated and a joint petition is not filed.)

NAME AND ADDRESS OF CREDITOR	DATE OF SETOFF	AMOUNT OF SETOFF

14. Property held for another person

None ☐

List all property owned by another person that the debtor holds or controls.

NAME AND ADDRESS OF OWNER	DESCRIPTION AND VALUE OF PROPERTY	LOCATION OF PROPERTY

15. Prior address of debtor

None ☐

If debtor has moved within **three years** immediately preceding the commencement of this case, list all premises which the debtor occupied during that period and vacated prior to the commencement of this case. If a joint petition is filed, report also any separate address of either spouse.

ADDRESS	NAME USED	DATES OF OCCUPANCY

16. Spouses and Former Spouses

None ☐

If the debtor resides or resided in a community property state, commonwealth, or territory (including Alaska, Arizona, California, Idaho, Louisiana, Nevada, New Mexico, Puerto Rico, Texas, Washington, or Wisconsin) within **eight years** immediately preceding the commencement of the case, identify the name of the debtor's spouse and of any former spouse who resides or resided with the debtor in the community property state.

NAME

---

17. Environmental Information.

For the purpose of this question, the following definitions apply:

"Environmental Law" means any federal, state, or local statute or regulation regulating pollution, contamination, releases of hazardous or toxic substances, wastes or material into the air, land, soil, surface water, groundwater, or other medium, including, but not limited to, statutes or regulations regulating the cleanup of these substances, wastes, or material.

"Site" means any location, facility, or property as defined under any Environmental Law, whether or not presently or formerly owned or operated by the debtor, including, but not limited to, disposal sites.

"Hazardous Material" means anything defined as a hazardous waste, hazardous substance, toxic substance, hazardous material, pollutant, or contaminant or similar term under an Environmental Law.

None ☐

a. List the name and address of every site for which the debtor has received notice in writing by a governmental unit that it may be liable or potentially liable under or in violation of an Environmental Law. Indicate the governmental unit, the date of the notice, and, if known, the Environmental Law:

SITE NAME AND ADDRESS	NAME AND ADDRESS OF GOVERNMENTAL UNIT	DATE OF NOTICE	ENVIRONMENTAL LAW

None ☐

b. List the name and address of every site for which the debtor provided notice to a governmental unit of a release of Hazardous Material. Indicate the governmental unit to which the notice was sent and the date of the notice.

SITE NAME AND ADDRESS	NAME AND ADDRESS OF GOVERNMENTAL UNIT	DATE OF NOTICE	ENVIRONMENTAL LAW

None ☐

c. List all judicial or administrative proceedings, including settlements or orders, under any Environmental Law with respect to which the debtor is or was a party. Indicate the name and address of the governmental unit that is or was a party to the proceeding, and the docket number.

NAME AND ADDRESS OF GOVERNMENTAL UNIT	DOCKET NUMBER	STATUS OR DISPOSITION

---

18 . Nature, location and name of business

None ☐

a. *If the debtor is an individual,* list the names, addresses, taxpayer-identification numbers, nature of the businesses, and beginning and ending dates of all businesses in which the debtor was an officer, director, partner, or managing

executive of a corporation, partner in a partnership, sole proprietor, or was self-employed in a trade, profession, or other activity either full- or part-time within **six years** immediately preceding the commencement of this case, or in which the debtor owned 5 percent or more of the voting or equity securities within **six years** immediately preceding the commencement of this case.

If the debtor is a partnership, list the names, addresses, taxpayer-identification numbers, nature of the businesses, and beginning and ending dates of all businesses in which the debtor was a partner or owned 5 percent or more of the voting or equity securities, within **six years** immediately preceding the commencement of this case.

If the debtor is a corporation, list the names, addresses, taxpayer-identification numbers, nature of the businesses, and beginning and ending dates of all businesses in which the debtor was a partner or owned 5 percent or more of the voting or equity securities within **six years** immediately preceding the commencement of this case.

NAME	LAST FOUR DIGITS OF SOCIAL-SECURITY OR OTHER INDIVIDUAL TAXPAYER-I.D. NO. (ITIN)/ COMPLETE EIN	ADDRESS	NATURE OF BUSINESS	BEGINNING AND ENDING DATES

None ☐ b. Identify any business listed in response to subdivision a., above, that is "single asset real estate" as defined in 11 U.S.C. § 101.

NAME	ADDRESS

The following questions are to be completed by every debtor that is a corporation or partnership and by any individual debtor who is or has been, within **six years** immediately preceding the commencement of this case, any of the following: an officer, director, managing executive, or owner of more than 5 percent of the voting or equity securities of a corporation; a partner, other than a limited partner, of a partnership, a sole proprietor, or self-employed in a trade, profession, or other activity, either full- or part-time.

(An individual or joint debtor should complete this portion of the statement ***only*** *if the debtor is or has been in business, as defined above, within six years immediately preceding the commencement of this case. A debtor who has not been in business within those six years should go directly to the signature page.)*

---

19. Books, records and financial statements

None ☐ a. List all bookkeepers and accountants who within **two years** immediately preceding the filing of this bankruptcy case kept or supervised the keeping of books of account and records of the debtor.

NAME AND ADDRESS	DATES SERVICES RENDERED

None ☐ b. List all firms or individuals who within **two years** immediately preceding the filing of this bankruptcy case have audited the books of account and records, or prepared a financial statement of the debtor.

NAME	ADDRESS	DATES SERVICES RENDERED

None ☐ c. List all firms or individuals who at the time of the commencement of this case were in possession of the books of account and records of the debtor. If any of the books of account and records are not available, explain.

NAME	ADDRESS

None ☐ d. List all financial institutions, creditors and other parties, including mercantile and trade agencies, to whom a financial statement was issued by the debtor within **two years** immediately preceding the commencement of this case.

NAME AND ADDRESS	DATE ISSUED

---

20. Inventories

None ☐ a. List the dates of the last two inventories taken of your property, the name of the person who supervised the taking of each inventory, and the dollar amount and basis of each inventory.

DATE OF INVENTORY	INVENTORY SUPERVISOR	DOLLAR AMOUNT OF INVENTORY (Specify cost, market or other basis)

None ☐ b. List the name and address of the person having possession of the records of each of the inventories reported in a., above.

DATE OF INVENTORY	NAME AND ADDRESSES OF CUSTODIAN OF INVENTORY RECORDS

---

21 . Current Partners, Officers, Directors and Shareholders

None ☐ a. If the debtor is a partnership, list the nature and percentage of partnership interest of each member of the partnership.

NAME AND ADDRESS	NATURE OF INTEREST	PERCENTAGE OF INTEREST

None ☐ b. If the debtor is a corporation, list all officers and directors of the corporation, and each stockholder who directly or indirectly owns, controls, or holds 5 percent or more of the voting or equity securities of the corporation.

NAME AND ADDRESS	TITLE	NATURE AND PERCENTAGE OF STOCK OWNERSHIP

---

22 . Former partners, officers, directors and shareholders

None ☐

a. If the debtor is a partnership, list each member who withdrew from the partnership within **one year** immediately preceding the commencement of this case.

NAME	ADDRESS	DATE OF WITHDRAWAL

None ☐

b. If the debtor is a corporation, list all officers or directors whose relationship with the corporation terminated within **one year** immediately preceding the commencement of this case.

NAME AND ADDRESS	TITLE	DATE OF TERMINATION

---

23 . Withdrawals from a partnership or distributions by a corporation

None ☐

If the debtor is a partnership or corporation, list all withdrawals or distributions credited or given to an insider, including compensation in any form, bonuses, loans, stock redemptions, options exercised and any other perquisite during **one year** immediately preceding the commencement of this case.

NAME & ADDRESS OF RECIPIENT, RELATIONSHIP TO DEBTOR	DATE AND PURPOSE OF WITHDRAWAL	AMOUNT OF MONEY OR DESCRIPTION AND VALUE OF PROPERTY

---

24. Tax Consolidation Group.

None ☐

If the debtor is a corporation, list the name and federal taxpayer-identification number of the parent corporation of any consolidated group for tax purposes of which the debtor has been a member at any time within **six years** immediately preceding the commencement of the case.

NAME OF PARENT CORPORATION	TAXPAYER-IDENTIFICATION NUMBER (EIN)

---

25. Pension Funds.

None ☐

If the debtor is not an individual, list the name and federal taxpayer-identification number of any pension fund to which the debtor, as an employer, has been responsible for contributing at any time within **six years** immediately preceding the commencement of the case.

NAME OF PENSION FUND	TAXPAYER-IDENTIFICATION NUMBER (EIN)

* * * * * *

[If completed by an individual or individual and spouse]

I declare under penalty of perjury that I have read the answers contained in the foregoing statement of financial affairs and any attachments thereto and that they are true and correct.

Date ____________________ Signature of Debtor ____________________

Date ____________________ Signature of Joint Debtor (if any) ____________________

[If completed on behalf of a partnership or corporation]

I declare under penalty of perjury that I have read the answers contained in the foregoing statement of financial affairs and any attachments thereto and that they are true and correct to the best of my knowledge, information and belief.

Date ____________________ Signature ____________________

Print Name and Title ____________________

[An individual signing on behalf of a partnership or corporation must indicate position or relationship to debtor.]

___continuation sheets attached

Penalty for making a false statement: Fine of up to $500,000 or imprisonment for up to 5 years, or both. 18 U.S.C. §§ 152 and 3571

DECLARATION AND SIGNATURE OF NON-ATTORNEY BANKRUPTCY PETITION PREPARER (See 11 U.S.C. § 110)

I declare under penalty of perjury that: (1) I am a bankruptcy petition preparer as defined in 11 U.S.C. § 110; (2) I prepared this document for compensation and have provided the debtor with a copy of this document and the notices and information required under 11 U.S.C. §§ 110(b), 110(h), and 342(b); and, (3) if rules or guidelines have been promulgated pursuant to 11 U.S.C. § 110(h) setting a maximum fee for services chargeable by bankruptcy petition preparers, I have given the debtor notice of the maximum amount before preparing any document for filing for a debtor or accepting any fee from the debtor, as required by that section.

____________________ ____________________

Printed or Typed Name and Title, if any, of Bankruptcy Petition Preparer Social-Security No. (Required by 11 U.S.C. § 110.)

If the bankruptcy petition preparer is not an individual, state the name, title (if any), address, and social-security number of the officer, principal, responsible person, or partner who signs this document.

____

Address

____________________ ____________________

Signature of Bankruptcy Petition Preparer Date

Names and Social-Security numbers of all other individuals who prepared or assisted in preparing this document unless the bankruptcy petition preparer is not an individual:

If more than one person prepared this document, attach additional signed sheets conforming to the appropriate Official Form for each person

A bankruptcy petition preparer's failure to comply with the provisions of title 11 and the Federal Rules of Bankruptcy Procedure may result in fines or imprisonment or both. 18 U.S.C. § 156.

UNITED STATES BANKRUPTCY COURT

In re ________________________________, Case No. ____________________
Debtor Chapter 7

CHAPTER 7 INDIVIDUAL DEBTOR'S STATEMENT OF INTENTION

PART A – Debts secured by property of the estate. *(Part A must be fully completed for **EACH** debt which is secured by property of the estate. Attach additional pages if necessary.)*

Property No. 1	
Creditor's Name:	**Describe Property Securing Debt:**

Property will be *(check one)*:
❒ Surrendered ❒ Retained

If retaining the property, I intend to *(check at least one)*:
❒ Redeem the property
❒ Reaffirm the debt
❒ Other. Explain ____________________________________ (for example, avoid lien using 11 U.S.C. § 522(f)).

Property is *(check one)*:
❒ Claimed as exempt ❒ Not claimed as exempt

Property No. 2 *(if necessary)*	
Creditor's Name:	**Describe Property Securing Debt:**

Property will be *(check one)*:
❒ Surrendered ❒ Retained

If retaining the property, I intend to *(check at least one)*:
❒ Redeem the property
❒ Reaffirm the debt
❒ Other. Explain ____________________________________ (for example, avoid lien using 11 U.S.C. § 522(f)).

Property is *(check one)*:
❒ Claimed as exempt ❒ Not claimed as exempt

PART B – Personal property subject to unexpired leases. *(All three columns of Part B must be completed for each unexpired lease. Attach additional pages if necessary.)*

Property No. 1		
Lessor's Name:	**Describe Leased Property:**	Lease will be Assumed pursuant to 11 U.S.C. § 365(p)(2): ❒ YES ❒ NO

Property No. 2 *(if necessary)*		
Lessor's Name:	**Describe Leased Property:**	Lease will be Assumed pursuant to 11 U.S.C. § 365(p)(2): ❒ YES ❒ NO

Property No. 3 *(if necessary)*		
Lessor's Name:	**Describe Leased Property:**	Lease will be Assumed pursuant to 11 U.S.C. § 365(p)(2): ❒ YES ❒ NO

_____ continuation sheets attached *(if any)*

I declare under penalty of perjury that the above indicates my intention as to any property of my estate securing a debt and/or personal property subject to an unexpired lease.

Date: ____________________

____
Signature of Debtor

____
Signature of Joint Debtor

CHAPTER 7 INDIVIDUAL DEBTOR'S STATEMENT OF INTENTION

(Continuation Sheet)

PART A - Continuation

Property No.	
Creditor's Name:	**Describe Property Securing Debt:**
Property will be *(check one)*: ❐ Surrendered ❐ Retained If retaining the property, I intend to *(check at least one)*: ❐ Redeem the property ❐ Reaffirm the debt ❐ Other. Explain ______________________ (for example, avoid lien using 11 U.S.C. § 522(f)). Property is *(check one)*: ❐ Claimed as exempt ❐ Not claimed as exempt	

PART B - Continuation

Property No.		
Lessor's Name:	**Describe Leased Property:**	Lease will be Assumed pursuant to 11 U.S.C. § 365(p)(2): ❐ YES ❐ NO

Property No.		
Lessor's Name:	**Describe Leased Property:**	Lease will be Assumed pursuant to 11 U.S.C. § 365(p)(2): ❐ YES ❐ NO

Form 16A. CAPTION (FULL)

United States Bankruptcy Court

_______________ District Of _______________

In re ____,)
[Set forth here all names including married,)
maiden, and trade names used by debtor within)
last 8 years.])
Debtor) Case No. _______________
)
Address ____)
)
____) Chapter __________
)
Last four digits of Social-Security or Individual Tax-
Payer-Identification (ITIN) No(s).,(if any): __________)
____)
Employer Tax-Identification (EIN) No(s).(if any): _____)
____)

[Designation of Character of Paper]

Official Form 20A
(12/03)

United States Bankruptcy Court

__________________ District Of __________________

In re ______________________________________, *Set forth here all names including married, maiden, and trade names used by debtor within last 6 years.]* Debtor	)	
	)	Case No. _____________
Address ______________________________________	)	
______________________________________	)	Chapter ________
Employer's Tax Identification (EIN) No(s). *[if any]:* ________ ______________________________________	)	
Last four digits of Social Security No(s).: _____________	)	

NOTICE OF [MOTION TO] [OBJECTION TO]

_________________has filed papers with the court to [relief sought in motion or objection].

<u>Your rights may be affected.</u> You should read these papers carefully and discuss them with your attorney, if you have one in this bankruptcy case. (If you do not have an attorney, you may wish to consult one.)

If you do not want the court to [relief sought in motion or objection], or if you want the court to consider your views on the [motion] [objection], then on or before (date), you or your attorney must:

[File with the court a written request for a hearing {*or, if the court requires a written response*, an answer, explaining your position} at:

{address of the bankruptcy clerk's office}

If you mail your {request}{response} to the court for filing, you must mail it early enough so the court will **receive** it on or before the date stated above.

You must also mail a copy to:

{movant's attorney's name and address}

{names and addresses of others to be served}]

[Attend the hearing scheduled to be held on (date), (year), at ____a.m./p.m. in Courtroom ____, United States Bankruptcy Court, {address}.]

[Other steps required to oppose a motion or objection under local rule or court order.]

If you or your attorney do not take these steps, the court may decide that you do not oppose the relief sought in the motion or objection and may enter an order granting that relief.

Date: ____________________

Signature: ____________________
Name:
Address:

UNITED STATES BANKRUPTCY COURT

In re ____,	)	
[Set forth here all names including married, maiden,	)	
and trade names used by debtor within last 8 years]	)	
	)	
Debtor	)	Case No. _______________
Address	)	
	)	Chapter _______________
	)	
Last four digits of Social-Security or Individual Taxpayer-	)	
Identification (ITIN) No(s).,(if any): ____________________	)	
	)	
Employer Tax-Identification (EIN) No(s).(if any):	)	
	)	

STATEMENT OF SOCIAL-SECURITY NUMBER(S)

*(or other Individual Taxpayer-Identification Number(s) (ITIN(s)))**

1.Name of Debtor (Last, First, Middle):___________________________________
(Check the appropriate box and, if applicable, provide the required information.)

☐ Debtor has a Social-Security Number and it is: _______________
(If more than one, state all.)

☐ Debtor does not have a Social-Security Number but has an Individual Taxpayer-Identification Number (ITIN), and it is: ________________
(If more than one, state all.)

☐ Debtor does not have either a Social-Security Number or an Individual Taxpayer-Identification Number (ITIN).

2.Name of Joint Debtor (Last, First, Middle):______________________________
(Check the appropriate box and, if applicable, provide the required information.)

☐ Joint Debtor has a Social-Security Number and it is: ______________
(If more than one, state all.)

☐ Joint Debtor does not have a Social-Security Number but has an Individual Taxpayer-Identification Number (ITIN) and it is: ________________
(If more than one, state all.)

☐ Joint Debtor does not have either a Social-Security Number or an Individual Taxpayer-Identification Number (ITIN).

I declare under penalty of perjury that the foregoing is true and correct.

X ____
Signature of Debtor Date

X ____
Signature of Joint Debtor Date

---

* *Joint debtors must provide information for both spouses.*

Penalty for making a false statement: Fine of up to $250,000 or up to 5 years imprisonment or both. 18 U.S.C. §§ 152 and 3571.

In re ______________________
Debtor(s)

Case Number: ______________
(If known)

According to the information required to be entered on this statement (check one box as directed in Part I, III, or VI of this statement):

☐ **The presumption arises.**
☐ **The presumption does not arise.**
☐ **The presumption is temporarily inapplicable.**

CHAPTER 7 STATEMENT OF CURRENT MONTHLY INCOME AND MEANS-TEST CALCULATION

In addition to Schedules I and J, this statement must be completed by every individual chapter 7 debtor, whether or not filing jointly. Unless the exclusion in Line 1C applies, joint debtors may complete a single statement. If the exclusion in Line 1C applies, each joint filer must complete a separate statement.

Part I. MILITARY AND NON-CONSUMER DEBTORS	
1A	**Disabled Veterans.** If you are a disabled veteran described in the Declaration in this Part IA, (1) check the box at the beginning of the Declaration, (2) check the box for "The presumption does not arise" at the top of this statement, and (3) complete the verification in Part VIII. Do not complete any of the remaining parts of this statement. ☐ **Declaration of Disabled Veteran.** By checking this box, I declare under penalty of perjury that I am a disabled veteran (as defined in 38 U.S.C. § 3741(1)) whose indebtedness occurred primarily during a period in which I was on active duty (as defined in 10 U.S.C. § 101(d)(1)) or while I was performing a homeland defense activity (as defined in 32 U.S.C. §901(1)).
1B	**Non-consumer Debtors.** If your debts are not primarily consumer debts, check the box below and complete the verification in Part VIII. Do not complete any of the remaining parts of this statement. ☐ **Declaration of non-consumer debts.** By checking this box, I declare that my debts are not primarily consumer debts.
1C	**Reservists and National Guard Members; active duty or homeland defense activity.** Members of a reserve component of the Armed Forces and members of the National Guard who were called to active duty (as defined in 10 U.S.C. § 101(d)(1)) after September 11, 2001, for a period of at least 90 days, or who have performed homeland defense activity (as defined in 32 U.S.C. § 901(1)) for a period of at least 90 days, are excluded from all forms of means testing during the time of active duty or homeland defense activity and for 540 days thereafter (the "exclusion period"). If you qualify for this temporary exclusion, (1) check the appropriate boxes and complete any required information in the Declaration of Reservists and National Guard Members below, (2) check the box for "The presumption is temporarily inapplicable" at the top of this statement, and (3) complete the verification in Part VIII. **During your exclusion period you are not required to complete the balance of this form, but you must complete the form no later than 14 days after the date on which your exclusion period ends, unless the time for filing a motion raising the means test presumption expires in your case before your exclusion period ends.** ☐ **Declaration of Reservists and National Guard Members.** By checking this box and making the appropriate entries below, I declare that I am eligible for a temporary exclusion from means testing because, as a member of a reserve component of the Armed Forces or the National Guard a. ☐ I was called to active duty after September 11, 2001, for a period of at least 90 days and ☐ I remain on active duty /or/ ☐ I was released from active duty on ______________, which is less than 540 days before this bankruptcy case was filed; OR b. ☐ I am performing homeland defense activity for a period of at least 90 days /or/ ☐ I performed homeland defense activity for a period of at least 90 days, terminating on ______________, which is less than 540 days before this bankruptcy case was filed.

Part II. CALCULATION OF MONTHLY INCOME FOR § 707(b)(7) EXCLUSION

Line		Column A Debtor's Income	Column B Spouse's Income
2	**Marital/filing status.** Check the box that applies and complete the balance of this part of this statement as directed. a. ☐ Unmarried. **Complete only Column A ("Debtor's Income") for Lines 3-11.** b. ☐ Married, not filing jointly, with declaration of separate households. By checking this box, debtor declares under penalty of perjury: "My spouse and I are legally separated under applicable non-bankruptcy law or my spouse and I are living apart other than for the purpose of evading the requirements of § 707(b)(2)(A) of the Bankruptcy Code." **Complete only Column A ("Debtor's Income") for Lines 3-11.** c. ☐ Married, not filing jointly, without the declaration of separate households set out in Line 2.b above. **Complete both Column A ("Debtor's Income") and Column B ("Spouse's Income") for Lines 3-11.** d. ☐ Married, filing jointly. **Complete both Column A ("Debtor's Income") and Column B ("Spouse's Income") for Lines 3-11.**		
	All figures must reflect average monthly income received from all sources, derived during the six calendar months prior to filing the bankruptcy case, ending on the last day of the month before the filing. If the amount of monthly income varied during the six months, you must divide the six-month total by six, and enter the result on the appropriate line.	**Column A Debtor's Income**	**Column B Spouse's Income**
3	**Gross wages, salary, tips, bonuses, overtime, commissions.**	$	$
4	**Income from the operation of a business, profession or farm.** Subtract Line b from Line a and enter the difference in the appropriate column(s) of Line 4. If you operate more than one business, profession or farm, enter aggregate numbers and provide details on an attachment. Do not enter a number less than zero. **Do not include any part of the business expenses entered on Line b as a deduction in Part V.** a. Gross receipts — $ b. Ordinary and necessary business expenses — $ c. Business income — Subtract Line b from Line a	$	$
5	**Rent and other real property income.** Subtract Line b from Line a and enter the difference in the appropriate column(s) of Line 5. Do not enter a number less than zero. **Do not include any part of the operating expenses entered on Line b as a deduction in Part V.** a. Gross receipts — $ b. Ordinary and necessary operating expenses — $ c. Rent and other real property income — Subtract Line b from Line a	$	$
6	**Interest, dividends and royalties.**	$	$
7	**Pension and retirement income.**	$	$
8	**Any amounts paid by another person or entity, on a regular basis, for the household expenses of the debtor or the debtor's dependents, including child support paid for that purpose.** Do not include alimony or separate maintenance payments or amounts paid by your spouse if Column B is completed.	$	$
9	**Unemployment compensation.** Enter the amount in the appropriate column(s) of Line 9. However, if you contend that unemployment compensation received by you or your spouse was a benefit under the Social Security Act, do not list the amount of such compensation in Column A or B, but instead state the amount in the space below: Unemployment compensation claimed to be a benefit under the Social Security Act — Debtor $ ________ — Spouse $ ________	$	$

10	**Income from all other sources.** Specify source and amount. If necessary, list additional sources on a separate page. **Do not include alimony or separate maintenance payments paid by your spouse if Column B is completed, but include all other payments of alimony or separate maintenance.** Do not include any benefits received under the Social Security Act or payments received as a victim of a war crime, crime against humanity, or as a victim of international or domestic terrorism. a. ___ $ b. ___ $ Total and enter on Line 10	$	$
11	**Subtotal of Current Monthly Income for § 707(b)(7).** Add Lines 3 thru 10 in Column A, and, if Column B is completed, add Lines 3 through 10 in Column B. Enter the total(s).	$	$
12	**Total Current Monthly Income for § 707(b)(7).** If Column B has been completed, add Line 11, Column A to Line 11, Column B, and enter the total. If Column B has not been completed, enter the amount from Line 11, Column A.	$	

Part III. APPLICATION OF § 707(b)(7) EXCLUSION

13	**Annualized Current Monthly Income for § 707(b)(7).** Multiply the amount from Line 12 by the number 12 and enter the result.	$
14	**Applicable median family income.** Enter the median family income for the applicable state and household size. (This information is available by family size at www.usdoj.gov/ust/ or from the clerk of the bankruptcy court.) a. Enter debtor's state of residence: ________ b. Enter debtor's household size: ______	$
15	**Application of Section 707(b)(7).** Check the applicable box and proceed as directed. ☐ **The amount on Line 13 is less than or equal to the amount on Line 14.** Check the box for "The presumption does not arise" at the top of page 1 of this statement, and complete Part VIII; do not complete Parts IV, V, VI or VII. ☐ **The amount on Line 13 is more than the amount on Line 14.** Complete the remaining parts of this statement.	

Complete Parts IV, V, VI, and VII of this statement only if required. (See Line 15.)

Part IV. CALCULATION OF CURRENT MONTHLY INCOME FOR § 707(b)(2)

16	**Enter the amount from Line 12.**	$
17	**Marital adjustment.** If you checked the box at Line 2.c, enter on Line 17 the total of any income listed in Line 11, Column B that was NOT paid on a regular basis for the household expenses of the debtor or the debtor's dependents. Specify in the lines below the basis for excluding the Column B income (such as payment of the spouse's tax liability or the spouse's support of persons other than the debtor or the debtor's dependents) and the amount of income devoted to each purpose. If necessary, list additional adjustments on a separate page. If you did not check box at Line 2.c, enter zero. a. ___ $ b. ___ $ c. ___ $ Total and enter on Line 17.	$
18	**Current monthly income for § 707(b)(2).** Subtract Line 17 from Line 16 and enter the result.	$

Part V. CALCULATION OF DEDUCTIONS FROM INCOME

Subpart A: Deductions under Standards of the Internal Revenue Service (IRS)

19A	**National Standards: food, clothing and other items.** Enter in Line 19A the "Total" amount from IRS National Standards for Food, Clothing and Other Items for the applicable household size. (This information is available at www.usdoj.gov/ust/ or from the clerk of the bankruptcy court.)	$

<table>
<tr><td>19B</td><td>National Standards: health care. Enter in Line a1 below the amount from IRS National Standards for Out-of-Pocket Health Care for persons under 65 years of age, and in Line a2 the IRS National Standards for Out-of-Pocket Health Care for persons 65 years of age or older. (This information is available at www.usdoj.gov/ust/ or from the clerk of the bankruptcy court.) Enter in Line b1 the number of members of your household who are under 65 years of age, and enter in Line b2 the number of members of your household who are 65 years of age or older. (The total number of household members must be the same as the number stated in Line 14b.) Multiply Line a1 by Line b1 to obtain a total amount for household members under 65, and enter the result in Line c1. Multiply Line a2 by Line b2 to obtain a total amount for household members 65 and older, and enter the result in Line c2. Add Lines c1 and c2 to obtain a total health care amount, and enter the result in Line 19B.
<table>
<tr><th colspan="3">Household members under 65 years of age</th><th colspan="3">Household members 65 years of age or older</th></tr>
<tr><td>a1.</td><td>Allowance per member</td><td></td><td>a2.</td><td>Allowance per member</td><td></td></tr>
<tr><td>b1.</td><td>Number of members</td><td></td><td>b2.</td><td>Number of members</td><td></td></tr>
<tr><td>c1.</td><td>Subtotal</td><td></td><td>c2.</td><td>Subtotal</td><td></td></tr>
</table></td><td>$</td></tr>
<tr><td>20A</td><td>Local Standards: housing and utilities; non-mortgage expenses. Enter the amount of the IRS Housing and Utilities Standards; non-mortgage expenses for the applicable county and household size. (This information is available at www.usdoj.gov/ust/ or from the clerk of the bankruptcy court).</td><td>$</td></tr>
<tr><td>20B</td><td>Local Standards: housing and utilities; mortgage/rent expense. Enter, in Line a below, the amount of the IRS Housing and Utilities Standards; mortgage/rent expense for your county and household size (this information is available at www.usdoj.gov/ust/ or from the clerk of the bankruptcy court); enter on Line b the total of the Average Monthly Payments for any debts secured by your home, as stated in Line 42; subtract Line b from Line a and enter the result in Line 20B. Do not enter an amount less than zero.
<table>
<tr><td>a.</td><td>IRS Housing and Utilities Standards; mortgage/rental expense</td><td>$</td></tr>
<tr><td>b.</td><td>Average Monthly Payment for any debts secured by your home, if any, as stated in Line 42</td><td>$</td></tr>
<tr><td>c.</td><td>Net mortgage/rental expense</td><td>Subtract Line b from Line a.</td></tr>
</table></td><td>$</td></tr>
<tr><td>21</td><td>Local Standards: housing and utilities; adjustment. If you contend that the process set out in Lines 20A and 20B does not accurately compute the allowance to which you are entitled under the IRS Housing and Utilities Standards, enter any additional amount to which you contend you are entitled, and state the basis for your contention in the space below:</td><td>$</td></tr>
<tr><td>22A</td><td>Local Standards: transportation; vehicle operation/public transportation expense. You are entitled to an expense allowance in this category regardless of whether you pay the expenses of operating a vehicle and regardless of whether you use public transportation.
Check the number of vehicles for which you pay the operating expenses or for which the operating expenses are included as a contribution to your household expenses in Line 8.
☐ 0 ☐ 1 ☐ 2 or more.
If you checked 0, enter on Line 22A the “Public Transportation” amount from IRS Local Standards: Transportation. If you checked 1 or 2 or more, enter on Line 22A the “Operating Costs” amount from IRS Local Standards: Transportation for the applicable number of vehicles in the applicable Metropolitan Statistical Area or Census Region. (These amounts are available at www.usdoj.gov/ust/ or from the clerk of the bankruptcy court.)</td><td>$</td></tr>
<tr><td>22B</td><td>Local Standards: transportation; additional public transportation expense. If you pay the operating expenses for a vehicle and also use public transportation, and you contend that you are entitled to an additional deduction for your public transportation expenses, enter on Line 22B the “Public Transportation” amount from IRS Local Standards: Transportation. (This amount is available at www.usdoj.gov/ust/ or from the clerk of the bankruptcy court.)</td><td>$</td></tr>
</table>

Line	Description	Amount
23	**Local Standards: transportation ownership/lease expense; Vehicle 1.** Check the number of vehicles for which you claim an ownership/lease expense. (You may not claim an ownership/lease expense for more than two vehicles.) ☐ 1 ☐ 2 or more. Enter, in Line a below, the "Ownership Costs" for "One Car" from the IRS Local Standards: Transportation (available at www.usdoj.gov/ust/ or from the clerk of the bankruptcy court); enter in Line b the total of the Average Monthly Payments for any debts secured by Vehicle 1, as stated in Line 42; subtract Line b from Line a and enter the result in Line 23. **Do not enter an amount less than zero.** a. IRS Transportation Standards, Ownership Costs — $ b. Average Monthly Payment for any debts secured by Vehicle 1, as stated in Line 42 — $ c. Net ownership/lease expense for Vehicle 1 — Subtract Line b from Line a.	$
24	**Local Standards: transportation ownership/lease expense; Vehicle 2.** Complete this Line only if you checked the "2 or more" Box in Line 23. Enter, in Line a below, the "Ownership Costs" for "One Car" from the IRS Local Standards: Transportation (available at www.usdoj.gov/ust/ or from the clerk of the bankruptcy court); enter in Line b the total of the Average Monthly Payments for any debts secured by Vehicle 2, as stated in Line 42; subtract Line b from Line a and enter the result in Line 24. **Do not enter an amount less than zero.** a. IRS Transportation Standards, Ownership Costs — $ b. Average Monthly Payment for any debts secured by Vehicle 2, as stated in Line 42 — $ c. Net ownership/lease expense for Vehicle 2 — Subtract Line b from Line a.	$
25	**Other Necessary Expenses: taxes.** Enter the total average monthly expense that you actually incur for all federal, state and local taxes, other than real estate and sales taxes, such as income taxes, self-employment taxes, social-security taxes, and Medicare taxes. **Do not include real estate or sales taxes.**	$
26	**Other Necessary Expenses: involuntary deductions for employment.** Enter the total average monthly payroll deductions that are required for your employment, such as retirement contributions, union dues, and uniform costs. **Do not include discretionary amounts, such as voluntary 401(k) contributions.**	$
27	**Other Necessary Expenses: life insurance.** Enter total average monthly premiums that you actually pay for term life insurance for yourself. **Do not include premiums for insurance on your dependents, for whole life or for any other form of insurance.**	$
28	**Other Necessary Expenses: court-ordered payments.** Enter the total monthly amount that you are required to pay pursuant to the order of a court or administrative agency, such as spousal or child support payments. **Do not include payments on past due obligations included in Line 44.**	$
29	**Other Necessary Expenses: education for employment or for a physically or mentally challenged child.** Enter the total average monthly amount that you actually expend for education that is a condition of employment and for education that is required for a physically or mentally challenged dependent child for whom no public education providing similar services is available.	$
30	**Other Necessary Expenses: childcare.** Enter the total average monthly amount that you actually expend on childcare—such as baby-sitting, day care, nursery and preschool. **Do not include other educational payments.**	$
31	**Other Necessary Expenses: health care.** Enter the total average monthly amount that you actually expend on health care that is required for the health and welfare of yourself or your dependents, that is not reimbursed by insurance or paid by a health savings account, and that is in excess of the amount entered in Line 19B. **Do not include payments for health insurance or health savings accounts listed in Line 34.**	$
32	**Other Necessary Expenses: telecommunication services.** Enter the total average monthly amount that you actually pay for telecommunication services other than your basic home telephone and cell phone service—such as pagers, call waiting, caller id, special long distance, or internet service—to the extent necessary for your health and welfare or that of your dependents. **Do not include any amount previously deducted.**	$
33	**Total Expenses Allowed under IRS Standards.** Enter the total of Lines 19 through 32.	$

Subpart B: Additional Living Expense Deductions
Note: Do not include any expenses that you have listed in Lines 19-32

34	**Health Insurance, Disability Insurance, and Health Savings Account Expenses.** List the monthly expenses in the categories set out in lines a-c below that are reasonably necessary for yourself, your spouse, or your dependents. a. Health Insurance $ b. Disability Insurance $ c. Health Savings Account $ Total and enter on Line 34	$
	If you do not actually expend this total amount, state your actual total average monthly expenditures in the space below: $ ____________	
35	**Continued contributions to the care of household or family members.** Enter the total average actual monthly expenses that you will continue to pay for the reasonable and necessary care and support of an elderly, chronically ill, or disabled member of your household or member of your immediate family who is unable to pay for such expenses.	$
36	**Protection against family violence.** Enter the total average reasonably necessary monthly expenses that you actually incurred to maintain the safety of your family under the Family Violence Prevention and Services Act or other applicable federal law. The nature of these expenses is required to be kept confidential by the court.	$
37	**Home energy costs.** Enter the total average monthly amount, in excess of the allowance specified by IRS Local Standards for Housing and Utilities, that you actually expend for home energy costs. **You must provide your case trustee with documentation of your actual expenses, and you must demonstrate that the additional amount claimed is reasonable and necessary.**	$
38	**Education expenses for dependent children less than 18.** Enter the total average monthly expenses that you actually incur, not to exceed $137.50 per child, for attendance at a private or public elementary or secondary school by your dependent children less than 18 years of age. **You must provide your case trustee with documentation of your actual expenses, and you must explain why the amount claimed is reasonable and necessary and not already accounted for in the IRS Standards.**	$
39	**Additional food and clothing expense.** Enter the total average monthly amount by which your food and clothing expenses exceed the combined allowances for food and clothing (apparel and services) in the IRS National Standards, not to exceed 5% of those combined allowances. (This information is available at www.usdoj.gov/ust/ or from the clerk of the bankruptcy court.) **You must demonstrate that the additional amount claimed is reasonable and necessary.**	$
40	**Continued charitable contributions.** Enter the amount that you will continue to contribute in the form of cash or financial instruments to a charitable organization as defined in 26 U.S.C. § 170(c)(1)-(2).	$
41	**Total Additional Expense Deductions under § 707(b).** Enter the total of Lines 34 through 40	$

Subpart C: Deductions for Debt Payment

42 **Future payments on secured claims.** For each of your debts that is secured by an interest in property that you own, list the name of the creditor, identify the property securing the debt, state the Average Monthly Payment, and check whether the payment includes taxes or insurance. The Average Monthly Payment is the total of all amounts scheduled as contractually due to each Secured Creditor in the 60 months following the filing of the bankruptcy case, divided by 60. If necessary, list additional entries on a separate page. Enter the total of the Average Monthly Payments on Line 42.

	Name of Creditor	Property Securing the Debt	Average Monthly Payment	Does payment include taxes or insurance?
a.			$	☐ yes ☐ no
b.			$	☐ yes ☐ no
c.			$	☐ yes ☐ no
			Total: Add Lines a, b and c.	

$

43 **Other payments on secured claims.** If any of debts listed in Line 42 are secured by your primary residence, a motor vehicle, or other property necessary for your support or the support of your dependents, you may include in your deduction 1/60th of any amount (the "cure amount") that you must pay the creditor in addition to the payments listed in Line 42, in order to maintain possession of the property. The cure amount would include any sums in default that must be paid in order to avoid repossession or foreclosure. List and total any such amounts in the following chart. If necessary, list additional entries on a separate page.

	Name of Creditor	Property Securing the Debt	1/60th of the Cure Amount
a.			$
b.			$
c.			$
			Total: Add Lines a, b and c

$

44 **Payments on prepetition priority claims.** Enter the total amount, divided by 60, of all priority claims, such as priority tax, child support and alimony claims, for which you were liable at the time of your bankruptcy filing. **Do not include current obligations, such as those set out in Line 28.** $

45 **Chapter 13 administrative expenses.** If you are eligible to file a case under chapter 13, complete the following chart, multiply the amount in line a by the amount in line b, and enter the resulting administrative expense.

a.	Projected average monthly chapter 13 plan payment.	$
b.	Current multiplier for your district as determined under schedules issued by the Executive Office for United States Trustees. (This information is available at www.usdoj.gov/ust/ or from the clerk of the bankruptcy court.)	x
c.	Average monthly administrative expense of chapter 13 case	Total: Multiply Lines a and b

$

46 **Total Deductions for Debt Payment.** Enter the total of Lines 42 through 45. $

Subpart D: Total Deductions from Income

47 **Total of all deductions allowed under § 707(b)(2).** Enter the total of Lines 33, 41, and 46. $

Part VI. DETERMINATION OF § 707(b)(2) PRESUMPTION

48	**Enter the amount from Line 18 (Current monthly income for § 707(b)(2))**	$
49	**Enter the amount from Line 47 (Total of all deductions allowed under § 707(b)(2))**	$
50	**Monthly disposable income under § 707(b)(2).** Subtract Line 49 from Line 48 and enter the result	$
51	**60-month disposable income under § 707(b)(2).** Multiply the amount in Line 50 by the number 60 and enter the result.	$
52	**Initial presumption determination.** Check the applicable box and proceed as directed. ☐ **The amount on Line 51 is less than $6,575** Check the box for "The presumption does not arise" at the top of page 1 of this statement, and complete the verification in Part VIII. Do not complete the remainder of Part VI. ☐ **The amount set forth on Line 51 is more than $10,950**. Check the box for "The presumption arises" at the top of page 1 of this statement, and complete the verification in Part VIII. You may also complete Part VII. Do not complete the remainder of Part VI. ☐ **The amount on Line 51 is at least $6,575, but not more than $10,950.** Complete the remainder of Part VI (Lines 53 through 55).	
53	**Enter the amount of your total non-priority unsecured debt**	$
54	**Threshold debt payment amount.** Multiply the amount in Line 53 by the number 0.25 and enter the result.	$
55	**Secondary presumption determination.** Check the applicable box and proceed as directed. ☐ **The amount on Line 51 is less than the amount on Line 54.** Check the box for "The presumption does not arise" at the top of page 1 of this statement, and complete the verification in Part VIII. ☐ **The amount on Line 51 is equal to or greater than the amount on Line 54.** Check the box for "The presumption arises" at the top of page 1 of this statement, and complete the verification in Part VIII. You may also complete Part VII.	

Part VII: ADDITIONAL EXPENSE CLAIMS

56 **Other Expenses.** List and describe any monthly expenses, not otherwise stated in this form, that are required for the health and welfare of you and your family and that you contend should be an additional deduction from your current monthly income under § 707(b)(2)(A)(ii)(I). If necessary, list additional sources on a separate page. All figures should reflect your average monthly expense for each item. Total the expenses.

	Expense Description	Monthly Amount
a.		$
b.		$
c.		$
	Total: Add Lines a, b and c	$

Part VIII: VERIFICATION

57 I declare under penalty of perjury that the information provided in this statement is true and correct. *(If this is a joint case, both debtors must sign.)*

Date: ____________ Signature: ____________________
(Debtor)

Date: ____________ Signature: ____________________
(Joint Debtor, if any)

UNITED STATES BANKRUPTCY COURT

In re ____,
Debtor

Case No. ____________________

Chapter ___________

DEBTOR'S CERTIFICATION OF COMPLETION OF POSTPETITION INSTRUCTIONAL COURSE CONCERNING PERSONAL FINANCIAL MANAGEMENT

Every individual debtor in a chapter 7, chapter 11 in which § 1141(d)(3) applies, or chapter 13 case must file this certification. If a joint petition is filed, each spouse must complete and file a separate certification. Complete one of the following statements and file by the deadline stated below:

❐ I, ____, the debtor in the above-styled case, hereby
(Printed Name of Debtor)
certify that on ____________________ *(Date)*, I completed an instructional course in personal financial management provided by ____, an approved personal financial
(Name of Provider)
management provider.

Certificate No. *(if any)*:________________________________.

❐ I, ____, the debtor in the above-styled case, hereby
(Printed Name of Debtor)
certify that no personal financial management course is required because of *[Check the appropriate box.]*:

❐ Incapacity or disability, as defined in 11 U.S.C. § 109(h);

❐ Active military duty in a military combat zone; or

❐ Residence in a district in which the United States trustee *(or bankruptcy administrator)* has determined that the approved instructional courses are not adequate at this time to serve the additional individuals who would otherwise be required to complete such courses.

Signature of Debtor: ___________________________________

Date: _____________

Instructions: Use this form only to certify whether you completed a course in personal financial management. (Fed. R. Bankr. P. 1007(b)(7).) Do NOT use this form to file the certificate given to you by your prepetition credit counseling provider and do NOT include with the petition when filing your case.

Filing Deadlines: In a chapter 7 case, file within 45 days of the first date set for the meeting of creditors under § 341 of the Bankruptcy Code. In a chapter 11 or 13 case, file no later than the last payment made by the debtor as required by the plan or the filing of a motion for a discharge under § 1141(d)(5)(B) or § 1328(b) of the Code. (See Fed. R. Bankr. P. 1007(c).)

UNITED STATES BANKRUPTCY COURT

In re ______________________________,
Debtor

Case No. ________________
Chapter ____

REAFFIRMATION AGREEMENT COVER SHEET

This form must be completed in its entirety and filed, with the reaffirmation agreement attached, within the time set under Rule 4008. It may be filed by any party to the reaffirmation agreement.

1. Creditor's Name:________________________________

2. Amount of the debt subject to this reaffirmation agreement:
$__________ on the date of bankruptcy $__________ to be paid under reaffirmation agreement

3. Annual percentage rate of interest: ______% prior to bankruptcy
______% under reaffirmation agreement (___ Fixed Rate ___ Adjustable Rate)

4. Repayment terms (if fixed rate): $_______ per month for _______ months

5. Collateral, if any, securing the debt: Current market value: $__________
Description: ____

6. Does the creditor assert that the debt is nondischargeable? ___Yes ___ No
(If yes, attach a declaration setting forth the nature of the debt and basis for the contention that the debt is nondischargeable.)

Debtor's Schedule I and J Entries

7A. Total monthly income from Schedule I, line 16 $________

8A. Total monthly expenses from Schedule J, line 18 $________

9A. Total monthly payments on reaffirmed debts not listed on Schedule J $________

Debtor's Income and Expenses as Stated on Reaffirmation Agreement

7B. Monthly income from all sources after payroll deductions $________

8B. Monthly expenses $________

9B. Total monthly payments on reaffirmed debts not included in monthly expenses $________

10B. Net monthly income $________
(Subtract sum of lines 8B and 9B from line 7B. If total is less than zero, put the number in brackets.)

11. Explain with specificity any difference between the income amounts (7A and 7B):

____

____

12. Explain with specificity any difference between the expense amounts (8A and 8B):

____

____

If line 11 or12 is completed, the undersigned debtor, and joint debtor if applicable, certifies that any explanation contained on those lines is true and correct.

____________________________	____________________________
Signature of Debtor (only required if line 11 or 12 is completed)	Signature of Joint Debtor (if applicable, and only required if line 11 or 12 is completed)

Other Information

☐ Check this box if the total on line 10B is less than zero. If that number is less than zero, a presumption of undue hardship arises (unless the creditor is a credit union) and you must explain with specificity the sources of funds available to the Debtor to make the monthly payments on the reaffirmed debt:

____

____

Was debtor represented by counsel during the course of negotiating this reaffirmation agreement?

_____Yes ______No

If debtor was represented by counsel during the course of negotiating this reaffirmation agreement, has counsel executed a certification (affidavit or declaration) in support of the reaffirmation agreement?

_____Yes ______No

FILER'S CERTIFICATION

I hereby certify that the attached agreement is a true and correct copy of the reaffirmation agreement between the parties identified on this Reaffirmation Agreement Cover Sheet.

____

Signature

____

Print/Type Name & Signer's Relation to Case

WARNING: Effective December 1, 2009, the 15-day deadline to file schedules and certain other documents under Bankruptcy Rule 1007(c) is shortened to 14 days. For further information, see note at bottom of page 2

UNITED STATES BANKRUPTCY COURT

NOTICE TO CONSUMER DEBTOR(S) UNDER §342(b) OF THE BANKRUPTCY CODE

In accordance with § 342(b) of the Bankruptcy Code, this notice to individuals with primarily consumer debts: (1) Describes briefly the services available from credit counseling services; (2) Describes briefly the purposes, benefits and costs of the four types of bankruptcy proceedings you may commence; and (3) Informs you about bankruptcy crimes and notifies you that the Attorney General may examine all information you supply in connection with a bankruptcy case.

You are cautioned that bankruptcy law is complicated and not easily described. Thus, you may wish to seek the advice of an attorney to learn of your rights and responsibilities should you decide to file a petition. Court employees cannot give you legal advice.

Notices from the bankruptcy court are sent to the mailing address you list on your bankruptcy petition. In order to ensure that you receive information about events concerning your case, Bankruptcy Rule 4002 requires that you notify the court of any changes in your address. If you are filing a **joint case** (a single bankruptcy case for two individuals married to each other), and each spouse lists the same mailing address on the bankruptcy petition, you and your spouse will generally receive a single copy of each notice mailed from the bankruptcy court in a jointly-addressed envelope, unless you file a statement with the court requesting that each spouse receive a separate copy of all notices.

1. Services Available from Credit Counseling Agencies

With limited exceptions, § 109(h) of the Bankruptcy Code requires that all individual debtors who file for bankruptcy relief on or after October 17, 2005, receive a briefing that outlines the available opportunities for credit counseling and provides assistance in performing a budget analysis. The briefing must be given within 180 days **before** the bankruptcy filing. The briefing may be provided individually or in a group (including briefings conducted by telephone or on the Internet) and must be provided by a nonprofit budget and credit counseling agency approved by the United States trustee or bankruptcy administrator. The clerk of the bankruptcy court has a list that you may consult of the approved budget and credit counseling agencies. Each debtor in a joint case must complete the briefing.

In addition, after filing a bankruptcy case, an individual debtor generally must complete a financial management instructional course before he or she can receive a discharge. The clerk also has a list of approved financial management instructional courses. Each debtor in a joint case must complete the course.

2. The Four Chapters of the Bankruptcy Code Available to Individual Consumer Debtors

Chapter 7: Liquidation ($245 filing fee, $39 administrative fee, $15 trustee surcharge: Total fee $299)

Chapter 7 is designed for debtors in financial difficulty who do not have the ability to pay their existing debts. Debtors whose debts are primarily consumer debts are subject to a "means test" designed to determine whether the case should be permitted to proceed under chapter 7. If your income is greater than the median income for your state of residence and family size, in some cases, the United States trustee (or bankruptcy administrator), the trustee, or creditors have the right to file a motion requesting that the court dismiss your case under § 707(b) of the Code. It is up to the court to decide whether the case should be dismissed.

Under chapter 7, you may claim certain of your property as exempt under governing law. A trustee may have the right to take possession of and sell the remaining property that is not exempt and use the sale proceeds to pay your creditors.

found to have committed certain kinds of improper conduct described in the Bankruptcy Code, the court may deny your discharge and, if it does, the purpose for which you filed the bankruptcy petition will be defeated.

Even if you receive a general discharge, some particular debts are not discharged under the law. Therefore, you may still be responsible for most taxes and student loans; debts incurred to pay nondischargeable taxes; domestic support and property settlement obligations; most fines, penalties, forfeitures, and criminal restitution obligations; certain debts which are not properly listed in your bankruptcy papers; and debts for death or personal injury caused by operating a motor vehicle, vessel, or aircraft while intoxicated from alcohol or drugs. Also, if a creditor can prove that a debt arose from fraud, breach of fiduciary duty, or theft, or from a willful and malicious injury, the bankruptcy court may determine that the debt is not discharged.

Chapter 13: Repayment of All or Part of the Debts of an Individual with Regular Income ($235 filing fee, $39 administrative fee: Total fee $274)

Chapter 13 is designed for individuals with regular income who would like to pay all or part of their debts in installments over a period of time. You are only eligible for chapter 13 if your debts do not exceed certain dollar amounts set forth in the Bankruptcy Code.

Under chapter 13, you must file with the court a plan to repay your creditors all or part of the money that you owe them, using your future earnings. The period allowed by the court to repay your debts may be three years or five years, depending upon your income and other factors. The court must approve your plan before it can take effect.

After completing the payments under your plan, your debts are generally discharged except for domestic support obligations; most student loans; certain taxes; most criminal fines and restitution obligations; certain debts which are not properly listed in your bankruptcy papers; certain debts for acts that caused death or personal injury; and certain long term secured obligations.

Chapter 11: Reorganization ($1000 filing fee, $39 administrative fee: Total fee $1039)

Chapter 11 is designed for the reorganization of a business but is also available to consumer debtors. Its provisions are quite complicated, and any decision by an individual to file a chapter 11 petition should be reviewed with an attorney.

Chapter 12: Family Farmer or Fisherman ($200 filing fee, $39 administrative fee: Total fee $239)

Chapter 12 is designed to permit family farmers and fishermen to repay their debts over a period of time from future earnings and is similar to chapter 13. The eligibility requirements are restrictive, limiting its use to those whose income arises primarily from a family-owned farm or commercial fishing operation.

3. Bankruptcy Crimes and Availability of Bankruptcy Papers to Law Enforcement Officials

A person who knowingly and fraudulently conceals assets or makes a false oath or statement under penalty of perjury, either orally or in writing, in connection with a bankruptcy case is subject to a fine, imprisonment, or both. All information supplied by a debtor in connection with a bankruptcy case is subject to examination by the Attorney General acting through the Office of the United States Trustee, the Office of the United States Attorney, and other components and employees of the Department of Justice.

WARNING: Section 521(a)(1) of the Bankruptcy Code requires that you promptly file detailed information regarding your creditors, assets, liabilities, income, expenses and general financial condition. Your bankruptcy case may be dismissed if this information is not filed with the court within the time deadlines set by the Bankruptcy Code, the Bankruptcy Rules, and the local rules of the court. The documents and the deadlines for filing them are listed on Form B200, which is posted at http://www.uscourts.gov/bkforms/bankruptcy_forms.html#procedure.

Many filing deadlines change on December 1, 2009. Of special note, 12 rules that set 15 days to act are amended to require action within 14 days, including Rule 1007(c), filing the initial case papers; Rule 3015(b), filing a chapter 13 plan; Rule 8009(a), filing appellate briefs; and Rules 1019, 1020, 2015, 2015.1, 2016, 4001, 4002, 6004, and 6007.

Check one.
☐ **Presumption of Undue Hardship**
☐ **No Presumption of Undue Hardship**
See Debtor's Statement in Support of Reaffirmation, Part II below, to determine which box to check.

UNITED STATES BANKRUPTCY COURT

In re ______________________________,
Debtor

Case No. ______________

Chapter ______________

REAFFIRMATION DOCUMENTS

Name of Creditor: ______________________________

☐ Check this box if Creditor is a Credit Union

I. REAFFIRMATION AGREEMENT

Reaffirming a debt is a serious financial decision. Before entering into this Reaffirmation Agreement, you must review the important disclosures, instructions, and definitions found in Part V of this Reaffirmation Documents packet.

1. Brief description of the original agreement being reaffirmed: ______________________
For example, auto loan

2. ***AMOUNT REAFFIRMED***: $______________________

The Amount Reaffirmed is the entire amount that you are agreeing to pay. This may include unpaid principal, interest, and fees and costs (if any) arising on or before the date you sign this Reaffirmation Agreement.

See the definition of "Amount Reaffirmed" in Part V.C below.

3. The ***ANNUAL PERCENTAGE RATE*** applicable to the Amount Reaffirmed is _________%.

See definition of "Annual Percentage Rate" in Part V.C below.

This is a *(check one)* ☐ Fixed rate ☐ Variable rate

If the loan has a variable rate, the future interest rate may increase or decrease from the Annual Percentage Rate disclosed here.

4. Reaffirmation Agreement Repayment Terms:

☐ If fixed term, $________ per month for ________ months starting on____________.

☐ If not fixed term, describe repayment terms: ______________________________.

5. Describe the collateral, if any, securing the debt:

Description:	______________________________
Current Market Value	$____________

6. Did the debt that is being reaffirming arise from the purchase of the collateral described above?

☐ Yes ☐ No

If yes, what was the purchase price for the collateral?	$____________
If no, what was the amount of the original loan?	$____________

7. Detail the changes made by this Reaffirmation Agreement to the most recent credit terms on the reaffirmed debt and any related agreement:

	Terms as of the Date of Bankruptcy	Terms After Reaffirmation
Balance due *(including fees and costs)*	$__________	$__________
Annual Percentage Rate	________%	________%
Monthly Payment	$__________	$__________

8. ☐ Check this box if the creditor is agreeing to provide you with additional future credit in connection with this Reaffirmation Agreement. Describe the credit limit, the Annual Percentage Rate that applies to future credit and any other terms on future purchases and advances using such credit:

II. DEBTOR'S STATEMENT IN SUPPORT OF REAFFIRMATION AGREEMENT

1. Were you represented by an attorney during the course of negotiating this agreement?

Check one. ☐ Yes ☐ No

2. Is the creditor a credit union?

Check one. ☐ Yes ☐ No

3. If your answer to EITHER question 1. or 2. above is "No" complete a. and b. below.

a. My present monthly income and expenses are:

i. Monthly income from all sources after payroll deductions (take-home pay plus any other income) $________

ii. Monthly expenses (including all reaffirmed debts except this one) $________

iii. Amount available to pay this reaffirmed debt (subtract ii. from i.) $________

iv. Amount of monthly payment required for this reaffirmed debt $________

If the monthly payment on this reaffirmed debt (line iv.) ***is greater than*** *the amount you have available to pay this reaffirmed debt (line iii.), you must check the box at the top of page one that says "Presumption of Undue Hardship." Otherwise, you must check the box at the top of page one that says "No Presumption of Undue Hardship."*

b. I believe this reaffirmation agreement will not impose an undue hardship on my dependents or on me because:

Check one of the two statements below, if applicable:

☐ I can afford to make the payments on the reaffirmed debt because my monthly income is greater than my monthly expenses even after I include in my expenses the monthly payments on all debts I am reaffirming, including this one.

☐ I can afford to make the payments on the reaffirmed debt even though my monthly income is less than my monthly expenses after I include in my expenses the monthly payments on all debts I am reaffirming, including this one, because:

Use an additional page if needed for a full explanation.

4. If your answers to BOTH questions 1. and 2. above were "Yes," check the following statement, if applicable:

☐ I believe this reaffirmation agreement is in my financial interest and I can afford to make the payments on the reaffirmed debt.

Also, check the box at the top of page one that says "No Presumption of Undue Hardship."

III. CERTIFICATION BY DEBTOR(S) AND SIGNATURES OF PARTIES

I (We) hereby certify that:

i. I (We) agree to reaffirm the debt described above.

ii. Before signing this reaffirmation agreement, I (we) read the terms disclosed in this Reaffirmation Agreement (Part I) and the Disclosure Statement, Instructions and Definitions included in Part V below;

iii. The Debtor's Statement in Support of Reaffirmation Agreement (Part II above) is true and complete;

iv. I am (We are) entering into this agreement voluntarily and fully informed of my (our) rights and responsibilities; and

v. I (We) have received a copy of this completed and signed Reaffirmation Documents packet.

SIGNATURE(S):

Date ______________ Signature ______________________________
Debtor

Date ______________ Signature ______________________________
Joint Debtor, if any

If a joint reaffirmation agreement, both debtors must sign.

Reaffirmation Agreement Terms Accepted by Creditor:

Creditor ______________________ ______________________
Print Name *Address*

______________________ ______________________ __________
Print Name of Representative *Signature* *Date*

IV. CERTIFICATION BY DEBTOR'S ATTORNEY (IF ANY)

To be filed only if the attorney represented the debtor during the course of negotiating this agreement.

I hereby certify that: (1) this agreement represents a fully informed and voluntary agreement by the debtor; (2) this agreement does not impose an undue hardship on the debtor or any dependent of the debtor; and (3) I have fully advised the debtor of the legal effect and consequences of this agreement and any default under this agreement.

☐ A presumption of undue hardship has been established with respect to this agreement. In my opinion, however, the debtor is able to make the required payment.

Check box, if the presumption of undue hardship box is checked on page 1 and the creditor is not a Credit Union.

Date ____________ Signature of Debtor's Attorney______________________________

Print Name of Debtor's Attorney ______________________________

V. DISCLOSURE STATEMENT AND INSTRUCTIONS TO DEBTOR(S)

Before agreeing to reaffirm a debt, review the terms disclosed in the Reaffirmation Agreement (Part I) and these additional important disclosures and instructions.

Reaffirming a debt is a serious financial decision. The law requires you to take certain steps to make sure the decision is in your best interest. If these steps, detailed in Part B below, are not completed, the reaffirmation agreement is not effective, even though you have signed it.

A. DISCLOSURE STATEMENT

1. **What are your obligations if you reaffirm a debt?** A reaffirmed debt remains your personal legal obligation. Your reaffirmed debt is not discharged in your bankruptcy case. That means that if you default on your reaffirmed debt after your bankruptcy case is over, your creditor may be able to take your property or your wages. Your obligations will be determined by the reaffirmation agreement, which may have changed the terms of the original agreement. If you are reaffirming an open end credit agreement, that agreement or applicable law may permit the creditor to change the terms of that agreement in the future under certain conditions.

2. **Are you required to enter into a reaffirmation agreement by any law?** No, you are not required to reaffirm a debt by any law. Only agree to reaffirm a debt if it is in your best interest. Be sure you can afford the payments that you agree to make.

3. **What if your creditor has a security interest or lien?** Your bankruptcy discharge does not eliminate any lien on your property. A ''lien'' is often referred to as a security interest, deed of trust, mortgage, or security deed. The property subject to a lien is often referred to as collateral. Even if you do not reaffirm and your personal liability on the debt is discharged, your creditor may still have a right under the lien to take the collateral if you do not pay or default on the debt. If the collateral is personal property that is exempt or that the trustee has abandoned, you may be able to redeem the item rather than reaffirm the debt. To redeem, you make a single payment to the creditor equal to the current value of the collateral, as the parties agree or the court determines.

4. **How soon do you need to enter into and file a reaffirmation agreement?** If you decide to enter into a reaffirmation agreement, you must do so before you receive your discharge. After you have entered into a reaffirmation agreement and all parts of this Reaffirmation Documents packet requiring signature have been signed, either you or the creditor should file it as soon as possible. The signed agreement must be filed with the court no later than 60 days after the first date set for the meeting of creditors, so that the court will have time to schedule a hearing to approve the agreement if approval is required.

5. **Can you cancel the agreement?** You may rescind (cancel) your reaffirmation agreement at any time before the bankruptcy court enters your discharge, or during the 60-day period that begins on the date your reaffirmation agreement is filed with the court, whichever occurs later. To rescind (cancel) your reaffirmation agreement, you must notify the creditor that your reaffirmation agreement is rescinded (or canceled). Remember that you can rescind the agreement, even if the court approves it, as long as you rescind within the time allowed.

6. **When will this reaffirmation agreement be effective?**

a. **If you** ***were represented*** **by an attorney during the negotiation of your reaffirmation agreement**

i. **if the creditor is not a Credit Union**, your reaffirmation agreement becomes effective upon filing with the court unless the reaffirmation is presumed to be an undue hardship in which case the agreement becomes effective only after the court approves it;

ii. **if the creditor is a Credit Union**, your reaffirmation agreement becomes effective when it is filed with the court.

b. **If you** ***were not represented*** **by an attorney during the negotiation of your reaffirmation agreement**, the reaffirmation agreement will not be effective unless the court approves it. To have the court approve your agreement, you must file a motion. See Instruction 5, below. The court will notify you and the creditor of the hearing on your reaffirmation agreement. You must attend this hearing, at which time the judge will review your reaffirmation agreement. If the judge decides that the reaffirmation agreement is in your best interest, the agreement will be approved and will become effective. However, if your reaffirmation agreement is for a consumer debt secured by a mortgage, deed of trust, security deed, or other lien on your real property, like your home, you do not need to file a motion or get court approval of your reaffirmation agreement.

7. **What if you have questions about what a creditor can do?** If you have questions about reaffirming a debt or what the law requires, consult with the attorney who helped you negotiate this agreement. If you do not have an attorney helping you, you may ask the judge to explain the effect of this agreement to you at the hearing to approve the reaffirmation agreement. When this disclosure refers to what a creditor "may" do, it is not giving any creditor permission to do anything. The word "may" is used to tell you what might occur if the law permits the creditor to take the action.

B. INSTRUCTIONS

1. Review these Disclosures and carefully consider the decision to reaffirm. If you want to reaffirm, review and complete the information contained in the Reaffirmation Agreement (Part I above). If your case is a joint case, both spouses must sign the agreement if both are reaffirming the debt.

2. Complete the Debtor's Statement in Support of Reaffirmation Agreement (Part II above). Be sure that you can afford to make the payments that you are agreeing to make and that you have received a copy of the Disclosure Statement and a completed and signed Reaffirmation Agreement.

3. If you were represented by an attorney during the negotiation of your Reaffirmation Agreement, your attorney must sign and date the Certification By Debtor's Attorney section (Part IV above).

4. You or your creditor must file with the court the original of this Reaffirmation Documents packet and a completed Reaffirmation Agreement Cover Sheet (Official Bankruptcy Form 27).

5. *If you are not represented by an attorney, you must also complete and file with the court a separate document entitled "Motion for Court Approval of Reaffirmation Agreement unless your reaffirmation agreement is for a consumer debt secured by a lien on your real property, such as your home.* You can use Form B240B to do this.

C. DEFINITIONS

1. **"Amount Reaffirmed"** means the total amount of debt that you are agreeing to pay (reaffirm) by entering into this agreement. The amount of debt includes any unpaid fees and costs arising on or before the date you sign this agreement that you are agreeing to pay. Your credit agreement may obligate you to pay additional amounts that arise after the date you sign this agreement. You should consult your credit agreement to determine whether you are obligated to pay additional amounts that may arise after the date of this agreement.

2. **"Annual Percentage Rate"** means the interest rate on a loan expressed under the rules required by federal law. The annual percentage Rate (as opposed to the "stated interest rate") tells you the full cost of your credit including many of the creditor's fees and charges. You will find the annual percentage rate for your original agreement on the disclosure statement that was given to you when the loan papers were signed or on the monthly statements sent to you for an open end credit account such as a credit card.

3. **"Credit Union"** means a financial institution as defined in 12 U.S.C. § 461(b)(1)(A)(iv). It is owned and controlled by and provides financial services to its members and typically uses words like "Credit Union" or initials like "C.U." or "F.C.U." in its name.

UNITED STATES BANKRUPTCY COURT

In re ______________________________,
Debtor

Case No.____________________

Chapter__________________

MOTION FOR APPROVAL OF REAFFIRMATION AGREEMENT

I (we), the debtor(s), affirm the following to be true and correct:

I am not represented by an attorney in connection with this reaffirmation agreement.

I believe this reaffirmation agreement is in my best interest based on the income and expenses I have disclosed in my Statement in Support of Reaffirmation Agreement, and because *(provide any additional relevant reasons the court should consider)*:

Therefore, I ask the court for an order approving this reaffirmation agreement under the following provisions *(check all applicable boxes)*:

☐ 11 U.S.C. § 524(c)(6) (debtor is not represented by an attorney during the course of the negotiation of the reaffirmation agreement)

☐ 11 U.S.C. § 524(m) (presumption of undue hardship has arisen because monthly expenses exceed monthly income, as explained in Part II of Form B240A, Reaffirmation Documents)

Signed:______________________________
(Debtor)

____
(Joint Debtor, if any)

Date: ____________________

United States Bankruptcy Court
_____________________District of ____________________

In re _______________________________________,
Debtor

Case No.________________
Chapter ________

ORDER ON REAFFIRMATION AGREEMENT

The debtor(s) _______________________ has (have) filed a motion for approval of the reaffirmation agreement dated ____________________ made between the debtor(s) and creditor ___________________________. The court held the hearing required by 11 U.S.C. § 524(d) on notice to the debtor(s) and the creditor on _________________ (date).

COURT ORDER:

☐ The court grants the debtor's motion under 11 U.S.C. § 524(c)(6)(A) and approves the reaffirmation agreement described above as not imposing an undue hardship on the debtor(s) or a dependent of the debtor(s) and as being in the best interest of the debtor(s).

☐ The court grants the debtor's motion under 11 U.S.C. § 524(k)(8) and approves the reaffirmation agreement described above.

☐ The court does not disapprove the reaffirmation agreement under 11 U.S.C. § 524(m).

☐ The court disapproves the reaffirmation agreement under 11 U.S.C. § 524(m).

☐ The court does not approve the reaffirmation agreement.

BY THE COURT

Date: ___________________

____
United States Bankruptcy Judge

APPENDIX

D

Pleadings

This appendix provides sample pleading forms for some of the more complicated procedures described in the book, such as avoiding a lien or reopening your case. The forms provided in this appendix are examples only: You may need to modify them to fit your situation, and you may need help from a lawyer for a few of these procedures.

Lien Avoidance

To avoid a lien, you claim the property as exempt on Schedule C, file a separate request (motion) with the bankruptcy court, and formally serve the motion on the creditor by mail. Filing a motion is simple and can be done without a lawyer. In most courts, you must file your motion with the court within 30 days after you file for bankruptcy. But some courts require you to file the motion before the creditors' meeting. Check your local rules.

Lien avoidance is covered in detail in Ch. 8.

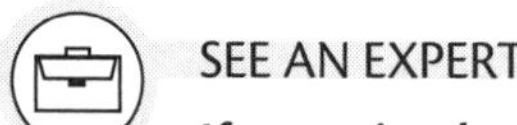

SEE AN EXPERT

If you miss the deadline, talk to a lawyer. You might not discover a lien until after the deadline passes for filing a motion. In fact, it's not uncommon to discover liens only after a bankruptcy case is closed. If this happens to you, you can file a motion asking the court to let you proceed even though you missed the deadline, or even to reopen the case if necessary. Talk to a lawyer right away if you want to avoid a lien after the deadline has passed.

What goes in your motion papers depends on the kind of lien you're trying to eliminate.

Nonpossessory, Non-Purchase-Money Security Interests

You will need to fill out one complete set of forms for each affected creditor—generally, each creditor holding a lien on that property. Sample forms are shown below. Some courts have their own forms; if yours does, use them and adapt these instructions to fit.

Checklist of Forms for Motion to Avoid Nonpossessory, Non-Purchase-Money Security Interest

- ☐ Motion to Avoid Nonpossessory, Non-Purchase-Money Security Interest
- ☐ Notice of Motion to Avoid Nonpossessory, Non-Purchase-Money Security Interest
- ☐ Order to Avoid Nonpossessory, Non-Purchase-Money Security Interest
- ☐ Proof of Service by Mail

Step 1: If your court publishes local rules, refer to them for time limits, format of papers, and other details of a motion proceeding.

Step 2: Type the top half of the pleading form (where you list your name, the court, the case number, and so on) following the examples shown below. This part of the form is known as the "caption." It is the same for all pleadings.

Step 3: If you're using a computer to prepare the forms, save the caption portion and reuse it for other pleadings. If you're using a typewriter to prepare the forms, stop when you've typed the caption and photocopy the page you've made so far, so you can reuse it for other pleadings.

Step 4: Using one of the copies that you just made, start typing again just below the caption and prepare a Motion to Avoid Nonpossessory, Non-Purchase-Money Security Interest, as shown in the example.

Step 5: Most courts require you only to file the motion with the court and serve the creditor with a notice explaining that the lien will be avoided by default if the creditor doesn't respond and request a hearing on your motion. (These are colorfully called "scream or die" motions—see the sample Notice of Motion and Motion to Avoid Judicial Lien on Real Estate, below, for language you can use instead of a formal notice if your district follows this procedure.) Because motions to avoid liens are usually pretty straightforward and are usually granted, many creditors don't bother to respond. If they do, however, either you or the creditor will have to schedule a hearing.

Step 6: If a hearing is required, call the court clerk and give your name and case number. Say you'd like to file a motion to avoid a lien and need to find out when and where the judge will hear arguments on your motion. Under some local rules the clerk will give you a hearing date; ask for one at least 31 days in the future, because you must mail notice of your motion to the creditor at least 30 days before the hearing (unless local rules set a different time limit). Write down the information. If the clerk won't give you the information over the phone, go to the bankruptcy court with a copy of your motion filled out. File that form and schedule the hearing. Write down the information about when and where your motion will be heard by the judge.

If there will be a hearing, prepare a Notice of Motion that lists the date, time, and place of the hearing. (See the sample Notice of Motion to Avoid Nonpossessory, Non-Purchase-Money Security Interest, below.) If you are filing in a district that requires a hearing only if the creditor requests one, use the language in the sample Notice of Motion and Motion to Avoid Judicial Lien on Real Estate, below, to give the creditor proper notice of this procedure.

Step 7: Prepare a proposed Order to Avoid Nonpossessory, Non-Purchase-Money Security Interest. This is the document the judge signs to grant your request. Specify exactly what property the creditor has secured in the space indicated in the sample. You can get this information from the security agreement you signed. Make two extra copies, and take them with you to the hearing if there is one. The court's local rules may require you to file the proposed order with the rest of your motion papers.

Step 8: Prepare at least two Proofs of Service by Mail, one for each affected creditor and one for the trustee. These forms state that a friend or relative of yours, who is at least 18 years old and not a party to the bankruptcy, mailed your papers to the creditor(s) or the trustee. Fill in the blanks as indicated. Have your friend sign and date the form at the end as shown on the sample. See "How to Serve the Creditor," below, for more information.

Step 9: Make at least three extra copies of all forms.

Step 10: Keep the proofs of service. Have your friend mail one copy of the motion, notice of motion, and proposed order to each affected creditor and the trustee.

Step 11: File (in person or by mail) the original (signed) notice of motion, motion (and proposed order, if required in your area), and proof of service with the bankruptcy court.

Step 12: The trustee or creditors affected by your motion may submit a written response. However, most courts will grant your motion if the trustee or creditor doesn't file a response to the motion and you ask the court to enter a default judgment in your favor (see Step 14, below).

Step 13: If there is a hearing, attend it. The hearing usually lasts ten minutes or less. Because you filed the motion, you argue your side first. Explain briefly how your property falls within the acceptable categories of exempt property, that the lien is a nonpossessory non-purchase-money security interest, and that the lien impairs your exemption. (11 U.S.C. § 522(f)(2).) "Impairs your exemption" means that because of the lien, your ownership interest in this item of exempt property has been reduced.

The trustee or creditor (or an attorney) responds. The judge either decides the matter and signs your proposed order or takes it "under advisement" and mails you the order in a few days.

Step 14: If the creditor doesn't show up at the hearing, or if the creditor doesn't file a response to your motion when it is required to do so (see Step 12, above), file and serve a Request for Entry of Order by Default. (See the sample request with the papers for avoiding a judicial lien, below, to get an idea of what this should look like. Of course, you'll have to change the language so it refers to a nonpossessory, non-purchase-money security interest rather than a judicial lien.) This document tells the court that you followed all of the proper procedures and gave the creditor notice of your motion, but the creditor didn't respond as it was required to do. The request asks the court to grant your motion by default. You must prepare another Proof of Service and serve this request on the creditor.

SEE AN EXPERT

Get an attorney, if you need one. If you are having trouble figuring out how to draft the necessary paperwork to avoid a lien, think about asking a lawyer for help—especially if the lien is substantial.

How to Serve the Creditor

Here are the rules for providing notice to the creditor:

- If the creditor provided you with a contact address and a current account number within the 90 days before you filed for bankruptcy, you must use that address and include the account number and the last four digits of your Social Security or taxpayer identification number with your papers.
- If the creditor was prohibited from communicating with you during this 90-day period, you must use the address and account number contained in the two written communications you received most recently from the creditor.
- If the creditor has filed a preferred contact address with the court, you must use that address.

If your creditor is a business, you must serve a live human being who represents the creditor—you can't just send your motion to "Visa" or "First Bank," for example. Here's how to find that warm body:

- Call the creditor and ask for the name and address of the person who accepts service of process for the business.
- If you don't know how to reach the creditor, contact your state's secretary of state office and ask for the name and address of the person who is listed as the registered agent for service of process for the company. Many states make this information available online, too.

Sample Motion to Avoid Nonpossessory, Non-Purchase-Money Security Interest

UNITED STATES BANKRUPTCY COURT

___*[Name of District]*___ DISTRICT OF ___*[Your State]*___

In re ______________________________)
[Set forth here all names including married, maiden, and trade names used by debtor within last 8 years.])
Debtor) Case No. ______________
) *[Special number for Avoidance of Lien motions, if any]*
Address ______________________________)
______________________________) Chapter 7
Last four digits of Social Security or Individual Taxpayer Identification (ITIN) No(s). (if any):__________)
Employer's Tax Identification (EIN) No(s). (if any): ______________________________)

MOTION TO AVOID NONPOSSESSORY,
NON-PURCHASE-MONEY SECURITY INTEREST

1. Debtors ___*[your name(s)]*___, filed a voluntary petition for relief under Chapter 7 of Title 11 of the United States Code on ___*[date you filed for bankruptcy]*___.

2. This court has jurisdiction over this motion, filed pursuant to 11 U.S.C. § 522(f), to avoid a nonpossessory non-purchase-money security interest held by ___*[name of lienholder]*___ on property held by the debtor.

3. On or about ___*[date you incurred the debt]*___, debtors borrowed $ ___*[amount of loan]*___ from ___*[name of creditor]*___. As security for loan, ___*[name of creditor]*___ insisted upon, and the debtors executed, a note and security agreement granting to ___*[name of creditor]*___ a security interest in and on the debtor's personal property, which consisted of ___*[items held as security as they are listed in your loan agreement]*___ which are held primarily for the family and household use of the debtors and their dependents.

4. All such possessions of debtors have been claimed as fully exempt in their bankruptcy case.

5. The money borrowed from ___*[name of creditor]*___ does not represent any part of the purchase money of any of the articles covered in the security agreement executed by the debtors, and all of the articles so covered remain in the possession of the debtors.

6. The existence of ___*[name of creditor]'s*___ lien on debtor's household and personal goods impairs exemptions to which the debtors would be entitled under 11 U.S.C. § 522(b).

Sample Motion to Avoid Nonpossessory, Non-Purchase-Money Security Interest (continued)

WHEREFORE, pursuant to 11 U.S.C. § 522(f), debtors pray for an order avoiding the security interest in their personal and household goods, and for such additional or alternative relief as may be just and proper.

Date: ______________________ Signed by: ______________________________
Debtor in Propria Persona

Date: ______________________ Signed by: ______________________________
Debtor in Propria Persona

Sample Notice of Motion to Avoid Nonpossessory, Non-Purchase-Money Security Interest

UNITED STATES BANKRUPTCY COURT

_______________ DISTRICT OF _______________

In re ______________________ *[Set forth here all names including married, maiden, and trade names used by debtor within last 8 years.]* Debtor	)	Case No. ______________
Address ______________________	)	*[Special number for Avoidance of Lien motions, if any]*
______________________	)	Chapter 7
Last four digits of Social Security or Individual Taxpayer Identification (ITIN) No(s). (if any): ________	)	
Employer's Tax Identification (EIN) No(s). (if any): ______________________	)	

NOTICE OF MOTION TO AVOID NONPOSSESSORY,
NON-PURCHASE-MONEY SECURITY INTEREST

Please take notice of motion set for a hearing on: ______ *[leave blank]* ______, 20____,

at ______ o'clock ____.m. at ______ *[leave blank]* ______, in

courtroom ______.

Sample Order to Avoid Nonpossessory, Non-Purchase-Money Security Interest

UNITED STATES BANKRUPTCY COURT

_______________ DISTRICT OF _______________

In re _______________)
[Set forth here all names including married, maiden, and trade names used by debtor within last 8 years.])
Debtor) Case No. _______________
) *[Special number for Avoidance of Lien motions, if any]*
Address _______________)
_______________) Chapter 7
)
Last four digits of Social Security or Individual Taxpayer Identification (ITIN) No(s). (if any):_______)
)
Employer's Tax Identification (EIN) No(s). (if any):)
_______________)

ORDER TO AVOID NONPOSSESSORY,
NON-PURCHASE-MONEY SECURITY INTEREST

The motion of the above-named debtor(s) ______*[your name(s)]*______, to avoid the lien of the respondent, ______*[name of creditor]*______, is sustained.

The lien is a nonpossessory, non-purchase-money lien that impairs the debtor's exemptions in the following property:

[list all items held as security as listed in your loan agreement]

Unless debtor's bankruptcy case is dismissed, the lien of the respondent is hereby extinguished and the lien shall not survive bankruptcy or affix to or remain enforceable against the aforementioned property of the debtor.

______*[name of creditor]*______ shall take all necessary steps to remove any record of the lien from the aforementioned property of the debtor.

Date: _______________ Signed by: ______*[leave blank for judge to sign]*______
U.S. Bankruptcy Judge

Judicial Lien

To eliminate a judicial lien, follow the steps to eliminate a nonpossessory, non-purchase-money security interest, above, but use the Sample Notice of Motion and Motion to Avoid Judicial Lien on Real Estate and Order to Avoid Judicial Lien on Real Estate forms as examples.

The sample forms are for eliminating a judicial lien on your home. To eliminate a lien on personal property, you will need to change the language accordingly.

Checklist of Forms for Motion to Avoid Judicial Lien

- ☐ Motion to Avoid Judicial Lien or Motion to Avoid Judicial Lien on Real Estate
- ☐ Notice of Motion to Avoid Judicial Lien
- ☐ Order to Avoid Judicial Lien
- ☐ Request for Entry of Order by Default and Proof of Service by Mail (if the creditor doesn't respond)
- ☐ Proof of Service

You may have to prove the value of the property in question. Typically, when you file for bankruptcy and assign a value to your property, the only person who may check your figures is the trustee—and that doesn't happen very often. However, if a creditor opposes your motion to avoid a judicial lien, the creditor can make you prove the property's value, because the more the property is worth, the less the lien impairs the exemption. For instance, if you listed property as worth $50,000 and the exemption is $45,000, a lien exceeding $5,000 would impair the exemption and entitle you to have the lien removed. But if the evidence you provide at the hearing shows that the property is worth $60,000, a lien of less than $15,000 wouldn't impair the exemption, because you would be able to take your $45,000 exemption and still pay the full lien. So be prepared to show how you determined the value of your property.

SEE AN EXPERT

Use an attorney, if necessary. If you are having trouble figuring out how to draft the necessary paperwork to avoid a lien, think about asking a lawyer for help—especially if the lien is substantial.

Sample Notice of Motion and Motion to Avoid Judicial Lien on Real Estate

UNITED STATES BANKRUPTCY COURT

[Name of District] DISTRICT OF *[Your State]*

In re ______________________________)
[Set forth here all names including married, maiden, and trade names used by debtor within last 8 years.])
Debtor) Case No. ________________
) *[Special number for Avoidance of Lien motions, if any]*
Address ______________________________)
______________________________) Chapter 7
Last four digits of Social Security or Individual Taxpayer Identification (ITIN) No(s). (if any): ________)
Employer's Tax Identification (EIN) No(s). (if any):)
______________________________)

NOTICE OF MOTION AND
MOTION TO AVOID JUDICIAL LIEN ON REAL ESTATE

PLEASE TAKE NOTICE that Debtor *[debtor's name]* is moving the court to avoid a judicial lien held by *[name of lien owner]* on certain real property owned by the Debtor.

This motion is being brought under procedures prescribed by *[local bankruptcy rule allowing motion to be decided without a hearing unless the creditor objects]* .

If you wish to object to the motion, or request a hearing on the motion, your objection and/or request must be filed and served upon Debtor within 20 days of the date this notice was mailed.

You must accompany any request you make for a hearing, or any objection to the relief sought by Debtor(s), with any declarations or memoranda of law you wish to present in support of your position.

If you do not make a timely objection to the requested relief, or a timely request for hearing, the court may enter an order granting the relief by default and either 1) set a tentative hearing date or 2) require that Debtors provide you at least 10 days written notice of hearing (in the event an objection or request for hearing is timely made).

1. Debtor *[debtor's name]* commenced this case on *[date of bankruptcy filing]* by filing a voluntary petition for relief under Chapter 7 of Title 11 of the United States Bankruptcy Code.

Sample Notice of Motion and Motion to Avoid Judicial Lien on Real Estate (continued)

2. This court has jurisdiction over this motion, filed pursuant to 11 U.S.C. Sec. 522(f), to avoid and cancel a judicial lien held by *[name of lien owner]* on real property used as the debtors' residence, under 28 U.S.C. Sec. 1334.

3. On *[date of lien being recorded]*, creditors recorded a judicial lien against the debtors' residence at *[address]*. The said judicial lien is entered of record as follows: *[describe how lien appears in public records]*.

4. The Debtors' interest in the property referred to in the preceding paragraph and encumbered by the lien has been claimed as fully exempt in their bankruptcy case.

5. The existence of *[lien owner's name]* lien on Debtors' real property impairs exemptions to which the Debtors would be entitled under 11 U.S.C. Sec. 522(b).

WHEREFORE, Debtors pray for an order against *[lien owner's name]* avoiding and canceling the judicial lien in the above-mentioned property, and for such additional or alternative relief as may be just and proper.

Date: ____________________ Signed by: ______________________________

Sample Request for Entry of Order by Default

UNITED STATES BANKRUPTCY COURT

[Name of District] DISTRICT OF *[Your State]*

In re ________________________)
[Set forth here all names including married, maiden, and trade names used by debtor within last 8 years.])
Debtor) Case No. ____________
) *[Special number for Avoidance of Lien motions, if any]*
Address ________________________)
________________________) Chapter 7
)
Last four digits of Social Security or Individual Taxpayer Identification (ITIN) No(s). (if any):________)
)
Employer's Tax Identification (EIN) No(s). (if any):)
________________________)

REQUEST FOR ENTRY OF ORDER BY DEFAULT AND PROPOSED ORDER

Now comes *[debtor's name]* who declares and says under penalty of perjury this *[date of request]* that the following statements are true and correct:

1. On *[date notice and motion served]*, Debtor *[debtor's name]* caused a Notice of Motion and Motion to Avoid Judicial Lien on Real Estate to be served on *[name of person served on behalf of lien owner]*.

2. A copy of the Notice of Motion and Motion and a proposed order are attached to this request. Also attached is a Proof of Service of this request on *[name of lien owner]*, the Trustee, and the U.S. Trustee.

3. The Trustee and the U.S. Trustee were also served with the Notice of Motion and Motion on *[date notice and motion served]*.

4. A proof of service duly executed by *[name of person who mailed the notice]* as to service of the Notice of Motion and Motion is on file with the court.

5. The Notice of Motion and Motion complies in all respects with *[local bankruptcy rule allowing motion to be decided without a hearing unless the creditor objects]*.

Sample Request for Entry of Order by Default (continued)

6. The Debtor has received no response from any of the served parties as of the date of this request, more than 20 days after the service of the Notice of Motion and Motion.

WHEREFORE, Debtor respectfully requests that the court enter by default the attached Order to Avoid Judicial Lien on Real Estate.

Date: ______________________ Signed by: ____

Redemption Agreements

If you want to redeem exempt or abandoned property, list the property on your Statement of Intention as property to be retained and check the column that says property will be redeemed. (More instructions are in Ch. 8.) You must pay the creditor the current replacement value of the property within 45 days after the creditors' meeting.

Before you can redeem property, you and the creditor must agree on what the property is worth. If you believe the creditor is setting too high a price for the property, tell the creditor why you think the property is worth less—it needs repair, it's falling apart, it's damaged or stained, or whatever. If you can't come to an agreement, you can ask the bankruptcy court to rule on the matter. But you will probably need an attorney to help you make this request, so it is not worth your while unless the property is worth more than the lawyer will cost, and you and the creditor are very far apart in your estimates of the property's value.

The creditor may refuse to let you redeem property, because the creditor claims that it isn't one of the types of property you can redeem or because you can't agree on the value. If so, you will need to file a formal complaint in the bankruptcy court to have a judge resolve the issue. You will need an attorney to help you, so think twice about whether you really want to redeem the property. It may be better just to let the creditor have it.

You and the creditor should sign a redemption agreement that sets forth the terms of your arrangement and the amount you are going to pay, in case there is a dispute later. Below are two sample redemption agreements you can use to type up your agreement with the creditor. Form 1 is for a lump sum and Form 2 is for installments payment. You should fill out a separate form for every item of property you want to redeem. Have the creditor sign it.

There is no need to file these agreements with the trustee. Keep them with your other bankruptcy papers, in case the trustee or the judge wants to see them.

Agreement for Lump Sum Redemption of Property

If you can afford to pay the full value of the property as agreed to between you and the creditor, use the form below to formalize your agreement.

Agreement for Installment Redemption of Property

If you can't raise enough cash to pay the creditor within 45 days after the creditors' meeting, try to get the creditor to let you pay in installments. Some creditors will agree if the installments are substantial and you agree to pay interest on them. But a creditor is not required to accept installments; it can demand the entire amount in cash.

If the creditor refuses to accept installments, you can ask the bankruptcy court to delay your deadline for making the payment for a month or two. But to do so, you will need to file a formal complaint in the bankruptcy court. Again, you will need an attorney to help you, so it may not be worth it.

Sample Agreement for Lump Sum Redemption of Property

AGREEMENT FOR LUMP SUM REDEMPTION OF PROPERTY

______________________________ (Debtor)

and ______________________________ (Creditor) agree that:

1. Creditor owns a security interest in ______________________ (Collateral).

2. The replacement value of Collateral is $______________.

3. Creditor's security interest is valid and enforceable despite the Debtor's bankruptcy case.

4. Debtor agrees to pay the full value of the collateral no later than ______________.

5. Upon receiving the payment specified in Paragraph 4, Creditor will take all steps necessary to terminate its security interest in Collateral.

Dated: ______________ ______________________
Debtor in Propria Persona

Dated: ______________ ______________________
Creditor

Sample Agreement for Installment Redemption of Property

AGREEMENT FOR INSTALLMENT REDEMPTION OF PROPERTY

____ (Debtor) and

____ (Creditor) agree that:

1. Creditor owns a security interest in ________________________ (Collateral).

2. The replacement value of Collateral is $________________.

3. Creditor's security interest is valid and enforceable despite the Debtor's bankruptcy case.

4. If Debtor continues to make payments of $__________ a month on Creditor's security interest, Creditor will take no action to repossess or foreclose its security.

5. Debtor's payments will continue until the amount of $________, plus interest (to be computed at the same annual percentage rate as in the original contract between the parties), is paid.

6. Upon being fully paid as specified in Paragraph 5, Creditor will take all steps necessary to terminate its security interest in Collateral.

7. If Debtor defaults, Creditor will have its rights under the original contract.

Dated: ________________ ________________________

Debtor in Propria Persona

Dated: ________________ ________________________

Creditor

Amending Your Bankruptcy Papers

As explained in Ch. 10, there may be situations that require you to amend some of your bankruptcy paperwork. Follow these steps to amend.

Step 1: Fill out the Amendment Cover Sheet below, if no local form is required. Otherwise, use the local form. If you use our form, here's how to fill it in:

- Put the appropriate information in the top blanks (for instance, Western District of Tennessee).
- After "In re," enter your name, the name of your spouse if you're married and filing jointly, and all other names you have used in the last eight years.
- Enter your address, the last four digits of your Social Security number, and a taxpayer ID number (if you have one for your business).
- On the right side, enter your case number.
- Check the boxes of the forms you are amending. If you are adding new creditors or changing addresses, check the box that you have enclosed the appropriate fee (currently $26).
- Sign the form.
- Continue to the declaration about the truth of the amendment.
- Enter your name (and the name of your spouse if you're filing jointly) after "I (we)."
- Enter the number of pages that will be accompanying the cover sheet.
- Enter the date you are signing the document.
- Sign at the bottom to swear under penalty of perjury that your amendment is true (your spouse should also sign, if you're filing jointly).

Step 2: Make copies of the forms affected by your amendment.

Step 3: Check your local court rules or ask the court clerk whether you must retype the whole form to make the correction, or whether you can just type the new information on another blank form. If you can't find the answer, ask a local bankruptcy lawyer or bankruptcy petition preparer who has done amendments in the past. If it's acceptable to just type the new information (this is the usual procedure), precede the information you're typing with "ADD," "CHANGE," or "DELETE" as appropriate. At the bottom of the form, type "AMENDED" in capital letters.

Step 4: Call or visit the court and ask what order the papers must be in and how many copies are required.

Step 5: Make the required number of copies, plus one copy for yourself, one for the trustee, and one for any creditor affected by your amendment.

Step 6: Have a friend or relative mail, first class, a copy of your amended papers to the bankruptcy trustee and to any creditor affected by your amendment.

Step 7: Enter the name and complete address of every new creditor affected by your amendment on the Proof of Service by Mail (a copy is below). Also enter the name and address of the bankruptcy trustee. Then have the person who mailed the amendment to the trustee and new creditors sign and date the Proof of Service.

Step 8: Mail or take the original amendment and Proof of Service and copies to the bankruptcy court. Enclose a money order for the filing fee, if required. If you use the mail, enclose a prepaid self-addressed envelope so the clerk can return a file-stamped set of papers to you.

Amendment Cover Sheet

UNITED STATES BANKRUPTCY COURT

________________ DISTRICT OF ________________

In re ________________)
[Set forth here all names including married, maiden, and trade names used by debtor within last 8 years.])
Debtor) Case No. ________________
)
Address ________________)
)
________________) Chapter 7
)
Last four digits of Social Security or Individual Taxpayer Identification (ITIN) No(s). (if any): ________)
)
Employer's Tax Identification (EIN) No(s). (if any):)
________________)

AMENDMENT COVER SHEET

Presented herewith are the original and one copy of the following:

- ☐ Voluntary Petition (Note: Spouse may not be added or deleted subsequent to initial filing.)
- ☐ Schedule A—Real Property
- ☐ Schedule B—Personal Property
- ☐ Schedule C—Property Claimed as Exempt
- ☐ Schedule D—Creditors Holding Secured Claims
- ☐ Schedule E—Creditors Holding Unsecured Priority Claims
- ☐ Schedule F—Creditors Holding Unsecured Nonpriority Claims
- ☐ Schedule G—Executory Contracts and Unexpired Leases
- ☐ Schedule H—Codebtors
- ☐ Schedule I—Current Income of Individual Debtor(s)
- ☐ Schedule J—Current Expenditures of Individual Debtor(s)
- ☐ Summary of Schedules
- ☐ Statement of Financial Affairs
- ☐ I have enclosed a $26 fee because I am adding new creditors or changing addresses after the original Meeting of Creditors Notice has been sent.

Amendment Cover Sheet (continued)

Signature of Debtor ______________________ Signature of Debtor's Spouse ______________________

I (we) ____

and ____,

the debtor(s) in this case, declare under penalty of perjury that the information set forth in the amendment attached hereto consisting of ________ pages is true and correct to the best of my (our) information and belief.

Dated: ______________________, 20______

Signature of Debtor ______________________ Signature of Debtor's Spouse ______________________

Notice of Change of Address

If you move while your bankruptcy case is still open, you must give your new address to the court, the trustee, and your creditors. Here's how to do it:

Step 1: Make one or two photocopies of the blank Notice of Change of Address and Proof of Service forms below.

Step 2: Fill in the Change of Address form with your old address, new address, and date you moved.

Step 3: Make one photocopy for the trustee, one for your records, and one for each creditor listed in Schedules D, E, and F, or the mailing matrix.

Step 4: Have a friend or relative mail a copy of the Notice of Change of Address to the trustee and to each creditor.

Step 5: Have the friend or relative complete and sign the Proof of Service by Mail form, listing the bankruptcy trustee and the names and addresses of all creditors to whom the notice was mailed.

Step 6: File the original notice and original Proof of Service with the bankruptcy court.

Voluntary Dismissal

If, for the reasons covered in Ch. 10, you decide that you must dismiss your bankruptcy case, follow these instructions:

Step 1: Check your court's local rules for time limits, format of papers, and other requirements for voluntary dismissals. (See Ch. 12 for information on finding local rules online.) If you can't find the information you need from reading your local rules, ask the court clerk, the trustee assigned to your case, a local bankruptcy petition preparer, or a bankruptcy lawyer for help.

Step 2: Refer to the sample Petition for Voluntary Dismissal and a sample Order Granting Voluntary Dismissal provided below. Follow along with the sample as you type your caption, inserting your own information in the blanks.

Step 3: If you're using a typewriter, make a few photocopies of what you have typed so far, so you can make two different documents with that one caption.

Step 4: On one copy of your caption, center and type "PETITION FOR VOLUNTARY DISMISSAL." The text of the petition will be similar to the sample but tailored to the facts of your case. In particular, you will put your filing date in paragraph 1; in paragraph 3 you will explain your own reason for wanting to dismiss the case.

Step 5: Sign and date the petition. If you filed together with your spouse, both of you must sign. Otherwise, leave the spouse's signature line blank.

Step 6: On another photocopy of the caption you made, center and type: "[PROPOSED] ORDER GRANTING VOLUNTARY DISMISSAL." Then type the text of the order from the sample at the end of this

Notice of Change of Address

UNITED STATES BANKRUPTCY COURT

____________________ DISTRICT OF ____________________

In re ____________________)	
[Set forth here all names including married, maiden, and trade names used by debtor within last 8 years.])	
Debtor)	Case No. ________________
Address ____________________)	Chapter 7
____________________)	
Last four digits of Social Security or Individual Taxpayer Identification (ITIN) No(s). (if any): ________)	
Employer's Tax Identification (EIN) No(s). (if any):)	
____________________)	

NOTICE OF CHANGE OF ADDRESS

MY (OUR) FORMER MAILING ADDRESS AND PHONE NUMBER WAS:

Name: ____________________

Street: ____________________

City: ____________________

State/Zip: ____________________

Phone: (______)____________________

PLEASE BE ADVISED THAT AS OF________________, 20____, MY (OUR) NEW MAILING ADDRESS AND PHONE NUMBER IS:

Name: ____________________

Street: ____________________

City: ____________________

State/Zip: ____________________

Phone: (______)____________________

____
Signature of Debtor

____
Signature of Debtor's Spouse

chapter. Include the blanks; the judge will fill them in.

Step 7: Make at least three copies of your signed petition and your blank order.

Step 8: Take your originals and copies to the bankruptcy court clerk. When you get to the court clerk, explain that you are filing a petition to dismiss your case. The clerk will take your originals and one or more of your copies. Ask the clerk the following:

What notice to your creditors is required?

If there is a problem, will you be contacted? If not, how will you learn of the problem?

If the judge signs the order, when can you expect to get it?

Once you have a signed order, who sends copies to your creditors—you or the court? If you send the copies, do you also have to file a Proof of Service?

Step 9: Once you receive the signed order, put it away for safekeeping if you don't have to notify your creditors. If you do, make copies and send one to each.

Step 10: If you have to file a Proof of Service, follow the instructions under "Lien Avoidance," above.

Reopening a Case

Here, we provide the forms necessary to ask the court to reopen your case to allow you to file Form 23, and to ask the court for a discharge (this process is briefly described in Ch. 10). There are four forms in all:

- a request to reopen the case
- an order reopening the case
- a request for a discharge, and
- an order that a discharge be entered.

If you want the court to reopen your case for a different reason, you'll have to change the forms. Describe why you need the case to be reopened and tailor the additional forms to request the ultimate relief you want the court to grant (for example, to avoid a lien). If you have trouble completing these forms or figuring out what to say, talk to a bankruptcy lawyer.

Petition for Voluntary Dismissal

UNITED STATES BANKRUPTCY COURT

_____[Name of District]_____ DISTRICT OF _____[Your State]_____

In re ______________________________)
[Set forth here all names including married,)
maiden, and trade names used by debtor)
within last 8 years.])
Debtor(s)) Case No. ______________
Address ______________________________)
)
______________________________) Chapter 7
)
Last four digits of Social Security or Individual)
Taxpayer Identification (ITIN) No(s). (if any): ______)
)
Employer's Tax Identification (EIN) No(s). (if any):)
______________________________)

PETITION FOR VOLUNTARY DISMISSAL

The debtor in the above-mentioned case hereby moves to dismiss his/her bankruptcy case for the following reasons:

1. Debtor filed a voluntary petition under Chapter 7 of the Bankruptcy Code on ______________, 20xx.

2. No complaints objecting to discharge or to determine the dischargeability of any debts have been filed in the case.

3. Debtor realizes that filing a Chapter 7 bankruptcy petition was erroneous. Debtor now realizes that a particular debt may not be dischargeable. Debtor would have to litigate this matter, and Debtor does not feel he/she has the ability to do so on his/her own nor the resources to hire an attorney to do it for him/her. Debtor intends to pursue other means of handling his/her debts.

4. No creditor has filed a claim in this case.

5. No creditor has requested relief from the automatic stay.

WHEREFORE, Debtor prays that this bankruptcy case be dismissed without prejudice.

Dated: ______________________ ______________________________
Signature of Debtor

Dated: ______________________ ______________________________
Signature of Debtor's Spouse

Order Granting Voluntary Dismissal

UNITED STATES BANKRUPTCY COURT

______*[Name of District]*______ DISTRICT OF ______*[Your State]*______

In re ________________________)
[Set forth here all names including married, maiden, and trade names used by debtor within last 8 years.])
Debtor(s)) Case No. ____________
Address ________________________)
________________________) Chapter 7
Last four digits of Social Security or Individual Taxpayer Identification (ITIN) No(s). (if any): ________)
Employer's Tax Identification (EIN) No(s). (if any):)
________________________)

[PROPOSED] ORDER GRANTING VOLUNTARY DISMISSAL

AND NOW, this __________ day of ____________, 20____, the Court having found that the voluntary dismissal of this case is in the best interests of the debtor and does not prejudice the rights of any of his or her creditors, it is hereby ordered that the petition for voluntary dismissal is approved.

Dated: __________________ ________________________
U.S. Bankruptcy Judge

Request to Reopen Case

UNITED STATES BANKRUPTCY COURT

[Name of District] DISTRICT OF [Your State]

In re ________________________)
[Set forth here all names including married, maiden, and trade names used by debtor within last 8 years.])
Debtor(s)) Case No. ____________
Address ________________________)
________________________) Chapter 7
Last four digits of Social Security or Individual Taxpayer Identification (ITIN) No(s). (if any): ________)
Employer's Tax Identification (EIN) No(s). (if any):)
________________________)

EX-PARTE APPLICATION TO REOPEN CLOSED CASE UNDER 11 U.S.C. SECTION 350(b)

To the Honorable [Name of Bankruptcy Judge]:

Debtor/Applicant [your name] herein applies to have [his/her] case reopened and respectfully represents:

1. On [date you filed your petition], Applicant filed a Petition for Relief under Chapter 7 of Title 11 of the United States Code, and on [date your case was closed] , said case was closed without an order of discharge under 11 U.S.C. Section 727.

2. The reason given for the Court's denial of a discharge was that the Court failed to timely receive Official Form 23, proof of personal financial management counseling under 11 U.S.C. Section 111.

3. Prior to closure of [his/her] case, Applicant had in fact undertaken and completed personal financial management counseling pursuant to 11 U.S.C. Section 111 but inadvertently failed to file a completed Official Form 23 with the court.

4. Applicant seeks to reopen [his/her] case in order to file Official Form 23 and to move the court to enter a discharge under 11 U.S.C. Section 727.

5. Attached to this application is a copy of Official Form 23 that Applicant will immediately file upon reopening of this case.

6. Reopening [his/her] case by ex-parte application for the purpose of filing Form 23 and seeking a discharge is authorized under 11 U.S.C. Section 350(b).

Request to Reopen Case (continued)

7. Wherefore Applicant prays that the above-entitled case be reopened for the purpose of permitting Applicant to file Official Form 23 and move the Court for a discharge in *[his/her]* Chapter 7 bankruptcy case.

Dated: ____________________ Signed: ______________________________
[*your name*]

Order Granting Request to Reopen Case

UNITED STATES BANKRUPTCY COURT

_____[*Name of District*]_____ DISTRICT OF _____[*Your State*]_____

In re ______________________________)
[Set forth here all names including married,)
maiden, and trade names used by debtor)
within last 8 years.])
Debtor) Case No. ____________
)
Address ______________________________)
)
______________________________) Chapter 7
)
Last four digits of Social Security or Individual)
Taxpayer Identification (ITIN) No(s). (if any):________)
)
Employer's Tax Identification (EIN) No(s). (if any):)
______________________________)

ORDER TO REOPEN CLOSED CASE

Based on debtor's Ex-Parte Application to Reopen Closed Case and applicable law, it is hereby ordered that Case No: [*case number*] be reopened for the purpose of permitting Applicant to file Official Form 23 and apply for an order of discharge under 11 U.S.C. Section 727.

Date: ______________ Signed: ______________________________
U.S. Bankruptcy Judge

Request for Discharge

UNITED STATES BANKRUPTCY COURT

______*[Name of District]*______ DISTRICT OF ______*[Your State]*______

In re ________________________________)
[Set forth here all names including married,)
maiden, and trade names used by debtor)
within last 8 years.])
Debtor) Case No. ________________
)
Address ________________________________)
)
____) Chapter 7
)
Last four digits of Social Security or Individual)
Taxpayer Identification (ITIN) No(s). (if any):________)
)
Employer's Tax Identification (EIN) No(s). (if any):)
____)

EX-PARTE APPLICATION FOR THE COURT TO ENTER
AN ORDER OF DISCHARGE UNDER 11 U.S.C. SECTION 727

To the Honorable *[Name of Bankruptcy Judge]*:

Debtor/Applicant *[your name]* herein applies to have an order of discharge entered in *[his/her]* case and respectfully represents:

1. On *[date you filed your petition]*, Applicant filed a Petition for Relief under Chapter 7 of Title 11 of the United States Code, and on *[date your case was closed]*, said case was closed without an order of discharge under 11 U.S.C. Section 727.

2. The reason given for the Court's denial of a discharge was that the Court failed to timely receive Official Form 23, proof of personal financial management counseling under 11 U.S.C. Section 111.

3. Applicant sought and obtained an Order to Reopen *[his/her]* case in order to refile Official Form 23 and move the court to enter a discharge under 11 U.S.C. Section 727.

4. On *[date you filed Form 23]*, Applicant filed Official Form 23 with the court clerk.

5. Wherefore Applicant prays that the honorable court enter an Order of Discharge in *[his/her]* case under 11 U.S.C. Section 727.

Date: __________________ Signed: ________________________________
[your name]

Order Granting Request for Discharge

UNITED STATES BANKRUPTCY COURT

_____*[Name of District]*_____ DISTRICT OF _____*[Your State]*_____

In re ______________________________)
[Set forth here all names including married,)
maiden, and trade names used by debtor)
within last 8 years.])
Debtor) Case No. ______________
)
Address ______________________________)
)
______________________________) Chapter 7
)
Last four digits of Social Security or Individual)
Taxpayer Identification (ITIN) No(s). (if any):__________)
)
Employer's Tax Identification (EIN) No(s). (if any):)
______________________________)

ORDER TO GRANT REQUEST FOR DISCHARGE

Based on debtor's Ex-Parte Application for the Court to Enter an Order of Discharge, it is hereby ordered that a discharge be entered under 11 U.S.C. Section 727 in Case No. *[case number]* .

Date: ____________________ Signed: ______________________________
U.S. Bankruptcy Judge

Supplemental Schedule for Property Acquired After Bankruptcy Discharge

As explained in Ch. 11, you must notify the trustee if you receive certain types of property after your bankruptcy case ends. To report this property to the trustee, use the form called Supplemental Schedule for Property Acquired After Bankruptcy Discharge, below. The form is self-explanatory. When you've filled it out, follow these steps:

Step 1: Photocopy a Proof of Service by Mail (see below) and fill it out, but don't sign it.

Step 2: Make three photocopies of the Supplemental Schedule and the Proof of Service.

Step 3: Have a friend or relative mail the original Supplemental Schedule and a copy of the Proof of Service to the trustee and the U.S. Trustee, and then sign the original Proof of Service.

Step 4: File a copy of the Supplemental Schedule and the original Proof of Service with the bankruptcy court. No additional filing fee is required.

Step 5: Keep a copy of the Supplemental Schedule and the Proof of Service for your records.

In some areas, the court may require you to file amended bankruptcy papers. If that happens, follow the instructions in "Amending Your Bankruptcy Papers," above.

Proof of Service

You must file a proof of service form along with any pleadings you file with the court. The proof of service lets the court know that your adversary has received notice of your pleading. The sections above explain how to complete a proof of service for various pleadings. Use the blank form, below.

Supplemental Schedule for Property Acquired After Bankruptcy Discharge

UNITED STATES BANKRUPTCY COURT

____________________ DISTRICT OF ____________________

In re ____________________ *[Set forth here all names including married, maiden, and trade names used by debtor within last 8 years.]* Debtor	Case No. ________________
Address ____________________ ____________________	Chapter 7
Last four digits of Social Security or Individual Taxpayer Identification (ITIN) No(s). (if any): __________	
Employer's Tax Identification (EIN) No(s). (if any): ____________________	

SUPPLEMENTAL SCHEDULE FOR PROPERTY
ACQUIRED AFTER BANKRUPTCY DISCHARGE

TO: ____________________________, Trustee

This is to inform you that I (we) have received the following item of property since my (our) discharge but within the 180-day period after filing my (our) Bankruptcy Petition under Bankruptcy Rule 1007(h):

____

____

This property was obtained through an inheritance, marital settlement agreement or divorce decree, death benefits or life insurance proceeds, or other (specify):

____

____

☐ I (we) claim this property exempt under the following law:

____

____

I (we) ____ and

____,

the debtor(s) in this case, declare under penalty of perjury that the foregoing is true and correct.

Dated: ________________, 20 _____

____
Signature of Debtor

____
Signature of Debtor's Spouse

Proof of Service by Mail

UNITED STATES BANKRUPTCY COURT
__________________ DISTRICT OF __________________

In re ______________________________)
[Set forth here all names including married, maiden, and trade names used by debtor within last 8 years.]
Debtor) Case No. ______________

Address ______________________________)
______________________________) Chapter 7

Last four digits of Social Security or Individual Taxpayer Identification (ITIN) No(s). (if any): __________)

Employer's Tax Identification (EIN) No(s). (if any):)
______________________________)

PROOF OF SERVICE BY MAIL

I, ______________________________, declare that: I am a resident or employed in the County of ______________, State of ______________. My residence/business address is ______________________________ ______________________________. I am over the age of eighteen years and not a party to this case.

On ______________, 20____, I served the enclosed ______________________________ ______________________________

on the following parties by placing true and correct copies thereof enclosed in a sealed envelope with postage thereon fully prepaid in the United States Mail at ______________________________, addressed as follows:

I declare under penalty of perjury that the foregoing is true and correct, and that this declaration was executed on

Date: ______________, 20____ at ______________________________
City and State

____
Signature

Index

A

B

D

E

F

J

N

O

P

Q

R

S

T

U

W